Lecture Notes in Computer Science 2709

Edited by G. Goos, J. Hartmanis, and J. van Leeuwen

Springer
Berlin
Heidelberg
New York
Barcelona
Hong Kong
London
Milan
Paris
Tokyo

Terry Windeatt   Fabio Roli (Eds.)

Multiple Classifier Systems

4th International Workshop, MCS 2003
Guildford, UK, June 11-13, 2003
Proceedings

 Springer

Series Editors

Gerhard Goos, Karlsruhe University, Germany
Juris Hartmanis, Cornell University, NY, USA
Jan van Leeuwen, Utrecht University, The Netherlands

Volume Editors

Terry Windeatt
University of Surrey, Centre for Vision, Speech and Signal Processing
Guildford, Surrey, GU2 7XH, UK
E-mail: T.Windeatt@surrey.ac.uk

Fabio Roli
University of Cagliari, Dept. of Electrical and Electronic Engineering
Piazza D'Ami, 09123 Cagliari, Italy
E-mail: roli@diee.unica.it

Cataloging-in-Publication Data applied for

A catalog record for this book is available from the Library of Congress

Bibliographic information published by Die Deutsche Bibliothek
Die Deutsche Bibliothek lists this publication in the Deutsche Nationalbibliografie;
detailed bibliographic data is available in the Internet at <http://dnb.ddb.de>.

CR Subject Classification (1998): I.5, I.4, I.2.10, I.2, F.1

ISSN 0302-9743
ISBN 3-540-40369-8 Springer-Verlag Berlin Heidelberg New York

Springer-Verlag Berlin Heidelberg New York
a member of BertelsmannSpringer Science+Business Media GmbH

http://www.springer.de

© Springer-Verlag Berlin Heidelberg 2003
Printed in Germany

Typesetting: Camera-ready by author, data conversion by Olgun Computergrafik
Printed on acid-free paper   SPIN 10928745   06/3142   5 4 3 2 1 0

Preface

The theory and practice of Multiple Classifier Systems (MCS) and related methods address the issues surrounding the optimality of decision-making in a multiple classifier framework. What contributes to the fascination of this field is that solutions have been developed by many diverse research communities, including machine learning, neural networks, pattern recognition, and statistics. The aim of the series of workshops on MCS is to create a common international forum for researchers of the diverse communities working in the field. The common thread running through the different approaches is the exploitation of methods involving several classifiers to obtain a better estimate of the optimal decision rule than can be obtained by trying to optimize the design of a single classifier.

The present volume contains the proceedings of the International Workshop on Multiple Classifier Systems MCS 2003 held at the University of Surrey, Guildford, Surrey, UK (June 11–13, 2003), which was organized to provide a forum for researchers to exchange views and report their latest results. It follows its predecessors: the third workshop, MCS 2002, held in the Hotel Chia Laguna, Cagliari, Italy (June 24–26, 2002, Springer, ISBN 3-540-43818-1); the second workshop, MCS 2001, held in Robinson College, Cambridge, UK (July 2–4, 2001, Springer, ISBN 3-540-42284-6); and the first workshop, MCS 2000, held in Santa Margherita di Pula, Sardinia, Italy (June 21–23, 2000, Springer, ISBN 3-540-67704-6).

This volume presents 40 papers selected by the scientific committee and organized into seven thematic sessions dealing with boosting, combination rules, multi-class methods, fusion schemes and architectures, neural network ensembles, ensemble strategies, and applications. The workshop program was enriched by invited talks from Jerry Friedman (Stanford University, USA) and Mohamed Kamel (University of Waterloo, Canada), the latter's paper appearing as the first in this volume.

The workshop was sponsored by the University of Surrey, UK and the University of Cagliari, Italy and was cosponsored by the International Association for Pattern Recognition through its Technical Committee TC1: Statistical Pattern Recognition Techniques. We also wish to express our gratitude to all those who helped to organize MCS 2003. First of all our thanks are due to the members of the Scientific Committee who selected the best papers from a large number of submissions to create excellent technical content. Special thanks are due to the members of the Organizing Committee, Josef Kittler, Rachel Gartshore, Giorgio Fumera and Giorgio Giacinto, for their indispensable contributions to local organization and Web site management.

June 2003

Terry Windeatt
Fabio Roli

Workshop Chairs

Terry Windeatt (Univ. of Surrey, UK)
Fabio Roli (Univ. of Cagliari, Italy)

Scientific Committee

J.A. Benediktsson (Iceland)
H. Bunke (Switzerland)
L.P. Cordella (Italy)
B.V. Dasarathy (USA)
R.P.W. Duin (The Netherlands)
C. Furlanello (Italy)
J. Ghosh (USA)
T.K. Ho (USA)
S. Impedovo (Italy)
N. Intrator (Israel)
A.K. Jain (USA)
M. Kamel (Canada)
J. Kittler (UK)
L.I. Kuncheva (UK)
L. Lam (Hong Kong)
D. Landgrebe (USA)
D.-S. Lee (USA)
D. Partridge (UK)
A.J.C. Sharkey (UK)
K. Tumer (USA)
G. Vernazza (Italy)

Local Committee

G. Fumera (Univ. of Cagliari, Italy)
R. Gartshore (Univ. of Surrey, UK)
G. Giacinto (Univ. of Cagliari, Italy)
J. Kittler (Univ. of Surrey, UK)

Sponsored By

University of Surrey, University of Cagliari
International Association for Pattern Recognition

Supported By

University of Surrey, University of Cagliari
Dept. of Electrical and Electronic Eng. of University of Cagliari

Table of Contents

Invited Paper

Data Dependence in Combining Classifiers 1
  Mohamed S. Kamel and Nayer M. Wanas

Boosting

Boosting with Averaged Weight Vectors 15
  Nikunj C. Oza

Error Bounds for Aggressive and Conservative AdaBoost............... 25
  Ludmila I. Kuncheva

An Empirical Comparison of Three Boosting Algorithms
on Real Data Sets with Artificial Class Noise 35
  Ross A. McDonald, David J. Hand, and Idris A. Eckley

The Beneficial Effects of Using Multi-net Systems That Focus
on Hard Patterns 45
  J. Arenas-García, A.R. Figueiras-Vidal, and A.J.C. Sharkey

Combination Rules

The Behavior Knowledge Space Fusion Method: Analysis of Generalization
Error and Strategies for Performance Improvement 55
  Šarunas Raudys and Fabio Roli

Reducing the Overconfidence of Base Classifiers
when Combining Their Decisions..................................... 65
  Šarunas Raudys, Ray Somorjai, and Richard Baumgartner

Linear Combiners for Classifier Fusion:
Some Theoretical and Experimental Results 74
  Giorgio Fumera and Fabio Roli

Comparison of Classifier Selection Methods
for Improving Committee Performance................................ 84
  Matti Aksela

Towards Automated Classifier Combination for Pattern Recognition 94
  Alper Baykut and Aytül Erçil

Multi-class Methods

Serial Multiple Classifier Systems Exploiting a Coarse
to Fine Output Coding 106
    Josef Kittler, Ali Ahmadyfard, and David Windridge

Polychotomous Classification with Pairwise Classifiers:
A New Voting Principle....................................... 115
    Florin Cutzu

Multi-category Classification by Soft-Max Combination
of Binary Classifiers 125
    *Kaibo Duan, S. Sathiya Keerthi, Wei Chu, Shirish Krishnaj Shevade,
    and Aun Neow Poo*

A Sequential Scheduling Approach
to Combining Multiple Object Classifiers Using Cross-Entropy 135
    Derek Magee

Binary Classifier Fusion Based on the Basic Decomposition Methods 146
    Jaepil Ko and Hyeran Byun

Fusion Schemes Architectures

Good Error Correcting Output Codes for Adaptive Multiclass Learning ... 156
    Elizabeth Tapia, José Carlos González, and Javier García-Villalba

Finding Natural Clusters Using Multi-clusterer Combiner Based
on Shared Nearest Neighbors 166
    Hanan Ayad and Mohamed Kamel

An Ensemble Approach for Data Fusion with Learn++ 176
    Michael Lewitt and Robi Polikar

The Practical Performance Characteristics
of Tomographically Filtered Multiple Classifier Fusion 186
    David Windridge and Josef Kittler

Accumulated-Recognition-Rate Normalization
for Combining Multiple On/Off-Line Japanese Character Classifiers Tested
on a Large Database 196
    Ondrej Velek, Stefan Jaeger, and Masaki Nakagawa

Beam Search Extraction and Forgetting Strategies on Shared Ensembles .. 206
    *V. Estruch, C. Ferri, J. Hernández-Orallo,
    and M.J. Ramírez-Quintana*

A Markov Chain Approach to Multiple Classifier Fusion 217
    S.P. Luttrell

Neural Network Ensembles

A Study of Ensemble of Hybrid Networks with Strong Regularization 227
 Shimon Cohen and Nathan Intrator

Combining Multiple Modes of Information
Using Unsupervised Neural Classifiers 236
 *Khurshid Ahmad, Matthew Casey, Bogdan Vrusias,
 and Panagiotis Saragiotis*

Neural Net Ensembles for Lithology Recognition 246
 *R.O.V. Santos, M.M.B.R. Vellasco, F.A.V. Artola,
 and S.A.B. da Fontoura*

Improving Performance of a Multiple Classifier System
Using Self-generating Neural Networks 256
 Hirotaka Inoue and Hiroyuki Narihisa

Ensemble Strategies

Negative Correlation Learning and the Ambiguity Family
of Ensemble Methods 266
 Gavin Brown and Jeremy Wyatt

Spectral Coefficients and Classifier Correlation 276
 Terry Windeatt, R. Ghaderi, and G. Ardeshir

Ensemble Construction *via* Designed Output Distortion 286
 Stefan W. Christensen

Simulating Classifier Outputs
for Evaluating Parallel Combination Methods 296
 H. Zouari, L. Heutte, Y. Lecourtier, and A. Alimi

A New Ensemble Diversity Measure Applied to Thinning Ensembles 306
 *Robert E. Banfield, Lawrence O. Hall, Kevin W. Bowyer,
 and W. Philip Kegelmeyer*

Ensemble Methods for Noise Elimination in Classification Problems 317
 Sofie Verbaeten and Anneleen Van Assche

Applications

New Boosting Algorithms for Classification Problems with Large Number
of Classes Applied to a Handwritten Word Recognition Task 326
 Simon Günter and Horst Bunke

Automatic Target Recognition Using Multiple Description Coding Models
for Multiple Classifier Systems 336
 Widhyakorn Asdornwised and Somchai Jitapunkul

A Modular Multiple Classifier System for the Detection of Intrusions
in Computer Networks... 346
  Giorgio Giacinto, Fabio Roli, and Luca Didaci

Input Space Transformations for Multi-classifier Systems Based
on n-tuple Classifiers with Application to Handwriting Recognition....... 356
  K. Sirlantzis, S. Hoque, and M.C. Fairhurst

Building Classifier Ensembles for Automatic Sports Classification 366
  Edward Jaser, Josef Kittler, and William Christmas

Classification of Aircraft Maneuvers for Fault Detection................. 375
  Nikunj C. Oza, Kagan Tumer, Irem Y. Tumer, and Edward M. Huff

Solving Problems Two at a Time: Classification of Web Pages
Using a Generic Pair-Wise Multiple Classifier System................... 385
  Hassan Alam, Fuad Rahman, and Yuliya Tarnikova

Design and Evaluation of an Adaptive Combination Framework
for OCR Result Strings 395
  Elke Wilczok and Wolfgang Lellmann

Author Index 405

Data Dependence in Combining Classifiers

Mohamed S. Kamel and Nayer M. Wanas

Pattern Analysis and Machine Intelligence lab
Department of Systems Design Engineering
University of Waterloo
Waterloo, Ontario, Canada, N2L-3G1
{mkamel,nwanas}@pami.uwaterloo.ca

Abstract. It has been accepted that multiple classifier systems provide a platform for not only performance improvement, but more efficient and robust pattern classification systems. A variety of combining methods have been proposed in the literature and some work has focused on comparing and categorizing these approaches. In this paper we present a new categorization of these combining schemes based on their dependence on the data patterns being classified. Combining methods can be totally independent from the data, or they can be implicitly or explicitly dependent on the data. It is argued that data dependent, and especially explicitly data dependent, approaches represent the highest potential for improved performance. On the basis of this categorization, an architecture for explicit data dependent combining methods is discussed. Experimental results to illustrate the comparative performance of some combining methods according to this categorization is included.

1 Introduction

The use of multiple classifiers has gained momentum in the recent years [1,2,3], and researchers have continuously argued for the benefits of using multiple classifiers to solve complex recognition problems [4]. It might be noted that a key issue in the use of multiple classifier systems is utilizing classifiers that demonstrate misclassification on different patterns. While most of the literature focus on new approaches to combine classifiers, little work has been focusing on categorizing these approaches.

The basic categorization of multiple classifier systems has been by the method these classifiers are arranged. The two basic categories in this regard are the serial suite and the parallel suite. The parallel expert architecture consists of a set of classifiers that are consulted in parallel. The decision of the various experts are combined by the fusion module. The experts, in this case, are capable of independent and simultaneous operation. On the other hand, the serial suite consists of a set of classifiers arranged in series, or in tandem. This architecture is well suited to deal with situations where the different experts have a ternary decision scheme. A scheme in which they can be undecided on the input pattern they are presented with. If the current expert is undecided, information is passed to the next expert in the sequence. The experts have to have a varying ability of

T. Windeatt and F. Roli (Eds.): MCS 2003, LNCS 2709, pp. 1–14, 2003.

generalizations. While parallel architectures are the most popular, there are also some complicated combinations of these basic schemes that can also be used, such as parallel-serial or serial-parallel architectures.

Multiple classifiers can also be categorized based on the method of mapping between the input and output of the fusion module. This mapping may be linear or non-linear. Linear combination are the simplest approaches, in which a weighting factor is assigned to the output of each expert being combined. This weighting factor can be specific to the input pattern, or can be specific to the expert. Weighted average, fuzzy integrals are among the linear combination methods. Non-linear methods include approaches such as the majority, or maximum votes. The feature-based approach [8], stacked generalization [9], or rank based methods [10], which involve a more complex mapping of the input, also use a nonlinear mapping in the combining method.

Combining methods can be divided into two different classes depending on the representation methodology. The classifiers can all use the same representation, and hence the classifiers themselves should be different. In multi-representation approaches [4] the different classifiers use different representations of the same inputs. This can be due to the use of different sensors or different features extracted from the same data set. Another categorization of classifier combining methods can be based on whether they encourage specialization in certain areas of the feature space, such are modular approaches [7]. Ensemble of classifiers [11,12,13] do not encourage such specialization and hence the classifiers themselves must have different classification powers. In other words, in an ensemble each base classifier can be used alone to provide a solution to the input pattern, while, a modular approach would need the coordination of all the classifiers to present a complete solution. Sharkey [5,6] presented an account of categorization of the various multiple classifier approaches. The basis of the categorization is the distinction between ensemble and modular approaches, as well as differentiating between cooperative and competitive approaches. Some research has also focused on comparing different types of multiple classifier systems, such as the work of Auda and Kamel [7] which focuses on modular approaches. In this work we are interested in shedding some light on how various combining methods depend on the data patterns being classified.

2   Data Dependence

Combining schemes can be categorized based on their dependence on the data patterns. They may be implicitly or explicitly dependent on the data, or lack any dependence on the data.

2.1   Data Independent Approaches

Voting methods that don't show any dependence on the data include methods such as the maximum, median, minimum, product and average votes [4,14,15]. The rank based methods, such as the borda count, are also independent of the

data. All such methods solely rely on the output of the base classifiers to produce
a final representative decision irrespective of the pattern being classified. In a
sense we can represent the confidence c_{ij}, of a classifier i in a given input pattern
x being a member in class y_j, $\forall j \in \Delta = \{1, 2, \cdots, K\}$ as a probability

$$c_{ij}(x) = P(y_j|x) \tag{1}$$

Then the data independent combining scheme will take the form

$$Q(x) = F_j(c_{ij}(x)) \tag{2}$$

Where Q is the final class assigned using the mapping F_j of the combining approach. In the case of the average vote, the function F_j would be a linear mapping, while, the product, maximum and majority votes would be represented
by a nonlinear mapping. Although such simple aggregation rules compete with
more complex aggregation schemes involving second-level training, they are susceptible to incorrect estimates of the confidence by the individual classifiers.
These confidences might be generated when using undertrained or overtrained
sub-optimal classifiers. Another key issues that pertain to the combining of such
classifiers, as well as other ensemble approaches, is the production of diverse
classifiers. Methods for creating or selecting classifiers for combining [6] depend
on the over-production of classifiers and applying diversity measures or selection
heuristics to choose which classifiers to use.

2.2   Data Dependent Approaches

Trained combining methods, in general, are data dependent [16]. This dependency can be either implicit or explicit. Implicit dependencies include methods
that train the combiner on the global performance of the data. The weighted
average [17,18], fuzzy integrals [19] and belief theory approaches [20] can be categorized as implicitly data dependent. In these approaches, the combiner is trained
on how the base classifiers perform collectively on a set of training data. Boosting [21] can also be categorized as implicitly data dependent since it depends
on clustering the data patterns into general clusters while training. Boosting,
however, is different in the sense that the dependence is inherent in the classifiers rather than in the combining method. Behaviour-Knowledge Space (BKS)
method [22] also clusters the data into a defined number of BKS units, and
in turn can also be considered implicitly data dependent. Modular approaches
and static classifier selection methods, such that certain classifiers are specified
for certain regions can be considered implicitly data dependent [7]. The predefined regions in which the classifiers are expected to excel are pre-defined during
training and do not dynamically change. Methods that post-process the output
of the base classifiers, or contain second-level training, while only considering the
desired final output are implicitly data dependent. Such methods also include
the stacked generalization approach [9], and hierarchical fusion [23,24]. Evolutionary algorithms [24,25] and Decision templates [26] have also been used to

determine the weights assigned to the different base classifiers, they in turn can be considered implicitly data dependent.

Dynamic Classifier Selection (DCS) [27], in which the choice of the base classifier is made during the classification phase, can be considered an explicitly data dependent approach. This is in contrast to static selection, in which the the input pattern is not considered when making the selection. In dynamic selection the "competence" of each classifier is estimated in the vicinity of the input pattern being classified. Woods et al. [28] used the DCS approach, in which the local accuracy is utilized to select the classifier of choice for a given pattern, while Giancinto and Roli [29] use a DCS approach based on multiple classifier behaviour (MCB). Both these approaches are explicitly data dependent. The mixture of experts [30], where the choice of the classifier is based on both its output and the input pattern being classified. Song et al. [31], use partial context maximum posterior (PCMP) decision rule, that includes contextual information about the pattern being classified. The feature-based approach [8] dynamically assigns weights to the individual classifier based on a given input pattern. Rather than making a selection, these weights are used to combine the output of the base classifiers in a non-linear mapping. The architecture learns these weights through a training phase and applied them to future patterns.

Implicitly Data Dependent Representation: Implicity dependent approaches can be represented by the following form

$$Q(x) = F_j(w_{ij}(c_{ij}(x)), c_{ij}(x)) \tag{3}$$

Where the weights, w_{ij}, assigned to any output c_{ij} depend on the output of the base classifiers. In the following we describe some of the key implicitly data dependent approaches in terms of the above representation.

– **Weighted Average:** Combining of the various classifiers is constructed by forming weighted sums of the classifier outputs. In this case, the combination weight w_{ij}, are obtained by minimizing the mean squared error of the correlation matrix. These weights need to be estimated from observed data. The function F_j, generally takes the form of the maximum operator across the various classes. Collinearity amongst the base classifiers can sometimes undermine the robustness of this approach.
– **Fuzzy Integral:** For a given input x, a fuzzy measure vector is calculated for each class. The measure is a combination of the the vectors associated with each classifier for a given class. The weights, w_{ij}, are generated by applying the fuzzy integral. The fuzzy measure that is most widely used is the Sugeno λ-fuzzy measure. The final output class is the one that maximizes the value of the fuzzy integral, hence, once again the function F_j is the maximum operator. Several researches have shown dramatic improvement using fuzzy integrals, but other data sets have shown it to perform poorly. It is safe to say that it is not a universal solution to combining classifiers.

– **Dempster Shafer Approach:** A belief in the final output class is generated based on the decisions of the individual base classifiers. For any given
output of the base classifiers, dependent on the input pattern, the degree
of belief in each class is generated to be the weight w_{ij}. F_j assigns, using
the maximum operator, the winning class to that which yields the largest
belief. This method has generally been reported to produce good results, but
involves more complex calculations compared to other approaches.
– **Boosting:** is a method of combining weak classifiers. Classifiers and training sets are obtained in a deterministic way. Boosting adaptively changes the
distribution of the training set based upon the performance of sequentially
constructed classifiers. Each classifier re-weights the training set, such that
the following classifier would preferably choose previously mis-classified patterns in its training set. The algorithm requires that each classifier performs
better than a random guess for it to be effective. In this case the weighting
function, w_{ij} and the combining function, F_j, are blended together into a
selection mechanism. The classifier expected to produce the suitable generalization for a given pattern is selected (In other words assigned a weight
$w_i = 1$, while all other classifiers are assigned a weight $w_m = 0, m \neq i$).
Boosting, generally requires large amounts of data to be effective. It also
can be paralyzed, when adding more classifiers rather than yield improved
performance, degrades the existing level of accuracy.
– **Behaviour-Knowledge Space (BKS):** The decisions generated by each
classifier are compared against a lookup table of all possible decision combinations. The class label most often encountered amongst the elements of
this table during training is assigned a weight $w_j = 1$, while all other classes
are assigned a weight $w_m = 0, m \neq j$. to the given pattern. The BKS is
prone to overtraining because it required large amounts of data to be properly composed. Generally, the BKS will perform well on the training data,
while performing poorly on the testing data.
– **Decision Templates (DT):** Similar to the BKS, the DT approach generates a template for given combination of classifier decision outputs. A similarity measure is used to compare the decision patterns of a certain given
input to the templates previously generated, hence assigning weights w_j for
every class. The DT are less likely to be overtrained than the BKS, but they
still rely on the presence of large training sets.
– **Stacked Generalization:** is an attempt to minimize the generalization error using the classifiers in higher layers to learn the type of errors made by
the classifiers immediately below (As seen in figure 1). From this perspective
stacked generalization can be seen as an extension to model selection methods such as cross validation, which uses a "winner takes all" strategy. The
single classifier with the lowest cross-validation error is selected. The idea behind stacked generalization is that there may be more intelligent ways to use
a set of classifiers. The role of the higher classifiers is to learn how previous
classifier have made mistakes, in which classes they agree or disagree, and
then use this knowledge for making predictions. The higher level classifier
can also be viewed as predicting the weights w_{ij}, while the combining func-

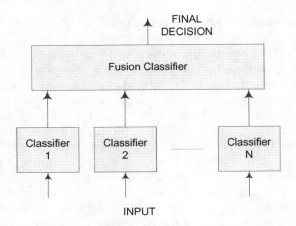

Fig. 1. Two-level stacked generalization architecture

tion, F_j, is the maximum operator. Again, the second-level and subsequent level training would be possible when large quantities of data be available. It is also prune to error due to unrealistic confidence by certain members of the base classifiers.

Explicitly Data Dependent Representation: In the case of either selection or combination explicitly dependent approaches can be defined as

$$Q(x) = F_j(w_{ij}(x), c_{ij}(x)). \tag{4}$$

Explaining some of the explicitly data-dependent approaches in terms of the above representation follows.

- **Dynamic Classifier Selection by Local Accuracy (DCS_LA):** estimates the accuracy of each classifier in local regions of the feature space. These regions are determined by k-NN approach using training data. If $k = 1$, then DCS_LA becomes equivalent to the BKS approach. The larger the value of k the more accurate an estimate that is generated for any given input pattern. However, the computational cost increases with the increased value of k. The classifier with the most patterns in the local region of the new pattern is selected. Therefore, the combination can be defined as $Q(x) = max_j(w_i(x) * c_{ij}(x))$, or the function F_j is the maximum operator, and the weights are assigned to the classifiers as the result of the clustering.
- **Dynamic Classifier Selection based on Multiple Classifier Behaviour (DCS_MCB):** tries to correct this dependence on the value of k. Determining the value of k is done dynamically depending on the degree of similarity the pattern considered is to neighbouring training patterns.

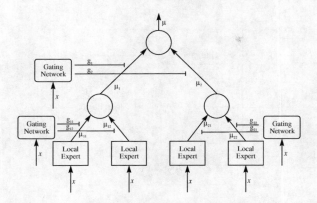

Fig. 2. Two-level hierarchical mixture of experts architecture

- **Hierarchical Mixture of Experts (HME):** is generally considered a
  modular approach (Figure 2). The various base classifiers are experts in
  local areas of the feature space, and classifier selection is done based on this
  pre-defined distribution. The misclassification of one classifier would immediately affect the overall performance of the approach.

The explicitly data dependent approaches presented above all perform classifier selection in local subspaces. The weights in these approaches demonstrate a
dependence on the input pattern, while the implicitly data dependent approaches
use weights that are dependent on the classifier output. In the following we will
discuss the feature based approach [8] which combines these two dependencies
together.

3   Feature Based Decision Aggregation Architecture

The feature based architecture [8], is a data dependent approach. It is a hierarchical architecture (Shown in Figure 3), that is composed of three different
modules. The classifier ensembles, the detector module and finally the aggregation module. In the following the various components of this architecture will
be introduced (We will also summarize the adaptive training algorithm of the
classifier ensembles in this section).

3.1   Classifier Ensembles

Each individual classifier, C_i, produces some output representing its interpretation of the input $y_i = f_i(x)$. We are interested in utilize sub-optimal classifiers in
the proposed architecture, to make the development overhead of such a system
worthwhile. The output of the classifiers are interpreted as a value and a confidence. These two values are used by the detectors and final aggregation schemes.
The members of the ensemble could be trained independently, or they can be
trained using the adaptive training algorithm proposed by Wanas et. al. [32].

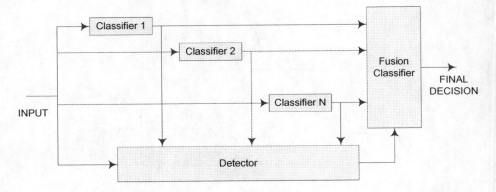

Fig. 3. Feature Based Architecture

3.2   Detector Module

The detectors uses the output of the ensemble of classifiers along with the input features to generate weights for the different classifiers. These weights reflect the degree of confidence in each classifier, this confidence is donated by D_i. The training of this module is performed on the training set after the individual classifiers are trained. These weights are then used in combining the output of the classifier ensemble.

3.3   The Aggregation Module

The aggregation procedure represents the fusion layer of all the different outputs to generate a more competent output. The aggregation procedure uses the detectors' output to guide the means of combining different classification results. The aggregation scheme can be divided into two phases: a learning phase and a decision making phase. The learning phase assigns a weight factor to each input to support each decision maker. This weighting factor represents a confidence in the output of each classifier. These confidences are then aggregated using standard classifier-combining methods.

Normally, each component is trained independently. This may lead to having each component optimized and achieve a high accuracy, while the final classification doesn't reflect this improvement. The presence of harmful collinearity or the correlation between the errors made by the component classifiers in an ensemble reduces the effectiveness of the ensemble itself [33]. The modules might also be over or under trained, and how these modules perform can only be determined through a process of testing the performance on a verification set. While the literature has suggested the use of overproduction of classifiers then performing a selection [29,34,35], based on the Evolving training algorithm suggested by Wanas et. al., adaptive training is performed. This algorithm, allows the ensemble to develop a diversity among themselves. Hence, reducing the correlation between the errors made by members of the ensemble. Similar to boosting, the algorithm allows re-training to focus on misclassified patterns. However, this re-training is performed on the classifier itself rather than adding more members to the ensemble as suggested in boosting. The detector and aggregation modules, in turn, have the re-training focused on feature sub-spaces with higher overall misclassifications. It also provides means to determine the duration for which the detector and aggregation modules should be trained. The algorithm is shown in Figure 4.

Let K be the number of classifiers in the ensemble, and M be the number of elements in the training set. Each classifier member of the ensemble is denoted by $C_i, 1 \leq i \leq K$, whereas the detector and the aggregation network are denoted by D,and A respectively. To avoid having the generalization ability of the classifier skewed by re-training, we maintain a ratio of correctly classified entries in the re-training set. This ratio is based on the pre-set modifier constant P. This modifier is normally between 10% to 45% and based on its own performance, is allowed to change for each classifier. This change is brought about by adding a factor δ that is calculated for each classifier. A real value constant Γ is assigned to be the threshold for minimum improvement in the performance of any component, CF. If the change is less than Γ, the training is terminated for this classifier. The algorithm is terminated when all the individual components do not require any further training.

The final classification output in the feature-based approach can be represented as

$$Q(x) = F_j(w_{ij}(x, c_{ij}), c_{ij}(x)). \tag{5}$$

where the weights w_{ij} are dependent on both the input pattern being classified and the individual confidence outputs of the classifiers. The detector provides a learning module for assigning these weights. The aggregation module is represented by F_j, where the combination of the weights w_{ij} and the confidence levels c_{ij} is performed. Based on this representation, the feature-based approach is a combination of both implicitly and explicitly data dependent approaches.

4   Results

In all the tests presented in this investigation, we compose an ensemble of five classifiers. Each classifier is a one-hidden layer backpropagation neural network with ten sigmoidal hidden units. These classifiers are trained using the error backpropagation algorithm. The training set is divided into five different parts. Each classifier in the ensemble is trained by using four parts of the training set, but a different part is omitted each time, which renders the different training sets partially disjointed. Each classifier is trained for 1000 epochs, and is tested on the verification set every 100 epochs. Next, the network instance that provides the best classification is saved.

The detector and aggregation modules are trained on the generated ensemble. Again, both modules are one-hidden layer backpropagation neural networks with ten sigmoidal hidden units. The classifiers are trained with the error backpropagation algorithm. The detector and aggregation modules are trained separately,

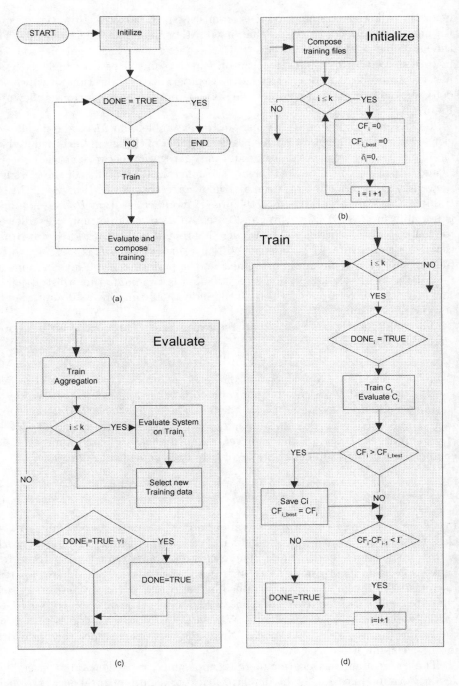

Fig. 4. Adaptive training algorithm, (a) Basic Algorithm which included (b) An Initialization Loop, (c) An Evaluation Algorithm, (d) A Training algorithm

Table 1. Error rates for the different data sets using various combining approaches

Data Set	20 Class	Clouds	Satimages
Single Net	13.82 ± 1.16	10.92 ± 0.08	14.06 ± 1.33
Oracle	5.42 ± 1.30	5.43 ± 0.11	5.48 ± 0.18
Data Independent Approaches			
Maximum	12.52 ± 1.53	11.20 ± 0.11	15.26 ± 0.47
Majority	11.76 ± 0.57	10.85 ± 0.05	14.03 ± 0.07
Average	11.75 ± 0.81	10.78 ± 0.03	13.79 ± 0.05
Borda	11.83 ± 0.70	10.85 ± 0.05	14.42 ± 0.12
Nash	11.72 ± 0.94	11.16 ± 0.14	16.75 ± 2.96
Implicitly Data Dependent Approaches			
Weighted Average	11.44 ± 0.64	10.81 ± 0.05	13.69 ± 0.06
Bayesian	11.40 ± 0.30	10.83 ± 0.04	14.05 ± 0.15
Fuzzy Integral	12.55 ± 1.62	11.17 ± 0.03	15.35 ± 0.49
Explicitly Data Dependent			
Feature-based	8.01 ± 0.19	10.06 ± 0.13	12.33 ± 0.14

and with the EVOL algorithm. For each set of ensembles, detector and aggregation modules are repeated six times. This experiment is conducted on two different sets of values for the learning rate and momentum (lr/m = 0.9/0.01 and 0.4/0.5). Then, the classification results are averaged across these different parameters and different runs. The algorithm uses the parameters $P = 0.35$ and $\Gamma = 0.1$. It may be noted that no parameter optimization is performed for the trained networks. The parameters of all the networks are maintained for all the classifiers that are trained. To reduce any external factors, the models are set up using the same platform, language, and implementation of the neural networks.

In this work, we use three different data sets to demonstrate the effectiveness of the feature-based architecture. These data sets are the Gaussian 20-Class problem [7], Clouds data, and Satimage database [36]. Table 1 compares average classification error of various combining approaches on the different data sets used.

We note that despite that the members of the ensemble generated by the adaptive algorithm demonstrate a deteriorated performance (compared to the single net), the combination approach yields improved results. This is due to the focused training achieved by the algorithm to improve the combined output rather than the individual classifier. The algorithm avoids the need for overproduction of classifiers to achieve a suitable level of diversity among the ensemble.

We can also note from the results that data dependent techniques generally perform better than data independent approaches. Although no clear winner can be found within these approaches that consistently outperforms other approaches. The feature based approach, on the other hand, produces results that are consistently higher than other approaches.

5   Conclusions

We have presented a categorization of the various combining methods based on their demonstration of data dependence. Simple techniques, which don't exhibit data dependence are vulnerable to incorrect confidence estimates. Static selection of classifiers in combining, or other approaches that are implicitly data dependent access the performance of each classifier on all of the feature-space or in comparison to one another. While this enhances the ability of the combining system to produce more reliable results, it doesn't take into account local superiority of certain classifiers. Such superiority enhances the performance of explicitly data dependent approaches. Most of the explicitly data dependent approaches focus on classifier selection methods, while the feature based approach presents a classifier combining approach. The feature based approach uses an Evolving training algorithm to enhance the diversity among the members of the ensemble, hence reducing harmful correlation among the classifiers.

Empirically, we find that in a direct comparison, the data dependent techniques perform better than data independent approaches. While the superiority of the explicitly data dependent approaches, namely the feature based approach, is also demonstrated showing at least 8% improvement over the single net performance.

References

1. J. Kittler, and F. Roli (Eds.), "Multiple classifier systems", First International Workshop, MCS2000, Cagliari, Italy, June 21-23, 2000, Proceedings, Vol. 1857 of Lecture Notes in Computer Science, Springer-Verlag, Berlin, 2000.
2. J. Kittler, and F. Roli (Eds.), "Multiple classifier systems", Second International Workshop, MCS2001, Cambridge, UK, July 2-4, 2001 Proceedings, Vol. 2096 of Lecture Notes in Computer Science, Springer-Verlag, Berlin, 2001.
3. F. Roli, and J. Kittler (Eds.), "Multiple classifier systems", Third International Workshop, MCS2002, Cagliari, Italy June 24-26, 2002, Proceedings, Vol. 2364 of Lecture Notes in Computer Science, Springer-Verlag, Berlin, 2002.
4. J. Kittler, M. Hatef, D. Robert, J. Matas, "On combining classifiers". IEEE Transactions on Pattern Analysis and Machine Intelligence, Vol. 20:3, pp. 226-239, 1998.
5. A. Sharakey, "Types of multinet systems", In: F. Roli, and J. Kittler (Eds.), "Multiple classifier systems", Third International Workshop, MCS2002, Cagliari, Italy June 24-26, 2002, Proceedings, Vol. 2364 of Lecture Notes in Computer Science, Springer-Verlag, Berlin, pp. 108-117, 2002.
6. A. Sharkey, "Multinet Systems", In: A. Sharkey (Ed.), "Combining Artificial Neural Nets", Springer-Verlag, Berlin, pp. 1-30, 1999.
7. G. Auda, and M. Kamel, "Modular neural network classifiers: A comparative study", Journal of Intelligent and Robotic Systems, Vol. 21, pp. 117-129, 1998.

8. N. Wanas, and M. Kamel, "Combining neural network ensembles", International Joint Conference on Neural Networks (IJCNN'01), Washington, D.C., Jul 15 - 19, pp. 2952-2957, 2001.

9. D. Wolpert, "Stacked generalization", Neural Networks, Vol. 5, pp. 241-259, 1992.

10. T. Ho, J. Hull, S. Srihari, "Decision combination in multiple classifier systems", IEEE Transactions on Pattern Analysis and Machine Intelligence, Vol. 16:1, pp. 66-75, 1994.

11. L. Kuncheva, "A theoritical study on six classifier fusion strategies", IEEE Transactions on Systems, Man and Cybernetics, Vol. 24:2, pp. 281-286, 2002.

12. A. Verikas, A. Lipnickas, K. Malmqvist, M. Bacauskiene, A. Gelzinis, "Soft combination of neural classifiers: A comparative study", Pattern Recognition Letters, Vol. 20, pp. 429-444, 1999.

13. R. Duin, and D. Tax, "Experiments with Classifier Combining Rules", In: J. Kittler, and F. Roli (Eds.), "Multiple classifier systems", First International Workshop, MCS2000, Cagliari, Italy, June 21-23, 2000, Proceedings, Vol. 1857 of Lecture Notes in Computer Science, Springer-Verlag, Berlin, pp. 16-29, 2000.

14. L. Alexandre, A. Campihlo, and M. Kamel, "On combining classifiers using sum and product rules", Pattern Recognition Letters, Vol. 22, pp. 1283-1289, 2001.

15. D. Tax, M. Breukelen, R. Duin, and J. Kittler, "Combining multiple classifiers by averaging or by mutliplying?", Pattern Recognition, Vol 33, pp. 1475-1485, 2000.

16. R. Duin, "The combining classifier: To train or not to train?", Proceedings of the 16th International Conference on Pattern Recognition (ICPR 2002), Quebec City, Canada, Vol 2, pp. 765-770, 2002.

17. S. Hashem, "Optimal linear combinations of neural networks", Neural Networks Vol. 10:4, pp. 599-614, 1997.

18. N. Ueda, "Optimal Linear Combination of neural networks for improving classification performance", Pattern Analysis and Machine Intelligence, Vol. 22, No. 2, pp. 207-215, 2000.

19. P. Gader, M. Mohamed, and J. Keller, "Fusion of handwritten word classifiers", Pattern Recognition Letters, Vol. 17, pp. 577-584, 1996.

20. L. Xu, A. Krzyzk, C. Suen, "Methods of combining multiple classifiers and their application to handwriting recognition", IEEE Transactions on Systems, Man and Cybernetics, Vol. 22:3, pp. 418-435, 1992.

21. Y. Freund, and R. Schapire, "Experiments with a new boosting algorithm", In Proceedings of the 13th International Conference on Machine Learning, Morgan Kaufmann, pp. 149-156, 1996.

22. Y. Huang, and C. Suen, "A method of combining multiple experts for recognition of unconstrained handwritten numerals", IEEE Transactions on Pattern Analysis and Machine Intelligence, Vol. 17:1, pp. 90-94, 1995.

23. S. Kumar, J. Ghosh, and M. Crawford, "Hierarchical fusion of multiple classifiers for Hyperspectral Data Analysis", Pattern Analysis and Applications, Vol. 5, pp. 210-220, 2002.

24. K. Sirlantzis, S. Hoque, and M. C. Fairhurst, "Trainable multiple classifier schemes for handwritten character recognition", In: F. Roli, J. Kittler (Eds.), "Multiple classifier systems", Third International Workshop, MCS2002, Cagliari, Italy June 24-26, 2002, Proceedings, Vol. 2364 of Lecture Notes in Computer Science, Springer-Verlag, Berlin, pp. 169-178, 2002.

25. L. Lam, and C. Suen, "Optimal combination of pattern classifiers", Pattern Recognition Letters, Vol. 16, pp. 945-954, 1995.

26. L. Kuncheva, J. Bezdek, and R. Duin, "Decsion templates for multiple classifier fusion: an experimental comparision", Pattern Recognition, Vol. 34, pp. 299-314, 2001.
27. L. Kuncheva, "Switching between selection and fusion in combining classifiers: An experiment", IEEE Transactions on Systems, Man and Cybernetics - Part B, Vol. 32:2, pp. 146-156, 2002.
28. K. Woods, W. Kegelmeyer, and K. Bowyer, "Combination of multiple classifiers using local accuracy estimates", Pattern Analysis and Machine Intelligence, Vol. 19, No. 4, pp. 405-410, 1997.
29. G. Giancinto, and F. Roli, "Dynamic classifier selection based on multiple classifier behaviour", Pattern Recognition, Vol. 34, pp. 1879-1881, 2001.
30. M. Jordon, and R. Jacobs, "Hierarchical mixtures of experts and the EM algorithm", Neural Computing Vol. 6:2, pp. 181-214, 1994.
31. X. Song, Y. AbuMostafa, J. Sill, H. Kasdan, and M. Pavel, "Robust image recognition by fusion of contextual information", Information Fusion, Vol. 3, pp. 277-287, 2002.
32. N. Wanas, L. Hodge, and M. Kamel, "Adaptive Training Algorithm for an Ensemble of Networks", International Joint Conference on Neural Networks (IJCNN'01), Washington, D.C., Jul 15 - 19, pp. 2590-2595, 2001.
33. S. Hashem, "Treating Harmful Collinearity in Neural Network Ensembles", In: A. Sharkey (Ed.), "Combing Artificial Neural Nets", Springer-Verlag, Berlin, pp. , 1999.
34. A. Sharkey, N. Sharkey, U. Gerecke, and G. Chandroth, "The test and select approach to ensemble combination", In: J. Kittler, and F. Roli (Eds.), "Multiple classifier systems", First International Workshop, MCS2000, Cagliari, Italy, June 21-23, 2000, Proceedings, Vol. 1857 of Lecture Notes in Computer Science, Springer-Verlag, Berlin, pp. 30-44, 2000.
35. Giorgio Giancinto, and Fabio Roli, "An approach to the automatic design of multiple classifier systems", Pattern Recognition Letters, Vol. 22, pp. 25-33, 2001
36. C. Blake, and C. Merz, "UCI Repository of machine learning databases [http://www.ics.uci.edu/~mlearn/MLRepository.html]", University of California, Irvine, Dept. of Information and Computer Sciences, 1998.

Boosting with Averaged Weight Vectors

Nikunj C. Oza

Computational Sciences Division
NASA Ames Research Center
Mail Stop 269-3
Moffett Field, CA 94035-1000, USA
oza@email.arc.nasa.gov

Abstract. AdaBoost [5] is a well-known ensemble learning algorithm
that constructs its constituent or *base* models in sequence. A key step
in AdaBoost is constructing a distribution over the training examples
to create each base model. This distribution, represented as a vector,
is constructed to be orthogonal to the vector of mistakes made by the
previous base model in the sequence [7]. The idea is to make the next
base model's errors uncorrelated with those of the previous model. Some
researchers have pointed out the intuition that it is probably better to
construct a distribution orthogonal to the mistake vectors of *all* the previous base models, but that this is not always possible [7]. We present an
algorithm that attempts to come as close as possible to this goal in an
efficient manner. We present experimental results demonstrating significant improvement over AdaBoost and the Totally Corrective boosting
algorithm [7], which also attempts to satisfy this goal.

1 Introduction

AdaBoost [5] is one of the most well-known and highest-performing ensemble
classifier learning algorithms [4]. It constructs a sequence of base models, where
each model is constructed based on the performance of the previous model on
the training set. In particular, AdaBoost calls the base model learning algorithm
with a training set weighted by a distribution[1]. After the base model is created,
it is tested on the training set to see how well it learned. We assume that the
base model learning algorithm is a weak learning algorithm [6]; that is, with
high probability, it produces a model whose probability of misclassifying an
example is less than 0.5 when that example is drawn from the same distribution
that generated the training set. The point is that such a model performs better
than random guessing[2]. The weights of the correctly classified examples and

---

[1] If the base model learning algorithm cannot take a weighted training set as input,
then one can create a sample with replacement from the original training set according to the distribution and call the algorithm with that sample.

[2] The version of AdaBoost that we use was designed for two-class classification problems. However, it is often used for a larger number of classes when the base model
learning algorithm is strong enough to have an error less than 0.5 in spite of the
larger number of classes.

T. Windeatt and F. Roli (Eds.): MCS 2003, LNCS 2709, pp. 15–24, 2003.
© Springer-Verlag Berlin Heidelberg 2003

misclassified examples are scaled down and up, respectively, so that the two groups' total weights are 0.5 each. The next base model is generated by calling the learning algorithm with this new weight distribution and the training set. The idea is that, because of the weak learning assumption, at least some of the previously misclassified examples will be correctly classified by the new base model. Previously misclassified examples are more likely to be classified correctly because of their higher weights, which focus more attention on them. Kivinen and Warmuth [7] have shown that AdaBoost scales the distribution with the goal of making the next base model's mistakes uncorrelated with those of the previous base model. It is well-known that ensembles need to have low correlation in their base models' errors in order to perform well [11].

Given this point, we would think, as was pointed out in [7], that AdaBoost would perform better if the next base model's mistakes were uncorrelated with those of all the previous base models instead of just the previous one. It is not always possible to construct a distribution consistent with this requirement. However, we can attempt to find a distribution that comes as close as possible to satisfying this requirement. Kivinen and Warmuth [7] devised the Totally Corrective algorithm (TCA), which attempts to do this. However, they do not present any empirical results. Also, they hypothesize that this algorithm will overfit and; therefore, not perform well. This paper presents a new algorithm, called AveBoost, which has the same goal as the TCA. In particular, AveBoost calculates the next base model's distribution by first calculating a distribution the same way as in AdaBoost, but then averaging it elementwise with those calculated for the previous base models. In this way, AveBoost takes all the previous base models into account in constructing the next model's distribution. In Section 2, we review AdaBoost and describe the TCA. In Section 3, we state the AveBoost algorithm and describe the sense in which our solution is the best one possible. In Section 4, we present an experimental comparison of AveBoost with AdaBoost and the TCA. Section 5 summarizes this paper and describes ongoing and future work.

2   AdaBoost and Totally Corrective Algorithm

Figure 1 shows AdaBoost's pseudocode. AdaBoost constructs a sequence of base models h_t for $t \in \{1, 2, \ldots, T\}$, where each one is constructed based on the performance of the previous base model on the training set. In particular, AdaBoost maintains a distribution over the m training examples. The distribution $\mathbf{d}_1$ used in creating the first base model gives equal weight to each example ($d_{1,i} = 1/m$ for all $i \in \{1, 2, \ldots, m\}$). AdaBoost now enters the loop, where the base model learning algorithm L_b is called with the training set and $\mathbf{d}_1$ [3]. The returned model h_1 is then tested on the training set to see how well it learned. Training examples misclassified by the current base model have their weights increased

---

[3] As mentioned earlier, if L_b cannot take a weighted training set as input, then we can give it a sample drawn with replacement from the original training set according to the distribution $\mathbf{d}$ induced by the weights.

AdaBoost($\{(x_1, y_1), \ldots, (x_m, y_m)\}, L_b, T$)
    Initialize $d_{1,i} = 1/m$ for all $i \in \{1, 2, \ldots, m\}$.
    For $t = 1, 2, \ldots, T$:
        $h_t = L_b(\{(x_1, y_1), \ldots, (x_m, y_m)\}, \mathbf{d_t})$.
        Calculate the error of h_t : $\epsilon_t = \sum_{i:h_t(x_i) \neq y_i} d_{t,i}$.
        If $\epsilon_t \geq 1/2$ then,
            set $T = t - 1$ and abort this loop.
        Calculate distribution $\mathbf{d}_{t+1}$:

$$d_{t+1,i} = d_{t,i} \times \begin{cases} \frac{1}{2(1-\epsilon_t)} & \text{if } h_t(x_i) = y_i \\ \frac{1}{2\epsilon_t} & \text{otherwise.} \end{cases}$$

Output the final hypothesis:
    $h_{fin}(x) = \text{argmax}_{y \in Y} \sum_{t:h_t(x)=y} log\frac{1-\epsilon_t}{\epsilon_t}$.

Fig. 1. AdaBoost algorithm: $\{(x_1, y_1), \ldots, (x_m, y_m)\}$ is the training set, L_b is the base model learning algorithm, and T is the maximum allowed number of base models

Totally Corrective AdaBoost($\{(x_1, y_1), \ldots, (x_m, y_m)\}, L_b, T$)
    Initialize $d_{1,i} = 1/m$ for all $i \in \{1, 2, \ldots, m\}$.
    For $t = 1, 2, \ldots, T$:
        $h_t = L_b(\{(x_1, y_1), \ldots, (x_m, y_m)\}, \mathbf{d_t})$.
        Calculate the mistake vector $\mathbf{u_t}$:

$$u_{t,i} = \begin{cases} 1 & \text{if } h_t(x_i) = y_i \\ -1 & \text{otherwise.} \end{cases}$$

    If $\mathbf{d_t} \cdot \mathbf{u_t} \leq 0$ then,
        set $T = t - 1$ and abort this loop.
    Calculate distribution $\mathbf{d_{t+1}}$:
        Initialize $\hat{\mathbf{d}}_1 = \mathbf{d_1}$.
        For $j = 1, 2, \ldots$:
            $q_j = \text{argmax}_{q_j \in \{1,2,\ldots,t\}} |\hat{\mathbf{d}}_\mathbf{j} \cdot \mathbf{u_{q_j}}|$.
            $\hat{\alpha}_j = \ln\left(\frac{1+\hat{\mathbf{d}}_\mathbf{j} \cdot \mathbf{u_{q_j}}}{1-\hat{\mathbf{d}}_\mathbf{j} \cdot \mathbf{u_{q_j}}}\right)$.
            For all $i \in \{1, 2, \ldots, m\}$,
                $\hat{d}_{j+1,i} = \frac{1}{\hat{Z}_j}\hat{d}_{j,i}exp(-\hat{\alpha}_j u_{q_j,i})$,
                where $\hat{Z}_j = \sum_{i=1}^m \hat{d}_{j,i}exp(-\hat{\alpha}_j u_{q_j,i})$.
    Output the final hypothesis:
    $h_{fin}(x) = \text{argmax}_{y \in Y} \sum_{t:h_t(x)=y} log\frac{1-\epsilon_t}{\epsilon_t}$.

Fig. 2. Totally Corrective Boosting algorithm: $\{(x_1, y_1), \ldots, (x_m, y_m)\}$ is the training set, L_b is the base model learning algorithm, and T is the maximum allowed number of base models

for the purpose of creating the next base model, while correctly-classified training examples have their weights decreased. More specifically, if h_t misclassifies the ith training example, then its new weight $d_{t+1,i}$ is set to be its old weight $d_{t,i}$ multiplied by $\frac{1}{2\epsilon_t}$, where ϵ_t is the sum of the weights of the examples that h_t misclassifies. AdaBoost assumes that L_b is a weak learner, i.e., $\epsilon_t < \frac{1}{2}$ with high probability. Under this assumption, $\frac{1}{2\epsilon_t} > 1$, so the ith example's weight increases $(d_{t+1,i} > d_{t,i})$. On the other hand, if h_t correctly classifies the ith example, then $d_{t+1,i}$ is set to $d_{t,i}$ multiplied by $\frac{1}{2(1-\epsilon_t)}$, which is less than one by the weak learning assumption; therefore, example i's weight is decreased. Note that $\mathbf{d}_{t+1}$ is already normalized:

$$\sum_{i=1}^m d_{t+1,i} = \frac{1}{2\epsilon_t} \sum_{i=1}^m d_{t,i} I(h_t(x_i) \neq y_i) + \frac{1}{2(1-\epsilon_t)} \sum_{i=1}^m d_{t,i} I(h_t(x_i) = y_i)$$

$$= \frac{1}{2\epsilon_t}\epsilon_t + \frac{1}{2(1-\epsilon_t)}(1-\epsilon_t) = 1.$$

Under distribution $\mathbf{d}_{t+1}$, the total weight of the examples misclassified by h_t and those correctly classified by h_t become 0.5 each. This is done so that, by the weak learning assumption, h_{t+1} will classify at least some of the previously misclassified examples correctly. As shown in [1], this weight update scheme is equivalent to the usual scheme [5] but is intuitively more clear. The loop continues, creating the T base models in the ensemble. The final ensemble returns, for a new example, the one class in the set of classes Y that gets the highest weighted vote from the base models.

Construct a vector $\mathbf{u}_t \in [-1,1]^m$ such that the ith element $u_{t,i} = 1$ if h_t classifies the ith training example correctly $(h_t(x_i) = y_i)$ and $u_{t,i} = -1$ otherwise. Kivinen and Warmuth [7] pointed out that AdaBoost finds $\mathbf{d}_{t+1}$ by minimizing $\Delta(\mathbf{d}_{t+1}, \mathbf{d}_t)$ subject to $\mathbf{d}_{t+1} \cdot \mathbf{u}_t = 0$, where $\Delta(a,b)$ is a distance measure such as relative entropy. That is, the new distribution is created to be orthogonal to the mistake vector of h_t, which can be intuitively described as wanting the new base model's mistakes to be uncorrelated with those of the previous model. This naturally leads to the question of whether one can improve upon AdaBoost by constructing $\mathbf{d}_{t+1}$ to be orthogonal to the mistake vectors of all the previous base models $h_1, h_2, \ldots, h_t$ (i.e., $\mathbf{d}_{t+1} \cdot \mathbf{u}_q = 0$ for all $q \in \{1, 2, \ldots, t\}$). However, there is no guarantee that a probability distribution $\mathbf{d}_{t+1}$ exists that satisfies all the constraints. Even if a solution exists, finding it appears to be a very difficult optimization problem [7]. The Totally Corrective Algorithm (figure 2) attempts to solve this problem using an iterative method. The initial parts of the algorithm are similar to AdaBoost: it uses the same $\mathbf{d}_1$ as AdaBoost in creating the first base model and the next statement checks that the base model error is less than 0.5. The difference is in the method of calculating the weight distribution for the next base model. The TCA starts with some initial distribution such as $\mathbf{d}_1$. It then repeatedly finds the $q_j \in \{1, 2, \ldots, t\}$ yielding the highest $|\hat{\mathbf{d}}_\mathbf{j} \cdot \mathbf{u}_{\mathbf{q}_\mathbf{j}}|$, and then projects the current distribution onto the hyperplane defined by $\hat{\mathbf{d}}_\mathbf{j} \cdot \mathbf{u}_{\mathbf{q}_\mathbf{j}} = 0$. This is similar to so-called row action optimization

---

AveBoost$(\{(x_1, y_1), \ldots, (x_m, y_m)\}, L_b, T)$
   Initialize $d_{1,i} = 1/m$ for all $i \in \{1, 2, \ldots, m\}$.
   For $t = 1, 2, \ldots, T$:
      $h_t = L_b(\{(x_1, y_1), \ldots, (x_m, y_m)\}, \mathbf{d}_t)$.
      Calculate the error of $h_t : \epsilon_t = \sum_{i:h_t(x_i) \neq y_i} d_{t,i}$.
      If $\epsilon_t \geq 1/2$ then,
         set $T = t - 1$ and abort this loop.
      Calculate orthogonal distribution:
         For $i = 1, 2, \ldots, m$:

$$c_{t,i} = d_{t,i} \times \begin{cases} \frac{1}{2(1-\epsilon_t)} & \text{if } h_t(x_i) = y_i \\ \frac{1}{2\epsilon_t} & \text{otherwise} \end{cases}$$

$$d_{t+1,i} = \frac{t d_{t,i} + c_{t,i}}{t + 1}$$

Output the final hypothesis:
   $h_{fin}(x) = \text{argmax}_{y \in Y} \sum_{t:h_t(x)=y} log \frac{1-\epsilon_t}{\epsilon_t}$.

Fig. 3. AveBoost algorithm: $\{(x_1, y_1), \ldots, (x_m, y_m)\}$ is the training set, L_b is the base model learning algorithm, and T is the maximum allowed number of base models

methods [3]. Kivinen and Warmuth show that, if there is a distribution that satisfies all the constraints, then at most $\frac{2 \ln m}{\gamma^2}$ iterations are needed so that $\max_{q_j \in \{1,2,\ldots,t\}} |\hat{\mathbf{d}}_\mathbf{j} \cdot \mathbf{u}_{\mathbf{q_j}}| \leq \gamma$ for any $\gamma > 0$. Of course, as mentioned earlier, we cannot generally assume that there is a distribution that satisfies all the constraints, in which case the bound is invalid. In fact, we are not even guaranteed to reduce $\max_{q_j \in \{1,2,\ldots,t\}} |\hat{\mathbf{d}}_\mathbf{j} \cdot \mathbf{u}_{\mathbf{q_j}}|$ at each iteration. To make the TCA usable for our experiments, we have added two stopping criteria not present in the original algorithm. Define $v_{t,j} = \max_{q_j \in \{1,2,\ldots,t\}} |\hat{\mathbf{d}}_\mathbf{j} \cdot \mathbf{u}_{\mathbf{q_j}}|$. The algorithm stops if either $|v_{t,j} - v_{t,j-1}| < 0.0001$ or both $j > m$ and $v_{t,j} > v_{t,j-1}$. The first constraint requires that the maximum dot product change by some minimum amount between consecutive iterations. The second constraint requires that, after iterating at least as many times as the number of training examples, the maximum dot product not increase. These are heuristic criteria devised based on our experiments with this algorithm.

3   AveBoost Algorithm

Figure 3 shows our new algorithm, AveBoost. Just as in AdaBoost, AveBoost initializes $d_{1,i} = 1/m$ for all $i \in \{1, 2, \ldots, m\}$. Then it goes inside the loop, where it calls the base model learning algorithm L_b with the training set and distribution $\mathbf{d}_1$ and calculates the error of the resulting base model h_1. It then calculates $\mathbf{c}_1$, which is the distribution that AdaBoost would use to construct the next base model. However, AveBoost averages this with $\mathbf{d}_1$ to get $\mathbf{d}_2$, and uses this $\mathbf{d}_2$ instead. Note that the $\mathbf{c}_t$'s for all $t \in \{1, 2, \ldots, T\}$ do not need to be normalized because they are calculated the same way as the $\mathbf{d}_t$'s in AdaBoost, which we showed to be distributions in Section 2. Showing that the $\mathbf{d}_t$'s in AveBoost are distributions is a trivial proof by induction. For the base case, $\mathbf{d}_1$ is constructed to be a distribution. For the inductive part, if $\mathbf{d}_t$ is a distribution, then $\mathbf{d}_{t+1}$ is a distribution because it is a convex combination of $\mathbf{d}_t$ and $\mathbf{c}_t$.

Returning to the algorithm, the loop continues for a total of T iterations. Then the base models are combined using the same weighted averaging used in AdaBoost. The vector $\mathbf{d}_{t+1}$ is a running average of $\mathbf{d}_1$ and the vectors $\mathbf{c_q}$ for $q \in \{1, 2, \ldots, t\}$, which are orthogonal to the mistake vectors of the previous t base models ($\mathbf{u_q}$ for $q \in \{1, 2, \ldots, t\}$), respectively. For ease of exposition, define $\mathbf{c}_0 \triangleq \mathbf{d}_1$ and $\mathbf{u}_0$ to be any vector in $[-1, 1]^m$ such that its elements sum to zero. Then we have $\mathbf{d}_{t+1} = \frac{1}{t+1} \sum_{q=0}^{t} \mathbf{c}_q$. This $\mathbf{d}_{t+1}$ has the least average Euclidian distance to the vectors $\mathbf{c}_q$ for $q \in \{0, 1, \ldots, t\}$. That is, $\mathbf{d}_{t+1}$ is the solution $\mathbf{d}$ that minimizes the least-squares error $\sum_{q=0}^{t} \sum_{i=1}^{m} (c_{q,i} - d_i)^2$. In this sense, AveBoost finds a solution that does the best job of balancing among the t constraints $\mathbf{c_q} \cdot \mathbf{u_q} = 0$ with much less computational cost than an optimization method such as that used in the TCA.

AveBoost can be seen as a relaxed version of AdaBoost. When training examples are noisy and therefore difficult to fit, AdaBoost is known to increase the weights on those examples to excess and overfit them [4] because many consecutive base models may not learn them properly. AveBoost tends to mitigate this overfitting by virtue of its averaging process. For this reason, we expect the range of training example weights to be narrower for AveBoost than AdaBoost. AveBoost's averaging process limits the range of training set distributions that are explored, which we expect will increase the average correlations among the base models. However, we expect their average accuracies to go up. We also hypothesize that AveBoost will tend to show greater advantage over AdaBoost for small numbers of base models. When AveBoost creates a large ensemble, the last few training set distributions cannot be too different from each other because they are prepared by averaging over many previous distributions.

4   Experimental Results

In this section, we compare AdaBoost, the TCA, and AveBoost on the nine UCI datasets [2] described in Table 1. We ran all three algorithms with three different values of T, which is the maximum number of base models that the algorithm is allowed to construct: 10, 50, and 100. Each result reported is the average over 50 results obtained by performing 10 runs of 5-fold cross-validation. Table 1 shows the sizes of the training and test sets for the cross-validation runs.

Table 2 shows how often AveBoost significantly outperformed, performed comparably with, and significantly underperformed AdaBoost and the TCA. For example, with 10 Naive Bayes base models, AveBoost significantly outper-

Table 1. The datasets used in the experiments

Data Set	Training Set	Test Set	Inputs	Classes
Promoters	84	22	57	2
Balance	500	125	4	3
Breast Cancer	559	140	9	2
German Credit	800	200	20	2
Car Evaluation	1382	346	6	4
Chess	2556	640	36	2
Mushroom	6499	1625	22	2
Nursery	10368	2592	8	5
Connect4	54045	13512	42	3

Table 2. Performance of AveBoost

Compared to	Base Model	10	50	100
AdaBoost	Naive Bayes	+6=1-2	+4=3-2	+4=2-3
Totally Corrective	Naive Bayes	+6=2-1	+6=2-1	+6=2-1
AdaBoost	Decision Trees	+2=7-0	+2=5-2	+2=5-2
AdaBoost	Decision Stumps	+2=6-1	+2=4-3	+2=3-4

formed[4] AdaBoost on six of the datasets, performed comparably on one dataset, and performed significantly worse on two, which is written as "+6=1-2." Figure 4 compares the error rates of AdaBoost and AveBoost with Naive Bayes base models. In all the plots presented in this paper, each point marks the error rates of two algorithms when run with the number of base models indicated in the legend and a particular dataset. The diagonal line in the plots contain points at which the two algorithms have equal error. Therefore, points below/above the line correspond to the error of the algorithm indicated on the y-axis being less than/greater than the error of the algorithm indicated on the x-axis, respectively. The scales for each plot were adapted for the error rates shown; therefore, they are different across the plots. We can see that, for Naive Bayes base models, AveBoost performs much better than AdaBoost overall. Figure 5 shows that AveBoost performs substantially better than the TCA. We examined the runs of the TCA in more detail and often found the overfitting that Kivinen and Warmuth thought would happen. Due to this poor performance, we did not continue experimenting with the TCA for the rest of this paper.

We compare AdaBoost and AveBoost using decision tree and decision stump base models in figures 6 and 7, respectively. With decision trees, AveBoost performs somewhat better than AdaBoost. With decision stumps, the differences in error rates vary much more, with AveBoost sometimes performing worse than AdaBoost.

We now analyze the performances of AdaBoost and AveBoost in more depth. Due to space limitations, we discuss our results with only Naive Bayes base mod-

---

[4] We use a t-test with $\alpha = 0.05$ to compare all the classifiers in this paper.

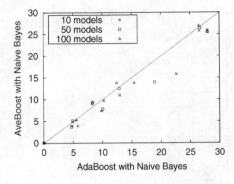

Fig. 4. Test set error rates of AdaBoost vs. AveBoost (Naive Bayes)

Fig. 5. Test set error rates of Totally Corrective Boosting vs. AveBoost (Naive Bayes)

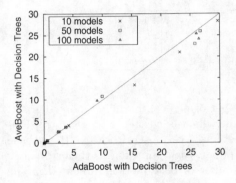

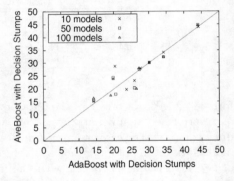

Fig. 6. Test set error rates of AdaBoost vs. AveBoost (Decision Trees)

Fig. 7. Test set error rates of AdaBoost vs. AveBoost (Decision Stumps)

els and for only two datasets: Promoters and Breast Cancer. We chose these two because the performances of AveBoost relative to AdaBoost are very different for these two datasets. On Promoters, AveBoost significantly outperformed AdaBoost, while on Breast Cancer, they performed comparably for 10 and 100 base models and AveBoost performed worse for 50 base models. Table 3 gives the results of our comparison. The top half of the table gives the Promoters dataset results while the bottom half gives the Breast Cancer results. For each dataset, the first row states the maximum allowed number of base models (this is T in Figures 1-3). The second row gives the average number of base models actually constructed over the 50 runs (recall that each algorithm has a stopping criterion that can result in fewer base models than what the user selects). AveBoost uses much fewer base models than AdaBoost on the Promoters dataset, but we found no correlation between number of base models and performance. The next two rows state the average ensemble performances on the training and test sets. Next are the average correlations of the outputs of all pairs of base models on

Table 3. Detailed comparison of AveBoost and AdaBoost on Promoters and Breast Cancer

PROMOTERS	AdaBoost NB			AveBoost NB		
Max. Base Models	10	50	100	10	50	100
Avg. Base Models	10	50	100	9.9	43.32	72.22
Ens. Train Perf.	0.9993	1.0	1.0	0.9998	1.0	1.0
Ens. Test Perf.	0.7736	0.8109	0.8455	0.8418	0.8600	0.8618
Avg. Corr. Train	0.3319	0.2901	0.2813	0.6229	0.5511	0.4277
Avg. Corr. Test	0.1877	0.1422	0.1395	0.4541	0.5159	0.5245
Base Train Perf.	0.7878	0.7597	0.7555	0.8917	0.9052	0.9085
Base Test Perf.	0.6514	0.6204	0.6210	0.7490	0.7613	0.7640
Min. Example Wt.	5.85e-05	3.40e-08	7.67e-10	0.0046	0.0024	0.0019
Max. Example Wt.	0.1748	0.2528	0.2821	0.0644	0.0670	0.0671
Sdev. Example Wt.	0.0177	0.0212	0.0217	0.0089	0.0098	0.0100

BREAST CANCER	AdaBoost NB			AveBoost NB		
Max. Base Models	10	50	100	10	50	100
Avg. Base Models	10	50	99.52	10	48.46	93.48
Ens. Train Perf.	0.9973	0.9998	1.0	0.9892	0.9985	0.9991
Ens. Test Perf.	0.9509	0.9506	0.9445	0.9509	0.9483	0.9470
Avg. Corr. Train	0.6409	0.4955	0.4638	0.9146	0.8688	0.7864
Avg. Corr. Test	0.6338	0.4960	0.4650	0.9210	0.9033	0.8958
Base Train Perf.	0.8918	0.8465	0.8340	0.9723	0.9727	0.9715
Base Test Perf.	0.8639	0.8209	0.8091	0.9429	0.9351	0.9324
Min. Example Wt.	7.06e-06	8.66e-15	4.96e-24	6.62e-04	3.25e-04	2.40e-04
Max. Example wt.	0.0934	0.1413	0.1643	0.0360	0.0434	0.0446
Sdev. Example Wt.	0.0073	0.0087	0.091	0.0039	0.0053	0.0056

the training and test sets. As expected, the correlations are higher for AveBoost than AdaBoost. However, the average training and test accuracies of the base models are also higher, as shown by the next two rows for each dataset. We then calculated, for each training example, the minimum and maximum weights ever assigned to it, and the standard deviation of all the weights assigned to it. The next three rows give the average, over all the training examples, of these minima, maxima, and standard deviations. As anticipated, the ranges of the weights for AveBoost are much lower than for AdaBoost.

5   Conclusions

We presented AveBoost, a boosting algorithm that trains each base model using a training example weight vector that is based on the performances of all the previous base models rather than just the previous one. We discussed the theoretical motivation for this algorithm and demonstrated empirical results that are superior overall to AdaBoost and the TCA that has the same goal as AveBoost.

We are currently analyzing AveBoost theoretically. The algorithmic stability-based framework [9] intuitively seems the most promising because of AveBoost's averaging process. We plan to empirically analyze the algorithms presented here for all the datasets in the style of Table 3 for a longer version of this paper. We also plan to devise synthetic datasets with various levels of noise to observe if AveBoost is more robust to noise than AdaBoost as we have hypothesized. Additionally, it has been pointed out [8,10] that ensembles work best when they are somewhat anti-correlated. We attempted to exploit this by implementing several boosting algorithms that, at each iteration, change the base model weights so that the correctly classified examples' weights add up to slightly less than 0.5. This scheme occasionally performed better and occasionally performed worse than AdaBoost. Depending on the available running time, it may be possible to create classifiers using several of these weight adjustment schemes and use the ones that look most promising for the dataset under consideration.

References

1. Eric Bauer and Ron Kohavi. An empirical comparison of voting classification algorithms: Bagging, boosting, and variants. *Machine Learning*, 36:105–139, Sep. 1999.
2. C. Blake, E. Keogh, and C.J. Merz. UCI repository of machine learning databases, 1999. (URL: http://www.ics.uci.edu/~mlearn/MLRepository.html).
3. Y. Censor and A. Lent. An iterative row-action method for interval convex programming. *Journal of Optimization Theory and Applications*, 34(3):321–353, 1981.
4. Thomas G. Dietterich. An experimental comparison of three methods for constructing ensembles of decision trees: Bagging, boosting, and randomization. *Machine Learning*, 40:139–158, Aug. 2000.
5. Y. Freund and R. Schapire. Experiments with a new boosting algorithm. In *Proceedings of the Thirteenth International Conference on Machine Learning*, pages 148–156, Bari, Italy, 1996. Morgan Kaufmann.
6. Michael J. Kearns and Umesh V. Vazirani. *Introduction to Computational Learning Theory*. MIT Press, Cambridge, MA, 1994.
7. Jyrki Kivinen and Manfred K. Warmuth. Boosting as entropy projection. In *Proceedings of the Twelfth Annual Conference on Computational Learning Theory*, pages 134–144, 1999.
8. A. Krogh and J. Vedelsby. Neural network ensembles, cross validation and active learning. In G. Tesauro, D. S. Touretzky, and T. K. Leen, editors, *Advances in Neural Information Processing Systems-7*, pages 231–238. M.I.T. Press, 1995.
9. Samuel Kutin and Partha Niyogi. The interaction of stability and weakness in adaboost. Technical Report TR-2001-30, University of Chicago, October 2001.
10. Nikunj C. Oza. *Online Ensemble Learning*. PhD thesis, The University of California, Berkeley, CA, Dec 2001.
11. K. Tumer and J. Ghosh. Analysis of decision boundaries in linearly combined neural classifiers. *Pattern Recognition*, 29(2):341–348, February 1996.

Error Bounds for Aggressive and Conservative AdaBoost

Ludmila I. Kuncheva

School of Informatics, University of Wales, Bangor
Bangor, Gwynedd, LL57 1UT, UK
`l.i.kuncheva@bangor.ac.uk`

Abstract. Three AdaBoost variants are distinguished based on the strategies applied to update the weights for each new ensemble member. The classic AdaBoost due to Freund and Schapire only decreases the weights of the correctly classified objects and is conservative in this sense. All the weights are then updated through a normalization step. Other AdaBoost variants in the literature update all the weights before renormalizing (aggressive variant). Alternatively we may increase only the weights of misclassified objects and then renormalize (the second conservative variant). The three variants have different bounds on their training errors. This could indicate different generalization performances. The bounds are derived here following the proof by Freund and Schapire for the classical AdaBoost for multiple classes (AdaBoost.M1), and compared against each other. The aggressive variant and the less popular of the two conservative variants have lower error bounds than the classical AdaBoost. Also, whereas the coefficients β_i in the classical AdaBoost are found as the unique solution of a minimization problem on the bound, the aggressive and the second conservative variants have monotone increasing functions of β_i ($0 \le \beta_i \le 1$) as their bounds, giving infinitely many choices of β_i.

1   Introduction

AdaBoost is an algorithm for designing classifier ensembles based on maintaining and manipulating a distribution of weights on the training examples. These weights are updated at each iteration to form a new training sample on which a new ensemble member is constructed.

Looking at the variety of implementations and interpretations, it seems that AdaBoost is rather a concept than a single algorithm. For example, a subject of debate has been the resampling versus reweighing when the distribution of weights has to be applied in order to derive the next ensemble member. Not only has the question not been resolved yet but sometimes it is impossible to tell from the text of a study which of the two methods has been implemented.

In this paper we are concerned with another "technicality": the way of updating the coefficients at each step. This detail is not always mentioned in the AdaBoost studies although as we show later, it makes a difference at least to the theoretical bounds of the algorithm.

T. Windeatt and F. Roli (Eds.): MCS 2003, LNCS 2709, pp. 25–34, 2003.
© Springer-Verlag Berlin Heidelberg 2003

Table 1. Three teaching strategies and the respective change in the weights w before the renormalization step

Strategy	Name	w – correct	w – wrong
Reward - Punishment	Aggressive	Smaller	Larger
Reward - No-action	Conservative.1	Smaller	The same
No-action - Punishment	Conservative.2	The same	Larger

There are three general teaching strategies shown in Table 1, which we, humans, experience since an early age. In the case of a successful outcome of an experiment, we can either be rewarded or no action be taken. In the case of an unsuccessful outcome, the possibilities are no-action or punishment. Obviously, if no action is taken in both cases, nothing will be learned from the experience. Thus there are three possible combinations which we associate with the three AdaBoost variants.

Error bounds on the training error have been derived in [3] for the Conservative.1 version. Following this proof, here we prove error bounds on the training error for the Aggressive and Conservaitve.2 version.

The rest of the paper is organized as follows. A general AdaBoost algorithm and the three variants are presented in Section 2. Section 3 contains the derivation of the bounds on the training error. A comparison is given in Section 4.

2   AdaBoost Variants

The generic algorithm of AdaBoost is shown in Figure 1.

Many versions of the above algorithm live under the same name in the literature on machine learning and pattern recognition. We distinguish between the following three (see Table 1)

$$
\begin{array}{lll}
\text{Aggressive AdaBoost } [2,4,5] & \xi(l_k^j) & = 1 - 2l_k^j; \\
\text{Conservative.1 AdaBoost } [1,3] & \xi(l_k^j) & = 1 - l_k^j; \\
\text{Conservative.2 AdaBoost} & \xi(l_k^j) & = -l_k^j.
\end{array}
\tag{5}
$$

The algorithm in Figure 1 differs slightly from AdaBoost.M1 [3] in that we do not perform the normalization of the weights as a separate step. This is reflected in the proofs in the next section.

3   Upper Bounds of Aggressive, Conservative.1 and Conservative.2 AdaBoost

Freund and Schapire prove an upper bound on the training error of AdaBoost [3] first for the case of two classes and (Conservative.1, $\xi(l_k^j) = 1 - l_k^j$). We will prove

---

ADABOOST

Training phase

1. Given is a data set $\mathbf{Z} = \{\mathbf{z}_1, \ldots, \mathbf{z}_N\}$.
Initialize the parameters
  · $\mathbf{w}^1 = [w_1, \ldots, w_N]$, the weights, $w_j^1 \in [0, 1]$, $\sum_{j=1}^{N} w_j^1 = 1$.
  $\left(\text{Usually } w_j^1 = \frac{1}{N} \right)$.
  · $\mathcal{D} = \emptyset$, the ensemble of classifiers.
  · L, the number of classifiers to train.
2. For $k = 1, \ldots, L$
  · Take a sample S_k from $\mathbf{Z}$ using distribution $\mathbf{w}^k$.
  · Build a classifier D_k using S_k as the training set.
  · Calculate the weighted error of D_k by

$$\epsilon_k = \sum_{j=1}^{N} w_j^k l_k^j, \tag{1}$$

  $\left(l_k^j = 1 \text{ if } D_k \text{ misclassifies } \mathbf{z}_j \text{ and } l_k^j = 0, \text{ otherwise.} \right)$.
  · If $\epsilon_k = 0$ or $\epsilon_k \geq 0.5$, the weights w_j^k are reinitialized to $\frac{1}{N}$.
  · Calculate

$$\beta_k = \frac{\epsilon_k}{1 - \epsilon_k}, \quad \text{where} \quad \epsilon_k \in (0, 0.5), \tag{2}$$

  · Update the individual weights

$$w_j^{k+1} = \frac{w_j^k \beta_k^{\xi(l_k^j)}}{\sum_{i=1}^{N} w_i^k \beta_k^{\xi(l_k^i)}}, \quad j = 1, \ldots, N. \tag{3}$$

  where $\xi(l_k^j)$ is a function which specifies which of the Boosting variants we use.
3. Return $\mathcal{D}$ and $\beta_1, \ldots, \beta_L$.

Classification phase

4. Calculate the support for class ω_t by

$$\mu_t(\mathbf{x}) = \sum_{D_k(\mathbf{x}) = \omega_t} \ln\left(\frac{1}{\beta_k}\right). \tag{4}$$

5. The class with the maximal support is chosen as the label for $\mathbf{x}$.

Fig. 1. A generic description of the Boosting algorithm for classifier ensemble design

the bound for c classes straight away and derive from it the bounds for c classes for the Aggressive version and the Conservative.2 version.

The following Lemma is needed within the proof.

Lemma. Let $a \geq 0$ and $r \in [0,1]$. Then

$$a^r \leq 1 - (1-a)r. \tag{6}$$

Proof. Take a^r to be a function of r for a fixed $a \geq 0$. The second derivative

$$\frac{\partial^2 (a^r)}{\partial r^2} = a^r (\ln a)^2, \tag{7}$$

is always nonnegative, therefore a^r is a convex function. The righthand side of inequality (6) represents a point on the line segment through points $(0,1)$ and $(1,a)$ on the curve a^r, therefore (6) holds for any $r \in [0,1]$. ∎

Theorem 1. (Conservative.1) $\boxed{\xi(l_k^j) = 1 - l_k^j}$ Let ϵ be the ensemble training error and let ϵ_i, $i = 1, \ldots, L$ be the weighted training errors of the classifiers in $\mathcal{D}$, as in (1). Then

$$\epsilon < 2^L \prod_{i=1}^{L} \sqrt{\epsilon_i(1 - \epsilon_i)}. \tag{8}$$

Proof. After the initialization, the weights are updated to

$$w_j^2 = \frac{w_j^1 \beta_1^{(1-l_j^1)}}{\sum_{k=1}^{N} w_k^1 \beta_1^{(1-l_k^1)}} \tag{9}$$

Denote the normalizing coefficient at step i by

$$C_i = \sum_{k=1}^{N} w_k^i \beta_i^{(1-l_k^i)} \tag{10}$$

The general formula for the weights is

$$w_j^{t+1} = w_j^1 \prod_{i=1}^{t} \frac{\beta_i^{(1-l_j^i)}}{C_i}. \tag{11}$$

Denote by $\mathbf{Z}^{(-)}$ the subset of elements of the training set $\mathbf{Z}$ which are misclassified by the ensemble. The ensemble error, weighted by the initial data weights w_j^1 is

$$\epsilon = \sum_{\mathbf{z}_j \in \mathbf{Z}^{(-)}} w_j^1. \tag{12}$$

(If we assign equal initial weights of $\frac{1}{N}$ to the objects, ϵ is the proportion of misclassifications on $\mathbf{Z}$ made by the ensemble.)

Since at each step, the sum of the weights in our algorithm equals one,

$$1 = \sum_{j=1}^{N} w_j^{L+1} \geq \sum_{\mathbf{z}_j \in \mathbf{Z}^{(-)}} w_j^{L+1} = \sum_{\mathbf{z}_j \in \mathbf{Z}^{(-)}} w_j^1 \prod_{i=1}^{L} \frac{\beta_i^{(1-l_j^i)}}{C_i}. \tag{13}$$

For the ensemble to commit an error in labeling of some $\mathbf{z}_j$, the sum of weighted votes for the wrong class label in (4) must be higher than any other score, including that of the right class label. Let us split the set of L classifiers into three subsets according to their outputs for a particular $\mathbf{z}_j \in \mathbf{Z}$

$\mathcal{D}^w \subset \mathcal{D}$, the set of classifiers whose output is the winning (wrong) label;
$\mathcal{D}^+ \subset \mathcal{D}$, the set of classifiers whose output is the true label;
$\mathcal{D}^- \subset \mathcal{D}$, the set of classifiers whose output is another (wrong) label.

The support for the winning class is

$$\sum_{D_i \in \mathcal{D}^w} \ln\left(\frac{1}{\beta_i}\right) \geq \sum_{D_i \in \mathcal{D}^+} \ln\left(\frac{1}{\beta_i}\right) \tag{14}$$

Add on both sides $\sum_{D_i \in \mathcal{D}^w}(.) + \sum_{D_i \in \mathcal{D}^-}(.)$ to get

$$2\sum_{D_i \in \mathcal{D}^w} \ln\left(\frac{1}{\beta_i}\right) + \sum_{D_i \in \mathcal{D}^-} \ln\left(\frac{1}{\beta_i}\right) \geq \sum_{i=1}^{L} \ln\left(\frac{1}{\beta_i}\right) \tag{15}$$

Then add $\sum_{D_i \in \mathcal{D}^-}(.)$ on the left side of the inequality. For the inequality to hold, the added quantity should be positive. To guarantee this, we require that all the terms in the summation are nonnegative, i.e., $\ln\left(\frac{1}{\beta_i}\right) \geq 0$, which is equivalent to $\beta_i \leq 1$.

Then the lefthand side of (15) is twice the sum of all weights for the wrong classes, i.e.,

$$2\sum_{i=1}^{L} l_j^i \ln\left(\frac{1}{\beta_i}\right) \geq \sum_{i=1}^{L} \ln\left(\frac{1}{\beta_i}\right), \tag{16}$$

$$\sum_{i=1}^{L} \ln(\beta_i)^{-l_j^i} \geq \sum_{i=1}^{L} \ln(\beta_i)^{-\frac{1}{2}} \tag{17}$$

$$\prod_{i=1}^{L} \beta_i^{(1-l_j^i)} \geq \prod_{i=1}^{L} \beta_i^{\frac{1}{2}}. \tag{18}$$

Taking (13), (18) and (12) together,

$$1 \geq \sum_{\mathbf{z}_j \in \mathbf{Z}^{(-)}} w_j^1 \prod_{i=1}^{L} \frac{\beta_i^{(1-l_j^i)}}{C_i} \tag{19}$$

$$\geq \left(\sum_{\mathbf{z}_j \in \mathbf{Z}^{(-)}} w_j^1\right) \prod_{i=1}^{L} \frac{\beta_i^{\frac{1}{2}}}{C_i} = \epsilon \cdot \prod_{i=1}^{L} \frac{\beta_i^{\frac{1}{2}}}{C_i}. \tag{20}$$

Solving for ϵ,

$$\epsilon \leq \prod_{i=1}^{L} \frac{C_i}{\beta_i^{\frac{1}{2}}}. \tag{21}$$

From the Lemma,

$$C_i = \sum_{k=1}^{N} w_k^i \beta_i^{(1-l_k^i)} \leq \sum_{k=1}^{N} w_k^i \left(1 - (1-\beta_i)(1-l_k^i)\right) \tag{22}$$

$$= \sum_{k=1}^{N} w_k^i \left(\beta_i + l_k^i - \beta_i l_k^i\right) \tag{23}$$

$$= \beta_i \sum_{k=1}^{N} w_k^i + \sum_{k=1}^{N} w_k^i l_k^i - \beta_i \sum_{k=1}^{N} w_k^i l_k^i \tag{24}$$

$$= \beta_i + \epsilon_i - \beta_i \epsilon_i = 1 - (1-\beta_i)(1-\epsilon_i). \tag{25}$$

Combining (21) and (25)

$$\epsilon \leq \prod_{i=1}^{L} \frac{1 - (1-\beta_i)(1-\epsilon_i)}{\sqrt{\beta_i}}. \tag{26}$$

The next step is to find β_i's that minimize the bound of ϵ in (26). Setting the first derivative to zero and solving for β_i, we obtain

$$\beta_i = \frac{\epsilon_i}{1 - \epsilon_i}. \tag{27}$$

The second derivative of the righthand side at $\beta_i = \frac{\epsilon_i}{1-\epsilon_i}$ is positive, therefore the solution for β_i is a minimum of the bound. Substituting (27) into (26) leads to the thesis of the theorem

$$\epsilon < 2^L \prod_{i=1}^{L} \sqrt{\epsilon_i(1-\epsilon_i)}. \tag{28}$$

∎

To illustrate the upper bound we generated a random sequence of individual errors $\epsilon_k \in (0, 0.5)$. for $L = 50$ classifiers. Plotted in Figure 2 is the average from 1000 such runs with one standard deviation on each side.

Note that the ensemble error is practically 0 at $L = 30$. Hoping that the generalization error will follow a corresponding pattern, in many experimental studies AdaBoost is run up to $L = 50$ classifiers.

To gurarantee $\beta_i < 1$, AdaBoost re-initializes the weights to $\frac{1}{N}$ if $\epsilon_i \geq 0.5$. Freund and Schapire argue that having an error greater than half is too strict a demand for a multiple-class weak learner D_i. Even though the concern about the restriction being too severe is intuitive, we have to stress that ϵ_k is not the conventional error of classifier D_k. It is its weighted error. This means that if we applied D_k on a data set drawn from the problem in question, its (conventional) error could be quite different from ϵ_k, both ways: larger or smaller.

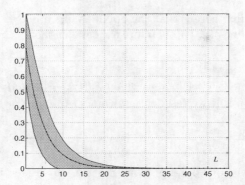

Fig. 2. A simulated upper bound of the training error of AdaBoost as a function of the number of classifier L and random individual errors in $(0, 0.5)$. The average of 1000 simulation runs is plotted with one standard deviation on each side

Theorem 2. (Aggressive) $\boxed{\xi(l_k^j) = 1 - 2l_k^j}$ Let ϵ be the ensemble training error and let ϵ_i, $i = 1, \ldots, L$ be the weighted training errors of the classifiers in $\mathcal{D}$ as in (1). Then

$$\epsilon \leq \prod_{i=1}^{L} 1 - (1 - \beta_i)(1 - 2\epsilon_i). \tag{29}$$

Proof. The proof matches that of Theorem 1 up to inequality (16). The only difference is that $\beta_i^{(1-l_j^i)}$ is replaced by $\beta_i^{(1-2l_j^i)}$. Adding $\sum_i \ln(\beta_i)$ on both sides of (16), and taking the exponent, we arrive at

$$\prod_{i=1}^{L} \beta_i^{(1-2l_j^i)} \geq 1. \tag{30}$$

From (20),

$$1 \geq \sum_{\mathbf{z}_j \in \mathbf{Z}^{(-)}} w_j^1 \prod_{i=1}^{L} \frac{\beta_i^{(1-2l_j^i)}}{C_i} \geq \left(\sum_{\mathbf{z}_j \in \mathbf{Z}^{(-)}} w_j^1 \right) \prod_{i=1}^{L} \frac{1}{C_i} = \epsilon \cdot \prod_{i=1}^{L} \frac{1}{C_i}. \tag{31}$$

Solving for ϵ,

$$\epsilon \leq \prod_{i=1}^{L} C_i. \tag{32}$$

Using the Lemma

$$\epsilon \leq \prod_{i=1}^{L} 1 - (1 - \beta_i)(1 - 2\epsilon_i). \tag{33}$$

∎

The curious finding here is that the bound is linear on β_i. The first derivative is positive if we assume $\epsilon < 0.5$, therefore the smaller the β_i, the better the bound. We can solve

$$1 - (1 - \beta_i)(1 - 2\epsilon_i) \quad \le \quad 2\sqrt{\epsilon_i(1 - \epsilon_i)} \tag{34}$$

for β_i to find out for which values the Aggressive bound is better than the Conservative.1 bound. If we restrict ϵ_i within $(0, 0.2)$ and use

$$\beta_i = \frac{\sqrt{\epsilon_i(1 - \epsilon_i)} - 2\epsilon_i}{1 - 2\epsilon_i}, \quad \text{(The restrcition guarantees } \beta > 0\text{)} \tag{35}$$

then we reduce the error bound of Conservative.1 by a factor of 2^L, i.e.,

$$\epsilon \quad < \quad \prod_{i=1}^{L} \sqrt{\epsilon_i(1 - \epsilon_i)}. \tag{36}$$

Theorem 3. (Conservative.2) $\boxed{\xi(l_k^j) = -l_k^j}$ Let ϵ be the ensemble training error and let ϵ_i, $i = 1, \ldots, L$ be the weighted training errors of the classifiers in $\mathcal{D}$ as in (1). Then for

$$\beta_i = \frac{\epsilon_i(1 - \epsilon_i)^2}{1 + \epsilon_i}, \tag{37}$$

$$\epsilon \quad < \quad \prod_{i=1}^{L} \sqrt{\epsilon_i(1 - \epsilon_i)}. \tag{38}$$

Proof. The proof follows these of Theorems 1 and 2 with $\beta_i^{(-l_j^i)}$ instead of $\beta_i^{(1-l_j^i)}$.

From (20) and (17),

$$1 \ge \sum_{\mathbf{z}_j \in \mathbf{Z}^{(-)}} w_j^1 \prod_{i=1}^{L} \frac{\beta_i^{(-l_j^i)}}{C_i} \ge \left(\sum_{\mathbf{z}_j \in \mathbf{Z}^{(-)}} w_j^1 \right) \prod_{i=1}^{L} \frac{\beta_i^{-\frac{1}{2}}}{C_i} = \epsilon \cdot \prod_{i=1}^{L} \frac{1}{C_i\sqrt{\beta_i}}. \tag{39}$$

Solving for ϵ,

$$\epsilon \quad \le \quad \prod_{i=1}^{L} C_i\sqrt{\beta_i}. \tag{40}$$

Using the Lemma

$$\epsilon \quad \le \quad \prod_{i=1}^{L} (1 + \epsilon_i - \beta_i\epsilon_i)\sqrt{\beta_i} \tag{41}$$

The bound has a maximum for $\beta_i = \frac{1 + \epsilon_i}{3\epsilon_i}$ but it is outside the range of interest (the interval $[0, 1]$) for β_i. If we pick β_i as in (37) and substitute into (41), the upper bound (38) is derived. As with the aggressive AdaBoost, this bound is better by a factor of 2^L and can be made arbitrarily better. ∎

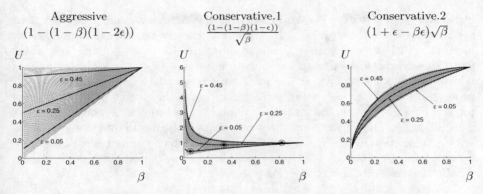

Fig. 3. Upper bounds on the training error for AdaBoost (one term in the product) for the three variants

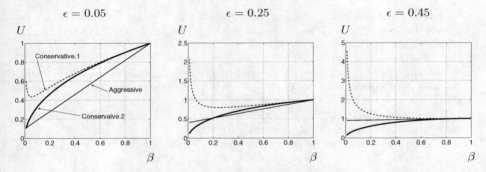

Fig. 4. Upper bounds on the training error for AdaBoost (one term in the product) for the three variants

4 Comparison

Figure 3 illustrates the bounds for the three AdaBoost versions as functions of $\beta \in [0,1]$. One term of the product is considered for each plot, so $\beta_i = \beta$, $\epsilon_i = \epsilon$, and U is the contribution of that term to the total error bound. ϵ was varied from 0 to 0.5. A gray line was plotted for each value of ϵ as a function $U(\beta)$. Do not be mislead by the scale: the most popular version (Conservative.1) has the worst bound. For reference we also plotted solid black lines for $\epsilon = \{0.05, 0.25, 0.45\}$. For the Conservative.1 version, the minima of U found by $\beta = \frac{\epsilon}{1-\epsilon}$ for the three values of ϵ are plotted as dots and encircled.

Figure 4 shows $U(\beta)$ for three values of ϵ. The bounds of the three AdaBoost versions are given on the same plot. The plots show that the conventional Conservative.1 version has the largest bound of the three AdaBoost variants.

5 Conclusions

Three AdaBoost variants are detailed and the error bounds on the training errors are derived (following the proof by Freund and Schapire [3] of the version called here Conservative.1). We found that the Aggressive and Conservative.2 versions have smaller error bounds. More importantly, whereas the bound $U(\beta)$ for Conservative.1 version has a unique minimum for $\beta = \frac{\epsilon}{1-\epsilon}$, the Aggressive and Conservative.2 AdaBoost are monotone for $\beta \in [0,1]$. This gives infinitely many choices for better error bounds than Conservative.1. Theorems 2 and 3 prove the bounds and give suggestions for β. An important point to be emphasized here is that the training error bounds do not guarantee anything about generalization. The results from this study that can be useful in real experiments are the suggestion for β (equations (35) and (37)) which guarantee training error bounds lower by a factor of 2^L than the training error bound of the conventional AdaBoost version (Conservative.1).

References

1. E. Bauer and R. Kohavi. An empirical comparison of voting classification algorithms: Bagging, boosting, and variants. *Machine Learning*, 36:105–142, 1999.
2. R.O. Duda, P.E. Hart, and D.G. Stork. *Pattern Classification*. John Wiley & Sons, NY, second edition, 2001.
3. Y. Freund and R.E. Schapire. A decision-theoretic generalization of on-line learning and an application to boosting. *Journal of Computer and System Sciences*, 55(1):119–139, 1997.
4. R.E. Schapire. Theoretical views of boosting. In *Proc. 4th European Conference on Computational Learning Theory*, pages 1–10, 1999.
5. R.E. Schapire. The boosting approach to machine learning. An overview. In *MSRI Workshop on Nonlinear Estimation and Classification*, 2002.

An Empirical Comparison
of Three Boosting Algorithms on Real Data Sets
with Artificial Class Noise

Ross A. McDonald[1], David J. Hand[1], and Idris A. Eckley[2]

[1] Imperial College London
[2] Shell Research Ltd.

Abstract. Boosting algorithms are a means of building a strong ensemble classifier by aggregating a sequence of weak hypotheses. In this paper we consider three of the best-known boosting algorithms: Adaboost [9], Logitboost [11] and Brownboost [8]. These algorithms are adaptive, and work by maintaining a set of example and class weights which focus the attention of a base learner on the examples that are hardest to classify. We conduct an empirical study to compare the performance of these algorithms, measured in terms of overall test error rate, on five real data sets. The tests consist of a series of cross-validatory samples. At each validation, we set aside one third of the data chosen at random as a test set, and fit the boosting algorithm to the remaining two thirds, using binary stumps as a base learner. At each stage we record the final training and test error rates, and report the average errors within a 95% confidence interval. We then add artificial class noise to our data sets by randomly reassigning 20% of class labels, and repeat our experiment. We find that Brownboost and Logitboost prove less likely than Adaboost to overfit in this circumstance.

1 Introduction

Boosting algorithms have their origins in the analysis of the theory surrounding the PAC (Probably Approximately Correct) learning model first introduced by Valiant in 1984 [23].

In the PAC framework, a data set is said to be strongly (PAC) learnable if there exists a classifier that can achieve an arbitrarily low error rate for all instances in the set. A weak learnable set requires only that the algorithm marginally outperform random guessing in terms of overall error rate. Kearns and Valiant [14] later proposed that these two definitions of learnability might be equivalent, and that this might be proven if it were shown to be possible to transform a weak learner into an arbitrarily strong one.

Schapire published the first hypothesis boosting algorithm in 1990 [20]. The more robust Boost-by-Majority (BBM) algorithm [7] was introduced by Freund at around the same time. The essential property of any boosting algorithm is that it is possible to derive an upper bound on the final training error rate. Both these precursor algorithms defined this upper bound in terms of γ, which is an

T. Windeatt and F. Roli (Eds.): MCS 2003, LNCS 2709, pp. 35–44, 2003.

amount by which the weak learner is guaranteed to outperform random guessing (so that in the two-class case, the weak learner would have to be guaranteed to yield an error rate below $\frac{1}{2} - \gamma$).

In practice it is usually unreasonable to assume that a base learning algorithm can always outperform a fixed error rate, and indeed the definition of a weak learner only requires that it should outperform random guessing by an arbitrarily small amount.

In 1995 Freund and Schapire published an adaptive algorithm known as Adaboost [9], which makes no prior assumptions about the base learner and has been the focus of much subsequent research. Adaboost is short for **Ada**ptive **Boost**ing, and the algorithm is characterised by the adaptive way that it generates and combines weak hypotheses. A monotonically decreasing upper bound on the training error can be derived, based on the performance of the individual component hypotheses. Thus if the base learner can consistently outperform random guessing, and we iterate long enough, we can eventually achieve any arbitrarily small error rate. It is also possible to derive an approximate upper bound for the the error rate of the fitted aggregate hypothesis when presented with new data.

It was subsequently observed [11] that Adaboost is in effect approximating a stagewise additive logistic regression model by optimising an exponential criterion. This leads us to new variants of Adaboost that fit additive models directly. One such variant is Logitboost, which uses the Newton-like steps to optimise the loss criterion.

In general terms, it has been observed that boosting algorithms do not tend to overfit within the number of iterations for which they are likely to be run. They are, however, particularly susceptible to class noise (where we take this to mean that a proportion of class labels have been redefined at random - but note that many authors use an alternative definition). Since the examples hardest to classify are very likely to be these noisy data, weak hypotheses induced at later iterations when such examples dominate will tend to be given undue influence in the final combined hypothesis, leading to a poor generalisation performance. In his empirical comparison of methods for constructing ensembles of decision trees [5], Dietterich concluded that 'the performance of Adaboost can be destroyed by classification noise'.

Brownboost [8], introduced by Freund and based on his Boost-by-Majority algorithm, may help to address this problem. It is derived by considering what happens to the BBM algorithm if the example reweighting is assumed to happen in continuous time. This leads us to an adaptive algorithm that resembles Adaboost, but which incorporates an extra parameter (the time parameter) that roughly corresponds to the proportion of noise in the training data. Because the algorithm knows in advance for how long it is to be run, it will not attempt to fit examples that are unlikely to be learnable in the remaining time. These are likely to be the noisy examples, so given a good estimate of the time parameter Brownboost is capable of avoiding overfitting. It can be shown [8] that Adaboost is a special case of Brownboost in the limit as the time parameter is allowed to tend to infinity.

In this paper, we conduct a series of empirical tests on four real data sets, using implementations of the Adaboost, Logitboost and Brownboost algorithms. We report our results in terms of overall test error rate. We then randomly reassign one in five class labels in each of the datasets and rerun the tests.

In Sections 2, 3 and 4 of this paper, we briefly describe each of the three boosting algorithms in turn. In setting out the Adaboost and Brownboost algorithms, we adopt notation that is consistent with the work of Freund and Schapire. The multi-class Logitboost algorithm is quoted from Friedman [11]. In Section 5, we describe our empirical study in detail, and report our findings. Finally, in Section 6 we summarise our conclusions.

2 Adaboost

Adaboost was the first adaptive boosting algorithm, and has received a good deal of attention since being introduced by Freund and Schapire in [9].

Our multi-class version of the algorithm uses the Hamming decoding and Error-Correcting Output Codes (ECOC) method of Allwein et al. (see [2] for a full description of this). The algorithm that we use is equivalent to the Adaboost.MH algorithm described in [22], and is an analogue of our own multi-class extension to the Brownboost algorithm [16].

Adaboost works by fitting a base learner to the training data using a vector or matrix of weights. These are then updated by increasing the relative weight assigned to examples that are misclassified at the current round. This forces the learner to focus on the examples that it finds harder to classify. After T iterations the output hypotheses are combined using a series of probabilistic estimates based on their training accuracy.

The Adaboost algorithm may be characterised by the way in which the hypothesis weights α are selected, and by the example weight update step. At iteration i, if γ_i is the gain of the weak learner over random guessing, then the hypothesis weight is chosen so that

$$\alpha_i = \frac{1}{2}\ln\left(\frac{1+\gamma_i}{1-\gamma_i}\right).$$

The weight update at step i multiplies the weights by an exponential function of the confidence of the prediction times the true label value, scaled by $-\alpha_i$.

In our multi-class adaptation of the algorithm, we maintain a separate weight for every example and class label. When calling our base learner, we take account of the possibility that this will either fit a binary (two-class) model, or a model that returns separate independent predictions for each of the k class labels. In the latter case, we assume that our coding matrix is the $k \times k$ matrix with 1 in all diagonal entries, and -1 everywhere else. We assume that hypotheses generated by base learners output confidence-rated predictions that are real values in the range $[-1, 1]$.

Adaboost Algorithm (Multi-Class Version)

Inputs:
ECOC Matrix: The $k \times \ell$ coding matrix $\mathbf{M}$.
Training Set: A set of m labelled examples: $T = (x_n, y_n), n = 1, ..., m$ where $x_n \in \mathbb{R}^d$ and $y_n \in \{y_1, y_2, ..., y_k\}$. Each y_n is associated via the matrix $\mathbf{M}$ with a set of ℓ binary labels $\{\lambda_1^n, ..., \lambda_\ell^n\}$, where $\lambda_j^n \in \{-1, 1\}$, $j = 1, ..., \ell$.
Weights: An $m \times \ell$ vector of initial weights, say, $W_{1,j}(x_n, y_n) = \frac{1}{m\ell}$, $n = 1, ..., m$, $j = 1, ..., \ell$
WeakLearn – A weak learning algorithm.

Do for $i = 1, 2, ..., T$

1.   **Binary base learner:** Call **Weaklearn** ℓ times $j = 1, ..., \ell$, each time passing it the weight distribution defined by normalizing $W_{i,j}(x_n, y_n)$ for fixed j, and the training data set alongside the binary labels defined by column j of the matrix $\mathbf{M}$.
     Multi-class base learner: Call **Weaklearn**, passing it the training data and the full set of weights.

     Receive from **Weaklearn** a set of ℓ hypotheses, $h_{i,j}(x)$, which have some advantage over random guessing

     $$\frac{\sum_{n=1}^m \sum_{j=1}^\ell W_{i,j}(x_n, y_n)(h_{i,j}(x_n)\lambda_j^n)}{\sum_{n=1}^m \sum_{j=1}^\ell W_{i,j}(x_n, y_n)} = \gamma_i > 0, \quad n = 1, ..., m, \quad j = 1, ..., \ell.$$

2.   Select $\alpha_i = \frac{1}{2}\ln\left(\frac{1+\gamma_i}{1-\gamma_i}\right)$.
3.   Weight update: $W_{i+1,j}(x_n, y_n) = \frac{W_{i,j}(x_n, y_n)\exp(-\alpha_i \ell_j^n h_{i,j}(x_n))}{\sum_{n=1}^m \sum_{j=1}^\ell W_{i,j}(x_n, y_n)}$.

Output Final hypotheses: $p_j(x) = \text{sign}\left(\sum_{i=1}^N \alpha_i h_{i,j}(x)\right)$, $j = 1, ..., \ell$.

Fig. 1. A multi-class Adaboost algorithm

3   Logitboost

The Logitboost algorithm [11] is based on the observation that Adaboost is in essence fitting an additive logistic regression model to the training data. An additive model is an approximation to a function $F(x)$ of the form

$$F(x) = \sum_{m=1}^M c_m f_m(x)$$

where the c_m are constants to be determined and the f_m are basis functions.

If we assume that $F(x)$ is the mapping that we seek to fit as our strong aggregate hypothesis, and the $f(x)$ are our weak hypotheses, then it can be shown that the two-class Adaboost algorithm is fitting such a model by minimising the criterion

$$J(F) = E(e^{-yF(x)})$$

where y is the true class label in $\{-1, 1\}$. Logitboost minimises this criterion by using Newton-like steps to fit an additive logistic regression model to directly optimise the binomial log-likelihood

$$-\log(1 + e^{-2yF(x)}).$$

This multi-class version of the algorithm is quoted from [11].

Logitboost Algorithm (Multi-Class Version)

1. Start with weights $w_{i,j} = 1/N, \quad i = 1, ..., N, \quad j = 1, ..., J, \quad F_j(x) = 0$ and $p_j(x) = 1/J \quad \forall j$.

2. Repeat for $m = 1, 2, ..., M$:

    (a) Repeat for $j = 1, ..., J$:
        i. Compute working responses and weights for the jth class

$$z_{i,j} = \frac{y_{i,j}^* - p_j(x_i)}{p_j(x_i)(1 - p_j(x_i))}$$

$$w_{i,j} = p_j(x_i)(1 - p_j(x_i))$$

        ii. Fit the function $f_{mj}(x)$ by a weighted least-squares regression of z_{ij} to x_i with weights w_{ij}.

    (b) Set $f_{mj}(x) \leftarrow \frac{J-1}{J}(f_{mj}(x) - \frac{1}{J}\sum_{k=1}^{J} f_{mk}(x))$, and $F_j(x) \leftarrow F_j(x) + f_{mj}(x)$.

    (c) Set $p_j(x) = \frac{e^{F_j(x)}}{\sum_{k=1}^{J} e^{F_k(x)}}$, enforcing the condition $\sum_{k=1}^{J} F_k(x) = 0$.

3. Output the classifier $\text{argmax}_j F_j(x)$.

Fig. 2. The multi-class Logitboost Algorithm, quoted from [11]

4 Brownboost

Brownboost is a continuous-time adaptive version of the Boost-by-Majority algorithm. Here we quote our own multi-class extension to this algorithm [16].

The derivation of the algorithm is beyond the scope of this paper, but we briefly summarise some of its key points.

The 'total time' parameter, c, sets the total amount of time for which the algorithm is set to run. At each iteration a quantity t is subtracted from this, and the algorithm terminates when the remaining time s reaches 0.

For every example (x_n, y_n) and class j, the algorithm maintains a margin. These are all initially set to 0, and at iteration i they are updated to:

$$r_{i+1,j}(x_n, y_n) = r_{i,j}(x_n, y_n) + \alpha_i h_{i,j}(x_n)\lambda_j^n$$

where λ_j^n is the label related to the example for class j by the ECOC matrix.

The hypothesis weights α_i are derived by solving a differential equation, and the weight updates are a function of these and the margin.

We can relate the parameter c to the final training error ϵ of the strong hypothesis via

$$\epsilon = 1 - \text{erf}(\sqrt{c}) \tag{4.1}$$

where 'erf' is the error function. Thus we can select c to guarantee any desired final error.

Brownboost Algorithm (Multi-Class Version)

Inputs:
ECOC Matrix: The $k \times \ell$ coding matrix **M**.
Training Set: A set of m labelled examples: $T = (x_n, y_n), n = 1, ..., m$ where $x_n \in \mathbb{R}^d$ and $y_n \in \{y_1, y_2, ..., y_k\}$. Each y_n is associated via the matrix **M** with a set of ℓ binary labels $\{\lambda_1^n, ..., \lambda_\ell^n\}$, where $\lambda_j^n \in \{-1, 1\}, j = 1, ..., \ell$.
WeakLearn – A weak learning algorithm.
c – a positive real valued parameter.
$\nu > 0$ – a small constant used to avoid degenerate cases.

Data Structures:
prediction value: With each example we associate a set of real valued margins. The margin of example (x_n, y_n) for label λ_j^n on iteration i is denoted $r_{i,j}(x_n, y_n)$. The initial value of all margins is zero: $r_{1,j}(x_n, y_n) = 0, n = 1, ..., m, j = 1, ..., \ell$.

Initialize 'remaining time' $s_1 = c$.
Do for $i = 1, 2, ...$

1. Associate with each example and label a positive weight
$$W_{i,j}(x_n, y_n) = e^{-(r_{i,j}(x_n,y_n)+s_i)^2/c}, n = 1, ..., m, j = 1, ..., \ell,$$

2. **Binary base learner:** Call **Weaklearn** ℓ times $j = 1, ..., \ell$, each time passing it the weight distribution defined by normalizing $W_{i,j}(x_n, y_n)$ for fixed j, and the training data set alongside the binary labels defined by column j of the matrix **M**.
    Multi-class base learner: Call **Weaklearn**, passing it the training data and the full set of weights.

    Receive from **Weaklearn** a set of ℓ hypotheses $h_{i,j}(x)$ which have some advantage over random guessing
    $$\frac{\sum_{n=1}^m \sum_{j=1}^\ell W_{i,j}(x_n,y_n)(h_{i,j}(x_n)\lambda_j^n)}{\sum_{n=1}^m \sum_{j=1}^\ell W_{i,j}(x_n,y_n)} = \gamma_i > 0.$$

3. Let γ, α and **t** be real valued
    variables that obey the following differential equation:
    $$\frac{d\mathbf{t}}{d\alpha} = \gamma = \frac{\sum_{n=1}^m \sum_{j=1}^\ell \exp(-\frac{1}{c}(r_{i,j}(x_n,y_n)+\alpha h_{i,j}(x_n)\lambda_j^n + s_i - \mathbf{t})^2)h_{i,j}(x_n)\lambda_j^n}{\sum_{n=1}^n \sum_{j=1}^\ell \exp(-\frac{1}{c}(r_{i,j}(x_n,y_n)+\alpha h_{i,j}(x_n)\lambda_j^n + s_i - \mathbf{t})^2)}.$$

    where $r_{i,j}(x_n, y_n)$, $h_{i,j}(x_n)$ and s_i are constants in this context.
    Given the boundary conditions $\mathbf{t} = 0, \alpha = 0$ solve the set of equations to find $t_i = \mathbf{t}^* > 0$ and $\alpha_i = \alpha^*$ such that either $\gamma^* \leq \nu$ or $\mathbf{t}^* = s_i$.

4. Margin update: $r_{i+1,j}(x_n, y_n) = r_{i,j}(x_n, y_n) + \alpha_i h_{i,j}(x_n)\lambda_j^n$.

5. Update 'remaining time' $s_{i+1} = s_i - t_i$.

Until $s_{i+1} \leq 0$
Output Final hypotheses: $p_j(x) = \mathrm{erf}\left(\frac{\sum_{i=1}^N \alpha_i h_{i,j}(x)}{\sqrt{c}}\right), j = 1, ..., \ell$.

Fig. 3. A multi-class Brownboost algorithm based on [8]

5   The Experiments

We conducted a series of tests using the four data sets summarised in Table 1. All of these data sets, with the exception of Credit were taken from the UCI Machine Learning Repository [1] and are available online.

Table 1. Summary table for the data sets used in experiments

Data Set	Entries	Attributes	Classes	Class Distribution
Wisconsin	699	9	2	241,458
Credit	500	–	2	–
KRKP	500	36	2	276,224
Wine	178	13	3	59,71,48
Balance	625	4	3	288,49,288

The Credit data set is a credit scoring data set of the type commonly found in commercial banking. Details of these data have been omitted from Table 1 for commercial reasons.

Wisconsin is the well-known diagnostic data set for breast cancer compiled by Dr William H. Wolberg, University of Wisconsin Hospitals [15].

King-Rook vs King-Pawn (KRKP) is a two-class data set based on chess endgames.

The Wine data, based on a chemical analysis of Italian wines, and Balance data, which records the results of a psychological experiment, are three-class data sets which have been included to test the multi-class versions of the algorithms.

In order to ensure algorithmic convergence in the time available, the Credit and KRKP data sets were each curtailed to 500 examples. Indicator variables were substituted for categorical variables where these occurred (see [12], Section 9.7 for more details).

We constructed a noisy version of each data set by assigning a randomly chosen, incorrect class label to 20% of training examples.

We implemented Adaboost, Logitboost and Brownboost in Matlab, using a purpose–written binary stump algorithm as our base learner.

Each experiment consisted of 100 trials. At each trial, one third of the data examples were selected at random and set aside as a test set. The remaining two thirds of examples were used to train the algorithm. We recorded the final error rates of the output hypothesis on both the training and test data.

We trained Adaboost and Logitboost on the original data to give us a benchmark for our comparison (recall that Adaboost is equivalent to Brownboost when the final training error is set to 0).

We then trained all three algorithms on the noisy data.

In all trials Adaboost was allowed to run until its training error matched the expected training error rate of that data set, or for a maximum of 100 iterations. We used the one-against-all approach, so our coding matrix was the $k \times k$ matrix whose diagonal entries are all 1, with all other entries -1.

Logitboost was also allowed to run until its training error matched the expected error rate, or up to a maximum of 100 iterations. We avoided numerical instabilities in this algorithm using the prescriptions in [11].

Table 2. Error rates for Adaboost and Logitboost on the unmodified data sets, 95% confidence intervals, 0% artificial class noise

0% Artificial Class Noise				
	Adaboost		Logitboost	
Data Set	Training Error	Test Error	Training Error	Test Error
Wisconsin	0.034 ± 0.002	0.048 ± 0.003	0.020 ± 0.001	0.040 ± 0.002
Credit	0.078 ± 0.002	0.105 ± 0.005	0.084 ± 0.002	0.085 ± 0.003
KRKP	0.030 ± 0.002	0.051 ± 0.003	0.039 ± 0.002	0.049 ± 0.003
Wine	0.000 ± 0.000	0.039 ± 0.005	0.000 ± 0.000	0.053 ± 0.006
Balance	0.076 ± 0.002	0.185 ± 0.005	0.089 ± 0.002	0.106 ± 0.004

Table 3. Error rates for Adaboost, Logitboost and Brownboost on the data sets with 20% artificial class noise, 95% confidence intervals

20% Artificial Class Noise						
	Adaboost		Logitboost		Brownboost	
Data Set	Training Error	Test Error	Training Error	Test Error	Training Error	Test Error
Wisconsin	0.216 ± 0.003	0.238 ± 0.005	0.206 ± 0.002	0.231 ± 0.004	0.188 ± 0.001	0.230 ± 0.004
Credit	0.239 ± 0.003	0.316 ± 0.010	0.241 ± 0.002	0.259 ± 0.006	0.177 ± 0.002	0.289 ± 0.005
KRKP	0.216 ± 0.004	0.269 ± 0.005	0.212 ± 0.003	0.240 ± 0.007	0.182 ± 0.001	0.243 ± 0.004
Wine	0.186 ± 0.002	0.279 ± 0.011	0.189 ± 0.001	0.255 ± 0.010	0.165 ± 0.003	0.248 ± 0.010
Balance	0.214 ± 0.003	0.337 ± 0.006	0.204 ± 0.002	0.235 ± 0.006	0.158 ± 0.002	0.280 ± 0.006

For Brownboost, we calculated the appropriate values for c using equation 4.1.

The training and test loss and error rates for each trial are recorded for a 95% confidence interval in Tables 2 and 3.

6   Discussion of Results and Conclusions

It appears that Logitboost was able to outperform Adaboost in terms of test error rate on all the unmodified data sets, despite achieving a higher training error rate on three of the five (and the same training error rate of zero on the wine data set, which is much smaller than the others). We speculate that since in implementation Logitboost imposes an upper limit on the magnitude of weight updates, since large updates can lead to numerical instabilities, it may be more resistant to overfitting. This is similar to the thinking behind the Madaboost (Modified Adaboost) algorithm of Domingo and Watanabe [6].

Broadly speaking, our results bear out claims that Adaboost is especially susceptible to class noise, while providing strong evidence that Brownboost is particularly robust in such situations. We were very surprised that Logitboost compares so favourably with Brownboost, clearly outperforming it on the credit and balance data sets, and appearing to do so on the KRKP data set (although the confidence intervals here overlap, as with the Wisconsin data). This may simply be due to the fact that Logitboost always terminated with a higher training error than Brownboost (since training loss does not quite equate to training error, Brownboost tends to overshoot the target error rate of 0.2). But it may be that Logitboost is itself especially robust to this kind of noise.

It is immediately evident from the test error rates in Tables 2 and 3 that the introduction of class noise to real data seriously impairs the generalisation performance of Adaboost. This would appear to tally with the observations made by Dietterich in [5].

When implementing Brownboost, we were able to calculate the value of c directly given our prior knowledge. Of course, in a real situation we would be very unlikely to know the level of class noise in advance. It remains to be seen how difficult it would prove to estimate c in practice.

Acknowledgements

RAM was supported in this work by Shell Research Ltd. and research grant number 0130322X from the Engineering and Physical Sciences Research Council.

References

1. *UCI Machine Learning Repository.*
   http://www.ics.uci.edu/~mlearn/MLRepository.html.
2. E. L. Allwein, R. E. Schapire, and Y. Singer. Reducing multiclass to binary: A unifying approach for margin classifiers. *Journal of Machine Learning Research*, 1:113 – 141, 2000.
3. E. Bauer and R. Kohavi. An empirical comparison of voting classification algorithms: Bagging, boosting and variants. *Machine Learning*, 36:105 – 142, 1999.
4. L. Breiman, J. H. Friedman, R. A. Olshen, and C. J. Stone. *Classification and Regression Trees*. Wadsworth, U.S., 1984.
5. T. G. Dietterich. An experimental comparison of three methods for constructing ensembles of decision trees: Bagging, boosting, and randomization. *AI Magazine*, 18:97 – 136, 1997.
6. C. Domingo and O. Watanabe. Madaboost: A modification of adaboost. In *Thirteenth Annual Conference on Computational Learning Theory*, 2000.
7. Y. Freund. Boosting a weak learning algorithm by majority. *Information and Computation*, 121, 1995.
8. Y. Freund. An adaptive version of the boost by majority algorithm. *Machine Learning 43*, 3:293 – 318, 2001.
9. Y. Freund and R. E. Schapire. A decision-theoretic generalization of on-line learning and an application to boosting. In *Second European Conference on Computational Learning Theory*, 1995.
10. Y. Freund and R. E. Schapire. A short introduction to boosting. *Journal of Japanese Society for Artificial Intelligence*, 14:771 – 780, 1999.
11. J. H. Friedman, T. Hastie, and R. Tibshirani. Additive logistic regression: A statistical view of boosting. *The Annals of Statistics*, 28:337 – 374, 2000.

12. D. J. Hand. *Construction and Assessment of Classification Rules*. John Wiley & Sons, Chichester, 1997.
13. W. Jiang. Some results on weakly accurate base learners for boosting regression and classification. In *Proceedings of the First International Workshop on Multiple Classifier Systems*, pages 87 – 96, 2000.
14. M. Kearns and L. G. Valiant. Learning boolean formulae or finite automata is as hard as factoring. *Technical Report TR-14-88, Harvard University Aiken Computation Laboratory*, 1988.
15. O. L. Mangasarian and W. H. Wolberg. Cancer diagnosis via linear programming. *SIAM News*, 23(5):1 – 18, 1990.
16. R. A. McDonald, I. A. Eckley, and D. J. Hand. A multi-class extension to the brownboost algorithm. *In Submission.*
17. J. R. Quinlan. The effect of noise on concept learning. In R. S. Michalski, J. G. Carbonell, and T. M. Mitchell, editors, *Machine Learning: An Artificial Intelligence Approach*, volume 2, San Mateo, CA, 1986. Morgan Kauffmann.
18. J. R. Quinlan. *C4.5: Programs for Machine Learning*. Morgan Kaufmann, 1993.
19. J. R. Quinlan. Bagging, boosting and c4.5. *AAAI/IAAI*, 1:725 – 730, 1996.
20. R. E. Schapire. The strength of weak learnability. *Machine Learning*, 5:197 – 227, 1990.
21. R. E. Schapire, Y. Freund, P. Bartlett, and W. S. Lee. Boosting the margin: A new explanation for the effectiveness of voting methods. *The Annals of Statistics*, 26:1651 – 1686, 1998.
22. R. E. Schapire and Y. Singer. Improved boosting algorithms using confidence-rated predictions. *Machine Learning*, 37:297 – 336, 1999.
23. L. G. Valiant. A theory of the learnable. *Artificial Intelligence and Language Processing*, 27:1134 – 1142, 1984.

The Beneficial Effects of Using Multi-net Systems That Focus on Hard Patterns

J. Arenas-García[1], A.R. Figueiras-Vidal[1], and A.J.C. Sharkey[2]

[1] Department of Signal Theory and Communications
Universidad Carlos III de Madrid, 28911 Leganés-Madrid, Spain
{jarenas,arfv}@tsc.uc3m.es
[2] Department of Computer Science
The University of Sheffield, Regent Court, 211 Portobello Street, S1 4DP, UK
A.Sharkey@dcs.shef.ac.uk

Abstract. Multi Net Systems have become very popular during the last decade. A great variety of techniques have been proposed: many of them resulting in excellent performance in recognition tasks. In this paper, we will show that focusing on the hardest patterns plays a crucial role in Adaboost, one of the most widely used multi net systems. To do this, we use a novel technique to illustrate how Adaboost effectively focuses its training in the regions near the decision border. Then we propose a new method for training multi net systems that shares this property with Adaboost. Both schemes are shown, when tested on three benchmark datasets, to outperform single nets and an ensemble system in which the training sets are held constant, and the component members differ only as a result of randomness introduced during training. Their better performance supports the notion of the beneficial effects that can result from an increasing focus on hard patterns.

1 Introduction

During the last decade there has been an increasing interest in combining Artificial Neural Networks. As discussed in [1], the theoretical advantages of multi net systems are numerous: high performance, fast training, improved understandability and easier design, among others. A number of different methods for combining neural nets have been proposed; methods which explore different issues such as specializing the base networks on certain regions of the input space (the divide-and-conquer approach) or using committees of redundant nets all of which offer a different solution to the same task. Closely related to this, is the issue of selecting the best network to use depending on the input pattern or, alternatively, fusing the outputs of all the component nets. Among all the approaches that have been proposed in the literature, in this paper we will pay attention to those fusing the outputs of all the classifiers forming the multi net system, and, in particular, to Adaboost [2].

T. Windeatt and F. Roli (Eds.): MCS 2003, LNCS 2709, pp. 45–54, 2003.
© Springer-Verlag Berlin Heidelberg 2003

The idea of boosting classifiers was first proposed by Schapire [3], as a way to improve the performance of any "weak" learning algorithm that obtains solutions which are simply better than a random guess. A more convenient algorithm for boosting classifiers, Adaboost.M1, was proposed in [2] and then improved in [4] (RealAdaboost). Adaboost works by refining the border of classification each time a base learner is added to the scheme, increasing the importance of the patterns that are hardest to classify.

To explain the good performance of Adaboost, the authors of the method originally proved that a bound on the training error is reduced as the number of nets in the Adaboost scheme grows. The fact that Adaboost concentrates on the hardest to classify patterns also seems to be very important, as Breimann [1] points out. Breimann [1] presents an alternative method (Arc-x4), that also focuses on the hardest patterns, and whose performance is similar to that of Adaboost. Later studies [5], [6] explained Adaboost's good performance in terms of its aggressive reduction of the margin of classification.

In this paper we will present a further investigation of the relevance of focusing on the hardest patterns for an explanation of the good performance of Adaboost. Towards this objective, we will first use a novel method to illustrate how Adaboost's reweighting scheme effectively serves to increase the importance of the patterns near the border of classification. Then, we will propose a new training scheme for multi net classifiers (based on Wald's Sequential Test [7]) which sequentially removes the easiest patterns from the training dataset, and so, also focuses on the difficult regions. We will show that it is possible to fuse the outputs of these base learners in an Adaboost manner obtaining performances similar to those of RealAdaboost. We will also show the superior performance of both systems in comparison to a third multi net approach that does not concentrate on the hard patterns. In addition, some advantages that the sequential scheme has over Adaboost will be identified and discussed. Finally, we will extend the idea of sequentially removing patterns to speed up the classification phase of the multi net systems that are considered in the paper.

The rest of the paper is organized as follows: the next Section reviews the RealAdaboost algorithm and includes some graphics showing how it focuses on the difficult instances. Then Section 3 introduces our sequential training algorithm. An extension of these ideas is presented in Section 4 with the objective of speeding up the classification phase. Section 5 is devoted to some experiments to compare the effectiveness of RealAdaboost, the Sequential scheme, and a simpler multinet system that does not vary the training set. Finally we present some conclusions, and outline plans for future work.

2   Boosting Classifiers: RealAdaboost (RA)

RealAdaboost (RA in the following) is a boosting algorithm which is able to improve the performance of a set of base learners with outputs in the real domain. We will use the implementantion described in [4].

To build up the RA classifier, it is necessary to train T base learners, each one implementing a function $o_t(\mathbf{x}) : X \rightarrow [-1, 1]$ for $t = 1, \ldots, T$. In order to introduce diversity, we train the classifiers to minimize different error functions:

$$E_t^2 = \sum_{i=1}^{l} D_t(i)\,(t_i - o_t(\mathbf{x}_i))^2 \tag{1}$$

where l is the size of the training dataset, $t_i \in \{-1, 1\}$ is the target for pattern $\mathbf{x}_i$, and $D_t(i)$ is a weight associated to the i-th pattern and the t-th classifier. In this way, diversity is introduced by giving different weights to the patterns for each base classifier.

All weights are initialized to the same value ($D_1(i) = 1/l, \forall i = 1, \ldots, l$, so $\sum_{i=1}^{l} D_1(i) = 1$), and the first base learner is trained. Then, at each round, RA increases the weights of patterns having a higher error in the last classifier:

$$D_{t+1}(i) = (D_t(i)\exp(-\alpha_t y_i o_t(\mathbf{x}_i)))\,/Z_t \tag{2}$$

where Z_t is a normalization factor that assures that $\sum_{i=1}^{l} D_{t+1}(i) = 1$, and α_t is the weight RA gives to the t-th classifier

$$\alpha_t = \frac{1}{2}\ln\left(\frac{1 + r_t}{1 - r_t}\right) \tag{3}$$

where

$$r_t = \sum_{i=1}^{l} D_t(i)y_i o_t(\mathbf{x}_i)\,. \tag{4}$$

Once all the classifiers have been set up, the overall output of the combined scheme is calculated as

$$y(\mathbf{x}) = \text{sign}(o(\mathbf{x})) = \text{sign}\left(\sum_{t=1}^{T} \alpha_t o_t(\mathbf{x})\right)\,. \tag{5}$$

To illustrate how RA effectively focuses on the hardest to classify patterns, we have depicted in Fig. 1 an example of the partitioning of the input space carried out for the kwok dataset (details about this problem and the base learner and settings used are given in Section 5). As RA does not make an explicit partitioning, we have developed a new method for showing its increasing focus on difficult patterns: for each round we place in a set X_h the patterns with the highest weights, so their sum is as close as possible (but higher) to 0.75. Then we color with dark grey the points in the input space where the nearest training pattern belongs to X_h. Therefore, we can say that the dark grey region has at least 0.75 influence in the error function used to train the corresponding base classifier. We have also depicted the border achieved by the RA classifier (up to each round) with a black line, while the border of the individual classifiers are depicted using white lines.

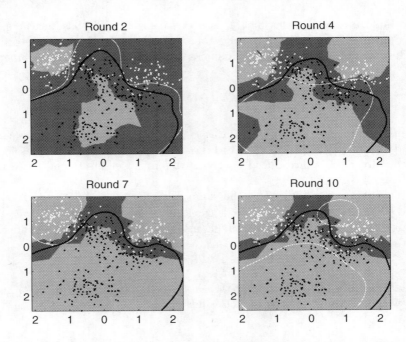

Fig. 1. Example of the implicit partitioning of the input space carried out by Real-Adaboost as the number of rounds increases. The dark region in each figure has an influence of at least 75% in the error function corresponding to each round. The light and dark dots are examples of the two classes that need to be separated. We have also depicted in the figures the decision border of each individual learner (white line) and that of the whole RA classifier up to each round (black line).

When examining the diagrams, it is apparent that the dark grey region (that with a higher influence on the error function) progressively shrinks as the rounds progress, correctly identifying the most difficult patterns. Notice that individual classifiers usually achieve poor borders, offering bad performances if used alone. However, RA fuses their outputs so the overall border is refined on each step.

3   Removing "Easy" Training Patterns: Sequential Training (ST)

We propose in this section a new method for assembling neural nets, sharing with Adaboost the property of focusing on the hard patterns. We will use this method, that we call Sequential Training (ST), to validate the importance of this characteristic for the good functioning of Adaboost. In this approach, the base learners are trained sequentially (see Fig. 2), and some thresholds (η_1^+, η_1^-, ... in the figure) are used to decide whether a training pattern should be passed to the following network (if the current network output is between its positive

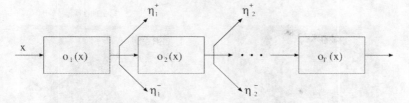

Fig. 2. Sequential Training of Classifiers.

and negative thresholds) or not; this implies that each classifier is trained with
a subset of the training dataset used by the previous classifier in the chain.

To be more precise, let us denote each classifier in the chain by C_t, with
$t = 1, \ldots, T$, T being the number of classifiers. Let $o_t(\mathbf{x})$ be the output of the
t-th base learner. Then the training of the scheme is as follows: the first learner
is trained with the whole training dataset $\mathcal{D}_1 = \{(\mathbf{x}_1, t_1), \ldots, (\mathbf{x}_l, t_l)\}$, and its
thresholds are selected. The training dataset for the second classifier is then:

$$\mathcal{D}_2 = \{(\mathbf{x}_i, t_i) \quad : \quad \eta_1^- \leq o_1(\mathbf{x}_i) \leq \eta_1^+\} .$$

We iterate the process, so the training set for the $(k+1)$-th classifier $(k < T)$ is

$$\mathcal{D}_{k+1} = \{(\mathbf{x}_i, t_i) \quad : \quad (\mathbf{x}_i, t_i) \in \mathcal{D}_k \text{ and } \eta_k^- \leq o_k(\mathbf{x}_i) \leq \eta_k^+\} .$$

In order to get a good performance from this combined scheme, the selection
of thresholds plays a crucial role. Our aim is that the training datasets are
increasingly restricted to the hardest patterns, so thresholds must be fixed to
remove the easiest patterns. To do this, we could set the thresholds to the highest
and lowest possible values guaranteeing that no misclassified training pattern is
removed, i.e., we could set the positive and negative thresholds to A_t^+ and A_t^-:

$$A_t^+ = \max\{o_t(\mathbf{x}_i) \quad : \quad o_t(\mathbf{x}_i) > 0 \text{ and } t_i = -1\}$$
$$A_t^- = \min\{o_t(\mathbf{x}_i) \quad : \quad o_t(\mathbf{x}_i) < 0 \text{ and } t_i = +1\} . \tag{6}$$

In order to relax this condition, we will finally use

$$\eta_t^+ = A_t^+ + (1 - A_t^+)D_t \quad ; \quad \eta_t^- = A_t^- - (1 + A_t^-)D_t$$

D_t being a factor that linearly decreases from v_i to v_f for the different rounds.
Thus, assuming that the outputs of the base learners are in the range $[-1, 1]$,
$D_t = 1$ ($\eta_t^+ = 1$ and $\eta_t^- = -1$) means that no training pattern is removed from
the dataset. On the other hand, if $D_t = 0$ ($\eta_t^+ = A_t^+$ and $\eta_t^- = A_t^-$) we just
guarantee that we never delete a misclassified training pattern. We will generally
use $v_i > v_f$, so we are more conservative for the first learners.

As for RealAdaboost, we show in Fig. 3 that the ST scheme also focuses
on the hardest patterns for an example using the kwok dataset. We show on
each diagram the region used to train each classifier in the scheme (dark grey).
Again, it can be seen that this region progressively shrinks and is restricted to

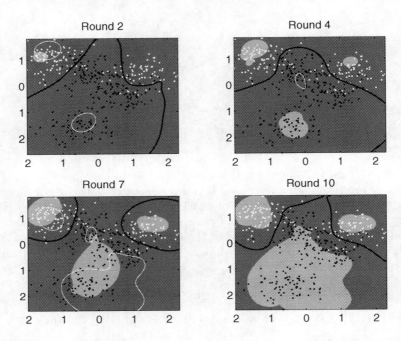

Fig. 3. Example of the partitioning of the input space carried out by ST as the number of rounds increases. The dark region is the region used to train each classifier. The light and dark dots represent patterns from the two classes that need to be separated. We have also depicted the borders achieved by each individual learner (black line) and the contours where the networks achieve the positive and negative thresholds (white lines).

the area near the frontier as the rounds progress. Comparing these illustrations to those in Fig. 1, we see that, with the settings we have used, the focus on hard patterns is less aggressive for the ST scheme, especially during the first rounds. This makes sense, as we have specified that a misclassified pattern can never be removed from the training dataset. This way, patterns lying in a region where the opposite class is clearly more likely, will make the selection of good thresholds difficult. We also observe that the decision borders obtained by the ST base learners seem to be better than those in Fig. 1. We will give numerical evidence for this in the experiments section.

Once all the base classifiers have been set up, we fuse their outputs using RealAdaboost scheme (so, we call the whole classifier ST-RA): to calculate the weights of each base classifier in the fusion, we simply run the RA algorithm using our base learners instead of training new ones.

In Section 5 we will use ST-RA to validate the importance of focusing on the hardest patterns for the good functioning of RA. Apart from this objective (which is the main topic of the paper), we want to point out that, as the training dataset sizes are reduced during the training, the setting up of ST-RA is faster than that of RA. In addition to this, the fact that base classifiers in the ST-RA net are more powerful than those in the RA scheme, opens the door to interesting approaches combining the fusion of all nets with the selection of the best one (or even the fusion of the best ones) depending on the patterns to be classified. This issue, however, goes beyond the scope of this paper.

4   Fast Classification (FC) Using Thresholds

As we have explained in the two previous sections, both RA and ST-RA schemes work by progressively refining the border of classification as the number of rounds increases. This way, it would be possible to correctly classify most of the patterns by fusing just the first or some of the first classifiers, while using the complete scheme only for the most difficult patterns.

In this section we propose to accelerate the classification process (both for the RA and ST-RA classifiers) by using thresholds in a way similar to that used for the sequential training. To do so, let us first denote with $h_t(\mathbf{x})$ the overall output given by a multi net system up to the t-th classifier. Then, to fix the thresholds, we will use the same procedure that was described for the sequential training, but considering only those training patterns that could be correctly classified at any step of the classification process, i.e., we will only consider patterns in the following subset of the training dataset:

$$\mathcal{D}_c = \{(\mathbf{x}_i, t_i) \quad : \quad \text{sign}(h_t(\mathbf{x}_i)) = t_i \text{ for any } t = 1, \ldots, T\} \ .$$

Once the thresholds are fixed, the classification process for pattern $\mathbf{x}$ stops as soon as $h_t(\mathbf{x})$ is above or below the corresponding positive and negative thresholds. We will show in the next section that this simple procedure can be used to save a lot of computation during the classification phase.

5   Experiments

In this section, we present numerical results supporting the ideas discussed earlier in the paper. In order to illustrate that focusing on the hardest patterns plays a crucial role in the good performance of RA classifiers, we compare the performances of 4 different classifiers on three benchmark datasets. Let us begin with a description of the classifiers used:

– Radial Basis Function Networks (RBFN) are the base learners that will be used by the multi net systems. Our implementation of RBFN initially selects at random 10% of the training data as centroids. We use Gaussian kernels as the basis function, and the sigma parameters are obtained by assigning each training pattern to its closest centroid and then computing the average distance of all patterns in a cluster to its centroid. This quantity is finally multiplied by a factor K. We use an hyperbolic tangent function to activate the output of the network. For training the weights in the output layer, we have used an stochastic gradient descent algorithm ($w_i(k+1) = w_i(k) - \frac{\mu}{2}\frac{\partial e^2}{\partial w_i}$) with learning step $\mu = 0.1$. 50 cycles through the training patterns have been shown to be enough for the networks to converge.

Table 1. Average Test errors and their standard deviations (inside brackets) obtained by RBFN, RA-RBFN, ST-RBFN and 10-RBFN classifiers.

	RBFN	RA-RBFN	ST-RBFN	10-RBFN
kwok	12.65 (0.34)	12.03 (0.23)	12.05 (0.18)	12.2 (0.19)
abalone	20.63 (0.38)	20.31 (0.35)	20.26 (0.39)	20.34 (0.31)
pima	24.64 (1)	22.97 (0.43)	23.31 (0.75)	23.78 (0.67)

- RA-RBFN is the RealAdaboost algorithm with RBFN as the base learner, setting the number of rounds to $T = 10$.
- ST-RBFN is the ST-RA algorithm having RBFN as the base learner. The settings for this net are $v_i = 0.97$, $v_f = 0$ and $T = 10$.
- 10-RBFN consists of 10 independent RBFN networks trained with the same dataset (note that, due to the randomness which is present in training, these networks will be different), fusing their outputs using the scheme inherent to RealAdaboost. This algorithm has been introduced in order to enable a comparison to other multi net system that does not pay special attention to the most difficult patterns.

Three binary problems will be used to test the different classifiers. Kwok is a 2 dimensional synthetic problem that was introduced in [8] and consists of 500 training and 10200 test patterns, 60% belonging to class +1 and 40% to class -1. Abalone is a multiclass problem from [9] that has been converted to binary according to [10]. Abalone has 8 dimensions and 2507 (1238/1269) training and 1670 (843/827) test patterns. Finally, pima is Pima Indian Diabetes from [9], a problem with a high amount of outliers. It is a 8 dimensional problem with 576 (375/201) training and 192 (125/67) test patterns.

Previous to their use, all training datasets were normalized to have zero mean and unit variance, with the same scaling being applied to the test data. In order to select the most appropriate parameter K for each problem and method, a 5-fold cross-validation procedure exploring values in range $[1, 5]$ was used.

Table 1 reports test errors for all methods and problems averaged over 50 runs. It can immediatly be seen that, as one would expect, all ensemble systems reduce the test error achieved by the weak learner (RBFN) alone. It is also interesting to notice that the standard deviations of the ensemble systems are generally lower, so we can conclude that the use of a combination of nets has improved the stability of the networks.

Restricting our analysis to the multi net systems, we notice that both RA-RBFN and ST-RBFN have achieved lower error rates than 10-RBFN for kwok and pima and are tied for abalone. This clearly indicates that focusing on the difficult patterns has had a positive effect in terms of test error. RA-RBFN and ST-RBFN are generally tied except for pima dataset. We think that the main reason for the better performance of RA-RBFN in pima is that our scheme for threshold selection is quite conservative, especially for this problem which is known to have a large number of outliers (the implementation of sequential training guarantees that no misclassified pattern is removed from the training

Table 2. Average size of the training datasets ($\overline{\#tr}$) and average test errors for the individual classifiers of the best RA-RBFN and ST-RBFN schemes (according to validation criterion).

	RA-RBFN		ST-RBFN	
	error	$\overline{\#tr}$	error	$\overline{\#tr}$
kwok	26.74	400	14.53	281.61
abalone	36.31	2005.6	20.79	1965.6
pima	34.63	460.8	24.81	413.18

dataset). Besides, Sequential Training can be considered to be a "hard" version of RealAdaboost, in the sense that it gives the same weight to all patterns used for the training of the base networks.

In any case, we argue that the results in Table 1 demonstrate that concentrating on the hardest patterns has beneficial effects, and is at least partially responsible for the good performances that have been reported in the literature concerning Adaboost. The Sequential Training method provides a different way of increasingly focusing on the hardest patterns in a classification task, and results in a similar improvement in performance than that achieved by Adaboost.

In Table 2 we have reported the average size of the training datasets used to train the base learners that compose both the RA-RBFN and ST-RBFN schemes. These results have been averaged over the 50 runs, over the 5 folds, and over the 10 learners forming the ensemble network. The lower figures from ST-RBFN mean that the training of base learners is faster in this case. Besides, as we always use 10% of training patterns as centroids, the lower number of centroids in the networks will also result in a computationally easier classification phase.

We also give in Table 2 the average test errors for the individual learners of RA-RBFN and ST-RBFN. As we have already pointed out, the better performance of the base learners in ST-RBFN could open the door to interesting approaches combining fusion and selection of base classifiers.

Finally, we have used the fast classification (FC) procedure both for the RA-RBFN and ST-RBFN schemes. Note that for the selection of the thresholds we have used both the training and validation data in each fold, but never the test dataset. In Table 3 we give average errors for the three datasets in this case, and the average number of classifiers ($\overline{T}$) that are used for the classification of a pattern when setting $v_i = 0.2$ and $v_f = 0$. When comparing these results with those in Table 1, we notice that the computational load is generally reduced by more than 60 % at no cost in terms of recognition error.

6   Conclusions

In this paper, we have studied the reasons for the good performance of one of the most widely used multi net systems: Adaboost. We have illustrated, by using a novel method, how Adaboost focuses its training in the regions near the decision border. Then we have investigated the importance of this property by proposing,

Table 3. Average Test errors and average number of classifiers used during the classification phase with the FC strategy. Standard deviations are given inside brackets.

	RA-RBFN		ST-RBFN	
	error	T	error	T
kwok	12 (0.21)	1.83 (0.19)	12.05 (0.18)	1.48 (0.2)
abalone	20.31 (0.35)	2.77 (0.44)	20.26 (0.39)	2.04 (0.5)
pima	22.97 (0.42)	3.4 (0.37)	23.31 (0.75)	2.59 (0.44)

and testing a new method for training multi net systems that also focuses on the hard patterns. The new sequential scheme results in similar performance to that of Adaboost: a demonstration that reinforces, by different means, Breiman's remarks in [1] about the role of Adaboost's increasing focus on difficult patterns.

The sequential scheme can also be seen to offer some advantages over Adaboost. It uses smaller training sets, reducing training times, and relies on an easier classification phase (using a lower number of centroids). The component nets in the scheme also show better individual classification performance. The ideas of sequential classification have also been useful to speed up the classification phase. Further research on the sequential scheme is planned. We are currently working on new methods for threshold selection. And, as a next step, we will use the sequential scheme as the basis for the development of architectures that are able to switch between selection and fusion, taking advantage of the good performances of the base learners.

References

1. A. J. C. Sharkey (ed.): Combining Artificial Neural Nets. Ensemble and Modular Multi-Net Systems. Perspectives in Neural Computing. Springer-Verlag, London, UK (1999).
2. Y. Freund and R. E. Schapire: Experiments with a new boosting algorithm. Machine Learning: Proceedings of the Thirteenth International Conference, (1996), 148–156.
3. R. E. Schapire: The strength of weak Learnability. 30th Annual Symposium on Foundations of Computer Science (1989), 28–33.
4. R. E. Schapire and Y. Singer: Improved boosting algorithms using confidence-rated predictions. Machine Learning, **37**(3) (1999) 297–336.
5. R. E. Schapire, Y. Freund, P. Bartlett and W. S. Lee: Boosting the margin: A new explanation for the effectiveness of voting methods. The Annals of Statistics, **26**(5) (1998) 1651–1686.
6. G. Ratsch, B. Scholkopf, S. Mika, and K. R. Muller: SVM and Boosting: One class. Technical Report 119, GMD FIRST, Berlin (2000).
7. A. Wald: Sequential Analysis. Wiley, New York, NY (1959).
8. J. T. Kwok: Moderating the Output of Support Vector Machine Classifiers. IEEE Trans. on Neural Networks, **10**(5) (1999) 1018–1031.
9. C. L. Blake and and C. J. Merz: UCI Repository of machine learning databases. http://www.ics.uci.edu/~mlearn/MLRepository.html. University of California, Irvine, Dept. of Information and Computer Sciences (1998).
10. A. Ruiz and P. E. López-de-Teruel: Nonlinear Kernels-Based Statistical Pattern Analysis. IEEE Trans. on Neural Networks, **12**(1) (2001) 16–32.

The Behavior Knowledge Space Fusion Method: Analysis of Generalization Error and Strategies for Performance Improvement

Šarunas Raudys[1] and Fabio Roli[2]

[1] Vilnius Gediminas Technical University
Sauletekio 11, Vilnius LT-2100, Lithuania 2006
raudys@ktl.mii.lt
[2] Dept. of Electrical and Electronic Engineering, University of Cagliari
Piazza díArmi, I-09123 Cagliari, Italy
roli@diee.unica.it

Abstract. In the pattern recognition literature, Huang and Suen introduced the "multinomial" rule for fusion of multiple classifiers under the name of Behavior Knowledge Space (BKS) method [1]. This classifier fusion method can provide very good performances if large and representative data sets are available. Otherwise over fitting is likely to occur, and the generalization error quickly increases. In spite of this crucial small sample size problem, analytical models of BKS generalization error are currently not available. In this paper, the generalization error of BKS method is analysed, and a simple analytical model that relates error to sample size is proposed. In addition, a strategy for improving performances by using linear classifiers in "ambiguous" cells of BKS table is described. Preliminary experiments on synthetic and real data sets are reported.

1   Introduction

Methods for fusing multiple classifiers can be subdivided according to the types of outputs that can be produced by the individual classifiers: abstract level or single class output, ranked list of classes, and measurement level outputs [2]. Among the methods that work with abstract-level outputs, the Behavior Knowledge Space (BKS) method became very popular [1]. In the BKS method, every possible combination of abstract-level classifiers outputs is regarded as a cell in a look-up table. The BKS table is designed by a training set. Each cell contains the samples of the training set characterized by a particular value of class labels. The training samples in each cell are subdivided per class, and the most representative class label ("majority" class) is selected for each cell. For each unknown test pattern, the classification is performed according to the class label of the BKS cell indexed by the classifiers outputs. From a statistical viewpoint, BKS method tries to estimate high order distribution of classifiers outputs from the frequencies of occurrence in the training set. Further details on BKS method are given in Section 2.1. Differently from other popular fusion methods, BKS does not require any model of classifiers' dependency; in particular, it does not assume conditional independence. On the other hand, some BKS drawbacks are well known. Among the others:

T. Windeatt and F. Roli (Eds.): MCS 2003, LNCS 2709, pp. 55–64, 2003.

- BKS suffers the small sample size problem. Large and representative data sets are required to estimate high order distribution of classifiers outputs. Otherwise overfitting is likely to occur, and the generalization error quickly increases;
- BKS produces high error for cells characterized by a low probability of the most representative class. (Hereafter, we'll use the adjective "ambiguous" for denoting this type of cells). This is an intrinsic limitation of BKS fusion method.

Some authors proposed techniques for dealing with BKS small sample size problem and limiting error. Reject option is basically used to limit error due to ambiguous cells [1]. Roli et al. showed that increasing the training set size by k-nn noise injection can reduce small sample size problem [4]. Kang and Lee proposed to approximate a high order distribution with a product of low order distributions [7,8]. It is worth noting that, in spite of BKS crucial small sample size problem, analytical models of BKS generalization error are currently not available.

In this paper, the generalization error of BKS method is analysed and a simple analytical model that relates error to sample size in a single cell is proposed (Section 2). In addition, a strategy for improving performances by using linear classifiers in "ambiguous" cells of BKS table is described (Section 3). Preliminary experiments on synthetic and real data sets are reported (Section 3).

2   Analysis of BKS Generalization Error

2.1   The BKS Fusion Method

Let us consider a classification task for K data classes $\omega_1,.., \omega_K$. Each class is assumed to represent a set of specific patterns, each pattern being characterised by a feature vector X. Let us also assume that L different classifiers, $e_j, j = 1,..,L$, have been trained separately to solve the classification task at hand. Let $e_j(X) \in \{1,.., K\}$ indicate the class label assigned to pattern X by classifier e_j. In the BKS method, only class labels are considered (i.e., it is a fusion method for abstract-level classifiers [2]). To simplify the notation, we replace $e_j(X)$ with e_j. For each pattern, X, the discrete-valued vector $E=(e_1, e_2....e_L)^T$ of classifiers' outputs can be computed. The number of possible combinations of L classifiers outputs is $m=K^L$. Therefore, the vector E can take one of these m values. In the BKS method proposed by Huang and Suen [1], every possible combination of L class labels is regarded as a cell in a look-up table (BKS table). The BKS table is designed by a training set. Each cell contains the samples of the training set characterized by the particular value of E. The training samples in each cell are subdivided per class, and the most representative class label is selected for each cell. For each unknown test pattern, the classification is performed according to the class label of the BKS cell indexed by $E=(e_1, e_2.... E_L)^T$. Obviously, reject option is used for test patterns that fall in empty cells. A threshold on the probability of the most representative class is also used to control the reliability of the decision made in each cell. Basically, the Chow's rule is used to reject patterns of BKS cells with a probability of the most representative class lower than a given threshold ("ambiguous" cells) [5].

For the purposes of this work, let us introduce the following probabilistic view on BKS method. As previously pointed out, each vector $E=(e_1, e_2.... e_L)^T$ can take one of m possible "states" $s_1, s_2, ... , s_{m-1}, s_m, m=K^L$. It is worth noting that, in statistical data analysis, it is supposed that values $s_1,...., s_m$ follow the Multinomial distribution.

The conditional distribution of the i-th class vector E is characterized by m probabilities:

$$P_1^{(i)}, P_2^{(i)}, ... , P_{m-1}^{(i)}, P_m^{(i)}, \text{ with } \sum_{j=1}^{m} P_j^{(i)} = 1, (i =1, ... , K). \tag{1}$$

To simplify the notation, we are indicating with the term $P_j^{(i)}$ the conditional probability $p_j(X/\omega_i)$, that is, the conditional distribution of the i-th class vector E for patterns falling in the state (BKS cell) s_j.

Let P_i be the prior probability of the class ω_i. According to Bayes rule, patterns falling into the state s_j (j=1,...,m) are assigned to the class that maximizes $P_i P_j^{(i)}$ (i =1,...., K). This points out that design of BKS rule needs the knowledge of $Kx(m-1)$ probabilities. If such probabilities are exactly known, this is the optimal fusion rule for abstract-level classifiers. In practice, the $Kx(m-1)$ probabilities are unknown and must be estimated from the data. One can use the maximum likelihood estimates (sample frequencies):

$$\hat{P}_j^{(i)} = n_j^{(i)} / N_i \tag{2}$$

where N_i is the number of training vectors belonging to the i-th pattern class, and $n_j^{(i)}$ is the number of vectors falling into the state s_j. If $\hat{P}_i = N_i / \sum_{i=1}^{L} N_i$ and estimate of prior probability P_i is proportional to N_i, we have the sample-based multinomial classifier, that Huang and Suen named BKS method [1]. It is worth remarking that BKS method coincides with the multinomial statistical classifier, that is the optimal statistical decision rule for discrete-valued feature vectors [9]. BKS should be therefore regarded as the application of the multinomial rule to fusion of abstract-level classifiers.

If the values of L and K are large, we have a great number of probabilities to be estimated. To design a good fusion rule, a sufficient number of training vectors should be available to estimate the probabilities in BKS cells. If the size of the data set is not sufficient, the BKS method becomes unreliable. An important issue is therefore to evaluate the size of data set that is necessary for reliable probability estimates. However, to the best of our knowledge, no model was proposed to analyse the generalization error of BKS method as function of sample size. Analysis of BKS generalization error could, first of all, contribute to improve the understanding of this popular fusion rule. In addition, guidelines on the number of samples necessary to limit BKS generalization error could be obtained. In the following section, a simple analytical model that relates BKS error to sample size is proposed for a two-class case, and some implications for BKS table design are discussed.

Finally, it is worth noting that, in small sample cases, small number of classifiers should be preferred. However, if the number of classifiers is small, the cells can become "large" and contain vectors of different classes, that is, ambiguous cells can exist. As pointed out in Section 1, BKS method does not work well for ambiguous cells. In Section 3, we propose a strategy for addressing this limitation of BKS method.

2.2   Analysis of Generalization Error in BKS Cells

Consider a two-class problem and N validation patterns belonging to such classes ($N = N_1 + N_2$). Let N_1 and N_2 be random variables whose distribution depends on class prior probabilities P_1 and P_2. Prior probabilities are estimated by $\hat{P}_i = N_i/N$. Consider the probability of misclassification for patterns falling into the j-th BKS cell ($j = 1, \ldots, m$). If the maximum likelihood estimates (equation 2) are used, the local generalization error $P_{err}^{BKS}(j)$ in the j-th BKS cell can be written as:

$$P_{err}^{BKS}(j) \quad = \quad Prob\{\,\hat{P}_1\hat{P}_j^{(1)} < \hat{P}_2\hat{P}_j^{(2)}\,\big|\,P_1, P_j^{(1)}, \qquad P_j^{(2)}\,\} \qquad P_1 P_j^{(1)} + \qquad (3)$$

$$Prob\{\,\hat{P}_1\hat{P}_j^{(1)} > P_2\,\hat{P}_2\hat{P}_j^{(2)}\,\big|\,P_1, P_j^{(1)}, P_j^{(2)}\,\} \quad P_2 P_j^{(2)} + \quad Prob\{\,\hat{P}_1\hat{P}_j^{(1)} = \hat{P}_2\hat{P}_j^{(2)}\,\big|\,P_1,$$

$$, P_j^{(1)}, P_j^{(2)}\,\}\;(P_1 P_j^{(1)} + P_2 P_j^{(2)})/2$$

Let us remark that we are assuming that an independent validation set is used to estimate probabilities, that is, the N validation patterns do not belong to the set used for training the L classifiers [3].

Random variables $n_j^{(i)}$ can take values 0, 1, 2, 3, ..., N (equation. 2). According to definitions given above, sample-based estimates $\hat{P}_i\hat{P}_j^{(i)} = n_j^{(i)}/N$ are multinomial random variables with parameters $q_j^{(1)} = P_1 P_j^{(1)}$, $q_j^{(2)} = P_2 P_j^{(1)}$, $1 - q_j^{(1)} - q_j^{(2)}$, and N ($j = 1, 2, \ldots, m$). Accordingly, the conditional probabilities in equation 3 can be expressed as follow:

$$Prob\{\,\hat{P}_1\hat{P}_j^{(1)} = r/N,\; \hat{P}_2\hat{P}_j^{(2)} = s/N\,\big|\,P_1, P_j^{(1)}, P_j^{(2)}\,\} = Prob\{\,n_j^{(1)} = r,\; n_j^{(2)} = s \qquad (4)$$

$$\big|\,q_j^{(1)}, q_j^{(2)}\,\} = \frac{N!}{r!s!(N-r-s)!}(q_j^{(1)})^r (q_j^{(2)})^s (1 - q_j^{(1)} - q_j^{(2)})^{N-r-s}.$$

Therefore, we can write the following equations:

$$Prob\{\,\hat{P}_1\hat{P}_j^{(1)} < \hat{P}_2\hat{P}_j^{(2)}\,\big|\,q_j^{(1)}, q_j^{(2)}\,\} = \qquad\qquad\qquad\qquad (5a)$$

$$\sum_{r=0}^{N-1}\sum_{s=r+1}^{N-r}\frac{N!}{r!s!(N-r-s)!}(q_j^{(1)})^r (q_j^{(2)})^s (1 - q_j^{(1)} - q_j^{(2)})^{N-r-s}$$

$$Prob\{\,\hat{P}_1\hat{P}_j^{(1)} > \hat{P}_2\hat{P}_j^{(2)}\,\big|\,q_j^{(1)},q_j^{(2)}\,\} = \tag{5b}$$

$$\sum_{s=0}^{N-1}\sum_{r=s+1}^{N-s}\frac{N!}{r!s!(N-r-s)!}(q_j^{(1)})^r(q_j^{(2)})^s(1-q_j^{(1)}-q_j^{(2)})^{N-r-s}$$

$$Prob\{\,\hat{P}_1\hat{P}_j^{(1)} = \hat{P}_2\hat{P}_j^{(2)}\,\big|\,q_j^{(1)},q_j^{(2)}\,\} = \tag{5c}$$

$$\sum_{r=0}^{N/2}\frac{N!}{r!r!(N-2r)!}(q_j^{(1)})^r(q_j^{(2)})^r(1-q_j^{(1)}-q_j^{(2)})^{N-2r}$$

Substituting equations 5a, 5b, and 5c in equation 3, one obtain the expression that allows evaluating generalization error as function of number of validation patterns, and probabilities $q_j^{(1)} = P_1\,P_j^{(1)}$, $q_j^{(2)} = P_2\,P_j^{(1)}$. Note that $q_j^{(i)}$ is the probability that patterns of i-th class fall in BKS cell j.

For the sake of brevity, let us analyze the derived expression of BKS cell generalization error by means of Figure 1. Figure 1 plots the BKS generalization error in a cell as function of the number N of samples used for estimating probabilities, that is, for designing the BKS table. The three plots refers to three different values of $q_j^{(1)} = P_1\,P_j^{(1)}$ and $q_j^{(2)} = P_2\,P_j^{(1)}$. Plot number 1: $q_j^{(1)} = 0.05$, $q_j^{(2)} = 0.05$. Plot number 2: $q_j^{(1)} = 0.05$, $q_j^{(2)} = 0.01$. Plot number 3: $q_j^{(1)} = 0.02$, $q_j^{(2)} = 0.01$.

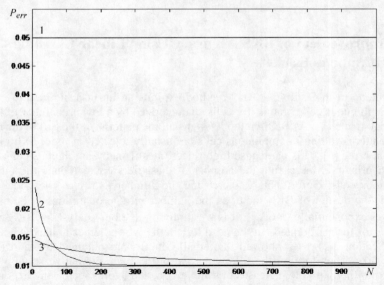

Fig. 1. BKS generalization error probability in a cell as function of the number N of samples used for estimating cell conditional probabilities $q_j^{(1)}$ and $q_j^{(2)}$.

For plots "2" and "3", generalization error decreases by increasing the number of samples, and converges to the minimum Bayes error, that is equal to 0.01. Note that $q_j^{(2)}$ =0.01 in the case of plots 2 and 3. BKS assigns all patterns in the cell to the most representative class; therefore, the Bayes error is equal to the probability of the minority class in the cell. The generalization error does not decrease in the case of plot 1 because $q_j^{(1)} = q_j^{(2)}$. It is worth noting that the generalization error decreases quicker for the plot number 2 than for the plot number 3. The reason is that the probability of the most representative class is higher for the case of plot 2 ($q_j^{(1)}$ =0.05 vs $q_j^{(1)}$ =0.02). On the other hand, the error is higher for small sample sizes in the case of the plot "2".

On the basis of this analysis of BKS generalization error, some preliminary comments can be made:

- Ambiguous cells, characterized by similar class probabilities, negatively affect BKS performances. In particular, our analysis points out that, for such cells, no benefit is obtained by increasing the sample size. Therefore, patterns falling in such cells should be rejected;
- Increasing the sample size is more effective for cells characterized by a class with very high probability, as the error decreases more quickly;
- On the other hand, error is higher for such cells in the small sample case.

With regard to the design of BKS table, our analysis of generalization error suggests that a good table should be made up of cells characterized by a class with very high probability, so that increasing the sample size can give benefits. Design of such a table depends on the selection of classifiers, and it is a topic of further investigations.

3   Improvement of BKS Accuracy Using Linear Classifiers in Ambiguous Cells

As pointed out in Section 1, BKS method exhibits an intrinsic limitation for the so called ambiguous cells, that is, for cells characterized by a low probability of the most representative class. As BKS method assigns all the patterns of the cell to the majority class, patterns falling in ambiguous cells are usually rejected in order to limit generalization error [1]. This can cause high reject rates if many ambiguous cells are present. In principle, increasing the number of classifiers could reduce the number of ambiguous cells. Unfortunately, increasing the number L of classifiers makes more difficult the design of BKS table, as the number m of probabilities to be estimated increases exponentially ($m=K^L$). It is worth noting that our analysis of BKS generalization error further pointed out the need for alternative strategies to handle ambiguous cells (Section 2.2), as it showed that small benefits are obtained by increasing the sample size. Therefore, in the following, we propose an alternative strategy that allows exploiting possible increases of sample size, and avoids increasing exponentially the number of probabilities.

First of all, let us indicate with $\{X_j\} \in s_j$ the set of patterns falling in BKS cell s_j, $j=1,\ldots,m$, $m=K^L$. Without loosing of generality, we can assume that such set falls in a region of the original feature space that can be indicated by $\{X_j\} \in \bigcup_{i=1}^{r_j} R_{ji}$. Namely, the set of pattern falling in BKS cell s_j belongs to the union of R_{ji} regions in the original feature space. Now, let us focus on ambiguous cells. For such cells, the majority decision rule of BKS method produces an intrinsic large error. However, it is easy to see that patterns falling in ambiguous cells might be discriminated correctly in the original feature space, supposed that an appropriate discrimination function is used, and enough training patterns are available. Consider, for example, the case of a two-class problem and an ambiguous cell s_{j*} with 49% of error (i.e., 49% of patterns belongs to the minority class). Assume that patterns of such cell belong to a single region R_{j*} (i.e., $\{X_{j*}\} \in R_{j*}$) in the original feature space, and they are linearly separable within R_{j*}. In such case, a simple linear classifier could discriminate with zero error the patterns of this ambiguous cell, so overcoming the intrinsic limitation of BKS method for such cell.

Therefore, we propose to discriminate patterns falling in ambiguous BKS cells by using additional "local" classifiers that work in the regions of the original feature space associated to such cells. The idea of refining BKS method by local analysis in the original feature space was originally proposed in [10]. In general, classifiers of appropriate complexity should be used. However, due to small sample size problems, we propose the use of linear classifiers. In particular, the use of single layer perceptrons (SLPs) according to the approach proposed in [9]. In order to handle the small sample size problem, data are first moved into the centre of coordinates, and data whitening, normalization of variances are performed. Then, SLP learning can start from weights with zero value, and a variety of classifiers of different complexity can be obtained while training proceeds. Details on this approach can be found in Chapter 5 of [9].

It is easy to see that the use of SLPs, according to the approach proposed in Chapter 5 of [9], can strongly reduce BKS error if patterns falling in ambiguous cells are almost linearly separable in the original feature space. This is more likely to happen for BKS cells whose patterns fall into a single compact region of the original feature space. For ambiguous cells whose patterns fall in a set of disjoint regions, the use of more complex classifiers should be investigated.

Finally, it is worth noting that our analysis of BKS generalization error pointed out that, for ambiguous cells, small benefits are obtained by increasing the sample size. Differently, SLPs can obviously benefit from the increase of sample size.

4   Experimental Results

Our experiments were aimed to assess the performance improvement achievable by the technique proposed in the previous section. For the sake of brevity, we report only two experiments, with an artificial data set and a real data set of remote sensing images.

4.1   Experiments with the Artificial Data set

The artificial data set was explicitly designed to assess the effectiveness of the proposed technique to increase BKS accuracy for ambiguous cells. Therefore, this data set was designed to favour the presence of ambiguous cells. The data set is shown in Figure 2. It is made up of five "balls", each ball containing patterns of two non-linearly separable classes. The data set is thirty dimensional, but all the discriminatory information is concentrated in only two dimensions. Figure 2 shows a projection of test data on the two-dimensional informative feature space. For training, we used two thousand 30-dimensional vectors. In order to favour the presence of ambiguous cells, we subdivided training data in five clusters by k-means clustering algorithm (k=5). Then, five multiplayer perceptron (MLP) classifiers, with two hidden nodes, were separately trained on each cluster by the Levenberg-Marquardt algorithm in order to obtain an ensemble of five "specialised" classifiers that were likely to generate ambiguous cells. (It is quite easy to see that classifiers trained on separate data sets are likely to generate ambiguous BKS cells on test data). To avoid over fitting of neural nets, we used an artificial validation set created by k-nn noise injection to control the training of MLPs [4, 11].

With $L=5$ classifiers and two classes, we have $m=32$ BKS cells. However, only eight cells were not empty and contained (224, 0), **(179, 204)**, (5, 0), **(196, 181)**, (1, 0), **(189, 202)**, **(206, 216)**, (0, 197) training vectors of the two classes, respectively. The fusion of the five classifiers with standard BKS method gave 37.00% of error on test data.

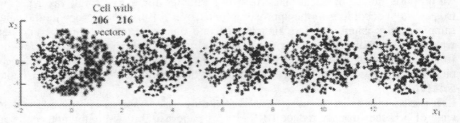

Fig. 2. Projection of test patterns of the artificial data set on the 2D informative feature space.

Then, we focused on the four ambiguous cells pointed out with bold characters. For example, Figure 2 points out test patterns falling in the **(206, 216)** cell in green and red colour. According to our strategy (Section 3), four single layer perceptrons were trained with patterns of each ambiguous cell, and then applied to test data falling in such cells. This allowed reducing the error to 4.95% (4.95% vs. 37.00%), that is a strong improvement of performances. Such result points out well the effectiveness of the proposed technique to increase BKS accuracy when ambiguous cells exist.

4.2   Experiments with the Remote Sensing Data Set

This data set consists of remote-sensing optical images [6]. Each pattern is characterised by an 8-dimensional feature vector. The data set consists of 15878 patterns belonging to two classes. We subdivided the data set into training set (4384+3555 patterns) and test set (4242+3606 patterns). The training set was sampled in order to create five disjoint subsets, that were used to perform ten independent trials. Each training subset was subdivided in four clusters by k-means clustering algorithm (k=4). Clustering was performed in the two-dimensional space obtained by principal component analysis. Four multiplayer perceptron (MLP) classifiers, with seven hidden nodes, were separately trained on each cluster by the Levenberg-Marquardt algorithm in order to obtain an ensemble of four specialized classifiers. The fusion of such four classifiers with standard BKS method provided 12.69% of error on test data. Then, six single layer perceptrons were trained with patterns of ambiguous cells, and applied to test data falling in such cells. We used single layer perceptrons only for ambiguous cells with a sufficient number of samples. This allowed reduce the error to 5.46% (5.46% vs. 12.69%). We did additional experiments using MLPs, with fifteen hidden units, trained on the entire training set (non specialised classifiers). In such case, the use of single layer perceptrons for ambiguous cells did not provide significant improvement, as such cells contained few patterns. Therefore, although definitive conclusions cannot be drawn on the basis of this limited set of experiments, the proposed technique seems to be effective for real data sets too, especially if ensembles made up of specialised classifiers are used.

5   Conclusions

The BKS method for fusing multiple classifiers was introduced in 1995 [1], and it is very popular in the pattern recognition literature. Reported experiments showed that it can provide good performances if large and representative data sets are available. Otherwise overfitting is likely to occur, and the generalization error quickly increases. In spite of this small sample size problem, analytical models of BKS generalization error are currently not available. BKS method also has an intrinsic limitation for the so called ambiguous cells, that is, for cells characterized by a low probability of the most representative class. So far the only strategy available to handle ambiguous cells is the reject option. In this paper, we proposed a simple analytical model that relates BKS generalization error to sample size for two-class cases. To the best of our knowledge, this is the first attempt to model BKS generalization error. We also discussed some implications of our model for BKS table design. Although this is a preliminary work limited to two class cases, such implications point out the practical relevance that the study of BKS generalization error can have. We also proposed to discriminate patterns falling in ambiguous BKS cells by using additional linear classifiers that work in the regions of the original feature space associated to such cells. Reported experiments showed that our technique could strongly improve BKS performances, especially when ensembles made up of specialised classifiers are used.

References

1. Huang, Y.S. and Suen, C.Y. A method of combining multiple experts for the recognition of unconstrained handwritten numerals. *IEEE Trans. On Pattern Analysis and Machine Intelligence* 17(1) (1995), pp. 90-94.
2. C.Y.Suen, L.Lam. Multiple classifier combination methodologies for different output levels. Springer-Verlag Pub., *Lecture Notes in Computer Science*, Vol. 1857 (J.Kittler and F.Roli Eds., 2000), pp. 52-66.

3. S.Raudys, Experts' boasting in trainable fusion rules, *IEEE Trans. on Pattern Analysis and Machine Intelligence*, in press, 2003.
4. F.Roli, S.Raudys, G. Marcialis, An experimental comparison of fixed and trained fusion rules for crisp classifiers outputs, Springer Pub., *Lecture Notes in Computer Science*, Vol. 2364 (F.Roli, J.Kittler Eds., 2002), pp. 232-241.
5. C. K. Chow, On optimum error and reject tradeoff, *IEEE Trans. on Information Theory*, 16 (1970) 41-46.
6. S.Raudys. Combining the expert networks: a review. *Proc. of the Int. Conference on Neural Networks and Artificial Intelligence*, (R. Sadykhov Ed.), 2-5 October 2001, Minsk, Belorus, pp. 81-91
7. H.J.Kang, S.W.Lee, A dependency-based framework of combining multiple experts for the recognition of unconstrained handwritten numerals, *Proc. 1999 Int. Conf. On Computer Vision and Pattern Recognition*, Fort Collins, Colorado, USA, June 1999, pp. 124-129
8. H.J.Kang, S.W.Lee, Combining classifiers based on minimization of a Bayes error rate, Proc. 5th int. Conf. On Document Analysis and Recognition, Bangalore, India, 1999, pp. 398-401
9. S.Raudys, *Statistical and Neural Classifiers: an integrated approach to design*, Springer, London, 2001
10. G. Giacinto, F. Roli , Dynamic cassifier selection based on multiple classifier behaviour, *Pattern Recognition*, 34(9), 2001, pp. 179-181.
11. M. Skurichina, S. Raudys, R.P.W. Duin. K-nearest neighbors directed noise injection in multilayer perceptron training, *IEEE Tr. on Neural Networks*, vol. 11, pp. 504–511, 2000.

Reducing the Overconfidence of Base Classifiers when Combining Their Decisions

Šarunas Raudys[1], Ray Somorjai[2], and Richard Baumgartner[2]

[1] Vilnius Gediminas Technical University, Sauletekio 11, Vilnius LT-2100, Lithuania 2006
raudys@ktl.mii.lt
[2] Institute for Biodiagnostics, National Research Council Canada, 435 Ellice Avenue
Winnipeg, MB, Canada, R3B 1Y6
{ray.somorjai,richard.baumgartner}@nrc-cnrc.gc.ca

Abstract. When the sample size is small, the optimistically biased outputs produced by expert classifiers create serious problems for the combiner rule designer. To overcome these problems, we derive analytical expressions for bias reduction for situations when the standard Gaussian density-based quadratic classifiers serve as experts and the decisions of the base experts are aggregated by the behavior-space-knowledge (BKS) method. These reduction terms diminish the experts' overconfidence and improve the multiple classification system's generalization ability. The bias-reduction approach is compared with the standard BKS, majority voting and stacked generalization fusion rules on two real-life datasets for which the different base expert aggregates comprise the multiple classification system.

Index Terms: multiple classification systems, fusion rule, BKS method, local classifiers, sample size, apparent error, complexity, stacked generalization.

1 Introduction

Multiple classifier systems (MCS) provide a useful approach for designing complex pattern recognition systems. In MCS, input pattern vectors are initially classified by several "simple" base (expert) classifiers. A combination rule aggregates the outputs of the experts and performs the ultimate classification. Dividing the decision-making procedure into two phases changes the training set size/complexity relations. A great deal of research in the pattern recognition community focused on combining rules [1-9]. Fixed combining rules (majority voting, sum, product, etc.) are based on quite strong assumptions, such as comparable performances of all members in the MCS, statistical independence between solutions of the experts, etc. [2, 3, 7].

Combining of the experts' outputs can be regarded as a problem of statistical pattern recognition. The most popular techniques used in classifier fusion include: linear weighted voting, the naïve Bayes classifiers, the kernel function approach, potential functions, the behavior-knowledge-space method, decision trees and multilayer perceptrons. Special approaches, such as bagging, boosting and arcing classifiers, mixture of experts, stacked generalization have been suggested [1, 9-13]. It was demonstrated that when the sample size is very small, simple, fixed, non-trainable rules

T. Windeatt and F. Roli (Eds.): MCS 2003, LNCS 2709, pp. 65–73, 2003.
© Springer-Verlag Berlin Heidelberg 2003

compete with or even outperform trainable ones [14, 15]. However, difficulties may arise in the finite sample size situation.

Sample size effects can be divided into three types: a) the generalization errors of the expert classifiers increase due to imperfect training; b) the generalization error of the combining rule increases due to imperfect training; c) if the same training set is used to train both the experts and the combiner, the designer is misled, since she/he utilizes biased resubstitution error estimates of the quality of each single expert, i.e. each expert classifier is overconfident.

The first effect necessitates using the simplest base classifiers. The second requires adapting the complexity of the fusion rule to the sample size: for small sample sizes, only simple fusion rules should be attempted. Complex combiners should only be employed for large sample sizes. The third effect compels the fusion rule designer to distrust the experts' "self-evaluations", if these expert classifiers are complex and the training set sizes are too small [3, 16, 17]. This paper deals with this last problem, not frequently considered in the literature.

In [13], leave-one-out estimates were used to design the combiner. In [17], Euclidean distance and standard linear Fisher classifiers were utilized as experts in a linearly weighted sum type of fusion. To improve the linear fusion rules, correction terms were derived to evaluate the experts' boasting. These corrections helped to improve the accuracy of MCS, however, the gain in classification error reduction was not appreciable. For the behaviour-space-knowledge (BKS) method and linear experts, such term was derived in [18]. Higher gain was demonstrated.

The objective of the present paper is to investigate different approaches to the aggregation of base classifiers (experts), extend the analysis of [18] for the case when non-linear classifiers are serving as experts and a nonlinear BKS rule is used for fusion, and present experimental comparison with standard BKS, majority voting and stacked generalization fusion rules on two real-life datasets for which the different base expert aggregates comprise the multiple classification system. Theoretical correction terms prove that expert overconfidence is responsible for an significant increase in the generalization error, and help elucidate consequences of expert boasting, allow to obtain *a better understanding* of the problem of combining classifiers, especially when the base classifiers are overtrained. It also gives a *useful procedure* for minimizing the undesired effects when this is the case.

2   The BKS Combining Rule

If the experts provide crisp outputs (class labels), then, as the sample size increases, the asymptotically optimal statistical decision rule is provided by the multinomial classifier [18 - 20] usually referred to by MCS proponents as the BKS method [21, 22]. In the pattern recognition literature, the use of the BKS method as the fusion rule was found very promising, but seriously limited when the training dataset size was small [8, 22].

First, we shall present a short description of the multinomial classifier, used here as the fusion method. More details can be found in [19]. For the MCS design problem, assume 2 pattern classes and L expert classifiers. Denote the decision made by the j-th expert by e_j. Suppose e_j can take one of the labels $\{0, 1\}$. Thus, for the design of the fusion rule, we have a discrete-valued binary vector $E = (e_1, e_2, \dots, e_L)^\tau$. The total number of possible combinations of L outputs (states) $e_1, e_2, \dots, e_L$ is $m = 2^L$. Each vector E can assume only one state, s_r, from the m possible ones, $s_1, s_2, \dots, s_{m-1}, s_m$. In the statistical approach, it is assumed that the values $s_1 \dots, s_m$ follow a multinomial distribution. The conditional distribution of the i-th class vector E, taking one of m "states", is characterized by m probabilities

$$P_1^{(i)}, P_2^{(i)}, \dots, P_{m-1}^{(i)}, P_m^{(i)}, \text{ with } \sum_{r=1}^{m} P_r^{(i)} = 1, (i = 1, 2).$$

Let P_i be the prior probability of the i-th pattern class, π_i. Then *Bayes rule* should allocate the vector E, falling into the r-th state, according to maximum of the products

$$P_1 P_r^{(1)}, P_2 P_r^{(2)}, \tag{1}$$

To use the allocation rule, we have to know $2 \times (m-1)$ probabilities $P_1^{(1)}, P_2^{(1)}, \dots,$ $P_{m-1}^{(2)}$ and the class priors P_1, P_2. If the fusion rule makes its prediction based only on *the class labels* $e_1, e_2, \dots, e_L$ supplied by the expert classifiers, and if all probabilities in Equation (1) are known, it is the *optimal classifier*. No other fusion rule can perform better. It is worth noting that the multinomial classifier-based fusion rule will fail compared to an *oracle*, an ideal fusion rule. The oracle is *a hypothetical rule*. It makes correct classification if at least one expert is exact. It commits an error, however, if all experts classify the vector x incorrectly. In comparison with the multinomial fusion rule, the oracle utilizes additional information (the vector x).

While solving real world problems, the $2 \times m$ probabilities $P_1^{(1)}, P_2^{(1)}, \dots, P_m^{(2)}$ are unknown. The standard method to estimate unknown state probabilities is the maximum likelihood (ML) method:

$$\hat{P}_r^{(i)} = n_r^{(i)} / N_i, \tag{2}$$

where N_i is the *a priori* fixed number of training vectors from the i-th pattern class, and of those, $n_r^{(i)}$ is the number of vectors falling into the state s_r.

In this case, we have a sample-based multinomial classifier (i.e., the BKS method). If the training set is used twice, to train both, the experts and the combiner (the fusion rule), the ML estimates (2) become optimistically biased. Inaccurate estimates of the cells' probabilities lead to an increase in the generalization error of MCS. In principle, an additional training set should to be used to design the fusion rule. Otherwise, special supplementary procedures have to be applied.

3   Fighting the Bias if Quadratic Classifiers Are Used as Experts

Correction Term. When we train the expert classifiers and use the training set to evaluate the cells' probabilities $P_1^{(1)}, P_2^{(1)}, \dots, P_m^{(2)}$, we deal with biased (apparent) error estimates. Is sample size is small and expert classifiers are complex, the bias can be significant and may bluff the fusion rule designer. One of possibilities to overcome the experts' the bias problem is to utilize leave one out method, another way is to derive bias correction terms analytically. For the standard linear classifier following bias correction term was used to correct the resubstitution error estimates [17 - 19]

$$\hat{P}_R^{corrected} = \hat{P}_R^C + (EP_{gen}^C - E\hat{P}_R^C) \tag{3}$$

where EP_{gen}^C and $E\hat{P}_R^C$ denote expectations of conditional probability of misclassification and that of the resubstitution error estimate of classifier "C": for Fisher classifier, "F", $EP_{gen}^C \approx \Phi\{ -\tfrac{1}{2}\hat{\delta} / \sqrt{T_{\mu\Sigma}} \}$ and $E\hat{P}_R^C \approx \Phi\{ -\tfrac{1}{2}\hat{\delta} \sqrt{T_{\mu\Sigma}} \}$, $T_{\mu\Sigma}$ is a term responsible to inexact sample estimation of mean vector and covariance matrix of the sample based discriminant function, $T_{\mu\Sigma} = (1+\dfrac{2n}{\delta^2 N})(1+\dfrac{n}{2\overline{N} - n})$, n is the input dimensionality (note that n can be different for each expert), and $\hat{\delta}$ is the sample estimate of δ, the Mahalanobis distance (for introduction to statistical pattern recognition see e.g. [23, 24]).

The parameter $\hat{\delta}$ can be evaluated from the resubstitution classification error estimate by interpolating the equation $\hat{P}_R^F = \Phi\{ -\tfrac{1}{2}\hat{\delta} \sqrt{T_{\mu\Sigma}} \}$. Our objective is to extend such approach to derive the correction term for quadratic discriminant function. In [25] (see also [26]), the generalization error of the standard quadratic classifier was expressed as $EP_{gen}^Q \approx \Phi\{ -\tfrac{1}{2}\hat{\delta} \, 1/\sqrt{T_{\mu\Sigma}} \}$, with

$$T_{\mu\Sigma}^* \approx \left(1+\frac{n+2}{\overline{N}-n-4}\right)\left(1+\frac{1}{\overline{N}}\left(1+\frac{2n}{\delta^2}\right)+\frac{n}{\overline{N}^2\delta^2}+\frac{(\delta^4/2)+ n+ n(\delta^2+ n)}{(\overline{N}-n-4)\delta^2}\right) \tag{4}$$

where it was assumed $N_2= N_1= N$.

Like in Equation (3) for expectation of the resubstitution error estimate we will use $EP_R^Q \approx \Phi\{ -\tfrac{1}{2}\hat{\delta} \sqrt{T_{\mu\Sigma}} \}$. To have the analytical bias correction term for the BKS fusion rule, we are assuming that the experts' outputs e_j $(j = 1, \dots , L)$ are independent binomial variables. The assumptions about independent solutions, Gaussian data seems very restrictive, however, simulation experiments show that even such rough approximation is useful. Following the independence assumption, the conditional probability $P_r^{(i)}$ of the i-th class, in the r-th cell $(0 < r = 1+e_1+ 2e_2+ 2^2 e_3 + \dots + 2^{L-1} e_L \le m)$ can be expressed as the product

$$P_r^{(i)} = \prod_{j=1}^{L}(P_{ij})^{1-e_j}(1-P_{ij})^{e_j-1}, \tag{5}$$

where P_{ij} is the probability that the j-th expert assigned the i-th class vector to the first class; P_{2j} and $1 - P_{1j}$ are conditional probabilities of misclassification of the first and second classes.

According to Equation (4), the conditional probability $P_r^{(i)}$ of the r-th cell is a function of the probabilities of incorrect classification, P_{2j} and $1 - P_{1j}$. Replacing P_{2j} and $1 - P_{1j}$ in Equation (4) by the *generalization error* estimates of each expert, $\hat{P}_{Rj}^{F*}$, we have an "unbiased" estimate of the conditional generalization error in the r-th cell, $\hat{P}_{Gr}^{(i)}$. Replacing P_{2j} and $1 - P_{1j}$ in Equation (5) by the *resubstitution error* estimates $\hat{P}_{Rj}^{F}$ ($j = 1, 2, \ldots, L$), we construct an almost unbiased estimate of the conditional resubstitution error in the r-th cell, $\hat{P}_{Rr}^{(i)}$ (for the sake of simplicity, we assume $P_{2r} = 1 - P_{1r}$). Thus, the modified term, $\hat{\Delta}_{ir} = \hat{P}_{Gr}^{(i)} - \hat{P}_{Rr}^{(i)}$, is utilized to reduce the bias of the r-th cell's probability estimate:

$$\hat{P}_{r \text{ unbiased}}^{(i)} = \hat{P}_r^{(i)} + (\hat{P}_{Gr}^{(i)} - \hat{P}_{Rr}^{(i)}). \tag{6}$$

4   Experiments with High-Variate Spectroscopic and Machine Vibration Data

The correction terms were derived for multivariate Gaussian datasets. Our aim here is to check whether the correction terms are useful in real-world situations, when standard quadratic and linear Fisher classifiers are used as base experts and the BKS rule is utilized for combining. Two high-dimensional, real-world, two-category datasets were considered.

Magnetic Resonance (MR) Spectral Data. The spectra were obtained from biofluids of cancer patients and normal subjects (dataset S300). Each sample consists of MR intensities measured at 300 frequencies, i.e., the original feature space is 300-dimensional. The training set comprises 31 cancer samples (class 1) and 40 normals (class 2). The test set contains 30 samples from class 1, 39 from class 2. Clearly, this presents a high-dimensionality, small sample size situation.

For analyzing dataset S300, we reduced the feature space by a genetic algorithm-based optimal feature selection (GA_ORS) method [27]. The GA_ORS method was required to find a prespecified number of optimal features (averages of adjacent spectral intensities). We created two different sets of 5 experts (Experts N 1 2 3 4 5). In one case, the feature sets were independent: they each comprised 60 *non-overlapping* original features, from which 4 new features were produced by the GA_ORS method. In the second, the 5 experts were *not independent* (Experts O 1 2 3 4 5), since some of the original feature spaces overlapped: 100 features comprised each expert's feature space: 1-100, 51-150, 101-200, 151-250, 201-300. From these, 2 new, optimal features were produced.

We also performed experiments with a stacked generalization (SG)-based fusion rule [13]. This rule produces expert fusion based on the individual experts' continuous output probabilities as input features to a simple linear Fisher classifier. This method was successful for solving a variety of difficult, real-life biomedical classification problems, characterized by high-dimensional but sparse datasets, such as the current one (see references in the review [28]).

The Machine Vibration Data. Three hundred spectral features of 400 electro motors were measured. The data were partitioned into two groups, good" and "bad" motors, 200 motors in each group. For each group, the dataset was randomly split into training and test sets. To have data somewhat closer to Gaussian, we used the square root of each spectral feature. In addition, a triangular filter (1 1.5 2.0 1.5 1) was utilized for smoothing. Preliminary analysis of scatter diagrams of 2D projections of spectral data showed that in general, the "good" motors were surrounded by the "bad" ones.

Therefore, quadratic discriminant functions were employed as experts. The term $T_{\mu\Sigma}^{*}$ shows that the standard quadratic classifier is extremely sensitive to the sample size / dimensionality ratio. For our pattern recognition problem, $N=100$. Calculations according to Equation (4) suggest that in order to have a "respectable" classification, we need to use a small number of features: if $p=50$ for asymptotic classification error $P_{\infty}=$ $\Phi\{-\frac{1}{2}\delta\}=0.1$, the expected value of the generalization error is $EP_{gen}^{Q}\approx0.312$; if $p=20$, $EP_{gen}^{Q}\approx0.182$. Therefore, in our experiments, the experts utilized feature subsets composed of approximately 25 features: after smoothing the spectra, only part of the features (typically every 4th) was used for classification (Table 1).

Table 1. Three expert groups considered in experiments with nonlinear experts 5. Comparison Experiments

Experts	1	2	3	4	5
1st group	5:4:100	55:4:150	105:4:200	155:4:250	2:16:298
2nd group	5:4:100	105:4:200	205:4:298	3:32:298	2:64:298
3rd group	5:4:100	55:4:150	105:4:200	155:4:250	202:4:298

Generalization errors, evaluated by a cross-validation method, are presented in Tables 2 and 3. Abbreviations: **BKSStand** is the standard, ideal BKS fusion rule (test set vectors were used to evaluate the cells' probabilities $P_1^{(1)}$, , ... , $P_{m-1}^{(2)}$). **MajorVot** stands for the fixed majority voting fusion rule. **BKSModif** denotes the modified BKS rule, when the ML sample-estimated cell probabilities (2) were corrected by Eq. (3), (4), (5), and the Fisher or quadratic classifiers were used as experts. **SG** designates expert fusion based on stacked generalization. All SG fusions were done with leave-one-out (LOO) cross-validation.

Experiments with machine vibration data were performed with a two-fold cross validation: The 200 vectors of each pattern class were split into 2 equal subsets. One of them was used for training the experts and the fusion rule, the other to estimate the generalization error. Then the data subsets were interchanged, the experiments repeated once more and the mean value of the two was calculated. This procedure was repeated 250 times (treatments), each time after new mixing of the data. Thus, in Table 3 we have mean values calculated of 500 training+testing experiments (left), standard deviations of 250 treatments (in brackets) and minimal values obtained of 250 treatments (right).

Table 2. Generalization error (in percents) of standard BKS, modified BKS, majority voting and stacked generalization (SG) rules in dataset S300 with 300 features. N indicates non-overlapping experts, O overlapping ones. Winning method is in bold. Linear expert classifiers.

Experts	BKSStand	BKSModif	MajorVot	0SG
S300 N 1 2 3 4 5	33.3	**24.6**	27.5	26.1
S300 N 1 2 3	34.8	**18.8**	**18.8**	30.4
S300 N 1 2 4	**26.1**	**26.1**	**26.1**	29.0
S300 N 1 2 5	33.3	33.3	31.9	**30.4**
S300 N 1 3 4	26.1	26.1	26.1	**24.6**
S300 N 1 3 5	29.0	29.0	29.0	**23.2**
S300 N 2 3 4	29.0	**24.6**	**24.6**	34.8
S300 N 2 3 5	40.6	**24.6**	**24.6**	29.0
S300 N 3 4 5	37.7	37.7	37.7	**33.3**
S300 O 1 2 3 4 5	40.6	31.9	30.4	**24.6**
S300 O 1 2 3	47.8	**26.1**	**26.1**	31.9
S300 O 1 2 4	33.1	**29.0**	**29.0**	33.1
S300 O 1 2 5	36.2	**34.8**	**34.8**	**34.8**
S300 O 1 3 4	34.8	**23.2**	**23.2**	31.9
S300 O 1 3 5	29.0	**26.1**	**26.1**	27.5
S300 O 2 3 4	30.4	29.0	29.0	**27.5**
S300 O 2 3 5	37.7	34.8	34.8	**24.6**
S300 O 3 4 5	**30.4**	**30.4**	**30.4**	**30.4**

Table 3. Generalization error (in percents) of standard BKS, modified BKS, majority voting and stacked generalization (SG) rules in dataset MV300 with 300 features. Winning method is in bold. Quadratic expert classifiers.

Experts	BKSStand	BKSModif	MajorVot	SG (LOO)
1 (O)	14.7 (2.0) / 9.3	**8.4** (1.4) / **5.2**	11.5 (1.3) / 7.5	10.1 (1.6) / 6.3
2 (N)	14.9 (2.4) / 7.5	**10.3** (1.5) / **5.5**	11.0 (1.1) / 8.5	11.1 (1.6) / 7.8
3 (O)	18.7 (2.2) / 12.3	14.4 (2.9) / 10.5	16.9 (1.3) / 13.5	**13.7** (1.8) / **9.7**

Experiments show that when the sample size is very small, the simple **MajorVot** fusion rule almost always outperforms the standard BKS (**BKSStand**). For larger sample sizes, more sophisticated rules perform better. The theoretical correction of the BKS method, **BKSModif**, frequently reduces the generalization error to the **MajorVot** rule's error rate or even lower. Based on Table 2, the pair-wise comparisons and winning scores are: **SG** vs. **BKSStand** 14 to 2 (2 ties), **MajorVot** vs. **BKSStand** 13 to 0 (5), **BKSModif** vs. **BKSStand** 13 to 0 (5), **SG** vs. **MajorVot** 8 to 8 (2), **SG** vs. **BKSModif** 7 to 9 (2) and **MajorVot** vs. **BKSModif** 2 to 1 (15). These results support the claim that **BKSModif** improves **BKSStand**. Interestingly, for linear experts, the simple **SG** (with leave-one-out crossvalidation) performs comparably to both **BKSModif** and **MajorVot**. As shown in Table 3, for the first two selections of the nonlinear experts, **BKSModif** always outperformed, and by wide margins, both **BKSStand** and **MajorVot**. Improper selection of the features for the experts (third expert group; it differs from the first group only in one expert) increased the generalization error notably, and reduced the effectiveness of **BKSModif** method: on average the SG method performed better in this situation. In general, the **BKSModif** and **SG** are comparable in performance, again with a slight edge to **BKSModif**.

5   Concluding Remarks

The expert boasting effect is present in all trainable combining rules if the training set is used twice, to train both the experts and the fusion rule. We derived new correction term for non-linear expert boasting, and justified theoretically and demonstrated experimentally that expert boasting can become harmful. If for Gaussian data the standard linear or quadratic classifiers are used as experts and a multinomial classifier is used for fusion, Equations (3), (4), (5) and (6) compensate for the increase in generalization error and, together with the correction terms derived in [17] and [18], provide a *theoretical explanation of the expert boasting phenomenon*: elimination of expert boasting (without reducing the variance!) helps diminish the generalization error of the trainable fusion rule.

Analytically derived correction terms cannot be used when the data are obviously multimodal, when more complex types of expert classification rules are employed, or when the number of pattern classes exceeds two. Due to the large variances of the statistical estimates of the classification error, the correction terms are also ineffective when the training set size is too small. In such cases, utilization of the leave-one-out method (**SG**) or a k - fold crossvalidation approach may be preferable. In future research, equations for unequal sample size will be derived, and experiments with more real-world datasets will be performed, including more detailed comparisons with SG-types of fusion rules.

Acknowledgements

We thank those authors who generously made their datasets public and Dr. Erinija Pranskeviciene for discussions.

References

1. J. Kittler, F. Roli (eds). Multiple Classifier Systems. *Lecture Notes in Computer Science*, Springer Vol. 1857 (2000), vol. 2096 (2001), Vol. 2364 (2002).
2. J. Kittler. Combining classifiers: a theoretical framework. *Pattern Analysis and Applications*, vol. 1, pp.18-27, 1998
3. J. Kittler. A framework for classifier fusion: is still needed? *Advances in Pattern Recognition,* Lecture Notes in Computer Science, Springer, vol. 1876, pp. 45–56, 2000.

4. J. Gosh. Multi-classifier systems: back to the future. Multiple Classifier Systems. *Lecture Notes in Computer Science*, Springer, vol. 2364 , pp. 1-15, 2002.
5. T.K. Ho. Data complexity analysis for classifier combination. Multiple Classifier Systems. *Lecture Notes in Computer Science*, Springer, vol. 2096, pp. 53-67, 2001.
6. S. Raudys. Multiple classifier systems in the context of feature extraction and selection. Multiple Classification Systems, *Lecture Notes in Computer Science*, Springer, vol. 2364, pp. 27-41, 2002.
7. J. Kittler, M. Hatef, R.P.W. Duin, J. Matas. On combining classifiers, *IEEE Trans. on Pattern Analysis and Machine Intelligence*, vol. 20, pp. 226-239, 1998.
8. L.I. Kuncheva, J.C.Bezdek, R.P.W. Duin. Decision templates for multiple classifier fusion: and experimental comparison. *Pattern Recognition,* vol. 34, pp. 299-314, 2001.
9. L. Breiman. Bagging predictors. *Machine Learning Journal,* vol. 24, pp. 123-140, 1996.
10. L. Breiman. Arcing classifiers. *Annals of Statistics*, vol. 26, pp. 801-849, 1998.
11. Y. Freund, R.E. Schapire. A decision-theoretic generalization of on-line learning and an application to boosting. *Journal of Computer and Systems Sci.*, vol. 55, pp. 119-139, 1997.
12. M. Jordan and R. Jakobs. Hierarchical mixture of experts and the EM algorithm. *Neural Computation*, vol. 6, pp. 181-214, 1994.
13. D. Wolpert. Stacked generalization. *Neural Networks*, vol. 5, pp. 241-260, 1992.
14. F. Roli, G. Fumera. Analysis of linear and order statistics combiners for fusion of imbalanced classifiers. Multiple Classification Systems, *Lecture Notes in ComputerScience,* Springer, vol. 2364, pp. 252-261, 2002.
15. F. Roli, S. Raudys, G.L. Marcialis. An experimental comparison of fixed and trained rules for crisp classifiers outputs, Multiple Classification Systems, *Lecture Notes in Computer Science*, Springer, vol. 2364, pp. 232-241, 2002.
16. C. Güler, B. Sankur, Y. Kahya, M. Skurichina, S. Raudys. Classification of respiratory sound patterns by means of cooperative neural networks. In: G. Ramponi, G. L. Sicuranza, S. Carrato, S. Marsi (eds), *Proc. of 8th European Signal Processing Conference* (isbn 88-86179-83-9). Edizioni Lint, Trieste, 1996.
17. A. Janeliunas, S. Raudys. Reduction of boasting bias' of linear expert. Multiple Classification Systems, Springer, *Lecture Notes in Comp. Science*, vol. 2364, pp. 242-251,2002.
18. S. Raudys. Experts' boosting in trainable fusion rules. *IEEE Transactions on Pattern Analysis and Machine Intelligence* (in press, 2003).
19. S. Raudys. *Statistical and Neural Classifiers: An integrated approach to design.* Springer, London, p. 312, 2001.
20. P.A. Lachenbruch, M. Goldstein. Discriminant analysis. *Biometrics,* vol. 5, pp. 9–85, 1979.
21. Y.S. Huang, C.Y. Suen. A method of combining multiple experts for the recognition of unconstrained handwritten numerals. *IEEE Trans. on Pattern Analysis and Machine Intelligence*, vol. 17, pp. 90-93, 1998.
22. L.I. Kuncheva, C.J. Whitaker. Feature subsets for classifier combination: An enumerative experiment. *Multiple Classifier Systems.* Lecture Notes in Computer Science, Springer, vol. 2096, pp. 228-237, 2001.
23. K. Fukunaga. *Introduction to Statistical Pattern Recognition.* 2nd ed. Academic Press, New York, 1990.
24.] R.O. Duda, P.E. Hart, D.G. Stork. *Pattern Classification.* 2nd ed. Wiley, NY, 2000.
25. S. Raudys, (1972). On the amount of a priori information in designing the classification algorithm. *Proc. Acad. of Sciences of the USSR,* 168-174, (in Russian).
26. S. Raudys and D. Young. A review of the former Soviet Union literature on small training sample problems in statistical discriminant analysis. *Journal of Multivariate Analysis.* (in press 2003).
27. A.E. Nikulin, B. Dolenko, T. Bezabeh, R.L. Somorjai. Near-optimal region selection for feature space reduction: novel preprocessing methods for classifying MR spectra. *NMR Biomed.* **11**, 209-216, 1998.
28. C.L. Lean, R.L Somorjai, I.C.P. Smith, P. Russell, C.E. Mountford. Accurate diagnosis and prognosis of human cancers by proton MRS and a three stage classification strategy. *Annual Reports on NMR Spectroscopy*, vol. 48, 71-111, 2002.

Linear Combiners for Classifier Fusion: Some Theoretical and Experimental Results

Giorgio Fumera and Fabio Roli

Department of Electrical and Electronic Engineering, University of Cagliari
Piazza d'Armi, 09123, Cagliari, Italy
{fumera,roli}@diee.unica.it

Abstract. In this paper, we continue the theoretical and experimental analysis of two widely used combining rules, namely, the simple and weighted average of classifier outputs, that we started in previous works. We analyse and compare the conditions which affect the performance improvement achievable by weighted average over simple average, and over individual classifiers, under the assumption of unbiased and uncorrelated estimation errors. Although our theoretical results have been obtained under strict assumptions, the reported experiments show that they can be useful in real applications, for designing multiple classifier systems based on linear combiners.

1 Introduction

Recently, some works started to analyze the theoretical foundations of techniques for combining multiple classifiers [7,10,6,11]. Some works also provided analytical comparisons between the performance of different techniques [4,5,3,1,9]. Because of the complexity of developing analytical models of combining rules, the focus was limited to the simplest and most used rules, like majority vote, linear combination of classifier outputs, and order statistics combiners.

In this paper, we focus on linear combiners. A theoretical framework for evaluating the performance improvement achievable by simple averaging the outputs of an ensemble of classifiers, was developed by Tumer and Ghosh [10,11]. In previous works, we extended this framework to weighted average [9,1], and to classification with reject option [2]. In these works, we focused on the comparison between the performance of simple and weighted average. In particular, we provided analytical results which showed how the difference between the accuracies of individual classifiers (performance "imbalance") affect the improvement achievable by weighted average over simple average, for classifier ensembles made up of three classifiers, and under the hypothesis of unbiased and uncorrelated estimation errors [9,1]. We also provided a preliminary analysis of the effects of correlated estimation errors.

In this work, we extend the above analysis of linear combiners. In particular, we determine the conditions on performance imbalance that affect the improvement of weighted average over simple average, and also over individual classifiers, for classifier ensembles of any size. We then analytically evaluate and compare such improvement. We also extend the experimental investigation with respect to our previous works. The behavior of simple and weighted average is evaluated on two real data sets, with the aim of assessing the usefulness of our theoretical results for the design of multiple classifier systems based on linear combiners.

T. Windeatt and F. Roli (Eds.): MCS 2003, LNCS 2709, pp. 74–83, 2003.

Our previous works are summarised in section 2. The new theoretical results are presented in section 3, while section 4 reports the experimental results.

2   Summary of Previous Results

Tumer and Ghosh developed a theoretical framework which allows to evaluate the added error probability, over Bayes error, of individual and multiple classifiers combined by simple average (SA), as a function of bias, variance and pair-wise correlation of estimation errors that affect the a posteriori probability estimates [10,11]. It turns out that the added error, for a given class boundary, is proportional to the sum of the variance and the squared bias of the estimation errors. For classifiers combined by SA, the variance component is also affected by pair-wise correlation between errors of different classifiers. It was shown that simple averaging the outputs of N classifiers reduces the variance component of the added error, while the bias component is not necessarily reduced. In particular, the reduction factor of the variance component is equal to N, if the errors are unbiased and uncorrelated, while it is lower (higher) than N if the errors are positively (negatively) correlated [10,11].

In [9,1], we extended the above framework to analyze and compare the performance of simple and weighted average (WA). We considered the case in which the estimate $\hat{P}(\omega_i \mid \mathbf{x})$ of the a posteriori probability of the i-th class, $P(\omega_i \mid \mathbf{x})$, is computed as a linear combination of the estimates provided by N individual classifiers, $\hat{P}(\omega_i \mid \mathbf{x}) = \sum_{m=1}^{N} w_m \hat{P}_m(\omega_i \mid \mathbf{x})$, where the weights are positive and sum up to 1: $\sum_{m=1}^{N} w_m = 1, w_m \geq 0 \; m = 1, \ldots, N$. If the errors $\varepsilon_i^m(\mathbf{x}) = \hat{P}_m(\omega_i \mid \mathbf{x}) - P(\omega_i \mid \mathbf{x})$ are unbiased and uncorrelated[1], we showed that the added error of a linear combination of classifiers is $E_{add}^{ave} = \sum_{m=1}^{N} E_{add}^m w_m^2$. It turns out that the optimal weights w_m (i.e., the ones which minimise E_{add}^{ave}) are inversely proportional to the added error E_{add}^m of the corresponding classifiers. Therefore, SA ($w_m = 1 / N$) provides the minimum of E_{add}^{ave} only if individual classifiers exhibit the same added error, or equivalently, the same overall error probability. Otherwise, WA provides a lower E_{add}^{ave}. Accordingly, it turned out that the minimum of E_{add}^{ave} is:

$$E_{add}^{WA} = \left(\sum_{m=1}^{N} 1 / E_{add}^m \right)^{-1} . \tag{1}$$

Simple average provides instead the following value of E_{add}^{ave}:

$$E_{add}^{SA} = \left(1 / N^2 \right) \sum_{m=1}^{N} E_{add}^m . \tag{2}$$

If the estimation errors of individual classifiers are correlated, by assuming that the variance and pair-wise correlations do not depend on the classes, E_{add}^{ave} is:

$$E_{add}^{ave} = \sum_{m=1}^{N} E_{add}^m w_m^2 + \sum_{m=1}^{N} \sum_{m \neq n} \rho^{mn} \sqrt{E_{add}^m E_{add}^n} \, w_m w_n , \tag{3}$$

---

[1] As in [T&G96, T&G99], we assume that only the errors of different classifiers on the same class, $\varepsilon_i^m(\mathbf{x})$ and $\varepsilon_i^n(\mathbf{x})$, can be correlated.

where ρ^{mn} is the correlation between the errors of classifiers m and n, on the considered class boundary. Even if in this case the optimal weights can not be computed analytically, it turns out that SA minimises E_{add}^{ave} only if the individual classifiers exhibit the same performance (i.e., equal values of E_{add}^{m}), and equal values of ρ^{mn}, $\forall m, n$. Otherwise, WA is needed.

In [9,1], we exploited the above results to analyse the performance improvement achievable by WA over SA, i.e., $E_{add}^{SA} - E_{add}^{WA}$, for ensembles of three classifiers ($N = 3$). Note that the difference between the added errors coincides with the difference between the overall error probabilities. In particular, we analysed how $E_{add}^{SA} - E_{add}^{WA}$ is affected by the difference between the performance and the pair-wise correlations of individual classifiers. Without loss of generality, consider the individual classifiers ordered for decreasing values of E_{add}^{m} : $E_{add}^{1} \geq E_{add}^{2} \geq E_{add}^{3}$. In the case of unbiased and uncorrelated errors (Eqs. (1),(2)), we proved that $E_{add}^{SA} - E_{add}^{WA}$ is maximum, for a given value of the error range $E_{add}^{1} - E_{add}^{3}$, if $E_{add}^{2} = E_{add}^{1}$. In other words, given the performance of the best and worst individual classifiers, WA provides the maximum improvement, with respect to SA, if the second best classifier exhibit the same performance of the worst classifier. We qualitatively denoted this condition as the maximum performance "imbalance" between individual classifiers, with respect to $E_{add}^{SA} - E_{add}^{WA}$. For correlated estimation errors (Eq. (3)), only a numerical analysis was possible (as pointed out above, the weights which minimise Eq. (3) can not be computed analytically). Consider any given value of the error range $E_{add}^{1} - E_{add}^{3}$, and of the correlation range $\rho_{max} - \rho_{min}$ (note that ρ_{max} and ρ_{min} depend on the number N of classifiers). $E_{add}^{SA} - E_{add}^{WA}$ turns out to be maximum, if $E_{add}^{2} = E_{add}^{1}$, and if $\rho^{23} = \rho_{min}$, $\rho^{12} = \rho^{13} = \rho_{max}$. In other words, we found the same conditions of maximum performance imbalance as for uncorrelated errors, and analogous conditions of maximum correlation imbalance.

Finally, using Eqs. (1)-(3), we evaluated $E_{add}^{SA} - E_{add}^{WA}$ under the above conditions of maximum performance and correlation imbalance, as a function of the error range $E_{add}^{1} - E_{add}^{3}$. To sum up, our model predicts that WA can achieve a significant improvement over SA only for ensembles of classifiers exhibiting highly imbalanced performance (that is, large error range and pair-wise correlations). However, in this case, WA tends to perform very similarly to the best individual classifier, and, therefore, combining provides little advantage.

The above results are limited to ensembles made up of three classifiers. In the following section, we extend our analysis to classifier ensembles of any size N. In particular, we provide the conditions under which $E_{add}^{SA} - E_{add}^{WA}$ is maximum and minimum, for any N. Moreover, we determine the conditions which affect the improvement achievable by simple and WA over individual classifiers. We then compare these conditions, and provide a quantitative evaluation for the case of unbiased and uncorrelated errors, based on Eqs. (1), (2).

3   Some Theoretical Results for Linear Combiners

Without loss of generality, consider N individual classifiers ordered for decreasing values of their added errors, $E_{add}^{1} \geq E_{add}^{2} \geq ... \geq E_{add}^{N}$. For unbiased and uncorrelated estimation errors (Eqs. (1) and (2)), it can be shown that $E_{add}^{SA} - E_{add}^{WA}$ is maximum, for any given error range $E_{add}^1 - E_{add}^N$, if k classifiers ($k < N$) have an added error equal to that of the best one (E_{add}^N), and the other $N - k$ have an added error equal to that of the worst one (E_{add}^1). The value of k can be either $\lfloor k^* \rfloor$ or $\lceil k^* \rceil$, where $k^* = N\left(E_{add}^N - \sqrt{E_{add}^1 E_{add}^N}\right) / \left(E_{add}^N - E_{add}^1\right)$ (which one depends on the particular values of the added errors). Note that, for $N = 3$, one always obtains $k = 1$, which is the condition found in our previous works (section 2). Moreover, $E_{add}^{SA} - E_{add}^{WA}$ is minimum, for any given $E_{add}^1 - E_{add}^N$, if classifiers $2, 3, \ldots, N-1$ exhibit the same added error, equal to $2E_{add}^1 E_{add}^N / \left(E_{add}^1 + E_{add}^N\right)$. These two conditions, depicted in Fig. 1(a),(b), can be denoted respectively as maximum and minimum performance imbalance, with respect to $E_{add}^{SA} - E_{add}^{WA}$.

The proof of the above results can be summarised as follows. The partial derivative of $E_{add}^{SA} - E_{add}^{WA}$ with respect to any E_{add}^m, $1 < m < N$, is $N^{-2} - \left(E_{add}^m\right)^{-2}\left(\sum_{n=1}^{N}\left(E_{add}^n\right)^{-1}\right)^{-2}$. By analyzing its sign, and noting that $E_{add}^1 \geq E_{add}^m \geq E_{add}^N$, it is easy to see that $E_{add}^{SA} - E_{add}^{WA}$ is convex with respect to E_{add}^m. In particular, the maximum of $E_{add}^{SA} - E_{add}^{WA}$ is achieved either when $E_{add}^m = E_{add}^1$, or when $E_{add}^m = E_{add}^N$. It follows that, for given E_{add}^1 and E_{add}^N, the maximum of $E_{add}^{SA} - E_{add}^{WA}$ with respect to $E_{add}^2, \ldots, E_{add}^{N-1}$ is achieved when some of the added errors (say, the first $N - k - 1$) are equal to E_{add}^1, and the other $k - 1$ are equal to E_{add}^N. The corresponding $E_{add}^{SA} - E_{add}^{WA}$ is:

$$E_{add}^{SA} - E_{add}^{WA} = \left((N-k)E_{add}^1 + kE_{add}^N\right)N^{-2} - \left((N-k)/E_{add}^1 + k/E_{add}^N\right)^{-1}. \qquad (4)$$

By minimising this expression with respect to k, one obtains the value of k given above. Let us consider the minimum of $E_{add}^{SA} - E_{add}^{WA}$, with respect to $E_{add}^2, \ldots, E_{add}^{N-1}$, for given E_{add}^1 and E_{add}^N. First, we recall that $E_{add}^{SA} - E_{add}^{WA}$ is convex with respect to any E_{add}^m, $1 < m < N$: it has therefore only one global minimum. By setting to zero the partial derivatives (given above) with respect to each E_{add}^m, $1 < m < N$, we obtain $N\left(E_{add}^m\right)^{-1} = \sum_{n=1}^{N}\left(E_{add}^n\right)^{-1}$. It easily follows that $E_{add}^{SA} - E_{add}^{WA}$ is minimum when $E_{add}^2, \ldots, E_{add}^{N-1}$ are all equal to $2E_{add}^1 E_{add}^N / \left(E_{add}^1 + E_{add}^N\right)$.

Consider now the improvement achievable by simple and WA over the best individual classifier. From Eqs. (1) and (2), it is easy to see that the maximum of $E_{add}^N - E_{add}^{SA}$ and $E_{add}^N - E_{add}^{WA}$, for any given $E_{add}^1 - E_{add}^N$, is achieved when classifiers $2, 3, \ldots, N-1$ exhibit an added error equal to E_{add}^N, while the minimum is achieved when the added error of classifiers $2, 3, \ldots, N-1$ is equal to E_{add}^1. Let us denote these conditions respectively as maximum and minimum performance imbalance, with respect to both $E_{add}^N - E_{add}^{SA}$ and $E_{add}^N - E_{add}^{WA}$. These conditions are depicted in Fig. 1(c),(d). By analysing Eq. (3), it is easy to see that these conditions also hold for correlated errors, when all correlation coefficients are non-negative.

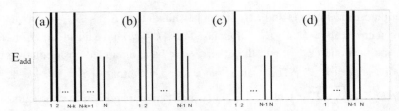

Fig. 1. Conditions of maximum and minimum performance imbalance, with respect to the added errors of individual classifiers, for $E_{add}^{SA} - E_{add}^{WA}$ (a), (b), and for $E_{add}^{N} - E_{add}^{SA}$ and $E_{add}^{N} - E_{add}^{WA}$ (c), (d).

We point out that the conditions of maximum performance imbalance for $E_{add}^{SA} - E_{add}^{WA}$, are different from the ones for $E_{add}^{N} - E_{add}^{SA}$ and $E_{add}^{N} - E_{add}^{WA}$ (see Figs. 1(a),(c)). This means that when simple and WA provide the maximum improvement over individual classifiers, the improvement of WA over SA is not maximum, and vice-versa. Let us now quantitatively evaluate and compare $E_{add}^{SA} - E_{add}^{WA}$, $E_{add}^{N} - E_{add}^{SA}$, and $E_{add}^{N} - E_{add}^{WA}$, for the case of unbiased and uncorrelated errors.

Fig. 2 shows their values, under the condition of maximum performance imbalance for $E_{add}^{N} - E_{add}^{SA}$ and $E_{add}^{N} - E_{add}^{WA}$ (i.e., $E_{add}^{1} E_{add}^{2} = ... = E_{add}^{N-1}$). We considered classifier ensembles of size $N = 3, 5, 7$, an error range between 0 and 0.15, and three different values of the added error of the best individual classifier, E_{add}^{N} (0.01, 0.05 and 0.10). Fig. 2(a) shows that SA can provide a remarkable improvement over the best individual classifier. In particular, the higher is the added error of the best individual classifier, E_{add}^{N}, the higher is the improvement achievable by SA. Such improvement decreases for increasing values of the error range, but this effect becomes negligible when the number of classifiers increases. This is reasonable, since $N - 2$ classifiers exhibit the same added error of the best one, E_{add}^{N}. Fig. 2(b) shows that the improvement achievable by WA over E_{add}^{N} is quite similar to that achievable by SA. This is evident from Fig. 2(c), where the values of $E_{add}^{SA} - E_{add}^{WA}$ are reported. Note that for $N > 3$, the improvement of WA over SA is always below 0.5%. Moreover, for $N = 3$, the improvement exceeds 1% only if the best individual classifier performs very well ($E_{add}^{3} = 0.01$), and the others perform very poorly ($E_{add}^{1} = E_{add}^{2} > 0.10$).

However, in this case, the performance of WA is very similar to E_{add}^{3}, and therefore, combining is useless. It is also worth pointing out that, for any fixed error range, and for any N, when the improvement of WA over the best individual classifier increases, the corresponding improvement over SA decreases (see Fig. 2(b), (c)).

In Fig. 3 we report the same comparison of Fig. 2, under the conditions of maximum performance imbalance for $E_{add}^{SA} - E_{add}^{WA}$ (see Fig. 1(a)). As expected, Fig. 3(a),(b) shows that the improvement of simple and WA, with respect to the best individual classifier, E_{add}^{N}, are lower than those reported in Fig. 2(a),(b), while the value of $E_{add}^{SA} - E_{add}^{WA}$ increases with respect to Fig. 2(c). However, even under the condition of maximum performance imbalance for $E_{add}^{SA} - E_{add}^{WA}$, Fig. 3(c) shows that $E_{add}^{SA} - E_{add}^{WA}$ is quite low. For $N = 3$, $E_{add}^{SA} - E_{add}^{WA}$ exceeds 1% only for highly imbalanced classifiers; for instance, if $E_{add}^{3} = 0.01$, the error range must be higher than 5%; in this case, the corresponding improvement over E_{add}^3 is near 0% (see Fig. 3(b)). Moreover, $E_{add}^{SA} - E_{add}^{WA}$ decreases when the number of classifiers increases. The results of the above comparison between simple and WA confirm the ones obtained in our previous works (see section 2), which were limited to ensembles of three classifiers. These results show that WA significantly outperforms both SA and individual classifiers, only for ensembles of few classifiers (say, $N = 3$), with highly imbalanced performances (for instance, one classifier with added error of about 5%, and two classifiers with added errors of at least 15%).

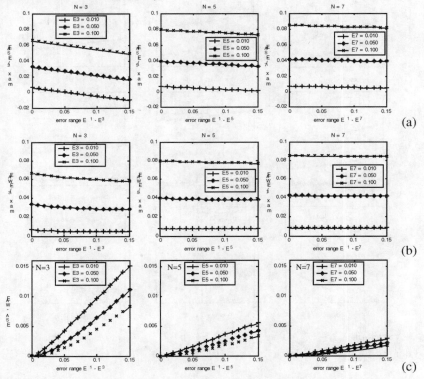

Fig. 2. Values of $E_{add}^N - E_{add}^{SA}$ (a), $E_{add}^N - E_{add}^{WA}$ (b), and $E_{add}^{SA} - E_{add}^{WA}$ (c), under the conditions of maximum performance imbalance for $E_{add}^N - E_{add}^{SA}$ and $E_{add}^N - E_{add}^{WA}$.

Let us now discuss briefly the practical relevance of the above results for the design of multiple classifier systems based on linear combiners. First of all, they show that the advantage of using WA, instead of SA, can be lower than one can expect. It is worth noting that, in real applications, the optimal weights of the linear combination can only be estimated from finite data. This means that, if the maximum theoretical improvement achievable by WA is low, it could be cancelled if a poor estimate from a small data set is done. Therefore, WA should be used only if large and representative data sets are available, in order to guarantee that its superiority over SA can be really exploited. For small data sets, WA can be used if the classifier ensemble at hand is likely to fit the conditions that guarantee the maximum advantage of WA over SA.

This work pointed out such conditions. Finally, it should be noted that the above results have been obtained under the assumption of unbiased and uncorrelated errors, which is likely to be violated in real applications. Therefore, it is interesting to compare the performance of simple and WA on real data sets. Such an experimental comparison is provided in the next section.

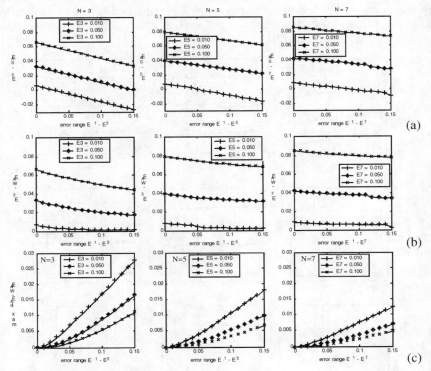

Fig. 3. Values of $E_{add}^{N} - E_{add}^{SA}$ (a), $E_{add}^{N} - E_{add}^{WA}$ (b), and $E_{add}^{SA} - E_{add}^{WA}$ (c), under the conditions of maximum performance imbalance for $E_{add}^{SA} - E_{add}^{WA}$.

4   Experimental Results

With the experiments presented in this section, we evaluated the performances of weighted and SA for two real applications. The aim was to compare their performances with that predicted by the theoretical model of section 3, which is based on the strict assumption of unbiased and uncorrelated errors. According to results of our model, we focused on the effects of the difference between the performance of individual classifiers.

We carried out our experiments on a remote-sensing image classification problem (Feltwell data set [8]), and on a character recognition problem (Letter data set, available at http://www.ncc.up.pt/liacc/ML/statlog). The Feltwell data set has five classes, and consists of 5,124 training patterns and 5,820 test patterns, characterised by fifteen

Table 1. Results for the Feltwell data set. Each row correspond to a different classifier ensemble, whose required percentage error rates are reported in the second column. The achieved error range is denoted as ΔE, while E^b, E^{sa} and E^{wa} denote, respectively, the test set error rate of the best individual classifier, and of simple and WA.

Ensemble		ΔE	E^{sa}	E^{wa}	$E^b - E^{sa}$	$E^b - E^{wa}$	$E^{sa} - E^{wa}$
1	10 10 10	0.51	9.91	9.67	0.49	0.73	0,24
2	15 15 15	0.16	12.67	11.94	2.26	3.00	0,73
3	20 20 20	1.33	15.98	14.43	1.9	3.45	1,55
4	25 25 25	0.97	25.11	24.23	-0.45	0.44	0,88
5	10 10 15	4.54	10.32	9.65	0.08	0.75	0,67
6	10 15 15	4.70	11.43	9.90	-1.03	0.51	1,53
7	15 15 20	4.27	13.45	12.42	1.49	2.52	1,03
8	15 20 20	4.27	14.71	12.83	0.23	2.11	1,88
9	20 20 25	6.13	16.44	15.13	2.09	3.40	1,31
10	20 25 25	6.15	21.82	17.77	-2.62	1.44	4,05
11	10 10 20	8.81	10.74	9.69	-0.34	0.71	1,05
12	10 20 20	8.81	12.33	9.80	-1.93	0.60	2,53
13	15 15 25	9.72	13.91	12.98	1.03	1.96	0,93
14	15 25 25	10.42	21.39	14.65	-6.45	0.29	6,74
15	10 10 25	14.26	11.21	9.97	-0.81	0.43	1,24
16	10 25 25	14.96	20.52	10.26	-10.11	0.14	10,26

features. The Letter data set is made up of 15,000 training patterns and 5,000 test patterns, belonging to 26 classes, and characterised by sixteen features. In our experiments, we used MLP neural network classifiers, with one hidden layer, and a number of input and output units equal to the number of features and classes, respectively. For each data set, in order to obtain classifiers exhibiting an error range at least of 15%, we trained fifty MLPs, characterised by five different numbers of hidden units (15, 5, 4, 3 and 2 for Feltwell, 110, 60, 40, 35 and 30 for Letter). We then constructed sixteen ensembles of three classifiers, each one characterised by a different pattern of the performances of individual classifiers. More precisely, we selected the MLPs exhibiting a test set error rate nearest to predefined values, which are reported in the second column of Tables 1,2. We repeated these experiments by using ten different training sets, obtained by randomly selecting the 80% of patterns from the original training sets. Reported results are averaged over ten runs.

The results are reported in Tables 1, 2. Note that ensembles 1-4 are "balanced" (i.e., the error range of the corresponding classifiers is low), while the others are "imbalanced", with error ranges of about 5%, 10% and 15%. For imbalanced ensembles, we considered the condition of maximum performance imbalance for $E_{add}^{SA} - E_{add}^{WA}$ (ensembles 6,8,10,12,14,16), and the one of maximum performance imbalance for $E_{add}^{N} - E_{add}^{SA}$ and $E_{add}^{N} - E_{add}^{WA}$ (ensembles 5,7,9,11,13,15).

Let us consider first whether the conditions of maximum performance imbalance, given in section 3, are verified. We recall that these conditions determine when $E_{add}^{SA} - E_{add}^{WA}$ is maximum, and when $E_{add}^{N} - E_{add}^{SA}$ and $E_{add}^{N} - E_{add}^{WA}$ are maximum, for fixed values of the error rate of the best and worst individual classifiers. Accordingly, we compared the ensembles of Tables 1 and 2, characterised by the same values of

Table 2. Results for the Letter data set.

Ensemble		ΔE	E^{sa}	E^{wa}	$E^{b}-E^{sa}$	$E^{b}-E^{wa}$	$E^{sa}-E^{wa}$
1	15 15 15	0.09	10.19	10.02	4.73	4.90	0,17
2	20 20 20	0.06	14.60	14.37	5.28	5.51	0,23
3	25 25 25	0.44	19.67	19.45	5.52	5.74	0,22
4	30 30 30	0.16	23.64	23.39	6.32	6.57	0,25
5	15 15 20	4.99	11.31	10.99	3.61	3.93	0,32
6	15 20 20	4.93	12.85	12.41	2.16	2.60	0,44
7	20 20 25	5.28	15.87	15.53.	4.03	4.37	0,34
8	20 25 25	5.51	17.50	16.95	2.4	2.95	0,55
9	25 25 30	4.83	20.77	20.34	4.42	4.84	0,43
10	25 30 30	4.83	21.79	21.24	3.4	3.94	0,55
11	15 15 25	10.26	12.01	11.37	2.92	3.55	0,64
12	15 25 25	10.41	14.95	13.74	0.06	1.27	1,21
13	20 20 30	10.10	16.51	15.88	3.39	4.03	0,63
14	20 30 30	10.10	19.43	18.23	0.48	1.67	1,20
15	15 15 30	15.09	12.27	11.42	2.65	3.50	0,85
16	15 30 30	15.00	16.47	14.24	-1.46	0.77	2,23

the error rate of the best and worst individual classifiers (for instance, ensembles 5 and 6). For all such ensembles, it is easy to see that $E_{add}^{SA} - E_{add}^{WA}$ is maximum when the second best individual classifier has the same error rate of the worst classifier. This is the condition of maximum performance imbalance for $E_{add}^{SA} - E_{add}^{WA}$, for $N = 3$, predicted by our theoretical model.

Analogously, the maximum of both $E_{add}^{N} - E_{add}^{SA}$ and $E_{add}^{N} - E_{add}^{WA}$ is achieved when the second best classifier exhibits the same error rate of the best one. Therefore, the theoretical results of section 3, concerning the conditions of maximum performance imbalance, showed to apply to the two real problems considered.

Let us now compare the performance of simple and WA. First, as expected, note that WA always outperformed the best individual classifier. However, consider the improvement achievable by WA over SA, $E_{add}^{SA} - E_{add}^{WA}$, and over the best individual classifier, $E_{add}^{N} - E_{add}^{WA}$, for the same classifier ensemble. Table 1 shows that, for the Feltwell data set, both values are higher than 1% only for five ensembles out of 16, while for the Letter data set (Table 2), this happens only for two ensembles. Moreover, for Letter, both simple and WA almost always outperform the best individual classifier, and exhibit a very similar error rate. By taking into account that the performance of WA can be worsened by weight estimation, these results show that it can be difficult to obtain a significant improvement over both SA and individual classifiers, as argued in section 3.

To sum up, the above experimental results show that the theoretical results of section 3 can be useful to predict the qualitative behaviour of linear combiners in real applications. Moreover, they also seem to confirm that the advantage of using the WA rule, instead of the SA, can be lower than one can expect.

References

1. Fumera, G., Roli, F.: Performance analysis and comparison of linear combiners for classifier fusion. In: Caelli, T., Amin, A., W. Duin, R.P., Kamel, M., de Ridder, D. (eds.): Proc. Joint Int. Workshops on Structural, Syntactic, and Statistical Pattern Recognition. LNCS, Vol. 2396. Springer-Verlag (2002) 424-432
2. Fumera, G., Roli, F., Vernazza, G.: Analysis of error-reject trade-off in linearly combined classifiers. In: Kasturi, R., Laurendeau, D., Suen, C. (eds.): Proc. 16th Int. Conf. on Pattern Recognition. Vol. 2 (2002) 120-123
3. Kittler, J., Alkoot, F. M.: Sum versus Vote Fusion in Multiple Classifier Systems. IEEE Trans. on Pattern Analysis and Machine Intelligence **25** (2003) 110-115
4. Kittler, J., Hatef, M., Duin, R.P.W., Matas, J.: On combining classifiers. IEEE Trans. on Pattern Analysis and Machine Intelligence **20** (1998) 226-239
5. Kuncheva, L. I.: A theoretical study on six classifier fusion strategies. IEEE Trans. on Pattern Analysis and Machine Intelligence **24** (2002) 281-286
6. Lam, L., Suen, C.Y.: Application of majority voting to pattern recognition: an analysis of its behavior and performance. IEEE Trans. on Systems, Man and Cybernetics - Part A **27** (1997) 553-568
7. Perrone, M.P., Cooper, L.N.: When Networks Disagree: Ensemble Methods for Hybrid Neural Networks. In: Mammone, R.J. (ed.): Neural Networks for Speech and Image Processing. Chapman-Hall, New York (1993)
8. Roli, F.: Multisensor image recognition by neural networks with understandable behaviour. Int. Journal of Pattern Recognition and Artificial Intelligence **10** (1996) 887-917
9. Roli, F., Fumera, G.: Analysis of Linear and Order Statistics Combiners for Fusion of Imbalanced Classifiers. In: Kittler, J., Roli, F. (eds.): Proc. of the 3rd Int. Workshop on Multiple Classifier Systems. LNCS, Vol. 2364. Springer-Verlag (2002) 252-261
10. Tumer, K., Ghosh, J.: Analysis of decision boundaries in linearly combined neural classifiers. Pattern Recognition **29** (1996) 341-348
11. Tumer, K., Ghosh, J.: Linear and order statistics combiners for pattern classification. In: Sharkey, A.J.C. (ed.): Combining Artificial Neural Nets. Springer, London (1999) 127-155

Comparison of Classifier Selection Methods for Improving Committee Performance

Matti Aksela

Helsinki University of Technology, Neural Networks Research Centre
P.O.Box 5400, Fin-02015 HUT, Finland
matti.aksela@hut.fi

Abstract. Combining classifiers is an effective way of improving classification performance. In many situations it is possible to construct several classifiers with different characteristics. Selecting the member classifiers with the best individual performance can be shown to be suboptimal in several cases, and hence there exists a need to attempt to find effective member classifier selection methods. In this paper six selection criteria are discussed and evaluated in the setting of combining classifiers for isolated handwritten character recognition. A criterion focused on penalizing many classifiers making the same error, the exponential error count, is found to be able to produce the best selections.

1 Introduction

In an attempt to improve recognition performance it is a common approach to combine multiple classifiers in a committee formation. This is feasible if the outputs of several classifiers contain exclusive information. Often the focus of the research is on methods for combining the classifiers in the most effective manner, but it should not be forgotten that the committee's performance is highly dependent on the member classifiers used. In fact these two fundamental aspects in committee performance enhancement are often referred to as decision optimization and coverage optimization [1].

Instead of selecting member classifiers based solely on their accuracy, it may often be more effective to attempt to select the members based on their diversity, for which several measures have been presented [2,3,4]. Measuring the diversity of the member classifiers is by no means trivial, and there is a trade-off between diversity and member accuracy. Standard statistics do not take into account that for classification purposes a situation where identical correct answers are given differs greatly from the situation where identical erroneous answers are suggested, with the former being generally the best case and the latter the worst. For classification purposes it may be useful to examine especially the errors made.

Here six approaches to deciding on what subset of a larger set of member classifiers to use are examined. Three very different committee structures are briefly explained and used for evaluation with application to handwritten character recognition. Due to space constraints, readers are directed to the references for more thorough discussion on each member classifier and committee method.

T. Windeatt and F. Roli (Eds.): MCS 2003, LNCS 2709, pp. 84–93, 2003.

2   Member Classifier Selection Criteria

Six different criteria for member classifier selection are presented here. The first three criteria are more traditional and have been gathered from literature. The latter three are novel and they have been designed based on the assumption of the significance of the classification errors being made. All except one of the presented approaches work in a pairwise fashion, where the result for a larger set is the mean of the pairwise measures for that set. The exception is the exponential error count in section 2.6, which compares all classifiers in the set simultaneously. As the minimum of the pairwise measures is always smaller or equal to the mean, the pairwise criteria are not suitable for selecting the size k of the classifier subset $C_1, \ldots, C_k$ from all of the K available classifiers. Hence it is assumed in all cases that the number of classifiers to be used is fixed in advance.

2.1   Correlation between Errors

As it is reasonable to expect that the independence of occurring errors should be beneficial for classifier combining, the correlation of the errors for the member classifiers is a natural choice for comparing the subsets of classifiers. Here the correlation $\rho_{a,b}$ for the binary vectors v_e^a and v_e^b of error occurrence in classifiers a and b respectively is calculated as

$$\rho_{a,b} = \frac{\text{Cov}[v_e^a, v_e^b]}{\sqrt{\text{Var}[v_e^a]\text{Var}[v_e^b]}}, \tag{1}$$

where Cov refers to covariance and Var variance. The best set is selected by choosing that with the minimal mean pairwise correlation.

2.2 Q Statistic

One statistic to assess the similarity of two classifiers is the Q statistic [2]. It is defined for two classifiers a, b as

$$Q_{a,b} = \frac{N^{11}N^{00} - N^{01}N^{10}}{N^{11}N^{00} + N^{01}N^{10}}, \tag{2}$$

where N^{11} is the number of times both classifiers are correct, N^{00} the number of times both classifiers are incorrect, and N^{10} and N^{01} the number of times when just the first or second classifier is correct, respectively. When the classifiers make just the same correct and incorrect decisions, it can be seen that the value of the Q statistic becomes one. Negative values indicate classifiers that make errors on different inputs. For sets of more than two classifiers the mean value of the pairwise Q statistics is considered to be the Q value for that set. The best subset of member classifiers is thus selected by minimizing the value of the Q statistic.

2.3   Mutual Information

As was suggested in [3], also a diversity measure based on calculating the mutual information of the classifiers results can establish a good set of member classifiers, as it by definition measures the amount of information shared between the classifiers. Hence minimizing the mutual information should produce a maximally diverse set of classifiers. The mutual information can be used for a measure of closeness and the pairwise mutual information between two classifiers a and b can be calculated as

$$I_{a,b} = \sum_{i=1}^{n} \sum_{j=1}^{n} p(c_i, c_j) \log \frac{p(c_i, c_j)}{p_a(c_i) p_b(c_j)} \ , \tag{3}$$

where n is the total number of classes and $c_i, i = 1, \ldots, n$ are the class labels.

In the experiments also the mutual information of the error occurrences has been calculated. There only two classes, correct or incorrect, are considered for each classifier. Both mutual information measures should be minimized to select the optimal subset of classifiers, again using the mean of the pairwise values for a larger set of classifiers.

2.4   Ratio between Different and Same Errors

The worst possible setting for classifier combination is the situation where several classifiers agree on an incorrect result, and it is not nearly as fatal if they make errors to different labels. To explore this let us denote the count of how many times two classifiers made different errors at the same sample with $N_{\text{different}}^{00}$ and the count of how many times both classifiers made the same error with N_{same}^{00}. Now we can examine the ratio

$$r_{a,b}^{DSE} = \frac{N_{\text{different}}^{00}}{N_{\text{same}}^{00}} \ . \tag{4}$$

Again for more than two members the mean of the pairwise ratios is used. The best subset of classifiers can be selected through maximizing this ratio.

2.5   Weighted Count of Errors and Correct Results

One should consider taking into account information on also correct decisions in addition to the incorrect results, with more emphasis placed on the situation where classifiers agree on either the correct or incorrect result. One may simply count the occurrences of the situations and place suitable emphasis on the "both correct", a positive situation, and "both same incorrect", a negative situation:

$$r_{a,b}^{WCEC} = N^{11} + \frac{1}{2}(N^{01} + N^{10}) - N_{\text{different}}^{00} - 5N_{\text{same}}^{00} \ . \tag{5}$$

The weighting is arbitrary, and the presented values have been chosen as they are deemed suitable based on the reasoning to penalize errors, and especially same errors. For multiple classifiers, the mean of the pairwise counts is used. The optimal subset can be selected by maximizing the measure.

2.6   Exponential Error Count

As it is assumed that the member classifiers will hinder the classification the most when they agree on the same incorrect result, that situation can be given even more emphasis in the selection criterion. The errors can be counted and weighted by the number of classifiers making the error in an exponential fashion. The count of errors made by a total of i classifiers is denoted $N^0_{i\text{ same}}$ and added to the sum after rising to the ith power, or

$$r^{EXP}_{C_1,\ldots,C_k} = \frac{\sum_{i=1}^{k}(N^0_{i\text{ same}})^i}{N^1_{\text{all}}} \ .$$ (6)

This measure considers all member classifiers of the set at the same time, and the best combination is selected by minimizing the measure. Here also the correct classifications are taken into account by scaling the result with N^1_{all}, the number of samples for which every member classifier was correct.

It should be noted that more than one $N^0_{i\text{ same}}$ can be increased while processing one sample – if m classifiers agree on one erroneous result and n classifiers on another, both $N^0_{m\text{ same}}$ and $N^0_{n\text{ same}}$ are increased.

3   Committee Methods

Three quite different combination methods are used to evaluate the member classifier selection criteria. The plurality voting committee is a very simple method, while the Behavior-Knowledge Space (BKS) method [5] uses a separate training phase. As our experiments have focused on adaptive committee classifiers, also the run-time adaptive Dynamically Expanding Context (DEC) committee [6] is used for evaluation. For default decisions in the BKS and DEC methods, ie. for the situations where no rules yet exist, all member classifiers had been run on an evaluation set and ranked in the order of decreasing performance.

3.1   Plurality Voting Committee

The committee classifier simply uses the plurality voting rule to decide the output of the committee. This basic committee structure has been included because of its widespread use and familiar behavior.

3.2   BKS Committee

The Behavior-Knowledge Space (BKS) method [5] is based on a K-dimensional discrete space that is used to determine the class labels, with each dimension corresponding to the decision of one classifier. The result is obtained by first finding the focal unit in the K-dimensional space, the unit which is the intersection of the classifiers' decisions of the current input. Then if the unit has gathered samples and for some class c the ratio between the number of samples for class c and all gathered samples is above a threshold, class c is selected.

In the training phase the focal unit had collected the count of recognitions and counts for each true class. The output of the committee was the class with the highest probability in the focal unit, the one that had received most samples, as suggested in [5]. If the focal unit had not received any samples, the default rule of using the highest-ranking single classifier's result was used.

3.3   DEC Committee

The adaptive committee used is based on the Dynamically Expanding Context (DEC) algorithm [7]. The DEC principle had to be slightly modified to suit the setting of combining classifiers [6]. For this setting, a list of member classifiers' results is taken as a one-sided context for the first member classifier's result. The classifiers are used in the order of decreasing performance. To correct errors transformation rules consisting of a list of member classifier results as the inputs and the desired recognition result as the output are generated. Only rules whose output is included in the inputs may be produced.

Each time a character is input to the system, the existing rules are first searched through and the most specific applicable rule is used. If no applicable rule is found, the default decision is applied. For these experiments the default decision was taken to be a plurality voting decision among all member classifiers.

The classification result is compared to the correct class. If the recognition was incorrect, a new rule is created. The created rule always employs the minimal amount of context, ie. member classifier results, sufficient to distinguish it from existing rules. To make the rules distinguishable every new rule employs more contextual knowledge, if possible, than the rule causing its creation. Eventually the entire context available will be used and more precise rules can no longer be written. In such situations selection among multiple rules is performed via tracking correctness of the rules' usage.

4   Data and Member Classifiers

The data used in the experiments were isolated on-line characters in three separate databases. The preprocessing is covered in detail in [8]. Database 1 consists of 10403 characters written by 22 writers without any visual feedback. Databases 2 and 3 were collected with the pen trace shown on-screen and characters recognized on-line, with also the recognition results being shown. They contain 8046 and 8077 character samples, respectively, both written by eight different writers. All databases featured 68 character classes.

Database 1 was used solely for member classifier construction and training. Database 2 was used for training the BKS, the only committee method used requiring a separate training phase, and database 3 was used as a test set. The adaptive DEC committee performs run-time adaptation and creates writer-dependent rules during classification. The DEC committee was not trained beforehand in any way. For all member classifiers the sizes of the characters were scaled so that the the longer side of their bounding box was constant and the

Table 1. Member classifier performance

Classifier index	Member classifier	Error rate	Classifier rank
1	DTW PL Bounding box	23.06	4
2	DTW PL Mass center	20.02	2
3	DTW PP Bounding box	21.16	3
4	DTW PP Mass center	19.30	1
5	Point-sequence SVM	23.93	5
6	Grid SVM	26.49	6
7	Point-sequence NN	50.22	8
8	Grid NN	35.74	7

aspect ratio was kept unchanged. The accuracies of the individual member classifiers to be described below have been gathered into table 1.

4.1 DTW Member Classifiers

Four individual classifiers were based on stroke-by-stroke distances between the given character and the prototypes. Dynamic Time Warping (DTW) [9] was used to compute one of two distances, point-to-line (PL) or point-to-point (PP) [8]. In the PL distance the points of a stroke are matched to lines interpolated between the successive points of the opposite stroke. The PP distance uses the squared Euclidean distance between two data points as the cost function. The second variation was the use of either the 'Mass center' as the input sample's mass center or by 'Bounding box' as the center of the sample's bounding box, for defining the characters centers, thus creating four combinations. Database 1 was used for constructing the initial user-independent prototype set which consisted of 7 prototypes for each class.

4.2 SVM Member Classifiers

Two member classifiers based on Support Vector Machines (SVMs) were also included. The support vector machine classifiers were implemented using the libsvm version 2.36 SVM package [10]. The routines were slightly modified to accommodate the data used and to return a more information, but the classification and training routines were directly from the toolbox. Database 1 was used for training the SVM models.

The first of the SVM member classifiers takes its data as a list of points from the character. For this classifier, first the strokes of the characters are joined by appending all strokes to the first one. Then the one-stroked characters are transformed via interpolation or decimation to have a fixed number of points, for these experiments the point number was set to 30. Then the x and y coordinates of each point were concatenated to form a 60 dimensional vector of point coordinates, which were then used as data for the SVM classifier.

The second SVM member classifier takes a feature vector of values calculated from a grid representation of the character. For this classifier, a grid was formed and 17 values were calculated for each grid cell. These values include the sums of both negative and positive sin and cos of the slope of the line between the current and next point, the neighboring 8-neighborhood grid location the stroke moves from this location, the count of points in the cell and the count of pen-ups in the cell and character-wise means of these. A 3×3 grid was found to be the most promising of those tested (3×3, 5×5, 7×7, 10×10), and resulted in 153 dimensional data vectors.

4.3   NN Member Classifiers

Two member classifiers based on neural networks (NNs) were used. A fully connected feed-forward network structure was created using the Stuttgart Neural Network Simulator (SNNS) version 4.2 [11]. Database 1 was used for training.

The first NN classifier used the same preprocessing and feature vector type as the first SVM classifier, the coordinates of the one-stroke fixed-length characters were concatenated to form a 60 dimensional input vector. The number of output neurons was determined by the number of classes in the data, 68. A network using one hidden layer consisting of 100 neurons was used with 5000 epochs of training with the BackpropMomentum [11] learning algorithm.

The second NN used the grid-based approach with the same features as the second SVM classifier. Here a 5×5 grid was used resulting in 425 dimensional data. A network with two hidden layers of 100 neurons each and 68 output neurons was trained with the BackpropMomentum method for 1000 epochs.

5   Results

It can be seen in table 1 that the DTW-based classifiers are all better in individual performance than the other methods here. This stems from the fact that our own custom DTW classifier has been tuned for a prolonged period of time, while the other member classifiers were created from existing toolkits without nearly as much effort. Especially the performance of the point-sequence NN classifier is in itself unacceptable, but was included to examine the effect of a significantly worse but different member classifier.

The experiments were run using a fixed member classifiers set size of $k = 4$ member classifiers. The best combinations from all eight possible member classifiers produced by the selection criteria and the resulting accuracies from the three committee structures used for evaluation have been gathered into table 2. Also results using the four individually best member classifiers have been included as 'Best individual rates'. The three best results for each combination method using the brute force approach of going through all 70 possible combinations with each decision method have been collected into table 3.

In this case the correlation, Q statistic, and mutual information or errors measure selected exactly the same set of member classifiers, which is not surprising considering their similar nature. The mutual information measure selected the worst performing classifiers. These criteria do not take into account the difference between errors and correct results – it is beneficial when members agree

Table 2. Comparison of selection criteria

Criterion	Members	Vote	BKS	DEC
Correlation	4,6,7,8	18.64	18.23	14.80
Q statistic	4,6,7,8	18.64	18.23	14.80
Mutual information	5,6,7,8	20.70	21.50	18.11
Mutual information of errors	4,6,7,8	18.64	18.23	14.80
Ratio between diff. and same errors	1,6,7,8	20.39	20.68	16.55
Weighted count of correct and err.	1,4,5,6	18.34	20.32	14.53
Exponential error count	4,5,6,8	16.45	18.13	14.12
Best individual rates	1,2,3,4	19.34	20.07	18.17

Table 3. Best brute force results

Method	Best		Second best		Third best	
	Members	Errors	Members	Errors	Members	Errors
Vote	4,5,6,8	16.45	2,5,6,8	16.66	3,5,6,8	17.14
BKS	2,3,4,7	17.46	2,3,6,8	17.83	3,4,6,8	17.85
DEC	4,5,6,8	14.12	2,5,6,8	14.44	4,5,6,7	14.49

on correct results, but not when they agree on errors. All these criteria selected also the worst-performing point-sequence NN member classifier, which is not surprising considering its less similar, albeit due to numerous errors, results.

The approach of comparing the ratios between different and same errors does not perform well, providing the second-worst results. Also this criterion uses the clearly worst point-sequence NN classifier. The weighted count of errors and correct results criterion provides a combination that is second best for both the voting and DEC committees but notably poor for the BKS committee.

The exponential error count approach finds the best selection of all criteria in table 2. As can be seen in table 3, this criterion found the best combination of classifiers for this given task with respect to both the voting and DEC committees. This is in accordance with the initial assumption of the importance of the classifiers not making exactly the same mistakes too often.

An interesting difference of behavior can be noted with the BKS in comparison to the two other combination methods. The best member classifier set from table 3 for BKS is $\{2, 3, 4, 7\}$, the three members with the best individual accuracies and one with the worst. Presumably the different behavior is at least partly due to the fact that the separate training phase teaches the committee the types of errors that commonly occur. Hence the overall diversity of the set becomes a less important factor and the effects of the training weigh more on the final result when using a separate training phase. Also with the voting and DEC approaches, the third-best combination was different, so clearly the optimal selection of member classifiers is also dependent on the combination method.

To evaluate the effect of just the one poorly performing, albeit diverse, classifier an additional experiment was run without using the point-sequence NN. The results are presented in table 4. It can be seen that the performance of the first five member selection criteria is greatly improved. Still the very simple ratio

Table 4. Comparison of selection criteria without member classifier 7

Criterion	Members	Vote	BKS	DEC
Correlation	4,5,6,8	16.45	18.13	14.12
Q statistic	4,5,6,8	16.45	18.13	14.12
Mutual information	1,5,6,8	17.75	19.82	15.04
Mutual information of errors	4,5,6,8	16.45	18.13	14.12
Ratio between diff. and same errors	2,4,6,8	18.57	18.11	14.53
Weighted count of correct and err.	1,4,5,6	18.34	20.32	14.53
Exponential error count	4,5,6,8	16.45	18.13	14.12
Best individual rates	1,2,3,4	19.34	20.07	18.17

between different and same errors is clearly not sufficient for selecting a member classifier set here, when the results of all methods but the BKS are compared. But the correlation, Q statistic, and mutual information of errors criteria, who are still in agreement on the best selection of members, are now able to find the combination that produces the best results with the voting and DEC committees. Hence it may be a logical conclusion that these criteria are less robust with regard to member classifiers making a large number of errors.

6   Conclusions

Several member classifier selection criteria were examined, including statistical, information-theoretic and error counting measures. It appears that the more general criteria may be suboptimal for the specific case of classifier combining, especially when also poorly performing classifiers are included. When combining classifiers it would seem that the most important factor is that the classifiers as rarely as possible make exactly same mistakes, as these situations are the most difficult for the combining methods to anticipate. But it is also important that the member classifiers perform well. The best trade-off between accuracy and diversity was obtained with the suggested exponential error count criterion, which weighs identical errors made by the classifiers in an exponential fashion and normalizes the count with the number of cases where all members were correct. This method also showed robustness with respect to a very poorly performing member classifier.

One may ask what benefit there is in using a diversity measure instead of the decision mechanism directly when examining all subsets of classifiers. If it is possible to form a diversity measure for any subset from the pairwise diversity measures of its members, noticeable computational benefits can be obtained. This is because going through all combinations of two classifiers results in significantly fewer possibilities than all combinations of a larger number of classifiers. For example in the presented experiments, with the subset size of 4 member classifiers from a total of 8 classifiers, the advantage is 28 vs. 70 combinations. The cost of forming the diversity measure of a subset from that of the pairs by averaging is insignificant. Naturally with very large numbers of member classifiers, a more evolved search scheme is necessary [4].

Still, if the objective is to optimize both the member classifier set and the decision method, the possibility of using a more general measure for the member classifier set selection should be considered. This may help refrain from excessive iteration of the two phases of optimization. But it must not be forgotten that the selection of member classifiers is dependent on the combination methods characteristics, a fact also concluded in [12] among others. A particular combination of classifiers, while optimal in some sense, does not guarantee the best results for all combination methods. However, a suitable measure may still provide some generalizational ability. Here the exponential error count has been shown to find a selection that consistently provides good results in the presented experiments.

References

1. Ho, T.K.: Multiple Classifier Combiation: Lessons and Next Steps. In: Hybrid Methods in Pattern Recognition. World Scientific Press (2002)
2. Kuncheva, L., Whittaker, C., Shipp, C., Duin, R.: Is independence good for combining classifiers. In: Proceedings of the 15th ICPR. Volume 2. (2000) 168–171
3. Kang, H., Lee, S.: An information-theoretic strategy for constructing multiple classifier systems. In: Proceedings of the 15th ICPR. Volume 2. (2000) 483–486
4. Roli, F., Giacinto, G.: Design of Multiple Classifier Systems. In: Hybrid Methods in Pattern Recognition. World Scientific Press (2002)
5. Huang, Y., Suen, C.: A method of combining multiple experts for the recognition of unconstrained handwritten numerals. IEEE Transactions on Pattern Analysis and Machine Intelligence **17** (1995) 90–94
6. Laaksonen, J., Aksela, M., Oja, E., Kangas, J.: Dynamically Expanding Context as committee adaptation method in on-line recognition of handwritten latin characters. In: Proceedings of ICDAR99. (1999) 796–799
7. Kohonen, T.: Dynamically expanding context. Journal of Intelligent Systems **1** (1987) 79–95
8. Vuori, V., Laaksonen, J., Oja, E., Kangas, J.: Experiments with adaptation strategies for a prototype-based recognition system of isolated handwritten characters. International Journal of Document Analysis and Recognition **3** (2001) 150–159
9. Sankoff, D., Kruskal, J.B.: Time warps, string edits, and macromolecules: the theory and practice of sequence comparison. Addison-Wesley (1983)
10. Chang, C.C., Lin, C.J.: Libsvm : a library for support vector machines version 2.36. http://www.csie.ntu.edu.tw/ cjlin/libsvm/ (2002)
11. Zell, A., Mache, N., et al, G.M.: Snns : Stuttgart neural network simulator. http://www-ra.informatik.uni-tuebingen.de/SNNS/ (2002)
12. Fumera, G., Roli, F.: Performance analysis and comparison of linear combiners for classifier fusion. In: Proceeding of S+SSPR2002. (2002) 424–432

Towards Automated Classifier Combination
for Pattern Recognition

Alper Baykut[1] and Aytül Erçil[2]

[1] Arçelik A.Ş. R & TD Department, Turkey
{alper.baykut@arcelik.com}
[2] Sabancı University, Turkey
{aytulercil@sabanciuniv.edu}

Abstract. This study covers weighted combination methodologies for multiple classifiers to improve classification accuracy. The classifiers are extended to produce class probability estimates besides their class label assignments to be able to combine them more efficiently. The leave-one-out training method is used and the results are combined using proposed weighted combination algorithms. The weights of the classifiers for the weighted classifier combination are determined based on the performance of the classifiers on the training phase. The classifiers and combination algorithms are evaluated using classical and proposed performance measures. It is found that the integration of the proposed reliability measure, improves the performance of classification. A sensitivity analysis shows that the proposed polynomial weight assignment applied with probability based combination is robust to choose classifiers for the classifier set and indicates a typical one to three percent consistent improvement compared to a single best classifier of the same set.

1   Introduction

The ultimate goal of designing pattern recognition systems is to achieve the best possible classification performance for the task at hand. It has been observed that different classifier designs potentially offer complementary information about the patterns to be classified, which could be harnessed to improve the performance of the selected classifier. A large number of combination methods have been proposed in the literature [1][3][7][8]. A typical combination method consists of a set of individual classifiers and a combiner, which combines the results of the individual classifiers to make the final classification. In this paper, we aim to build a robust classifier combination system given a classifier set. For this purpose, current trends in classifier combination are studied and various classifier combination schemes have been devised. To study classifier combination techniques, 10 classical classifiers are gathered to form a classifier set [2].

It is very difficult to make sense of the multitude of empirical comparisons for classifier performances that have been made. There are no agreed objective criteria by which to judge algorithms. The situation is made more difficult because rapid advances are being made in all fields of pattern recognition. Any comparative study that does not include the majority of the algorithms is clearly not aiming to be complete. Also, any comparative study that looks at limited number of data sets cannot

T. Windeatt and F. Roli (Eds.): MCS 2003, LNCS 2709, pp. 94–105, 2003.
© Springer-Verlag Berlin Heidelberg 2003

give reliable indicators of performance. In this study, an extensive comparative study is realized among a wealth of classifiers applied on different data sets. Their performances are evaluated using a variety of performance measures. This comparative study builds the base of the study on combining classifiers to improve the classification performance.

The set of classifiers that are used in this study are fixed, i.e. they are not optimized especially for the application at hand. Different combination schemes are developed hoping to reach reasonable classification accuracy, which is independent of the characteristic of the application. Section 2 summarizes the different classifiers used in the study, section 3 reviews the performance measures that are proposed and used throughout the study, section 4 outlines the different weighted combination algorithms that are proposed, section 5 summarizes the data sets used and section 6 gives the experimental results.

2   Classifier Set Used in the Study

This study focuses on the weighted combination of classification algorithms, in which the weights are optimized based on the performance in the training data set. To have a classifier combination, following classifiers with the given parameters are designed.

KMClus: K-means clustering (max iteration=10; max error=0.5).
SOM: Self organizing map clustering (max iteration=1000; learning rate=1).
FANN: Fuzzy neural network classifier (fuzzification level=3; fuzzification type=0; hidden layer units=25; learning rate=0.001; max iteration=1000; min error=0.02).
ANN: Artificial neural network classifier (hidden layer units=25; learning rate=0.001; max iteration=1000; min error=0.02).
KMClas: K-means classifier.
Parzen: Parzen classifier (alfa=1).
KNN: K-nearest neighbour classifier (k=3).
PQD: Piecewise quadratic distance classifier.
PLD: Piecewise linear distance classifier.
SVM: Support vector machine using radial basis kernel with (p=1).

The design parameters of classifiers are chosen as typical values used in the literature or by experience. The classifiers are not specifically tuned for the data set at hand even though they may reach a better performance with another parameter set, since the goal is to design an automated classifier combination based on any classifier in the classifier set. The aim of this study is to combine the classifiers' results in a robust way to achieve almost the performance of the best classifier in the classifier set or better.

In this study, the classifiers are modified to produce class probability estimates besides their class labels for all classes. For that purpose, their distance measures or belief values are normalized in the training set as probabilities and applied on the test set. For some classifiers such as fuzzy neural network classifier, artificial neural network classifier and support vector machine, their belief values are converted to posterior probabilities using a normalized mapping. For K-means classifier, Parzen, K-nearest neighbour, piecewise quadratic and piecewise linear distance classifiers their implicit distance measures are explicitly calculated and converted to posterior probabilities for each class. One of the main contributions of this study is that all the classifiers and clustering based classifier algorithms in the classifier set are modified to produce posterior probabilities for their class assignments for all classes.

For clustering, standard k-means clustering and self-organizing map algorithms are applied on the data in a usual way. After the final step of clustering a one-to-one assignment algorithm is applied on the final clusters of the leave-one-out technique to convert them into a classification problem by solving an optimization problem to assign clusters to class (1). The resulting mapping criteria of clusters to classes are then applied on the test sample.

$$\text{minimize} \quad \sum_{c=1}^{C}\sum_{n=1}^{N} z_{nc} x_{nc}$$

$$\text{subject to} \quad \sum_{n=1}^{N} x_{nc} = 1 \; c = 1...C \; (C \text{ is the number of classes})$$

$$\sum_{c=1}^{C} x_{nc} = 1 \; n = 1...N \; (N \text{ is the number of samples})$$

$$\text{where} \quad x_{nc} = \begin{cases} 1 \text{ if sample } n \text{ is assigned to class } c \\ 0 \text{ otherwise} \end{cases}$$

$$z_{nc} = \begin{cases} 1 \text{ if sample } n \text{ is wrongly assigned to class } c \\ 0 \text{ otherwise} \end{cases}$$

(1)

3   Performance Measures for Evaluating Classifier Combination Methods

To compare different classification algorithms and combination methods, performance measures should be defined. There are different performance measures which evaluate different performances of classifiers: generalization performance, learning performance, correct and wrong classification performance, real time performance, etc. Performance measures are given in equations (2). The proposed "reliability" is the probability of correct classification for that class. Classification accuracy based on classes (CAC) is the ratio of correct classifications to the sample size. Generally, this is the only performance measure used in the literature. Classification accuracy based on probabilities (CAP) is based on distances of the posterior probabilities p'_i of the classification result and the true classification probability p_i. The proposed overall classification performance (OP) is a measure, which combines the products of performance (P_i) and reliability (R_i) with the counts of samples (N_i) for corresponding class c as a weight. CR_i is the number of correct assignments for class i, WR_{ij} is the number of wrong assignments of class i to class j and UN_i is the number of unclassified samples of class i.

$$P_i = \frac{CR_i}{N_i}, \; R_i = \frac{CR_i}{CR_i + \sum_{\substack{j=1 \\ j \neq i}}^{C} WR_{ji}}, \; CAC = \frac{\sum_{i=1}^{C} CR_i}{\sum_{i=1}^{C} N_i}, \; CAP = 1 - \frac{\sum_{i=1}^{N} |p'_i - p_i|}{\sum_{i=1}^{C} N_i}, \; OP = \frac{\sum_{i=1}^{C} P_i \times R_i \times N_i}{\sum_{i=1}^{C} N_i}$$

(2)

4   Weighted Combination Algorithms

This study focuses on combining the results of several different classifiers in a way that provides a coherent inference, which performs a reasonable classification performance for the data set at hand. Therefore four different weighted combination algorithms with three different weight assignment are applied on the data sets. Combination algorithm based on class labels uses the classifiers' class label assignments to combine [1]. For each class, the weights of the classifier is added to the decision value of the classifier combination, if the classifier has decided on that class. The classifier combination decides the assigned class based on the maximum of these decision values.

$$\text{Assign } x_n \to w_c \text{ if } \sum_{k=1}^{K} W_k \Delta_{cnk} = \max_{i=1..C} \sum_{k=1}^{K} W_k \Delta_{ink} \tag{3}$$

If the weights are equal, this combination algorithm is the classical majority vote. The classifiers are forced to produce binary valued function Δ_{cnk} using the posterior probabilities as: $\Delta_{cnk}=1$ if $P(w_c \mid x_{nk}) = \max_{i=1..C} P(w_i \mid x_{nk})$ and 0 otherwise.

The reliability of the classifier for the assigned class, as proposed in (2), is also integrated to the combination by multiplying the reliability value with the weighted class label. This idea is intuitive, if we handle the classifiers as experts in the decision theory. That is, each classifier has different reliabilities on deciding on different classes. This reliability value increases the influence on the final decision, if the classifier reliability is high for deciding this class, and decreases the influence, if it is unreliable.

$$\text{Assign } x_n \to w_c \text{ if } \sum_{k=1}^{K} W_k R_{kc} \Delta_{cnk} = \max_{i=1..C} \sum_{k=1}^{K} W_k R_{ki} \Delta_{ink} \tag{4}$$

Combination algorithm based probabilities uses the posterior probabilities of classifiers to carry out the combination. As in the case of combination based class labels on they are weighted with the classifier's weights.

$$\text{Assign } x_n \to w_c \text{ if } \sum_{k=1}^{K} W_k P(w_c \mid x_{nk}) = \max_{i=1..C} \sum_{k=1}^{K} W_k P(w_i \mid x_{nk}) \tag{5}$$

The reliability of the classifier for the assigned class is also integrated to the combination by multiplying the reliability value with the assignment probability.

$$\text{Assign } x_n \to w_c \text{ if } \sum_{k=1}^{K} W_k R_{kc} P(w_c \mid x_{nk}) = \max_{i=1..C} \sum_{k=1}^{K} W_k R_{ki} P(w_i \mid x_{nk}) \tag{6}$$

Different algorithms are used to calculate the weights of the classifiers for weighted combination. The easiest way is to combine the classifiers using equal weights, well known as simple majority. This performs a good result if the classifiers in the set are independent and unbiased [1]. The weight of classifier m_k is: $W_k=1/K$.

A better way for assigning weights to classifiers is, to assign their performance values in the training phase. In this study, it is proposed that the defined overall performance values, "OP"s, found in the leave-one-out training phase are assigned as weights. These results are also integrated with the reliability of the classifiers. The weight of a classifier m_k is its weighted OP value.

Another proposal is to assign weights using a linear fit on the posterior probabilities of leave-one-out results. Better and reliable performance is reached with the weight assignment where the true class probabilities of the training data set and the posterior probabilities found by the classifiers are used to find a linear regression parameters for them. Least square fit parameters for the training data set is used as weights of the classifiers in the combination. The constant term which may be in the equation is not used since shifting will not affect the relative values for classification. The weights are the solution of the following equation (7).

$$
\begin{bmatrix} P(w_1|x_1) \\ \vdots \\ P(w_1|x_N) \\ P(w_2|x_1) \\ \vdots \\ P(w_C|x_N) \end{bmatrix} = \begin{bmatrix} W_1 \\ \vdots \\ W_k \\ \vdots \\ W_K \end{bmatrix} \begin{bmatrix} P(w_1|x_1,m_1) & .. & P(w_1|x_1,m_2) & .. & P(w_1|x_1,m_K) \\ \vdots & & \vdots & & \vdots \\ P(w_1|x_N,m_1) & .. & P(w_1|x_N,m_2) & .. & P(w_1|x_N,m_K) \\ P(w_2|x_1,m_1) & .. & P(w_2|x_1,m_2) & ... & P(w_2|x_1,m_K) \\ \vdots & & \vdots & & \vdots \\ P(w_C|x_N,m_1) & .. & P(w_C|x_N,m_2) & .. & P(w_C|x_N,m_K) \end{bmatrix} \quad (7)
$$

The extension of this polynomial weight assignment proposal is to integrate the reliability of the classifier for the assigned class (8).

$$
\begin{bmatrix} P(w_1|x_1) \\ \vdots \\ P(w_1|x_N) \\ P(w_2|x_1) \\ \vdots \\ P(w_C|x_N) \end{bmatrix} = \begin{bmatrix} W_1 \\ \vdots \\ W_k \\ \vdots \\ W_K \end{bmatrix} \begin{bmatrix} R(w_1|m_1)P(w_1|x_1,m_1) & .. & R(w_1|m_K)P(w_1|x_1,m_K) \\ \vdots & & \vdots \\ R(w_1|m_1)P(w_1|x_N,m_1) & .. & R(w_1|m_K)P(w_1|x_N,m_K) \\ R(w_2|m_1)P(w_2|x_1,m_1) & .. & R(w_2|m_K)P(w_2|x_1,m_K) \\ \vdots & & \vdots \\ R(w_C|m_1)P(w_C|x_N,m_1) & .. & R(w_C|m_K)P(w_C|x_N,m_K) \end{bmatrix} \quad (8)
$$

5   Data Sets Used in the Study

Popular data sets from the literature are used for evaluating the different combination schemes proposed and comparing them with existing techniques. The data sets used are summarized below:

BIO: Data from cariers and non cariers of a rare genetic disorder. 5 inputs, 2 outputs (127+67) 194 case.

DIB: Pigma Indians Diabetes Database. 8 inputs, 2 outputs (500+268) 768 case.

D10:   Two class data set, with Duin 10 dimensional distribution. 10 inputs, 2 outputs (100+100) 200 case.

GID: Glass Identification Databas. 9 inputs, 6 outputs (70+76+17+13+9+29) 214 case.

IMX: IEEE data file of letters I, M, O, X. 8 inputs, 4 outputs (48+48+48+48) 192 case.

SMR: Sonar data set. 60 inputs, 2 outputs (97+111) 208 case.

2SD: Two spirals two dimensional data set. 2 inputs, 2 outputs (97+97) 194 case.

WQD: Wine data set. 13 inputs, 3 outputs (59+71+48) 178 case.

80X: IEEE 80X data set. 8 inputs, 3 outputs (15+15+15) 45 case.

ZMM: Data set of 6 Zernike moments of 8 characters. 6 inputs, 8 outputs (12+12+12+12+12+12+12+12) 96 case.

BEM: Two class data set, with equal mean but different variance(20 percent Bayes error). 2 inputs, 2 outputs (100+100) 200 case.

BEV: Two class data set, with different mean but equal variance (20 percent Bayes error). 2 inputs, 2 outputs (100+100) 200 case.
HRD: Highleyman distributed random patterns. 2 inputs, 2 outputs (100+100) 200 case.
IFD: Classical data set of Fisher with 150 iris flowers. 4 inputs, 3 outputs (50+50+50) 150 case.

6   Experimental Results

6.1   Classifier Results

Classifiers' individual performances are given in Tables 1 and 2. In these tables the best performances for the data sets are marked as bold face. The number of the marked items in the last column, titled "Best" indicates the number of times the classifier has outperformed the others for 14 data sets. The standart deviations are given in last rows.

Table 1. Classification accuracy of classifiers based on class labels

CAC	BIO	DIB	D10	GID	IMX	SMR	2SD	WQD	80X	ZMM	BEM	BEV	HRD	IFD	Best
KMClus	71.1	65.9	69.0	50.5	81.8	48.1	42.3	51.7	28.9	34.4	59.0	48.5	73.0	90.0	0
SOM	84.0	64.8	75.5	45.3	72.4	54.3	37.1	84.3	71.1	52.1	45.5	87.0	**84.0**	89.3	1
FANN	70.6	74.7	70.0	36.0	68.8	74.5	36.6	93.3	28.9	8.3	34.0	86.0	81.5	71.3	0
ANN	**87.6**	**76.8**	**78.0**	50.5	86.5	77.9	45.9	96.6	82.2	66.7	53.0	85.5	81.5	82.7	3
KMClas	75.3	46.1	76.0	33.2	88.5	65.4	47.4	62.9	**93.3**	69.8	48.5	74.5	82.5	91.3	1
Parzen	58.8	62.2	21.0	28.5	15.6	24.5	57.7	32.6	35.6	63.5	47.5	82.0	59.5	76.0	0
kNN	84.5	67.6	69.0	**73.4**	**94.3**	**82.2**	**76.3**	76.4	**93.3**	**88.5**	70.0	**92.0**	74.5	95.3	7
PQD	13.9	72.8	72.5	1.9	**94.3**	75.0	43.3	**99.4**	88.9	26.0	**79.5**	65.0	82.0	92.0	3
PLD	84.5	75.7	77.0	57.5	90.6	72.6	47.4	98.3	88.9	85.4	56.5	84.0	81.5	**97.3**	1
SVM	6.2	7.6	70.5	37.4	**94.3**	71.2	26.8	25.8	91.1	36.5	73.5	86.0	80.5	94.7	1
STD	2.4	1.5	2.9	3.0	1.7	2.7	3.1	0.6	3.7	3.3	2.9	1.9	2.6	1.3	

Table 2. Classification accuracy of classifiers based on probabilities

CAP	BIO	DIB	D10	GID	IMX	SMR	2SD	WQD	80X	ZMM	BEM	BEV	HRD	IFD	Best
KMClus	52.9	50.6	53.1	72.6	64.7	49.2	50.9	57.1	50.6	78.3	49.2	49.3	54.5	60.9	0
SOM	84.0	64.8	**75.5**	81.8	86.2	54.3	37.1	**89.5**	80.7	88.0	45.5	87.0	**84.0**	92.9	3
FANN	69.2	64.3	60.3	77.0	68.4	63.1	44.7	72.5	54.1	77.7	45.6	60.8	66.8	70.0	0
ANN	63.9	58.3	59.3	75.6	69.0	60.6	50.6	70.9	64.8	79.5	50.2	58.6	63.0	65.4	0
KMClas	50.3	50.1	54.2	72.6	65.1	51.4	52.2	58.4	60.1	78.5	49.9	51.0	58.6	60.9	0
Parzen	71.9	66.2	52.7	76.6	65.5	58.2	71.4	60.6	63.0	84.8	55.8	81.6	65.7	74.5	0
kNN	**84.2**	**67.4**	67.0	**90.6**	**97.3**	**81.8**	**77.9**	82.6	**96.2**	**97.2**	69.0	**91.9**	75.8	**97.0**	10
PQD	50.5	50.9	53.7	73.1	64.7	51.9	51.2	57.9	58.9	78.2	53.3	52.0	57.8	58.7	0
PLD	52.0	50.9	56.2	72.2	64.4	52.7	51.7	59.2	60.8	79.4	49.3	53.1	64.0	64.8	0
SVC	53.1	52.8	71.3	82.4	97.3	76.0	29.9	66.8	95.6	86.1	**75.9**	87.2	82.5	96.9	1
STD	2.6	1.7	3.0	2.0	1.2	2.7	3.0	2.3	2.9	1.7	3.0	1.9	2.6	1.4	

In Table 1 the results show that k-nearest neighbour classifier has the best result seven times out of 14 different data sets. All classifiers show different performance on different data set, for example the k-nearest neighbour classifier, which is the best classifier based on Table 1, has at least 10 percent lower performance compared with other classifiers in some data sets like DIB, D10, WQD, BEM and HRD.

In Table 2 the results indicate that the k-nearest neighbour classifier is more successful than the case in Table 1; 10 times out of 14 different data sets, k-nearest neighbour classifier outperforms the others. This improvement can be explained by the fact that the artificial neural networks' CAP is lower compared to its CAC. For example for the DIB data set with 76.8 percent CAC, which is higher than the k-nearest neighbour classifier's 67.6 percent, drops to 58.3 percent CAP, which is lower than the k-nearest neighbour classifier's 67.4 percent CAP value.

The decrease of performance can be explained by the nature of the training data set, since the training data set for supervised learning only have the class values given. The probabilities are in fact a mapping of class information to probabilities as zero or one, so the artificial neural network does not have the real probability information to train.

For the sake of this study, all classifiers are like experts with different back-grounds, who try to conclude the class of the sample at hand via decision combination with an acceptable reliability. As stated before, the classifiers are not especially tuned for the training set. The results show that k-nearest neighbour classifier outperforms the others for this classifier set with the current setting of parameters for individual classifiers. Another point is that the k-means clustering and Parzen classifiers are the worst ones. The results also validate that the data sets have different characteristics, since their performance are different for different classifiers. Based on the classifier set with current parameter settings, the data sets DIB, D10, GID, SMR and 2SD are relatively hard to classify.

6.2   Classifier Combination Results

As the first combination algorithm, defined weight assignment algorithms are used on class label based classifier combination, where the classifiers have produced only the class assignment results. The results for this combination can be summarized as in Table 3. The performance of the combination is marked as bold face, if it is better than the average of the top three best performance of the classifier set. Results are grouped for three different performance measures (OP, CAC, CAP). Results of different weight assignments are given in rows. Simple majority voting results are given in rows with "MV" title and the results next to "MV" rows, titled "xR", tabulate the integration of reliability for combination. For the weight assignment titled "OP", overall performance values are assigned as weights. The results integrated with the reliability of the classifiers are given in the rows next to it. The last rows are for weight assignment titled "Poly", where linear regression values are assigned as weights and reliabilities are integrated in the last row.

The results in Table 3 of the majority voting are not so promising as expected, since the classifiers in the set are not specifically chosen to be independent and unbi-ased. The "Best" column indicates the number of times the combination algorithm performs better than the average of the top three classifiers. The results show that even this performance can be improved using the classifier reliability for the class label assignments. For the class label based combination algorithm, the integration of the reliability of the classifiers improves the performance of the combination. The results show that the performance assignment as weights is better than the other methods of combination weight assignments. If we consider the standart deviations of the results, we can say that BIO, DIB and WQD datasets can be better classified using class label based combination method.

Table 3. Class label based classifier combination

OP Class	BIO	DIB	D10	GID	IMX	SMR	2SD	WQD	80X	ZMM	BEM	BEV	HRD	IFD	Best
MV	77.0	52.7	54.3	33.2	85.1	61.6	21.0	93.3	87.0	60.8	39.0	77.9	69.0	91.5	1
xR	77.4	54.9	58.1	41.1	86.7	66.3	24.6	96.1	93.5	69.2	48.7	80.3	68.4	91.5	5
OP	78.9	56.7	58.8	47.1	86.7	66.6	39.3	96.7	93.5	75.5	54.6	78.7	68.8	90.9	5
xR	79.6	55.1	59.1	51.6	87.6	67.9	59.6	97.2	93.5	75.5	58.0	79.3	68.8	91.5	9
Poly	60.8	56.1	60.8	34.7	90.9	65.9	46.7	93.4	66.0	65.9	58.8	54.9	55.8	88.0	4
xR	77.7	57.0	61.6	35.7	90.1	62.1	43.8	90.7	73.3	70.1	47.6	74.3	67.9	87.9	2
CAC Class	BIO	DIB	D10	GID	IMX	SMR	2SD	WQD	80X	ZMM	BEM	BEV	HRD	IFD	Best
MV	85.6	68.0	69.5	53.7	90.6	72.1	45.4	94.9	91.1	71.9	56.0	86.5	80.5	94.0	0
xR	87.6	74.0	76.0	62.6	92.7	80.8	49.5	97.8	95.6	82.3	68.0	89.0	82.5	94.7	6
OP	87.6	75.1	76.5	67.3	92.7	81.3	62.4	97.8	95.6	85.4	72.5	88.0	82.5	94.7	6
xR	87.1	74.1	76.5	71.0	92.7	81.3	76.8	98.3	95.6	85.4	75.5	88.0	82.5	94.7	8
Poly	76.3	74.3	77.0	57.0	94.8	80.8	61.9	96.1	80.0	79.2	75.5	66.0	73.5	93.3	5
xR	86.1	75.1	77.5	57.5	94.8	75.5	47.4	99.4	84.4	82.3	67.5	86.0	80.5	93.3	4
CAP Class	BIO	DIB	D10	GID	IMX	SMR	2SD	WQD	80X	ZMM	BEM	BEV	HRD	IFD	Best
MV	82.6	70.4	73.6	84.2	93.2	70.4	49.3	88.3	85.1	90.8	59.4	83.2	80.7	94.2	5
xR	83.3	70.9	73.9	86.1	93.9	72.4	55.4	91.9	92.6	93.9	62.9	85.1	80.9	94.9	9
OP	83.2	71.1	74.0	85.6	94.0	73.2	59.6	92.8	91.9	94.0	65.3	86.0	81.1	94.8	9
xR	83.8	71.6	74.2	87.4	94.6	74.5	65.7	94.6	94.6	95.1	68.1	86.9	81.3	95.4	11
Poly	76.1	74.8	77.8	86.0	96.8	81.6	67.7	96.1	78.9	94.3	76.8	76.0	73.8	94.4	9
xR	87.0	74.6	78.2	84.5	97.0	79.5	71.6	90.8	84.5	95.4	68.6	83.2	78.9	94.9	9

Table 4. Probability based classifier combination

OP Prob	BIO	DIB	D10	GID	IMX	SMR	2SD	WQD	80X	ZMM	BEM	BEV	HRD	IFD	Best
MV	80.0	54.5	55.3	42.1	89.0	64.4	39.1	77.1	93.5	65.4	48.5	80.3	71.3	91.6	6
xR	78.0	51.4	55.6	52.8	89.4	67.6	56.2	84.9	93.5	71.9	58.5	79.7	71.3	91.6	8
OP	79.5	54.3	55.8	53.2	89.9	68.9	62.5	82.6	91.3	76.2	61.3	80.3	70.9	91.6	9
xR	78.5	51.0	55.8	54.3	89.9	71.0	66.5	84.5	91.3	78.1	61.0	78.7	70.9	91.6	8
Poly	81.8	59.5	61.2	56.7	90.8	72.0	98.5	90.8	93.5	81.7	64.7	87.4	70.1	92.2	12
xR	79.1	58.1	61.4	56.0	90.8	73.2	67.8	87.6	97.8	81.6	60.8	87.9	70.4	92.2	12
CAC Prob	BIO	DIB	D10	GID	IMX	SMR	2SD	WQD	80X	ZMM	BEM	BEV	HRD	IFD	Best
MV	89.2	73.6	74.0	63.1	93.8	79.3	62.4	87.1	95.6	79.2	69.0	89.0	84.0	95.3	7
xR	87.1	71.5	74.0	71.5	93.8	81.7	74.7	91.0	95.6	83.3	76.0	88.0	84.0	95.3	8
OP	88.7	73.4	74.5	71.0	93.8	82.2	78.9	90.4	93.3	86.5	77.5	89.0	84.0	95.3	9
xR	88.1	71.4	74.5	72.9	93.8	83.7	80.9	91.6	93.3	87.5	77.5	88.0	84.0	95.3	8
Poly	90.2	77.1	78.0	74.3	94.3	84.6	99.0	94.9	95.6	89.6	79.0	93.0	83.5	95.3	12
xR	88.7	76.2	78.0	72.9	94.3	85.1	70.6	93.3	97.8	89.6	76.5	93.5	83.5	95.3	12
CAP Prob	BIO	DIB	D10	GID	IMX	SMR	2SD	WQD	80X	ZMM	BEM	BEV	HRD	IFD	Best
MV	63.2	57.6	60.4	77.5	74.3	59.9	51.8	67.6	68.5	82.8	54.4	67.2	67.3	74.2	0
xR	63.6	58.9	60.3	79.7	75.2	60.9	56.5	68.3	72.0	84.1	56.1	68.3	67.3	74.3	0
OP	65.8	58.2	60.8	79.3	75.5	61.8	60.2	68.4	72.2	84.4	57.4	69.8	67.5	74.6	0
xR	65.5	59.4	60.8	82.0	76.0	62.6	64.7	68.5	73.6	85.1	58.9	70.3	67.6	74.7	0
Poly	81.0	67.5	68.3	86.6	96.1	77.7	92.5	86.4	95.0	94.6	67.9	88.3	75.0	94.4	10
xR	76.6	70.7	69.7	84.9	96.5	85.1	83.8	86.4	89.8	97.3	76.2	92.4	74.4	94.7	8

In Table 4 the classifiers' class probability estimates are used to combine using all the weight assignment algorithms. We note that the integration of the reliability improves the performance. The results compared to the class label based combination ones show us a different behaviour, the polynomial weight assignment is better than the others. This can be explained by the discrete type of function values of the class based combination compared to continuous type of function values for polynomial weight assignment.

Based on CAC, the proposed polynomial weight assignment for weighted classifier combination outperforms the other combination methods. Comparing single classifier

Table 5. Sum of squared errors on probabilities of classifier set

SSE	BIO	DIB	D10	GID	IMX	SMR	2SD	WQD	80X	ZMM	BEM	BEV	HRD	IFD	Best
KMClu	74.3	89.7	56.5	370.5	174.6	70.4	71.6	141.6	135.3	520.1	85.1	91.4	65.2	109.1	0
SOM	32.0	70.3	49.0	109.3	55.2	91.3	125.8	31.5	57.8	95.8	109.0	26.0	32.0	**21.3**	1
FANN	32.6	**33.8**	**38.0**	116.2	56.1	**34.0**	69.2	**27.3**	85.8	224.0	62.4	34.3	**29.0**	35.1	5
ANN	**31.3**	41.1	39.9	80.8	69.9	38.4	58.5	29.7	48.2	131.4	54.4	40.6	34.2	48.3	1
KMCla	95.0	95.4	53.1	380.7	165.2	65.3	71.4	143.0	92.4	528.5	83.1	85.2	52.4	109.1	0
Parzen	72.9	70.2	96.8	86.2	95.2	93.5	79.2	87.0	92.7	82.4	86.4	59.3	76.7	84.4	0
kNN	41.6	54.7	55.5	**51.9**	**33.7**	43.1	**37.0**	49.1	**33.0**	**36.0**	52.9	32.9	45.7	33.1	5
PQD	95.8	80.5	53.6	386.0	195.0	74.7	72.3	147.3	129.3	639.0	75.3	87.5	53.9	140.4	0
PLD	53.0	51.9	42.1	183.6	121.0	56.4	56.0	76.0	69.2	190.3	51.9	56.4	30.6	51.5	0
SVC	53.1	54.7	77.9	69.4	73.7	46.0	128.6	75.5	85.9	68.4	**47.6**	**21.2**	34.5	68.9	2

and combination results, except for the data sets WQD, BEM and IFD, the combination performance is even higher than the best classifier's performance. For example for the DIB data set, the best possible class performance is 76.8 percent, which is increased to 77.1 percent. Considering the standart deviations of the single classifier results we can even state that the BIO, DIB, SMR, 2SD, and 80X data sets are classified better than the single best classifiers.

The analysis of removing the worst and best classifiers improves the classification performance for some data sets. For the worst classifier removal, improvements are better than the case of removing the best classifier. A detailed study [2] shows that the behaviour is different depending on the characteristics of the data sets. In fact the removal of worst classifier improves the performance as expected, but the result for the best classifier was an unexpected result. A closer look at the k-nearest neighbour classifier based on the sum of squared errors of posterior probabilities is given in Table 5. The bold face values indicate the best sum of squared errors among the classifiers on the same data set on that column. The last column titled "Best" indicates the number of times the classifier has the best sum of squared error of posterior probability among the classifier collection. The results show that the k-nearest neighbour classifier is one of the best ones, but not in all cases.

To have an automated classifier, we may have a collection of fuzzy neural networks, artificial neural networks, k-nearest neighbour and support vector machine based classifiers, and combine them. The design of this subset of classifiers is based on their sum of squared error on posterior probabilities in Table 5. The four classifiers chosen, have the lowest sum of squared errors. The results of this set were almost as good as the original classifier set with all the classifiers. The probability based combination with overall performance values assigned as weights performs better than the whole classifier set for classification accuracy based on probability.

A more detailed sensitivity analysis is done on data sets separately [2]. For each data set the classifiers are sorted based on the sum of squared errors, respectively. Beginning with the best classifier, all classifiers are incrementally added to the classifier set. Their performance changes are graphically presented in Figure 1 and Figure 2.

As can be seen in Figure 1, the classification accuracy based on class labels for the majority vote of the classifier set, after the best classifier is in the subset, the performance first drops by adding the second or third best classifier and then it begins to improve sometimes to its initial level and sometimes above it. This is due to the fact that the best classifiers in the classifier set are not independent of each other, that is

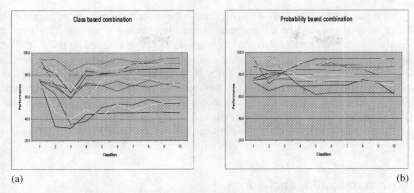

Fig. 1. Classification accuracy based on class labels of simple majority vote

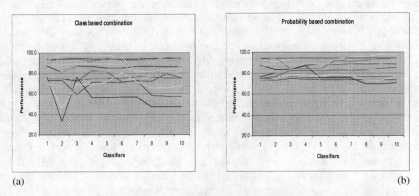

Fig. 2. Class performance of polynomial weight assignment with reliability

they are correlated in the misclassification of the same test samples. A complete search for the best classifier subset may also be carried out by considering all possible subsets of the original classifier set. A further research should be done on the class characteristics of the data sets, since the performance of classifiers are not just data set dependent, their performance also depend on the different classes of the data set. For some classifiers, certain classes of some data sets may be classified more reliably than the other classes of the same data set. In fact in this study, this kind of analysis is added to the combination by the proposed reliability factors.

Comparing the sensitivity of adding classifiers to the set in the figures 1 and 2 show that polynomial weight assignment is more robust for addition of new classifiers. Another point is that probability based classifier combination is more robust to class label based combination algorithms, as can be noticed by the smaller variability in the performance, which ranges between 70 percent and 100 percent (Figure 2(b)), compared to the large variation of the simple majority vote case of 60-100 percent range (Figure 1(b)). Based on this analysis we can outline a guide for designing a classifier set for combination.

Assuming that at the design time of the classifier set, the time is not a critical issue, all available classifiers should be trained. If possible, they may be tuned for better performance. At training phase the time costly leave-one-out algorithm should be used. The reliabilities after this training should be recorded for testing phase. Than a sensitivity analysis should be carried out: either beginning with best classifier based on the sum of squared probability errors, all classifiers are added to the classifier set and the new performance is traced after each step till all classifiers are added, or all possible subsets of classifiers for classifier set should be considered. Either the best set or if the performance difference is not so high, all classifiers should be selected for classifier set. Finally using results of leave-one-out, the polynomial weights and the class reliabilities of classifiers should be calculated and used for the testing phase. The probability based combination algorithm is more robust as the combination algorithm.

7   Summary and Conclusions

In this study different classifier combination schemes are proposed and realized in an integrated framework. All classifiers and combination schemes are evaluated using a variety of performance measures. When combining different classifiers, the weighted combination methods are applied as the combination schemes. The two basic questions concerning the weighting methods: what to weight and how to weight, direct us to new ideas of alternatives for combination methods and for weight assignments. Class and probability based combination methods are applied on the data set and experimentally demonstrated that the proposed probability based weighted combination method is a robust way of combining classifiers. The weights of classifiers are basically based on their performances in the training phase, assuming that they will achieve almost the same performance for the test samples. Overall performance values, originated by the class performance and reliability values proportional to the class population for a specific class after the leave-one-out training phase, is proposed for weight assignment. A better way of assigning weights is proposed by using the least square fit parameters of true and estimated posterior probabilities in the leave-one-out training, and it is called polynomial weight assignment. The classical equal weight assignment is also implemented and tested in the framework to compare the effectiveness of proposed methods.

Sensitivity analysis of selecting a classifier subset to achieve best performance possible with the current classifier set is performed. The basic idea behind selection of a classifier for the classifier set is that, the individual classifier which will be added in the set should not be strongly correlated in the misclassification of the current classifiers in the classifier set. This criterion is not easily satisfied, since even different classes of the same data set may have different characteristics. That is, the classifier's performance may vary for the different classes of the same data set. The results of different sensitivity analysis show that the probability based combination with polynomial weights is a robust way to combine classifiers. Probability based combination with polynomial weights achieves the best possible performance with the current set of classifiers at hand.

To have a complete comparative study, all the proposed combination schemes and weight assignments are applied on the data sets and their performances are evaluated using the proposed performance measures. Some of the performance measures proposed in this study include the reliabilities of the classifiers for their decisions based on their training performances. The reliability values integrate their trust for their decisions, which is used with the assigned weights, to improve the performance of correct classification and reduce the overall misclassification error. Hence, the integration of the reliability measure in the combination improves the classification performance; even the simplest combination scheme of equal weight assignment for classifiers is improved. The main observation of this study is that a typical one to three percent consistent improvement compared to a single best classifier is seen when combining classifiers using the polynomial weight assignment applied with probability based combination.

References

1. Alexandre, L., A. Campilho and M. Kamel, 2000, "Combining Unbiased and Independent Classifiers Using Weighted Average", *11th Portuguese Conference on Pattern Recognition*, pp. 495-498, Porto, Portugal.
2. Baykut, A., 2002, "Classifier Combination Methods in Pattern Recognition", PhD. Thesis, Bogaziçi University, Istanbul, Turkey.
3. Bauer, E. and R. Kohavi, 1999, "An Empirical Comparison of Voting Classification Algorithms: Bagging", *Boosting and Variants, Machine Learning*, Vol. 36.
4. Christianini, N. and J. S. Taylor, 2000, *Support Vector Machines and other kernel-based learning methods*, Cambridge University Press, UK.
5. Cortes, C. and V. Vapnik, 1995, "Support Vector Networks", *Machine Learning*, Vol. 20, pp. 273-297.
6. Duda, R. O. and P. E. Hart, Stork, D.G. 2001, *Pattern Classification*, John Wiley&Sons.
7. Kittler, J., 1998, "Combining Classifiers: A Theoretical Framework", *Pattern Analysis and Applications*, Vol. 1, No. 1, pp. 18-28.
8. Kittler, J., M. Hatef, R. P. W. Duin and J. Matas, 1998, "On Combining Classifiers", *IEEE Trans. on Pattern Analysis and Machine Intelligence*, Vol. 20, No. 3, pp. 226-240.
9. Shalkoff, R. J., 1992b, Pattern Recognition: Statistical, Structural and Neural Approaches, John Wiley&Sons.

Serial Multiple Classifier Systems Exploiting a Coarse to Fine Output Coding

Josef Kittler, Ali Ahmadyfard, and David Windridge

Centre for Vision, Speech and Signal Processing
University of Surrey, Guildford, Surrey GU2 7XH, UK

Abstract. We investigate serial multiple classifier system architectures which exploit a hierarchical output coding. Such architectures are known to deliver performance benefits and are widely used in applications involving a large number of classes such as character and handwriting recognition. We develop a theoretical model which underpins this approach to multiple classifier system design and show how it relates to various heuristic design strategies advocated in the literature. The approach is applied to the problem of 3D object recognition in computer vision.

1   Introduction

There are several papers [3,10,11,12,13,6,8,7] concerned with multiple classifier system architectures which suggest that complex architectures, in which the decision process is decomposed into several stages involving coarse to fine classification, result in an improved recognition performance. For example, by grouping classes and performing initially coarse classification, followed by fine classification refinement which disambiguates the classes of the coarse group, one can achieve significant gains in performance. [7] applies this approach to the problem of handwritten character recognition and suggests that class grouping should maximise an entropy measure. Similar strategies have been advocated in [3,10,11,12,13]. The popular decision tree methods can be seen to exploit the same phenomenon.

The aim of the current study is to demonstrate that these heuristic processes do indeed have a theoretical basis by developing a very general framework for analysing the benefit of hierarchical class grouping. The outcome of the analysis will be to indicate and elucidate a number of differing strategies that can be adopted to build serial multiple classifier systems architectures. Finally, we select one such strategy and apply it to the practical problem of 3D object recognition using 2D views.

The paper is organised as follows. In Section 2 the problem of pattern recognition using hierarchical class grouping is formulated. We derive an expression for the additional decision error over and above the Bayes error, as a function of estimation error. In Section 3 we discuss various strategies that naturally stem from this analysis. In Section 4 one of these strategies is applied to the problem of 3D object recognition using a two stage classifier. Section 5 draws the paper to conclusion.

T. Windeatt and F. Roli (Eds.): MCS 2003, LNCS 2709, pp. 106–114, 2003.

2   Problem Formulation and Mathematical Notation

Consider a multi-class pattern recognition problem where pattern Z is to be assigned to one of m possible classes $\{\omega_i, \ i = 1, ...m\}$. Let us assume that the given pattern is represented by a measurement vector, $\mathbf{x}$. In the measurement space each class ω_k is modelled by the probability density function $p(\mathbf{x}|\omega_k)$, and let the a priori probability of class occurrence be denoted by $P(\omega_k)$. We shall consider the models to be mutually exclusive, meaning that only one model can be associated with each pattern.

Now according to the Bayesian decision theory, given measurements $\mathbf{x}$, the pattern Z should be assigned to class ω_j, i.e. its label θ should assume value $\theta = \omega_j$, if the a posteriori probability of that interpretation is a maximum, i.e.

$$assign \qquad \theta \to \omega_j \qquad if$$

$$P(\theta = \omega_j|\mathbf{x}) = \max_k P(\theta = \omega_k|\mathbf{x}) \tag{1}$$

In practice, for each class ω_i, a classifier will provide only an estimate $\hat{P}(\omega_i|\mathbf{x})$ of the true a posteriori class probability $P(\omega_i|\mathbf{x})$ given pattern vector $\mathbf{x}$, rather than the true probability. Let us denote the error on the estimate of the ith class a posteriori probability at point $\mathbf{x}$ as $e(\omega_i|\mathbf{x})$ and let the probability distribution of the errors be $p_i[e(\omega_i|\mathbf{x})]$.

In order to investigate the effect of sequential decision making by class grouping, let us examine the class a posteriori probabilities at a single point $\mathbf{x}$. Suppose the a posteriori probability of class ω_s is maximum, i.e. $P(\omega_s|\mathbf{x}) = \max_{i=1}^m P(\omega_i|\mathbf{x})$ giving the local Bayes error $e_B(\mathbf{x}) = 1 - \max_{i=1}^m P(\omega_i|\mathbf{x})$. However, our classifier only estimates these a posteriori class probabilities. The associated estimation errors may result in suboptimal decisions, and consequently in an additional classification error. In order to precisely quantify this additional error we have to establish what the probability is for the recognition system to make a suboptimal decision. This situation will occur when the a posteriori class probability estimates for one of the other classes becomes maximal. Let us derive the probability $e_{S_i}(\mathbf{x})$ of the event occurring for class ω_i, $i \neq s$, i.e. when

$$\hat{P}(\omega_i|\mathbf{x}) - \hat{P}(\omega_j|\mathbf{x}) > 0 \ \forall j \neq i \tag{2}$$

Note the left hand side of (2) can be expressed as

$$P(\omega_i|\mathbf{x}) - P(\omega_j|\mathbf{x}) + e(\omega_i|\mathbf{x}) - e(\omega_j|\mathbf{x}) > 0 \tag{3}$$

Equation (3) defines a constraint for the two estimation errors $e(\omega_k|\mathbf{x})$, $k = i, j$ as

$$e(\omega_i|\mathbf{x}) - e(\omega_j|\mathbf{x}) > P(\omega_j|\mathbf{x}) - P(\omega_i|\mathbf{x}) \tag{4}$$

The event in (2) will occur when the estimate of the a posteriori probability of class ω_i exceeds the estimate for class ω_s, while the other estimates of the a posteriori class probabilities ω_j, $\forall j \neq i, s$ remain dominated by $\hat{P}(\omega_i|\mathbf{x})$.

The first part of the condition will happen with the probability given by the integral of the distribution of the error difference in (4) under the tail defined by the margin $\Delta P_{si}(\mathbf{x}) = P(\omega_s|\mathbf{x}) - P(\omega_i|\mathbf{x})$. Let us denote this error difference by $\eta_\omega(\mathbf{x})$. Then the

108   Josef Kittler, Ali Ahmadyfard, and David Windridge

distribution of error difference $p[\eta_\omega(\mathbf{x})]$ will be given by the convolution of the error distribution functions $p_i[e(\omega_i|\mathbf{x})]$ and $p_s[e(\omega_s|\mathbf{x})]$, i.e.

$$p[\eta_\omega(\mathbf{x})] = \int_{-\infty}^{\infty} p_i[\eta_\omega(\mathbf{x}) + e(\omega_s|\mathbf{x})]p_s[e(\omega_s|\mathbf{x})]de(\omega_s|\mathbf{x}) \qquad (5)$$

Note that errors $e(\omega_r|\mathbf{x})$, $\forall r$ are subject to various constraints (i.e. $\sum_r e(\omega_r|\mathbf{x}) = 0$, $-P(\omega_r|\mathbf{x}) \leq e(\omega_r|\mathbf{x}) \leq 1 - P(\omega_r|\mathbf{x})$). We will make the assumption that the constraints are reflected in the error probability distributions themselves and therefore we do not need to take them into account elsewhere (i.e. integral limits, etc). However, the constraints also have implications for the validity of assumptions about the error distributions in different parts of the pattern space. For instance, in regions where all the classes are overlapping, the Gaussian assumption may hold, but as we move to the parts of the space where the a posteriori class probabilities are saturated, such an assumption would not be justified. At the same time, however, one would not be expecting any errors to arise in such regions, and the breakdown of the assumption would not be critical to the validity of the argument.

Returning to the event indicated in (2), the probability of the first condition being true may thus be stated to be $\int_{\Delta P_{si}(\mathbf{x})}^{\infty} p[\eta_\omega(\mathbf{x})]d\eta_\omega(\mathbf{x})$.

With regard to equation (4), treating each j individually, we observe that the second condition will hold (for $j \neq s, i$) with probability $\int_{-\infty}^{P(\omega_i|\mathbf{x})+e(\omega_i|\mathbf{x})} p_j[e(\omega_j|\mathbf{x})]de(\omega_j|\mathbf{x})$, the exception being the last term, say $e(\omega_k|\mathbf{x})$, which is constrained by:

$$e(\omega_k|\mathbf{x}) = - \sum_{\substack{j=1 \\ j \neq k}}^{m} e(\omega_j|\mathbf{x}) \qquad (6)$$

Thus, finally, the probability of assigning point $\mathbf{x}$ to class ω_i in place of the Bayes optimal class ω_s, will be given by:

$$e_{S_i}(\mathbf{x}) = \int_{\Delta P_{si}(\mathbf{x})}^{\infty} p[\eta_\omega(\mathbf{x})]d\eta_\omega(\mathbf{x})$$
$$\bullet \int_{-\infty}^{\Delta P_{ij}(\mathbf{x})+e(\omega_i|\mathbf{x})} p_j[e(\omega_j|\mathbf{x})]de(\omega_j|\mathbf{x})........$$
$$... \int_{-\Delta P_{ik}(\mathbf{x})-e(\omega_i|\mathbf{x})-\sum_{\substack{t=1 \\ t \neq k}}^{m} e_t(\omega_t|\mathbf{x})}^{\Delta P_{il}(\mathbf{x})+e(\omega_i|\mathbf{x})} p_l[e(\omega_l|\mathbf{x})]de(\omega_l|\mathbf{x}) \qquad (7)$$

and the total probability of label switching will be given by:

$$e_S(\mathbf{x}) = \sum_{\substack{i=1 \\ i \neq s}}^{m} e_{S_i}(\mathbf{x}) \qquad (8)$$

Now how do these labelling errors translate to classification error probabilities? We know that for the Bayes minimum error decision rule the error probability at point $\mathbf{x}$ will be $e_B(\mathbf{x})$. If our pseudo Bayesian decision rule, i.e. the rule that assigns patterns according to the maximum estimated a posteriori class probability, deviates from the Bayesian rule with probability $e_S(\mathbf{x})$, the local error of the decision rule will be given by

$$\alpha(\mathbf{x}) = e_B(\mathbf{x})[1 - e_S(\mathbf{x})] + e_S(\mathbf{x})[1 - e_B(\mathbf{x})] \qquad (9)$$

Suppose that we divide the classes into two groups and perform a coarse classification of the input pattern to one of these two groups, and then, in the next stage, refine the classification further, by considering the remaining alternatives, the number of which will be reduced by one half. To be specific, let us consider a four class case. Then the probability of label switching in (7) will become:

$$e_{S_i}(\mathbf{x}) = \int_{\Delta P_{si}(\mathbf{x})}^{\infty} p[\eta_\omega(\mathbf{x})] d\eta_\omega(\mathbf{x})$$
$$\bullet \int_{-\Delta P_{ik}(\mathbf{x}) - 2e(\omega_i|\mathbf{x}) - e(\omega_s|\mathbf{x})}^{\Delta P_{ij}(\mathbf{x}) + e(\omega_i|\mathbf{x})} p_j[e(\omega_j|\mathbf{x})] de(\omega_j|\mathbf{x}) \qquad (10)$$

The *total* probability of switching will be defined as in (8). Here the total probability will involve three terms $e_{S_r}(\mathbf{x})$, $r = i, j, k$.

After grouping the classes to super classes $\Omega_1 = \{\omega_s, \omega_i\}$ and $\Omega_2 = \{\omega_j, \omega_k\}$ the probability of label switching will be given by the probability of choosing the incorrect super class, Ω_2, plus the probability of picking Ω_1 times the probability of not selecting the Bayes optimal decision during the decision refinement. Let us denote the former term by $w(\mathbf{x})$, i.e.

$$w(\mathbf{x}) = \int_{\Delta \Pi_{12}(\mathbf{x})}^{\infty} p[\eta_\Omega(\mathbf{x})] d\eta_\Omega(\mathbf{x}) \qquad (11)$$

where $\Delta \Pi_{12}(\mathbf{x}) = P(\Omega_1|\mathbf{x}) - P(\Omega_2|\mathbf{x})$. Then the total probability of label switching can be written as

$$\epsilon_S(\mathbf{x}) = w(\mathbf{x}) + [1 - w(\mathbf{x})] \int_{\Delta Q_{si}(\mathbf{x})}^{\infty} p[\eta_\omega(\mathbf{x})] d\eta_\omega(\mathbf{x}) \qquad (12)$$

In equation (12) we implicitly denote the a posteriori probabilities for classes ω_s and ω_i by different symbols to indicate that these functions differ from $P(\omega_r|\mathbf{x})$, $r = i, s$ by a scaling factor $P(\omega_s|\mathbf{x}) + P(\omega_i|\mathbf{x})$ since they are required to sum to unity. Note that if functions $Q(\omega_r|\mathbf{x})$ are estimated via probability densities, the estimation errors will be scaled up versions of the original errors $e(\omega_r|\mathbf{x})$. However, if these functions are estimated directly from the training data, the errors will be different and can be assumed to have the same distribution as the original unscaled errors $e(\omega_r|\mathbf{x})$. If this is the case, then one can see why this two stage approach may produce better results. If the error distributions are the same but the margins increase by scaling, the probability of label switching will accordingly go down.

In general, there will be m classes that can be gathered hierarchically into binary groups at each stage of the hierarchy. Let us denote the two groups created at stage k by Ω^k and $\bar{\Omega}^k$. Thus, the set Ω^k will be divided at the next stage into two subsets, and so on. The class sets Ω^k will hence satisfy the condition:

$$\Omega^k \epsilon \Omega^j \quad j < k \qquad (13)$$

Further, let the additional error of classifying pattern $\mathbf{x}$ from superclass Ω^k be denoted $w^k(\mathbf{x})$. Then by analogy to (12), the total additional error of the hierarchical decision making process can be written as

$$e_S(\mathbf{x}) = w^1(\mathbf{x}) + \sum_{i=2}^{n-1}[\Pi_{j=1}^{i-1}(1 - w^j(\mathbf{x}))]w^i(\mathbf{x}) + \Pi_{j=1}^{n-1}(1 - w^j(\mathbf{x}))w^n(\mathbf{x}) \quad (14)$$

3   Discussion

Let us consider the implication of expression (14). Assuming that the estimation errors have identical distribution at all the stages of the sequential decision making process, the label switching error $w^i(\mathbf{x})$ at stage i will be determined entirely by the margin (difference) between the a posteriori probabilities of classes $P(\Omega^i|(\mathbf{x}))$ and $P(\bar{\Omega}^i|(\mathbf{x}))$. By grouping classes at the top of the hierarchy we can increase this margin and therefore control the additional error. In this way we can ensure that the additional errors $w^i(\mathbf{x})$ in all but the last stage of the decision making process are negligible. In the limiting case, when $w^i(\mathbf{x}) \to 0$, $i = 1, ..., n - 1$, the switching error $e_S(\mathbf{x})$ will be equal to $w^n(\mathbf{x})$. At that point the set Ω^n is likely to contain just a single class. Thus the last stage decision will involve two classes only. Note that whereas the margin between the a posteriori probabilities of the two classes, say ω_t and ω_r, at the top of the hierarchy, was $P(\omega_t|\mathbf{x}) - P(\omega_r|\mathbf{x})$, in the last stage, it will become

$$\Delta = \frac{P(\omega_t|\mathbf{x}) - P(\omega_r|\mathbf{x})}{P(\omega_t|\mathbf{x}) + P(\omega_r|\mathbf{x})} \quad (15)$$

Thus the margin will be significantly magnified and consequently the additional error $e_S(\mathbf{x})$ significantly lower than it would otherwise have been in a single stage system.

The expression (14) immediately suggests a number of grouping strategies. For instance, in order to maintain as large a margin as possible in all stages of the decision making process, it would clearly be most effective to group all but one class in a single super class with the weakest class constituting the complement super class. This strategy has in fact been suggested, based on heuristic arguments, in [2]. The disadvantage of this strategy is that it would involve $m - 1$ decision steps.

Computationally more effective is to arrive at a decision after $log_2\ m$ steps. This would lead to grouping which maintains a greater balance of the two class sets Ω^i and $\bar{\Omega}^i$. Another suggestion [7] is to split the classes so as to minimise an entropy criterion. However, all these strategies would have in common that they exploit the same underlying principle embodied by our model.

4   Experimental Results

In the following section, we set out to test the idea of grouping thus elucidated within the context of 3-D object recognition. Hence, we consider two particular recognition experts in tandem, the first of which will perform a course grouping of the object hypotheses based on an entropy criterion. This initial classification is performed using colour cues via the *MNS* method of Matas et al [9], whereby the colour structure of an image is captured in terms of a set of colour descriptors computed on multimodal neighbourhoods of the image. We use the similarity between the descriptors from the scene image and each of the K object models to find a posteriori probabilities of the object in the scene image belonging to each class in the database.

Having provided the set of a posteriori probabilities $\mathcal{P} = \{p(\omega_i|\overline{x}), \forall i \in \{1 \cdots K\}\}$, we rank them in the descending order, our objective being to compile a list of hypothesised objects based on their likelihood of being in the scene ($\mathcal{P}$). For this purpose we use the entropy of the system as a criterion. Let us consider the list, $\mathcal{O}$ of objects arranged according to the descending order of their probabilities of being in the scene. If $\mathcal{O}$ is split into two groups O_1 and O_2, corresponding to the m most likely objects in the scene and the remaining objects of the database, respectively, the entropy of the system is evaluated as follows [5]:

$$E = \alpha E(O_1) + (1 - \alpha)E(O_2) \tag{16}$$

where $E(O_1)$ and $E(O_2)$ are the entropies associated with groups O_1 and O_2 respectively, and α is the probability that the present object in the scene exists in the group O_1. By searching the range of possible configurations, $(m = \{1 \cdots K\})$, the grouping with the minimum entropy is selected and the group of the hypothesised objects, O_1, is passed to the next expert (ARG).

The second expert establishes the object identity by considering only the subset of candidate models contained in the most probable of the coarse groups. We opt for the region-based matching proposed in [1] as the second expert in our recognition system. In this method an object image is represented by its constituent regions segmented from the image, the regions being represented in the form of the Attributed Relational Graph. Hence, this expert takes into account geometric relations between object primitives and determines the winning hypothesis by means of relaxation labelling [1]: we refer to this method as the *ARG* method. Thus the recognition system as a whole is denoted the MNS-ARG method.

In seeking to experimentally demonstrate the effect of model pruning in this context, we are thus interested in determining the effect of the first classifier (MNS) on the performance of the ARG method in terms of the recognition rate. The experiment was hence conducted on the SOIL-47 (Surrey Object Image Library) database which contains 47 objects, each of which has been imaged from 21 viewing angles spanning a range of up to ± 90 degrees. Fig1(a) shows the frontal view of the objects in the database, the whole of which is available online [4]. We model each object using its frontal image, leaving the other 20 views of the objects to be used as test images (Fig 1(b)): the size of images used in this experiment is 288×360 pixels.

For each test image we applied the MNS method to determine the hypothesised objects matching to it, the outcome of which is depicted in Fig 2. In this figure we plot the percentage of cases in which the list of hypothesised objects includes the correct model, the rate being shown as a function of object pose. For comparison, we plot the percentage of cases in which the correct object has the highest probability among the other candidates (i.e. the recognition rate): the results illustrate that the recognition rate for the MNS method is not particularly high despite the fact that in the majority of cases

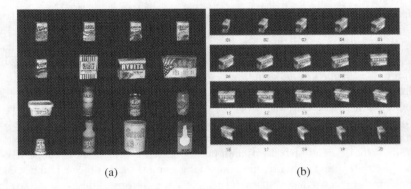

(a)   (b)

Fig. 1. a) The frontal view of sample objects from the SOIL47 database b) Database objects imaged from 20 viewing angles

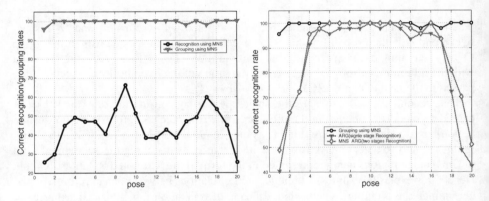

Fig. 2. The likelihood of the correct model being in the list of hypothesised objects generated by the MNS method

Fig. 3. The percentage of correct recognition for the ARG and the MNS-ARG methods

the hypothesised list *does* include the correct object (though note that the average size of the list of hypothesised objects is 16, near to one third of the database size (47 objects)).

The ARG method was then applied to identify the object model based on the list of hypothesised objects generated by the MNS method, this recognition procedure being applied to all test images in the database. In Fig 3 we have plotted the recognition rate for the MNS-ARG method as a function of object pose: for comparison we add the recognition rate when ARG method is applied as a stand alone expert. As a base line we have also included the rate of correct classification for the MNS method. The results show that the object grouping using the MNS method uniformly improves the recognition rate, particularly for extreme object views. In these cases, the hypotheses at a node of the test graph do not receive good support from their neighbours (due to the problem of distortion in image regions). Moreover, we observe that a large number of labels involved in the matching tends to increase the entropy of labelling, while, when the number of candidate labels for a test node declines by virtue of model pruning, the entropy of labelling correspondingly diminishes. Consequently it is more likely for a test node to take its proper label (instead of the null label).

It is, furthermore, worth noting that grouping using the MNS method not only improves the recognition rate, but also reduces the computational complexity of the entire recognition system. Specifically, the MNS-ARG method executes, in the outlined scenario, at almost three times the rate of the stand alone ARG method.

5   Conclusion

We have set out a theoretical basis for the commonly employed heuristic method of class coarse-graining in order to improve classification performance by considering the question in terms of the composite error margin and the associated probability of label switching.

As such, we have additionally been able to indicate the existence a range of such approaches, which would allow the balancing of execution time with classification performance as appropriate to the user's specifications. A practical example of one such process was given, which demonstrated the real utility of this type of approach by applying an entropy criterion to the coarse-graining of object targets in a 3-D object recognition problem, substantially improving recognition for the most ambiguous classes.

References

1. A. Ahmadyfard and J. Kittler. Enhancement of ARG object recognition method. In *Proceeding of 11 the European Signal Processing Conference*, volume 3, pages 551–554, September 2002.
2. A. R. Ahmadyfard and J. Kittler. A multiple classifier system approach to affine invariant object recognition. In *3rd International Conference on Computer Vision Systems, 2003 (accepted)*.
3. M C Fairhurst and A F R Rahman. Generalised approach to the recognition of structurally similar handwritten characters using multiple expert classifiers. *IEE Proc. on Vision, Image and Signal Processing*, 144(1):15–22, 2 1997.
4. http://www.ee.surrey.ac.uk/Research/VSSP/demos/colour/soil47/.
5. Ianakiev K. and V. Govindaraju. Architecture for classifier combination using entropy measures. In *IAPR International Workshop on Multiple Classifier Systems*, Lecture Notes in Computer Science, pages 340–350, June 2000.
6. G Kim and V Govindaraju. A lexicon driven approach to handwritten word recognition. *IEEE Transactions on PAMI*, 19(4):366–379, 1997.
7. I Krassimir and V Govindaraju. An architecture for classifier combination using entropy measure. In J Kittler and F Roli, editors, *Proceedings of Multple Classifier Systems 2000*, pages 340–350, 2000.
8. S Madhvanath, E Kleinberg, and V Govindaraju. Holistic verification for handwritten phrases. *IEEE Transactions on PAMI*, 21(12):1344–1356, 1999.
9. J. Matas, D. Koubaroulis, and J. Kittler. Colour image retrieval and object recognition using the multimodal neighbourhood signature. In D. Vernon, editor, *Proceedings of ECCV*, volume Springer, pages 48–64, 2000.
10. A F R Rahman and M C Fairhurst. Exploiting second order information to design a novel multiple expert decision combination platform for pattern classification. *Electronic Letters*, 33:476–477, 1997.

11. A F R Rahman and M C Fairhurst. A new hybrid approach in combining multiple experts to recognise handwritten numerals. *Pattern Recognition Letters*, 18:781–790, 1997.
12. A F R Rahman and M C Fairhurst. An evaluation of multi-expert configurations for for the recognition of handwritten numerals. *Pattern Recognition*, 31:1255–1273, 1998.
13. A F R Rahman and M C Fairhurst. Enhancing multiple expert decision combination strategies through exploitation of a priori information sources. In *IEE PROCEEDINGS-VISION IMAGE AND SIGNAL PROCESSING*, volume 146, pages 40–49, 1999.

Polychotomous Classification with Pairwise Classifiers: A New Voting Principle

Florin Cutzu

Dept. of Computer Science, Indiana University
Bloomington, IN 47405, USA
florin@indiana.edu

Abstract. A new principle for performing polychotomous classification with pairwise classifiers is introduced: if pairwise classifier $\mathcal{N}_{ij}$, trained to discriminate between classes i and j, responds "i" for an input $\boldsymbol{x}$ from an unknown class (not necessarily i or j), one can at best conclude that $\boldsymbol{x} \notin j$. Thus, the output of pairwise classifier $\mathcal{N}_{ij}$ can be interpreted as a vote against the losing class j, and not, as existing methods propose, as a vote for the winning class i. Both a discrete and a continuous classification model derived from this principle are introduced.

1 Introduction

1.1 Problem Statement

Consider the problem of m-way classification ($m \geq 2$) of the random variable $\boldsymbol{x} \in \mathcal{R}^d$. The probability density function of $\boldsymbol{x}$ is a mixture of m partially overlapping components corresponding to the classes of interest in the classification problem: $p(\boldsymbol{x}) = \sum_1^m w_k p(\boldsymbol{x} \mid k)$ where the weights are the prior class probabilities: $w_k = P(k)$, $\sum_1^m w_k = 1$. The training data consists of n input vectors $\boldsymbol{x}_i$, which usually are typical representatives of the classes, and the corresponding class labels $y_i \in \{1, \ldots, m\}$. The goal is to assign class labels to novel inputs.

The direct approach is to use a single m-way classifier; an alternative approach is to employ several k-way classifiers ($k < m$) and combine their outputs in a m-way classification decision. In this paper the case $k = 2$ (pairwise classifiers) is explored.

1.2 Current Approaches

The idea of performing complex multi-way classification tasks by combining multiple simpler, specialized classifiers is not new and various approaches based on this principle have been presented in the research literature as well as in pattern recognition textbooks such as [6].

Of particular interest in the context of this paper are Friedman's method [2], the pairwise coupling model of Hastie & Tibshirani [3] and the related approach presented in [6].

T. Windeatt and F. Roli (Eds.): MCS 2003, LNCS 2709, pp. 115–124, 2003.
© Springer-Verlag Berlin Heidelberg 2003

Friedman's Voting Method. The Bayesian solution to the classification of x requires that estimates of the m class posterior probability densities $P(k \mid x)$ be obtained in the training stage.

Friedman's approach reformulates the Bayesian solution to reduce the m-way classification problem to $m(m-1)/2$ pairwise discrimination problems, as follows. During training, possibly using neural network techniques, estimates of the following ratios of probability densities are obtained:

$$r_{ij}(x) = \frac{P(i \mid x)}{P(j \mid x) + P(i \mid x)} \quad (i,j = 1,\ldots,m) \tag{1.1}$$

The functions r_{ij} learned in the training phase are then used in the testing phase. If for input vector x, $r_{ij}(x) > 0.5$ then $P(i \mid x) > P(j \mid x)$, and class i is the "winner" of the $i - j$ comparison. Thus, the output of pairwise estimator (i, j) can be interpreted as a vote for either class i or for class j. There are $m(m-1)/2$ non-trivially distinct functions r_{ij}, one for each pair of classes. Input vector x is assigned to class k if class k wins the most votes, or two-class classifier decisions $k - i$ $(i = 1,\ldots,m)$.

Pairwise Coupling and Similar Models. The pairwise coupling model [3] assumes that, for input x, the output of pairwise classifier (i, j) is given by:

$$s_{ij}(x) = P(i \mid x, i \vee j) \tag{1.2}$$

and that

$$s_{ij}(x) = \frac{P(i \mid x)}{P(i \mid x) + P(j \mid x)} \tag{1.3}$$

which is the same relation as in Eq. 1.1. The authors then proceed to find the set of probabilities $P(i \mid x)$ that best fit the set of classier outputs s_{ij} via Eq. 1.3. Thus, while Friedman determines only the class with maximum posterior probability, the pairwise coupling model estimates the class posterior probabilities of all classes.

A similar model is given in [6]. For input x, the output of pairwise classifier (i, j) is given, as in the pairwise coupling model, by:

$$s_{ij}(x) = P(i \mid x, i \vee j)$$

By Bayes law

$$s_{ij}(x) = \frac{w_i P(x \mid i)}{w_i P(x \mid i) + w_j P(x \mid j)} \tag{1.4}$$

where w_i is the prior probability of class i. Note that, as opposed to Eq. 1.3 of the pairwise coupling model, this is an exact relation.

Given the classifier outputs s_{ij}, using Eq. 1.4 and Bayes' law

$$P(i \mid x) = \frac{w_i P(x \mid i)}{\sum_{j=1}^{m} w_j P(x \mid j)}$$

one can compute all class posterior probabilities.

More Complex Schemes. The literature contains a relatively large number of papers on the problem of combining simpler classifiers into multi-way classifiers: [1,4,5,7]. These papers will not be discussed any further, since they generalize the problem and its solution in various ways, but, as far as the focus of the present paper is concerned, do not fundamentally change the principles introduced by Friedman.

2   The Proposed Approach

2.1   Problems with Current Approaches

Friedman's method, being a form of Bayesian classification, requires estimates of the probabilities of the various classes at the input vector. Unfortunately, class probability estimation is a difficult problem. Thus, it is desirable to design a classification method that retains the advantage of reducing the multi-way problem to a set of two-way decisions but does not require pairwise class density comparison.

The problem with with the pairwise coupling and related models is more basic. According to these models, the output of classifier (i, j) for input vector $\boldsymbol{x}$ is given by $s_{ij}(\boldsymbol{x}) = P(i \mid \boldsymbol{x}, i \vee j)$. In other words, the input vector is assumed to belong to class i or to class j. However, in the testing phase, it is impossible to ensure that input vector $\boldsymbol{x}$ fed to classifier (i, j) belongs to either class i or j. If the input belongs to some other class, $\boldsymbol{x} \in k \neq i, j$, then the output of classifier (i, j) can no longer be interpreted as in Eqs 1.2, 1.3, 1.4, and these models cannot be applied.

2.2   "Non-probabilistic" Pairwise Classifiers

The goal of this paper is to formulate a multi-way classification scheme based on pairwise classifiers that do not estimate the pairwise class probability ratios of the type 1.1 for the input vector. Such classifiers will be hereafter termed "non-probabilistic". A typical example of such a classifier is the multilayer perceptron.

A non-probabilistic classifier performs certain calculations on the components of the input vector. For example, such a pairwise classifier may discriminate between two classes by comparing a certain continuous feature with a threshold, or by detecting the presence of one of two distinguishing features, or by performing more complex calculations on the vector components in the case of the neural networks. In vision application, one may differentiate between two image classes by detecting one or two image templates at certain positions in the image.

In the training stage, using neural networks or related techniques as pairwise classifiers is attractive because, in general, learning one m-way classification is more expensive computationally than learning $m(m - 1)/2$ two-way classifications.

For input $\boldsymbol{x} \in i \vee j$, the output of a pairwise neural network $\mathcal{N}_{i,j}$ trained to discriminate between classes i and j (by outputting 0 for class i and 1 for class

j) can be interpreted as deciding whether $p_i(\boldsymbol{x}) > p_j(\boldsymbol{x})$ (despite the fact that such networks do not actually estimate class probabilities).

One is therefore tempted to try to apply Friedman's voting method to the outputs of neural, non-probabilistic pairwise classifiers. However, the output of pairwise network $\mathcal{N}_{ij}(\boldsymbol{x})$ has the same meaning as $r_{ij}(\boldsymbol{x})$ in Eq. 1.1 only if the input $\boldsymbol{x} \in i \vee j$, condition that can be verified only for the training set.

This is a problem, since in practical classification problems the different classes have finite extents and overlap only partially in input space. Consequently, there usually exist regions in input space where only one single class is present, and consequently the ratio $r_{ij}(\boldsymbol{x})$ may be undefined, since both $P_i(\boldsymbol{x})$ and $P_j(\boldsymbol{x})$ may be 0. At these locations the neural network pairwise classifier $\mathcal{N}_{i,j}$ will have some output in $[0,1]$; however, comparing this output to 0.5 to determine whether $p_i > p_j$ is no longer legitimate. The meaning of the output of $\mathcal{N}_{ij}(\boldsymbol{x})$ for $\boldsymbol{x} \notin i \vee j$ is not obvious, and applying Friedman's voting scheme is not justified.

2.3   A Novel Voting Principle: Vote against, Not for

To correctly use the pairwise non-probabilistic classifiers $\mathcal{N}_{ij}$ for classification of novel inputs one must interpret the outputs of these classifiers for inputs from untrained-for classes $k \neq i, j$.

The problem with directly applying the Friedman [2] or Hastie-Tibshirani [3] approaches to non-probabilistic pairwise classifiers is the following. Consider classifier $\mathcal{N}_{ij}$, trained to discriminate between classes i and j. If, for input $\boldsymbol{x}$ of unknown class membership, the output of the classifier is "i", applying the Friedman algorithm results in a vote for class i. Similarly, the Hastie-Tibshirani algorithm increases the probability of class i.

However, since the true class of $\boldsymbol{x}$ can be other than i or j, such an interpretation of the output of classifier $\mathcal{N}_{ij}$ can result in false positive errors–i.e., falsely attributing $\boldsymbol{x} \notin i \cup j$ to class i or j. On the other hand, one can expect that, if properly trained, the pairwise classifiers do not make (many) false negative errors—i.e., give the wrong response to inputs from trained-for classes. Thus, false positive errors are much more likely than false negative errors.

This observation leads to the following classification rule. If, for input $\boldsymbol{x}$ of unknown class membership, classifier $\mathcal{N}_{ij}$ responds "i", one can not conclude that $\boldsymbol{x} \in i$. Due to the possibility of false positive errors, one can only conclude that $\boldsymbol{x} \notin j$, because, if the input was from class j, the classifier $\mathcal{N}_{ij}$ would have responded "j" (assuming no false negative errors). In other words, one votes against j, not for i.

Formally, $(\boldsymbol{x} \in i \rightarrow \mathcal{N}_{ij}$ responds "i"$) \equiv (\boldsymbol{x} \notin i \rightarrow \mathcal{N}_{ij}$ does not respond "i"$) \not\equiv (\mathcal{N}_{ij}$ responds "i" $\rightarrow \boldsymbol{x} \in i)$.

2.4   A Model for the Class Posterior Probabilities

Let y_{ij} denote the output of non-probabilistic pairwise classifier $\mathcal{N}_{ij}$ for an input $\boldsymbol{x}$ from an arbitrary class. y_{ij} is a random variable. Using solely the principle formulated above, a model for the class posterior probabilities $P(k \mid y_{ij})$ can be formulated, as follows. This model represents a conservative (maximum ignorance) interpretation of the outputs of the classifiers when nothing is known about the class membership of the input.

Discrete Output Classifiers. To simplify, assume first the classifiers $\mathcal{N}_{ij}$, $i, j = 1, \ldots, m$ output binary decisions: either i or j.

Given that classifier $\mathcal{N}_{ij}$ outputs j, what are the probabilities of each of the m classes?

It can reasonably be assumed that the classifiers are properly trained, and thus very few false negative errors occur. Therefore, if classifier N_{ij} outputs j, the posterior probability of class i is reduced to zero, or more generally, to a very small fraction ϵ_{ji} of its prior probability w_i, that is, $P(i \mid y_{ij} = j) = \epsilon_{ji} w_i$.

All the other classes $k \neq i$ (not only class j!) are possible, it is hypothesized, with probabilities that sum up to $1 - \epsilon_{ji} w_i$ and are in ratios equal to the ratios of their prior probabilities w_k.

Therefore:

$$P(i \mid y_{ij} = j) = \epsilon_{ji} w_i; \tag{2.1}$$

$$P(j \mid y_{ij} = j) = \frac{w_j(1 - \epsilon_{ji} w_i)}{1 - w_i}; \tag{2.2}$$

$$\text{Generally, } \forall k \neq i : P(k \mid y_{ij} = j) = \frac{w_k(1 - \epsilon_{ji} w_i)}{1 - w_i}; \tag{2.3}$$

As desired, $\forall k, h \neq i$, $P(k \mid y_{ij} = j)/P(h \mid y_{ij} = j) = w_k/w_h$. As required, $\sum_{k=1}^{m} P(k \mid \mathcal{N}_{ij} = j) = 1$.

The factor ϵ_{ji} determines the probability that classifier $\mathcal{N}_{ij}$ outputs "i" for an input of class j, and it can be estimated in the training stage. Similarly, ϵ_{ij} measures the probability that classifier $\mathcal{N}_{ij}$ outputs "j" for an input of class i. If ϵ_{ji} is sufficiently small, $\forall k \neq i, P(k \mid y_{ij} = j) > w_k$.

Note that if w_i increases for w_j constant $P(j \mid y_{ij} = j)$ increases nonlinearly. This is a consequence of the fact that class i is excluded and the "missing probability" is made up for in part by class j. If $w_i + w_j = \text{constant}$ then $P(j \mid y_{ij} = j)$ decreases with increasing w_i.

It will be shown later that if the prior probabilities w_i are equal, and all ϵ_{ij} are equal, the voting-against method is equivalent to Friedman's voting-for method. Intuitively, voting against class j is equivalent to voting equally for each of the other classes $j \neq i$ — in other words, if $\mathcal{N}_{ij}$ classifier responds "i", the true class can be any class except j, with the same probability.

Continuous Output Classifiers. If classifier outputs y_{ij} are not binary but continuous in $[0, 1]$ a simple possibility is to interpolate between the limiting cases $P(k \mid y_{ij} = 0)$ and $P(k \mid y_{ij} = 1)$ to obtain $P(k \mid y_{ij} \in (0, 1))$. Assuming that for classifier $\mathcal{N}_{ij}$, $y_{ij} = 0$ corresponds to $y_{ij} = j$ and $y_{ij} = 1$ corresponds to $y_{ij} = i$, these limiting probabilities are given, for the various values of k, by Eqs 2.1, 2.2, 2.3. By linear interpolation:

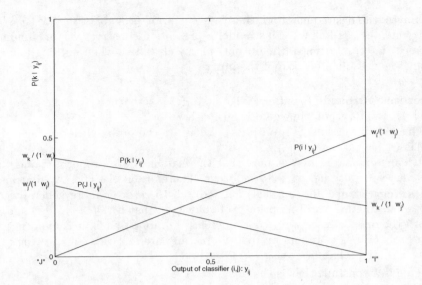

Fig. 1. A model for the probabilities of the m classes as functions of y_{ij}, the output of classifier $\mathcal{N}_{ij}$. For simplicity, the figure displays the case where the false negative rate is zero ($\epsilon = 0$).

$$P(k \mid y_{ij}) = (1 - y_{ij})\frac{w_k(1 - \epsilon_{ji}w_i)}{1 - w_i} + y_{ij}\frac{w_k(1 - \epsilon_{ij}w_j)}{1 - w_j}, \ k \neq i,j \quad (2.4)$$

$$P(i \mid y_{ij}) = (1 - y_{ij})\epsilon_{ji}w_i + y_{ij}\frac{w_i(1 - \epsilon_{ij}w_j)}{1 - w_j},$$

$$P(j \mid y_{ij}) = (1 - y_{ij})\frac{w_j(1 - \epsilon_{ji}w_i)}{1 - w_i} + y_{ij}\epsilon_{ij}w_j.$$

It can be verified that $\sum_{k=1}^{m} P(k \mid y_{ij}) = 1$. Figure 1 illustrates class posterior probabilities $P(k \mid y_{ij})$ conditional on the output of classifier $\mathcal{N}_{ij}$.

Determining the Joint Classifier Class-Posterior Probability. The next step is to determine the joint $P(i \mid \boldsymbol{y})$, where $\boldsymbol{y} = [y_{1,2}, \ldots, y_{m-1,m}]$. By Bayes

$$p(y_{ij} \mid i) = \frac{P(i \mid p_{ij})p(y_{ij})}{w_i}.$$

If the assumption is made that the outputs of the classifiers in the classifier bank are (conditionally) independent, the conditional joint probability $p(\boldsymbol{y} \mid i)$ of the output of the full classifier bank is:

$$p(\boldsymbol{y} \mid i) = \prod_{k,j} p(y_{kj} \mid i) = w_i^{-m(m-1)/2} \prod_{k,j} P(i \mid y_{kj})p(y_{kj}).$$

By Bayes, the desired class posterior probability is:

$$P(i \mid \boldsymbol{y}) = \frac{p(\boldsymbol{y} \mid i)w_i}{p(\boldsymbol{y})} = w_i^{1-m(m-1)/2} \frac{\prod_{k,j} P(i \mid y_{kj})p(y_{kj})}{p(\boldsymbol{y})} \tag{2.5}$$

Given that $p(\boldsymbol{y})$ and $\prod_{k,j} p(y_{kj})$ are the same for all class posterior probabilities $P(i \mid \boldsymbol{y})$, $i = 1, \ldots, m$, they can be ignored. Therefore

$$P(i \mid \boldsymbol{y}) \sim w_i^{1-m(m-1)/2} \prod_{k,j} P(i \mid y_{kj}) \tag{2.6}$$

Taking logarithm:

$$\log P(i \mid \boldsymbol{y}) = c + (1 - m(m-1)/2) \log w_i + \sum_{k,j} \log P(i \mid y_{kj}) \tag{2.7}$$

where c is a constant that is the same for all classes i. The logarithm exists for $P(i \mid y_{kj}) > 0$, and this requires that $\epsilon_{ij} > 0$, condition which can always be met.

Discrete Case. For classifiers with binary outputs $y_{ij} = i$ or j, replacing the probabilities $P(i \mid y_{kj})$ with the expressions given in Eq. 2.1, 2.2, 2.3, gives:

$$\log P(i \mid \boldsymbol{y}) = c + \log w_i + \tag{2.8}$$
$$\sum_{j \neq i} \log \left(\epsilon_{ji}, \text{ if } y_{ij} = j \ ; \ \frac{1-\epsilon_{ij}w_j}{1-w_j}, \text{ if } y_{ij} = i \right) +$$
$$\sum_{k,j \neq i} \log \left(\frac{1-\epsilon_{kj}w_j}{1-w_j}, \text{ if } y_{kj} = k \ ; \ \frac{1-\epsilon_{jk}w_k}{1-w_k}, \text{ if } y_{kj} = j \right)$$

This equation indicates that each pairwise classifier contributes "votes" for class i. If a classifier of type $\mathcal{N}_{ij}$ outputs j, its vote is negative ($\epsilon < 1$); otherwise the votes are positive ($(1-\epsilon w_j)/(1-w_j) > 1$), the strength of the vote depending on the network output, prior class probabilities, and the false negative error rates ϵ_{ij}.

If all classes have the same prior probability $w_i = 1/m$ and if all ϵ_{ij} are equal, then the classifiers of type $\mathcal{N}_{kj}$, $k, j \neq i$ become irrelevant to classifying class i, and the relation above is equivalent to Friedman's voting formula, which thus obtains as a special case:

$$\log P(i \mid \boldsymbol{y}) = c + \sum_{j \neq i} \log \left(\epsilon, \text{ if } y_{ij} = j \ ; \ \frac{m-\epsilon}{m-1}, \text{ if } y_{ij} = i \right) \tag{2.9}$$

Since $\log \frac{m-\epsilon}{m-1} > \log \epsilon$, the probability of class i increases with the proportion of the $m - 1$ classifiers of type $\mathcal{N}_{ij}$ that respond i (as opposed to j).

Continuous Case. For continuous-output classifiers, using Eq. 2.4, and assuming that classifier $\mathcal{N}_{ij}$ outputs 1 for class i and 0 for class j:

$$\log P(i \mid \boldsymbol{y}) = c + \log w_i + \tag{2.10}$$
$$\sum_{j \neq i} \log \left(\epsilon_{ji}(1 - y_{ij}) + \frac{1 - \epsilon_{ij} w_j}{1 - w_j} y_{ij} \right) +$$
$$\sum_{k, j \neq i} \log \left(\frac{1 - \epsilon_{kj} w_j}{1 - w_j} y_{kj} + \frac{1 - \epsilon_{jk} w_k}{1 - w_k} (1 - y_{kj}) \right).$$

This equation is the one of the main results of this paper.

If all classes have the same prior probability $w_i = 1/m$ and if all ϵ_{ij} are equal, then the classifiers of type $\mathcal{N}_{kj}$, $k, j \neq i$ become irrelevant to classifying class i:

$$\log P(i \mid \boldsymbol{y}) = c + \sum_{j \neq i} \log \left(\epsilon(1 - y_{ij}) + \frac{m - \epsilon}{m - 1} y_{ij} \right) \tag{2.11}$$

which is a continuous analogue of the Friedman voting rule (soft voting).

2.5   Classifying with an Incomplete Pairwise Classifier Set

From a computational standpoint it is important to study the situation in which only a subset of all $m(m-1)/2$ pairwise classifiers are used.

Here only the simplest situation is considered, namely, binary output pairwise classifiers that do not make false negative errors ($\epsilon = 0$).

Consider a subset of the complete classifier set consisting of $b \leq m(m-1)/2$ classifiers, and consider class i. Assume there are $n(i) \leq (m-1)$ classifiers of type $\mathcal{N}_{i(*)}$, trained to discriminate class i from other classes $(*)$. Assume that for input $\boldsymbol{x}$ of indeterminate class membership, a number $v(i) \leq n(i)$ of these classifiers will respond "i". Because voting against class $j \neq i$ is equivalent to voting for all classes $k \neq j$, including i, the number of votes for class i resulting from the votes against classes $j \neq i$ is, for input $\boldsymbol{x}$:

$$f(i) = b - n(i) + v(i) \tag{2.12}$$

Therefore, the vote-against method results in $f(i)$ votes for class i; under usual voting-for method class i receives $v(i)$ votes. The voting-against and the voting-for methods are equivalent if $n(i)$ does not depend on i, and in particular if all $m(m-1)/2$ pairwise classifiers are used in the classification process.

The voting-against method is superior if not all classifiers are used. Unlike the voting-for method, regardless of the number of pairwise classifiers employed, the voting-against method never selects the wrong class: it never casts a vote against the true class (assuming no false negative errors occur). If $\boldsymbol{x} \in i$ is input to classifier $\mathcal{N}_{ij}$, the vote-for method will correctly vote for class i; the vote-against method will, also correctly, vote against class j. However, if $\boldsymbol{x} \in i$ is input to classifier $\mathcal{N}_{kj}$, the vote-for method will incorrectly vote for either class k or j; the vote-against method will correctly vote against either class j or k. The vote-for method fails if the classifiers trained on the true class are not used in the classification process; the vote-against method correctly selects the true class even if none of these are used. Both methods give the same, correct results if only the classifiers trained on the true class are used. The vote-against method, while never voting against the true class i, can however fail to cast votes against some classes $j \neq i$, resulting in a non-unique solution. However, this happens if the only classifiers used are a subset of the classifiers $\mathcal{N}_{ij}$ trained on the true class, i.

3 Summary and Conclusions

This paper addresses the problem of polychotomous classification with pairwise classifiers. The essential difference from previous methods such as [2] and [3] is that the pairwise classifiers considered in the present paper are common classifiers such as the multilayer perceptron which do not require class probability estimation to perform classification.

To handle such classifiers the paper introduces a new, conservative interpretation of the output of a pairwise classifier for inputs of unknown class membership. The observation at the basis of the proposed method is that, while an adequately-trained classifier will inevitably falsely recognize inputs from unknown classes, it will not fail to recognize inputs from trained-for classes. This approach has not only the theoretical advantage of being logically correct, but is also, unlike other methods, robust to reducing the number of pairwise classifiers used in the classification process.

Interpreting the output of a pairwise, or more generally, n-way classifier as evidence against (rather than for) a trained-for class has the advantage that it allows, conceptually, the classification of an input in an "unknown" class if there is evidence against all known classes.

Two practical classification models based on this principle were proposed: one for discrete-output pairwise classifiers, in Equation 2.8 and another for continuous-output classifiers, in Equation 2.10. The Friedman voting scheme is as a particular case of the proposed model.

In practice it should be possible to use a less conservative interpretation of the outputs of the pairwise classifiers. The idea is to use the training data not only for training the pairwise classifiers, but also for testing them and getting an idea, in probabilistic terms, of their behavior for inputs from untrained-for classes.

References

1. Erin L. Allwein, Robert E. Schapire, and Yoram Singer. Reducing multiclass to binary: A unifying approach for margin classifiers. In *Proc. 17th International Conf. on Machine Learning*, pages 9–16. Morgan Kaufmann, San Francisco, CA, 2000.
2. Jerome H. Friedman. Another approach to polychotomous classification. Technical report, Stanford University, 1996.

3. Trevor Hastie and Robert Tibshirani. Classification by pairwise coupling. In Michael I. Jordan, Michael J. Kearns, and Sara A. Solla, editors, *Advances in Neural Information Processing Systems*, volume 10. The MIT Press, 1998.
4. Eddy Mayoraz and Ethem Alpaydin. Support vector machines for multi-class classification. In *IWANN (2)*, pages 833–842, 1999.
5. Volker Roth. Probabilistic discriminative kernel classifiers for multi-class problems. *Lecture Notes in Computer Science*, 2191:246–266, 2001.
6. Jürgen Schürmann. *Patern Classification. A Unified View of Statistical and Neural Principles*. John Wiley & Sons, Inc, New York, NA, 1996.
7. B. Zadrozny. Reducing multiclass to binary by coupling probability estimates, 2001.

Multi-category Classification
by Soft-Max Combination of Binary Classifiers

Kaibo Duan[1], S. Sathiya Keerthi[1], Wei Chu[1],
Shirish Krishnaj Shevade[2], and Aun Neow Poo[1]

[1] Control Division, Department of Mechanical Engineering
National University of Singapore, Singapore 119260
{engp9286,mpessk,engp9354,mpepooan}@nus.edu.sg
[2] Department of Computer Science and Automation
Indian Institute of Science, Bangalore 560 012
shirish@csa.iisc.ernet.in

Abstract. In this paper, we propose a multi-category classification method that combines binary classifiers through soft-max function. Posteriori probabilities are also obtained. Both, one-versus-all and one-versus-one classifiers can be used in the combination. Empirical comparison shows that the proposed method is competitive with other implementations of one-versus-all and one-versus-one methods in terms of both classification accuracy and posteriori probability estimate.

1   Introduction

Multi-category classification is a central problem in machine learning. While binary classification methods are relatively well-developed, how to effectively extend these binary classification methods for multi-category classification is an important but still on-going research issue. For methods such as support vector machines (SVMs) [6] the most common approaches to multi-category classification are binary-classifier-based methods, such as "one-versus-all" (1va) and "one-versus-one" (1v1), that make direct use of binary classifiers to tackle multi-category classification tasks. For SVMs, some researchers also proposed "all-together" approaches [6] [7] that solve the multi-category classification problem in one step by considering all the examples from all classes together at once. However, the training speed of "all-together" methods is usually slow.

One-versus-all method is usually implemented using a "Winner-Takes-All" (WTA) strategy. It constructs M binary classifier models where M is the number of classes. The ith binary classifier is trained with all the examples from ith class ω_i with positive labels (typically +1), and the examples from all other classes with negative labels (typically -1). For an example $\mathbf{x}$, WTA strategy assigns it to the class with the largest decision function value.

One-versus-one method is usually implemented using a "Max-Wins" voting (MWV) strategy. This method constructs one binary classifier for every pair of distinct classes and so, all together it constructs $M(M-1)/2$ binary classifiers. The binary classifier C_{ij} is trained with examples from ith class ω_i and jth class

T. Windeatt and F. Roli (Eds.): MCS 2003, LNCS 2709, pp. 125–134, 2003.

ω_j only, where examples from class ω_i take positive labels while examples from class ω_j take negative labels. For an example $\mathbf{x}$, if classifier C_{ij} says $\mathbf{x}$ is in class ω_i, then the vote for class ω_i is added by one. Otherwise, the vote for class ω_j is increased by one. After each of the $M(M-1)/2$ binary classifiers makes its vote, MWV strategy assigns $\mathbf{x}$ to the class with the largest number of votes.

For binary classifiers with probabilistic outputs, such as kernel logistic regression (kLOGREG) [5], a "pairwise coupling" (PWC) procedure was proposed in [2] to implement the one-versus-one method. The central idea is to couple the $M(M-1)/2$ pairwise class probability estimates to obtain estimates of posteriori probabilities for the M classes. PWC assigns an example $\mathbf{x}$ to the class with the largest posteriori probability among the M classes.

In this paper, we present a multi-category classification method by combining one-versus-all or one-versus-one binary classifiers, through a soft-max function. Posteriori probabilities obtained from the combination are used to do multi-category classification.

In section 2 we present various designs of soft-max combining functions for one-versus-all and one-versus-one binary classifiers. Practical implementation issues associated with these designs are given in section 3. Numerical experiments are given in section 4 where the proposed methods are compared with other implementations of one-versus-all and one-versus-one methods with different binary classification techniques. Finally, results are analyzed and conclusions are made in section 5.

2   Soft-Max Combination of Binary Classifiers

In this section, we present soft-max combination of one-versus-all and one-versus-one binary classifiers. The relation of the methods with some previous work is also briefly discussed.

2.1   Soft-Max Combination of One-versus-All Classifiers

Suppose there are M classes and l labelled training data $(\mathbf{x}_1, y_1), \cdots, (\mathbf{x}_l, y_l)$, where $\mathbf{x}_i \in \mathbf{R}^m$ is the ith training example and $y_i \in \{1, \cdots, M\}$ is the class label of $\mathbf{x}_i$. For an example $\mathbf{x}_i$, let us denote the output (decision function value) of the kth binary classifier (class ω_k versus the rest) as r_k^i; r_k^i is expected to be large if $\mathbf{x}_i$ is in class ω_k and small otherwise.

After M one-versus-all binary classifiers are constructed, we can obtain the posteriori probabilities through a soft-max function

$$P_k^i = \mathrm{Prob}(\omega_k | \mathbf{x}_i) = \frac{e^{w_k r_k^i + w_{ko}}}{z^i} , \tag{1}$$

where $z^i = \sum_{k=1}^{M} e^{w_k r_k^i + w_{ko}}$ is a normalization term that ensures that $\sum_{k=1}^{M} P_k^i = 1$. The parameters of the soft-max function, $(w_1, w_{1o}), \cdots, (w_M, w_{Mo})$, can be designed by minimizing a penalized negative log-likelihood (NLL) function , i.e.,

$$\min \quad E = \tfrac{1}{2}\|\mathbf{w}\|^2 - C\sum_{i=1}^l \log P_{y_i}^i \tag{2}$$
$$\text{subject to} \quad w_k, w_{ko} > 0 \ , \ k = 1, \cdots, M \tag{3}$$

where $\|\mathbf{w}\|^2 = \sum_{k=1}^M (w_k^2 + w_{ko}^2)$ and C is a positive regularization parameter. Note that positiveness constraints are placed on weight factor w_k and bias factor w_{ko}. We place positiveness constraints on w_k because we assume that r_k^i is large if $\mathbf{x}_i$ is in class ω_k and small otherwise. We place positiveness constraints on w_{ko} simply to reduce redundancy, since adding a same constant to all w_{ko} does not change the posteriori probability estimates in (1).

The above constrained optimization problem can be transformed to an unconstrained one by using the following substitute variables

$$s_k = \log(w_k) \text{ and } s_{ko} = \log(w_{ko}) \ , \ k = 1, \cdots, M \ . \tag{4}$$

The unconstrained optimization problem can be solved using gradient based methods, such as BFGS [3]. The first-order derivatives of E with respect to the substitute variables can be computed using the following formulas

$$\frac{\partial E}{\partial s_k} = \frac{\partial E}{\partial w_k}\frac{\partial w_k}{\partial s_k} = \left(w_k + C\sum_{y_i=k} \left(P_k^i - 1\right) r_k^i + C\sum_{y_i \neq k} P_k^i r_k^i \right) w_k \ , \tag{5}$$

$$\frac{\partial E}{\partial s_{ko}} = \frac{\partial E}{\partial w_{ko}}\frac{\partial w_{ko}}{\partial ds_{ko}} = \left(w_{ko} + C\sum_{y_i=k} \left(P_k^i - 1\right) + C\sum_{y_i \neq k} P_k^i \right) w_{ko} \ . \tag{6}$$

2.2   Soft-Max Combination of One-versus-One Classifiers

Following the same idea as in the previous subsection, posteriori probabilities can also be obtained by soft-max combination of one-versus-one binary classifiers. For an example $\mathbf{x}_i$, let us denote the outputs of one-versus-one classifier C_{kt} as r_{kt}^i. Obviously we have $r_{tk}^i = -r_{kt}^i$. The following soft-max function is used to combine the one-versus-one binary classifiers

$$P_k^i = \text{Prob}(\omega_k|\mathbf{x}_i) = \frac{e^{\sum_{t \neq k} w_{kt} r_{kt}^i + w_{ko}}}{z^i} \ , \tag{7}$$

where $z^i = \sum_{k=1}^M e^{\sum_{t \neq k} w_{kt} r_{kt}^i + w_{ko}}$ is a normalization term. The soft-max function parameters can be determined by solving the following optimization problem

$$\min \quad E = \tfrac{1}{2}\|\mathbf{w}\|^2 - C\sum_{i=1}^l \log P_{y_i}^i \tag{8}$$
$$\text{subject to} \quad w_{kt}, w_{ko} > 0 \ , \ k, t = 1, \cdots, M \text{ and } t \neq k \tag{9}$$

where $\|\mathbf{w}\|^2 = \sum_{k=1}^M(\sum_{t \neq k} w_{kt}^2 + w_{ko}^2)$ and C is a positive regularization parameter. Note that, as in soft-max combination of one-versus-all classifiers, positiveness constraints are placed on w_{kt} and w_{ko} for the same reason.

As before, we can transform the above constrained optimization problem to an unconstrained one by using the following substitute variables

$$s_{kt} = \log(w_{kt}) \quad \text{and} \quad s_{ko} = \log(w_{ko}) \,, \ k, t = 1, \cdots, M \text{ and } t \neq k \qquad (10)$$

The first-order derivatives of E with respect to the substitute variables are

$$\frac{\partial E}{\partial s_{kt}} = \frac{\partial E}{\partial w_{kt}} \frac{\partial w_{kt}}{\partial s_{kt}} = \left(w_{kt} + C \sum_{y_i = k} \left(P_k^i - 1 \right) r_{kt}^i + C \sum_{y_i \neq k} P_k^i r_{kt}^i \right) w_{kt} \,, \ (11)$$

$$\frac{\partial E}{\partial s_{ko}} = \frac{\partial E}{\partial w_{ko}} \frac{\partial w_{ko}}{\partial s_{ko}} = \left(w_{ko} + C \sum_{y_i = k} \left(P_k^i - 1 \right) + C \sum_{y_i \neq k} P_k^i \right) w_{ko} \,. \qquad (12)$$

The proposed soft-max combination method can be used with any binary classification technique with non-probabilistic outputs. In our numerical study, SVMs are mainly used as the binary classification method.

2.3   Relation to Previous Work

For binary classification, Platt [4] proposed a method to map the outputs of SVMs into probabilities by fitting a sigmoid function after the SVMs are designed. The following parametric model is used by Platt to fit the posteriori probability

$$\text{Prob}(\omega_1 | \mathbf{x}_i) = \frac{1}{1 + e^{A f_i + B}} \,, \qquad (13)$$

where f_i is the output of the SVMs associated with example $\mathbf{x}_i$. The parameters A and B are determined by minimizing the NLL function of the validation data. We refer to the combination of SVM plus a sigmoid function post-fitted using Platt's method as PSVM .

Let us look at our soft-max combination of one-versus-all classifiers for the case $M = 2$. In this case, we have $r_1^i = f_i$, $r_2^i = -r_1^i$, and

$$\text{Prob}(\omega_1 | \mathbf{x}_i) = \frac{1}{1 + e^{-(w_1 + w_2) f_i + (w_{2o} - w_{1o})}} \,. \qquad (14)$$

In soft-max combination of one-versus-one classifiers, in the case $M = 2$, we have $r_{12}^i = f_i$, $r_{21}^i = -r_{12}^i$, and

$$\text{Prob}(\omega_1 | \mathbf{x}_i) = \frac{1}{1 + e^{-(w_{12} + w_{21}) f_i + (w_{2o} - w_{1o})}} \,. \qquad (15)$$

Note that (14) and (15) are exactly in the same form as (13). Therefore, our soft-max combination methods can be viewed as natural extensions of Platt's sigmoid-fitting idea to multi-category classification. To design A and B of the sigmoid function (13), Platt used some simple ideas from Parzen windows design because there were only two parameters. We employ penalized likelihood for our designs because there are many parameters in (1) and (7).

3 Practical Issues in the Soft-Max Function Design

In this section we discuss two important practical issues in the soft-max function design, i.e., how to get the training examples for the soft-max function design and how to tune the regularization parameter C.

3.1 Training Examples for the Soft-Max Function Design

We use 5-fold cross-validation (CV) to get unbiased training data (r_k^i or r_{kt}^i) for soft-max function design. The original training data ($\mathbf{x}$) are partitioned into 5 almost equal folds with each fold contains almost equal percentage of examples of one particular class.

Let us first consider the soft-max combination of one-versus-all classifiers. Take one k. The r_k^i of examples ($\mathbf{x}_i$) in the left-out fold is determined by a binary classifier trained on all other examples except those in the left-out fold, where training examples from class ω_k take positive labels and other examples take negative labels.

Now consider the soft-max combination of one-versus-one classifiers. Take one k and t. The r_{kt}^i of examples ($\mathbf{x}_i$) in the left-out fold from class ω_k and class ω_t are determined by a binary classifier trained on examples of only class ω_k and class ω_t, in all the other folds, where examples from ω_k take positive labels and those from class ω_t take negative labels. For the examples ($\mathbf{x}_i$) not from either class ω_k or class ω_t, the r_{kt}^i are determined by a binary classifier trained on the full examples, in all folds, from class ω_k and class ω_t, where examples from class ω_k and class ω_t respectively take positive and negative labels.

The cross-validation determination of unbiased training data mentioned above adds almost no extra cost to the overall design process since it is also used to tune the hyperparameters of the binary classifiers.

3.2 Regularization Parameter C

Let us now discuss the choice of parameter C for use in (2) and (8). Since designing the soft-max combining function is a relatively small optimization problem with only $2M$ or M^2 variables, we can use k-fold cross-validation to tune this regularization parameter with little extra computation cost.

We can do k-fold cross-validation at various values of C and then choose one C value based on measurements, of the multi-category classifier's performance, estimated from cross-validation. In our study, we do 5-fold cross-validation and try the set of C values: $C = \{2^{-15}, 2^{-14}, \cdots, 2^{15}\}$. Let us denote the cross-validation estimates of error rate and NLL with $cvErr$ and $cvNLL$. In order to get a good classification accuracy as well as good posteriori probability estimates, instead of choosing the C associated with the least $cvErr$, we do the following. First, let us denote the least $cvErr$ with Err_Least and define the C set: $SC_{LeastErr} = \{C : cvErr(C) \leq 1.05Err\_Least\}$. Second, let us define the least cvNLL, with $C \in SC_{LeastErr}$, as NLL_Least. Based on NLL_Least, the relaxed C set is defined: $SC_{LeastNLL} = \{C : cvNLL(C) \leq 1.05NLL\_Least, C \in$

$SC_{LeastErr}$}. The smallest $C \in SC_{LeastNLL}$ is chosen as the final regularization parameter value.

3.3 Simplified Soft-Max Function Design

We may simplify the soft-max function design by minimizing only the second term in (2) and (8), i.e., omit the use of regularization; equivalently, set $C = +\infty$. The only change in solving the optimization problem is that, the gradient expression of (5), (6), (11) and (12) are appropriately modified. In the next section, we will evaluate this simplified design against the one designed with regularizer, as well as against standard multi-category methods.

4 Numerical Study

In this section, we numerically study the performance of the soft-max combination methods and compare it with other implementations of one-versus-all and one-versus-one methods. For the basic binary classifier the following three methods were used: (a) the support vector machine (SVM)[6]; (b) support vector machine with Platt's posterior probabilities (PSVM)[4]; and (c) kernel logistic regression (kLOGREG) [5]. SVM, PSVM and kLOGREG all are kernel-based classification methods. The Gaussian kernel, $K(\mathbf{x}_i, \mathbf{x}_j) = e^{-\|\mathbf{x}_i - \mathbf{x}_j\|^2 / 2\sigma^2}$ was employed. The following multi-category classification methods were studied:

- **Soft-max combination of SVM one-versus-all classifiers:** The soft max functions may be designed with the regularizer or without it (the simplified design); we refer to the corresponding methods as SM C1va and SSM C1va (the first "S" denotes "simplified").
- **Soft-max combination of SVM one-versus-one classifiers:** The method in which the combination function is designed with the regularizer is referred as SM C1va; the method which did not use the regularizer (the simplified design) is referred as SSM C1v1.
- **Winner-Takes-All implementation of one-versus-all classifiers:** Using SVM, PSVM and kLOGREG for binary classification with WTA we obtain 3 methods: W TA_SVM , W TA_PSVM and W TA_KLR. For WTA_PSVM and WTA_KLR, we can obtain posteriori probability estimates crudely by simple normalization, i.e., $\text{Prob}(\omega_k|\mathbf{x}) = p_k / \sum_{t=1}^M p_t$, where p_k is the probabilistic output of kth binary classifier (class ω_k versus the rest).
- **Max-Wins voting implementation of one-versus-one classifiers:** Using SVM, PSVM and kLOGREG for binary classification with MWV we obtain 3 methods: M W V_SVM , M W V_PSVM and M W V_KLR.
- **Pairwise coupling implementation of one-versus-one classifiers:** We refer to the PWC implementations with PSVM and kLOGREG methods respectively as PW C_PSVM and PW C_KLR.

Each binary classifier (whether it is SVM, PSVM or kLOGREG) requires the selection of two hyperparameters (a regularization parameter C and kernel

Table 1. Basic information about the datasets and training sizes used in the numerical study

Dataset	#Classes	#Inputs	#Training Examples	#Total Examples
ABE	3	16	560	2,323
DNA	3	180	500	3,186
Satellite Image (SAT)	6	36	1,500	6,435
Image Segmentation (SEG)	7	19	500	2,310
Waveform (WAV)	3	21	300	5,000

parameter σ^2). Every multi-category classification method mentioned above involves several binary classifiers. We take the C and σ^2 of each of the binary classifiers within a multi-category method to be the same. The two hyperparameters are tuned using 5-fold cross-validation estimation of the multi-category classification performance. We select the optimal hyperparameter pair by a two-step grid search. First we do a coarse grid search using the following sets of values: $C = \{$ 1.0e-3, $\cdots$, 1.0e+3$\}$ and $\sigma^2 = \{$ 1.0e-3, $\cdots$, 1.0e+3$\}$. Thus 49 combinations of C and σ^2 are tried in this step. An optimal pair (C_o, σ_o^2) is selected from this coarse grid search. In the second step, a fine grid search is conducted around (C_o, σ_o^2), where $C = \{0.2C_o, 0.4C_o, \cdots, 0.8C_o, C_o, 2C_o, 4C_o, \cdots, 8C_o\}$ and $\sigma^2 = \{0.2\sigma_o^2, 0.4\sigma_o^2, \cdots, 0.8\sigma_o^2, \sigma_o^2, 2\sigma_o^2, 4\sigma_o^2, \cdots, 8\sigma_o^2\}$. All together, 81 combinations of C and σ^2 are tried in this step. The final optimal hyperparameter pair is selected from this fine search. In grid search, especially in the fine search step, it is quite often the case that there are several pairs of hyperparameters that give the same cross validational classification accuracy. So, some principles have to be used to select one pair of C and σ^2 from these short-listed combinations. For the methods with posteriori probability estimates, where cross-validation estimated error rate (cvErr) and NLL (cvNLL) are both available, the following strategies are applied sequentially until we find one unique parameter pair: (a) select the pair with smallest cvErr value; (b) select the pair with smallest cvNLL value; (c) select the pair with smaller C and larger σ^2; (d) select the pair with smallest 8-neighbor average cvErr value; (e) select the pair with smallest 8-neighbor average cvNLL value; (f) select the pair with smallest C value. For the methods without posteriori probability estimates, only step (a), (c), (d) and (f) are sequentially applied.

When the training size is large enough, probably all the methods may perform as well as Bayes-optimal algorithm. So, to clearly see differences in the performance of various methods, reasonably sparse training sets at which there is still room for performance improvement should be used. For this purpose, we run all the methods on 5 datasets with training sets that are somewhat smaller than those which are usually used. The training set sizes are chosen based on the suggestions in [1]. The 5 standard datasets used are: ABE, DNA, Satellite Image (SAT), Image Segmentation (SEG) and Waveform (WAV). ABE is a dataset that we extract from the dataset Letter by using only the classes corresponding to the characters "A", "B" and "E". All the continuous inputs of these datasets are normalized to have zero mean and unit standard deviation. Table 1 summarizes the basic information about the datasets and the training set sizes used. For each dataset, we randomly partition the whole dataset into a training set

Table 2. The mean and standard deviation of test error rate (in percentage) over 20 partitions, of the methods based on the one-versus-all binary classifiers

	SMC1va	SSMC1va	WTA_SVM	WTA_PSVM	WTA_KLR
ABE	0.91±0.37	0.95±0.30	0.91±0.33	0.90±0.35	0.90±0.34
DNA	7.66±0.73	7.54±0.64	7.80±0.74	7.73±1.00	7.74±0.73
SAT	10.07±0.44	10.16±0.49	10.02±0.41	10.13±0.43	10.28±0.47
SEG	6.01±0.80	5.91±0.94	6.56±0.88	6.18±0.96	5.72±0.80
WAV	15.17±0.77	15.33±0.76	15.29±0.74	15.40±0.99	14.82±0.59

Table 3. The mean and standard deviation of test error rate (in percentage) over 20 partitions, of the methods based on one-versus-one binary classifiers

	SMC1v1	SSMC1v1	MWV_SVM	MWV_PSVM	MWV_KLR	PWC_PSVM	PWC_KLR
ABE	1.20±.0061	0.99±0.40	1.01±0.41	0.98±0.38	0.97±0.36	0.87±0.28	0.93±0.37
DNA	7.81±.0096	7.96±0.77	7.65±0.93	7.89±0.93	7.81±0.70	7.65±0.77	7.56±0.73
SAT	10.31±.0064	10.03±0.37	10.37±0.71	10.18±0.50	10.23±0.43	9.98±0.41	10.21±0.39
SEG	5.92±.0156	5.66±0.93	5.41±1.02	5.38±0.96	4.85±0.69	5.42±0.90	4.82±0.68
WAV	14.47±.0087	14.55±1.08	16.01±1.06	14.62±0.82	14.63±0.66	14.66±0.76	14.66±0.67

Table 4. mean and standard deviation of test NLL value over 20 partitions, of the methods with posteriori probability estimates

	SMC1va	SSMC1va	SMC1v1	SSMC1v1	WTA_PSVM	WTA_KLR	PWC_PSVM	PWC_KLR
ABE	.0452±.0378	.0392±.0226	.0661±.0413	.0460±.0368	.0316±.0096	.0257±.0068	.0361±.0057	.0306±.0142
DNA	.2250±.0346	.2153±.0123	.2295±.0386	.2154±.0212	.2326±.0235	.2315±.0290	.2105±.0166	.2165±.0195
SAT	.3129±.0103	.3017±.0116	.2911±.0134	.2763±.0110	.3231±.0093	.2887±.0462	.2976±.0078	.2915±.0144
SEG	.2080±.0496	.2221±.0413	.2353±.0985	.2723±.0782	.2392±.0226	.2098±.0294	.2923±.0200	.1752±.0134
WAV	.3808±.0452	.3664±.0198	.3584±.0522	.3448±.0231	.3617±.0229	.4353±.0698	.3553±.0154	.4132±.0436

and a test set 20 times by stratified sampling. For each partition of one dataset, after each multi-category classifier is designed using the training set, it is tested on the test set. Then the mean and the standard deviation of the test set error rate of each method is computed using the results of the 20 runs. These values are reported in Table 2-3 for the five datasets. For the methods with posteriori probability estimates, the mean and the standard deviation values of the test set NLL are reported in Table 4.

5   Results and Conclusions

Let us now analyze the results of our numerical study. First, it is easy to see from Tables 2–4 that all the methods included in the numerical study give competitive performance. However, some methods show overall betterness over other methods. We do a finer analysis and comparison to see this.

Suppose we want to compare method 1 against method 2 on a given dataset. The pairwise t-test is conducted to analyze if the (test set) error of method 1 is greater than that of method 2. Assuming normality of the populations and using the hypothesis that the mean errors of the two methods are same, we compute the p-value, which is the probability that the mean error of method 1 is greater than that of method 2. Thus, a large p-value (say > 0.9) indicates that method 1 is clearly worse than method 2, while a small value (say < 0.1) indicates that method 1 is clearly better than method 2. Since there are five datasets, we compute a set of five p-values, using the following order for the datasets: ABE, DNA, SAT, SEG and WAV. Similar to (test set) error, we can also conduct the above analysis for (test set) NLL. Unless mentioned otherwise, all p-values will refer to the (test set) error.

For the WTA implementations of one-versus-all methods, WTA_KLR has a slightly better classification accuracy than WTA_SVM and WTA_PSVM. The sets of p-values of WTA_KLR against WTA_SVM and WTA_PSVM are {0.4005, 0.3121, 0.9995, 2.5044e-5, 1.1164e-4} and {0.4818, 0.5433, 0.9557, 0.0015, 0.0078}. The set of p-values of WTA_PSVM against WTA_SVM is {0.4225, 0.3360, 0.9323, 0.0092, 0.7166}; these two methods give close performance.

For the MWV implementation of one-versus-one methods, MWV_KLR and MWV_PSVM have slightly better classification accuracy than MWV_SVM. The sets of p-values of MWV_KLR and MWV_PSVM against MWV_SVM are {0.3278, 0.9300, 0.1887, 0.0133, 1.0282e-5} and {0.2574, 0.8499, 0.0749, 0.3617, 1.4880e-7}. The classification accuracies of MWV_KLR and MWV_PSVM are close; the set of p-values of MWV_KLR against MWV_PSVM is {0.4846, 0.3713, 0.7442, 0.0082, 0.5160}.

For soft-max combination of one-versus-all classifiers, SSMC1va and SMC1va give close classification accuracy. But SSMC1va has a better probability estimate. The set of p-values of SSMC1va against SMC1va, from the pairwise t-test on (test set) NLL, is {0.2242, 0.1088, 9.9571e-6, 0.9070, 0.0610}. It should be noted that the design of the combination function for SSMC1va is also much simpler than that of SMC1va.

For soft-max combination of one-versus-one classifiers, SSMC1v1 is better than SMC1v1, both, in terms of classification accuracy as well as probability estimate. The sets of p-values from pairwise t-test on (test set) error and (test set) NLL, of SSMC1v1 against SMC1v1, are {0.0088, 0.1808, 0.0141, 0.1830, 0.6939} and {0.0053, 0.0652, 1.0274e-4, 0.9233, 0.1437}.

Overall, the two PWC implementations, PWC_PSVM and PWC_KLR, are the best. The variance of PWC_KLR is smaller than that of PWC_PSVM for (test set) error while the variance of PWC_PSVM is smaller than that of PWC_KLR for (test set) NLL. The variances of PWC_PSVM and PWC_KLR are also smaller than those of other methods. Given below are the p-values, from the t-test of (test set) error on five datasets, of PWC_PSVM and PWC_KLR against the rest of the methods:

	PWC_PSVM				PWC_KLR				
	ABE	DNA	SAT	SEG	WAV	ABE	DNA	SAT	SEG	WAV
WTA_SVM	0.1613	0.1470	0.2604	1.5271e-6	1.4349e-4	0.6248	9.2922e-20	6.0812e-25	2.0127e-16	3.8722e-26
WTA_PSVM	0.2994	0.3629	0.0183	3.5621e-4	0.0016	0.8127	0.2274	0.7764	5.8390e-7	6.3759e-4
WTA_KLR	0.3001	0.2742	7.6409e-5	0.0570	0.1989	0.6858	0.0849	0.1823	1.1105e-6	0.0822
MWV_SVM	0.0124	0.4869	0.0054	0.5111	3.0141e-7	0.1892	0.1950	0.1432	0.0040	1.0058e-5
MWV_PSVM	0.0421	0.0375	0.0077	0.6686	0.6191	0.2977	0.0673	0.6182	0.0019	0.5838
MWV_KLR	0.0525	0.1572	2.2732e-4	0.9960	0.5539	0.2319	0.0027	0.3458	0.3473	0.6276
SMC1va	0.2785	0.4609	0.1310	0.0012	0.0011	0.6116	0.2159	0.9468	1.2190e-7	0.0045
SSMC1va	0.0656	0.7975	0.0026	0.0016	0.0014	0.4209	0.5673	0.7105	7.0694e-7	0.0041
SMC1v1	0.0011	0.1920	0.0120	0.0277	0.8451	0.0012	0.0924	0.1992	0.0016	0.8008
SSMC1v1	0.0410	0.3818	0.2655	0.1022	0.6799	0.1786	0.1423	0.9896	8.5907e-5	0.6631

To conclude, we can say the following. WTA_KLR seems to be the best WTA implementation among all one-versus-all classifiers. MWV_KLR seems to be the best MWV implementation among all one-versus-one classifiers. The two PWC implementations, PWC_PSVM and PWC_KLR are the best overall. The proposed soft-max combination methods with simplified combination function design, SSMC1va and SSMC1v1, are better than their 'regularized' counterparts, SMC1va and SMC1v1; they are also much simpler to design. The proposed soft-max combination methods provide new good ways of doing multi-category classification with binary classification methods, and more importantly, new ways of obtaining posteriori probability estimates from binary classifiers whose outputs are not probabilistic values.

References

1. Bauer, E., R. Kohavi, R.: An Empirical Comparison of Voting Classification Algorithms: Bagging, Boosting and Variants. Machine Learning, 36 (1999) 105–142.
2. Hastie, T., Tibshirani, R.: Classification by Pairwise Coupling. In: Jordan, M.I., Kearns, M.J., Solla, A.S. (eds.): Advances in Neural Information Processing Systems, Vol. 10. MIT Press (1998)
3. Liu, D.C., Nocedal, J.: On the Limited Memory Method for Large Scale Optimization. Mathematical Programming B, 45 (1989) 503-528
4. Platt, J.: Probabilistic Outputs for Support Vector Machines and Comparison to Regularized Likelihood Methods. In: Smola, A.J., Bartlett, P., Schölkopf, B., Schuurmans, D. (eds.): Advances in Large Margin Classifiers. MIT Press (1999) 61–74
5. Roth, V.: Probabilistic Discriminant Kernel Classifiers for Multi-class Problems. In: Radig, B., Florczyk, S. (eds.): Pattern Recognition-DAGM'01. Springer (2001) 246–253
6. Vapnik, V.: Statistical Learning Theory. Wiley, New York, NY (1998)
7. Weston, J., Watkins, C.: Multi-class Support Vector Machines. Technical Report CSD-TR-98-04, Royal Holloway, University of London, Egham, UK (1998)

A Sequential Scheduling Approach to Combining Multiple Object Classifiers Using Cross-Entropy

Derek Magee

University of Leeds, Leeds, UK
drm@comp.leeds.ac.uk

Abstract. A method for multiple classifier selection and combination is presented. Classifiers are selected sequentially on-line based on a context specific (data driven) formulation of classifier optimality. A finite subset of a large (or infinite) set of classifiers is used for classification resulting not only in a computational saving, but a boost in classification performance. Experiments were carried out using single class binary classifiers on multi-class classification problems. Classifier outputs are combined using a Bayesian approach and results show a significant improvement in classification accuracy over the AdaBoost.MH method.

1 Introduction

The combination of multiple classifiers to improve classification performance is currently a popular research area. It is often desirable (for computational, as well as accuracy, reasons) to select a subset of a large (or infinite) set of classifiers. Typical methods (such as boosting [1]) select a fixed subset of classifiers prior to classification, however the optimal approach to classification sometimes differs from this. As an example the game 'Animal, Vegetable, Mineral' (also known as '20 questions') demonstrates well an alternative approach to classification. One player picks an object, which is kept secret from the other. The second player asks a fixed number of questions in order to determine the identity of this object. The nature of these questions (especially in the latter stages of the game) is determined by the answers given to previous questions and the resultant hypotheses formulated by the second player. Applying boosting type methods to this problem would result in a fixed list of questions that would be asked by the player without reference to the answers of the previous questions. Experience tells us that this is not a good strategy for playing this game. In this paper we develop a strategy for automatic (object) classification inspired by the human method for playing this game and demonstrate that such a technique can outperform static boosting type algorithms in this domain also. The technique is (currently) limited to binary output classifiers, however the concept could potentially be extended to continuous output classifiers. It is advantageous to use single class classifiers as they require no re-training if an additional class is added to the problem.

The statistical learning algorithm presented in this paper is divided into two parts; 1) Selection of a finite set of classifiers from an infinite (or prohibitively

T. Windeatt and F. Roli (Eds.): MCS 2003, LNCS 2709, pp. 135–145, 2003.
© Springer-Verlag Berlin Heidelberg 2003

large) set, and 2) Learning an optimal classifier selection strategy, based on observations of a random selection strategy. Part 1) is based around a stochastic select and replace strategy. This relies on a multi-class extension of boosting (AdaBoost.MH [2]) to order, and assign a quality measure to, a selected sub-set of classifiers. Part 2) is based on a statistical analysis of the likelihood of a particular classifier resulting in a true positive classification given some knowledge obtained from the outputs of previously used classifiers. The cross-entropy between the probability distribution of a given parameter ($P(X)$) and that parameter conditioned on subsequent true positive classification ($P(X|T.P.)$) is used to select parameters / parameter values that give information about a likely true positive classification for a given classifier. This information is combined across multiple parameters and multiple classifiers to make a selection of the next classifier that is most likely to result in a true positive classification.

2   Background

The problem of multi-classifier combination may be divided into three main sub-problems; Multiple Classifier Training, Classifier Selection and Classifier Output Combination. In this paper we focus on Classifier Selection and Output Combination, however here we present a brief review of all three areas.

Multiple Classifier Training: Several methods have been presented for multiple classifier training given a single learning algorithm and a training/ example data set. These are essentially based around obtaining classifiers with different properties which, when combined, result in a better classification than using a single application of the learning algorithm. Perhaps the simplest of these is Bagging [3]. This involves training the learning algorithm with different subsets of the complete training set. This can lead to improved performance, however if the training set is not sufficiently large 'over-fitting' of the classifiers to the training data may occur. An alternative approach is boosting [1] (see section 2.1), in which the entire training set is used. The training set is re-weighted after each time a new classifier is trained to emphasise examples where past classification performance has been poor. Hierarchical Mixtures of Experts [4] is an architecture where all learning algorithms are trained simultaneously using the iterative Expectation Maximisation algorithm. The hierarchical architecture used means that individual instances of the learning algorithm work together, and may not be used as individual classifiers as in the case of Boosting or Bagging. Gating networks 'dynamically' change the way node outputs are combined based on the input data being classified.

Classifier Selection: Many methods for classifier combination ignore the classifier selection problem by using just a single machine learning algorithm and training it with different representations/subsets of a training set (e.g. Boosting and Bagging). Viola and Jones [5] point out classifier learning is analogous to classifier selection and many instances of classifier training may be replaced with an optimal classifier selection. This allows classifiers of many different forms to be combined using methods such as Boosting or Bagging. AdaBoost [1] (a form of boosting) ranks classifiers in order with an associated weight. This may be used to select an 'optimal' subset of classifiers from a finite set by picking the first N or putting a lower limit on the weight. It does not allow the selection of a subset of classifiers from an infinite set (see section 4). Mertz takes a data driven approach to classifier selection called 'Dynamic Selection' [6]. This involves selecting (and possibly weighting) classifiers based on the input being classified. This selection is based on cross-validation results from a training set. This is much in common with the Gating networks used in the Hierarchical Mixtures of Experts scheme described previously. Woods et al. [7] present an approach in which the single classifier used to perform classification is selected based on the output of a K-nearest neighbours classifier (to obtain the 'locally best' classifier). Kuncheva [8] presents a method where the output of a relatively general classifier is used to determine whether a more specific classifier is used. If so the outputs of the two (or more) classifiers are combined to give the final classification. Our work is along similar lines to that of Kuncheva, however classifier selection is based on learned statistics rather than heuristics, and the outputs of all previously used classifiers (plus estimated class probabilities) are used to select the next classifier to use.

Classifier Output Combination: Several approaches have been taken to the combination of multiple classification methods. Perhaps the simplest are voting and weighted voting [9]. In this scheme each classifier casts a vote (in weighted voting the votes of some classifier are worth more than others). The final classification is given as the class with the largest vote (essentially a sum rule). Empirical and theoretical work [10,11] has compared the sum rule with a product rule approach (essentially multiplying continuous classifier outputs). The conclusion was that essentially the product rule should perform better (as it more closely maps to Bayesian combination), however it is more sensitive to noise than the sum rule. This is because erroneous near zero outputs effect the result disproportionately. Alkoot and Kittler [10] present a method for improving product rule combination by dynamically putting a lower bound on classifier outputs. Mertz re-defines the classifier combination problem as nearest neighbour classification problem in a space calculated using Correspondence analysis [12]. This approach incorporates prior information about the nature of classifier outputs, which gives improved performance over voting approaches.

2.1 AdaBoost

The AdaBoost algorithm [1] is useful for multiple classifier training and also for multiple classifier selection [5] and combination. Empirical studies [13] suggest AdaBoost is a good baseline method to use (and make comparison with). In this paper an extension of the basic AdaBoost algorithm is used for classifier selection and ranking. The basic algorithm for selection using AdaBoost (taken from [5]) is as follows:

- Consider a set of labelled training examples $(x_1, y_1), ... (x_n, y_n)$, where $y_i = 0, 1$ for negative and positive examples respectively.
- Initialise data weights equal (or using some other sensible weighting).
- Repeat (until sufficient/all classifiers selected):

    1. Normalise the weights $w_i \leftarrow \frac{w_i}{\sum_{j=1}^{n} w_j}$
    2. select the classifier h_j with the lowest error $\epsilon = \sum_{i=1}^{n} w_i |h_j(x_i) - y_i|$.
    3. Update the weights $w_{i_{new}} = w_i \beta_t^{1-e_i}$ where $e_i = 0$ if example x_i is classified correctly, or $e_i = 1$ otherwise, and $\beta_t = \frac{\epsilon}{1-\epsilon}$

- The final classifier is:

$$h(x) = \begin{cases} 1 \sum_{t=1}^{T} \alpha_t h_t(x) \geq \frac{1}{2} \sum_{t=1}^{T} \alpha_t \\ 0 \text{ otherwise} \end{cases} \qquad \text{Where } \alpha_t = \log \frac{1}{\beta_t}$$

2.2   Multi-Class Extensions of AdaBoost

Adaboost [1] may be extended to multi-class classification scenarios in a number of ways. The simplest of these is AdaBoost.M1 (see [1]). In this method the classifier output (y_i) is now assumed to be one of a finite set of class labels. The original AdaBoost algorithm is then applied in much the same way as detailed in section 2.1. This method cannot be applied when multiple binary classifiers, with knowledge of only a single class, are applied to a multi-class classification problem. This is because the definition of 'classified correctly' is not easily specified in these cases. In fact there are four scenarios for a single binary classifier output (true positive, false positive, true negative and false negative). It is obvious that true positive and true negative classifications are 'correct' and false positive and false negative classifications are 'incorrect', however true positive classifications are more important than true negative classifications in actually determining to which class an object belongs. There is no mechanism within AdaBoost.M1 for encoding this and, as such, this approach can favour classifiers that are good at telling that an object is NOT of a certain class rather than that it IS of a particular class. This is a particular problem if there are a large number of classes.

An alternative multi-class extension of AdaBoost is AdaBoost.MH [2,1]. This is effectively a set of single class Adaboost implementations (one per class) that are combined to give a multi-class classification. This method is better suited to combining multiple single class classifiers, has theoretically less limitations [1], and appears to perform better than AdaBoost.M1 in our ad-hoc experiments. As presented in [2] AdaBoost.MH simply provides a yes/no classification of an object for each class (as with standard AdaBoost), however the classifications can also be ranked by considering the magnitude of the classification:

$$mag(t) = \frac{\sum_{t=1}^{T} \alpha_t h_t(x)}{\sum_{t=1}^{T} \alpha_t} \qquad (1)$$

3   A Novel Framework for Multiple Classifier Selection and Combination

The following sections detail a framework in which multiple classifiers are selected and combined in a novel way. Initially a finite set of classifiers are selected from a large or infinite set using a method based on AdaBoost.MH (section 4). Classifiers are selected sequentially on-line based on (statistical) context specific optimality criteria (section 5), and their outputs combined using a Bayesian approach (section 6).

4   Selection of Optimal Classifiers from an Infinite Set Using AdaBoost.MH

AdaBoost [1], and a number of related algorithms for classifier combination (Boosting, Bagging etc [13]), are based on training multiple instances of a learning mechanism (e.g. a neural network) using different weightings of a training data set to produce a set of 'weak' classifiers. When combined these can result in a more robust classification in comparison to using a single instance of the learning algorithm. Viola and Jones [5] suggested that classifier learning is analogous to classifier selection and presented a method in which a finite set of classification methods are selected (and combined) based on the AdaBoost principle. In practice there may be an infinite (or prohibitively large) set of possible classification methods, such as with our chosen example exemplars. Exemplars may be chosen from a large (if represented in a discrete space) or infinite (if represented in a continuous space) set. Classification using exemplars may also involve various thresholds which are usually continuous and thus come from an infinite set. For example the selection of a simple colour exemplar classifier would be as follows:

- Select a colour exemplar (i.e. A point in RGB or YUV colourspace)
- Select a distance (in colourspace) from exemplar threshold.
- Select a minimum (or maximum, or both) proportion of the object that should be within this threshold for a true classification

AdaBoost alone cannot select an optimal subset of classifiers from an infinite set. To achieve this we have implemented the novel stochastic select and evaluate process detailed below:

1. Select (randomly or stochastically) a subset of N_c classifiers from the infinite set of classifiers for each class
2. Use AdaBoost.MH to rank these classifiers (within each class) and assign a weight (α_t)
3. Replace classifiers with a weight below W_{min} (and the classifier with lowest weight)
4. Repeat from 2 until replacement doesn't occur for M iterations

5   Sequential Classifier Scheduling: Context Specific Classifier Selection

In section 1 we discussed the differences between the static approach to classification typical of algorithms such as AdaBoost, and the dynamic, context sensitive, approach taken by humans. The challenge is to replicate the approach taken by human beings without adding significant computational expense to the system. We pose the problem in a statistical framework as a problem of successively selecting the classifier that is most likely to result in a true positive classification. An alternative approach would be to select the classifier that is most likely to result in a correct classification, however in practice this results in a less efficient strategy as it is usually easier to pick a classifier that results in a true negative classification than a true positive one if the number of classes $\gg 2$.

We consider our knowledge so far (K_t) as a conditioning variable on the likelihood of a true positive outcome for a given classifier. This knowledge may consist of previous classifier outputs, estimates of class probabilities and any other relevant information. Our aim is to estimate the conditional density of a true positive classification for a given classifier (C_n) over all possible K_t:

$$P_{TP}(n) = P(C_n = \text{True positive (T.P.)}|K_t) \qquad (2)$$

Classifier scheduling / selection is then simply a matter of selecting the classifier with the highest value of $P_{TP}(n)$ as the next classifier to use. In our implementation we constrain each classifier to a single use (for each object classification) to retain classifier diversity.

There are standard techniques for estimating multivariate densities such as $P_{TP}(n)$ from training data, such as Gaussian Mixture models [14]. Alternatively a neural network could be used to approximate these densities. In practice modelling such a multivariate distribution is hard because 1) K_t may contain both discrete and continuous elements, and 2) The dimensionality of K_t may be high which can put a prohibitively high cost on the estimation and evaluation of $P_{TP}(n)$. In many cases human data fusion discounts the covariance terms between information and simply adds information, for example: "f it is orange AND spherical AND bounces it is likely to be a basketball". This is not true in every case, but we propose this is a good simplifying model. This allows the problem to be broken up into a set of low dimensional density estimation problems (one for each element of K_t) and a data fusion problem.

5.1   Cross-Entropy for Data Fusion

Estimation of $P_{TP}(n)$ (equation 2) directly is not possible as probabilities are not directly observable. Methods such as Expectation Maximisation [14] or histograms may be used, but an alternative is to reformulate the problem using Bayes rule as:

$$P_{TP}(n) = \frac{P(K_{t_m}|C_n = \text{T.P.})}{P(K_{t_m})} P(C_n = \text{T.P.}) \qquad (3)$$

As $P(C_n = \text{T.P.})$ is independent of K_{t_m} this may be regarded as a constant and so the information available from K_{t_m} depends only on $P(K_{t_m}|C_n = \text{T.P.})$ and $P(K_{t_m})$, which may be easily approximated from a training set.

Our approach to the data fusion problem is to use the cross-entropy between these distributions to formulate a weighted voting process between knowledge variables (K_{t_m}). Cross entropy (XE) is defined as the difference in information content between two probability densities (i.e. identical densities have zero cross-entropy), calculated as:

$$\text{XE(t,m)} = \int P(K_{t_m}|C_n = \text{T.P.}) \log \frac{P(K_{t_m}|C_n = \text{T.P})}{P(K_{t_m})} dx \qquad (4)$$

For discrete distributions (i.e. where K_{t_m} is the output of a particular binary classifier at step t) this simplifies to a sum. In our implementation distributions over continuous variables (i.e. where K_{t_m} is the estimated probability of the object being of a given class at step t, see section 6) are approximated by Gaussian distributions. It can be shown for 1D Gaussians (proof available on request) that cross-entropy may be calculated as:

$$XE(t,m) = \log_e \left(\frac{\sigma_p}{\sigma_q}\right) + \frac{\sigma_q^2 - \sigma_p^2}{2\sigma_p^2} + \frac{2\sigma_p^2 \bar{x}_q^2 + \sigma_q^2(\bar{x}_q^2 - \bar{x}_p^2 - \bar{x}_p \bar{x}_q)}{2\sigma_p^2 \sigma_q^2} \qquad (5)$$

Where:
$\bar{x}_q$ = The mean of the Gaussian approximation to $P(K_{t_m}|C_n = \text{T.P.})$
σ_q^2 = The std. deviation of the Gaussian approximation to $P(K_{t_m}|C_n = \text{T.P.})$
$\bar{x}_p$ = The mean of the Gaussian approximation to $P(K_{t_m})$
σ_p^2 = The std. deviation of the Gaussian approximation to $P(K_{t_m})$

5.2   Efficient Scheduling

As some knowledge variables (K_{t_m}) convey little or no information about the likely outcome of a given classifier an efficient approach is to only evaluate those K_{t_m} that are likely to add knowledge. In this paper we formulate this by ordering the knowledge variables for each classifier and selecting a fixed number (N) of K_{t_m}s as **pre-condition variables** for each classifier. An alternative approach would be to put a lower limit on the cross-entropy.

Classifier selection is performed by adding the cross-entropy information for all pre-condition variables K_{t_m} where K_{t_m} is better represented by the $P(K_{t_m}|C_n = \text{T.P.})$ distribution than the $P(K_{t_m})$ distribution over all classifiers (this may be implemented very efficiently for discrete and Gaussian distributions).

$$TCI(t,n) = \sum_{m=1}^{N} XE(t,m)S(m) \qquad (6)$$

Where: $S(m) = \begin{cases} 1 \; P(K_{t_m}|C_n = \text{T.P.}) > P(K_{t_m}) \\ 0 \; \text{otherwise} \end{cases}$

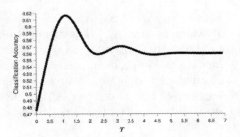

Fig. 1. Effect of varying constant T to include $P(C_n = \text{correct})$ information

The final selection may be based on the highest value of this 'total conditional information' (TCI) alone, however significantly better results may be achieved by considering the a-priori probability of a correct classification ($P(C_n = \text{correct})$) for each classifier as follows:

- Calculate the highest value of 'total conditional information' TCI_{max}
- Determine the subset of classifiers for which 'total conditional information' is within T of XE_{max}
- Select the classifier from this subset that has the highest value for $P(C_n = \text{correct})$

Note: $P(C_n = \text{correct})$ is estimated from a training data set. Figure 1 shows the effect of using different values of T for the basketball scene data used in section 7 (Note: majority voting is used to combine classifier outputs in this experiment, as this emphasises changes in T).

From figure 1 it is clear that there is an optimal value of T. This matches with intuition, as zero T makes the classifier selection decision entirely dependant on the 'total conditional information' and increasing T makes the decision increasingly dependant on the a-priori probability of a correct classification. An optimal selection is based on both these variables. For this example the optimum is around 1. This may be determined for an arbitrary data set using cross-validation.

6   Bayesian Classifier Output Combination

Bayesian combination is an alternative to the classifier output combination techniques detailed in section 2 when information is available about the likelihood of correct and incorrect classification for each classifier. The scheme detailed in this section is specific to binary output classifiers. Using Bayes law:

$$
\begin{aligned}
P(class|C_{out}) &= \frac{P(C_{out}|class)P(class)}{P(C_{out})} \\
&= \frac{P(C_{out}|class)}{P(C_{out}|class) + \frac{P(!class)}{P(class)}P(C_{out}|!class)}
\end{aligned}
\tag{7}
$$

Where: C_{out} is the outputs of the classifiers. For a binary classifier we can define:

$$P_{is_n} = \begin{cases} P_{TP_n} & \text{if classifier output is true/yes} \\ P_{FN_n} & \text{if classifier output is false/no} \end{cases} \quad (8)$$

$$P_{not_n} = \begin{cases} P_{FP_n} & \text{if classifier output is true/yes} \\ P_{TN_n} & \text{if classifier output is false/no} \end{cases} \quad (9)$$

The probabilities (P_{TP_n}, P_{FN_n}, P_{FP_n}, and P_{TN_n}) may be estimated by application of the classifiers to a training data set. Thus:

$$P(C_{out}|class) = \prod_{n=1}^{N} P_{is_n} \qquad P(C_{out}|!class) = \prod_{n=1}^{N} P_{not_n} \quad (10)$$

Substituting these into equation 7 gives:

$$P(class|C_{out}) = \frac{\prod_{n=1}^{N} P_{is_n}}{\prod_{n=1}^{N} P_{is_n} + \frac{P(!class)}{P(class)} \prod_{n=1}^{N} P_{not_n}} \quad (11)$$

$P(class)$, and thus $P(!class)$, may be estimated from a training set. $P(class)$ = $P(!class)$ = 0.5 is often a useful approximation. This allows probabilities that an object is of a given class to be estimated and compared across the set of possible classes. It should be noted that this approach differs from voting in that classifier output information is combined as a product rather than a sum. The use of a probabilistic formulation overcomes many of the shortcomings of product based combination discussed by Alkoot and Kittler [10] as zero values of P_{is_n} never occur in practice as this would imply a perfect classifier and thus a classifier combination scheme would not be necessary. (In practice the data may suggest a perfect or a perfectly imperfect classifier due to small sample size. In such circumstances P_{is_n} and P_{not_n} can be set to sensible defaults.).

7   Experimental Evaluation

For two data sets cross-validation tests were carried out. A set of classifiers was formed for each experiment using the method described in section 4. Training of our scheduling method and AdaBoost.MH was carried out on the same training set as used in this initial phase. The methods were then applied to unseen data and the relative performance compared. The first data set used was from a scene of three people playing basketball, tracked and segmented using an object tracker [15] (training set and test set sizes were 4x50 examples of 3 people plus ball). The second data set was the CogVis project image library (41 views/images each of 10 examples each of 8 classes - 3280 segmented images). A set of 80 leave-one-(example)-out tests were performed.

A set of colour exemplar classifiers (as described in section 4) was used to classify each segmented example by its colour distribution alone. Classification results for our method using Bayesian Output combination (see section 6) and simple voting are compared to those for AdaBoost.MH in figure 2.

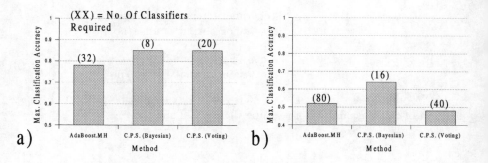

Fig. 2. Classification Accuracy of Cross-entropy Precondition Selection (C.P.S. - 10 Pre-conditions/classifier) with Bayesian and Simple Voting output combination, and AdaBoost.MH for a) Basketball scene data and b) CogVis Image Library Data

8   Discussion

The results presented in section 7 show the method of Cross-entropy Pre-condition selection (C.P.S.) results in an overall performance increase (of 7-12%) when compared to the static AdaBoost.MH method, and also that the maximum performance for C.P.S. requires a significantly lower number of classifiers than AdaBoost.MH. This is due to a more optimal subset of classifiers being selected dynamically in our method than the fixed set selected by AdaBoost.MH. However, the performance of C.P.S. reduces after an optimum peak as increasing numbers of poorer classifiers are used. In contrast, the drop in performance of AdaBoost.MH is near insignificant as later classifiers are associated with increasingly smaller weights. Bayesian combination outperforms simple voting combination, as this captures the information present in negative classifications as well as positive ones, as well as assigning greater significance to classifiers that are more likely to output a correct result. The disadvantage of C.P.S. over static scheduling methods, such as AdaBoost, is the extra computational expense involved at run-time. While this is small if small numbers of classifiers are used for classification, the complexity grows with approximately order 2. This is a significant extra cost when using larger numbers of classifiers, however for the examples we are currently using it is optimal to use a relatively small number of classifiers. For the future we hope to develop a method of combining the information from TCI and $P(C_n = \text{correct})$ (section 5.2) in an information theoretic way, and determine a way of automatically deciding on the number of classifiers to use (possibly on-line). Evaluation with more data sets and different classification methods is also the subject of current work.

Acknowledgements

This work is part of the EU Cognitive Vision Project (Contract IST-2000-29375).

References

1. Schapire, R.: The boosting approach to machine learning: An overview. In: Proc. MSRI Workshop on Nonlinear Estimation and Classification. (2002)
2. Schapire, R., Singer, Y.: Improved boosting algorithms using confidence-rated predictions. Machine Learning **37(3)** (1999) 297–336
3. Breiman, L.: Bagging predictors. Machine Learning **24** (1996) 123–140
4. Jordan, M.: Hierarchical mixtures of experts and the EM algorithm. Neural Computation **6** (1994) 181–214
5. Viola, P., Jones, M.: Rapid object detection using a boosted cascade of simple features. In: Proc. IEEE C.V.P.R. (2001) 1.511–1.518
6. Merz, C.: Dynamical selection of learning algorithms. In Fisher, D., Lenz, H., eds.: Learning from Data: Artificial Intelligence and Statistics, 5. (1996)
7. Woods, K., Kegelmeyer, W., Bowyer, K.: Combination of multiple classifiers using local accuracy estimates. IEEE Trans. on P.A.M.I. **19** (1997) 405–410
8. Kuncheva, L.: 'change-glasses' approach in pattern recognition. Pattern Recognition Letters **14** (1993) 619–623
9. Parhami, B.: Voting algorithms. IEEE Trans. on Reliability **43(4)** (1994) 617–629
10. Alkoot, F., Kitler, J.: Improving performance of the product fusion strategy. In: Proc. International Conference on Pattern Recognition. (2000)
11. Schiele, B.: How many classifiers do I need? In: Proc. I.C.P.R. (2002) 176–179
12. Merz, C.: Using correspondance analysis to combine classifiers. Machine Learning **0** (1997) 1–26
13. Bauer, E., Kohavi, R.: An empirical comparison of voting classification algorithms: Bagging, boosting and variants. Machine Learning **36** (1999) 105–142
14. Dempster, A., N. Laird, D.R.: Maximum likelihood from incomplete data via the EM algorithm. Journal of the Royal Statistical Society. Series B **39** (1977) 1–38
15. Magee, D.: Tracking multiple vehicles using foreground, background and motion models. In: Proc. ECCV: Statistical Methods in Video Processing. (2002) 7–12

Binary Classifier Fusion Based
on the Basic Decomposition Methods

Jaepil Ko and Hyeran Byun

Dept. of Computer Science, Yonsei Univ.
134 Shinchon-dong, Seodaemun-gu, Seoul 120-749, Korea
{nonezero,hrbyun}@cs.yonsei.ac.kr

Abstract. For a complex multiclass problem, it is common to construct the multiclass classifier by combining the outputs of several binary ones. The two basic methods for this purpose are known as one-per-class (OPC) and pairwise coupling (PWC) and their general form is error correcting output code (ECOC). In this paper, we review basic decomposition methods and introduce a new sequential fusion method based on OPC and PWC according to their properties. In the experiments, we compare our proposed method with each basic method and ECOC method. The experimental results show that our proposed method can improve significantly the classification accuracy on the real dataset.

1   Introduction

For a complex multiclass problem, it is common to construct the multiclass classifier by combining the outputs of several binary ones. They first decompose a multiclass problem into a set of separated two class problems and then reconstruct the outputs of the binary classifiers in order to solve the original polychotomy [1]. The problem complexity can be reduced through the decomposition of the polychotomy into less complex subproblems. The two basic methods for this purpose are known as one-per-class (OPC) and pairwise coupling (PWC) [2], and their general form is error correcting output code (ECOC) [3]. OPC separates one class from all other classes and PWC separates only two classes for each possible pair of classes. ECOC consists of several dichotomizers with class redundancy to get robustness in case some dichotomizers fail.

OPC suffers from the problems of having complex dichotomizers and PWC has a problem that nonsense outputs from unrelated dichotomizers are considered in the final decision. To improve the performance of PWC, Moreira and Mayoraz suggested PWC+OPC and correcting classifier (CC) [4]. In PWC+OPC, the outputs of PWC are weighted with the outputs of OPC. However, it failed to improve the classification accuracy because of combining all the outputs of PWC without regarding to the confidence level of OPC outputs. CC itself is a good decomposition method in the aspect of ECOC and showed significant improvement of classification accuracy in their experiments, however the method generates more complex dichotomies than that of OPC and needs much more training time than those of both OPC and PWC.

T. Windeatt and F. Roli (Eds.): MCS 2003, LNCS 2709, pp. 146–155, 2003.

In this paper, we review briefly the properties of OPC and PWC and propose a new combining method strongly motivated from PWC+OPC. The proposed method is to combine OPC and PWC subsequently according to the strength and weakness of them. The main difference of PWC+OPC and our proposed method is as follows. First, we consider only one machine instead of all the machines in PWC whereby the one machine is selected by the OPC outputs with the two highest confidence values. Second, we adopt support vector machines (SVM) as base binary learning machines. SVM is recently proposed by Vapnik [5] and is well known for optimal binary classifier that can give complex decision boundary.

The paper is organized as follows. We will briefly review output coding methods in section 2. In section 3, we will introduce sequential fusion of basic decomposition schemes. In the next section, we will show that our proposed method generates more accurate classification through the experiments on the real dataset. Finally, conclusions will be given in section 5.

2   Output Coding Methods

2.1   Fundamental

Learning machines implementing decomposition methods are composed of two parts; one is decomposition (encoding) and the other is reconstruction (decoding) [1]. For more detailed summary, refer to [6], [7].

In decomposition step, we generate decomposition matrix $D \in \{-1, 0, +1\}^{L \times K}$ that specify the K classes to train L dichotomizers, $f_1, ..., f_L$. The dichotomizer f_l is trained according to row $D(l, \cdot)$. If $D(l, k) = +1$, all examples of class k are positive and if $D(l, k) = -1$, all examples of class k are negative, and if $D(l, k) = 0$ none of the examples of class k participates in training of f_l [6]. The columns of D are called *codewords* [7].

In reconstruction step, a simple nearest-neighbor rule is commonly used. The class output is selected that minimizes the some similarity measure $S : R^L \times \{-1,0,1\}^L \rightarrow [0, \infty]$, between $f(\mathbf{x})$ and column $D(\cdot, k)$ [7].

$$class\_output = \arg \min_k S(f(\mathbf{x}), D(\cdot, k)) \qquad (1)$$

When the similarity measure is defined based on *margin* the method is called *margin decoding*. The *margin* of an example $(\mathbf{x}, y)$ with respect to f is defined as $y \cdot f(\mathbf{x})$ where $f(\mathbf{x})$ is a function of binary linear classifier like SVM and $\mathbf{x}$ is an input vector and y is the class label.

$$S(f(\mathbf{x}), D(\cdot, k)) = \sum_l f_l(\mathbf{x}) D(l, k) \qquad (2)$$

When the classifier outputs hard decision, $h(\mathbf{x}) \in \{-1, 1\}$, the method is called *hamming decoding*.

$$S_H(h(\mathbf{x}), D(\cdot, k)) = 0.5 \times \sum_l (1 - h_l(\mathbf{x}) D(l, k)) \tag{3}$$

Theoretical and experimental results indicate that *margin decoding* is better than *hamming decoding* [8].

2.2   One Per Class (OPC)

Each dichotomizer f_i has to separate a single class from all the others. Therefore, if we have K classes, we need K dichotomizers. In reconstruction step, *max-win* decoding is commonly used for this scheme, i.e., a new input $\mathbf{x}$ can be classified as class j such that f_j gives the highest value as we use similarity measure. In real applications, the decomposition of a polychotomy gives rise to complex dichotomies and we need in turn complex dichotomizers [7]. One of the merits of OPC is to train all the classes at once, however it can give complex dichotomies because it groups various classes into one, so the performance of OPC depends heavily on the performance of base classifier.

2.3   PairWise Coupling (PWC)

Each dichotomizer f_{ij} is to separate a class i from a class j for each possible pair of classes therefore a dichotomizer is trained on the samples related to the two classes only. The merit is that simpler dichotomy can be made, but the demerit is when we consider decoding procedure. If an input $\mathbf{x}$ which belongs neither to class i nor to class j is fed into f_{ij}, nonsense output can come out [4]. As the number of classes increases, the performance becomes lowered by the nonsense outputs. The number of dichotomizer is $_KC_2 = K(K-1)/2$ and hamming decoding is frequently used. To reduce decoding time, *tree-structured* decoding is applied in [9].

2.4   Correcting Classifier (CC)

Correcting classifier is proposed in [4] to handle the problem of nonsense output of PWC. Each dichotomizer f_{ij} is to separate two classes i and j from the other classes for each possible pair of classes, so the number of dichotomizer is the same as PWC. The performance of this method shows significant improvement than OPC or PWC in the experiments on some dataset in UCI repository [10]. This is because of its error correcting ability based on large hamming distance, $\Delta = 2(K-2)$. The disadvantage is that all the data is used for the training of each dichotomizer, as a result it needs a considerable amount of total training time.

On the other side, PWC+OPC method is also referenced in [4] to handle the nonsense output problem of PWC. However, it performs worse than PWC for most of the dataset. In this scheme, the class probability of a class i is estimated as follows:

$$
\begin{bmatrix}
+1 & -1 & -1 & -1 \\
-1 & +1 & -1 & -1 \\
-1 & -1 & +1 & -1 \\
-1 & -1 & -1 & +1
\end{bmatrix}
\qquad
\begin{bmatrix}
+1 & -1 & 0 & 0 \\
+1 & 0 & -1 & 0 \\
+1 & 0 & 0 & -1 \\
0 & +1 & -1 & 0 \\
0 & +1 & 0 & -1 \\
0 & 0 & +1 & -1
\end{bmatrix}
\qquad
\begin{bmatrix}
+1 & +1 & -1 & -1 \\
+1 & -1 & +1 & -1 \\
+1 & -1 & -1 & +1 \\
-1 & +1 & +1 & -1 \\
-1 & +1 & -1 & +1 \\
-1 & -1 & +1 & +1
\end{bmatrix}
$$

      (a) OPC   (b) PWC   (c) CC

Fig. 1. Decomposition matrix of OPC, PWC and CC schemes for $K=4$, Each row corresponds to one dichotomy and each column to one class. In (a) and (c), all the columns are filled with 1 or -1 for each dichotomy; all the classes are trained for each dichotomy. In (b) one dichotomy involves two classes except for the classes with elements of value 0.

$$
p_i = \frac{2}{K(K-1)} \sum_{j \neq i} p_{ij} \cdot (q_i + q_j) \tag{4}
$$

where, p_{ij} assumes that an input **x** is in class i or in class j and computed from PWC and q_i assumes that an input **x** is in class i and computed from OPC.

From (4), we can see that all the outputs of PWC are still involved in computing class probability with regard to q_i and q_j. However, q_i and q_j might have low confidence because OPC make complex dichotomies, and low confidence value cannot have any information. The decomposition matrix of OPC, PWC and CC schemes, for $K = 4$, are given in Fig. 1.

3   Sequential Fusion of Output Coding Methods

OPC and PWC are frequently used as a decomposition method for multiclass problem. However, they have their own problems due to their intrinsic decomposition algorithm. OPC suffers from the problems of having complex dichotomizers and PWC has a problem that nonsense outputs from unrelated dichotomizers are considered in the final decision.

In decoding stage, if a simple nearest-neighbor rule with hamming distance is used, then OPC is more apt to generate uncertain codes that do not match exactly the code words in decoding matrix than PWC is. Uncertain codes correspond to uncertain regions in Fig. 2. OPC has more uncertain regions than PWC, and uncertain outputs of OPC are another useless information as well as nonsense outputs of PWC in final decision.

Based on the ground explained above, we propose a new decoding scheme that only uses certain outputs of OPC and PWC by combining OPC and PWC subsequently. We find two classes according to the two largest confident outputs of OPC on a given input, and then consult on a proper PWC. The framework of our proposed method is illustrated in Fig. 3.

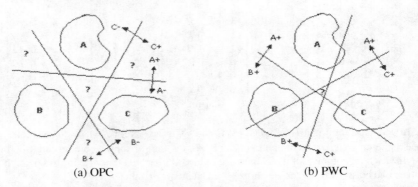

(a) OPC   (b) PWC

Fig. 2. 2D dataset with 3 classes: The questions marks indicate the uncertain regions. OPC has more uncertain regions than PWC

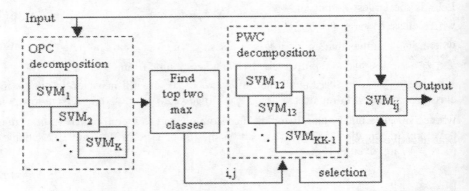

Fig. 3. Reconstruction flow of our proposed method. In final class decision, only one relative machine training class i and class j is used. Class i and class j are determined by OPC outputs with the two largest confidence values

The proposed strategy can be supported by the *error bound* concept. The training error bound of OPC and PWC are presented respectively in [7]:

$$\varepsilon_K = K\varepsilon_b \tag{5}$$

$$\varepsilon_K \leq (K-1)\varepsilon_b \tag{6}$$

where ε_b is the error rate of dichotomizers that is average of the number of training examples misclassified and K is the number of classes. The confidence level of the complex dichotomizer might be lower than that of simple dichotomizer. In other words, since each PWC dichotomizer is trained on only two classes, one would expect that classification error rate of PWC is lower than the corresponding error rate of OPC. This agrees with the fact that the bound in (6) is lower than in (5) [7].

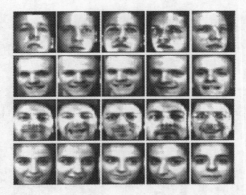

Fig. 4. Example of normalized face images in the ORL face images

Let s_1 is the largest output and s_2 is the second largest output among $\{f_1(\mathbf{x}),...,f_L(\mathbf{x})\}$ where class $c_i = \arg_i\{s_1 = f_i(\mathbf{x})\}$ and class $c_j = \arg_j\{s_2 = f_j(\mathbf{x})\}$, then final decision is done as (7):

$$class\_output = \begin{cases} c_i & if\ SVM_{ij} \geq 0 \\ c_j & if\ SVM_{ij} < 0 \end{cases} \tag{7}$$

where SVM_{ij} is a binary classifier that is trained with class i as positive class and class j as negative class.

4   Experimental Results

We will use *satimage* from the dataset presented in [10] and the ORL face dataset to show the performance comparison of our proposed method and the representative existing methods. We choose satimage because of its high dimension and large number of samples and it is divided into two parts; one is for training and the other is for testing.

The ORL dataset is one of the popular public datasets in face recognition. The image sets consist of 400 images, ten images per each individual. Each image for one person differs from each other in lighting, facial expression and pose. We get the final training and testing dataset by applying image preprocessing and principal component analysis (PCA). That procedure is presented in FERET, face recognition evaluation protocol [11]. Fig. 4 shows examples of the normalized face images after the pre-processing.

The characteristics of these datasets are given in Table 1. The datasets for SVM, base learner we adopt, are shifted using the mean and scaled by their standard deviation. We used SMOBR that is one of the SVM implementations [12]. We performed SVM by radial basis function (RBF) kernel with various C that is the trade-off between margin maximization and training error minimization.

Table 1. Dataset characteristics

Dataset	# set	# train	# test	# class	# dim
satimage	1	4435	2000	6	36
ORL face	5	200	200	40	50

We made datasets for the ORL face images by dividing 400 images into two equal parts; 5 images per person for training and the other 5 images for testing randomly and repeat it five times.

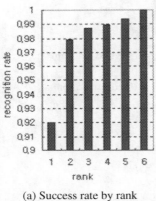
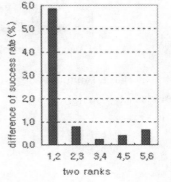

(a) Success rate by rank   (b) Difference of success rate between ranks

Fig. 5. Test on the satimage dataset using OPC with margin decoding, In (b) difference of success rate between rank 1 and 2 is 5.9%

4.1   Experiments on Difference of Success Rate between Ranks

Our proposed method considers only the highest and second highest ranked candidates. It means that the right answer should be one of those two candidates. Fig. 5 shows the success rate according to the rank change on the satimage dataset. OPC with margin decoding and RBF kernel with $\sigma=0.2$ and $C=8$ were used for this experiment. We can see that success rate increases as the rank increases in Fig. 5(a). Moreover, shown in Fig. 5(b), the difference of success rate between rank *1* and rank *2* is distinguishable from other pairs

The similar results from the test on the ORL dataset are given in Table 2. The averaged results are collected with the same parameters; OPC with margin decoding and RBF kernel with $\sigma=0.8$ and $C=2$. We also see that the difference of recognition rate between rank *1* and rank *2* is distinguishable.

From the results, we show that most of the right answer is the top two candidates in OPC with margin decoding.

4.2   Performance Comparison

In this section, we compare the recognition performance of OPC, PWC, CC and our proposed method. OPC and PWC are basic decomposition method and CC is one of

Table 2. Preliminary Test on the ORL dataset

Rank	Average recognition rate	Variance	Difference of recognition rate between ranks (%)
1	0.93	0.00015	-
2	0.97	0.00017	**3.9**
3	0.98	0.00013	0.9
4	0.98	0.00011	0.6
5	0.99	0.00004	0.4
6	0.99	0.00005	0.4
7	0.99	0.00003	0.1
8	0.99	0.00003	0.2
9	1.00	0.00001	0.2
10	1.00	0.00002	0.1

Table 3. Classificaton / Recognition Accuracy Rate (%)

Method (# machines)	Satimage dataset		ORL dataset	
	Hamming decoding (C, σ)	Margin decoding (C, σ)	Hamming decoding (C, σ)	Margin decoding (C, σ)
OPC (6, 40)	90.30	92.05 (8, 0.2)	68.50	93.40 (2, 0.8)
PWC (12, 780)	92.00 (3, 0.3)	91.70	91.70 (5, 1.0)	88.20
CC (12, 780)	91.50	92.00	90.50	93.60
Our Method (18, 820)	**97.40**		**96.00**	

The number of machines is for satimage and ORL respectively.

the representative ECOC methods. We calculated the recognition rate varying C from 1 to 10 and RBF kernel with dispersion from 0.2 to 1.2. For satimage, we choose the best recognition rate among them and for ORL dataset we tested on the 5 datasets with the same parameters for each dataset and averaged the results. We got the results of our proposed method by combining OPC with margin decoding and PWC with hamming decoding using the best parameters for each method. We summarized the results in Table 3.

Our proposed method shows significantly better performance than OPC, PWC, and CC, which is representative ECOC method.

The main difference between OPC and PWC is the number of classes that are concerned in training. In OPC, all the classes are trained for one machine, on the other hand just two classes are trained for one machine in PWC. When we compare the two methods, in case of hamming decoding, PWC shows significantly better performance than OPC, but in case of margin decoding, OPC shows better performance. Overall OPC with margin decoding shows slightly better performance than PWC with hamming decoding.

Each machine in OPC and CC trains all the classes at once. In this case, CC shows significantly better performance than OPC in hamming decoding like PWC due to its large number of machines, however when it comes to margin decoding, the performance of the two is almost the same regardless of the quite difference of the number of machines.

5   Conclusions

OPC and PWC are frequently used as a decomposition method for multiclass problem. However, they have their own problems due to their intrinsic decomposition algorithm. OPC suffers from the problems of having complex dichotomizers and PWC has a problem that nonsense outputs from unrelated dichotomizers are considered in the final decision. To solve the problem, we proposed a new sequential fusion method based on OPC and PWC according to their properties.

In the experiments, we showed that we had margin for improvement in OPC method. Our proposed method is one of the strategies that use the margin.

From the comparison results, we showed promising results of our proposed method to solve the complex multiclass problem like face recognition. Face recognition suffers from small number of training samples for their high dimensional feature space. In such a case, OPC can be preferred for its advantage of training all the samples at once. However, it also causes the problem of generating complex dichotomy. PWC can be effectively used for this situation.

We also showed that PWC suited with hamming decoding and OPC suited with margin decoding.

The disadvantage of our methods is to require more binary machines and more elaboration for selecting suitable model parameters in both PWC and OPC.

Acknowledgments

This work was supported in part by Biometrics Engineering Research Center, (KOSEF).

References

1. Valentini G.: Upper bounds on the training error of ECOC-SVM ensembles. Technical Report TR-00-17, DISI-Dipartimento di Informatica Scienze dell Informazione (2000)
2. Hastie T., Tibshirani R.: Classification by Pairwise Coupling. Advances in Neural Information Processing Systems, Vol. 10, MIT Press (1998)

3. Dietterich T. G., Bakiri G.: Solving Multiclass Learning Problems via Error-Correcting Output Codes. Journal of Artificial Intelligence Research, Vol. 2 (1995) 263-286
4. Moreira M., Mayoraz E.: Improved Pairwise Coupling Classification with Correcting Classifiers. Proc. of European Conference on Machine Learning (1998) 160-171
5. Vapnik, V. N.: Statistical Learning Theory. John Wiley & Sons, New York (1998)
6. Masulli F., Valentini G.: Comparing Decomposition Methods for Classification. Proc. of International Conference on Knowledge-based Intelligent Engineering Systems & Allied Technologies, Vol. 2 (2000) 788-791
7. Klautau A., Jevtic N., Orlisky A.: Combined Binary Classifiers with Applications to Speech Recognition. Proc. of International Conference on Spoken Language Processing (2002) 2469-2472
8. Allwein E. L., Schapire R. E., Singer Y.: Reducing Multiclass to Binary: A Unifying Approach for Margin Classifiers. Proc. of International Conference on Machine Learning (2000) 9-16
9. Guo G., Li S. Z., and Chan K. L.: Support vector machines for face recognition. Image and Vision Computing, Vol. 19 (2001) 631-638
10. Merz C. J. and Murphy P. M.: UCI repository of machine learning databases. Department of Computer Science, University of California at Irvine, (1998).
http://ics.uci.edu/~mlearn/mlrepository.html
11. Phillips P. J., Moon H., Rizvi S. A., Rauss P. J.: The FERET evaluation methodology for face-recognition algorithms. IEEE Trans. PAMI, Vol. 22, No. 10 (2000) 1090-1104
12. Almedia M. B.: SMOBR-A SMO program for training SVM. Univ. of Minas Gerais, Dept. of Electrical Engineering. http://www.cpdee.ufmg.br/~barros/

Good Error Correcting Output Codes
for Adaptive Multiclass Learning

Elizabeth Tapia[1], José Carlos González[2], and Javier García-Villalba[3]

[1] Department of Electrical Engineering, National Univ. of Rosario, Argentina
etapia@eie.fceia.unr.edu.ar
[2] Department of Telematics Engineering - Technical Univ. of Madrid, Spain
jgonzalez@dit.upm.es
[3] Department of Computer Systems and Programming - Complutense Univ. of Madrid, Spain
javiergv@sip.ucm.es

Abstract. In recent work, we introduced a generalization of ECOC learning under the theory of recursive error correcting codes. We named it RECOC (Recursive ECOC) learning. If long output codewords are allowed, as in the case of problems involving a large number of classes, standard recursive codes such as LDPC or Turbo can be used. However, if the number of classes is moderated, neither good LDPC nor Turbo codes might exist due to the small block lengths involved. In this paper, RECOC learning based on the recently introduced ensemble of Product Accumulated codes is analyzed. Due to their native data storage oriented design, smaller block lengths are allowed. In addition, because of their simplicity, all key concepts regarding RECOC learning can be easily explained.

1 Introduction

There is a strong Machine Learning community consensus [1] that good Error Correcting Output Codes (ECOC) [2] should resemble random ones. In addittion, since standard ECOC codes construction is NP-hard [3], one should not expect further generalizations of ECOC learning by keeping the paradigm changeless. In fact, past ECOC developments are far from being coherent. Both ad-hoc codes (standard ECOC), and algebraic codes (BCH codes used in [4]) have been used. Furthermore, completely random codes, dense and sparse, have been used [5]. In all cases and disregarding the underlying coding structure (none, algebraic, dense or sparse random), trivial[1] decoding algorithms based on Minimum Hamming Distance have been used. It should be noted, however, that the important fact about the ECOC framework is that coding theory results can be used for explaining and improving ECOC behavior. A first attempt in this line of research can be found in [6].

In recent work [7][8], we introduced a generalization of ECOC learning under the theory of recursive codes [9]. We named it Recursive ECOC (RECOC) learning. Roughly speaking, recursive codes are codes constructed from component subcodes. Subcodes might be weak when working on their own, but strong when working alto-

---

[1] We rule-out brute-force search decoding algorithms

T. Windeatt and F. Roli (Eds.): MCS 2003, LNCS 2709, pp. 156–165, 2003.
© Springer-Verlag Berlin Heidelberg 2003

gether...RECOC learning reduces multiclass problems to multiclass ones. Reduction is achieved by means of recursive error correcting codes with each component subcode defining a local multiclass learner. In addition at each local multiclass learner, reduction proceeds until binary learning is required. It might be argued that if at the end binary learning is performed, a multiclass-to-multiclass reduction might be useless in view of the standard ECOC approach. It should be noted, however, that local multiclass learners are constrained to follow some rules of consistency, commonly expressed in a coding theory language. Therefore, despite of local binary learners' weaknesses, learning as a whole can still be good.

Recursive codes allow a "regulated" degree of randomness in their core design. Randomness is the holy grail of Shannon's coding theory. A random code is the ideal way to protect information against noise. However, it is also the most expensive way to do it. By preserving native coding structures in component subcodes and allowing some degree of randomness, recursive codes permit crucial but efficient soft iterative decoding algorithms to be used. In ECOC learning terms, soft iterative decoding implies iterative error adaptative learning.

RECOC learning for classification problems involving a large number of classes can be solved by means of standard recursive codes such as LDPC [10] or Turbo [11]. However, finding good LDPC or Turbo codes becomes difficult with small block lengths. In this paper, we present a RECOC learning approach based on recently discovered ensemble of Product Accumulated (PA) [12] codes. Their high channel rates[2] (at least 0.5) and relative short codewords turn them suitable for classification problems involving a modest number of classes. We give experimental evidence, supported in well-known coding theory results, that RECOC learning based on PA codes is highly competitive even when resting on simple Decision Stump binary learners. Similarly to all RECOC counterparts, RECOC PA learning subtleties can be explained by means of graphical models [13].

The remainder of this paper is organized as follows. In section 2, we revisit RECOC learning models. In section 3, we present a RECOC instance based on PA codes. In section 4, we present experimental results. Finally, in Section 5 conclusions and further work are presented.

2   RECOC Learning

The ECOC algorithm is applicable to the supervised learning of target concepts c belonging to target classes $C : X \rightarrow Y$, $|Y| = M \succ 2$, i.e. non-binary classification problems. Let $E : Y \rightarrow \Theta$ be an output-encoding mapping based on some Θ recursive-coding scheme. Recursive error correcting codes, can be modeled by means of Tanner graphs [14] . A Tanner graph is a bipartite graph i.e. only two type of nodes exist and there is no connection between nodes of the same type. Variable nodes model codeword symbols. Check nodes model coding constraints on subsets of variable nodes. Each check node can be understood as a component subcode. Undirected edges are put between check nodes and participating variable nodes. Clearly, the Sin-

---

[2] We want to transmit blocks of k source symbols in presence of noise. We pack them into blocks of n symbols, n > k. Hence, we are transmitting information at a channel rate r= k/n

gle Parity Check[3] (SPC) code is the simplest coding constraint that we can impose. Because component subcodes are low complexity error correcting codes, they are easy to decode. Overall decoding of recursive codes is approximated by means of a message-passing algorithm between decoding algorithms on component subcodes. In **Fig. 1.**, a simple recursive code built from two SPC component subcodes $S_j, 0 \leq j \leq 1$, on codeword bits $c_i, 0 \leq i \leq 5$, is shown.

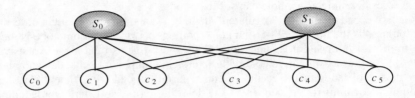

Fig. 1. Tanner graph for a simple recursive code built from two component subcodes

Now, let us consider how Tanner graphs can be used for the design of distributed ECOC learning strategies when an underlying recursive code is used. Without loss of generality, let us consider the output encoding of $M = 2^k$ classes by means of binary linear block codes (n, k, d)[4]. For the sake of simplicity, let $M = 2^{16}$ so that any linear block code with $k = 16$ and satisfying standard ECOC constraints will suffice. Assume we could not find such a good block code but found one for $k' = 4$, $M' = 2^4$. For the sake of simplicity, let us assume such code be a $(n'= 7, k'= 4, d'= 3)$[5] Hamming code. Now, we must tackle the following, purely constructivist, problem

The Recursive Learning Problem: *Let c be a target concept, $c \in C : X \rightarrow Y, |Y| = M = 2^k \succ 2$. Let S, $|S| = m$, be a training sample. Let $\theta_i : \{0,1\}^{k'(i)} \rightarrow \{0,1\}^{n'(i)}$, $k'(i) \prec k$, $n'(i) \prec n$, $k \prec n$, $0 \leq i \leq r-1$, a set of output encoding mappings. Construct an n-ECOC algorithm A in terms of the $n'(i)$- ECOC algorithms A_i arising from S and $[\theta_i]$, $0 \leq i \leq r-1$.*

To some extent, the recursive learning problem captures the greedy way we proceed when learning difficult concepts. We argue that a nice solution for the recursive learning problem can be obtained by performing recursive error correcting output encoding. By doing so, simpler ECOC versions of the target learning problem can be obtained at the encoding stage. Similarly, a combination mechanism on the set of available ECOC solutions can be obtained at a recursive decoding stage.

---

[3] Sum mod 2 of involved bits equals zero
[4] In standard coding notation, it refers to block codes with codeword length n, each codeword carrying k informative bits and Minimum Hamming Distance d
[5] $(n = 2^r - 1, k = 2^r - 1 - r, d = 3)$

A simple way for constructing an $(n,k = 16,d)$ block code from $(n' = 7, k' = 4,$ $d' = 3)$ Hamming subcodes is the product form [9]. Blocks of $k = 16$ information bits are arranged in matrices of four rows and four columns. Both rows and columns, each one carrying $k' = 4$ informative bits, are Hamming encoded (see Fig. 2.). The resulting product code is $(n = 49, k = 16, d = 9)$ block code. Its minimum distance $d = 9$, can be derived using graph theory based arguments. In its construction, exactly 7×7 simple $(n' = 7, k' = 4, d' = 3)$ Hamming subcodes are used. General product $(n_1 \cdot n_2, k_1 \cdot k_2, d_1 \cdot d_2)$ codes can be constructed taking n_1 Hamming (n_2, k_2, d_2) subcodes and n_2 Hamming (n_1, k_1, d_1) subcodes.

$$
\begin{array}{c}
Block \\
Data
\end{array}
\left[
\begin{array}{cccc|ccc}
1 & 0 & 1 & 1 & 0 & 0 & 0 \\
0 & 0 & 0 & 0 & 0 & 0 & 0 \\
1 & 0 & 1 & 1 & 0 & 0 & 0 \\
\hline
1 & 0 & 1 & 1 & 0 & 0 & 0 \\
0 & 0 & 0 & 0 & 0 & 0 & 0 \\
0 & 0 & 0 & 0 & 0 & 0 & 0 \\
0 & 0 & 0 & 0 & 0 & 0 & 0
\end{array}
\right]
\begin{array}{c}
Horizontal \\
Encoding
\end{array}
$$

$$
\begin{array}{c}
Vertical \\
Encoding
\end{array}
\qquad\qquad\qquad\qquad\qquad
\begin{array}{c}
Parity\ on \\
Parity
\end{array}
$$

Fig. 2. Product codeword (49, 16, 9) from 7×7 component Hamming (7,4,3) codes

For our learning problem involving $M = 2^{16}$ classes, output coding by means of an $(n = 49, k = 16, d = 9)$ product code implies ECOC learning based on $n = 49$ binary learners. Alternatively, it also implies 7×7 ECOC learning instances, each of them involving only $M' = 2^4$ classes and requiring only $n' = 7$ binary learners. Hence, recursive coding is one solution for our recursive-learning problem. Its formulation leads us to the Recursive ECOC (RECOC) learning approach.

RECOC learning algorithms arise when observing that at the ECOC prediction stage only noisy versions of transmitted binary concepts are available. If binary predictions are independent, it follows that RECOC learning can be analyzed as a decoding problem over an *additive Discrete Memoryless Channel* [15]. In addition, required channel statistics can be gathered at the ECOC training stage.

The existence of recursive codes of the product type above provides a nice theoretical solution for the recursive learning problem. However, it does not guarantee the fundamental ECOC requirement about rows and columns Hamming distances. Roughly speaking, it only guarantees good separations between rows (codewords) disregarding column separation issues. In the worst case of identical columns, identical binary learners might be obtained and hence secure dependency between their errors. As a result, ECOC training error performance [6] will be seriously degraded. However, coding theory deserves a surprising notice for our thoughts: *recursive codes can be enriched with randomness!* Furthermore, these are the codes coding theorists have been searching for almost the last 50 years. C. Berrou *et al* [16] discovered them by 1993 when presenting the amazing Turbo codes. Regarding our learning framework, Turbo output encoding might be feasible only for high dimensional output spaces, where the so-called interleaver gain [11] could be strongly expressed. At relative low dimensional output spaces, we found the class of Product Accumulated Codes (PA) proposed by Li *et al* [12], as a good researching alternative. These codes might be also a good choice for ECOC learning with bounded redundancy (a constraint that may arise in real time processing applications). Due to the high channel rates involved by PA codes (at least 0.5), the number of redundant binary learners cannot be greater than k.

3   RECOC Learning Based on Product Accumulated Codes

Product Accumulated codes are a class of simple, soft decodable, high rate codes based on SPC Turbo Product codes. Information to be encoded, binary expansions of class labels must be first arranged into a matrix of p rows and t columns. Thus, at a first attempt only classification problems involving $M \leq 2^{p \times t}$ classes $(k = p \times t)$ can be considered. Initially, a round of p SPC encoding operations is computed on each of input data row so that a p-column vector is obtained. Following the well-known Turbo approach, the same input data matrix is passed through an interleaver[6] π_1. A second round of p SPC encoding operations is performed again so that a new p-column vector is obtained. The concatenation of the input data matrix with the two p-columns of SPC bits defines a SPC Turbo Product codeword with length $n = p \times (t + 2)$. Finally, a serial concatenation with a rate *one* inner code through a new interleaver π_2 is performed.

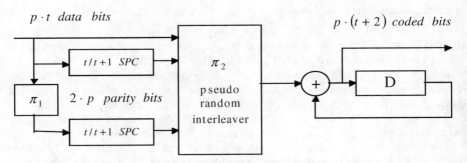

Fig. 3. A Product Accumulated encoder. The D unit stands for bit delay

The introduction of interleaving stages gives SPC product codes the required degree of randomness so that they become suitable candidates for the design of good RECOC learning algorithms. Clearly, PA codes work at channel rates $r = \dfrac{k}{n} = \dfrac{t}{t+2}$. Because the minimum t value is two, it follows that PA codes allow only channel rates $r \geq 0.5$. In RECOC learning terms, such high channel rates imply stronger re-

---

[6] A device which permutes the order of matrix elements in a pseudorandom way

quirements on underlying binary learners in order to keep learning generalization error within acceptable limits.

Decoding of PA codes does not differ from the way we decode general recursive codes. We apply a message-passing algorithm on the associated Tanner graph. The message-passing algorithm is a generalization of Pearl's Belief Propagation algorithm in loopy Bayesian networks [17]. We recall here that Pearl's belief propagation algorithm is an artificial intelligence development, suitable for modeling human inference in presence of distributed sources of knowledge. Loopy belief propagation results in coding theory should not be confused with those developed in the Artificial Intelligence field [18]. Coding theory results are mainly limited to the binary case and rely on the presence of certain combinatorial properties in the underlying loopy Bayesian network or Tanner graph.

For the sake of brevity, we refer the interested reader to [12] and references therein for details of iterative decoding of PA codes. For purposes of RECOC PA implementation, we only need to characterize the additive Discrete Memoryless Channel at the end of which, binary weak learners $WL_i, 0 \le i \le n-1$, make their noisy predictions. Under this learning-coding theory setting, binary learners' training errors $p_i, 0 \le i \le n-1$, are a good approximation for true probabilities of bit error at bit positions $0 \le i \le n-1$. Following is the algorithmic formulation of RECOC PA learning.

RECOC PA Algorithm

Input

$BSpan_M : Y \to \{0,1\}^k$, k bits per input label in $Y = \left\{1,..., M \le 2^k\right\}$

PA encoder $t = 2$, $k = p \times t$, $n = p \times (t+2)$

Training Sample S, $|S| = m_S$, Binary Weak Learner WL

Number of iterations I for BP and T for inner boosting

Processing

$RECOC(S, PA, T, WL_0, \ldots, WL_{n-1}, p_0, \ldots, p_{n-1})$

Output

$h_f(\boldsymbol{x}) = BSpan_M^{-1}(BP(PA, \boldsymbol{x}, I, T, WL_0, \ldots, WL_{n-1}, p_0, \ldots, p_{n-1}))$

End

The RECOC procedure performs the standard ECOC encoding-training stage based on PA codes with the additional computation of training error responses p_i achieved by binary learners $WL_i, 0 \le i \le n-1$. Binary learners are improved with T

inner AdaBoost [19] boosting steps. A prediction on an unseen feature vector x requires an iterative decoding stage on a received noisy codeword under the assumption of a given Discrete Memoryless Channel. The received noisy codeword is provided by the set of binary predictions WL_i, $0 \leq i \leq n-1$, on the given x. The Discrete Memoryless Channel is characterized by probabilities $p_i, 0 \leq i \leq n-1$. The decoding stage is performed by the well-known Belief Propagation (BP) algorithm based on at most I iterative steps. As a result, k binary predictions are estimated. A concluding hypothesis is obtained by application of the inverse $BSpan_M^{-1}$ to the latter binary predictions. Note that if $M \prec 2^k$, the latter step might fail because of an unrecognized k-binary pattern. In such cases, a random decision could be applied.

Before moving on to experimental results, we would like to make a few remarks about the expected performance of RECOC PA learning. Consistent with their recursive coding nature, performance of PA codes does not depend on the Minimum Hamming distance between codewords [20]. Roughly speaking, the code may have low weight codewords, and hence poor error correcting capabilities in classical coding theory, but with low probability of appearance, so that on the whole it might behave as good error correcting code. From a coding theory point of view of the learning problem, we could conjecture a negligible fraction of knowledge concentrated in the neighborhood of low weight codewords.

4   Experimental Results

Learning algorithms were developed using the public domain Java WEKA library [21]. Therefore, AdaBoost and Decision Stump (DS) implementation details can be fully determined from WEKA documentation. PA coding and decoding routines were implemented based on [12].

Learning performance was measured by the 10-fold crossvalidation error for I=1, 30 iterative decoding steps and T=10, 50, 100 AdaBoost steps for DS learners and T=1, 10, 50 for C4.5 learners. For purposes of fair comparisons, experimental results are shown only for five small datasets regarding the limitations of boosting C4.5 learners on big datasets[7]. Results confirm that RECOC PA learning can tackle learning complexity. Clear learning improvements are observed when boosting or improving base binary learners i.e. error adaptation holds. Similarly, improvements are observed when performing iterative decoding i.e. greedy learning is achieved in the temporal domain. For questions of stability of iterative decoding algorithms, a threshold value of 0.01 was assumed for all binary-training errors characterizing the underlying channel. This fact is particularly important with binary learners achieving tiny binary training errors. Belief propagation algorithms cannot manage them. Hence, abnormal learning behavior might be observed i.e. iterations might increase the training error instead of lowering it. In addition, when dealing with a small number of classes, interleavers cannot provide good Tanner Graph structures for efficient belief propagation, which might result is an sticking effect with no further iterative decoding improvement (the Lymph case).

---

[7] See Conclusions and Further Work

Regarding further comparisons with other ECOC learning schemes, one may argue that better results have been obtained in [5]. It should be noted, however, that results in [5] are based in a hard preprocessing stage for hunting good random codes at clearly lower channel rates (0.06 and 0.1). We do not perform any preprocessing stage. Also we work at clearly higher channel rates (0.5). In addition, results in [7] do not provide experimental evidence of how error adaptation takes place when augmenting the strength of binary learners. Their results assume either an AdaBoost DS binary learner with T=10 inner boosting steps or an unboosted SVM learner, with the former one providing better results despite of its smaller complexity.

Table 1. RECOC PA 10-fold cross validation on UCI datasets using AdaBoost DS learners

Dataset	Size	Attrib-utes	M	T=10 I=1	T=10 I=30	T=50 I=1	T=50 I=30	T=100 I=1	T=100 I=30
Audiology	226	69	24	0.433	0.460	0.429	0.429	0.424	0.424
Primary Tumor	339	17	22	0.707	0.707	0.716	0.710	0.716	0.710
Glass	214	10	7	0.471	0.471	0.453	0.453	0.434	0.434
Anneal	798	38	6	0.044	0.052	0.026	0.027	0.017	0.066
Lymph	148	18	4	0.236	0.229	0.1891	0.189	0.189	0.189

Table 2. RECOC PA 10-fold cross validation on UCI datasets using AdaBoost C4.5 learners

Dataset	Size	Attrib-utes	M	T=1 I=1	T=1 I=30	T=10 I=1	T=10 I=30	T=50 I=1	T=50 I=30
Audiology	226	69	24	0.331	0.327	0.234	0.230	0.207	0.194
Primary Tumor	339	17	22	0.707	0.699	0.710	0.699	0.672	0.657
Glass	214	10	7	0.415	0.406	0.345	0.579	0.303	0.570
Anneal	798	38	6	0.017	0.11	0.003	0.113	0.003	0.113
Lymph	148	18	4	0.25	0.25	0.162	0.162	0.141	0.141

5   Conclusions and Further Work

RECOC learning brings light into an important widespread phenomenon in nature: random structures can easily achieve certain combinatorial properties that are very hard to achieve deterministically. In this paper, we propose RECOC learning models based on PA codes to be one expression of randomized learning strategies. Clearly, any other code comprising some degree on randomness and defining short codewords is a good candidate for RECOC learning in low dimensional output spaces. In this line of research, array codes [22] appear to be a good option for surveying.

Regarding practical applications, RECOC learning emerge as an important line of research for the development of low complexity learning algorithms for classification problems in Functional Genomics [23]. In such setting, learning is constrained by a hierarchical, multilabel output space with either vast or small datasets. A moment of thought reveals that all these learning constraints could be tackled uniformly under a RECOC approach. Vast datasets could be broken down into smaller ones and each of them could be further independently binary expanded. Similarly, multiple independent binary expansions could be used for obtaining independent replicas for small datasets. For each binary expansion, a RECOC instance could be computed. From a set of RECOC instances a new RECOC stage can be applied...Hopefully, both manifest and subtle learning factors could be captured in this way.

Acknowledgments

Elizabeth Tapia's work was supported by an Argentinean Government FOMEC grant and the National University of Rosario, Argentina. Javier García-Villalba's work was supported by the Spanish Ministry of Science and Technology (MCYT, Spain) under Projects TIC2002-04516-C03-03 and TIC2000-0735. During this work he was with the Information Storage Group at the IBM Almaden Research Center, San Jose, California, USA (javiervi@almaden.ibm.com).

References

1. James, G., Hastie, T.: The error coding method and PiCTs. Journal of Computational and Graphical Statistics, 7:3:377-387 (1997)
2. Dietterich, T., Bakiri, G.: Error-correcting output codes: A general method for improving multiclass inductive learning programs. Proceedings of the Ninth National Conference on Artificial Intelligence (AAAI-91), pp. 572-577, Anaheim, CA: AAAI Press (1991)
3. Crammer, K., Singer, Y.: On the Learnability and Design of Output Codes for Multiclass Problems. 35-46. Nicolò Cesa-Bianchi, Sally A. Goldman (Eds.): Proceedings of the Thirteenth Annual Conference on Computational Learning Theory (COLT 2000), pp. 35-46, Palo Alto, California. Morgan Kaufmann (2000)
4. Kong, E., Dietterich, T.: Error-correcting output coding corrects bias and variance. In Proceedings of the 12 th International Conference on Machine Learning, pp. 313-321, (1995)
5. Allwein, E., Schapire, R., Singer, Y.: Reducing Multiclass to Binary: A Unifying Approach for Margin Classifiers. Journal of Machine Learning Research 1, pp. 113-141 (2000)
6. Guruswami, V., Sahai, A.: Multiclass Learning, Boosting, and Error-Correcting Codes. Proceedings of the Twelfth Annual Conference on Computational Learning Theory (COLT 99), pp. 145-155, Santa Cruz, CA, USA (1999)
7. Tapia, E., González, J.C., García Villalba, J., Villena, J.: Recursive Adaptive ECOC models. Proceedings of the 10th Portuguese Conference on Artificial Intelligence, EPIA 2001. Springer Lecture Notes in Artificial Intelligence, LNAI 2258, Oporto, Portugal (2001)
8. Tapia, E., González, J.C., García Villalba, J.: Recursive Classifiers. Proceedings of the 2002 IEEE International Symposium on Information Theory ISIT 2002, Lausanne, Switzerland (2002)
9. Tanner, M.: A recursive Approach to Low Complexity Error Correcting Codes. IEEE Transactions on Information Theory, Vol. IT-27, pp. 533-547 (1981)
10. Richardson, T., Urbanke, R.: The Capacity of Low Density Parity Check Codes under Message Passing Decoding. IEEE Transactions on Information Theory, Vol. 47, No. 2, pp. 599-618 (2001)

11. Benedetto S., Montorsi G.: Unveiling Turbo Codes: Some Results on Parallel Concatenated Coding Schemes. IEEE Transactions on Information Theory, Vol. 42, No. 2, pp. 409-428, (1996)
12. Li, J., Narayanan K. R., Georghiades C. N.: Product Accumulate Codes: A class of Capacity-Approaching, Low Complexity Codes. Department of Electrical Engineering, Texas A&M University. Submitted (2001) IEEE Transactions on Information Theory. http://ee.tamu.edu/~jingli/pub/paper/IT_1.pdf
13. Kschischang, F., Frey, B.: Iterative decoding of compound codes by probability propagation in graphical models. IEEE Journal on Selected Areas in Communications, Vol. 16-2, pp. 219-230 (1998)
14. Wiberg, N.: Codes and Decoding on General Graphs. Doctoral Dissertation, Department of Electrical Engineering, Linköping University, Sweden (1996)
15. Csiszár, I., Körner J.: Information Theory: Coding Theorems for Discrete Memoryless Systems. Academic Press, Inc. (London) LTD (1981)
16. Berrou, C., Glavieux, A.: Near Optimum Error Correcting Coding and Decoding: Turbo Codes. IEEE Transactions on Communications, Vol. 44, No. 10, pp. 1261-1271 (1996)
17. McEliece, R. J., MacKay, D. J.: Turbo Decoding as an Instance of Pearl's Belief Propagation Algorithm. IEEE Journal on Selected Areas in Communications, Vol. 16, No. 2, pp. 140-152 (1998)
18. Weiss, Y.: Belief propagation and revision in networks with loops. Technical Report 1616, MIT AI lab (1997)
19. Schapire, R. E., Singer, Y.: Improved Boosting Algorithms Using Confidence - rated Predictions. Machine Learning, Vol. 37, No. 3, pp. 277-296 (1999)
20. Sason, I., Shamai, S.: Improved Upper bounds on the ML decoding error probability of parallel and serial concatenated turbo codes via their ensemble distance spectrum. IEEE Trans. on Information Theory, Vol. 46, No. 1, pp. 24 – 47 (2000)
21. Witten, I., Frank E.: Data Mining, Practical Machine Learning Tools and Techniques with JAVA Implementations. Morgan Kaufmann Publishers, San Francisco, California (2000)
22. Blaum M., Fan J. L., Xu L.: Soft Decoding of Several Classes of Array Codes. Proceedings of the 2002 IEEE International Symposium on Information Theory ISIT 2002, Lausanne, Switzerland (2002)
23. Kell, D. B., King, R. D.: On the optimization of classes for the assignment of unidentified reading frames in functional genomics programs: the need for machine learning. Trends in Biotechnology 18, pp. 93- 98 (2000)

Finding Natural Clusters Using Multi-clusterer Combiner Based on Shared Nearest Neighbors

Hanan Ayad and Mohamed Kamel

Pattern Analysis and Machine Intelligence Lab
Systems Design Engineering, University of Waterloo
Waterloo, Ontario N2L 3G1, Canada
{hanan,mkamel}@pami.uwaterloo.ca
http://pami.uwaterloo.ca/

Abstract. In this paper, we present a multiple data clusterings combiner, based on a proposed *Weighted Shared nearest neighbors Graph (WSnnG)*. While combining of multiple classifiers (supervised learners) is now an active and mature area, only a limited number of contemporary research in combining multiple data clusterings (un-supervised learners) appear in the literature. The problem addressed in this paper is that of generating a reliable clustering to represent the natural cluster structure in a set of patterns, when a number of different clusterings of the data is available or can be generated. The underlying model of the proposed shared nearest neighbors based combiner is a weighted graph, whose vertices correspond to the set of patterns, and are assigned relative weights based on a ratio of a balancing factor to the size of their *shared nearest neighbors population*. The edges in the graph exist only between patterns that share a pre-specified portion of their nearest neighborhood. The graph can be further partitioned into a desired number of clusters. Preliminary experiments show promising results, and comparison with a recent study justifies the combiner's suitability to the pre-defined problem domain.

1 Introduction

1.1 Motivations

Cluster analysis is an un-supervised learning method used in exploratory data analysis. It provides a means to explore and uncover the clustering structure of a set of patterns. However, the variety of techniques for representing data, measuring similarity between patterns, and grouping data elements, have produced "a rich and often confusing assortment of clustering methods" [1]. Without a priori knowledge about the structure of the data, which after all, is what cluster analysis all about, it is very difficult to choose the best clustering method.

It is further well known that no clustering method can adequately handle all sorts of cluster shapes and structures. In fact, the cluster structure produced by a clustering method is sometimes an artifact of the method itself that is actually imposed on the data rather than discovered about its true structure.

T. Windeatt and F. Roli (Eds.): MCS 2003, LNCS 2709, pp. 166–175, 2003.

This is a very real problem in the application of clustering methods [2]. Moreover, natural clusters present in a set of patterns may be of different sizes, densities and shapes, making it more difficult for a clustering method to discover natural cluster structures.

While combining multiple classifiers (supervised learners) is a mature area, and an approach that is proved to enhance the quality of classification results, research in combining multiple data clusterings has only started to emerge. In [3], the reasons that impede the study of clustering combination are: (1) It is believed that the quality of clustering combination algorithms can not be evaluated as precisely as combining classifiers. A priori knowledge or user's judgement always play a critical role in clustering performance estimation. This problem gives an obstacle to propose a mathematical theory to design clustering combination algorithms. (2) As various clustering algorithms produce results with large difference due to different clustering criteria, directly combining the clustering results with integration rules, such as sum, product, median and majority vote can not generate a good meaningful result. In [4], combining multiple clusterings is regarded as a more difficult problem than combining multiple classifiers, since cluster labels are symbolic and one must also solve a correspondence problem. Additionally, there are other difficulties pertaining to the variability of the number and shape of clusters provided by individual solutions, and the desired or the unknown "right" number.

However, as noted in [4,5], combining multiple clusterings can lead to improved quality and robustness of clustering solutions across a wider variety of data sets, enable knowledge reuse, and distributed clustering both in terms of objects or features. Moreover, we believe that one of the potential benefits of combining multiple clusterings lies in leveraging the ability of cluster analysis to uncover the natural or difficult cluster structures inherent in the data, rather than imposing one that is an artifact of the clustering method itself.

1.2   Related Work

Representative work in combining multiple clusterings is found in [6]. The idea of evidence accumulation for combining multiple clusterings which follows a split and merge strategy is used. The data is decomposed into a large number of compact clusters using the k-means with different initializations. The data organization present in the multiple clusterings is mapped into a co-association matrix which provides a measure of similarity between patterns. The final clusters are obtained by clustering this new matrix, corresponding to merging of clusters. The proposed method was able to identify arbitrary shaped clusters. The method relies on the repeated use of a single technique (the K-means), at different fine grain levels.

Another key contribution found in [5], introduced the problem of combining multiple clusterings of a set of objects without accessing the original features. Several application scenarios for the resultant "knowledge reuse" framework, referred to as "cluster ensemble" were identified. A formal definition of the cluster ensemble problem as an optimization of normalized mutual information is proposed, in which the optimal combined clustering is defined as the one that has maximal average mutual information with all individual clusterings. Three consensus functions (combiners) were presented for solving it. An un-supervised "supra-consensus" function evaluates all three functions and selects the best clustering as the combined one. In general, the consensus functions, and the normalized mutual information criterion favor well-balanced clusters. For example the normalized mutual information between two identical clusterings will be less than 1.0 unless all categories have equal prior probabilities. While the generation of well-balanced clusters is desirable in many applications, natural clusters present in a set of patterns may be of different probability distributions, and the ability to find such clusters remains important in other scenarios.

In an earlier contribution [7], we observed the different clustering solutions produced using different clustering methods on high dimensional text data (the Reuters-21578). We proposed an aggregation scheme that consolidates two different clusterings of given sets of documents into one combined clustering. The combiner algorithm works by tracking the overlaps between the two different clusterings and chooses to either merge or separate overlapping clusters, based on the levels of overlaps, and by accessing the original input patterns.

1.3   Contribution of This Paper

In this paper, we address the problem of combining multiple clusterings in order to generate a reliable partitioning that helps reveal the natural cluster structure of a set of patterns.

We believe that some of the difficulties encountered when combining different clusterings concern (1) the construction of multi-fold similarity relationships between various objects (i.e. construction of clusters) based on evidence of direct similarity between sets of objects as determined from different partitionings and (2) the reliability of such induced relationships. For example, Let there be evidence of similarity - as determined by the consensus among different clusterings - between pattern i and pattern j, and between pattern j and pattern k. However, no (enough) evidence of similarity between patterns i and k was determined. So, should all three patterns i, j, and k be merged in the same cluster? Or, are objects i and j "really" similar, if they are not both similar to the same object k? The idea of shared nearest neighbors provides a reliable way to analyze the similarities between objects and therefore ideas based on this concept, such as those used in this paper, can help in determining the cluster structure of the data, beyond applying strict consensus or transitivity on similarity relationships.

At the representation level of the clusterings, we use the same approach as in [6], and [5] to induces a pairwise similarity measure between objects from the different partitionings based on their co-occurrence in the given clusterings. At the combiner level, we emphasize the shared neighborhood relationships between the objects based on shared nearest neighbors, an approach to similarity proposed in 1973 by Jarvis and Patrick [8] and recently extended in [9]. We further define the shared nearest neighbors population associated with each object i as the number of objects with a "relatively significant" sharing of nearest neighbors with object i. We use this number in determining the relative weights of objects. A Weighted Shared nearest neighbors Graph (WSnnG) is constructed, in which weights are assigned on both edges and vertices.

In preliminary experiments, we compare the results of the proposed combiner based on the $WSnnG$, and referred to as the Snn-based combiner, to the supra-consensus function described in [5] on a number of data sets. Preliminary results show improvement in the case of unbalanced data, and are as good as the supra-consensus function on well balanced data.

2   Shared Nearest Neighbors Based Combiner

2.1   Formulation

Let $X = \{x_1, x_2, \cdots, x_n\}$ denote a set of objects, and $C = \{C_1, C_2, \cdots, C_r\}$ is a set of r clusterings (partitionings) of the n objects. The number of clusters in clustering C_i is denoted by k_i. From the given ensemble of clusterings C of the n data objects , we construct a $WSnnG = (V, E)$, where $V = \{v_1, v_2, \cdots v_n\}$ is the set of weighted vertices corresponding to the set of objects. $E = \{e_1, e_2, \cdots, e_m\}$ represents the set of weighted edges connecting the objects, where m is the number of edges. An edge between any pair of vertices is counted only once, i.e. edge connecting object i to object j is not counted separately from edge connecting j to i. The evaluation of weights assigned to the vertices and edges of the $WSnnG$, are described in Section 2.2.

The graph $WSnnG = (V, E)$ is partitioned using the graph partitioning package METIS [10], in which the underlying algorithms are described in [10,11,12], and are known for robustness and scalability. METIS can partition a graph in the presence a balancing constraint. The idea is that each vertex has a weight associated with it, and the objective of the partitioning algorithm is to minimize the edge-cut subject to the constraint that the weight of the vertices is equally distributed among the domains.

2.2   Weighted Shared Nearest Neighbors Graph

A reliable way to define similarity between objects is in terms of their shared nearest neighbors. In other words, one can confirm the similarity between two objects by their common (i.e shared) nearest neighbors. For instance, if object i is similar to object j and if they are both similar to a set of objects S, then one can have greater confidence in the similarity between objects i and j, since their similarity is confirmed by the objects in set S.

In order to construct the $WSnnG = (V, E)$, we proceed as follows:

1. **Computation of co-associations (direct-similarities):** Similar to the voting mechanism described in [6], a similarity measure between patterns is summarized in the $co - assoc$ matrix:

$$co - assoc(i, j) = \frac{votes_{ij}}{r}$$

where $votes_{ij}$ is the number of times, the objects i and j are assigned to the same cluster among the r clusterings. That is $0 \leq co - assoc(i, j) \leq 1.0$.

2. **Sparsification of the similarity matrix:** Sparsify the $co - assoc$ matrix, by keeping only the most similar neighbors to each object. We determine those neighbors based on a $vote_{Thresh}$. We maintained a value of 0.5 for this threshold throughout the experiments, which corresponds to enforcing a majority vote.

   Increasing the value of this threshold corresponds to imposing stricter consensus among the clusterings, and revealing of fewer nearest neighbors for each object. For instance a value of 1.0 means agreement among "all" clusterers. On the other hand, decreasing this value, corresponds to reducing the number of votes needed for a consensus and leads to revealing of more nearest neighbors. This is analogous to selecting K in a K-nearest neighbors approach, but the number of nearest neighbors for each object is not fixed.

3. **Constructing the skeleton of the WSnnG:** For each pair of objects i and j, determine the size of their shared nearest neighbors, that is, the size of intersection $|A \cap B|$ of their respective nearest neighbors lists A and B. The strength σ_{ij} of the association between the two objects i and j is given by:

$$\sigma_{ij} = 2 \times \frac{|A \cap B|}{|A| + |B|}$$

   If σ_{ij} satisfies a strength threshold $\sigma_{ijThresh}$, where this threshold is evaluated dynamically for each pair of objects i and j, and is given as, $\sigma_{ijThresh} = \mu \times max(|A|, |B|)$. The parameter μ determines the required ratio of overlap. In the reported experiments $\mu = 0.5$, indicating that objects must share at least 50% of their nearest neighbors in order to satisfy the strength threshold. **Then**
   – Create an edge between i and j with weight σ_{ij}
   – Increment shared nearest neighbors populations θ_i, θ_j for objects i and j

4. **Assignment of Vertices Weights:** The weight ω_i of each object i is computed as the ratio of a balancing factor l (we choose $l = n$), where n is the number of objects, to the shared nearest neighbors population θ_i associated with object i. That is, $\omega_i = \frac{l}{\theta_i}$

The $WSnnG$ is then partitioned into k clusters, so as to minimize the edge-cut subject to the constraint that the weight on the vertices is equally distributed among the domains. The issue of how to determine k is not the focus of this work. It is rather assumed that k is available to all clustering methods, and to the combiner. However, this issue will be investigated in a future study. In fact, the $WSnnG$ itself, without partitioning, would represent a partitioning of the data objects at a given level of granularity. If one want to see it at a specific level, the graph is partitioned into the desired number of clusters k.

By assigning relative weights ω_i to the vertices based on the their respective number of shared nearest neighbors, we embed in the graph information about the densities and sizes of neighborhood around each object, thus accommodating

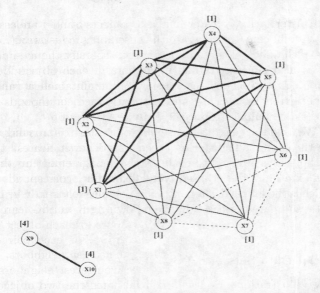

Fig. 1. $WSnnG = (V, E)$ for the example given in Section 2.3

for structure imbalances. The weights σ_{ij} on the edges, are based on the strength of link with respect to the connected objects i and j. Stronger links are less likely to be cut, again subject to the balance constraint.

2.3   Example

Let $X = \{x_1, x_2, \cdots x_{10}\}$ be a set of 10 objects, whose true cluster structure is $C_0 = \{\{x_1, x_2, x_3, x_4, x_5, x_6, x_7, x_8\}, \{x_9, x_{10}\}\}$. Let $C = \{C_1, C_2, C_3\}$ be a given set of 3 clusterings of the objects, with three different misplacements of the objects x_8, x_7, x_6 as shown below. The generated $WSnnG$ for this example is shown in Figure 1.

$C_1 = \{\{x_1, x_2, x_3, x_4, x_5, x_6, x_7\}, \{x_8, x_9, x_{10}\}\}$,
$C_2 = \{\{x_1, x_2, x_3, x_4, x_5, x_6, x_8\}, \{x_7, x_9, x_{10}\}\}$, and
$C_3 = \{\{x_1, x_2, x_3, x_4, x_5, x_7, x_8\}, \{x_6, x_9, x_{10}\}\}$.

The strength of the edges is reflected by the thickness of the lines. The weights are assigned to the vertices so as to ensures the balance between the clusters. The graph combines all three clusterings and represents a partitioning of the objects into two clusters that perfectly match the true clusters C_0.

3   Experimental Analysis

In order to assess the proposed Snn-based combiner, preliminary experiments are performed on a number of balanced and unbalanced data sets, which are described below. Both artificial and real data sets are used.

We used ClusterPack, a cluster analysis package by Alexander Strehl available at http://strehl.com/ to generate the ensemble of clusterings, using a total of 9 different techniques. The combined clustering, using the supra-consensus function [13] is also generated. The individual clustering techniques used are graph partitioning and k-means, each using 4 different similarity measures (Euclidean, cosine, extended Jaccard and correlation), in addition to hypergraph partitioning. The techniques represent a diverse collection of clusterers as proposed by [5]. We used the generated ensemble of clusterings to build the $WSnnG$, and generate the combined clustering based on the partitioning of the $WSnnG$.

We used the F-measure [14] to evaluate the quality of all clusterings. The F-measure is an external criteria based on additional information not given to the clusterer, which is the labelled categorization assigned externally by humans. The experimental results are discussed in the following subsections and summarized in Table 1.

3.1   Artificial Data Sets

In the first two illustrations, we used artificial data sets used in [13], and downloaded from http://strehl.com/. The first is the 2D2K, containing 1000 points from two 2D Gaussian clusters (500 points each), with means $(-0.227, 0.077)$ and $(0.095, 0.322)$ and equal variance of 0.1. A test is performed on a random sample of 200 points, (100 from each distribution). The value of the F-measure for both clusterings generated by the supra-consensus function [13] and by the Snn-based combiner is 0.98.

In the second illustration, we used the data set (8D5K), which contains 1000 points from 5 multivariate Gaussian distributions (200 points each) in 8D space. All clusters have the same variance (0.1), but different means. Means were drawn from a uniform distribution within the unit hypercube. A test performed on a random sample of 250 points (equally distributed among the five classes) yields an F-measure value of 1.0 using both the supra-consensus and Snn-based combiner.

We artificially generate the data set (2D-2C) shown in Figure 2 (a). Note that the clusters are of different sizes and densities. The value of the F-measure for the clustering generated using the supra-consensus is 0.76, and 0.94 for the clustering generated using the Snn-based combiner, an improvement of 23%.

Another artificially generated data set (2D-3C) is shown in Figure 2 (b), in which the three clusters of points are of different sizes, shapes and densities. The values of the F-measure for the clustering generated using the supra-consensus and the Snn-based combiner are 0.68 and 0.87 respectively, that is an improvement of 27%.

3.2   Real Data Sets

Experiments are performed on the Iris Plant Database, one of the best known databases in the pattern recognition literature, downloaded from the UCI machine learning repository. The data set contains 3 classes of 50 instances each,

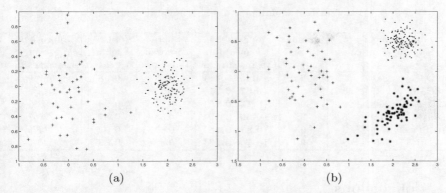

Fig. 2. (a) Data set (2D-2C) consists of two clusters of points of sizes (50, 150) sampled from two Gaussian distributions with different means and variances. (b) Data Set (2D-3C) consists of three clusters of points of sizes (50, 150, 75) sampled from three Gaussian distributions with different means, and co-variance matrices

where each class refers to a type of iris plant, and the data is represented by 4 attributes. One class is linearly separable from the other 2; the latter are not linearly separable from each other. An F-measure value of 0.95 was obtained using both the supra-consensus and Snn-based combiner. The ensemble's averge F-measure is 0.81.

The second real dataset used is the Wisconsin Diagnostic Breast Cancer Database (WDBC) [15], also downloaded from the UCI machine learning repository. The Data contains 569 instances, described by 30 real-valued input features. The sets are linearly separable using all the 30 input features. Each instance has one of 2 possible classes: benign or malignant. The class distribution is 357 benign, and 212 malignant (that's about 63% to 37%). The F-measure values obtained are 0.81 and 0.89 using the supra-consensus function and Snn-based combiner, respectively. It is noted that using the supra-consensus function, two equal size clusters were generated (that is a balance of 50% to 50%). The Snn-based combiner, on the other hand, generated two clusters with 70% to 30% distribution, which is closer to the actual class distribution. Interestingly, it is further noticed that the distribution of the individual clusterings was as follows: 5 out of the 9 clustering techniques generated two equal clusters, one generated a cluster distribution of 99% to 1%, that is almost one cluster, two were 78% to 22% and one was 72% to 28%. The experiment demonstrates the ability of the Snn-based combiner to recover a better clustering structure from a collection of clusterings with different biases. Moreover it flexibly handles class distributions that are not necessarily well balanced, making it a clustering combining method that is adequate for finding natural clusters.

Table 1 summarizes the results of all the experiments described above, with more details on the F-measure of the individual clusterings. It is noticed from the results in Table 1 that the quality of the clustering generated using the Snn-based combiner always surpasses the average quality of the basic individual clusterings.

174 Hanan Ayad and Mohamed Kamel

Table 1. Summary of experimental results

Data Set	sample size	# classes	ensemble size r	ensemble F-measure (Mean, Std-Dev)	Supra-consensus F-measure	Snn-based combiner F-measure	Improvement over ensemble's mean
2D2K	200	2	9	**(0.86, 0.18)**	0.98	**0.98**	13%
8D5K	250	5	9	**(0.87, 0.21)**	1.0	**1.0**	14%
2D-2C	200	2	9	**(0.73, 0.15)**	0.76	**0.94**	28%
2D-3C	275	3	9	**(0.69, 0.19)**	0.68	**0.87**	26%
Iris Plant	150	3	9	**(0.81, 0.18)**	0.95	**0.95**	17%
WDBC	569	2	9	**(0.74, 0.13)**	0.81	**0.89**	20%

4 Conclusions

In conclusion, we introduced in this paper a multiple data clusterings combiner based on a weighted shared nearest neighbors graph. The shared nearest neighbors approach to similarity provides an alternative, or rather a complement, to direct similarities between objects and is a reliable approach to analyze and extract complex similarity relationships among sets of patterns. We believe that this approach is particularly useful in combining clusterings.

We used the strength of neighborhood sharing to measure the association between objects and defined the shared nearest neighbors population to assign relative weights to objects. The combiner based on the $WSnnG$ is characterized by the ability to reveal natural cluster structures. Preliminary experiments are showing promising results.

In Future work, we would like to further analyze the $WSnnG$ both theoretically and experimentally. Moreover, we want to extend the Snn-based combiner and explore its applicability in the domain high dimensional data, overlapping clusters, and multi-class patterns. Finally, it is worth noting that in this work, we emphasized the underlying model and process for combining a given number of different data partitionings, while the issue of which clustering techniques to use, as an ensemble, is not emphasized. Nonetheless, the study of which clustering techniques would produce the best results with the proposed combiner, could be addressed in future work.

Acknowledgements

This work was partially funded by an NSERC strategic grant. The breast cancer databases available on the UCI machine learning repository are obtained from the University of Wisconsin Hospitals, Madison from Dr. William H. Wolberg.

References

1. A. K. Jain, M. N. Murty, and P. J. Flynn. Data clustering: a review. *ACM Computing Surveys*, 31(3):264–323, 1999.
2. B. S. Everitt, S. Landau, and M. Leese. *Cluster Analysis*. Arnold and Oxford University Press Inc., fourth edition, 2001.

3. Y. Qian and C. Suen. Clustering combination method. In *International Conference on Pattern Recognition. ICPR 2000*, volume 2, Barcelona, Spain, September 2000.

4. J. Ghosh. Multiclassifier systems: Back to the future. In J. Kittler F. Roli, editor, *Multiple Classifier Systems: Third International Workshop, MCS 2002, Proceedings*, volume 2364, Cagliari, Italy, June 2002. Springer.

5. A. Strehl and J. Ghosh. Cluster ensembles - a knowledge reuse framework for combining partitionings. In *Conference on Artificial Intelligence (AAAI 2002)*, Edmonton, July 2002. AAAI/MIT Press.

6. A. Fred and A.K. Jain. Data clustering using evidence accumulation. In *Proceedings of the 16th International Conference on Pattern Recognition. ICPR 2002*, Quebec City, Quebec, Canada, August 2002.

7. H. Ayad and M. Kamel. Topic discovery from text using aggregation of different clustering methods. In R. Cohen and B. Spencer, editors, *Advances in Artificial Intelligence: 15th Conference of the Canadian Society for Computational Studies of Intelligence. Proceedings*, AI 2002 Calgary, Canada, May 27-29 2002.

8. R.A. Jarvis and E.A. Patrick. Clustering using a similarity measure based on shared nearest neighbors. *IEEE Transactions on Computers*, C-22(11), November 1973.

9. L. Ertoz, M. Steinbach, and V. Kumar. Finding clusters of different sizes, shapes, and densities in noisy, high dimensional data. Technical report, Department of Computer Science, University of Minnesota, 2002.

10. George Karypis and Vipin Kumar. A fast and high quality multilevel scheme for partitioning irregular graphs. Technical Report TR 95-035, Department of Computer Science and Engineering, University of Minnesota, 1995.

11. George Karypis and Vipin Kumar. Multilevel k-way partitioning scheme for irregular graphs. Technical Report TR 95-064, Department of Computer Science and Engineering, University of Minnesota, 1995.

12. George Karypis and Vipin Kumar. Multilevel algorithms for multi-constraint graph partitioning. In *Conference on High Performance Networking and Computing. Proceedings of the 1998 ACM/IEEE conference on Supercomputing*, San Jose, CA, 1998.

13. A. Strehl. *Relationship-based Clustering and Cluster Ensembles for High-dimensional Data Mining*. PhD thesis, The University of Texas at Austin, May 2002.

14. M. Steinbach, G. Karypis, and V. Kumar. A comparison of document clustering techniques. In *KDD Workshop on Text Mining*, 2000.

15. O. L. Mangasarian and W. H. Wolberg. Cancer diagnosis via linear programming. *SIAM News*, 23(5):1–18, September 1990.

An Ensemble Approach for Data Fusion with Learn++

Michael Lewitt and Robi Polikar

Electrical and Computer Engineering, Rowan University
136 Rowan Hall, Glassboro, NJ 08028, USA
mlewitt@ieee.org,   polikar@rowan.edu

Abstract. We have recently introduced Learn++ as an incremental learning algorithm capable of learning additional data that may later become available. The strength of Learn++ lies with its ability to learn new data without forgetting previously acquired knowledge and without requiring access to any of the previously seen data, even when the new data introduce new classes. Learn++, inspired in part by AdaBoost, achieves incremental learning through generating an ensemble of classifiers for each new dataset that becomes available and then combining them through weighted majority voting with a distribution update rule modified for incremental learning of new classes. We have recently discovered that Learn++ also provides a practical and a general purpose approach for multisensor and/or multimodality data fusion. In this paper, we present Learn++ as an addition to the new breed of classifier fusion algorithms, along with preliminary results obtained on two real-world data fusion applications.

1   Introduction

1.1   Incremental Learning and Data Fusion

A common, and often painful, characteristic of classification algorithms is that they require the availability of an adequate and representative set of training examples for satisfactory generalization performance. Often, acquisition of such data is expensive and time consuming. Consequently, it is not uncommon for the entire data to become available in small batches over a period of time. Furthermore, the datasets acquired in later batches may introduce instances of new classes that were not present in previous datasets. In such settings, it is necessary to update an existing classifier in an incremental fashion to accommodate new data without compromising classification performance on old data. The ability of a classifier to learn under this setting is usually referred to as *incremental* (also called *cumulative* or *lifelong*) *learning*.

Incremental learning however, is conceptually related to data fusion, as new data may be obtained using a different set of sensors, or simply be composed of a different set of features. In such cases, the classifier is expected to learn and integrate the novel information content provided by new features, hence data fusion.

Ensemble or multiple classifier systems (MCS) have attracted a great deal of attention over the last decade due to their reported superiority over single classifier systems on a variety of applications. MCS combines an ensemble of generally weak classifiers to take advantage of the so-called *instability* of the weak classifier. This instability causes the classifiers to construct sufficiently different decision boundaries for minor modifications in their training datasets (or other parameters), causing each classifier to make different errors on any given instance. A strategic combination of these classifiers then eliminates the individual errors, generating a strong classifier.

A rich collection of algorithms have been developed using multiple classifiers with the general goal of improving the generalization performance of the classification system. Using multiple classifiers for incremental learning, however, has been largely unexplored. Learn++ was developed in response to recognizing the potential feasibility of ensemble of classifiers in solving the incremental learning problem.

In our previous work, we have shown that Learn++ is indeed capable of incrementally learning from new data, without forgetting previously acquired knowledge and without requiring access to previous data even when additional datasets introduce new classes [1]. The general approach in Learn++, much like those in other MCS algorithms, such as AdaBoost [2], is to create an ensemble of classifiers, where each classifier learns a subset of the dataset. The classifiers are then combined using weighted majority voting [3]. Learn++ differs from other techniques, however, in the way the data subsets are chosen to allow incremental learning of new data.

Recognizing that data fusion also involves combining different datasets consisting of new features or modalities, we have evaluated Learn++ on two real world applications requiring data fusion. Learn++ was used to generate additional ensembles of classifiers from datasets comprising of different features/sensors/modalities, which were then combined using weighted majority voting. While the algorithm certainly has much room for improvement when used in data fusion mode, the initial results utilizing the existing version of the algorithm have been very promising. In this paper, we describe the Learn++ algorithm and how it can be used as a general purpose approach for a variety of data fusion applications, along with our preliminary results on two such applications.

1.2   Ensemble Approaches for Data Fusion

Several approaches have been developed for data fusion, for which ensemble approaches constitute a relatively new breed of algorithms. Traditional methods are generally based on probability theory, such as the Dempster-Schafer (DS) theory of evidence and its many variations. However, algorithms based on DS require specific knowledge of the underlying probability distribution, which may not be readily available. The majority of these algorithms have been developed in response to the needs of military applications, most notably target detection and tracking [4-6]. Ensemble approaches seek to provide a fresh and a more general solution for a broader spectrum of applications. Such approaches include simpler combination schemes such as majority vote, threshold voting, averaged Bayes classifier, maximum/minimum rules, and linear combinations of posterior probabilities [6-8]. More complex data fusion schemes are also widely used in practice including ensemble based variations of DS, neural network and fuzzy logic classifiers, and stacked generalization [9-14].

A related approach to data fusion and classifier combination schemes is input decimation, the use of feature subsets in multiple classifiers [15, 16]. In addition to the simpler combination methods of majority vote, maximum, minimum, average, and product, slightly more complex combination schemes such as behavior-knowledge space or decision templates can be employed [15, 16]. Input decimation can be useful in allowing different modalities, such as Fourier coefficients and pixel averages, to be naturally grouped together for independent classifiers [15]. Input decimation can also be used to lower the dimensionality of the input space by "weeding out input features that do not carry strong discriminating information" [16]. A useful addition to this list of classifier ensembles is a more general structure capable of using a variety of different basic network architectures and containing the ability to combining their outputs for (a) a stronger overall classifier, (b) a classifier capable of incremental learning, and (c) a classifier capable of easily fusing its outputs with other ensembles.

2   Learn++

The power of Learn++ as an ensemble of classifiers approach lies in its ability to learn incrementally additional information from new data. Specifically, for each database that becomes available, Learn++ generates an ensemble of relatively weak classifiers, whose outputs are combined through weighted majority voting to obtain the final classification. The weak classifiers are trained based on a dynamically updated distribution over the training data instances, where the distribution is biased towards those novel instances that have not been properly learned or seen by the previous ensemble(s). The pseudocode for the Learn++ algorithm is provided in Figure 1.

For each database $\mathcal{D}_k$, $k=1,...,K$ that is submitted to Learn++, the inputs to the algorithm are (i) $S_k = \{(x_i, y_i) | i = 1, \cdots, m_k\}$, a sequence of m_k training data instances x_i along with their correct labels y_i, (ii) a weak classification algorithm **BaseClassifier** to generate weak hypotheses, and (iii) an integer T_k specifying the number of classifiers (hypotheses) to be generated for that database. The only requirement on the **BaseClassifier** algorithm is that it can obtain a 50% correct classification performance on its own training dataset. **BaseClassifier** can be any supervised classifier such as a multilayer perceptron, radial basis function, or a support vector machine, whose weakness can be achieved by reducing their size and increasing their error goal with respect to the complexity of the problem. Using weak classifiers allows generating sufficiently different decision boundaries based on slightly different training datasets. Weak classifiers also have the advantage of rapid training because, unlike stronger classifiers, they only generate a rough approximation of the decision boundary, further helping to prevent overfitting of the training dataset.

Learn++ starts by initializing a set of weights for the training data, w, and a distribution D obtained from w, according to which a training subset TR_t and a test subset TE_t are drawn at the tth iteration of the algorithm. Unless apriori information indicates otherwise, this distribution is initially set to be uniform, giving equal probability to each instance to be selected into the first training subset.

At each iteration t, the weights adjusted at iteration t-1 are normalized to ensuring a legitimate distribution, D_t, is obtained (step 1). Training and test subsets are then drawn according to D_t (step 2), and the weak classifier is trained with the training subset (step 3). A hypothesis h_t is obtained as the tth classifier, whose error ε_t is computed on the entire (current) database $S_k=TR_t + TE_t$, simply by adding the distribution weights of the misclassified instances (step 4)

Input: For each dataset drawn from $\mathcal{D}_k$ $k=1,2,...,K$
- Sequence of m_k examples $S_k = \{(x_i, y_i) | i = 1, \cdots, m_k\}$
- Weak learning algorithm **BaseClassifier**
- Integer T_k, specifying the number of iterations

Initialize $w_i(i) = D_i(i) = 1/m_k$, $\forall i$, $i=1,2,...,m_k$

Do for each $k=1,2,...,K$:

  Do for $t= 1,2,...,T_k$:

    1. Set $D_t = \mathbf{w_t} \Big/ \sum_{i=1}^{m} w_t(i)$ so that D_t is a distribution

    2. Draw training TR_t and testing TE_t subsets from D_t.

    3. Call **BaseClassifier** to be trained with TR_t.

    4. Obtain a hypothesis h_t: $X \rightarrow Y$, and calculate the error of h_t:
$$\varepsilon_t = \sum_{i:h_t(x_i) \neq y_i} D_t(i) \text{ on } TR_t + TE_t. \text{ If } \varepsilon t > \tfrac{1}{2}, \text{ discard ht and go to step 2.}$$

    Otherwise, compute normalized error as $\beta_t = \varepsilon_t / (1 - \varepsilon_t)$.

    5. Call weighed majority voting and obtain the composite hypothesis
$$H_t = \arg\max_{y \in Y} \sum_{t:h_t(x)=y} \log(1/\beta_t)$$

    6. Compute the error of the composite hypothesis
$$E_t = \sum_{i:H_t(x_i) \neq y_i} D_t(i) = \sum_{i=1}^{m} D_t(i) \big[|H_t(x_i) \neq y_i| \big]$$

    7. Set $B_t = E_t / (1 - E_t)$, and update the weights:
$$w_{t+1}(i) = w_t(i) \times \begin{cases} B_t, & if \ H_t(x_i) = y_i \\ 1, & otherwise \end{cases} = w_t(i) \times B_t^{1-\|H_t(x_i) \neq y_i\|}$$

Call Weighted majority voting and **Output** the final hypothesis:
$$H_{final}(x) = \arg\max_{y \in Y} \sum_{k=1}^{K} \sum_{t:h_t(x)=y} \log(1/\beta_t)$$

Fig. 1. Learn++ Algorithm

$$\varepsilon_t = \sum_{i:h_t(x_i) \neq y_i} D_t(i) \tag{1}$$

The error, as defined in Equation (1), is required to be less than ½ to ensure that a minimum reasonable performance can be expected from h_t. If this is the case, the hypothesis h_t is accepted and the error is normalized to obtain the normalized error

$$\beta_t = \varepsilon_t / (1 - \varepsilon_t), \qquad 0 < \beta_t < 1 \tag{2}$$

If $\varepsilon_t \geq \tfrac{1}{2}$, then the current hypothesis is discarded, and a new training subset is selected by returning to step 2. All hypotheses generated thus far are then combined using the weighted majority voting to obtain the composite hypothesis H_t (step 5).

$$H_t = \arg\max_{y \in Y} \sum_{t:h_t(x)=y} \log(1/\beta_t) \qquad (3)$$

The voting scheme used by Learn++ is less than democratic, however, as the algorithm chooses the class receiving the highest vote from all hypotheses, where the voting weight for each hypothesis is inversely proportional to its normalized error. Therefore, those hypotheses with good performances are awarded a higher voting weight. The error of the composite hypothesis is then computed in a similar fashion as the sum of distribution weights of the instances that are misclassified by H_t (step 6)

$$E_t = \sum_{i:H_t(x_i) \neq y_i} D_t(i) = \sum_{i=1}^{m} D_t(i) \left[\!\left[H_t(x_i) \neq y_i \right]\!\right] \qquad (4)$$

where $[\![\cdot]\!]$ evaluates to 1, if the predicate holds true.

$$B_t = E_t / (1 - E_t), \quad 0 < B_t < 1 \qquad (5)$$

The normalized composite error B_t is computed for the weight update rule (step 7):

$$w_{t+1}(i) = w_t(i) \times \begin{cases} B_t, & \text{if } H_t(x_i) = y_i \\ 1 & , \text{ otherwise} \end{cases}$$

$$= w_t(i) \times B_t^{1-[\![H_t(x_i) \neq y_i]\!]} \qquad (6)$$

Equation (6) reduces the weights of those instances that are correctly classified by the composite hypothesis H_t, lowering their probability of being selected into the next training subset. In effect, the weights of misclassified instances are increased relative to the rest of the dataset. We emphasize that, unlike AdaBoost and its variations, the weight update rule in Learn++ looks at the classification of the composite hypothesis, not of a specific hypothesis. This weight update procedure forces the algorithm to focus more and more on instances that have not been properly learned by the ensemble. When Learn++ is learning incrementally, the instances introduced by the new database (and in particular from new classes, if applicable) are precisely those not learned by the ensemble, and hence the algorithm quickly focuses on these instances. At any point, a final hypothesis H_{final} can be obtained by combining all hypotheses that have been generated thus far using the weighed majority voting rule

$$H_{final}(x) = \arg\max_{y \in Y} \sum_{k=1}^{K} \sum_{t:h_t(x)=y} \log \frac{1}{\beta_t}. \qquad (7)$$

Simulation results of Learn++ on incremental learning using a variety of datasets as well as comparisons to the AdaBoost algorithm and other methods of incremental learning including ensemble of classifier approaches can be found in [1] and references within.

3   Simulation Results on Learn++ for Data Fusion

Similar to other classifier fusion algorithms, Learn++ seeks to acquire novel and additional information content by selectively distributing the information to individual elements of the ensemble and then strategically combining them. While Learn++ was originally developed as an incremental learning algorithm, its ensemble structure allows it to be used in data fusion applications as well. This is because, the algorithm does not assume that instances in consecutive databases are composed of the same features as those seen previously. When used in data fusion mode, Learn++ seeks to incrementally learn additional information provided by consequent databases, where the instances of the new data still come from the same application but are composed of different features.

We have tested Learn++ on two real world classification problems which required data fusion. In the first, additional databases provided sensor measurements obtained with different sensors. In the second application, additional databases were constructed by taking different transforms of a time domain signal. These applications, how they relate to data fusion, and Learn++ simulation results are presented next.

3.1   Gas Identification Database

The gas identification database used in this study consisted of responses of quartz crystal microbalances to twelve volatile organic compounds (VOC), including acetone, acetonitrile, toluene, xylene, hexane, octane, methanol, ethanol, methyethylketone, tricholoroethylene, tricholoroethane, and dicholoroethane. The task was identification of an unknown VOC from the sensor responses to that VOC. A total of 12 sensors were used, where each sensor was coated with a different polymer to alter its sensitivity and selectivity to different VOCs. The entire data was available in three databases S_1, S_2, S_3, where each database consisted of responses of 4 of the 12 sensors. More information on this database, including the experimental setup, names of the polymers, and sample instances are available on the web [17].

Sensor responses were acquired in response to seven different concentrations for each VOC, producing a total of 84 instances for each database. Thirty instances from each database were used for training and the remaining 54 were used for validation. We note that the validation data was not used by Learn++ during training. At any iteration t, the test subset, TR_t mentioned above is a different subset of the 30 instance training data. We have randomly mixed the sensors for four separate trials of the algorithm, where the sensors were combined in mutually exclusive groups of four. For each run, R_1, R_2, R_3, R_4, three ensembles E_1, E_2, E_3, were generated by Learn++, one for each database. Table 1 summarizes sensor (feature) selection for each run. For the results shown in Table 2, each ensemble consisted of a multilayer perceptron network with a single 8-node hidden layer and an error goal of 0.005. The individual performances indicate the generalization performance of Learn++ when trained with only four features. Results for binary combination of ensembles indicate the generalization performance when two ensembles were combined by Learn++ to effectively fuse information from two four-feature datasets. Finally, the tertiary combination of ensembles show how the algorithm performed when three datasets were combined to fuse information from three four-feature datasets.

Table 1. Ensemble features for each run were determined randomly to form three ensembles with four mutually exculsive sets of features.

Dataset features	E_1	E_2	E_3
R_1	12, 7, 6, 3	10, 4, 5, 9	8, 1, 2, 11
R_2	2, 9, 4, 3	10, 11, 5, 1	6, 8, 7, 12
R_3	3, 2, 10, 12	7, 5, 9, 8	1, 11, 4, 6
R_4	3, 7, 12, 11	1, 8, 9, 10	4, 5, 6, 2

Table 2. Learn++ generalization performance on the validation dataset.

	Individual Performance			Combined Performance			
	E_1	E_2	E_3	$E_1 E_2$	$E_1 E_3$	$E_2 E_3$	$E_1 E_2 E_3$
R_1	69.0%	79.8%	66.7%	82.1%	**83.3%**	82.1%	82.1%
R_2	79.8%	79.8%	75.0%	82.1%	91.7%	83.3%	**95.2%**
R_3	78.6%	77.4%	76.2%	76.2%	84.5%	81.0%	**84.5%**
R_4	81.0%	82.1%	77.4%	86.9%	84.5%	90.5%	**92.9%**

The results indicate a general improvement in the generalization performance when the ensembles are combined. The best performance is indicated in bold for each run. It is interesting to note that in R_1, the best performance was achieved when combining ensembles E_1 and E_3. In all other cases, combining all three ensembles produced a performance increase over performances of any individual ensemble or any binary combination of other ensembles. Furthermore, no combination ever performed worse than an individual ensemble, demonstrating the ability of Learn++ in fusing information from three different datasets and acquiring additional information from each consecutive database.

3.2   Ultrasonic Weld Inspection (UWI) Database

The UWI database consists of ultrasonic scans of nuclear power plant pipes for the purpose of distinguishing between three types of pipe wall defects. The three defects of interest in this database are intergranular stress corrosion cracking (IGSCC), counterbores, and weld roots. IGSCCs are usually found in an area immediately neighboring the welding region, known as the heat affected zone, and form a discontinuity in the pipe that can be detected by using ultrasonic (or eddy current) techniques. The counterbore and weld roots also appear as discontinuities in the pipe wall, but they do not degrade the structural integrity of the pipe. These two *geometric reflectors* often generate signals that are very similar to those generated by cracks, making the defect identification a very challenging task. The cross section in Figure 2 helps illustrate the ultrasonic testing procedure, employing 1 MHz ultrasonic transducers, used to generate the first database analyzed in this study.

The goal of the classification algorithm is to distinguish between the three different types of pipe wall defects from the ultrasonic scans. The database consists of 1845 instances, specifically 553 crack, 615 counterbore, and 677 weld root instances. A subset of these instances was given to the first ensemble of each run as the time domain information. The Fourier Transform of each instance was obtained and the same subset as before was given to the second ensemble of each run as frequency domain information. Finally, the discrete wavelet transform coefficients from a Daubechies-4 mother wavelet were computed to form the third ensemble of each run as a time-scale representation of the data. Training three ensembles of Learn++ on the time, frequency, and time-scale data provided three modalities of information to be fused for final classification. Table 3 shows the base classifier architecture and number of classifiers generated for five different runs, whereas Table 4 presents the results obtained by Learn++ on the UWI database when used in data fusion mode.

As before, combinations of ensembles performed better than individual ensembles. In general, the combination of all three ensembles (that is combining time, frequency and time-scale information) performed better than any individual or other binary combination, with the exceptions of R_3 and R_5, where the frequency and time-scale combination performed only slightly better then the combination of all. The results given in Table 4 provides further promising results indicating that the algorithm is able to combine information of different features from different datasets.

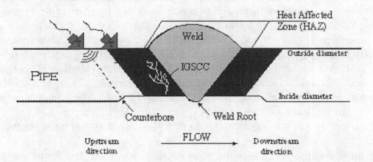

Fig. 2. Ultrasonic testing of nuclear power plant pipes for identification of hazardous *crack* vs non-hazardous *weld root* and *counterbore*.

Table 3. UWI Database: Ensemble parameters for individual runs

Run #	Hidden Layer nodes	Error goal	Training size	# of classifiers/ensemble		
				E_1	E_2	E_3
R_1	8	0.1	500	15	20	23
R_2	20	0.1	500	23	19	25
R_3	30	0.1	500	8	8	9
R_4	10	0.1	500	6	10	7
R_5	20	0.1	500	10	8	9

4 Discussion and Conclusions

Learn++ has been evaluated as a potential data fusion algorithm capable of combining data from ensembles trained on separate uncorrelated features, as well as ensembles trained on different correlated modalities such as time, frequency, and wavelet domain data. The algorithm relies on the weighted voting scheme inherent to Learn++ to take advantage of the synergistic knowledge acquisition property of an ensemble of classifiers. In essence, the incremental learning algorithm is used in a data fusion seting, where the consecutive databases use instances of different features.

Table 4. Learn++ Datafusion performance on the test dataset

	Individual Performance			Combined Performance			
	E_1	E_2	E_3	E_1E_2	E_1E_3	E_2E_3	$E_1E_2E_3$
R_1	87.36%	81.41%	87.36%	89.29%	88.84%	89.77%	**91.52%**
R_2	86.84%	80.52%	86.47%	88.69%	87.36%	90.93%	**91.30%**
R_3	82.97%	79.03%	81.04%	85.80%	82.16%	**85.80%**	85.72%
R_4	82.01%	78.74%	82.01%	84.24%	81.19%	84.01%	**85.58%**
R_5	80.74%	80.30%	80.30%	86.10%	80.59%	**86.62%**	85.13%

The two datasets presented here show improved performance when the ensemble's information are combined, forming a joint classification. However, the datasets also show that not all combinations are necessarily better than a single ensemble's performance. This information could be used to help select the features and modalities for future ensembles. A related advantage of Learn++ used in a data fusion setting is the ability of the algorithm to add or remove modalities or feature groups from the overall system without having to retrain the complete system. The algorithm has already been shown to be capable of incremental learning [1], so the combination of incremental learning of new data with the flexibility of adding or removing features and/or modalities makes for an extremely versatile algorithm.

Further testing on the algorithm is currently underway, along with the following future directions:

- Determine whether the algorithm can be used to obtain the optimum subset of a large number of features
- Since the algorithm is independent of the base classifiers, determine whether using different classifier structures particularly suited to a specific set of features may also be combined for improved data fusion performance (Learn++ has already demonstrated that it can work with a variety of base classifiers when running in the incremental learning mode [18]).

In summary, the unique characteristics of the Learn++ algorithm make it a potentially powerful and versatile system that can not only incrementally learn additional knowledge, but also can combine ensembles generated by training with different features for a diverse set of data fusion applications.

Acknowledgement

This material is based upon work supported by the National Science Foundation under Grant No. ECS-0239090.

References

[1] R. Polikar, L. Udpa, S. Udpa, V. Honavar, "Learn++: An incremental learning algorithm for supervised neural networks," *IEEE Trans Systems, Man and Cybernetics*, vol.31, no.4, pp.497-508, 2001.

[2] Y. Freund and R. Schapire, "A decision theoretic generalization of online learning and an application to boosting," *Computer and System Sciences*, vol. 57, no. 1, pp. 119-139, 1997.

[3] N. Littlestone and M. Warmuth, "Weighted majority algorithm," *Information and Computation*, vol. 108, pp. 212-261, 1994.

[4] D. Hall and J. Llinas, "An intrododuction to multisensor data fusion", *IEEE Proceedings*, vol. 85, no. 1, 1997.

[5] D. Hall and J. Llinas (editors), Handbook of Multisensor Data Fusion, CRC Press: Boca Raton, FL, 2001.

[6] L. A. Klein, Sensor and Data Fusion Concepts and Applications, SPIE Press, vol. TT35: Belingham, WA, 1999.

[7] J. Grim, J. Kittler, P. Pudil, and P. Somol, "Information analysis of multiple classifier fusion," *2nd Intl Workshop on Multiple Classifier Systems*, MCS 2001, pp. 168-177.

[8] J. Kittler, M. Hatef, R.P. Duin, J. Matas, "On combining classifiers," *IEEE Trans on Pattern Analysis and Machine Intelligence,* vol. 20, no.3, pp. 226-239, 1998.

[9] L.O. Jimenez, A.M. Morales, A. Creus, "Classification of hyperdimensional data based on feature and decision fusion approaches using projection pursuit, majority voting and neural networks, *IEEE Trans Geoscience and Remote Sensors*, vol. 37, no. 3, pp 1360-1366, 1999.

[10] G.J. Briem, J.A. Benediktsson, and J.R. Sveinsson, "Use of multiple classifiers in classification of data from multiple data sources," *Proc. of IEEE Geoscience and Remote Sensor Symposium*, vol. 2, pp. 882-884, Sydney, Australia, 2001.

[11] A. Krzyzak, C.Y. Suen, L. Xu. "Methods of combining multiple classifiers and their applications to handwriting recognition," *IEEE Trans Systems, Man, and Cybernetics*, vol.22, no.3, pp. 418-435, 1992.

[12] F.M. Alkoot.; J. Kittler. "Multiple expert system design by combined feature selection and probability level fusion," *Proc of the 3rd Intl Conf on FUSION 2000,* vol. 2, pp. 9-16, 2000.

[13] D. Wolpert, "Stacked Generalization," *Neural Networks*, vol. 2, pp 241-259, 1992.

[14] B.V. Dasarathy, "Adaptive fusion processor paradigms for fusion of information acquired at different levels of detail," Optical Engineering, vol 35, no 3 pp 634-649, 1996.

[15] L. Kuncheva and C. Whitaker, "Feature subsets for classifier combination: an enumerative experiment," *2nd Intl Workshop on Multiple Classifier Systems*, MCS 2001, pp. 228-237.

[16] N. Oza and K. Tumer, "Input decimation ensembles: decorrelation through dimensionality reduction," *2nd Intl Workshop on Multiple Classifier Systems*, MCS 2001, pp. 238-247.

[17] R. Polikar, VOC Identification database available at http://engineering.eng.rowan.edu/ ~polikar/RESEARCH/voc_database.doc

[18] R. Polikar, J. Byorick, S. Krause, A. Marino, M. Moreton, "Learn++: a classifier independent incremental learning algorithm for supervised Neural Networks," *Proc. of Intl Joint Conf on Neural Networks*, vol.2, pp. 1742-1747, 2002.

The Practical Performance Characteristics of Tomographically Filtered Multiple Classifier Fusion

David Windridge and Josef Kittler

Dept. of Electronic and Electrical Engineering
University of Surrey, Guildford, Surrey, GU2 7XH, UK
{D.Windridge,J.Kittler}@surrey.ac.uk

Abstract. In this paper we set out to give an indication both of the classification performance and the robustness to estimation error of the authors' 'tomographic' classifier fusion methodology in a comparative field test with the sum and product classier fusion methodologies.
In encompassing this, we find evidence to confirm that the tomographic methodology represents a *generally* superior fusion strategy across the entire range of problem dimensionalities, final results indicating an as much as 25% improvement on the next nearest performing combination scheme at the extremity of the tested range.

1 Introduction

In a series of previous papers [1-6], we have mathematically elaborated a metaphor between, respectively, the processes of feature selection and classifier fusion, and the processes of Radon transformation and back-projection (the latter familiar from, in particular, medical imaging cf eg [23-25]). The entity which is thus implicitly reconstructed by back-projection/classifier-combination is the prior probability density function pertaining to the entirety of the pattern-space before feature-selection took place and gave rise to a series of predominantly disjoint feature sub-sets represented within individual classifiers (see [7-10] for experimental evidence of the likelihood of this configuration when feature-selection is explicitly carried out with respect to the combined classifier output).

It is consequently possible to consider the individual classifiers as being, in a mathematically definable sense, morphological probes of the underlying composite pattern space PDF, since, intuitively, we expect feature selection to occur on the basis of the representative ability of the classifiers. The earlier papers in this series [1-6] consequently sought to m orphologically optimise the process of classifier combination by introducing a pre-combination filtration process to eliminate the artifacts generated by the mechanics of specifically linear back-projection upon on the recovered composite PDF that are implied by all existing combination schemes.

The principle motivation behind the tomographic approach to classifier combination is thus to derive and optimise the classifier-combination process on

T. Windeatt and F. Roli (Eds.): MCS 2003, LNCS 2709, pp. 186–195, 2003.

purely a priori grounds (as opposed to seeking optimisation from within a pre-existing combination strategy selected on contingent or heuristic grounds; cf eg [11-15]).

In the particular case of sum rule combination scheme, the mathematical analogy with back-projection is exact (the remaining combination schemes (eg [16-21]) having been demonstrated to constitute specically constrained forms of back-projection), and the proposed 'tomographically-filtered' combination scheme thus acts in relation to this particular fusion methodology. Precise algorithmic details of the methodology arising from this approach are set out in [4], the main results of which are reprinted in appendix 1, which will thus serve in the current context as the test-bed tomographic combination methodology through which we shall address the paper's objectives. (It should be noted in passing that the appendix's technique is highly optimised, and superficially betrays little of its tomographic pedigree: interested readers are thus referred to [4] for precise details of its derivation and relation to tomography. Cursory inspection of the economised procedure should, however, reveal that it seeks, like tomography, to correlate related morphology across all of the classifiers' feature spaces in a manner not feasible for any simply linear combination).

1.1   Objective of the Current Paper

We have argued before [1-6] that the expected error resilience of the tomographic method ought to be similar to that of the sum rule, the optimal combination strategy in terms of robustness to estimation error [1], since the back-projection aspect of the tomographic fusion technique imposes exactly the same averaging process with respect to stochastic variation. However, a precise calculation was omitted since it depends critically on the interaction between the filtering mechanism and the morphological characteristics of the classifier (which is not something we would wish to specify in advance, the tomographic method being intended as a 'black box' approach, to which novel methods of classification may be appended as developed). Given this theoretical limitation on characterising the error resilience of the proposed method, it will be necessary to base the attempted quantification of the resilience to estimation error instead on a practical investigation.

More generally, though, we have yet to fully establish the most significant performance statistic for the tomographic combination method in relation to the conventional alternatives: the effect on the misclassification rate. A very limited example of such statistics within an applications context were given in [1] for the two-dimensional case (that is, the combination of two classifiers containing a single feature). However, an inspection of the methodology set out in the appendix would indicate that it is not possible to guarantee an equivalent performance response for combinations of higher dimensionality without a great deal of further analysis. Indeed, this is self-evidently not the case if the classifiers constituting the combination exhibit any degree of estimation error, since error resilience scales differently with dimensionality for the sum and product rule combination schemes (see discussion in [22]). It is therefore necessary, in any reasonable attempt to quantify the general performance of tomographic combination, to establish performance across the range of feature-space dimensionalities: we should in particular like an assurance that the tomographic method remains the optimal choice at higher dimensionalities within a representative range of scenarios. The following section will therefore set-out our attempts to achieve this on a practical level.

2   Investigation of Relative Real-World Performance of Tomographic Classifier Fusion

Giving any comparative performance benchmark for the tomographic combination method requires that we test it against a representative sample of the remaining combination schemes. Kittler et al. [17] have demonstrated that the majority of commonly used decision rules can be considered to derive from either the sum or the product decision rules: It is therefore these two methodologies, in particular, against which we shall choose to benchmark the tomographic combination system of appendix 1.

The 'real-world' data upon which we shall perform this experimental comparison derives from a set of expertly-classified geological survey images, with the 26 dimensions of the pattern vectors corresponding to 26 distinct cell-based processes for texture characterisation. The arbitrary nature of these processes means that the data simultaneously exhibits all three of the distinct characteristics of, respectively; large-scale feature redundancy, feature independence and its converse, feature dependency within its various feature subsets: that is, very largely the full range of possible behaviours with regard to feature selection, classification and classifier combination.

Also, since we are primarily interested in testing the relative capabilities of the combination schemes, we shall seek both to homogenise the classifiers constituting the combination, and to make them as representative of the pattern-data as possible. Thus, rather than the customary arrangement in which feature sets are allocated to a morphologically disparate set of classifiers on the basis of their individual representative strengths, we shall instead artificially impose a uniform classification scheme, a probability density function derived by regularly-spaced block-density histogramming of the pattern-data, upon each of the tested feature subsets constituting the combination.

Furthermore, in order that we might establish a direct measure of the classification performance of the various combination schemes, we shall impose the condition that the composite feature space PDF of i-dimensions which we are implicitly reconstructing by classifier combination is that obtained by a block density histogramming of the original i-dimensional space. In other words, we are designating the i-dimensional PDF thus derived as the underlying prior probability density function of the i-dimensional space.

For this approach to have general validity it is necessary that a large number of pattern vectors are sampled per histogram, even at the extremity of the tested dimensionality range. Thus we are also required to impose a relatively small

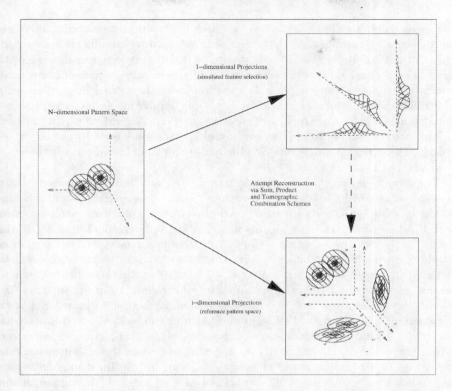

Fig. 1. Experimental format, indicating (in three-dimensional terms) the principle types of data involved in the performance measurement: the original unprojected 3-D pattern-space, three pseudo-Bayesian 2-D reference spaces to be reconstructed, and three 1-dimensional spaces representing feature-selected classifiers.

number of bins per feature (r) in order to maintain reasonable count statistics at the extremity of the range: of the order of $r = 4$, given our ≈ 125000 pattern vectors and 8 dimensional range.

Because of the need to establish a meaningful performance comparison across the dimensional range, it is additionally necessary to derive each of the tested multi-dimensional composite reference feature-space PDFs from the same experimental source. Hence we obtain the various i-dimensional spaces via projection of the complete n-dimensional pattern-space, finally averaging over all ^nC_i performance figures thus obtained. Clearly, as the dimensionality i varies, the averages thus obtained are subject to a statistical fluctuation associated with low number statistics (becoming asymptotic at $i = n$ when only one subspace exists), and hence the tested sequence is required to terminate well short of this value (coupled with the aforementioned consideration of avoiding under-sampling of the prior PDF at higher dimensionalities).

The reason it shall only prove necessary to consider the combination configuration consisting of i one-dimensional classifiers (that is, combinations with one feature per classifier), is that we are principally interested in characterising the variation of combination performance in relation to a uniform 'morphological information shortfall'. That is, we are primarily interested in the extent to which a combination scheme can make use of the ri possible classifier ordinate values to reconstruct the r^i possible co-ordinates of the prior PDF: introducing additional combinations of classifiers containing differing numbers of features would tend only to obscure this perspective without generating any additional insight into the combination processes not already encompassed by the latter approach. The experimental format for the real-world combination test is therefore as illustrated in figure 1.

We should clarify that the test scenario in no way intended to represent a plausible real-world situation when feature-selection is explicitly taken into consideration: Given that we are in a position to obtain sufficient pattern-vectors as to be able to constrain a plausible model of the i-dimensional prior PDF, the most effective feature selection strategy (presuming a reasonably flexible set of classifier morphologies to choose from) would, most naturally, be to allocate the maximal i features to the best performing classifier of the ensemble in order to guarantee retention of the maximal quantity of discrimination information. We have, however, imposed the one-feature-per-classifier limitation in order that we might mimic the generalised situation in which any one-classifier parameterisation of the whole i-dimensional space would likely be subject to serious over-parameterisation error, and therefore disposed to reduce the classification rate in relation to a combination of classifiers of lower, but better sampled, feature dimensionalities. Of course, this condition being an external restriction means that, in fact, we do have access to a plausible model for the i-dimensional prior PDF as required for the purposes of performance evaluation.

The specified experimental scenario should thus be considered from the context of the broader tomographic perspective, within which feature-selection can be envisaged as seeking an appropriate balance between the mutually exclusive requirements of maximising the retention of class-discriminant morphology information through the allocation of spaces of higher feature dimensionalities to the classifiers, and the minimisation of the dangers of over-classification through the allocation of lower feature-space dimensionalities to classifiers.

The remaining aspect of the investigation, the assessment of the resilience to estimation error of the three fusion methods, is addressed in the above experimental context by the straightforward simulation of classifier error through adding uniform stochastic noise to each of the classifier density histograms (simulating, in effect, estimation-error arising from an insufficient degree of parameter-freedom amongst the classifiers, rather than estimation-error attributable to, say, incorrect, or over, parameterisation).

The performance results for the 'real-world' geological survey data are thus as depicted in figure 2 (with an appropriate horizontalising log-space offset added for clarity), and which will consequently constitute the basis of the following assessment of tomographic fusion performance in the field.

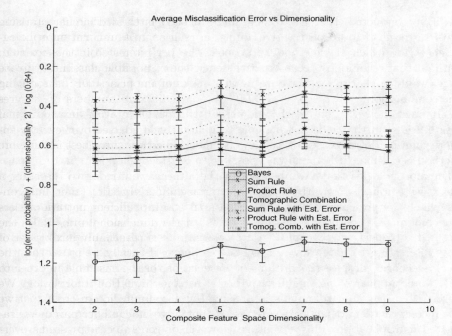

Fig. 2. Misclassification Rate vs Dimensionality for the Real-World Data

3   Analysis of Results

The performance results for the 2-class rock-strata data quantified in figure 2 would indeed appear to indicate that the ability of the tomographic combiner to correlate morphology between the i discrete classifiers is of concrete utility in a practical context, with a clear performance advantage over the sum and product rules developing with increasing dimensionality.

In terms of the point-by-point relationship between the three combining methodologies, it would appear that the tomographic method more closely mimics the performance of the product rule than the sum rule, despite its origins in the latter technique. We hypothesise that this is a consequence of actual feature independence in the original PDFs being recovered by the tomographic method (which is feasible, given that, on inspection, the prior PDFs have an approximately similar morphology to the Gaussian distribution of uniform covariance). It should be noted, however, that the tomographic estimation-error graph more closely mimics that of the sum rule than the product rule.

4   Conclusions

From the point of view of advocating a generally superior combination strategy for non-specific classification problems, it would appear, on the basis of the tests we have conducted, that the tomographic method is the indicated approach, both in terms of its reconstructive ability, as well as in its estimation error resilience (for which the method approaches the performance of the sum rule, without that technique's reconstructive deficiencies). In particular, these advantages would appear to scale favourably with the number of classifiers constituting the combination.

It must, however, be clearly understood that the scatter of data points in figure 2 is such that it is not possible to guarantee in all cases (or even much more than half of the cases for the lower dimensionalities) that the tomographic method is optimal (it being always possible to consider composite pattern-space PDF morphologies that favour either of the alternative strategies). Our argument, we emphasise, is with respect to arbitrary underlying PDF morphologies, for which the presence of back-projection artifacts implied by conventional linear combination methods (the gamut of which the sum and product rules are deemed to collectively encompass) are taken to be generally unrepresentative. It is interesting to note, however, on the evidence of figure 2, that in the real world scenario, despite the presumed presence of these artifacts, the product rule would appear to be significantly better at composite PDF morphology recovery than the sum rule. This is presumably a consequence of the fact that the reconstruction artifacts are suppressed (but, note, not fully removed) via repeated multiplication. This advantage, however, is generally suppressed by the multiplicative cumulation of estimation-error effects for all but ideal classifiers.

With respect to the prospects for further improving the tomographic combination methodology, one possibility is to note that the modified Högbom method specified in the appendix inherently regards the rectanguloid hypercube as its deconvolution primitive, and thus constitutes only a partial realisation of the potential for applying tomographic filtration to combined classifiers, the central idea of which is removal of all axial bias from back-projected radon data. Clearly, while the rectanguloid hypercube primitive serves to remove much of the the feature-axial alignment imposed by classifier combination (in particular, the elongated striations depicted in fig 2 of [1]), it still exhibits an obvious axial alignment on the local scale. Thus there is scope for future methodological improvement by introducing more rotationally symmetric primitives (for instance hyper-ovoids, which would be capable of reconstructing complete Gaussians).

Another, complementary, approach is to seek to increase the computational performance of the tomographic method, which at present, though considerably economised [4] (and parametrically tunable to a high degree), falls significantly behind the linear sum and product methods. To remedy this situation, it is necessary to employ a pre-filtration approach. That is, we should have to apply a filtering convolution to the individual classifier PDFs and combine via the sum rule, imposing a positivity condition on the output. Such a method, while conjectured to be of somewhat less accuracy than the current approach, would have the benefit of scaling linearly in terms of operation time with the number of classifiers. To determine exactly what the accuracy deficit might be for such a procedure would be the basis of further empirical and theoretical investigation.

In sum, then, we have provided performance statistics to complement the earlier theoretical assertion that tomographic combination recovers the greatest degree of the composite pattern space PDF morphology lost during feature selection (the precise quantity of recoverable information being indicated by the relative disparity of the Bayesian and tomographic error rates in figure 2).

Moreover, we have demonstrated that the tomographic method, as well as having the best underlying performance rate, has also a similar error resilience to the sum-rule combination methodology, thereby combining the best of both of the aspects of combination through which classification performance can improve, namely, the morphologically reconstructive and the error-negating: these two aspects being previously partially, though separately, represented within the product and sum rules, respectively.

Acknowledgement

This research was carried out at the University of Surrey, UK, supported by, and within the framework of, EPSRC research grant number GR/M61320.

Appendix 1: Step-by-Step Approach to Procedurally Implementing Tomographic Classifier Combination

1. Assemble experts constituting the combination as a series of PDFs ranging over n discrete feature spaces of respective dimensionality; $a_1, a_2 \ldots a_n$ for the class set; $\omega_1, \omega_2, \ldots \omega_m$.
2. Select the first class of the series, ω_1, and establish peak probability density value(s), P_{a_i}, for of each expert's individual representation of that class.
3. Specify a pair of accuracy parameters, Δz and Δx, that respectively denote the probability density and feature-space resolutions.
4. Establish the 'hyper-area' between the probability density ordinates representing the peak value and (peak value$-\Delta z$) for each of the classifier PDFs: ie, the scalar number of $(\Delta x)^{a_i} \times \Delta z$ units between the two probability density values for each of the classifiers in the fusion.
5. Specify a matrix of dimension; $a_1 + a_2 + \ldots + a_n$ with each element designating an (initially zero) probability density value attributable to every $(\Delta x)^{a_1+a_2+\ldots+a_n}$ unit of the composite feature-space[1]. Add a value, N, to those points representing all combinations of n concatenations of the respective (co-)ordinates established in 4: That is, the Cartesian product $\{X_1\} \times \{X_2\} \times \{X_3\} \times \ldots \times \{X_n\}$. ($N$ must be $> \sum_{i=1}^n P_{a_i}$).

[1] In a memory-restricted environment, it is alternatively possible to perform iterations 7-11 *simultaneously* for the respective classes, retaining only those *points of coincidence* between the various class probabilities: a significantly smaller set than the matrix specified in 5. The total memory footprint for this configuration is of the order $\{X\}^{a_1} + \{X\}^{a_2} + \ldots \{X\}^{a_n}$, rather than the former; $\{X\}^{a_1+a_2+\ldots+a_n}$ (for feature-spaces of uniform dimensional size X); which is to say, an equivalent memory requirement to conventional linear methods of combination.

6. Subtract the resolution parameter Δz from each peak value P_{a_i}; $\forall i$, and set an iteration parameter (say, t) to zero.

7. Subtract a quantity $|X_1| \times |X_2|... \times |X_{i-1}| \times |X_{i+1}| \times ... \times |X_n| \times dz$ from the current peak value of each classifier, P_{a_i}; $|X_j|$ being the scalar values derived in **5**, ie: the number of coordinate vectors $\{X_i\}$ of dimensionality a_i counted by the PDF hyper-area establishing procedure above. Note, especially, the absence of $|X_i|$ in the product entity.

8. Establish the new hyper-area value associated with the subtraction **7**, that is: the hyper-area between the probability density ordinates representing the previous and current peak-values (as per **4**).

9. Allocate a value $N - t.\Delta z$ to those points in the deconvolution matrix representing novel coordinates established after the manner of **4**. That is, the Cartesian product difference:

$$[(\{X_1\}_{old} \cup \{X_1\}_{new}) \times (\{X_2\}_{old} \cup \{X_2\}_{new}) \times ... \times (\{X_n\}_{old} \cup \{X_n\}_{new})] - [\{X_1\}_{old} \times \{X_2\}_{old} ... \{X_n\}_{old}]$$

(t the cycle count number, N as above).

10. Increment the cycle counter, t, by 1 and go to **7** while $P_{a_i} > 0$, $\forall i$.

11. After termination of the major cycle **7-11**, subtract a value $t.\Delta z$ from each point of the deconvolution matrices to establish true PDFs, if required (see footnote 5).

12. Repeat from **2** for the remaining classes in the sequence $\omega_1, \omega_2 ... \omega_m$.

References

1. D. Windridge, J. Kittler, "A Morphologically Optimal Strategy for Classifier Combination: Multiple Expert Fusion as a Tomographic Process", IEEE PAMI, Vol 25, no. 3, March 2003
2. D. Windridge, J. Kittler, "Classifier Combination as a Tomographic Process", Multiple Classifier Systems, LNCS. Vol. 2096, 2001.
3. D. Windridge, J. Kittler, "A Generalised Solution to the Problem of Multiple Expert Fusion", Univ. of Surrey Technical Report: VSSP-TR-5/2000)
4. D. Windridge, J. Kittler, "An Efficient Algorithmic Implementation of Tomographic Classifier Combination", PR journal, Submitted
5. D. Windridge, J. Kittler, "Morphologically Unbiased Classifier Combination Through Graphical PDF Correlation", LNCS 2396, August 2002
6. D. Windridge, J. Kittler, "On the General Application of the Tomographic Classifier Fusion Methodology, LNCS. Vol. 2364, June 2002
7. Windridge D., Kittler J., "Combined Classifier Optimisation via Feature Selection", Proceedings "Advances in Pattern Recognition", Lecture Notes in Computer Science. Vol. 1876
8. K. M. Ali and M.J. Pazzani, "On the link between error correlation and error reduction in decision tree ensembles", *Technical Report 95-38*, ICS-UCI, 1995
9. T.K. Ho, J.J. Hull, and S.N. Srihari, "Decision combination in multiple classifier systems", *IEEE Transactions on Pattern Analysis and Machine Intelligence*, vol. 16, no. 1, 1994, 66-75.

10. L. Xu, A. Krzyzak and C.Y. Suen, "Methods of combining multiple classifiers and their application to handwriting recognition", *IEEE Trans. SMC*, vol. 22, no. 11, 1994, 1539-1549

11. Neal R., Probabilistic inference using Markov chain Monte Carlo methods. Tech. rep. CRG-TR-93-1 1993, Dept. of Computer Science, University of Toronto, Toronto, CA.

12. Breiman L., Bagging predictors, Machine Learning 1996; vol. 24, no. 2:123-140.

13. Drucker H., Cortes C., Jackel L. D., Lecun Y., and Vapnik V., Boosting and other ensemble methods, Neural Computation, 1994; vol. 6, no. 6:1289-1301

14. Windridge D., Kittler J., "Combined Classifier Optimisation via Feature Selection", Proceedings "Advances in Pattern Recognition", Lecture Notes in Computer Science.VOL. 1876

15. Dieterich T. G., Bakiri G. "Solving Multiclass Learning Problems via Error-Correcting Output Codes." Journal of Artificial Intelligence Research, 1995; Vol 2.: 263-286.

16. R A Jacobs, "Methods for combining experts' probability assessments", Neural Computation, 3, pp 79-87, 1991

17. J. Kittler, M. Hatef, R.P.W. Duin, and J. Matas, "On combining classifiers", IEEE Transactions on Pattern Analysis and Machine Intelligence, vol. 20, no. 3, 1998, 226-239

18. L. Lam and C.Y. Suen, "Optimal combinations of pattern classifiers", Pattern Recognition Letters, vol. 16, no. 9, 1995, 945-954.

19. A F R Rahman and M C Fairhurst, "An evaluation of multi-expert configurations for the recognition of handwritten numerals", Pattern Recognition Letters, 31, pp 1255-1273, 1998

20. A F R Rahman and M C Fairhurst, "A new hybrid approach in combining multiple experts to recognise handwritten numerals", Pattern Recognition Letters, 18, pp 781-790, 1997

21. K Woods, W P Kegelmeyer and K Bowyer, "Combination of multiple classifiers using local accuracy estimates", IEEE Trans. Pattern Analysis and Machine Intelligence, 19, pp 405-410, 1997

22. J. Kittler, "Improving Recognition Rates by Classifier Combination: A Review", 1st IAPR TC1 Workshop on Statistical Techniques in Pattern Recognition, 205-210, June 1997

23. F. Natterer, Proc. "State of the Art in Numerical Analysis", York, April 1-4, 1996.

24. S. Webb, "The Physics of Medical Imaging", Institute of Physics Publishing, Bristol and Philadelphia, 1993.

25. G. T. Herman, "Image Reconstruction from Projections, The Fundamentals of Computerized Tomography", Computer science and Applied Mathematics, 1980.

Accumulated-Recognition-Rate Normalization for Combining Multiple On/Off-Line Japanese Character Classifiers Tested on a Large Database

Ondrej Velek, Stefan Jaeger, and Masaki Nakagawa

Graduate School of Technology, Tokyo University of Agriculture and Technology
2-24-16 Naka-cho Koganei-shi, Tokyo, 184-8588, Japan
{velek,stefan}@hands.ei.tuat.ac.jp
nakagawa@cc.tuat.ac.jp

Abstract. This paper presents a technique for normalizing likelihood of multiple classifiers, allowing their fair combination. Our technique generates for each recognizer one general or several stroke-number specific characteristic functions. A simple warping process maps output scores into an ideal characteristic. A novelty of our approach is in using a characteristic based on the accumulated recognition rate, which makes our method very robust and stable to random errors in training data and requires no smoothing prior to normalization. In this paper we test our method on a large database named Kuchibue_d, a publicly available benchmark for on-line Japanese handwritten character recognition and very often used for benchmarking new methods.

1 Introduction

Combining different classifiers for the same classification problem has become very popular during the last years [7,9]. In handwriting recognition, classifier combinations are of particular interest since they allow bridging the gap between on-line and off-line handwriting recognition. An integrated on-line/off-line recognition system can exploit valuable on-line information while off-line data guarantees robustness against stroke order and stroke number variations. Since the different nature of on-line and off-line data complicates their combination, most approaches combine both types of information either during pre-processing; i.e. feature computation [1-3] or, like this paper, in post-processing [5-8].

In this paper, we report experiments on the combination of on-line and off-line recognizers for on-line recognition of Japanese characters. Multiple classifiers, especially on-line and off-line classifiers, very often generate likelihood values that are incompatible. The focus of this paper lies on our accumulated-recognition-rate normalization technique, which tries to overcome this problem by aligning the likelihood values with the actual performance of each classifier. At first we define the accumulated recognition rate, which is normalized to a linearly growing function. Using normalized likelihood ensures a fair combination of classifiers.

We have introduced our warping technique in [13, 16], and tested its efficiency on a small NTT-AT database. That database is a collection of patterns written by elderly people, usually by incorrect writing style. We have achieved improvement of the

T. Windeatt and F. Roli (Eds.): MCS 2003, LNCS 2709, pp. 196–205, 2003.
© Springer-Verlag Berlin Heidelberg 2003

recognition rate from 89.07% for the best single classifier to 94.14% by combining seven classifiers in our combination system [13] and in [16] 93.68% by combining two classifiers. However, since the NTT-AT database is not a collection of typical character patterns and the number of samples and categories is low, a good perform-ance cannot be easily generalized for common Japanese character patterns. In this paper we experiment with the benchmark database Kuchibue_d, which contains on-line Japanese handwritten characters for which many researchers have already pub-lished recognition rates.

This paper is structured as follows: Section 2 and 3 outline the work described in our previous paper [13] and describe the general theoretical framework of our nor-malization technique based on accumulated recognition rate. In Section 4 we intro-duce our improved approach utilizing information about stroke number, firstly pub-lished in [16]. Section 5 describes single classifiers and combination schemes used in our experiments. Section 6 presents our new results on the Kuchibue_d benchmark set, which allows comparison of our recognition results on the same benchmark with other research groups or with our previous results on the NTT-AT database (Section 7). Finally, Section 8 concludes this paper with a general discussion of our results.

2   Comparability of Different Classifiers

Let A be a classifier that maps an unknown input pattern x to one of m possible classes $(\omega_1, ..., \omega_m)$, and returns values $a_i = A(x, \omega_i)$ denoting its confidence that x is a mem-ber of class ω_i. For an ideal classifier, each returned value a_i corresponds to the true probability of ω_i given x: $P_i(\omega_i|x)$, also called a-posteriori probability, with $0 \leq a_i = P_i(\omega_i|x) \leq 1$. In real practice, however, the output values a_i can merely be approxi-mations of the correct a-posteriori probabilities. Many classifiers do not even output approximations but only values related to the a-posteriori probabilities. For instance, $A(x, \omega_i) = a_i$ very often denotes the distance between the input pattern x and the class ω_i in a high-dimensional feature space under a given metric, sometimes with $a_i \in [0;\infty]$. In this case, the best candidate is not the class with the maximum value among all a_i, but the class having the smallest a_i; i.e., the class with the shortest dis-tance. Also, the scale of output values is generally unknown. For example, from $a_r = 2a_p$ one cannot predict that class ω_r is twice as likely as class ω_p.

These inadequacies generally pose little problem for a single classifier that needs to find only k-best candidates. If a single classifier rejects patterns with confidence val-ues below a certain threshold, a relation between confidence and a-posteriori probabil-ity is useful for setting the threshold. However, for combining several classifiers {A, B, C...} we necessarily need some relation among candidates stemming from differ-ent classifiers {$a_i = A(x, \omega_i)$, $b_i = B(x, \omega_i)$, ...} in order to compare them and to select the best class.

To better describe the output of classifiers, we define two auxiliary functions, $n(a_k)$ and $n_{correct}(a_k)$ counting the overall number of samples and correctly recognized sam-ples for each output value respectively: Function $n(a_k)$ returns the number of test pat-terns classified with output value a_k and function $n_{correct}(a_k)$ returns the number of cor-rectly recognized test patterns. We begin by counting the number of correctly and incorrectly recognized samples for each value: $n_{correct}(a_k)$ and $n_{incorrect}(a_k) = n_i(a_k) -$

$n_{correct}(a_k)$. Graph 1 and Graph 2 show two exemplary histograms of these numbers for off-line and on-line recognition respectively.

An ideal classifier returns only correct answers with likelihood values covering the whole range of possible values. As a matter of fact, most practical classifiers also return incorrect answers and do not cover all output values. Graph 1 and Graph 2 illustrate this for the off-line classifier - most of the correct output is around $a = 600$ -, while the on-line classifier has most of its correct answers around $a=900$. The peak of $n_{correct}(a)$ differs from $n_{incorrect}(i)$ in both classifiers. Also, both classifiers use only a small range of the output interval [0;1000] intensively.

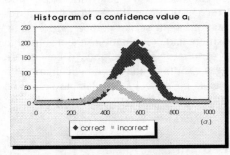
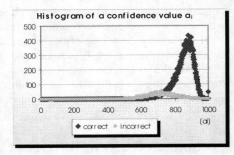

Graph 1. Histogram for an off-line recognizer   **Graph 2.** Histogram for an on-line recognizer

For a single classifier system, only the recognition rate; i.e., the number of correctly recognized patterns $\sum_i n_{correct}(i)$ divided by the number of overall patterns, is of importance. However, for combining multiple classifiers, not only the recognition rate, but also the distribution of $n_{correct}(a_k)$ and $n_{incorrect}(a_k)$ is of interest. If some classifiers provide better recognition rates than the best single recognition rate on several sub-intervals, then we can suppose that by combining multiple classifiers the combined recognition rate will outperform the single best rate. Graph 3 and Graph 4 show the recognition rates corresponding to Graph 1 and 2 respectively.

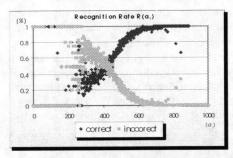
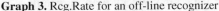
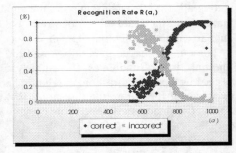

Graph 3. Rcg.Rate for an off-line recognizer   **Graph 4.** Rcg.Rate for an on-line recognizer

3   Normalization and Warping

Our goal is to normalize the output of each classifier so that it better reflects the actual classifier performance for each output value and allows direct comparison and combination with outputs from other classifiers. The main idea is to turn confidence values into a monotone increasing function depending on the recognition rate. After normalization, the highest output should still define the most likely class of an unknown input pattern x; $a_i > a_j$ should imply that $P(\omega_i|x) > P(\omega_j|x)$. However straightforward normalization of classifier outputs to a monotone increasing function is not possible, because classifier confidence is neither a continuous nor a monotone function.

In our new approach we solve this problem by defining the accumulated recognition rate (which is always a continuous function) and applying a warping process on it. This process expands and compresses local subintervals of the horizontal likelihood-axis to better match the practical recognition rates achieved, without changing the order and without adding artificial error by additive smoothing.

The confidence value is often either smaller than the value suggested by the recognition rate, which means that the confidence value is "too pessimistic," or it is higher than the actual recognition rate suggests, which is then a "too optimistic" value. We proposed using a second training set to measure the classifier performance for each likelihood value, given an appropriate quantization of likelihood, and then calibrate likelihood in a post-processing step according to the performance measured. Let $A = \{a_0, \ldots, a_i, \ldots, a_{max}\}$ be a set of likelihood values with a_0 being the lowest and a_{max} being the highest likelihood assigned by the classifier. In our experiments, the likelihood values span the integer interval ranging from 0 to 1000, and thus $A = [0;1000]$, $max = 1000$, and $a_k = k$. The calibration replaces the old likelihood values a_i by their corresponding recognition rates $r_i = a_i^{new}$ so that after normalization likelihood and recognition rate are equal: $A_i = R_i$.

Using our auxiliary functions, we can state this as follows:

$$a_i^{new} = \frac{n_{correct}(a_i) * a_{max}}{n(a_i)} \quad \forall i .$$

Graph 5 and Graph 6 show the accumulated recognition rates before and after normalization computed for the off-line and on-line recognition rates shown in Graph 3 and Graph 4 respectively.

The error rates depicted in Graph 5 and Graph 6 show the remaining percentage of misclassified patterns for likelihood values higher than a particular value a_i.

Note that the accumulated recognition rate is a monotone growing function over classifier output. Our normalization method equals the accumulated likelihood mass with the corresponding accumulated recognition rate. Using the nomenclature introduced above, our normalization ensures the following equation: $A_0^i = R_0^i$, which translates as $\frac{1}{L}\sum_{k=0}^{i} n(a_k) * a_k = \frac{1}{N}\sum_{k=0}^{i} n_{correct}(a_k)$ for all i, with N being the overall number of patterns and L being the overall likelihood mass; i.e.,

$$L = \sum_{k=0}^{max} n(a_k) * a_k .$$

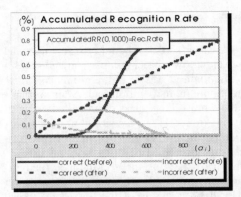 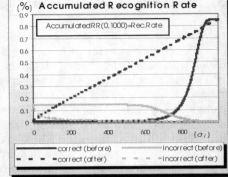

Graph 5. R($<0,a_i>$) Accumulated Recognition Rate for an off-line recognizer before and after normalization

Graph 6. R($<0,a_i>$) Accumulated Recognition Rate for an on-line recognizer before and after normalization

For each classifier, we thus normalize the output so that the accumulated probability function R($<0,a_i>$) becomes a function proportional to the classifier output. Accordingly, we adjust each classifier's output by adding the following adjustment $charf(a_i)$:

$$a'_i = a_{max} * \frac{\sum_{k=0}^{i} n_{correct}(a_k)}{N} = a_i + \left[a_{max} * \frac{\sum_{k=0}^{i} n_{correct}(a_k)}{N} - a_i \right] = a_i + charf(a_i)$$

where a_{max} is the maximum possible output of a classifier (a_{max} = 1000 in our experiments), N is the number of overall patterns, and r_i stands for the partially accumulated recognition rate. We call this classifier-specific adjustment "the characteristic function [$charf_i$]" of a classifier. To compute the [$charf_i$] of a classifier, we need another sample set, which should be independent from the training set. Hence, we use data independent from the training set to ensure a proper evaluation, although we observed that a characteristic function depends mostly on the classifier and not the data.

To illustrate the effects of normalization we now compare the graphs 1-4 with the corresponding graphs computed after normalization; i.e., after adding the adjustment. Graph 7 and Graph 8 nicely illustrate the uniform distribution of output values after normalization, compared to Graph 1 and Graph 2. In both Graphs 7-8, we see that, after normalization, the whole output spectrum is used for correct answers. Moreover, incorrect answers concentrate in the left, low-value part with a peak near zero. Since both off-line and on-line recognizers show the same output behavior after normalization, this provides us with a standard measure for classifier combination.

Finally, Graph 9 and Graph 10 show the likelihood-dependent recognition rates for each likelihood value after normalization, which correspond to the recognition rates shown in Graph 3 and Graph 4 before normalization.

In Graph 9 and Graph 10, the recognition performance quickly increases to a high level, and except for very small likelihood values, the recognition rate is about the same for each likelihood value. The number of correctly recognized patterns is higher than the number of falsely recognized ones, from likelihood values greater than 50 onwards. Again, both off-line and on-line classifiers behave similarly here.

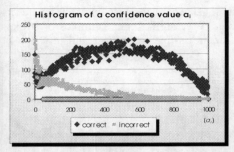

Graph 7. Histogram for an off-line recognizer after normalization

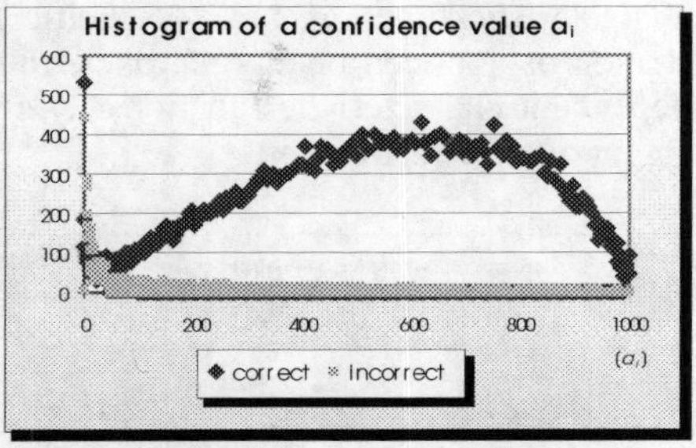

Graph 8. Histogram for an on-line recognizer after normalization

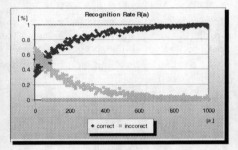
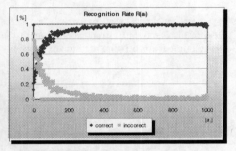

Graph 9. Recognition Rate for an off-line recognizer after normalization

Graph 10. Recognition Rate for an on-line recognizer after normalization

4   Characteristic of On/Off Classifiers According to Stroke Number

Number of strokes is the basic feature of Chinese and Japanese characters. The right stroke number can be found in a dictionary and varies from 1 to about 30. However, for fluently and quickly written characters, the number of strokes is often lower because some strokes are connected. In some cases the number of strokes can be higher than they should be. An interesting characteristic of stroke number variations is given in [11]. Graph 11-12 show the recognition rate according to the stroke number for an on-line and off-line recognizer respectively. Even from a brief view, we see the big difference between both classifiers. An off-line recognizer is weaker in recognizing characters written with a low number of strokes. The recognition rate grows with increasing complexity of patterns. This is in accordance with the well-known fact that for off-line classifiers it is more difficult to recognize simple patterns like Kana than difficult Kanji. On the contrary, on-line recognizers are very efficient for one-stroke patterns.

From Graph 12 we see that although an average rate of the on-line recognizer is about 5% worse than that of the off-line recognizer, for characters written by one, two, or three strokes the recognition rate is better, or at least similar. Since classifiers efficiency depends on the strokes number, we tried to make not only one general characteristic function, but 14 specific functions, where the last one is for patterns written by fourteen or more strokes. In Graph 13 we show some examples of stroke-dependent characteristic functions [$charf_i$] for an on-line recognizer and in Graph 14 for an off-line recognizer.

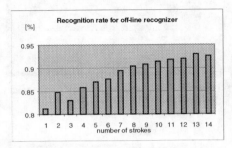

Graph 11. Recognition rate according to the stroke number for off-line recognizer

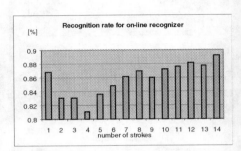

Graph 12. Recognition rate according to the stroke number for on-line recognizer

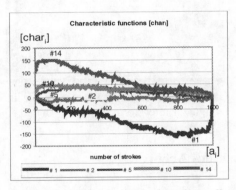

Graph 13. Characteristic functions for on-line recognizer

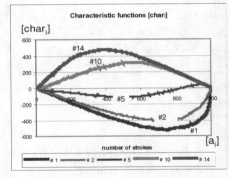

Graph 14. Characteristic functions for off-line recognizer

5   On-Line & Off-Line Classifiers and Combination Schemes

Our off-line recognizer represents each character as a 256-dimensional feature vector. Every input pattern is scaled to a 64x64 grid by non-linear normalization and smoothed by a connectivity-preserving procedure. Then, a normalized image is decomposed into 4 contour sub-patterns, one for each main orientation. Finally, a 64-dimensional feature vector is extracted for each contour pattern from its convolution with a blurring mask (Gaussian filter). A pre-classification step precedes the actual final recognition. Pre-classification selects the 50 candidates with the shortest Euclidian distances between the categories' mean vectors and the test pattern. The final classification uses a modified quadratic discriminant function (MQDF2) developed by Kimura et al. [5] from traditional QDF. The off-line classifier is trained with the off-line HP-JEITA database (3,036 categories, 580 patterns per category).

The on-line recognizer presented in [12] by Nakagawa et al. employs a two-step coarse classification based on easily extractable on-line features in the first step and four-directional features in the second step. An efficient elastic matcher exploiting hierarchical pattern representations performs the main classification. The recognizer is trained with the on-line Nakayosi_t database[6] (163 patterns for each of 4,438 categories).

We investigate two different combination strategies for combining our on-line and off-line recognizers: max-rule and sum-rule. Max-rule takes the class with the maximum output value among each classifier, while the sum-rule adds up the output for each class and selects the one with the highest sum[7].

6   Benchmarking with the Kuchibue_d Database

This section presents experiments evaluating our proposed normalization with respect to the Kuchibue_d database [6], [14], which is a widely acknowledged benchmark for Japanese character recognition. It contains handwritten sentences from a Japanese newspaper. In total, Kuchibue contains more than 1.4 million characters written by 120 writers (11,962 Kanji samples per writer). Kuchibue covers 3,356 Kanji categories including the two phonetic alphabets Hiragana and Katakana, plus alphanumerical characters. Since our recently published results were based on the ETL9B benchmark-database, which does not cover Katakana and alphanumerical characters, we confine our experiments to the 3036 categories of Kuchibue (Kanji and Hiragana) included in ETL9B. On-line patterns processed by the off-line classifier are converted to bitmaps by our calligraphic method [15] painting realistic off-line patterns.

Table 1. Combination of an on-line and an off-line recognizer, tested on Kuchibue_d

Benchmark: Kuchibue_d	Single classifier		Combination of single classifiers			
	On-line	Off-line	AND	OR	Max	Sum
without normalization					91.44	96.29
Normalization by 1 characteristic function	91.06	94.69	86.88	98.88	95.61	97.13
Normalization by 14 characteristic function					96.27	97.71

The efficiency of our two single recognizers are 91.06% (on-line) and 94.69% (off-line); Table 1, column 1 and 2. The higher recognition rate of the off-line recognizer is partially result of more training patterns per category (580 against 163) and smaller scope of recognizable categories (3036 against 4438). The next two columns show the theoretical worst (AND - a pattern was recognized by both classifiers) and best (OR - a pattern was recognized at least by one recognizer) combination schemes, which are the theoretical bounds for any combination rule. Especially the OR combination scheme is important. Although it can never be utilized in a real application, the best theoretical boundary is important for comparing the efficiency of other combination schemes.

Column 5 and Column 6 of Table 1 show the recognition rates for the max-rule and sum-rule respectively. The sum-rule performs better than max-rule. A theoretical explanation why the sum-rule outperforms the max-rule is given in [7]. The sum-rule is also more resistant to problems of non-normalized likelihood.

We have achieved improvements of single recognition rates from 91.06% and 94.69% up to 97.71%. And what is also important, our result is very near to the theoretical maximum 98.88% of the OR combination scheme.

7   Benchmarking with the NTT-AT Database

In this section we compare the results based on Kuchibue_d from Section 6 with results based on the NTT-AT database published in [16]. The NTT-AT database contains data written by elderly people with an average age of 70.5 years, with the oldest writer being 86 years old. These patterns are casually written, very often with an untypical stroke order.

Table 2 shows that our normalization significantly improves the recognition rate. From 85.67% (on-line classifier) and 89.07% (off-line classifier) to 93.68%.

Table 2. Combination of on-line and off-line recognizers tested on NTT-AT

Benchmark: NTT-AT	Single classifier		Combination of single classifiers			
	On-line	Off-line	AND	OR	Max	Sum
without normalization					92.04	92.08
Normalization by 1 characteristic function	85.67	89.07	79.03	95.71	92.11	93.40
Normalization by 14 characteristic function					92.19	93.68

8   Discussion

In this paper we presented an updated version of our accumulated-recognition-rate-based normalization for combining multiple classifiers, which was introduced at IWFHR 2001 [13,16]. A simple warping process aligns confidence values according to the accumulated recognition rate, so that the normalized values allow a fair combination. In our previous experiments on the NTT-AT database, which contains casually written characters often written in untypical writing order, we improved the recognition rate from 89.07% for the best single recognizer to 93.68%.

In this paper we used the Kuchibue_d database, which is the well-established benchmark of common casually written Japanese characters. Its size is 23 times bigger than that of the NTT-AT database. The improvement of the recognition rate is from 94.69% for the best single recognizer to 96.29% for the sum-rule combination prior to our normalization, 97.13% when normalized by one common characteristic function, and finally 97.71% if normalized by 14 stroke-number-specific characteristic functions.

The main advantages of our normalization based on the accumulated-recognition-rate are as follows: Firstly, the possibility to combine any number of classifiers, without having weaker classifiers degrade the final result. Secondly, it allows easy combination of classifiers with incompatible confidence values. Thirdly, normalizing is a completely automatic process, without empirical parameter settings. And fourthly, normalization is performed only once and does not consume time during recognition.

Normalization based on stroke numbers better reflects the nature of each recognizer and thus leads to better results; it requires more training patterns for computing multiple characteristic functions though.

Although our accumulated-recognition-rate-based normalization was tested on combined on-line/off-line classifiers for on-line Japanese handwritten characters, it should be useful for combinations in various fields of pattern recognition.

References

1. M. Hamanaka, K. Yamada, J. Tsukumo, On-Line Japanese Character Recognition Experiments by an Off-Line Method Based on Normalization-Cooperated Feature Extraction, Proc. 2nd ICDAR (1993) 204-207
2. M. Okamoto, A. Nakamura, K. Yamamoto, Direction-Change Features of Imaginary Strokes for On-Line Handwriting Character Recognition, 14th ICPR (1998) 1747-1751
3. S. Jaeger, S. Manke, J. Reichert, A. Waibel, On-Line Handwriting Recognition: The Npen++ Recognizer, IJDAR 3(3) (2001) 169-180
4. F. Kimura, et al., Modified quadratic discriminant function and the application to Chinese characters, IEEE Pattern Analysis and Machine Intelligence, 9(1), pp.149-153, 1987
5. H. Kang, K. Kim and J. Kim, A Framework for Probabilistic Combination of Multiple Classifiers at an Abstract Level, EAAI 10 (4) (1997) 379-385
6. Distribution of the on-line databases Kuchibue_d and Nakayosi_t, Nakagawa laboratory, TUAT, Japan: http://www.tuat.ac.jp/~nakagawa/ipdb/
7. J.Kittler, M.Hatef, R.Duin, J.Matas, On Combining Classifiers, *IEEE PAMI 20(3)* (1998) 222-239
8. H. Tanaka, K. Nakajima, K. Ishigaki, K. Akiyama, M. Nakagawa, Hybrid Pen-Input Character Recognition System Based on Integration of On-Line – Off-Line Recognition, Proc. 5th ICDAR (1999) 209-212
9. T. Ho, J. Hull, S. Srihari, Decision Combination in Multiple Classifier Systems, IEEE Trans. on Pattern Analysis and Machine Intelligence, vol. 16, no. 1, pp. 66-75, 1994
10. M. Oberländer, German Patent DE 44 36 408 C1 (in German), 1995, on-line available on the website of the German Patent and Trade Mark Office: www.depatisnet.de
11. K. Matsumoto, T. Fukushima, M. Nakagawa, Collection and analysis of on-line handwritten Japanese character patterns, Proc. 6th ICDAR, Seattle, 2001, pp.496-500.
12. M. Nakagawa, K. Akiyama, L.V. Tu, A. Homma, T. Higashiyama, Robust and Highly Customizable Recognition of On-Line Handwritten Japanese Characters, Proc. 13th ICPR (1996), volume III, 269-273
13. O. Velek, S. Jaeger, M. Nakagawa, A New Warping Technique for Normalizing Likelihood of Multiple Classifiers and its Effectiveness in Combined On-Line/Off-Line Japanese Character Recognition, Proc. 8th IWFHR(2002), pp. 177-182
14. S. Jaeger, M. Nakagawa, Two On-Line Japanese Character Databases in Unipen Format, Proc. 6th ICDAR(2001), pp. 566-570
15. O. Velek, M. Nakagawa, C.-L.Liu, Vector-to-Image Transformation of Character patterns for On-line and Off-line Recognition, International Journal of Computer Processing of Oriental Languages, Vol.15, No2 (2002) 187-209
16. O. Velek, M.Nakagawa, Using Stroke-Number Characteristics for Improving Efficiency of Combined On-Line and Off-Line Japanese Character Classifiers, 5th DAS (2002), 115-118

Beam Search Extraction and Forgetting Strategies on Shared Ensembles[*]

V. Estruch, C. Ferri, J. Hernández-Orallo, and M.J. Ramírez-Quintana

DSIC, Univ. Politècnica de València , Camí de Vera s/n, 46020 València, Spain
{vestruch,cferri,jorallo,mramirez}@dsic.upv.es

Abstract. Ensemble methods improve accuracy by combining the predictions of a set of different hypotheses. However, there is an important shortcoming associated with ensemble methods. Huge amounts of memory are required to store a set of multiple hypotheses. In this work, we have devised an ensemble method that partially solves this problem. The key point is that components share their common parts. We employ a multi-tree, which is a structure that can simultaneously contain an ensemble of decision trees but has the advantage that decision trees share some conditions. To construct this multi-tree, we define an algorithm based on a beam search with several extraction criteria and with several forgetting policies for the suspended nodes. Finally, we compare the behaviour of this ensemble method with some well-known methods for generating hypothesis ensembles.

Keywords: Ensemble Methods, Decision Trees, Randomisation, Search Space, Beam Search.

1 Introduction

Ensemble methods [7] are used to improve the accuracy of machine learning models. Basically, this technique combines a finite set of hypotheses into a new hypothesis, which is usually more accurate than any of the ensemble components. Examples of well-known ensemble methods are boosting [11], bagging [2], randomisation [8], etc. Although accuracy is significantly increased, a large amount of computational resources is necessary to generate, store, and employ the ensemble due to the large number of different hypotheses that make up the ensemble. For this reason, there are several contexts where these techniques are hard to apply.

Since ensemble methods construct a set of models, one way to overcome the above mentioned drawbacks could be to share the common parts of the models. In a previous work [10], we presented an algorithm which is able to obtain more than one tree. It is based on a structure, called multi-tree, which can contain a set of decision trees that have some of their conditions in common. A multi-tree is generated by applying a splitting criterion on a node and then storing the

---

[*] This work has been partially supported by CICYT under grant TIC2001-2705-C03-01 and Acción Integrada Hispano-Austríaca HA2001-0059.

T. Windeatt and F. Roli (Eds.): MCS 2003, LNCS 2709, pp. 206–216, 2003.

splits which have not been selected into a list of suspended nodes. The selected split is pursued until a complete tree is constructed. Later, alternative models can be generated by exploring the nodes of the list. This way of exploring the space for generating an ensemble of hypotheses can be considered a beam search [15].

The use of an auxiliary data structure (list of suspended nodes) must lead to establishing a policy to manage it. This policy must cover several aspects such as the definition of a criterion to extract a node in order to further populate the multi-tree. In this paper, we focus on the study of some strategies for selecting the nodes to be explored from the list of suspended nodes. We introduce some methods, and we then study these strategies experimentally. We also compare the performance of this ensemble method with other well-known methods such as bagging [2] and boosting [11].

Despite the advantages of the multi-tree approach, there is a great number of suspended nodes that are never employed. Thus, they occupy memory needlessly and it would be interesting to forget these nodes. We study some techniques to keep only one subset of the nodes under consideration. This forgetting technique leads to a better use of resources as we experimentally demonstrate.

This work can be considered as a continuation of [10]. In that work, we presented the basis for and main features of a multi-tree as an ensemble method. An experimental study of some fusion strategies and vector modification techniques was made. In this work, we investigate some multi-tree search and exploration policies, and we present an important optimisation in the algorithm.

The paper is organised as follows. In section 2, we introduce the multi-tree structure. Section 3 includes some experimental evaluations on multi-tree construction. It also explains different forgetting strategies and shows the results of several experiments related to this technique. Finally, section 4 closes the paper with conclusions and future work.

2 Shared Ensembles

Ensemble methods require the generation, storage and application of a set of models in order to predict future cases. This represents an important use of resources in both scenarios: the learning process and the prediction of new cases.

In our previous work [10], we presented a method that allows a set of decision trees to be generated from a single evidence. A collection of trees is called a forest, but our approach is based on a shared ensemble, namely, a collection of trees that share their common parts (decision multi-tree). The idea is to generate an AND/OR tree structure, called multi-tree, from which it is possible to extract a set of hypotheses. We perform a greedy search for each solution, but once the first solution is found, the following ones can be obtained keeping in mind that computation time is limited. Therefore, in a certain way, our algorithm can be considered anytime. An anytime algorithm is one that can be interrupted at any point during computation to return a result whose quality increases as the computation time increases [6].

Since a multi-tree can contain a set of hypotheses, we employ an ensemble method that combines the individual components of the multi-tree. This ensemble method takes advantage of the internal structure of the multi-tree by sharing common parts of the components of the ensemble. In this way the amount of resources required for the learning and the application of the ensemble is reduced. We called this ensemble method: shared ensemble.

A decision multi-tree structure is similar to an option tree [3,4,12]. The main difference between these methods is the construction strategy. In the multi-tree method, we store all the rejected splits as suspended nodes, and later we continue the multi-tree construction selecting one of these suspended nodes according to a criterion. Option trees are constructed as usual. However, when the difference between the best test and the other alternatives is small at a level, these alternatives are also explored as optional tests (OR-nodes). The creation of optional nodes is limited at the upper levels to restrict the size of the option tree. Therefore, while option trees are constructed by a breadth search, a multi-tree is generated by a beam search, i.e. we store the discarded alternatives in a list of suspended nodes, and later, if we want to further populate the multi-tree, we select one node from the list according to one selection criterion, and at this point the search is continued.

As we have just seen in Section 1, the decision multi-tree can be populated by selecting one suspended OR-node from the list of suspended OR-nodes by means of a selection criterion (suspended OR-node selection criterion). The *optimality* computed by the splitting criterion can be used to choose the OR-node to be explored. We have introduced the following suspended OR-node selection criteria:

- **Rival Absolute:** The node with the highest optimality is selected from the list of suspended OR-nodes.
- **Rival Ratio:** For every suspended OR-node, a rival ratio value is computed as the relation between the *optimality* of the OR-node and the best *optimality* of its sibling OR-nodes (i.e. the children of the same AND-node). The suspended OR-node with the highest rival ratio value is chosen.
- **Random:** This criterion just selects nodes pseudo-randomly (uniform distribution) from the list.
- **TopMost:** Select the topmost node with the highest optimality first.
- **Bottom:** Selects the bottom node with the highest optimality first.

Once a multi-tree is constructed, it contains a set of hypotheses which depends on the number of suspended OR-nodes which have been explored. Note that the number of hypotheses increases exponentially w.r.t. the number of nodes explored. Since it could be prohibitive to combine all these models at the top, the combination is performed inside the multi-tree by a majority vote. A study of some fusion methods, most of them based on [13], was presented in [10].

2.1   Node Forgetting

Despite the advantages of the multi-tree structure, many suspended nodes are never 'woken', occupying memory needlessly. An additional criterion can be specified to forget some of the suspended nodes and, hence, to use less memory.

Table 1. Datasets used in the experiments.

#	Datasets	Size	Classes	Nom. Attr.	Num. Attr.
1	Balance Scale	325	3	0	4
2	Breast Cancer	699	2	0	9
3	Breast Cancer Wisconsin	569	2	1	30
4	Chess	3196	2	36	0
5	Contraceptive Method Choice	1473	3	7	2
6	Dermatology	366	6	33	1
7	Hayes-Roth	106	3	5	0
8	Heart Disease	920	5	8	5
9	Hepatitis	155	2	14	5
10	Horse-colic-outcome	366	3	14	8
11	Horse-colic-surgical	366	2	14	8
12	House Congressional Voting	435	2	16	0
13	Iris Plan	158	3	0	4
14	MONK's1	566	2	6	0
15	MONK's2	601	2	6	0
16	MONK's3	554	2	6	0
17	New Thyroid	215	3	0	5
18	Postoperative Patient	90	3	7	1
19	Segmentation Image Database	2310	7	0	14
20	Teaching Assistant Evaluation	151	3	2	3
21	Thyroid ANN	7200	3	15	0
22	Tic-Tac-Toe Endgame	958	2	8	0
23	Wine Recognition	178	3	0	13

We have studied several methods for restricting the nodes to be selected:

- **Constant:** We only store a constant minimum number of nodes.
- **Logarithmic:** A logarithmic number of nodes is selected (a constant minimum is also applied).
- **Logarithmic + depth:** A logarithmic number of nodes is selected but corrected by the depth of the nodes (a constant minimum is also applied). This correction tends to store more nodes at the top positions, where the exploration of suspended nodes permits models to become more diverse.

In the following section, we perform an experimental evaluation of forgetting strategies.

3   Experiments

In this section, we present an experimental evaluation of our approach, as is implemented in the SMILES system [9]. SMILES is a multi-purpose machine learning system which (among many other features) includes the implementation of a multiple decision tree learner.

For the experimental evaluation, we have employed 23 datasets from the UCI dataset repository [1]. Some details of the datasets are included in Table 1.

For the experiments, we used GainRatio [16] as a splitting criterion. Pruning is not enabled. The experiments were performed on a Pentium III-800 Mhz with 180MB of memory running Linux 2.4.2. The results present the mean accuracy of the 10×10-fold cross-validation for each dataset, and finally the geometric

Table 2. Accuracy of combination depending on the second tree criterion.

#	Bottom	Optimal	Random	Rival Ratio	Top most
1	78.18	79.00	82.61	77.63	86.60
2	93.84	94.70	94.88	93.45	94.45
3	92.43	92.55	93.07	93.75	93.75
4	99.62	99.58	99.38	99.64	99.62
5	48.35	48.23	49.73	48.31	51.70
6	91.86	92.92	94.03	92.17	91.31
7	76.44	76.75	76.75	73.06	76.75
8	52.23	52.48	54.43	52.20	59.13
9	76.07	75.87	81.40	75.93	83.67
10	62.72	62.78	67.28	62.69	75.28
11	78.53	78.00	83.36	78.33	85.83
12	94.70	95.53	95.67	94.35	95.23
13	94.13	94.13	95.33	94.20	94.67
14	95.20	95.91	99.78	99.73	100.00
15	75.42	75.33	75.67	71.05	77.55
16	98.02	98.02	97.85	97.38	97.95
17	92.14	93.38	93.29	93.14	92.43
18	64.63	63.75	63.25	69.88	63.00
19	95.91	95.91	96.40	96.06	96.06
20	60.47	60.60	62.93	60.07	63.40
21	99.24	99.37	99.26	99.23	99.19
22	77.21	76.97	82.01	78.13	84.94
23	92.94	92.59	93.06	94.00	90.00
Geomean	80.56	80.70	82.45	80.69	83.61

mean of all the datasets. First, we analyse the behaviour of the quality of the shared ensemble depending on some criteria to populate the multi-tree: Bottom, Optimal, Random, Rival Ratio and Top Most

Table 2 shows the accuracy comparison between these methods for populating the multi-tree. According to the results, the best methods for building the shared ensemble seem to be Random and Top Most The Top Most method has an important drawback: the decision trees do not share many components, so the construction and use of the shared structure is slower. This fact is perceived if one observes the consumption of time. Table 3 shows the average learning time for each dataset depending on the method employed to populate the multi-tree. The difference in time between Random and Top Most is important because the Top Most method selects the nodes to be explored at the top positions in the multi-tree. This leads to the generation of very different models because they do not share many conditions. However, this criterion also produces large multi-trees where the advantages in resource saving of the multi-tree structure are practically lost. Consequently, the Random criterion can be considered as an optimal trade-off between efficiency and accuracy.

3.1   Node Forgetting

In this section, we study the effect of the forgetting optimisation in the performance of the ensemble method. Since we have seen that a good criterion is to select the nodes to be explored randomly, a random strategy of node forgetting will not alter the suspended node selection criterion, and therefore the accuracy of the multi-classifier will not be degraded.

Table 3. Average learning time (in seconds) depending on the second tree criterion.

#	Bottom	Optimal	Random	Rival Ratio	Top most
1	0.05	0.06	1.10	0.08	31.41
2	0.81	0.34	2.47	0.29	21.92
3	0.09	0.56	11.86	8.77	136.39
4	0.39	0.63	5.78	0.91	0.30
5	0.56	0.46	5.64	40.11	939.99
6	0.30	0.33	3.51	1.09	16.03
7	0.04	0.02	0.07	0.03	0.03
8	0.40	0.36	5.00	5.64	255.20
9	0.06	0.07	1.52	0.13	7.92
10	0.21	0.18	3.59	0.58	83.75
11	0.17	0.14	3.19	0.26	41.93
12	0.02	0.08	0.54	0.07	2.62
13	0.03	0.12	0.35	0.05	1.59
14	0.16	0.02	0.16	0.04	0.26
15	0.02	0.03	0.29	0.07	1.05
16	0.03	0.02	0.15	0.02	0.18
17	0.01	0.16	0.91	0.96	6.93
18	0.01	0.02	0.21	0.03	0.49
19	1.32	2.71	15.92	28.78	15.82
20	0.03	0.04	0.85	11.40	118.58
21	1.24	2.17	11.31	7.56	14.62
22	0.05	0.05	0.46	0.06	9.02
23	0.06	0.57	1.99	0.68	880.00
Geomean	0.10	0.14	1.34	0.46	9.12

A comparison of some of these criteria according to the accuracy of the classifiers obtained is presented in Table 4. These criteria are: no forgetting, limiting a constant number of nodes (5) in each OR-node, leaving a logarithmic number of nodes, and finally a correction of the last method depending on the node depth. The results of Table 4 indicate that, as expected, the forgetting process does not produce significant modifications on the quality of the classifiers.

Table 5 contains the average learning time for each classifier and dataset, and the geometric mean of all the datasets. The experiments demonstrate the usefulness of node forgetting, because it reduces the learning time. The best forgetting method is the one based on the selection of a logarithmic number of all possible nodes. The corrected version (log + depth) is a bit slower because it selects nodes at the top of the multi-tree. The method based on a constant number also improves the learning time. However, the results in accuracy are slightly worse than the logarithmic method.

With regard to the improvement in memory, Table 6 shows the memory (in Kilobytes) required by the system for learning the multi-tree for some datasets. We also include the percentage of memory employed by the forgetting method with respect to the original method (no forgetting). For large and medium problems (4, 28) the use of forgetting drastically reduces the required memory. However, for small problems (15) the reduction is more limited. The forgetting method that requires less memory is the "logarithmic" method.

According to these experiments, the best suspended-node forgetting criterion seems to be to randomly leave a logarithmic number of nodes, without taking depth into account.

Table 4. Accuracy of the combination in the multi-tree depending on the forgetting method.

#	No forgetting	Const=5	Logarithmic	Log. + depth
1	82.61	81.40	82.24	85.11
2	94.88	95.16	94.93	94.81
3	93.07	93.36	93.41	93.80
4	99.38	99.39	99.37	99.34
5	49.73	49.30	49.51	52.65
6	94.03	94.53	94.42	94.39
7	76.75	76.75	76.44	75.94
8	54.43	54.09	54.26	55.58
9	81.40	81.53	80.67	81.67
10	67.28	66.00	67.42	67.06
11	83.36	83.36	83.19	83.67
12	95.67	95.86	95.91	95.79
13	95.33	95.07	95.00	95.13
14	99.78	99.78	99.89	97.56
15	75.67	75.67	76.38	71.50
16	97.85	97.85	97.75	97.67
17	93.29	93.29	93.57	92.29
18	63.25	62.00	61.88	62.13
19	96.40	96.31	96.61	96.43
20	62.93	62.40	62.87	63.40
21	99.26	99.28	99.33	99.24
22	82.01	82.22	81.78	83.96
23	93.06	92.88	93.76	92.76
GeoMean	82.45	82.22	82.38	82.55

3.2   Comparison with Other Ensemble Methods

Let us compare the behaviour of the shared ensemble technique (random extraction + logarithmic forgetting) with other popular ensemble methods: bagging and boosting (Adaboost). We have employed the Weka (version 3.2.3)[1] implementation of these two ensemble methods. The ensemble methods use $J48$ as base classifier (the Weka version of C4.5), and we have used the default settings. Pruning is only enabled for boosting since this method requires pruning to get good results.

Figure 1 shows the average accuracy (10×10-fold cross-validation) obtained by the three methods depending on the number of iterations. Initially, the best results are obtained by boosting, whereas bagging and Multi-tree results are slightly lower. This is probably due to the fact that they do not use pruning. As expected, when the number of iterations of the ensemble methods is increased, all the methods improve in accuracy. In this case, we can see that the multi-tree method is the one that most enhances the results. It even surpasses boosting at 80 iterations or more. Note that the accuracy of bagging with 100 classifiers is not shown in the figure. The reason for this is that the computer ran out of memory for such a configuration.

Finally, although the shared ensemble method has suitable properties in terms of accuracy of the combined classifier, the most attractive feature of this algorithm is the sharing of some parts of the ensemble. This fact allows for a good allocation of computational resources. Figure 2 shows the average train-

---

[1] http://www.cs.waikato.ac.nz/~ml/weka/

Table 5. Average learning time for the combined solution in the multi-tree depending on the forgetting method.

#	No forgetting	Const=5	Logarithmic	Log + depth
1	1.10	0.60	0.62	1.71
2	2.47	1.62	1.66	2.82
3	11.86	12.47	12.00	15.20
4	5.78	5.68	4.77	9.97
5	5.64	3.74	2.48	12.49
6	3.51	3.36	3.10	4.02
7	0.07	0.07	0.02	0.01
8	5.00	2.66	2.64	5.54
9	1.52	1.38	1.36	1.87
10	3.59	2.34	2.45	3.70
11	3.19	2.33	2.28	3.58
12	0.54	0.51	0.47	0.94
13	0.35	0.30	0.27	0.53
14	0.16	0.17	0.14	0.04
15	0.29	0.30	0.29	0.08
16	0.15	0.16	0.12	0.03
17	0.91	0.90	0.74	1.27
18	0.21	0.18	0.16	0.08
19	15.92	17.34	16.17	17.44
20	0.85	0.63	0.57	1.28
21	11.31	12.14	9.79	15.36
22	0.46	0.44	0.37	0.55
23	1.99	2.06	1.70	2.05
GeoMean	1.34	1.16	0.99	1.23

Table 6. Average memory (in Kbytes) for the combined solution in the multi-tree depending on the forgetting method.

#	Original	Const=5	%	Logarithmic	%	Log + depth	%
4	49512.00	10892.00	22.0%0	6388.00	12.90%	8328.00	16.82%
15	4880.00	4820.00	98.77%	1484.00	30.41%	3472.00	71.15%
23	18800.00	3268.00	17.38%	2272.00	12.09%	2608.00	13.87%

ing time of bagging, boosting, and Multi-tree (shared ensemble) depending on the size of the ensemble. While bagging and boosting[2] show a linear increase in time, the shared ensemble technique shows a sub-linear increase. Note that the implementation features of the methods clearly affect the training time (Weka is implemented in Java, while SMILES is implemented in C++). However, this does not produce significant changes in the asymptotic behaviour of the algorithms when varying the number of iterations.

4   Conclusions

This work has presented some strategies for constructing an ensemble based on a beam search. This search considers the alternative options that are rejected by classical greedy decision-tree construction algorithms. The main feature of the technique is the use of a structure called multi-tree that permits sharing

---

[2] The observed non-linear behaviour of Boosting is due to a technique implemented in it that stops the algorithm when the accuracy does not improve further from iteration to iteration.

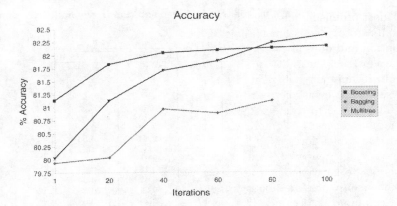

Fig. 1. Accuracy obtained by the ensemble methods depending on the number of iterations.

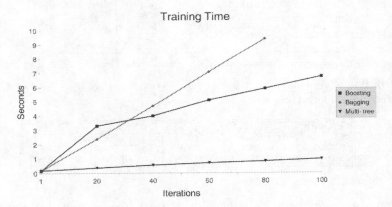

Fig. 2. Training time required by the ensemble methods depending on the number of iterations.

common parts of the single components of the ensemble. For this reason, we call it shared ensemble.

We have introduced some criteria to populate the multi-tree. These criteria are variations of a beam search over the multi-tree structure. We have implemented this algorithm and an experimental evaluation has been performed in order to analyse the performance of these criteria. We have also studied an optimisation that permits a better use of resources based on a filter of the nodes to be stored (forgetting).

The beam search employed for the generation of the multi-tree structure is related to the rule learning system CN2 [5]. This algorithm performs a search in which the algorithm maintains a list of k candidates at each selection, instead of considering just a single option. On each search step, the algorithm generates descendants from these k candidates, and the resulting set is again reduced to the k most promising members. This can be seen as a global forgetting technique that only stores a constant number k of options. Additionally, CN2 just explores one option and does not perform combination.

We construct the multi-tree by a random extraction from the node list. Therefore, our technique is also related to randomisation [8]. This technique constructs an ensemble of decision trees by injecting randomness into the splitting criterion. The idea is to randomly select among the top 20 best splits. In this way, the method generates a different decision tree for each iteration. However, randomisation builds forests, i.e. an ensemble of completely independent decision trees.

Lastly, we have included a comparison of the ensemble method with some well-known ensemble methods, namely boosting and bagging. Due to the sharing of the common parts, much less time is required than with classical ensemble approaches to perform the same number of iterations. Consequently, our system is very appropriate for complex problems where other ensemble methods such as boosting or bagging require huge amounts of memory and time.

As future work, we propose the study of a new strategy for generating trees. This strategy would be different from the current random technique we have employed to explore OR-nodes, and would probably be based on the semantic discrepancy of classifiers (using kappa function [14], for instance). This technique would provide a way to improve the results of our ensemble method with fewer iterations.

References

1. C.L. Blake and C.J. Merz. UCI repository of machine learning databases, 1998.
2. L. Breiman. Bagging predictors. *Machine Learning*, 24(2):123–140, 1996.
3. W. Buntine. *A Theory of Learning Classification Rules*. PhD thesis, School of Computing Science in the University of Technology, Sydney, February 1990.
4. W. Buntine. Learning classification trees. In D. J. Hand, editor, *Artificial Intelligence frontiers in statistics*, pages 182–201. Chapman & Hall,London, 1993.
5. P. Clark and T. Niblett. The CN2 induction algorithm. *Machine Learning*, 3:261–283, 1989.
6. T. Dean and M. Boddy. An analysis of time-dependent planning. In *Proc. of the 7th National Conference on Artificial Intelligence*, pages 49–54, 1988.
7. T. G Dietterich. Ensemble methods in machine learning. In *First International Workshop on Multiple Classifier Systems*, pages 1–15, 2000.
8. T. G. Dietterich. An experimental comparison of three methods for constructing ensembles of decision trees: Bagging, Boosting, and Randomization. *Machine Learning*, 40(2):139–157, 2000.
9. V. Estruch, C. Ferri, J. Hernández, and M. J. Ramírez. SMILES: A multi-purpose learning system. In *Logics in Artificial Intelligence, European Conference, JELIA*, volume 2424 of *Lecture Notes in Computer Science*, pages 529–532, 2002.
10. V. Estruch, C. Ferri, J. Hernández, and M.J. Ramírez. Shared Ensembles using Multi-trees. In *the 8th Iberoamerican Conference on Artificial. Intelligence, Iberamia'02*, volume 2527 of *Lecture Notes in Computer Science*, pages 204–213, 2002.

11. Y. Freund and R.E. Schapire. Experiments with a new boosting algorithm. In *Proc. 13th International Conference on Machine Learning*, pages 148–146. Morgan Kaufmann, 1996.
12. R. Kohavi and C. Kunz. Option decision trees with majority votes. In *Proc. 14th International Conference on Machine Learning*, pages 161–169. Morgan Kaufmann, 1997.
13. L. Kuncheva. A Theoretical Study on Six Classifier Fusion Strategies. *IEEE Trans. on Pattern Analysis and Machine Intelligence*, 24(2):281–286, 2002.
14. L. Kuncheva and C. J. Whitaker. Measures of diversity in classifier ensembles and their relationship with the ensemble accuracy. Submitted to Machine Learning, 2002.
15. N.J. Nilsson. *Artificial Intelligence: a new synthesis*. Morgan Kaufmann, 1998.
16. J. R. Quinlan. *C4.5: Programs for Machine Learning*. Morgan Kaufmann, San Mateo, CA, 1993.

A Markov Chain Approach to Multiple Classifier Fusion

S.P. Luttrell

QinetiQ
Malvern, Worcestershire, UK
S.Luttrell@signal.QinetiQ.com

Abstract. The aim of this paper is to show how the problem of optimising the processing chain in a classifier combiner network can be recast as a Markov chain optimisation problem. A summary of the application of coding theory to Markov chains and to encoder networks is presented, and the key idea of optimising the *joint* probability density of the state of the processing chain is stated. An example of the application of these ideas to processing data from multiple correlated sources (i.e. a hierarchically correlated phase screen) is then given.

1 Introduction

The aim of this paper is to show how the problem of optimising the processing chain in a classifier combiner network can be recast as a Markov chain optimisation problem, where the input to the chain is the original data (possibly derived from multiple sensors) that needs to be classified, and the stages of the Markov chain progressively process and combine the data as it passes along the chain.

The key problem is to choose a suitable objective function for optimising the properties of the Markov chain. In this paper the joint PDF of the states in the chain is represented in two ways corresponding to forwards and backwards passes through the chain. The objective is to maximise the log-likelihood that the backwards pass generates states that look as if they were derived from the forward pass, which is equivalent to minimising the number of bits per symbol needed to specify the state of the chain (forward pass) using a model (backward pass). This idea was originally proposed in [1]. The objective function can be interpreted as imposing a self-consistency condition on the forwards and backwards passes through the Markov chain. Note that although these two directions are related by Bayes theorem, in this approach they are treated as being independent, although they must satisfy the above self-consistency condition.

It turns out that this type of Markov chain is very useful for implementing classifier combiner networks, because if the forward pass through the chain is arranged to compress the data (e.g. by progressively reducing the size of the state space as the data passes along the chain), then the above optimisation is forced to find efficient ways of encoding the data. Typically, as the data passes along the chain its small degrees of freedom and its internal correlations are progressively removed, and by the time the data emerges from the far end of the chain only a few large degrees of freedom remain. In the classifier combiner context the data is encoded in great detail

T. Windeatt and F. Roli (Eds.): MCS 2003, LNCS 2709, pp. 217–226, 2003.
© Springer-Verlag Berlin Heidelberg 2003

near the start of the chain, whereas it is encoded in coarse outline near the far end of the chain, and the progressive compression of the fine detail into coarse outline has exactly the form of a familiar (and possibly hierarchical) classifier combiner network.

In Sect. 2 a brief summary of the relevant parts of coding theory is given, focusing on coding of sources and then generalising to Markov sources. In Sect. 3 these results are applied to Markov chains used as encoder networks, and the results obtained are shown to be equivalent to the self organising network introduced in [2] and used for some simple classifier combiner applications in [3]. In Sect. 4 these results are applied to the problem of designing classifier combiner networks, and this is illustrated by a simulation in which hierarchically correlated phase screen data causes the self-organising network to develop a hierarchical data processing architecture.

2   Coding Theory

The purpose of this section is to firmly establish the underlying principles on which the later derivations depend. In Sect. 2.1 a brief summary of source coding theory is given, and in Sect. 2.2 this is generalised to Markov chain sources. A useful reference work on coding theory is [4], the original papers on information theory are [5], and for a discussion on the number of bits required to encode a source see [6].

2.1   Source Coding

A source of symbols (drawn from an alphabet of M distinct symbols) is modelled by a vector of probabilities P

$$P \equiv (P_1, P_2, \cdots, P_M) \tag{1}$$

which describes the relative frequency with which each symbol is drawn independently from the source P. An ordered sequence of symbols may be partitioned into long subsequences of N symbols, and each such subsequence will be called a message. A message from P will be called a P-message. The number of times n_i that each symbol i occurs in a P-message of length N is $n_i = N P_i$, where $\sum_{i=1}^{M} P_i = 1$ guarantees that the normalisation condition $\sum_{i=1}^{M} n_i = N$ is satisfied. Define the entropy $H(P)$ of source P as the logarithm of the number of different P-messages (per message symbol)

$$H(P) \equiv -\sum_{i=1}^{M} P_i \log P_i \geq 0 \tag{2}$$

where $H(P)$ is the number of bits per symbol (on average) that is required to encode the source assuming a perfect encoder.

The mathematical model of P may be derived from a vector of probabilities Q, whose M elements model the probability of each symbol drawn from an alphabet of M distinct symbols. The log-probability $\Pi_N(P, Q)$ that a Q-message is a P-message is

$$\Pi_N(P, Q) \approx -N \sum_{i=1}^{M} P_i \log \frac{P_i}{Q_i} \leq 0 \tag{3}$$

which is negative because the model Q generates P-messages with less than unit probability. The model Q must be used to generate enough Q-messages to ensure that all of the P-messages are reproduced. This requires the basic $H(P)$ bits per symbol that would be required if $Q = P$, plus some extra bits to compensate for the less than 100 % efficiency (because $Q \neq P$) with which Q generates P-messages. The number of extra bits per symbol is the relative entropy $G(P, Q)$ which is defined as

$$G(P, Q) \equiv \sum_{i=1}^{M} P_i \log \frac{P_i}{Q_i} \geq 0 \qquad (4)$$

Thus $G(P, Q)$ is $-\frac{\Pi_N (P,Q)}{N}$, which is minus the log-probability (per symbol) that a Q-message is a P-message. Thus Q is used to generate exactly the number of extra Q-messages that is required to compensate for the fact that the probability that each Q-message is a P-message is less than unity (i.e. $\Pi_N (P, Q) \leq 0$). $G(P, Q)$ (i.e. relative entropy) is the amount by which the number of bits per symbol exceeds the lower bound $H(P)$ (i.e. source entropy). For convenience, define the *total* number of bits per symbol $H(P) + G(P, Q)$ as $L(P, Q)$

$$L(P, Q) \equiv H(P) + G(P, Q) = -\sum_{i=1}^{M} P_i \log Q_i \geq 0 \qquad (5)$$

The expression for $G(P, Q)$ provides a means of optimising the model Q. Ideally the number of extra bits that is required to compensate for the inefficiency of the model should be as small as possible, which requires that the optimum model Q_{opt} should minimise the objective function $G(P, Q)$ with respect to Q, thus

$$Q_{opt} = \frac{\arg \min}{Q} G(P, Q) = \frac{\arg \max}{Q} \log(Q_1^{n_1} Q_2^{n_2} \cdots Q_M^{n_M}) \qquad (6)$$

where $\log(Q_1^{n_1} Q_2^{n_2} \cdots Q_M^{n_M})$ is the log-probability that a message of length N generated by Q is a P-message. $G(P, Q)$ is frequently used as an objective function in density modelling. The optimum model Q_{opt} is chosen as the one that maximises the log-probability of generating the observed data $(n_1, n_2, \cdots, n_M)$. Since Q_{opt} must, in some sense, be close to P, this affords a practical way of ensuring that the optimum model probabilities Q_{opt} are similar to the source probabilities P, which is the goal of density modelling.

2.2 Markov Chain Coding

The above scheme for using a model Q to code symbols derived from a source P may be extended to the case where the source and the model are L-stage Markov chains as discussed in [1]. Thus P and Q can be split into separate pieces associated with each stage

$$\begin{aligned}
P &= P^0 P^{1|0} \cdots P^{L-1|L-2} P^{L|L-1} = P^{0|1} P^{1|2} \cdots P^{L-1|L} P^L \\
Q &= Q^0 Q^{1|0} \cdots Q^{L-1|L-2} Q^{L|L-1} = Q^{0|1} Q^{1|2} \cdots Q^{L-1|L} Q^L
\end{aligned} \qquad (7)$$

where $P^{k|l}$ ($Q^{k|l}$) is the matrix of transition probabilities from layer l to layer k of the Markov chain of the source (model), P^0 (Q^0) is the vector of marginal probabilities in layer 0, and P^L (Q^L) is the vector of marginal probabilities in layer L. These two ways of decomposing P (and Q) are equivalent, because a forward pass through a

Markov chain may be converted into a backward pass through another Markov chain, where the transition probabilities in the two chains are related via Bayes' theorem.

The *total* number of bits per symbol required to code the source P with the model Q is $L(P, Q)$ (i.e. $H(P) + G(P, Q)$) is given by

$$L(P, Q) = \sum_{l=0}^{L-1} \sum_{i_{l+1}=1}^{M_{l+1}} P_{i_{l+1}}^{l+1} L_{i_{l+1}} (P^{l|l+1}, Q^{l|l+1}) + L(P^L, Q^L) \tag{8}$$

where the suffix i_{l+1} appears on the $L_{i_{l+1}} (P^{l|l+1}, Q^{l|l+1})$ because the state of layer $l + 1$ is fixed during the evaluation of $L_{i_{l+1}} (P^{l|l+1}, Q^{l|l+1})$.

This result has a very natural interpretation. Both the source P and the model Q are Markov chains, and corresponding parts of the model are matched up with corresponding parts of the source. First of all, the number of bits that is required to encode the Lth layer of the source is $L(P^L, Q^L)$. Having done that, the number of bits that is required to encode the $L - 1^{th}$ layer of the source, given that the state of the Lth layer is already known, is $L_L (P^{L-1|L}, Q^{L-1|L})$, which must then be averaged over the alternative possible states of the Lth layer to yield $\sum_{i_L=1}^{M_L} P_{i_L}^L L_L (P^{L-1|L}, Q^{L-1|L})$. This process is then repeated to encode the $L - 2^{th}$ layer of the source, given that the state of the $L - 1^{th}$ layer is already known, and so on back to layer 0. This yields precisely the expression for $L(P, Q)$ given above.

Now evaluate the expression for $L(P, Q)$ in the case where P and Q run in opposite directions through the Markov chain. Define $K_{i_l} (P^{l+1|l}, Q^{l|l+1})$ as

$$K_{i_l} (P^{l+1|l}, Q^{l|l+1}) \equiv - \sum_{i_{l+1}=1}^{M_{l+1}} P_{i_{l+1},i_l}^{l+1|l} \log Q_{i_l,i_{l+1}}^{l|l+1} \tag{9}$$

which allows the $P_{i_{l+1}}^{l+1} L_{i_{l+1}} (P^{l|l+1}, Q^{l|l+1})$ terms in $L(P, Q)$ to be rewritten as

$$\sum_{i_{l+1}=1}^{M_{l+1}} P_{i_{l+1}}^{l+1} L_{i_{l+1}} (P^{l|l+1}, Q^{l|l+1}) = \sum_{i_l=1}^{M_l} P_{i_l}^l K_{i_l} (P^{l+1|l}, Q^{l|l+1}) \tag{10}$$

whence $L(P, Q)$ may be written as

$$L(P, Q) = \sum_{l=0}^{L-1} \sum_{i_l=1}^{M_l} P_{i_l}^l K_{i_l} (P^{l+1|l}, Q^{l|l+1}) + L(P^L, Q^L) \tag{11}$$

3   Encoder Networks

The purpose of this section is to translate the Markov chain theory results that were summarised in the previous section into a notation that is more appropriate for processing vectors of input data, and which also makes contact with previous results on encoder networks. In Sect. 3.1 the results of Sect. 2.2 are shown to be equivalent to stochastic vector quantiser (SVQ) theory (which is a particular instance of ACEnet - the adaptive cluster expansion network [7]), and in Sect. 3.2 this is generalised to multi-stage stochastic vector quantiser theory.

3.1   1-Stage Markov Chain

Use the expression for $L(P, Q)$ in equation 11 to obtain the objective function for a 1-stage (i.e. $L = 1$) Markov chain

$$L(P, Q) = \sum_{i_0=1}^{M_0} P_{i_0}^0 K_{i_0} (P^{1|0}, Q^{0|1}) + L(P^1, Q^1) \tag{12}$$

Now change notation in order to make contact with previous results on autoencoders [2]: $i_0 \longrightarrow x$ (input vector), $i_1 \longrightarrow y$ (output code index vector), $\sum_{i_0=1}^{M_0} \longrightarrow \int dx$, $\sum_{i_1=1}^{M_1} \longrightarrow \sum_y$, $P_{i_0}^0 \longrightarrow \Pr(x)$ (input PDF), $P_{i_1,i_0}^{1|0} \longrightarrow \Pr(y \mid x)$ (encoder), $Q_{i_0,i_1}^{0|1} \longrightarrow V \frac{1}{(\sqrt{2\pi}\,\sigma)^{\dim x}} \exp\left(-\frac{\|x - x'(y)\|^2}{2\sigma^2}\right)$ (decoder, where V is an infinitesimal volume element). This allows $L(P, Q)$ to be written as

$$L(P, Q) = \frac{1}{4\sigma^2} D_{SVQ} - \log \frac{V}{(\sqrt{2\pi}\,\sigma)^{\dim x}} + L(P^1, Q^1) \tag{13}$$

where D_{SVQ} is the objective function for a stochastic vector quantiser (SVQ) defined as in [2]

$$D_{SVQ} \equiv 2 \int dx\, \Pr(x) \sum_y \Pr(y \mid x) \|x - x'(y)\|^2 \tag{14}$$

If the cost of coding the output (i.e. $L(P^1, Q^1)$) is ignored, then provided that V and σ are fixed quantities, the 2-layer Markov source coding objective function $L(P, Q)$ can be minimised by minimising the SVQ objective function D_{SVQ}.

If $y = (y_1, y_2, \cdots, y_n)$ where $y_i = 1, 2, \cdots, M$, and $\Pr(y \mid x) = \Pr(y_1 \mid x)\Pr(y_2 \mid x)\cdots\Pr(y_n \mid x)$, then $D_{SVQ} \leq D_1 + D_2$ where D_1 and D_2 are defined as in [2]

$$D_1 \equiv \frac{2}{n} \int dx\, \Pr(x) \sum_{y=1}^M \Pr(y \mid x) \|x - x'(y)\|^2 \tag{15}$$

$$D_2 \equiv \frac{2(n-1)}{n} \int dx\, \Pr(x) \left\|x - \sum_{y=1}^M \Pr(y \mid x)\, x'(y)\right\|^2$$

$x'(y)$ is used to approximate $x'(y)$ thus

$$x'(y) \approx \frac{1}{n} \sum_{i=1}^n x'(y_i) = \sum_{y=1}^M n(y)\, x'(y) \tag{16}$$

where $n(y)$ is the number of times that the term $x'(y)$ appears in the sum $\sum_{i=1}^n x'(y_i)$, so $n = (n(1), n(2), \cdots, n(M))$ (where $n = \sum_{y=1}^M n(y)$) is the histogram derived from the vector of samples $y = (y_1, y_2, \cdots, y_n)$ drawn from $\Pr(y \mid x)$. Similarly $\Pr(y \mid x)$ may be written as

$$\Pr(y \mid x) = \prod_{i=1}^n \Pr(y_i \mid x) = \prod_{y=1}^M \Pr(y \mid x)^{n(y)} \tag{17}$$

so $\Pr(y \mid x)$ is a function of only the histogram n of samples independently drawn from $\Pr(y \mid x)$ (i.e. n is a sufficient set of statistics for $\Pr(y \mid x)$). This fact allows the histogram n to be used instead of the vector of samples y where convenient. Note that the normalised histogram $\frac{n}{n}$ is also a sufficient statistic, because the value of n is known so it can later be removed to recover n.

3.2 Multi-Stage Markov Chain

The results will now be generalised to an L-stage (i.e. $L+1$ layers) Markov chain to yield

$$L(P, Q) = \sum_{l=0}^{L-1} \left(\frac{D_{SVQ}^l}{4(\sigma^l)^2} - \log \frac{V^l}{(\sqrt{2\pi}\,\sigma^l)^{\dim x^l}} \right) + L(P^L, Q^L) \tag{18}$$

where x^l is the input vector to stage l, which is chosen to be the sufficient statistic $\frac{n^{l-1}}{n^{l-1}}$ derived from the output vector y^{l-1} from stage $l-1$. Unlike the original Markov chain, this sufficient statistic prescription causes the input to stage l to be *different from* the output from stage $l-1$, but this difference does not affect the statistical properties of the Markov chain, as would be expected since suffcient statistics have been used. Note that other sufficient statistics (such as n itself) could be used instead of the above prescription.

$L(P, Q)$ is a sum of 1-stage SVQ objective functions (where each term is weighted by $(\sigma^l)^{-2}$), plus an output coding cost $L(P^L, Q^L)$. If the cost of coding the final output is ignored, then the multi-stage Markov chain objective function $L(P, Q)$ is minimised by minimising the sum of 1-stage SVQ objective functions $\sum_{l=0}^{L-1} \frac{D_{SVQ}^l}{(\sigma^l)^2}$.

These main benefit of the results is that they provide a unifying framework for a wide variety of previous results (e.g. [2, 3, 7, 8]). For instance, in [3] a simple classifier combiner problem was addressed, in which the stages of the chain were linked together, not by the normalised histogram $\frac{n}{n}$, but by the vector of probabilities $(\Pr(y=1\,|\,x), \Pr(y=2\,|\,x), \cdots, \Pr(y=M\,|\,x))$. In the limit $n \longrightarrow \infty$ these are equivalent prescriptions, because the normalised histogram represented by $\frac{n}{n}$ has a limiting form that is identical to the underlying probabilities $(\Pr(y=1\,|\,x), \Pr(y=2\,|\,x), \cdots, \Pr(y=M\,|\,x))$ that are used to generate it. When n is finite the histogram fluctuates in shape about the limiting form of histogram, and provided these fluctuations are not too large it turns out that they are ignored by the encoder in the next stage of the Markov chain. Thus, for Markov chains that progressively compress the data as it passes along the chain, it is valid to use the vector of probabilities $(\Pr(y=1\,|\,x), \Pr(y=2\,|\,x), \cdots, \Pr(y=M\,|\,x))$ to link the stages of the chain *even though* more generally the normalised histogram (with its fluctuations) $\frac{n}{n}$ should be used. This comment assumes that each encoder in the chain ignores (i.e. is invariant to) the degrees of freedom that comprise the fluctuations about the limiting form of each normalised histogram (see [8] for detailed analysis of invariance).

A useful side effect of using the vector of probabilities to link the stages of the chain is that the effect of later stages of the chain is to soften the probabilities used by the earlier stages, which encourages the development of separate information processing channels in intermediate stages of the processing chain.

4   Classifier Combiner Networks

The purpose of this section is to show how the encoder network results of the previous section are applicable to problems of combining classifiers, and to give an example to illustrate how this approach works in practice. In Sect. 4.1 the problem of combining classifiers is recast as a problem of designing Markov chains of the type discussed in Sect. 2 and Sect. 3, and in Sect. 4.2 these results are illustrated by a simulation.

4.1   Augmented Input Space

The L stage Markov chain has the objective function given in Eq. 18, which is (up to an additive constant) the weighted sum of L SVQ objective functions (D_{SVQ}^l, $l = 0, 1, \cdots, L - 1$), corresponding to the individual stages of the chain leading from layer 0 (the original input layer) to layer L (the final output layer), plus a term $L(P^L, Q^L)$ corresponding to the final output from the chain. The sum of all of these contributions (i.e. the overall objective function) is $L(P, Q)$ for the whole chain, whose relevance to the problem of combining classifiers will now be discussed.

In pattern processing the basic problem is to characterise the PDF of the input P^0. The simplest approach is to introduce a model Q^0, and to optimise it by minimising the number of bits $L(P^0, Q^0)$ needed to specify the input (as specified by P^0) using a model (as specified by Q^0). This approach is widely used but it has limited flexibility because the model is used to *directly* characterise the input, rather than *indirectly* characterise it by modelling its underlying causes (for instance). More flexibility is possible if the input is augmented to include properties derived from the original input, and then a model is used to characterise the *whole* augmented input (i.e. original input *and* derived properties). If these properties of the input are obtained by applying an L-stage Markov chain of processing to the original input, then the PDF P^0 is augmented to become the *joint* PDF $P^0 P^{1|0} \cdots P^{L-1|L-2} P^{L|L-1}$ and PDF Q^0 becomes the *joint* PDF $Q^0 Q^{1|0} \cdots Q^{L-1|L-2} Q^{L|L-1}$, which is exactly the same as the Markov chain model in Eq. 7.

In the approach described in this paper the objective function is applied to the *whole* Markov chain (i.e $L(P, Q)$) rather than to *only* its input (i.e. $L(P^0, Q^0)$) as is usually the case in PDF modelling, because this leads more naturally to many useful self-organising properties. $L(P, Q)$ has two types of contribution. The sum of SVQ objective functions (D_{SVQ}^l, $l = 0, 1, \cdots, L - 1$) acts to encourage the augmented input to encode useful information about the original input. The term $L(P^L, Q^L)$ acts to encourage the formation of a good model Q^L of the final encoded output P^L. Typically the properties of P^L are much simpler than those of the original input P^0, so the problem of minimising $L(P^L, Q^L)$ is much simpler than minimising $L(P^0, Q^0)$. Also optimising the Markov chain reduces to a number of simpler coupled optimisation problems. In the simulation presented in Sect. 4.2 the $L(P^L, Q^L)$ term is omitted from the objective function.

There is a lot of flexibility in controlling the type of Markov chain that is used to augment the input space. The properties of each encoder (i.e. each stage of the chain) can be controlled by selecting its code book size M (i.e. the size of the stage output layer), number of samples n (i.e. the number of code indices that are independently sampled), and standard deviation σ (i.e. the smaller σ is the larger the stage weighting is in the objective function). The interaction between the stages depends on the choice of these parameters in all of the stages of the chain.

Optimisation of the objective function for the whole Markov chain leads to the self-organising emergence of classifier combiner networks. Each stage of the chain automatically *splits* into a number of separate information processing channels, and the stages of the chain automatically connect together to progressively *merge* the information flowing along these channels. This splitting and merging of information is the origin of the classifier combiner properties of the approach described in this paper.

4.2   Example of Combining Classifiers

The properties of the objective function $L(P, Q)$ are difficult to derive analytically, so a numerical simulation will now be used to illustrate the key property (i.e. splitting and merging of information channels) of the self-organising design of classifier combiner networks.

A hierarchical model will be used to generate the training data. The specific model will be a hierarchically generated vector of phases $(\phi_1, \phi_2, \phi_3, \phi_4)$ (i.e. "phase screen") that is generated from a single randomly chosen initial phase ϕ_{1234} using the following splitting processes: $\phi_{1234} \longrightarrow (\phi_{12}, \phi_{34})$, $\phi_{12} \longrightarrow (\phi_1, \phi_2)$, $\phi_{34} \longrightarrow (\phi_3, \phi_4)$. ϕ_{12} is uniformly distributed in the interval $[\phi_{1234} - \frac{\pi}{2}, \phi_{1234}]$, ϕ_{34} is uniformly distributed in the interval $[\phi_{1234}, \phi_{1234} + \frac{\pi}{2}]$, ϕ_1 is uniformly distributed in the interval $[\phi_{12} - \frac{\pi}{2}, \phi_{12}]$, ϕ_2 is uniformly distributed in the interval $[\phi_{12}, \phi_{12} + \frac{\pi}{2}]$, ϕ_3 is uniformly distributed in the interval $[\phi_{34} - \frac{\pi}{2}, \phi_{34}]$, and ϕ_4 is uniformly distributed in the interval $[\phi_{34}, \phi_{34} + \frac{\pi}{2}]$.

The phase screen $(\phi_1, \phi_2, \phi_3, \phi_4)$ must be pre-processed in order to convert it into a form that is suitable for input to a chain of encoders. Each phase variable parameterises a circular manifold that needs to be embedded in a 2-dimensional space (i.e. $\phi \longrightarrow (\cos \phi, \sin \phi)$). Thus the phase screen is embedded in an 8-dimensional space $\qquad (\phi_1, \phi_2, \phi_3, \phi_4) \longrightarrow (x_1, x_2, x_3, x_4, x_5, x_6, x_7, x_8) \qquad$ where $(x_{2i-1}, x_{2i}) = (\cos \phi_i, \sin \phi_i)$ for $i = 1, 2, 3, 4$.

The phase screen $(\phi_1, \phi_2, \phi_3, \phi_4)$ is parameterised by 4 phase variables, so it lives on a 4-torus manifold. The embedding $(x_1, x_2, x_3, x_4, x_5, x_6, x_7, x_8)$ of the phase screen is thus an embedding of a 4-torus in an 8-dimensional space. Each possible phase screen $(\phi_1, \phi_2, \phi_3, \phi_4)$ is represented by one point on this 4-torus manifold. The presence of correlations between the phase variables means that the probability density assigned to each point on the 4-torus manifold is non-uniform. The hierarchical structure of these correlations causes a characteristic pattern of probability density variations on the 4-torus manifold, which then influences the way in which a chain of encoders decides how to encode such data.

Ideally, although this is not guaranteed, a 3-stage chain of encoders will attempt to invert the process whereby the phase screen data was generated. Thus it will first encode the data as 4 separate phase variables (corresponding to $(\phi_1, \phi_2, \phi_3, \phi_4)$), which it will then encode as 2 separate phase variables (corresponding to (ϕ_{12}, ϕ_{34})), which it will then encode as 1 phase variable (corresponding to ϕ_{1234}). Each successive encoding stage reduces the dimensionality of the encoded representation of the original data. This is achieved by progressively introducing invariances (i.e. removing degrees of freedom from the encoded representation) into the overall encoder. The stage 1 encoder removes no degrees of freedom, the stage 2 encoder removes 2 phase degrees of freedom, and finally the stage 3 encoder removes 1 more phase degree of freedom. This particular sequence of invariances is not guaranteed, but must be discovered by choosing appropriate parameter values (i.e. code book size, number of samples, and weighting in the objective function) for each encoder in the chain. In general, different choices of the encoder parameters will lead to different encoding schemes.

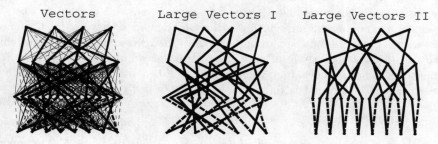

Fig. 1. Reconstruction vectors in a trained 3-stage network. The left hand diagram shows all of the reconstruction vectors, using thickness to indicate absolute value and dashing to indicate negative values. The centre diagram shows only the reconstruction vector components with the largest absolute value. The right hand diagram is the same as the centre diagram except that the order of the code indices in layers 1, 2, and 3 have been permuted (together with their connections) to show more clearly the overall network connectivity.

The chosen Markov chain network has layer sizes (4 layers) chosen so as to compress the data as it flows along the chain: $M = (8, 16, 8, 4)$, numbers of samples (3 stages) $n = (20, 20, 20)$, and has stage weightings (3 stages) $\frac{1}{4\sigma^2} = (1.0, 5.0, 0.1)$. In Eq. 15 (for each stage of the network) the posterior probability is parameterised as $P(y \mid x) = \frac{Q(y|x)}{\sum_{y'} Q(y'|x)}$ where $Q(y \mid x) = \frac{1}{1+\exp(-w(y).x-b(y))}$, and all the components of the weight vectors $w(y)$, biases $b(y)$, and reconstruction vectors $x'(y)$ are initialised to random numbers uniformly distributed in the interval $[-0.1, +0.1]$. The network is trained by a simple gradient descent algorithm using the derivatives of $D_1 + D_2$ obtained from Eq. 15. The detailed derivatives are given in [2].

Fig. 1 shows the reconstruction vectors in the trained 3-stage network. The right hand diagram clearly shows that the network has configured itself into a hierarchical processing architecture which processess the input in separate information channels that are progressively fused as the data passes upwards through the network.

5 Conclusions

The problem of optimising a classifier combiner network has been recast as a Markov chain optimisation problem [3]. The input to the chain is the original data (possibly derived from multiple sensors) that needs to be classified, and the stages of the Markov chain progressively process and combine the data as it passes along the chain, as illustrated by a simulation using hierarchically correlated phase screen data. This approach has been shown to be equivalent to multi-stage stochastic vector quantiser theory [2, 7, 8].

This approach is based on optimising the *joint* probability density of the states of *all* of the layers in the Markov chain that processes the input data [1], rather than optimising only the probability density of the input layer, as is usually the case. The objective function used to achieve this is the *total* number of bits needed to code the forward pass through the chain using a model of the reverse pass through the chain. The fact that the state space of each layer of the network is predefined (i.e. fixed number of samples drawn from a code book of fixed size) ensures that when the Markov chain is optimised useful properties emerge by self-organisation.

6 Acknowledgement

This work was carried out as part of Technology Group 10 of the MoD Corporate Research Programme.

References

1. Luttrell, S. P.: A Unified Theory of Density Models and Auto-Encoders. Isaac Newton Institute for Mathematical Sciences, Preprint Series, No. NI97039-NNM (1997)
2. Luttrell, S. P.: A Theory of Self-Organising Neural Networks. In: Ellacott, S. W., Mason, J. C., and Anderson, I. J. (eds.): Mathematics of Neural Networks: Models, Algorithms and Applications, Kluwer (1997) 240-244
3. Luttrell, S. P.: A Self-Organising Approach to Multiple Classifier Fusion. Lecture Notes in Computer Science, Vol. 2096. Springer-Verlag (2001) 319-328
4. McEliece, R. J.: The Theory of Infomation and Coding. Addison-Wesley (1977)
5. Shannon, C. E.: The Mathematical Theory of Communication. Bell Systems Technical Journal **27** (1948) 379-423 and 623-656
6. Rissanen, J., Stochastic Complexity in Statistical Enquiry. Series in Computer Science, Vol. 15. World Scientific (1989)
7. Luttrell, S. P.: A Discrete Firing Event Analysis of the Adaptive Cluster Expansion Network. Network: Computation in Neural Systems **7** (1996) 285-290
8. Luttrell, S. P.: Using Stochastic Vector Quantisers to Characterise Signal and Noise Subspaces. In: McWhirter, J. G., and Proudler, I. K. (eds.): Mathematics in Signal Processing V. OUP (2002) 193-204

A Study of Ensemble of Hybrid Networks
with Strong Regularization

Shimon Cohen and Nathan Intrator*

School of Computer Science, Tel Aviv University
Ramat Aviv 69978, Israel
shimon_cohen2000@yahoo.com, nin@cs.tau.ac.il
www.cs.tau.ac.il/~nin

Abstract. We study various ensemble methods for hybrid neural networks. The hybrid networks are composed of radial and projection units and are trained using a deterministic algorithm that completely defines the parameters of the network for a given data set. Thus, there is no random selection of the initial (and final) parameters as in other training algorithms. Network independent is achieved by using bootstrap and boosting methods as well as random input sub-space sampling. The fusion methods are evaluated on several classification benchmark data-sets. A novel MDL based fusion method appears to reduce the variance of the classification scheme and sometimes be superior in its overall performance.

1 Introduction

Hybrid neural networks that are composed of radial basis functions and perceptrons have been recently introduced [5,4]. Such networks employ a deterministic algorithm that computes the initial parameters from the training data. Thus, networks that have been trained on the same data-set produce the same solution and therefore, a combination of such classifiers can not enhance the performance over a single one.

Fusion of experts has been studied extensively recently. One of the main results is that experts have to be partially independent for the fusion to be effective [13,14]. The bagging algorithm [1] can be used to de-correlate between classifiers as well as to obtain some performance measure on the accuracy of the classifiers using the "out of bag" sub-set of the data. Another technique Arcing – adaptive re-weighting and combining – refers to reusing or selecting data in order to improve classification [2]. One popular arcing procedure is AdaBoost [10], in which the errors on the training data-sets are used to train more specific classifiers. Sub-sampling of the input space as well as the training patters is extensively used in the random forest algorithm [3]. A different flavor of combination of classifiers use dynamic class combination (DCS) [11] and Classifiers Local Accuracy (CLA) in order to select the best classifier when making a predication.

---

* Corresponding author's address: Institute for Brain and Neural Systems, Box 1843, Brown University, Providence, RI 02912, USA

T. Windeatt and F. Roli (Eds.): MCS 2003, LNCS 2709, pp. 227–235, 2003.

This is done at the cost of saving the whole training set and then selecting the predication of the best classifier at the vicinity of a given pattern.

The hybrid Perceptron Radial Basis Function Network (PRBFN) is constructed with strong regularization and with initial parameters that are estimated from the data and not random. The strong regularization and excellent approximation properties of a hybrid of projection and radial units leads to a relatively small architecture, which, in addition to the strong regularization leads to an estimator with low variance. Thus, ensemble combination, which is known to reduce the variance portion of the error is more challenging. In this paper, we investigate the use of ensemble fusion methods on a collection of low variance classifiers with a deterministic training algorithm. Several ways to increase the classifiers' independence are studied as well as different combination strategies.

In addition, we use the MDL approach for expert fusion, and estimate the accuracy of each classifier by using its description length. The description length, is then used as a weight in a convex combination of the experts, where a shorter description length, gives higher weight.

2   Training an Ensemble

Training of individual elements in an ensemble for improved independence can be done in several ways. The random forest algorithm [3] uses sub-space re-sampling for each node in the tree. AdaBoost [10] uses a fraction of the data (which earlier classifiers performed poorly on) to train a classifier, thus different classifiers train on different data-sets. We use both techniques to increase classifier's independence.

The output of the ensemble is given by:

$$f(x) = \sum_{k=1}^{M} a_k f_k(x) \qquad a_k \geq 0, \qquad \sum_{k=1}^{M} a_k = 1, \tag{1}$$

where a_k is the weight of the kth expert. Other forms of combination will be discussed below.

2.1   Ensemble Generation

We have used "boosting" to generate data sets for the classifiers in the ensemble. In boosting, the first classifier is created with accuracy on the training set greater than chance, and then add new component classifiers to form an ensemble whose joint decision rule has arbitrary high accuracy on the training set. This technique trains successive components classifiers with the subset of data that is most informative. Given a data set $D = \{x_i, y_i\}_{i=1}^{N}$ where $x_i \in R^d$ and y_i is the class label. The input to the algorithm includes the maximum number of classifiers k_{max}, the size of re-sampled sub set of D $n < N$, and $\gamma \in [0, 1]$ the fraction of features for the random subspace selection. We use the following boosting algorithm:

- Initialize: empty ensemble, k=0
- while $k \leq k_{max}$
  - test the ensemble on the full training-set.
  - add to the current dataset D_k the misclassified patterns
  - select randomly $n - |D_k|$ from $D - D_k$ and add them to D_k
  - re-sample D_k on the features by using $\gamma * d$ features.
- end-loop

The above algorithm differs from the AdaBoost algorithm [10], as **all** the misclassified patterns are added to the next subset (with probability 1). Each classifier receives a different subsample of the training data and a different subsample of the input variables as in Random Forests. Thus, dependency between experts is greatly reduced.

2.2 Using MDL for Experts Fusion

The minimum description length (MDL) concept is typically used for model evaluation and selection. It is used here for weighting the different experts for optimal combination. In the MDL formulation, the coding of the data is combined with the coding of the model itself to provide the full description of the data [16]. MDL can be formulated for an imaginary communication channel, in which a sender observes the data D and thus can estimate its distribution, and form an appropriate model for that distribution. The sender then transmits the data using the code that is appropriate for the observed distribution (data model) but since the receiver does not observe the full data, the model has to be transmitted to the receiver (in a predefined coding). Noise and insufficient data to estimate the correct model lead to modeling errors. MDL has been constructed for the purpose of reducing such modeling errors. The MDL principle asserts that the best model of some data is the one that minimizes the combined cost of describing the model and the misfit between the model and the data.

This approach is formulated as follows: The sender composes a message which is consists of the model description with the length $\ell(M)$, and $\ell(D|M)$ specifies the length of the data given the model. The goal of the sender is to find the model that minimizes the length of this encoded message $\ell(M, D)$, called the description length:

$$\ell(M, D) = \ell(D|M) + \ell(M). \tag{2}$$

According to Shannon's theory, to encode a random variable X with a known distribution by the minimum number of bits, a realization of x has to be encoded by $-\log(p(x))$ bits [18,6]. Thus, the description length is:

$$\ell(M, D) = -\log(p(D|M)) - \log(p(M)), \tag{3}$$

where $p(M|D)$ is the probability of the output data given the model, and $p(M)$ is $a - priori$ model probability. Typically the MDL principle is used to select the model with the shorter description length. In this work we combine the experts by using the description length as a weight for the convex combination in Eq. (1). Hinton and Camp [12] used zero-mean Gaussian distribution for the neural network weights. We follow this idea, and define the simplest Gaussian model prior,

$$p(M) = \frac{1}{(2\pi)^{1/2}\beta^d} exp(-\frac{\sum_{i=1}^{d} w_i^2}{2\beta^2}), \tag{4}$$

where d is the number of weights in the second layer and β is the standard deviation. Hinton and Camp [12] used a Gaussian with standard deviation α for encoding the output errors. In addition, we assume that the errors that the model makes are i.i.d with normal distribution. Clearly, a better assumption is that the error are binomial, but for purpose of estimating the relative probability of different methods the Gaussian assumption is good enough and easier to handle mathematically. We also assume that the patterns in the training set are independent.

Thus, the likelihood of the data given the model is:

$$p(D|M) = \frac{1}{(2\pi)^{\frac{NC}{2}} \alpha^{NC}} \exp(-\frac{\sum_{n=1}^{N} \sum_{k=1}^{C} (y_{kn} - t_{kn})^2}{2\alpha^2}), \tag{5}$$

where t_{kn} is the target value for the nth pattern at the k'th class, y_{kn} is the respected output of the expert and α is the standard deviation. Under these assumptions the description length of the model is:

$$\ell(M, D) = \frac{NC}{2} \log(2\pi) + NC \log(\alpha) + \frac{\sum_{n=1}^{N} \sum_{k=1}^{C} (y_{kn} - t_{kn})^2}{2\alpha^2} +$$
$$\frac{d}{2} \log(2\pi) + d \log(\beta) + \sum_{i=1}^{d} \frac{w_i^2}{2\alpha^2}. \tag{6}$$

Differentiating Eq. (6) with respect to α and equating to zero, we obtain:

$$\alpha^2 = \frac{1}{NC} \sum_{n=1}^{N} \sum_{k=1}^{C} (y_{kn} - t_{kn})^2. \tag{7}$$

Differentiating Eq. (6) with respect to β and equating to zero, we obtain:

$$\beta^2 = \frac{1}{d} \sum_{i=1}^{d} w_i^2. \tag{8}$$

Substituting Eq. (7) and Eq. (8) into Eq. (6) and discarding the constant terms we arrive at:

$$\ell(M, D) = NC \log(\alpha) + d \log(\beta) + \frac{d}{2}(1 + \log(2\pi)). \tag{9}$$

Equation (9) shows that the description length of the model is a tradeoff between the errors and the number of parameters d and their average value. Considering description length as an energy and following Gibbs distribution formulation, we use the description length as a weight for each classifier in the convex combination as follows:

$$a_k = \frac{\exp(-\ell_k(M, D))}{\sum_{k=1}^{M} \exp(-\ell_k(M, D))}, \tag{10}$$

where M is the number of classifiers. Thus, a classifier with a shorter description length gets higher weight when combining the output of the ensemble. This is in contrast to other fusion methods when only the error is considered.

2.3   Other Expert Fusion Methodologies

In addition to the MDL fusion method, we have used five more classifier combination rules. They are described in this section.

I. Majority Rule: The first is the familiar majority vote; Here, the final decision is made by selection of the class with maximum number of votes in the ensemble.

II. Convex Combination: The second strategy relies on a convex combination using the error values from the first stage of training [17]. Let e_i be the classification error of the $i'th$ classifier. We set the weight of this classifier as follows:

$$a_k = \frac{1/e_k}{\sum_{i=1}^{M} 1/e_i}, \tag{11}$$

where M is the number of classifiers in the ensemble. The output of the ensemble is define as in Eq. (1).

III. Convex Combination: The third strategy relies on a convex combination using the error values from the first stage of training. Let e_i be the classification error of the $i'th$ classifier. To maximize the entropy of the ensemble, we set the weight associated with this classifier in accordance with Gibbs distribution as follows:

$$a_k = \frac{\exp(-e_k)}{\sum_{i=1}^{M} \exp(-e_i)}, \tag{12}$$

where M is the number of classifiers in the ensemble. The output of the ensemble is define as in Eq. (1).

IV. Dynamic Selection: The forth strategy involves dynamic selection of the best classifier for prediction of the output value when a novel pattern is given [11]. When the confidence of the best classifier (to be explained below) is below a given threshold, we use a dynamic combination of the classifiers to produce the output of the ensemble. We define a local accuracy for each classifier as follows. Let $k > 0$ and $x \in R^d$ be a novel pattern. Let $D_k(x)$ be the $k-nearest$ patterns in the training set to x. Set the local accuracy of the current classifier on x the to be:

$$l(x) = \frac{\sum_{x_j \in D_k(x)} \delta(\arg\max_i p(y_i|x_j) - \arg\max_j(t_j))}{k}, \quad (13)$$

where $\delta(x)$ is one for $x = 0$ and zero otherwise, and t_j is the target for pattern x_j. Thus, the local accuracy is the number of correct classified patterns in the $k - neighborhood$ of x. Let $l_1(x)$ be the maximum local accuracy and let $l_2(x)$ be the next highest accuracy. Define the confidence level as follows:

$$cl(x) = \frac{l_1(x) - l_2(x)}{l_1(x)}. \quad (14)$$

We further define the weights for each classifier as follows:

$$a_k(x) = \frac{\exp(l_k(x))}{\sum_{i=1}^{M} \exp(l_i(x))}, \quad (15)$$

The combination rule in this case is given by:

- Compute the local accuracy for each classifier as in Eq. (13).
- Compute the confidence level $cl(x)$ from Eq. (14).
- If $\max cl(x) > threshold$, select the output of the best classifier, otherwise use Eq. (1).

V . A daptive B oosting A daB oost: The fifth strategy uses the AdaBoost algorithm [10]. The boosting algorithm AdaBoost - from adaptive boosting - allows the designer to continue adding weak learners until some desired low training error has been achieved. In AdaBoost each training pattern receives a weight which determines its probability of being selected for a training set for an individual component classifier. If a pattern is accurately classified then its chance to be selected again in a subsequent component classifier is reduced. In this way AdaBoost focuses on the difficult-to-classify patterns. We start by initialize the weights to be uniform. On each iteration we draw a training set at random according to these weights. Next we increase weights of misclassified patterns and decrease weights of patterns correctly classified. The new distribution of patterns is used to train the next classifier.

3   Results

The following methods of combination were used:

- ENS1-PRBFN Ensemble using a majority vote strategy.
- ENS2-PRBFN Ensemble using a convex combination (II) as in [17].
- ENS3-PRBFN Ensemble using a convex combination (III) of classifiers where the errors affect the weight of the different classifiers in the ensemble.

Table 1. Comparison of correct classification (percentage) of several ensemble fusion methods using 10 folds cross validation. Ensemble training is done by boosting.

Method	Breast-cancer	Glass	Iris	Vowel	Pima	Image
ENS1-PRBFN	96.5±1.4	96.2±3.5	95.3±4.5	85.2±3.2	77.4±3.2	91.2±6.5
ENS2-PRBFN	96.7±1.4	94.8±4.7	96.7±5.3	86.7±3.9	77.0±3.3	89.4±6.9
ENS3-PRBFN	96.8±1.8	94.2±4.6	96.0±4.5	87.1±4.0	74.9±4.4	90.4±5.6
ENS4-PRBFN	96.4±2.3	94.2±5.2	95.3±5.3	89.3±4.5	76.7±3.7	90.6±5.8
ENS5-PRBFN	97.0±1.5	95.2±3.8	96.0±4.5	87.3±2.7	78.8±2.8	91.9±3.8
ENS6-PRBFN	96.7±1.7	95.0±4.2	96.3±4.5	86.4±2.8	75.8±3.7	92.3±5.6
PRBFN	96.0±2.0	92.8±3.9	95.3±4.6	81.8±2.6	76.6±3.4	88.6±5.4

- ENS4-PRBFN The ensemble using k nearest neighbors (IV) to select the best classifier [11].
- ENS5-PRBFN Ensemble using MDL to set the weight of each classifier in the convex combination.
- ENS6-PRBFN Ensemble using AdaBoost algorithm (V) as describe in [10].
- PRBFN the single classifier as described in [4].

Data Sets Description

The Breast-cancer dataset from the UCI repository was obtained from Dr. William H. Wolberg at the University of Wisconsin Hospitals. This dataset has 9 attributes and two classes and the number of training patterns is 699. The task is to classify the patterns to Benign or Malignant.

The Glass dataset from the UCI repository has 10 attributes and 7 types of glasses. The study of classification of types of glass was motivated by criminological investigation. At the scene of the crime, the glass left can be used as evidence if it is correctly identified! Ripley's best result on this data-set is 80% correct classification [15].

The Iris data-set [8] contains three classes, each with 50 instances. The classes refer to a type of iris plant. Each pattern is composed of four attributes. We used ten folds of cross validation in order to estimate the performance of the different classifiers.

The Deterding vowel recognition data [7,9] is a widely studied benchmark. This problem may be more indicative of a real-world modeling problem. The data consists of auditory features of steady state vowels spoken by British English speakers. There are 528 training patterns and 462 test patterns. Each pattern consists of 10 features and belongs to one of 11 classes that correspond to the spoken vowel. The speakers are of both genders. This data, unlike the other data-sets that have been studied, has a fixed training and test set. We provide results with cross validation in Table 1, where we compare experts on cross validated test set. Previous best score on the fixed test set was reported by Flake using SMLP units. His average best score was 60.6% [9] and was achieved with 44 hidden units. The single PRBFN network surpasses this result and achieves 68.4% correct classification with only 22 hidden units [4]. Thus, the additional improvement that is obtained here using ensemble, puts this result at the top of performance for the vowel data set.

The Image Segmentation data from the UCI repository is composed of 210 instances for train. The instances were drawn randomly from a database of 7 outdoor images. The images were hand-segmented to create a classification for every pixel. Each instance is a 3x3 region and has 19 continuous attributes. The task is to classify to one of the seven classes: brickface, sky, foliage, cement, window, path and grass.

The results in Table 1 are the average of three to ten times cross validation tests of ten folds on each of the data sets. The average performance is given in each entry as well as the variance of each predictor.

4   Discussion

The performance of ensemble methods on a tight architecture, which has been shown to have a low variance portion of the error, was evaluated on several benchmark data-sets. Partial independence of the experts was achieved via boosting or cross validation, and several methods were used for expert fusion. PRBFN is a deterministic classifier with a tightly controlled variance, therefore, simple fusion methods do not improve its performance. For instance, the best known result on the Glass data set is 80% accuracy [15], while PRBFN obtained 92.8% accuracy. We considered few approaches, to enhance the independence of several PRBFN, on the same data set. We note that the improvement of ensemble of such architectures is smaller than improvement that can be achieved on other architectures which posses higher variance, nevertheless, improvement still exists, and is sometimes quite significant.

Most of the fusion methods we have studied, do not appear to be significantly different in their improvement over a single expert. The key factor affecting the improvement is the degree of decorrelation of experts, which in this case, due to the deterministic nature of the architecture, depends on data re-sampling methods. The DCS fusion (ENS4) achieved a noticeable improvement on the Vowel data set. However, we note that this fusion method has large variance. This is due to the fact that quite often, prediction of a single expert (the best classifier) is selected, and thus there is no averaging that reduces the variance. The fusion based on the MDL principle (ENS5-PRBFN) appears to have a lower variance compared with other fusion methods. This is due to the higher emphasis that the MDL approach gives to lower description length and, thus, to simple models with a lower variance. The MDL fusion does not have to store the training data for future prediction and is thus faster in recognition compared with the DCS method.

References

1. L. Breiman. Bagging predictors. *Machine Learning*, 24:123–140, 1996.
2. L. Breiman. Arcing classifiers. *The Annals of Statistics*, 26(3):801–849, 1998.

3. L. Breiman. Random forests. Technical Report, Statistic Department University of California, Berkeley, 2001.
4. S. Cohen and N. Intrator. Automatic model selection in a hybrid perceptron/radial network. *Information Fusion Journal*, 3(4), December 2002.
5. S. Cohen and N. Intrator. A hybrid projection based and radial basis function architecture: Initial values and global optimization. *Pattern Analysis and Applications special issue on Fusion of Multiple Classifiers*, 2:113–120, 2002.
6. T. Cover and J. Thomas. *Elements of Information Theory*. Wiley, 1991.
7. D.H. Deterding. *Speaker Normalisation for Automatic Speech Recognition*. PhD thesis, University of Cambridge, 1989.
8. R. A. Fisher. The use of multiple measurements in taxonomic problems. *Annals of Eugenics*, 7:179–188, 1936.
9. G.W. Flake. Square unit augmented, radially extended, multilayer percpetrons. In G. B. Orr and K. Müller, editors, *Neural Networks: Tricks of the Trade*, pages 145–163. Springer, 1998.
10. Y. Freund and R.E. Schapire. A decision theorethic generalization of on-line learning and application to boosing. *Journal of Computer and System Sciences*, 55(1):119–139, 1995.
11. G. Giacinto and F. Roli. Dynamic classifier selection. In *First International workshop on Multiple Classifier Systems*, pages 177–189, 2000.
12. G. E. Hinton and D. van Camp. Keeping neural networks simple by minimizing the description length of the weights. In *Sixth ACM conference on Computational Learning Theory*, pages 5–13, July 1993.
13. M. P. Perrone and Leon N Cooper. When networks disagree: Ensemble method for neural networks. In R. J. Mammone, editor, *Neural Networks for Speech and Image processing*. Chapman-Hall, 1993.
14. Y. Raviv and N. Intrator. Bootstrapping with noise: An effective regularization technique. *Connection Science, Special issue on Combining Estimators*, 8:356–372, 1996.
15. B. D. Ripley. *Pattern Recognition and Neural Networks*. Oxford Press, 1996.
16. J. Rissanen. A universal prior for integers and estimation by minimum description length. *The Annals of Statistics*, 11:416–431, 1983.
17. F. Roli and G. Fumera. Analysis of linear and order statistic for combiners for fusion of imbalanced classifiers. In *Third International workshop on Multiple Classifier Systems*, pages 252–261, 2002.
18. C. E. Shannon. A mathematical theory of communication. *Bell Syst. Tech. J.*, 27:379–423 and 623–656, 1948.

Combining Multiple Modes of Information Using Unsupervised Neural Classifiers

Khurshid Ahmad, Matthew Casey, Bogdan Vrusias, and Panagiotis Saragiotis

Neural Computing Group, Department of Computing
School of Electronics and Physical Sciences
University of Surrey, Guildford, Surrey, GU2 7XH, UK
{K.Ahmad,M.Casey,B.Vrusias,P.Saragiotis}@surrey.ac.uk
www.computing.surrey.ac.uk

Abstract. A modular neural network-based system is presented where the component networks learn together to classify a set of complex input patterns. Each pattern comprises two vectors: a primary vector and a collateral vector. Examples of such patterns include annotated images and magnitudes with articulated numerical labels. Our modular system is trained using an unsupervised learning algorithm. One component learns to classify the patterns using the primary vectors and another classifies the same patterns using the collateral vectors. The third combiner network correlates the primary with the collateral. The primary and collateral vectors are mapped on a Kohonen self-organising feature map (SOM), with the combiner based on a variant of Hebbian networks. The classification results appear encouraging in our attempts to classify a set of scene-of-crime images and in our attempts to investigate how pre-school infants relate magnitude to articulated numerical quantities. Certain features of SOM's, namely the topological neighbourhoods of specific nodes, allow for one to many mappings between the primary and collateral maps, hence establishing a broader association between the two vectors when compared with the association due to synchrony in a conventional Hebbian association.

1   Introduction

There are a number of problems currently advocated in the image understanding / retrieval literature and in the developmental psychology literature, which will benefit from the use of a system comprising a set of classifiers, capable of learning key features in the input, and using a decision combination function that can learn to combine the output of the different classifiers.

1.1   Image Recognition and Multiple Classifiers

Image understanding and retrieval systems, especially those discussed under the rubric of content-based image retrieval (CBIR) systems, focus on how a system can identify the components of an image by dealing, almost exclusively, on physical

T. Windeatt and F. Roli (Eds.): MCS 2003, LNCS 2709, pp. 236–245, 2003.

and/or perceptual features of the image. Typical multiple classifier ensembles used so far comprise individual 'expert' classifiers that can deal with one physical feature at a time: colour, texture, shape or illumination. The CBIR literature is increasingly using image external features, for instance, texts collateral to the image – a caption, or a news story in which the image is embedded. Schettini et al [15] have used the CART methodology to construct tree classifiers, which in turn use a majority voting rule, for classifying a set of indoor, outdoor and close up images.

In an oft-cited paper, Kittler et al have presented 'a common theoretical framework for combining classifiers which use distinct pattern representation' ([10] p.226). The framework uses the Bayesian relationship between the posterior and prior probability density functions that model one of the many possible classes, to the measurement vectors used by a given classifier. What is of interest to us here is the use of multiple classifiers that deal with perceptually (quasi-) independent biometric sensing modalities, such as frontal facial features, face profile features and (characteristic) voice features, and a combination function that is expected to lead to the establishment of personal identity. Each classifier matches an input with a stored template and an identity is produced. In a handwriting recognition experiment, Kittler et al use four different classifiers operating on the same input, with the sum rule again achieving one of the best combining schemes. Here, the authors have used a large feed forward neural network as one of the classifiers.

Jing and Zhang [8] have used genetic algorithms for evaluating the 'correctness of the result from [...] combined classifiers' (p. 486) in dealing with recognition of faces. The authors use four classifiers dealing with sub-images based on low frequency filtered images and three orientation sub-images: horizontal, vertical and diagonal. A genetic algorithm is used for determining the weights for combining the output from the classifiers. The authors show that individual classifiers, except for low frequency filtered sub-image classifiers, perform poorly when compared to a majority voting method combined classifier – and the results of a generic-algorithm (GA) weighted classifier shows a 96% recognition rate.

The use of neural networks in the classification of complex images, for instance, human faces, is limited to less than 20 classes. There are exceptions to such a limited approach: Lawrence *et al* [12] have developed a multiple neural network system comprising a Kohonen self-organising feature map (SOM) [11], for quantizing a set of input image samples into a topological space, and a backpropagation network, also called a *convolution network*, that learns to incorporate constraints that allow it to deal with an image in an invariant manner. Such multiple neural network systems have been termed *multi-net* systems by Sharkey [16], but there are some nuances added to concept of multi-nets [17].

A backpropagation network is in itself multi-layered (planes in parallel) and capable of detecting multiple features in an image. Lawrence *et al* have compared the performance of their multi-net system with another combined classifier comprising a principal component analysis (PCA) system and multi-layer perceptron (MLP). The convolutional approach outperforms the MLP in the classification of 400 images of 40 individuals. The performance of the MLP, containing up to 200 hidden nodes, is not surprising. The interesting thing for us is that this multi-net system, convolutional plus Kohonen, with substantial *ab initio* unsupervised learning capability performs well in the difficult task of face recognition.

1.2   Combining Unsupervised Classifiers

In a recent paper on the limitations on research in multiple classifier systems, Sharkey [17] suggests that this may be due to a lack of 'awareness of the range of modular designs that could be employed' (p. 108). Sharkey advocates a modular approach and illustrates the advantages with a system of classifiers that only provides a partial solution to the classification task and the combination of the partials providing the full solution. She uses a number of neural networks, multi-layer perceptrons (MLP), organised in different topologies as unitary classifiers of fault patterns in diesel engines, and compares these with modular and ensemble approaches. An approximately 2% improvement in performance is achieved with both modular and ensemble systems over the unity solutions, not quite advocating the use of modular and ensemble systems. However, intuitively we believe that modular networks should outperform ensemble networks.

In this paper, we describe a modular co-operative network, where the component networks learn through an unsupervised process, in contrast to other supervised approaches, such as Sharkey's. The unsupervised learning regimen is used to train networks that classify the input patterns and a combiner network that produces the output.

Willshaw & von der Malsburg [20] developed a model that applied Hebbian learning [6] between a two-dimensional pre-synaptic (input) layer and a post-synaptic (output) layer of neurons to form a topological map of activations; Hebbian learning is based on the postulate that to affect learning in connections (synapses) between two neuronal cells, the strengths of the connections are increased when both sides of the connection are active. This associative learning pre-empts the use of a teacher. The production of a topological map as a consequence of a learning rule can be regarded as a rule that maximises the average mutual information between input and output signals. Kohonen's [11] SOM is based upon a similar principle to Willshaw & von der Malsburg's, producing a statistical approximation of the input space by mapping the input to a two-dimensional output layer. The approximation is achieved by selection of features (or prototypes) that characterise the data, which are output in a topologically ordered map.

In this paper we discuss how a multi-net system can learn to classify a set of complex input patterns; the complexity lies in the fact that the input comprises a number of independent components. Each component has different information about a given input pattern. Consider, for example the case of an annotated image – an image plus its collateral description. The image features may include a texture vector together with a textual description. The texture vector informs a system about the idiosyncratic visual features of an image independently of the description and in a different manner. Collateral information helps to sharpen the query to an image database [19].

Our combination of neural networks is so organised that one network each can learn to classify an input pattern based on the sole knowledge of one component only, in contrast to other such schemes such as the so-called mixture-of-experts (ME) network [7] in which a number of networks are trained on the same set of input patterns. The behaviour of the individual networks, taken two at a time, is learnt by another network which, in turn, learns to associate classes in the individual network that are active at a given time. This synchronous activity is used to interrelate two independent components and is learnt through association *whilst* the individual classifiers learn.

The co-operative multi-net architecture that we propose extends both Willshaw & von der Malsburg [20] paradigm and Kohonen's [11] formulation, this time by connecting two SOMs together with a Hebbian network. A multi-net system that uses a Hebbian network to interrelate the output of two (or more) SOMs, can exploit some or all of the properties of Hebbian synapses. The properties of time dependence, local modification, interaction between pre- and post-synaptic signals and their correlation provides justification for the combination of independent modalities of information (images and collateral text or numbers and articulation). When combining two SOMs, the clustering of activation in either map relates an input signal to similar prototype inputs. This local information on either side of the Hebbian connection allows local modification of signals to be achieved through corresponding interaction at pre-set time steps. Furthermore, since inputs to both SOMs are related during training, the Hebbian connection modification provides correlation between the two modalities, which can be exploited during recall. These properties enable information modalities to be combined effectively to improve classification of signals through multiple, distinct classifiers, allowing the translation of classification from one modality to another.

2   Self-organised Combinations

A SOM uses an algorithm that transforms a continuous n-dimensional input signal onto a one- or two-dimensional discrete space of neurons. For each input pattern, the weight vectors in the SOM that connect the input layer to the output layer, attempt to relate to the input by computing respective values of a discriminant function. The weight vector closest to the input is deemed the winner and represents the non-linear transformation of the input onto the output. The process of competition complete, the co-operative phase takes over with the winning neuron determining the spatial location of a set of (less) excited neurons accompanying the highly excited winner. The winner's 'halo', visually created by a Gaussian neighbourhood function, displays co-operation. The topological neighbourhood is of considerable import to our method.

The input vectors for the cases we discuss comprise two vectors – a *primary* vector and a *collateral* vector; for example, an annotated image's primary vector may comprise the visual features of colour, texture and shape, and the collateral vector holds indications of the presence or absence of keywords in the image's collateral text. We train two SOMs: one for classifying input patterns based *entirely* on the basis of the primary vectors, one on the collateral vectors (Fig 1). Here, the primary vector is

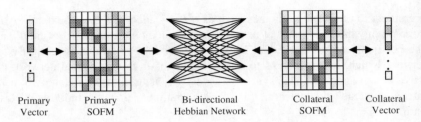

Fig. 1. Architecture showing the connections between the primary and collateral SOMs. Note that training is performed in-situ with association between neighbourhoods.

presented to the primary SOM, which is then trained on the input using Kohonen's weight update rule [11], using a Gaussian neighbourhood function, an exponentially decreasing learning rate and neighbourhood radius. Similarly, the collateral vector is presented to the collateral SOM, which in turn is trained on the input.

Subsequent to this, the output of both the primary and collateral SOMs are input to the Hebbian network. In order to preserve the topological information provided by both SOMs, the output from each is represented as a range of activations centred on the winning neuron, demonstrating the active neighbourhood of the winner and allowing a cluster of activity to be presented to the Hebbian network. This is achieved by using the Euclidean distance for each unit in the SOM for an input, and inverting this via the function $f(x) = e^{-x}$, which provides a sufficient radius around the winner. With both primary and collateral SOM output represented in this way, the Hebbian connections were allowed to train on both of these patterns, with the cycle continuing for subsequent input patterns until sufficient learning has occurred in the SOMs to form clusters.

Each SOM shows the effects of the competition and co-operation processes used in training by assigning each pattern's neuron in the output layer. Each winning neuron has a topological neighbourhood of active neurons. The neighbours may or may not be associated with other patterns. Therefore, if during the testing phase, the presentation of a test pattern leads to its recognition by the excitation of a neuron that has won similar or the same pattern during training, the neighbourhood will also be activated.

Recall that we link the primary and collateral vectors through Hebbian learning. During the training phase, the presentation of the two vectors comprising a pattern trivially leads to a weighted one-to-one association simply because both patterns are present at the same time. However, in addition to this association by synchrony, the winning unit of a primary vector gets associated not only with the winning unit of the collateral (and vice versa), but also the neighbourhood of the winner gets associated with that of the neighbourhood of the winning unit of the collateral (and vice versa).

2.1   Classifying Images and Collateral Text

We first look at the combination of image and text classifiers, the image forming the primary vector, and the text associated with the image the collateral vector, taken from the scene-of-crime domain. An image is represented by a 112-dimensional vector that consists of extracted physical features. The intention when extracting these 112 components was to create vectors that described various properties such as colours, edges and textures. In these vectors we used 21 dimensions to describe the colour distribution as an intensity histogram, 19 dimensions to describe edges by applying an edge filter and the water-filling algorithm [21], and 72 dimensions to describe texture using Grey Level Co-occurrence Matrices [5]. Here, the primary 15 by 15 unit SOM is intended to organise the images into clusters that share similar image features.

Collateral text is represented by a 50-dimensional (term based) binary vector. These are generated by extracting significant terms from the text, ignoring punctuation, numerical expressions and closed-class words. These significant terms are generated using the frequency of a term and a *weirdness* coefficient describing the subject-specificity of a term [2]. Textual vectors with common key-terms are clustered together in a 15 by 15 unit SOM.

To evaluate the proposed architecture, we trained three separate systems to allow for a comparison of results: the combined architecture, two separate SOMs, one each for images and texts, and a single SOM trained on combined image and text vectors. A total of 66 images and associated texts where used, pre-classified into 8 ideal classes by experts on the scene-of-crime domain: 'bar area', 'exhibits', 'fingerprints', 'footmarks', 'fruit machine area', 'body', 'window area' and 'general'. One vector was then selected at random from each class for use in testing and the remaining 58 were used for training.

Each system was trained for 1000 epochs with training vectors, with initial random weights, Gaussian neighbourhood function with initial radius 8, reducing to 1, and exponential learning rate starting at 0.9 reducing to 0.1. The Hebbian weight connections were normalised and a learning rate of 10 was used. For the combined system, we first tested the performance of the Hebbian network on the training data by translating one SOM's output to the other SOM (image to text, text to image). We calculated the Euclidean distance of the actual SOM's winning node for a particular input, to the node that the Hebbian link activated. The results showed that the Hebbian network managed to identify all images correctly for a given textual input, and only missed 1 out of 58 texts for a given image input.

The system was then tested for its accuracy on classifying each of the 8 test inputs. Here, of the 8 test vectors, the image SOM correctly classified 4. For the remaining misclassified vectors, the collateral text vectors were input to the text SOM, and subsequently provided activation through the Hebbian link to obtain an image classification. This technique correctly classified 3 of the remaining 4 vectors. A similar approach was applied to the text SOM, giving 5 initially correct classifications, and 2 more via the image SOM and Hebbian linkage.

In comparison, the independently trained SOMs were tested with the same test vectors. The image SOM showed correct classification of 4 out of 8 test vectors, the text SOM 5 out of 8. The combined system therefore shows the benefit of combining modalities of information to improve classification, allowing an improved response by selecting the best possible via the Hebbian connection. However, the multi-net approach shows benefit over a monolithic solution, as demonstrated by the single SOM that was trained with the input vectors formed by concatenating the image and text vectors together. Test results show worse classification ability, with only 3 out of 8 correctly classified, demonstrating that combined modalities can only be used if appropriate selection of response and separation of signals is possible. Whilst building a monolithic network to process combined modality vectors may not seem intuitive, this is one approach to using multiple modalities of information for classification. Our multi-net approach is an alternative that seems to offer benefit.

2.2   Classifying Number Magnitude and Articulation

The combination of modalities to improve classification is a subject that has relevance to developmental psychology. For example, the study of mathematical abilities has concentrated on the way different numerical modalities are processed [4], [13], [14]. Dehaene's *triple code* model of numerical abilities includes processing of Arabic and spoken numbers, together with an internalised magnitude representation of number [4]. Such an internal representation of number can be obtained through a process of subitization or estimation [9]. Of specific interest here is the way in which the internal magnitude representation of number interacts with number articulation. We simulate the linkage of the internal representation of number and its phonetic representation [1], [3].

We use number magnitude as the primary vector, using a 1-dimensional SOM with 66 neurons as a number line. Input to the SOM is formed as a 66-dimensional binary vector where each magnitude is identified with a block of three digits. The collateral vector is formed as a number articulation, with a SOM consisting of 16 by 16 neurons, showing the representation between the spoken form of the numbers one to twenty-two. For example, the numbers seven, seventeen and eleven all have similar sounds, and are hence clustered together within the SOM. Input to the SOM is formed as a 16-dimensional vector representing the phonemes used in the number word, with value taken as the order found within the Collins English Dictionary and Thesaurus [18], with zero representing the absence of a phoneme for shorter number words.

The training and testing data sets where selected randomly from the numbers 1 to 22, with 16 numbers in the training set and 6 in the test set (2,3,10,14,15,19). The entire system was trained for 1000 epochs on the training data, with initial random weights, Gaussian neighbourhood function with initial radius for the primary map as 33, and the collateral 8, reducing to 1, and exponential learning rate starting at 0.5. The Hebbian weight connections were normalised and a learning rate of 0.5 was used.

Once trained, the system was tested on both the magnitude and phonetic forms of all 22 numbers. Looking at the magnitude SOM in isolation, the system correctly ordered all 22 magnitudes such that 1 was at one end of the map and 22 at the other, with all intermediate values in ascending order, including those that were not in the training set. This demonstrates the SOMs ability to generalise to new patterns based upon their apparent magnitude. However, the testing of the phonetic SOM shows the inability to correctly classify 2, 3, 10, 14, 15 and 19 (those not in the training set). The SOM is able to associate these values with those based upon their phonetic similarity, for example 2 is classified as 1, however the SOM cannot distinguish between values, attempting to provide an existing specific label rather than a distinct value.

To determine if the combined system can improve upon this classification, the six misclassified values were presented to the magnitude SOM, and its output used to activate the Hebbian link to produce a corresponding articulation output. The corresponding Hebbian output provides new associations for the six values. Here 14, 15 and 19 are now distinct whilst being associated with the 'teens' cluster, improving classification by distinguishing these values whilst retaining their similarity to their phonetic counterparts. However, 2, 3 and 10 are associated with 20, 12 and 21, respectively, a worse classification than previously achieved. The improvement in classification is marginal, having both beneficial and detrimental affects. However, the combined system has the advantage that we can improve classification with another modality of information.

To understand if this can be achieved in a monolithic solution rather than the multi-net we describe, we trained a single SOM on a combined set of input modalities. Here, both the magnitude and phonetic representations for the training and testing sets described above where combined into appropriate 82-dimensional vectors. A single SOM consisting of 16 by 16 units was trained using the same parameters as above for 1000 epochs, with an initial neighbourhood radius of 8 units. The results show a map that demonstrates the relationship between the phonetic representations alone, with no magnitude information portrayed. The responses for the six test values gives a similar level of classification as that for the single phonetic SOM described above, with all six values being associated with those that are phonetically similar. However, the loss of magnitude information means that there is no understanding of the relationship between the numbers, nor how to translate between a magnitude and an articulation, or vice-versa. This loss of modality information supports the use of split modalities in a combined system, such as we have described.

3   Conclusion

We have presented a modular co-operative neural network system that incorporates unsupervised networks, of the same architecture and topology, that learn to classify a set of patterns based on partial information, either primary information or collateral information, about the patterns. The combiner, a Hebbian network, learns to associate not only the two winning units on the primary and collateral maps, but between the respective neighbourhoods of the two winners.

Note that the number of units in our networks is smaller than, say, in Sharkey's supervised multi-net simulations. We have been parsimonious perhaps compensating for manually assigning the classifiers to the primary or the collateral sub-vectors. However, this manual assignment is offset partially by the fact that the two classifying networks have exactly the same topology and aspects of the training, including regimen, that is the way the neighbourhood distances and learning rates are changed, for the two networks are exactly the same. The combiner in our system shares the same learning paradigm, unsupervised learning, and indeed the SOM architecture is a variant of the Hebbian architecture [20].

A comparison between our modular system and that of a unity network demonstrates improvement. In classifying images and text the unity network does not demonstrate any linkage between images and text, whereas the modular system allow the neighbourhood of images to be associated with neighbourhoods of text. For magnitudes and articulated numerical labels, a unity network provides a comparable classification to that of just the phonetic representations, demonstrating that the phonetic information dominates the magnitude information.

Acknowledgements

The authors acknowledge the support of the EPSRC sponsored *Scene of Crime Information System* project (Grant No.GR/M89041) jointly undertaken by the Universities of Sheffield and Surrey and supported by five police forces in the UK. The authors would also like to thank the UK Police Training College at Hendon for supplying the scene-of-crime images and Mr C. Handy for transcribing the image collateral text. Lastly, the authors would like to thank the anonymous reviewers of this paper for their constructive comments.

References

1. Ahmad, K., Casey, M. & Bale, T. (2002). Connectionist Simulation of Quantification Skills. *Connection Science*, vol. 14(3), pp. 165-201.
2. Ahmad, K., Vrusias, B. & Tariq, M. (2002). Co-operative Neural Networks and 'Integrated' Classification. *Proceedings of the 2002 International Joint Conference on Neural Networks (IJCNN'02)*, vol.2, pp. 1546-1551.
3. Bale, T.A. (1998). *Modular Connectionist Architectures and the Learning of Quantification Skills*. Unpublished doctoral thesis. Guildford, UK: University of Surrey.
4. Dehaene, S. (1992). Varieties of Numerical Abilities. In *Numerical Cognition* (1993), pp.1-42. Cambridge, MA.: Blackwell Publishers.
5. Haralick, R.M., Shanmugam, K. & Dinstein, I. (1973). Textural Features for Image Classification. *IEEE Transactions on Systems, Man, and Cybernetics*, vol. SMC-3(6), pp.610-621.
6. Hebb, D.O. (1949). *The Organization of Behavior: A Neuropsychological Theory*. New York: John Wiley & Sons.
7. Jacobs, R.A., Jordan, M.I., & Barto, A.G. (1991). Task Decomposition through Competition in a Modular Connectionist Architecture: The What and Where Vision Tasks. *Cognitive Science*, vol. 15, pp. 219-250.
8. Jing, X., & Zhang, D. (2003) Face recognition based on linear classifiers combination. *Neurocomputing*, vol. 50, pp. 485-488.

9. Kaufman, E.L., Lord, M.W., Reese, T.W. & Volkmann, J. (1949). The Discrimination of Visual Number. *American Journal of Psychology*, vol. 62, pp. 498-525.

10. Kittler, J., Hatef, M. Duin, R.P.W. & Matas, J. (1998). On Combining Classifiers. *IEEE Transactions on Pattern Analysis and Machine Intelligence*, vol. 20(3), pp. 226-239.

11. Kohonen, T. (1997). *Self-Organizing Maps*, 2nd Ed. Berlin, Heidelberg, New York: Springer-Verlag.

12. Lawrence, S., Giles, C.L., Ah Chung Tsoi & Back, A.D. (1997). Face Recognition: A Convolutional Neural Network Approach. *IEEE Transactions on Neural* Networks, vol. 8 (1) pp 98-113.

13. McCloskey, M. (1992). Cognitive Mechanisms in Number Processing and Calculation: Evidence from Dyscalculia. In Dehaene, S. (Ed), *Numerical Cognition* (1993), pp. 107-157. Cambridge, MA.: Blackwell Publishers.

14. McCloskey, M., Caramazza, A. & Basili, A. (1985). Cognitive Mechanisms in Number Processing and Calculation: Evidence from Dyscalculia. *Brain and Cognition*, vol. 4, pp. 171-196.

15. Schettini, R., Brambilla, C. & Cusano, C. (2002). Content-based Classification of Digital Photos. In Roli, F. & Kittler, J. (Eds), *Proceedings of the Third International Workshop on Multiple Classifier Systems (MCS 2002)*, LNCS 2364, pp. 272-282.

16. Sharkey, A.J.C. (1999). Multi-net Systems. In Sharkey, A.J.C. (Ed), *Combining Artificial Neural Nets: Ensemble and Modular Multi-Net Systems*, pp.1-30. Berlin, Heidelberg, New York: Springer-Verlag.

17. Sharkey, A.J.C. (2002). Types of Multinet System. In Roli, F. & Kittler, J. (Eds), *Proceedings of the Third International Workshop on Multiple Classifier Systems (MCS 2002)*, LNCS 2364, pp. 108-117.

18. Sinclair, J. M. (Ed.) (1993) Collins English Dictionary and Thesaurus. Harper Collins.

19. Srihari R.K., (1995). *Use of Collateral Text in Understanding Photos*, Artificial Intelligence Review, special issue on Integrating Language and Vision, Volume 8, pp. 409-430.

20. Willshaw, D.J. & von der Malsburg, C. (1976). How Patterned Neural Connections can be set up by Self-Organization. *Proceedings of the Royal Society, Series B*, vol. 194, pp. 431-445.

21. Zhou, X.S., Rui Y. & Huang S.T. (1999). Water-filling: A Novel Way for Image Structural Feature Extraction. *Proceedings of the IEEE International Conference on Image Processing*, pp. 570-574.

Neural Net Ensembles for Lithology Recognition

R.O.V. Santos[1], M.M.B.R. Vellasco[1], F.A.V. Artola[2], and S.A.B. da Fontoura[2]

[1] DEE / PUC-Rio – ICA: Laboratório de Inteligência Computacional Aplicada,
Pontifícia Universidade Católica do Rio de Janeiro
{rafael,marley}@ele.puc-rio.br
[2] GTEP / PUC-Rio – Grupo de Tecnologia em Engenharia de Petróleo,
Pontifícia Universidade Católica do Rio de Janeiro
{rvsantos,fontoura,artola}@civ.puc-rio.br

Abstract. Lithology recognition is a common task found in the petroleum exploration field. Roughly speaking, it is a problem of classifying rock types,
based on core samples obtained from well drilling programs. In this paper we
evaluate the performance of different ensemble systems, specially developed
for the task of lithology recognition, based on well data from a major petroleum
company. Among the procedures for creating committee members we applied
Driven Pattern Replication (DPR), Bootstrap and ARC-X4 techniques. With respect to the available combining methods, Averaging, Plurality Voting, Borda
Count and Fuzzy Integrals were selected. The paper presents results obtained
with ensembles derived from these different methods, evaluating their performance against the single neural network classifier. The results confirm the effectiveness of applying ensembles in real world classification problems.

1 Introduction

As mentioned in [1], the solution of the lithology recognition problem has many potential utilities in the petroleum field. If well succeeded, this kind of analysis leads to
drilling path optimization, a desirable achievement for all the exploration industry.

One of the first references of Artificial Intelligence systems applied to the lithology
recognition problem was settled by H. Doveton [2]. After that, other researchers have
presented contributions where single Neural Networks (NNs) are applied as rock
classifier systems [3], [4], [5]. In a recent work [1], we addressed the problem by
using MLP Classifier Ensembles, in a way similar to the one suggested in [6]. Now,
handing a different well data interpretation from those applied in [1], our aim is to
improve and extend the started analysis, supplying results from others ensemble
methods, for the task of classifying rocks over a Brazilian offshore well.

Many approaches for the design of committee members, as well as for the combination strategy of the individual outputs have been proposed [7], [8], [9], [10], [11],
[12], [13]. In particular, we chose to assess here the following techniques: Driven
Pattern Replication (*DPR*) [1] , *ARC-X4* [7] and Bootstrap [10] as member-forming
procedures, and Fuzzy Integrals [14], Plurality Voting [8], Borda-Count [13] and
Averaging [15], as combining methods.

The next section describes the lithology recognition problem; section 3 briefly presents the proposed ensemble procedures. Section 4 describes the experiments in de-

T. Windeatt and F. Roli (Eds.): MCS 2003, LNCS 2709, pp. 246–255, 2003.

tails, while section 5 brings the performance results obtained and a short discussion. The final conclusions are presented in section 6.

2   Lithology Recognition

The characterization of the vertical and lateral distribution of the diverse types of lithology in a petroleum field plays relevant role in the processes of thickness and rock quality mapping. Usually, these variations are estimated during well drilling programs, directly from the analysis and interpretation of some types of well logs – roughly speaking, electrical signals collected by instruments attached to the drill system. These variations constitute what is called lithological records.

To provide an automatic way to form lithology records, some algorithm must be set to map an efficient relation between physical responses (well logs) and lithology types (rock types). MLP classifiers are clearly suitable to this mapping task. This approach delivers lithologic distributions over diverse locations in the petroleum field, where the only existing information comes from well logs. Results like that can be used in the set up of spatial lithology distribution maps, especially of the lithologies associated with reservoir rocks levels.

3   MLP Ensembles

A committee of MLP neural networks is composed of independent classifiers that are designed to be later integrated in an ensemble. The committee is formed with the objective of achieving complementary performance in different regions of the feature space.

3.1   Forming Members with Driven Pattern Replication (*DPR*)

Let the number of available training patterns in a dataset, N, be given by:

$$N = \sum_{i=1}^{M} n_i \tag{1}$$

where M is the number of pattern classes present in the application, and n_i (for $1 \leq i \leq M$) is the number of training patterns belonging to class i. The *Driven Pattern Replication (DPR)* method creates one expert neural network for each class in the training set; the M specialized neural networks are then combined. To build an expert network for class k, the n_k available training patterns belonging to that class are replicated by an integer factor $\gamma > 1$, so that the resulting training set will have a total of $N + (\gamma-1) n_k$ patterns. Therefore, in each epoch, the training patterns not belonging to class k are presented to the network only once, while the patterns belonging to class k are presented γ times. The choice of a suitable value for γ shall be guided by some metric to determine how class-expert are the created networks. As will be seen later in section 5.2, the *specialization level* is a possible metric.

3.2   Forming Members with ARC-X4

The *ARC-x4* method assigns sampling probabilities for each pattern of the original training set and then performs an iterative pattern selection algorithm. In each new iteration, a new training set is sampled and a new neural network is trained with the current selected patterns. The selection probabilities of misclassified patterns are increased for the next iteration, based on an empirical relationship that takes into account the number of times each pattern has been wrongly classified until the present iteration.

3.3   Forming Members with Bootstrap

In the *Bootstrap* method each committee member is trained with a bootstrap version of the available training patterns. A Bootstrap [24] version of a data set with N patterns is a set of N patterns created by a simple random sampling with replacement (SRSR) from the original data set. Although the training sets built in this way are completely random, the Bootstrap method may produce good practical results [7], [10].

3.4   Combining by Average

When combining by *Average* the ensemble output is simply given by the average of the corresponding outputs of its members.

3.5   Combining by Plurality Voting

Given a pattern in a *Plurality Voting* scheme, if there is a class that is more assigned by the ensemble members to that pattern than any other is, than this class is selected as the combined response. If there is no such a class, a *rejection* label is assigned to that pattern.

3.6   Combining by Borda Count

The *Borda Count* decision procedure is based on a *ranking* computation. Given a pattern, each ensemble member response is ranked in a class pertinence degree order. The class that has the overall better ranking is selected as the consensual response. If there is more than one class in this condition a rejection label is applied.

3.7   Combining by Fuzzy Integrals

As in evidence theory [16], the combination of classifiers using Fuzzy Integrals relies on some measure relative to the pair classifier/class (e_k / c). In this technique such measures are called *Fuzzy Measures*.

A fuzzy measure is defined as a function that assigns a value in the [0,1] interval to each crisp set of the universal set [17]. In the context of classifier combination, a fuzzy measure expresses the level of competence of a classifier in assigning a pattern to a particular class.

A fuzzy integral [18] is a non-linear operation defined over the concept of fuzzy measure. In the framework of combining classifiers this can be explained as follows.

Let L = {1, 2, ..., M} be the set of labels (classes) and ε = {e_1, e_2, ..., e_K} the set of available classifiers. A set of $K{\times}M$ fuzzy measures $g_c(e_i)$ is calculated, for c varying between 1 and M and i varying from 1 to K, denoting the competence of each classifier e_i in relation to each class c. These measures can be estimated by an expert or through an analysis of the training set (section 3.7.1 shows how competence may be computed). Fuzzy integrals are computed pattern by pattern, class by class, using mathematical relations considering competences and classifiers outputs. A pattern **x** will be assigned to the class with the highest value for the fuzzy integral; this class is selected as the response of the committee.

There are many interpretations for fuzzy integrals; they may be understood here as a methodology to rate the agreement between the response of an entity and its competence in doing so.

3.7.1   Estimating Competence

Competence of a classifier e_k in relation to a class i is estimated in this work by a ratio known as *local classification performance* [19], defined as:

$$g_i(e_k) = \frac{o_{ii}}{o_{ii} + \sum_{j, j \neq i} o_{ij} + \sum_{j, j \neq i} o_{ji}} \qquad (2)$$

where o_{ij} is the number of patterns (observations) from class i assigned by the classifier e_k to the class j.

4   Experiments Description

Every ensemble classifier system assessed here is based on single hidden layers MLP architectures. The general input vector is composed of *five* log registers - GAMMA RAY, SONIC, DENSITY, RESISTIVITY and CALIPER – plus the observation's DEPTH, totalizing *six* attributes. As usual for classification tasks, the network outputs are binary vectors, with as many entrances as there are classes to be considered in 5the problem at hand - each classifier is trained so that if output j is "on", the others are "off" and the observation is said to belong to class j. The number of hidden processors along the networks was set to 12, following the *Hecht-Nielsen* metric [20].

4.1   The Data Set

The experiments were carried out over data from a Brazilian offshore well, located in the northeast coast. The raw data consists of 3330 observations, each of which joining, for a given well depth, the five log signals mentioned before plus the associated

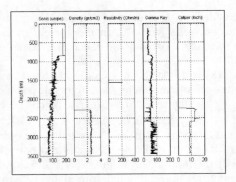

Fig. 1. Well logs

rock type. The information ranges from 130 to 3500m in depth. The log signals can be seen from Fig. 1. It can be seen from the figure that some log signals are missing for upper depths. This is a common situation and a test of robustness for the methodology – the logs with missing values were presented to the MLP networks as zero-valued attributes.

Each observation is assigned to one of three rock classes, known as: RESERVOIR (1), SEAL (2) and SOURCE (3) (besides each class name is its numeric label).

4.2   Selected Subsets and Reference Network

The complete dataset has the following class distribution:

Table 1. Class distribution

Label	1	2	3
#Observ.	683	2023	624
Total %	20.51	60.75	18.74

A practical training rule adopted from other classification problems [21], suggests that for a D dimensional input space a minimum of 10×D samples per class is desirable, with 100×D being highly desirable if it can be attained. On this way, the number of training patterns available here should be not restrictive at all. Despite that, to prove the advantages of a multi-classifier system when the training set is restrictive, we settled, for all the experiments performed, a base training set with 60 randomly chosen patterns per class. As the methods implemented here require changing the original training set, this base training set will be referred to as the *reference training set*, or simply TREF.

Having the training set being formed by 180 patterns, the remaining 3150 patterns were used as testing sample.

Next, a proper *reference network* was created. The reference network serves as a starting point from where all the experiments in the case study are carried out. Its single performance over the testing set is used for comparison with each subsequent experiment.

As the reference network is used as a starting point for all the experiments, the experiments are started from the same initial weights. This condition intends to provide fair comparisons. In this paper, the initial weights and biases were chosen using a simple cross-validation over the training set, splitting it in two parts - 50% for *estimation*, 50% for *validation* [22]. The number of epochs was fixed at 1000 (one thousand), a number that showed to be sufficient for convergence during the reference network training.

Finally, it should be observed that in all the experiments the input information was normalized to standard scores [23].

5   Results

The results obtained over the testing set will be measured with confusion matrixes, average hit ratio percentages (AH%) and rejection percentages (RE%), if there are rejections. As we are only dealing with stratified sets [24] (sets with the same number of patterns per class), the average hit ratio per class equals the total pattern hit ratio.

5.1   Reference

The reference network, trained with the reference training set, TREF, delivered the following results:

Table 2. Results from TREF

Confusion Matrix			
	SIMULATED		
TARGET	**79.61**	5.78	14.61
	4.79	**80.59**	14.62
	3.55	10.11	**86.35**
AH%	**81.43**		

Being the reference result established, the next sections analyze the ensemble methods performances.

5.2   DPR

The DPR application over TREF was tested with six different γ values: 5, 8, 10, 12, 15 and 20. The chosen of an appropriate value were guided by the *specialization level metric* [25], a simple metric based on the concept of *local classification performance* (section 3.7.1). When a the set of $g_i(e_k)$'s are calculated for all possible classes i and classifiers k, these results can be arranged in matrix called the competence matrix, G, where each line corresponds to a classifier and each column corresponds to a class. When specialized networks formed by the DPR method are trained and tested with the training set itself, the correspondent G matrix must have the higher values (close to 1) over its main diagonal. At that point, the specialization level SL (Eq.3) can be applied as a metric to evaluate the DPR effectiveness.

$$SL = \frac{trace(G)}{\sum \sum G} \qquad (3)$$

The DPR application with $\gamma = 8$ over TREF resulted in the following G matrix and SL value, after test with TREF itself:

Table 3. Results from TREF

G Matrix			
	CLASSES		
	0.92	0.81	0.81
CLASSIFIERS	0.83	**0.90**	0.76
	0.83	0.80	**0.85**
	SL = 0.3552		

The SL values for $\gamma = 5$, 10, 12, 15 and 20 were respectively 0.3399, 0.3445, 0.3487, 0.3484 and 0.3455.

Once the specialized networks were available, the results obtained from the four combining techniques are as follows (for the fuzzy integrals combination, the competences used were just the ones exposed in Table 3, taken from the TREF testing performance):

Table 4. Results for DPR

Combining Technique	Fuzzy	Avg.	Voting	BC
AH%	88.38	87.52	79.14	79.49
RE%	0.00	0.00	7.27	1.43

5.3   ARC-X4

The ARC-X4 method applied to TREF allows the user to form ensembles with as many networks as he or she wishes. Several numbers of networks were assessed (Table 5), with the combination phase being always performed with the averaging technique. Averaging was selected due to its good performance, together with the fact that, as realized in [25], fuzzy integrals become processing prohibitive when the numbers of ensemble members increases beyond 15.

Table 5. Results for ARC-X4

#Nets	3	15	25	50	75	100
AH%	87.87	87.81	87.52	87.84	88.06	88.25

5.4   Bootstrap

As for the ARC-X4 procedure, the results for Bootstrap/Averaging:

Table 6. Results for Bootstrap

#Nets	3	15	25	50	75	100
AH%	88.06	87.33	88.83	88.22	88.03	88.06

5.5   Discussion

In the best case, the reference average hit ratio was increased in about 7.4%, by the Bootstrap ensemble formed with 25 members, combined by averaging:

Table 7. Best x Reference

BEST Confusion Matrix				REFERENCE Confusion Matrix		
	SIMULATED				SIMULATED	
TARGET	**80.90**	4.17	14.93	**TARGET**	**79.61**	5.78	14.61
	3.82	**91.49**	4.69		4.79	**80.59**	14.62
	2.48	9.22	**88.30**		3.55	10.11	**86.35**
AH%	**88.83**			AH%	**81.43**		

Concerning the methods involving many nets, namely ARC-X4 and Bootstrap, as the number of combined nets increased, ARC-X4 presented a growth tendency in its performance, while bootstrap had greater oscillations. Booth facts were theoretically expected.

Concerning the DPR method, the fuzzy integrals combination presented the best performance, overcoming the reference in 6.95%. The Voting and Borda Count combination schemes delivered results of 2.9% and 1.94% below the reference, respectively.

6   Conclusions

The experiments carried out assessed the performance of some MLP Neural Network ensemble systems applied to the lithology recognition problem, using well data furnished by a major petroleum exploration company. Considering a single classifier output as reference value, a performance increase of 7.4% was achieved by the multi-classifier system, using the same cross-validated initial weights for fair comparison.

As opposed to a previous work with similar information [1], the study case in this paper had stratified datasets [24]. This can be considered a major difference, since the behavior of the techniques are almost opposite – while in [1] the ensemble methods involving many nets are inefficient, here they show good results. This reinforces the feeling that, being the involved training set stratified, techniques like ARC-X4 or Bootstrap tend to deliver similar results – in many cases better – when compared to DPR.

It has to be noticed that, despite of not being the best result for this case, the result achieved by DPR with fuzzy integrals is truly positive - increase of 6.95% in performance, a value close to the best achieved, 7.4%; even more if we consider, in face of the many-nets methods presented, the lower randomness involved and the almost always less training time required (depending on gamma). The DPR results with Voting and Borda Count were poor.

References

[1] Santos, R.O.V., Artola, F.A.V, Fontoura, S.A.B., Vellasco, M. M. B. R., "Lithology Recognition by Neural Network Ensembles", Advances in Artificial Intelligence, proceedings of the 16th Brazilian Symposium on Artificial Intelligence, SBIA 2002, Porto de Galinhas / Recife Brazil, November 2002. Lecture Notes in Artificial Intelligence, 2507, Springer, pp. 302-312.

[2] Doveton, J. H., Log Analysis of Subsurface Geology: Concepts and Computer Methods, 1986, John Wiley & Sons, 1986.

[3] Saggaf, M. M., I Marhoon, M., and Toksöz, M. N., "Seismic facies mapping by competitive neural networks", SEG/San Antonio 2001, San Antonio, 2001, CD-ROM.

[4] Ford, D. A., Kelly, M. C., "Using Neural Networks to Predict Lithology from Well Logs", SEG/San Antonio 2001, San Antonio, 2001, CD-ROM.

[5] Taner, M. T., Walls, J. D., Smith, M., Taylor, G., Carr, M. B., Dumas, D., "Reservoir Characterization by Calibration of Self-Organized Map Clusters", SEG/San Antonio 2001, San Antonio, 2001, CD-ROM.

[6] Bhatt, A., Helle, H. B., Ursin, B., "Determination of facies from well logs using modular neural networks", EAGE 64th Conference and Exhibition, Florence, Italy, 27-30 May 2002, CD-ROM.

[7] L. Breiman, "Combining predictors", in Combining Artificial Neural Nets: Ensemble and Modular Multi-Net System – Perspectives in Neural Computing, ed. A. J. C.Sharkey, Springer Verlag, 1999, pp. 31-51.

[8] L. K. Hansen, and P. Salamon, "Neural network ensembles", IEEE Transactions on Pattern Analysis and Machine Intelligence 12 (1990), pp. 993-1001.

[9] Y. Liu and X. Yao, "Evolutionary ensembles with negative correlation learning", IEEE Transactions on Evolutionary Computation, 4 (2000), pp. 380-387.

[10] D. Opitz and R. Maclin, "Popular ensemble methods: an empirical study", Journal of Artificial Intelligence Research 11 (1999), pp. 169-198.

[11] Santos, R.O.V., Vellasco, M. M. B. R., Feitosa, R. Q., Simões, M., and Tanscheit, R., "An application of combined neural networks to remotely sensed images", Proceedings of the 9th International Conference in Central Europe on Computer Graphics, Visualization and Computer Vision, Pilsen, Czech Republic, 2001, pp. 87-92.

[12] N. Ueda, "Optimal linear combination of neural networks for improving classification performance", IEEE Transactions on Pattern Analysis and Machine Intelligence **22** (2000), pp. 207-215.

[13] Cho, S., Kim, J.H.: "Combining Multiple Neural Networks by Fuzzy Integral for Robust Classification", IEEE Transactions on Systems, Man and Cybernetics, Vol.25, No.2, 1995.

[14] M. Sugeno, "Fuzzy measures and fuzzy integrals: a survey", in Fuzzy Automata and Decision Processes, North Holland, Amsterdam, 1977, pp. 89-102.

[15] Kittler, J., Hatef, M., Duin, R.P.W., Matas, J.: "On Combining Classifiers" – IEEE Transactions on Pattern Analysis and Machine Intelligence, Vol.20, No.3, 1998.

[16] G. A. Shafer, "A Mathematical Theory of Evidence", Princeton University Press, 1976.

[17] G. Klir and T. Folger, "Fuzzy Sets, Uncertainty and Information", Prentice-Hall, 1988.

[18] M. Sugeno, "Fuzzy measures and fuzzy integrals: a survey", in Fuzzy Automata and Decision Processes, North Holland, Amsterdam, 1977, pp. 89-102.

[19] N. Ueda, "Optimal linear combination of neural networks for improving classification performance", IEEE Transactions on Pattern Analysis and Machine Intelligence **22** (2000), pp. 207-215.

[20] Hecht-Nielsen, R., "Neurocomputing", Addison Wesley, 1990

[21] Richards, J. A., Jia, X., "Remote Sensing Digital Analysis – An Introduction", Third Edition. Springer, 1999.

[22] S. Haykin, "Neural Networks: A Comprehensive Foundation", Prentice Hall, New Jersey, 1999.
[23] R. A. Johnson, D. W. Wichern, "Applied Multivariate Statistical Analysis - 5th Edition", Prentice-Hall, 2002
[24] R. Kohavi, "A study of cross-validation and bootstrap for accuracy estimation and model selection", Proceedings of the International Joint Conference on Artificial Intelligence (IJCAI), 1995, pp. 1137-1145.
[25] Santos, R.O.V., "Combining MLP Neural Networks in Classification Problems", MSc dissertation, Decision Support Methods, Electrical Engineering Department, PUC-Rio, 2001, 105 pages (in Portuguese).

Improving Performance of a Multiple Classifier System Using Self-generating Neural Networks

Hirotaka Inoue[1] and Hiroyuki Narihisa[2]

[1] Department of Electrical Engineering and Information Science
Kure National College of Technology
2-2-11 Agaminami, Kure-shi, Hiroshima, 737-8506 Japan
hiro@kure-nct.ac.jp
[2] Department of Information and Computer Engineering
Okayama University of Science
1-1 Ridai-cho, Okayama-shi, Okayama, 700-0005 Japan
narihisa@ice.ous.ac.jp

Abstract. Recently, multiple classifier systems (MCS) have been used for practical applications to improve classification accuracy. Self-generating neural networks (SGNN) are one of the suitable base-classifiers for MCS because of their simple setting and fast learning. However, the computational cost of the MCS increases in proportion to the number of SGNN. In an earlier paper, we proposed a pruning method for the structure of the SGNN in the MCS to reduce the computational cost. In this paper, we propose a novel pruning method for effective processing. The pruning method is constructed from an on-line pruning method and an off-line pruning method. We implement the pruned MCS with two sampling methods. Experiments have been conducted to compare the pruned MCS with the unpruned MCS, the MCS based on C4.5, and k-nearest neighbor method. The results show that the pruned MCS can improve its classification accuracy as well as reducing the computational cost.

1 Introduction

Classifiers need to find hidden information in the given large data effectively and classify unknown data as accurately as possible [1]. Recently, to improve the classification accuracy, multiple classifier systems (MCS) such as neural network ensembles, bagging, and boosting have been used for practical data mining applications [2,3]. In general, the base classifiers of the MCS use traditional models such as neural networks (backpropagation network and radial basis function network) [4] and decision trees (CART and C4.5) [5].

Neural networks have great advantages of adaptability, flexibility, and universal nonlinear input-output mapping capability. However, to apply these neural networks, it is necessary to determine the network structure and some parameters by human experts, and it is quite difficult to choose the right network structure suitable for a particular application at hand. Moreover, they require

T. Windeatt and F. Roli (Eds.): MCS 2003, LNCS 2709, pp. 256–265, 2003.

a long training time to learn the input-output relation of the given data. These drawbacks prevent neural networks being the base classifier of the MCS for practical applications.

Self-generating neural networks (SGNN) [6] have simple network design and high speed learning. SGNN are an extension of the self-organizing maps (SOM) of Kohonen [7] and utilize the competitive learning which is implemented as a self-generating neural tree (SGNT). The abilities of SGNN make it suitable for the base classifier of the MCS. In order to improve in the accuracy of SGNN, we proposed ensemble self-generating neural networks (ESGNN) for classification [8] as one of the MCS. Although the accuracy of ESGNN improves by using various SGNN, the computational cost, that is, the computation time and the memory capacity increases in proportion to the increase in number of SGNN in the MCS. Therefore, we proposed a pruning method for the structure of the SGNN in the MCS to reduce the computational cost [9].

In this paper, we propose a novel MCS pruning method for effective processing. This pruning method is intended to reduce the computational cost for the previous one. This pruning method is constructed from two stages. At the first stage, we introduce an on-line pruning method to reduce the computational cost by using class labels in learning. At the second stage, we optimize the structure of the SGNT in the MCS to improve the generalization capability by pruning the tedious leaves after learning. In the optimization stage, we introduce a threshold value as a pruning parameter to decide which subtree's leaves to prune and estimate with 10-fold cross-validation [10]. After the optimization, the MCS can improve its classification accuracy as well as reducing the computational cost. We use two sampling methods for the optimizing MCS; shuffling and bagging. Shuffling uses all the training data by changing randomly the order of the training data on each classifier. Bagging [11] is a resampling technique which permits the overlap of the data. We investigate the improvement performance of the pruned MCS by comparing it with the MCS based on C4.5 [12] using ten problems in the UCI repository [13]. Moreover, we compare the pruned MCS with k-nearest neighbor (k-NN) [14] to investigate the computational cost and the classification accuracy. The optimized MCS demonstrates higher classification accuracy and faster processing speed than k-NN on average.

2   Pruning Method for the Multiple Classifier System

In this section, we describe how to prune tedious leaves in the MCS. First, we mention the on-line pruning method in learning of SGNN. Second, we describe the optimization method in constructing the MCS. Finally, we show a simple example of the pruning method for a two dimensional classification problem.

2.1   Self-generating Neural Networks

SGNN are based on SOM and implemented as a SGNT architecture. The SGNT can be constructed directly from the given training data without any intervening human effort. The SGNT algorithm is defined as a tree construction problem of how to construct a tree structure from the given data which consist of multiple attributes under the condition that the final leaves correspond to the given data.

Before we describe the SGNT algorithm, we denote some notations.

- input data vector: $e_i \in \mathbb{R}^m$.
- root, leaf, and node in the SGNT: n_j.
- weight vector of n_j: $w_j \in \mathbb{R}^m$.
- the number of the leaves in n_j: c_j.
- distance measure: $d(e_i, w_j)$.
- winner leaf for e_i in the SGNT: n_{win}.

The SGNT algorithm is a hierarchical clustering algorithm. The pseudo C code of the SGNT algorithm is given as follows:

Algorithm (SGNT Generation)

```
Input:
  A set of training examples E = {e_i}, i = 1, ... , N.
  A distance measure d(e_i,w_j).
Program Code:
  copy(n_1,e_1);
  for (i = 2, j = 2; i <= N; i++) {
    n_win = choose(e_i, n_1);
    if (leaf(n_win)) {
      copy(n_j, w_win);
      connect(n_j, n_win);
      j++;
    }
    copy(n_j, e_i);
    connect(n_j, n_win);
    j++;
    prune(n_win);
  }
Output:
 Constructed SGNT by E.
```

In the above algorithm, several sub procedures are used. Table 1 shows the sub procedures of the SGNT algorithm and their specifications.

In order to decide the winner leaf n_{win} in the sub procedure choose(e_i,n_1), competitive learning is used. If an n_j includes the n_{win} as its descendant in the SGNT, the weight w_{jk} ($k = 1, 2, \ldots, m$) of the n_j is updated as follows:

$$w_{jk} \leftarrow w_{jk} + \frac{1}{c_j} \cdot (e_{ik} - w_{jk}), \quad 1 \leq k \leq m. \tag{1}$$

After all training data are inserted into the SGNT as the leaves, the leaves have each class label as the outputs and the weights of each node are the averages

Table 1. Sub procedures of the SGNT algorithm

Sub procedure	Specification
$copy(n_j, \boldsymbol{e}_i/\boldsymbol{w}_{win})$	Create n_j, copy attributes of $\boldsymbol{e}_i/\boldsymbol{w}_{win}$ as weights $\boldsymbol{w}_j$ in n_j.
$choose(\boldsymbol{e}_i, n_1)$	Decide n_{win} for $\boldsymbol{e}_i$.
$leaf(n_{win})$	Check n_{win} whether n_{win} is a leaf or not.
$connect(n_j, n_{win})$	Connect n_j as a child leaf of n_{win}.
$prune(n_{win})$	Prune leaves if the leaves have the same class.

of the corresponding weights of all its leaves. The whole network of the SGNT reflects the given feature space by its topology. For more details concerning how to construct and perform the SGNT, see [6]. Note, to optimize the structure of the SGNT effectively, we remove the threshold value of the original SGNT algorithm in [6] to control the number of leaves based on the distance because of the trade-off between the memory capacity and the classification accuracy. In order to avoid the above problem, we introduce a new pruning method in the sub procedure `prune(n_win)`. We use the class label to prune leaves. For leaves connected to the n_{win}, if those leaves have the same class label, then the parent node of those leaves is given the class label and those leaves are pruned.

2.2   Optimization of the Multiple Classifier System

The SGNT has the capability of high speed processing. However, the accuracy of the SGNT is inferior to the conventional approaches, such as nearest neighbor, because the SGNT has no guarantee to reach the nearest leaf for unknown data. Hence, we construct an MCS by taking the majority of plural SGNT's outputs to improve the accuracy.

Although the accuracy of the MCS is superior or comparable to the accuracy of conventional approaches, the computational cost increases in proportion to the increase in the number of SGNTs in the MCS. In particular, the huge memory requirement prevents the use of MCS for large datasets even with latest computers.

In order to improve the classification accuracy as well as reducing the computational cost, we propose an optimization method of the MCS for classification. This method has two parts, the merge phase and the evaluation phase. The merge phase is performed as a pruning algorithm to reduce dense leaves (Figure 1). This phase uses the class information and a threshold value α to decide which subtree's leaves to prune or not. For leaves that have the same parent node, if the proportion of the most common class is greater than or equal to the threshold value α, then these leaves are pruned and the parent node is given the most common class.

The optimum threshold values α of the given problems are different from each other. The evaluation phase is performed to choose the best threshold value by introducing 10-fold cross validation.

```
1 begin    initialize j = the height of the SGNT
2    do for each subtree's leaves in the height j
3       if the ratio of the most class ≥ the threshold value α,
4       then merge all leaves to parent node
5       if all subtrees are traversed in the height j,
6       then j ← j − 1
7    until j = 0
8 end.
```

Fig. 1. The merge phase

2.3   An Example of the Pruning Method

We show an example of the pruning method in Figure 2. This is a two-dimensional classification problem with two equal circular Gaussian distributions that have an overlap. The shaded plane is the decision region of class 0 and the other plane is the decision region of class 1 by the SGNT. The dotted line is the ideal decision boundary. The number of training samples is 200 (class0: 100,class1: 100) (Figure 2(a)).

The unpruned SGNT is given in Figure 2(b). In this case, 200 leaves and 120 nodes are automatically generated by the SGNT algorithm. In this unpruned SGNT, the height is 7 and the number of units is 320. In this, we define the unit to count the sum of the root, nodes, and leaves of the SGNT. The root is the node which is of height 0. The unit is used as a measure of the memory requirement in the next section. Figure 2(c) shows the pruned SGNT after the on-line pruning stage. In this case, 272 units are pruned away from Figure 2(b) and 48 units remain (the height is 3). The decision boundary is the same as the unpruned SGNT. Figure 2(d) shows the pruned SGNT after the optimization stage in $\alpha = 0.6$. In this case, 27 units are pruned away from Figure 2(c) and 21 units remain (the height is 2). Moreover, the decision boundary is improved more than the unpruned SGNT because this case can reduce the effect of the overlapping class by pruning the SGNT.

In the above example, we use all training data to construct the SGNT. The structure of the SGNT is changed by the order of the training data. Hence, we can construct the MCS from the same training data by changing the input order. We call this approach "shuffling". We investigate the pruning method for more complex problems in the next section.

3   Experimental Results

We investigate the computational cost (the memory capacity and the computation time) and the classification accuracy of the MCS based on SGNN with two sampling methods, shuffling and bagging for ten benchmark problems in the UCI repository [13]. We evaluate how the MCS is pruned using 10-fold cross-validation for the ten benchmark problems. In this experiment, we use a modified Euclidean distance measure for the MCS. To select the optimum threshold value α, we set the different threshold values α which are moved from 0.5 to 1;

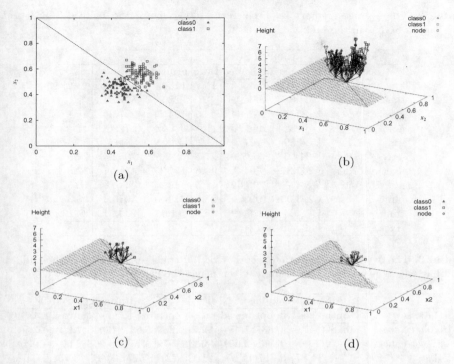

Fig. 2. An example of the SGNT's pruning algorithm, (a) a two dimensional classification problem with two equal circular Gaussian distribution, (b) the structure of the unpruned SGNT, (c) the structure of the pruned SGNT after the on-line pruning stage, and (d) the structure of the pruned SGNT after the optimization stage ($\alpha = 0.6$). The shaded plane is the decision region of class 0 by the SGNT and the doted line shows the ideal decision boundary

$\alpha = [0.5, 0.55, 0.6, \ldots, 1]$. We set the number of SGNT K in the MCS as 25 and execute 100 trials by changing the sampling order of each training set. All computations of the MCS are performed on an IBM PC-AT machine (CPU: Intel Pentium II 450MHz, Memory: 323MB).

Table 2 shows the average memory requirement of 100 trials for the MCS based on shuffled SGNN and the MCS based on bagged SGNN. As the memory requirement, we count the number of units which is the sum of the root, nodes, and leaves of the SGNT. The memory requirement is reduced from 55.4% to 96.2% in shuffling, and from 64.9% to 96.8% in bagging, by optimizing the MCS. It is found that the bagged SGNT can be a higher memory compression than the shuffled SGNN. This supports that the pruned MCS can be effectively used for all datasets with regard to both the computational cost and the classification accuracy. These results are reduced 18% and 17.4% for shuffing and bagging on average than the previous results in [9].

Table 3 shows the average classification accuracy of 100 trials for the MCS with shuffling and bagging. It is clear that over 10 datasets, both optimized MCS

Table 2. The average memory requirement of 100 trials for the shuffled SGNT and the bagged SGNT in the MCS

Dataset	shuffled SGNT			bagged SGNT		
	pruned	unpruned	ratio	pruned	unpruned	ratio
balance-scale	133.42	846.43	15.7	113.62	860.61	13.2
breast-cancer-w	34.65	889.05	3.8	28.9	897.81	3.2
glass	125.66	295.64	42.5	104.77	297.95	35.1
ionosphere	68.32	454.16	15	54.52	472.18	11.5
iris	16.59	207.7	7.9	14.65	208.7	7
letter	7312.68	26537.91	27.5	6213.52	27052.43	22.9
liver-disorders	207.37	464.3	44.6	155.17	471.71	32.8
new-thyroid	54.41	296.52	18.3	49.6	298.4	16.6
pima-diabetes	263.06	1023.88	25.6	212.81	1045.4	20.3
wine	18.34	229.19	8	14.69	239.21	6.1
Average	823.45	3124.48	20.8	696.22	3184.44	16.8

Table 3. The average classification accuracy of 100 trials for the MCS with shuffling and bagging. The standard deviation is given inside the bracket ($\times 10^{-3}$)

Dataset	MCS with shuffled SGNT			MCS with bagged SGNT		
	optimized	unoptimized	ratio	optimized	unoptimized	ratio
balance-scale	0.864(6.19)	0.837(7.45)	+2.7	0.869(5.68)	0.848(7.93)	+2.1
breast-cancer-w	0.972(1.89)	0.968(2.05)	+0.4	0.972(2.45)	0.968(2.66)	+0.4
glass	0.728(11.87)	0.717(11.95)	+1.1	0.721(11.77)	0.716(13.73)	+0.5
ionosphere	0.912(5.63)	0.882(5.53)	+3	0.893(8.24)	0.868(7.79)	+2.5
iris	0.964(4.05)	0.964(3.94)	0	0.965(4.83)	0.961(4.74)	+0.4
letter	0.959(0.69)	0.958(0.68)	+0.1	0.956(0.76)	0.956(0.75)	0
liver-disorders	0.621(12.69)	0.605(13.03)	+1.6	0.624(14.88)	0.608(17.01)	+1.6
new-thyroid	0.958(5.19)	0.957(5.92)	+0.1	0.952(6.32)	0.949(6.76)	+0.3
pima-diabetes	0.747(6.28)	0.72(8.18)	+2.7	0.749(7.34)	0.730(8.71)	+1.9
wine	0.964(4.08)	0.958(5.29)	+0.6	0.965(4.73)	0.96(4.2)	+0.5
Average	0.868	0.856	+1.2	0.866	0.856	+1

with shuffled and bagged SGNT lead to more accurate or comparable classifiers than the unoptimized MCS. In comparison with shuffling, bagging is superior or comparable to shuffling on 6 of the 10 datasets. In short, bagging is better than shuffling in terms of the computational cost and the classification accuracy in the MCS.

To evaluate the pruned MCS's performance, we compare the pruned MCS with the MCS based on C4.5. We set the number of classifiers K in the MCS as 25 and we construct both MCS by bagging. Table 4 shows the improved performance of the pruned MCS and the MCS based on C4.5. The results of the SGNT and the pruned MCS are the average of 100 trials. The pruned MCS has a better performance than the MCS based on C4.5 for 6 of the 10 datasets. Although the MCS based on C4.5 degrades the classification accuracy for iris, the pruned MCS can improve the classification accuracy for all problems. Therefore,

Table 4. The improved performance of the pruned MCS and the MCS based on C4.5 with bagging

	MCS based on SGNT			MCS based on C4.5		
Dataset	SGNT	MCS	ratio	C4.5	MCS	ratio
balance-scale	0.781	**0.869**	+8.8	0.795	0.827	+3.2
breast-cancer-w	0.957	**0.972**	+1.5	0.946	0.963	+1.7
glass	0.641	0.721	+8	0.664	**0.757**	+9.3
ionosphere	0.853	0.894	+4.1	0.897	**0.92**	+2.3
iris	0.949	**0.965**	+1.6	0.953	0.947	−0.6
letter	0.879	**0.956**	+7.7	0.880	0.938	+5.8
liver-disorders	0.58	0.624	+4.4	0.635	**0.736**	+10.1
new-thyroid	0.935	**0.952**	+1.7	0.93	0.94	+1
pima-diabetes	0.699	0.749	+5	0.749	**0.767**	+1.8
wine	0.95	**0.965**	+1.5	0.927	0.949	+2.2
Average	0.822	0.866	+4.4	0.837	**0.874**	+3

Table 5. The classification accuracy, the memory requirement, and the computation time of ten trials for the best pruned MCS and k-NN

	classification acc.		memory requirement		computation time (s)	
Dataset	MCS	k-NN	MCS	k-NN	MCS	k-NN
balance-scale	0.882	**0.899**	**100.41**	562.5	**1.27**	2.52
breast-cancer-w	**0.977**	0.973	**26.7**	629.1	1.69	**1.31**
glass	**0.756**	0.706	**115.97**	192.6	0.48	**0.04**
ionosphere	**0.915**	0.875	**25.62**	315.9	1.7	**0.25**
iris	**0.973**	0.960	**10.9**	135	0.18	**0.05**
letter	0.958	**0.961**	**6273.15**	18000	**220.52**	845.44
liver-disorders	**0.666**	0.647	**150.28**	310.5	0.77	**0.6**
new-thyroid	0.968	0.968	**53.57**	193.5	0.34	**0.05**
pima-diabetes	**0.768**	0.753	**204.11**	691.2	**2.47**	3.41
wine	**0.978**	0.977	**12.2**	160.2	0.36	**0.13**
Average	**0.884**	0.872	**697.29**	2119.1	**22.98**	85.38

the pruned SGNT is a good base classifier for the MCS on the basis of both the scalability for large scale datasets and the robust improving generalization capability for the noisy datasets comparable to the MCS with C4.5.

To show the advantages of the pruned MCS, we compare it with k-NN on the same problems. In the pruned MCS, we choose the best classification accuracy of 100 trials with bagging. In k-NN, we choose the best accuracy where k is 1,3,5,7,9,11,13,15,25 with 10-fold cross-validation. We use the modified Euclidean distance measure for the equivalent evaluation. All methods are compiled by using gcc with the optimization level -O2 on the same computer.

Table 5 shows the classification accuracy, the memory requirement, and the computation time achieved by the pruned MCS and k-NN. Next, we show the results for each category.

First, with regard to the classification accuracy, the pruned MCS is superior to k-NN for 7 of the 10 datasets and gives 1.2% improvement on average. Second,

in terms of the memory requirement, even though the pruned MCS includes the
root and the nodes which are generated by the SGNT generation algorithm,
this is less than k-NN for all problems. Although the memory requirement of
the pruned MCS is totally used K times in Table 5, we release the memory of
SGNT for each trial and reuse the memory for effective computation. Therefore,
the memory requirement is suppressed by the size of the single SGNT. Finally,
in view of the computation time, although the pruned MCS consumes the cost of
K times of the SGNT, the average computation time is faster than k-NN. In the
case of letter, in particular, the computation time of the pruned MCS is faster
than k-NN by about 3.8 times. We need to repeat 10-fold cross validation many
times to select the optimum parameters for α and k. This evaluation consumes
much computation time for large datasets such as letter. Therefore, the pruned
MCS based on the fast and compact SGNT is useful and practical for large
datasets. Moreover, the pruned MCS has the ability of parallel computation
because each classifier behaves independently. In conclusion, the pruned MCS is
practical for large-scale data mining compared with k-NN.

4   Discussion

In this paper, we proposed a new pruning method for the MCS based on SGNN
and evaluated the computational cost and the accuracy. We introduced an on-
line and off-line pruning method and evaluated the pruned MCS by 10-fold
cross-validation.

We discuss the difference between this pruning method and previously described methods. The classical cost complexity pruning method is proposed
in [15]. This method defines a cost complexity measure that has a complexity parameter. The complexity parameter is gradually increased. To search the
optimal pruned tree is complicated for large tree. Our proposed method is simple since the on-line pruning eliminate leaves on training using the class label.
Cohen and Intrator introduced the pruning method for hybrid network of RBF
and MLP with BIC and LRT [16]. The difference of their method and our proposed method is a main purpose. Their method aims to improve the accuracy
by pruning unnecessary weights for reducing the effect of over-fitting for small
datasets. Our proposed method aims to reduce the computational cost, that is
the memory capacity and the computation time, for large datasets.

Experimental results showed that the memory requirement reduces remark-
ably, and the accuracy increases by using the pruned SGNT as the base classifier
of the MCS. The pruned MCS based on SGNN is a useful and practical tool to
classify large datasets. In future work, we will study an incremental learning and
a parallel and distributed processing of the MCS for large scale data mining.

Acknowledgements

We would like to thank the anonymous referees for their helpful comments.

References

1. Han, J. and Kamber, M.: Data Mining: Concepts and Techniques. Morgan Kaufmann Publishers, San Francisco, CA (2000)
2. Quinlan, J. R.: Bagging, Boosting, and C4.5. Proceedings of the Thirteenth National Conference on Artificial Intelligence, AAAI Press and the MIT Press, Portland, OR (1996) 725–730
3. Rätsch, G., Onoda, T. and Müller, K.-R.: Soft margins for AdaBoost. Machine Learning **42**(3) (2001) 287–320
4. Bishop, C. M.: Neural Networks for Pattern Recognition. Oxford University Press, New York (1995)
5. Duda, R. O., Hart, P. E. and Stork, D. G.: Pattern Classification. 2nd ed. John Wiley & Sons Inc., New York (2000).
6. Wen, W. X., Jennings, A. and Liu, H.: Learning a neural tree. Proceedings of the International Joint Conference on Neural Networks **2**, Beijing, China (1992) 751–756
7. Kohonen, T.: Self-Organizing Maps. Springer-Verlag, Berlin (1995)
8. Inoue, H. and Narihisa, H.: Improving generalization ability of self-generating neural networks through ensemble averaging. In: Terano, T., Liu, H., and Chen, A. L. P. (eds.): The Fourth Pacific-Asia Conference on Knowledge Discovery and Data Mining, LNAI 1805, Springer-Verlag, Berlin (2000) 177–180
9. Inoue, H. and Narihisa, H.: Optimizing a multiple classifier system. In: Ishizuka, M. and Sattar, A. (eds.): PRICAI2002: Trends in Artificial Intelligence, LNAI 2417, Springer-Verlag, Berlin (2002) 285–294
10. Stone, M.: Cross-validation: A review. Math. Operationsforsch. Statist., Ser. Statistics **9**(1) (1978) 127–139
11. Breiman, L.: Bagging predictors. Machine Learning **24** (1996) 123–140
12. Quinlan, J. R.: C4.5: Programs for Machine Learning. Morgan Kaufmann, San Mateo, CA (1993)
13. Blake, C. L. and Merz, C. J.: UCI repository of machine learning databases, University of California, Irvine, Dept of Information and Computer Science (1998) Datasets is available at `http://www.ics.uci.edu/~mlearn/MLRepository.html`
14. Patrick, E. A. and Fischer, F. P.: A generalized k-nearest neighbor rule. Information and Control **16**(2) (1970) 128–152
15. Breiman, L., Friedman, J., Olshen, R. and Stone, C.: Classification and Regression Trees. Wadsworth, Belmont, CA (1984)
16. Cohen, S. and Intrator, N.: Forward and backward selection in regression hybrid network. In: Roli, F. and Kittler, J. (eds.): Multiple Classifier Systems, Third International Workshop, LNCS 2364, Springer-Verlag, Berlin (2002) 98–107

Negative Correlation Learning and the Ambiguity Family of Ensemble Methods

Gavin Brown and Jeremy Wyatt

School of Computer Science, University of Birmingham
Edgbaston Park Road, Birmingham, B15 2TT
{g.brown,j.l.wyatt}@cs.bham.ac.uk
http://www.cs.bham.ac.uk/~gxb

Abstract. We study the formal basis behind Negative Correlation (NC) Learning, an ensemble technique developed in the evolutionary computation literature. We show that by removing an assumption made in the original work, NC can be shown to be a derivative technique of the Ambiguity decomposition by Krogh and Vedelsby. From this formalisation, we calculate parameter bounds, and show significant improvements in empirical tests. We hypothesize that the reason for its success lies in rescaling an estimate of ensemble covariance; then show that during this rescaling, NC varies smoothly between a single neural network and an ensemble system. Finally we unify several other works in the literature, all of which have exploited the Ambiguity decomposition in some way, and term them the *Ambiguity Family*.

1   Introduction

Error 'diversity' is now widely recognised as a desirable characteristic in multiple classifier systems. Though still an ill-defined concept, it is related to statistical correlation, and a number of methods designed to encourage low correlation between classifiers have matured over the last decade. Our framework for this investigation hinges on regarding these methods as dichotomous: explicit and implicit diversity methods. Explicit methods measure diversity (correlation) in some manner and directly incorporate this knowledge into the construction or combination of the estimators; for example Input Decimation Ensembles [10], which measure correlation between features before assigning them to particular networks. Implicit methods utilise purely stochastic perturbations to encourage diversity; for example, Bagging or similar data resampling techniques. In this paper we are concerned with explicit methods, in particular those which share a common root in the Ambiguity decomposition from [4], widely recognised as one of the most important theoretical results obtained for ensemble learning. It states that the mean-square error of the ensemble estimator is guaranteed to be less than or equal to the average mean-square error of the component estimators; the details of this will be expanded upon later.

T. Windeatt and F. Roli (Eds.): MCS 2003, LNCS 2709, pp. 266–275, 2003.
© Springer-Verlag Berlin Heidelberg 2003

1.1   Negative Correlation Learning

After this initial branching, both explicit and implicit methods can be further divided as manipulating either: the initial weights of the networks, the network architectures, the training data, or the learning algorithm. Some authors, taking the latter approach, have found benefit from using a regularisation term in the learning. Negative Correlation[1] (NC) Learning [5], an extension of Rosen's decorrelated networks [11], is an ensemble learning technique which incorporates such a regularisation term into the backpropagation error function. The regularisation term is meant to quantify the amount of error correlation, so it can be minimised explicitly during training—as such, it is an explicit diversity method. In NC the error ϵ_i of network i is:

$$\epsilon_i = \frac{1}{2}(f_i - d)^2 + \lambda p_i \tag{1}$$

where f_i is the output of the ith network on a single input pattern, d is the target, and λ is a weighting parameter on the penalty function p_i. Strictly, this notation should include input, so $f_i(n)$ and $d(n)$ for the nth input pattern, but we omit this for notational simplicity. The λ parameter controls a trade-off between objective and penalty functions; when $\lambda = 0$, the penalty function is removed and we have an ensemble with each network training independently of the others, using plain backpropagation. NC has a penalty function of the form:

$$p_i = (f_i - \bar{f}) \sum_{j \neq i} (f_j - \bar{f}) \tag{2}$$

where $\bar{f}$ is the average output of the whole ensemble of M networks at the previous timestep, defined as $\bar{f} = \frac{1}{M} \sum_{i=1}^{i=M} f_i$. NC has seen a number of empirical successes [5,6,7], consistently outperforming a simple ensemble system, but so far has had very little formal analysis to explain why it works when it does; this leads naturally to our first question.

1.2   Why Does the Algorithm Work?

The mean-square error (MSE) of an ensemble system can be decomposed into bias, variance and covariance components [12]. The strength parameter λ in NC provides a way of controlling the trade-off between these three components: a higher value encourages a decrease in covariance, as has been demonstrated empirically [5]. However we do not yet have a clear picture of the exact dynamics of the algorithm.

When $\lambda = 1$, we have a special situation. This was described by Liu [5] to show a theoretical justification for NC-Learning. It should be noted that, in the calculation of the derivative, Liu has: "... made use of the assumption that the output of the ensemble $\bar{f}$ has constant value with respect to f_i" [5, p.29].

---

[1] So-called because it has demonstrated on a number of occasions that it is able to generate estimators with *negatively correlated* errors.

We have:

$$\epsilon_i = \frac{1}{2}(f_i - d)^2 + \lambda(f_i - \bar{f})\sum_{j \neq i}(f_j - \bar{f})$$

$$\frac{\partial \epsilon_i}{\partial f_i} = f_i - d + \lambda\sum_{j \neq i}(f_j - \bar{f})$$

$$= f_i - d - \lambda(f_i - \bar{f})$$

$$= \bar{f} - d$$

However, although the assumption of constant $\bar{f}$ is used, so is the property that $\sum_{j \neq i}(f_j - \bar{f}) = -(f_i - \bar{f})$, the sum of deviations around a mean is equal to zero; obviously the sum of deviations around a constant does not have this property. Using this apparently contradictory assumption, and the fact that the overall ensemble error function is defined as $\epsilon = \frac{1}{2}(\bar{f} - d)^2$, it was stated:

$$\frac{\partial \epsilon}{\partial f_i} = \frac{1}{M}\left[\frac{\partial \epsilon_i}{\partial f_i}\right] \tag{3}$$

showing that the gradient of the individual network error is directly proportional to the gradient of the ensemble error. Though this is obviously a useful property, the justification for the assumption is unclear. To understand this further, as with all algorithms, it would be useful to first understand a framework into which NC can fit. What is the theoretical grounding of NC? What are other similar algorithms? In the following sections we address these questions.

2   Formalising NC-Learning

In this section we show how NC can be related to the work by Krogh and Vedelsby [4], which showed the ensemble error could be broken down into two terms, one of which is dependent on the correlations between network errors.

2.1   NC Uses the Ambiguity Decomposition

Note that the penalty function is actually a sum of pairwise correlations; if we remember again that the MSE of an ensemble decomposes into bias plus variance plus covariance [12], then including some measure of correlation to be minimised seems like an intuitive thing to do (first noted by Rosen [11]). However this intuition is not enough. We note that the penalty function can be rearranged to:

$$p_i = -(f_i - \bar{f})^2 \tag{4}$$

which is again due to the property that the sum of deviations around a mean is equal to zero. This rearrangement is only possible if we remove Liu's assumption ([5], p29) of constant $\bar{f}$. As can be seen, each network minimises its penalty function by moving its output away from the ensemble output, the mean response of all the other networks. So why should increasing distance from the mean, or optimising equation (1), necessarily lead to a decrease in ensemble error? An examination of the proof by Krogh and Vedelsby can answer this question, and also raise some new questions on the setting for the λ parameter. Their work showed that the following statement about ensemble error was true:

$$(\bar{f} - d)^2 = \sum_i w_i (f_i - d)^2 - \sum_i w_i (f_i - \bar{f})^2 \qquad (5)$$

This stems from a number of definitions, one of which is the ambiguity of a single member of the ensemble:

$$v_i = (f_i - \bar{f})^2 \qquad (6)$$

Remembering that the individual networks in NC-learning minimise the penalty function, and looking at equations (4) and (6) we can see $p_i = -v_i$ and so the networks are in fact maximising this ambiguity term, equation (6). This in turn of course affects the total ensemble error. Please note this result for NC only holds if the weightings on the networks are all $\frac{1}{M}$, as equation (2) cannot be rearranged to (4) without this constraint.

To understand this further we take equation (5), multiply through by $\frac{1}{2}$ and rearrange slightly assuming our ensemble is uniformly weighted, we then have:

$$\frac{1}{2}(\bar{f} - d)^2 = \frac{1}{M} \sum_i \left[\frac{1}{2}(f_i - d)^2 - \frac{1}{2}(f_i - \bar{f})^2 \right] \qquad (7)$$

We see that the mean squared error of an ensemble can be decomposed into a weighted summation, where the ith term is the backpropagation error function plus the NC-Learning penalty function.

Now, since we have removed the constraint of assuming constant $\bar{f}$ to allow a link to the ambiguity decomposition, it seems more rigorous to differentiate the network error again without this assumption. What happens in this case? We have a partial derivative:

$$\frac{\partial \epsilon_i}{\partial f_i} = f_i - d - \lambda \left[2\frac{M-1}{M}(f_i - \bar{f}) \right] \qquad (8)$$

where M is the number of networks in the ensemble. Keeping the assumption of constant $\bar{f}$ causes this term $2\frac{M-1}{M}$ to disappear. However, it does seem sensible to retain this, as it takes account of the number of networks. In all of Liu's experiments [5,6,7], the λ parameter was thought to be problem dependent. Now we understand that it has a deterministic component, this $2\frac{M-1}{M}$. To avoid confusion, from this point on, we shall refer to the λ parameter in the following context, where γ is still a problem-dependent scaling parameter:

$$\lambda = \gamma \left[2\frac{M-1}{M} \right] \qquad (9)$$

In understanding the role of the strength parameter a natural question to ask is, what are the bounds?

2.2   What Are the Bounds of λ and γ?

As with any problem-dependent parameter, we would like to know bounds, to allow us to set it sensibly. Liu stated that the bounds of λ should be $[0, 1]$, based on the following calculation:

$$\frac{\partial \epsilon_i}{\partial f_i} = f_i - d + \lambda \sum_{j \neq i}(f_j - \bar{f})$$
$$= f_i - d - \lambda(f_i - \bar{f})$$
$$= (1 - \lambda)(f_i - d) + \lambda(\bar{f} - d)$$

He states: "the value of parameter λ lies inside the range $0 \leq \lambda \leq 1$ so that both $(1-\lambda)$ and λ have non-negative values" ([5], p29). However this justification is questionable, and again here we see the assumption of constant $\bar{f}$ is violated.

We have to ask therefore, why would it be a problem if $(1 - \lambda)$ and λ were negative values? Maybe the bounds of λ should not be $[0, 1]$. How can we determine what the true bounds should be? We can simply take the second partial derivative of ϵ_i with respect to f_i:

$$\frac{\partial^2 \epsilon_i}{\partial f_i^2} = 1 - \lambda(1 - \frac{1}{M})$$

If the second derivative becomes negative, then our function contains only local maxima or points of inflexion, and we have lost any useful gradient information from our original objective function. Rearranging this, to maintain a positive second derivative, we have an upper bound for λ and also γ:

$$\lambda_{upper} = \frac{M}{M - 1} \qquad\qquad \gamma_{upper} = \frac{M^2}{2(M - 1)^2}$$

Figure 1 plots λ_{upper} and the equivalent γ_{upper} for different numbers of networks. We see that in the infinite networks case, λ_{upper} converges to 1, and γ_{upper} converges to 0.5. It should be noted that with a smaller number of networks λ_{upper} is greater than 1.

2.3   An Empirical Study

With our new understanding of the bounds of the parameter in NC, we now perform an empirical evaluation, and show that it is critical to consider values for the strength parameter outside the originally specified range.

Table 1 shows the classification error rates and standard errors of two empirical tests, on the Wisconsin breast cancer data from the UCI repository (699 patterns), and the heart disease Statlog dataset (270 patterns). An ensemble consisting of two networks, each with five hidden nodes, was trained for 2000 iterations with and without NC. We use 5-fold cross-validation and 40 trials from uniform random weights in $[-0.5, 0.5]$ for each setup; in total 200 trials were conducted for each experimental configuration. It should be noted that with 2

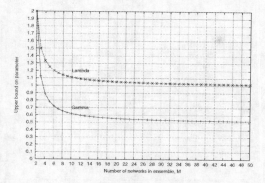

Fig. 1. The Upper bound on γ and λ

Table 1. Mean classification error rates (200 trials) using NC on two UCI datasets

	$\gamma = 0$	$\gamma = 0.5$	$\gamma = 1$
BREAST CANCER	0.0408 (0.0006)	0.0410 (0.0007)	0.0383 (0.0009)
HEART DISEASE	0.2022 (0.0028)	0.1995 (0.0027)	**0.1802** (0.0020)

networks, $\gamma = \lambda$. The γ values tested are those considered in the original work on NC: 0.0, 0.5 and 1.0. When γ was set appropriately, results on the heart data showed NC significantly better than a simple ensemble (equivalent to $\gamma = 0$) at $\alpha = 0.05$ on a two-tailed t-test. On the breast cancer data, although the mean was lower, it was not statistically significant.

Figure 2 shows the results of repeating our experiment, but illustrating the full range of the strength parameter. Mean error rate over the 200 trials is plotted, and 95% confidence intervals shown. We see that performance on the breast cancer data can be improved significantly by considering the upper bounds beyond those previously specified; on the heart disease data (not shown due to space considerations), stable performance was observed beyond $\gamma = 1$.

As a further measure of comparison, we calculated the percentage reduction in the mean error rate, in relation to when $\gamma = 0$, equivalent to a simple backpropagation ensemble. On the breast cancer data, using $\gamma = 1$ gave a 6% reduction, but using the optimum value at $\gamma = 1.7$ gave a 21% reduction.

We have shown a significant performance improvement by reconsidering the bounds of the strength parameters. It should be noted that, even though the theoretical upper bound is known, in practise it seems error can rise rapidly long before this bound is reached. On the breast cancer data, error became uncontrollable beyond $\gamma = 1.8$, and on the heart disease data at $\gamma = 1.45$; it remains to be seen if it is possible to empirically characterise when this rapid increase will occur.

We know from figure 1 that the upper bound reduces as we add more networks; from this it is reasonable to assume that the optimal value would follow a similar trend. But why? What role does γ play?

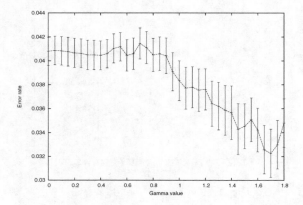

Fig. 2. Breast cancer dataset results

3   What Is the Relation of NC to Bias and Variance?

In this section we ask the question, how does NC relate to the bias-variance decomposition? Can this tell us what role the strength parameter plays?

The second term on the right handside of equation 5 is the *ensemble ambiguity*; this is maximised when training an ensemble with NC. When $w_i = \frac{1}{M}$ for all i, it can be shown:

$$-E\Big\{ \sum_i w_i (f_i - \bar{f})^2 \Big\} = E\Big\{ \frac{1}{M} \sum_i (f_i - \bar{f}) \sum_{j \neq i} (f_j - \bar{f}) \Big\}$$

$$= \frac{1}{M} \sum_i \sum_{j \neq i} E\Big\{ (f_i - \bar{f})(f_j - \bar{f}) \Big\}$$

The expected value of the ensemble ambiguity term is an approximation to the average covariance of the ensemble members. It is an approximation because with a finite number of networks, $\bar{f} \neq E\{f\}$, and also because the sum is multiplied by $\frac{1}{M}$ instead of $\frac{1}{M(M-1)}$. We can see that when we are increasing ambiguity, we are reducing this covariance term. When training an ensemble with NC, we use the γ parameter, directly attempting to reduce covariance by over-emphasising this component. A larger γ parameter will be needed when our approximation is not very good: this is will most likely occur when we have a small number of networks, but it could also be due to noise in the training data. It is hoped that with further analysis we will be able to mathematically characterise this, and provide further guidelines for setting the strength parameter.

4   Viewing the Ensemble as a Single Estimator

In this section we briefly show how NC-Learning works on a search landscape that, using the λ parameter, can be smoothly scaled between that of a fully par-

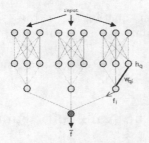

Fig. 3. A typical ensemble architecture

allel ensemble system, and a single large neural network. Regard the architecture in figure 3.

This is an ensemble of three networks, each with three hidden nodes, using a simple average combination rule for the ensemble output. We desire to update the weight, w_{qi}, marked in bold—this is one of the output layer weights for the ith network (connected to the qth hidden node). If we use NC-Learning, we need the derivative of the error ϵ_i with respect to w_{qi}. If $\lambda = 0$, we have:

$$\frac{\partial \epsilon_i}{\partial w_{qi}} = \left[(f_i - d)\right] \cdot \left[f_i(1 - f_i)\right] \cdot \left[h_q\right] \tag{10}$$

And if $\lambda = 1$, we have:

$$\frac{\partial \epsilon_i}{\partial w_{qi}} = \left[(\bar{f} - d)\right] \cdot \left[f_i(1 - f_i)\right] \cdot \left[h_q\right] \tag{11}$$

If we now consider the ensemble architecture as one large network (with fixed output layer weights), then our output node is marked in dark gray, and has a linear output function $\bar{f}$:

$$\bar{f} = a_i \tag{12}$$

and its activation function a_i:

$$a_i = \frac{1}{M} \sum_i f_i \tag{13}$$

The error of this large network on a single pattern is:

$$\epsilon = \frac{1}{2}(\bar{f} - d)^2 \tag{14}$$

Now, as before, we find the derivative of ϵ with respect to the weight w_{qi}:

$$\frac{\partial \epsilon}{\partial w_{qi}} = \frac{\partial \epsilon}{\partial \bar{f}} \frac{\partial \bar{f}}{\partial a_i} \frac{\partial a_i}{\partial f_i} \frac{\partial f_i}{\partial a_i} \frac{\partial a_i}{\partial w_{qi}} \tag{15}$$

$$\frac{\partial \epsilon}{\partial w_q} = \left[(\bar{f} - d))\right] \cdot \left[1\right] \cdot \left[\frac{1}{M}\right] \cdot \left[f_i(1 - f_i)\right] \cdot \left[h_q\right] \tag{16}$$

The only difference from equation (11) is the $\frac{1}{M}$. All the minima are in the same locations, but the landscape is M times shallower—the effect of which could be duplicated with a smaller learning rate in the update rule. When we change λ, we can scale smoothly between a single network with a linear output function, and a parallel ensemble system.

5   Related Work: The Ambiguity Family

In this section we briefly review some other techniques which have exploited the ambiguity decomposition in some way, either to create or combine a set of predictors. In the last few years, the ambiguity decomposition has quietly been utilised in almost every aspect of ensemble construction. Krogh and Vedelsby themselves developed an active learning scheme [4], based on the method of query by committee, selecting patterns to train on that had a large ambiguity; this showed significant improvements over passive learning in approximating a square wave function.

[8] selected feature subsets for the ensemble members to train on, using a genetic algorithm with an ambiguity-based fitness function; this showed gains over Bagging and Adaboost on several classification datasets from the UCI repository. A precursor to this work was Opitz and Shavlik's Addemup algorithm [9], which used the same fitness function to optimise the network topologies composing the ensemble. Interestingly, both these GA-based approaches also used a strength parameter, λ, to vary the emphasis on diversity. The difference between their work and NC is that NC incorporates ambiguity into the backpropagation weight updates, while Addemup trains with standard backpropagation, then selects networks with a good error diversity.

The original ambiguity paper [4] also used an estimate of ambiguity to optimise the ensemble combination weights, showing in some cases it is optimal to set a network weight to zero—essentially removing it from the ensemble. In [1] bootstrap resamples of training data are used to estimate ambiguity, in order to approximate the optimal training time; this minimises the overall ensemble generalisation error.

We can see that ambiguity has been utilised in many ways: pattern selection [4], feature selection [8], optimising the topologies [9] of networks in the ensemble, optimising the combination function [4], and also optimising training time [1]. NC fits neatly into the gap as the first technique to directly use ambiguity for network weight updates.

6   Conclusions

We analyzed an ensemble technique, Negative Correlation Learning[5], that extended from Rosen[11], and developed in the evolutionary computation literature. We show a link to the bias-variance decomposition, and hypothesise that NC succeeds by rescaling an estimate of the ensemble covariance. This formalisation of NC is a step towards placing it in a solid statistical framework. In showing how NC uses its strength parameter to scale smoothly between an ensemble system and a single network, it serves to partially unify the concepts of training an ensemble and training a single estimator.

In addition this work highlights the need for collaboration between communities, as a technique grown in the artificial intelligence and evolutionary computation community can be of interest to the pattern recognition community. Several other works on artificial speciation[3] and multi-objective evolutionary algorithms[2] are highly relevant, and are slowly formulating a solid statistical grounding, and it is hoped future cross-disciplinary links can be fostered.

References

1. J. Carney and P. Cunningham. Tuning diversity in bagged neural network ensembles. Technical Report TCD-CS-1999-44, Trinity College Dublin, 1999.
2. Kalyanmoy Deb. Multi-objective genetic algorithms: Problem difficulties and construction of test problems. *Evolutionary Computation*, 7(3):205–230, 1999.
3. Vineet Khare and Xin Yao. Artificial speciation of neural network ensembles. In J.A.Bullinaria, editor, *Proc. of the 2002 UK Workshop on Computational Intelligence (UKCI'02)*, pages 96–103. University of Birmingham, UK, September 2002.
4. Anders Krogh and Jesper Vedelsby. Neural network ensembles, cross validation, and active learning. *NIPS*, 7:231–238, 1995.
5. Yong Liu. *Negative Correlation Learning and Evolutionary Neural Network Ensembles*. PhD thesis, University College, The University of New South Wales, Australian Defence Force Academy, Canberra, Australia, 1998.
6. Yong Liu and Xin Yao. Negatively correlated neural networks can produce best ensembles. *Australian Journal of Intelligent Information Processing Systems*, 4(3/4):176–185, 1997.
7. Yong Liu and Xin Yao. Ensemble learning via negative correlation. *Neural Networks*, 12(10):1399–1404, 1999.
8. David Opitz. Feature selection for ensembles. In *Proceedings of 16th National Conference on Artificial Intelligence (AAAI)*, pages 379–384, 1999.
9. David W. Opitz and Jude W. Shavlik. Generating accurate and diverse members of a neural-network ensemble. *NIPS*, 8:535–541, 1996.
10. Nikunj C. Oza and Kagan Tumer. Input decimation ensembles: Decorrelation through dimensionality reduction. *LNCS*, 2096:238–247, 2001.
11. Bruce E. Rosen. Ensemble learning using decorrelated neural networks. *Connection Science - Special Issue on Combining Artificial Neural Networks: Ensemble Approaches*, 8(3 and 4):373–384, 1996.
12. N. Ueda and R. Nakano. Generalization error of ensemble estimators. In *Proceedings of International Conference on Neural Networks*, pages 90–95, 1996.

Spectral Coefficients and Classifier Correlation

Terry Windeatt, R. Ghaderi, and G. Ardeshir

Centre for Vision, Speech and Signal Processing (CVSSP)
University of Surrey, Guildford, Surrey, GU2 5XH, UK
T.Windeatt@eim.surrey.ac.uk

Abstract. Various counting measures, such as Margin and Bias/Variance, have been proposed for analysing Multiple Classifier Systems (MCS) performance. In this paper a measure based on counting votes to estimate first order spectral coefficients for two-class problems is described. Experiments employing MLP base classifiers, in which parameters are fixed but systematically varied, demonstrate how the proposed measure varies with test error. Estimated spectral coefficients are used to design a weighted vote combiner, which is shown experimentally to be less sensitive than majority vote to base classifier complexity.

1 Introduction

Various counting measures have been proposed for analysing the Multiple Classifier Systems (MCS) framework. The Margin concept (section 3.1) was used to help explain Boosting. Bias and Variance (section 3.3) are concepts from regression theory that have motivated modified definitions for 0/1 loss function for characterising Bagging and other ensemble techniques. Classifier diversity measures [6] are variously defined in an attempt to quantify the notion of diversity which is known to be a necessary condition for improvement of MCS performance. However, it is not clear how to use the information available from any of these measures in MCS design. The most common approach is to rely on either a validation set or cross-validation techniques to select MCS parameter values.

In this paper, we propose a vote counting measure based on spectral representation of a Boolean function for characterising correlation of a set of binary base classifiers with respect to binary class labels (Section 2). The relationship between this measure and test error is observed experimentally as classifier complexity is varied. Experiments use Multi-layer Perceptron (MLP) base classifiers since their complexity can be independently changed in a smooth fashion, which is not possible, for example, with decision tree classifiers [12]. Also the estimated first order spectral coefficients are used to design a weighted vote combiner which is compared experimentally with majority vote as number of training epochs is reduced.

Estimation of spectral coefficients is based on the assumption that spectral contribution with respect to a pair of patterns is inversely proportional to Hamming Distance (equation (3) Section 2). Hamming Distance was used as a measure of closeness between binary patterns in the decision-making stage of

Error-Correcting Output Coding (ECOC) . The principle behind ECOC is that individual classification errors can be tolerated if codes with large Hamming distance are employed. In ECOC however, L_1 norm usually replaces Hamming Distance if it can be shown that base classifiers provide good probability estimates [13].

2   Spectral Representation

Assume that we are dealing with a two-class problem having b parallel binary base classifiers in the MCS framework. If a binary decision is taken for each classifier, the mapping defined by the classifier outputs with respect to target labels is binary-to-binary. Therefore the mth training pattern may be represented as a vertex in the b-dimensional binary hypercube

$$X_m = (x_{m1}, x_{m2}, \dots x_{mb}) \tag{1}$$

where x_{mj} and $f(X_m) \in \{+1,-1\}$. The following equations assume $\{+1,-1\}$ coding and a simple modification is required for $\{0,1\}$. Consider the following change of representation of a completely specified Boolean function, which assigns σ_{mj} to the jth pattern component x_{mj} for $j = 1, 2, \dots b$.

$$\sigma_{mj} = \frac{1 - x_{mj}x_{nj}}{2}, \quad f(X_m) \neq f(X_n), \sum_{j=1}^{b} \left(\frac{1 - x_{mj}x_{nj}}{2} \right) = 1 \tag{2}$$

where Hamming Distance $D_H(X_m, X_n) = \sum_{j=1}^{b} \left(\frac{1-x_{mj}x_{nj}}{2} \right)$. Equation (2) is just the first stage of logic minimisation [14], and requires finding, for each pattern X_m, all patterns of the other class that are unit D_H apart. We refer to σ_{mj} as sensitivity [11] and write as $x_{mj}^{\sigma_{mj}}$ for convenience. In words, x_{mj} is sensitive ($\sigma_{mj} = 1$) if a change in x_{mj} leads to a change in $f(X_m)$. In order to keep positive and negative contributions separate σ_{mj} is defined as excitatory (σ_{mj}^+) if $x_{mj} = f(X_m)$ and inhibitory (σ_{mj}^-) if $x_{mj} \neq f(X_m)$. Using spectral summation [3] the difference between $\sum_X \sigma_j^+$ and $\sum_X \sigma_j^-$ gives first order spectral coefficient s_j, where $\sum_X$ is the sum over all training patterns.

To understand the proposed representational change and its relation to the calculation and meaning of spectral coefficients, consider the following example of a Boolean function $f(X) = (\bar{x}_1 \wedge x_2) \vee (x_1 \wedge \bar{x}_2) \vee (x_2 \wedge x_3)$. The truth table is given by

x_1	1	-1	1	-1	1	-1	1	-1
x_2	1	1	-1	-1	1	1	-1	-1
x_3	1	1	1	1	-1	-1	-1	-1
f(X)	1	-1	-1	1	1	-1	-1	-1

and matrix multiplication using an appropriate transform [3] gives the spectral coefficients as follows

$$
\begin{bmatrix}
1 & 1 & 1 & 1 & 1 & 1 & 1 & 1 \\
1 & -1 & 1 & -1 & 1 & -1 & 1 & -1 \\
1 & 1 & -1 & -1 & 1 & 1 & -1 & -1 \\
1 & -1 & -1 & 1 & 1 & -1 & -1 & 1 \\
1 & 1 & 1 & 1 & -1 & -1 & -1 & -1 \\
1 & -1 & 1 & -1 & -1 & 1 & -1 & 1 \\
1 & 1 & -1 & -1 & -1 & -1 & 1 & 1 \\
1 & -1 & -1 & 1 & -1 & 1 & 1 & -1
\end{bmatrix}
\begin{bmatrix}
1 \\ -1 \\ -1 \\ 1 \\ 1 \\ -1 \\ -1 \\ -1
\end{bmatrix}
=
\begin{bmatrix}
-2 \\ +2 \\ +2 \\ +6 \\ +2 \\ -2 \\ -2 \\ +2
\end{bmatrix}
\begin{matrix}
s_0 \\ s_1 \\ s_2 \\ s_{12} \\ s_3 \\ s_{13} \\ s_{23} \\ s_{123}
\end{matrix}
$$

By comparing the truth table and the transformation matrix, we can see that first order coefficients s_i where $i = 1, 2, 3$ represent the correlation between $f(X)$ and x_i. Similarly the second order coefficients s_{ij} represent correlation between $f(X)$ and $x_i \oplus x_j$ and s_{ijk} between $f(X)$ and $x_i \oplus x_j \oplus x_k$, where $\oplus$ is logic exclusive-OR. Applying equation (2) to the three class 1 patterns in the example function:

$$
\begin{array}{c|ccc}
x_1 & 1^1 & -1^1 & 1^1 \\
x_2 & 1^1 & -1^1 & 1^1 \\
x_3 & 1^0 & 1^1 & -1^0
\end{array}
$$

We now demonstrate by example that this representational change leads to an alternative calculation of the spectral coefficients. The three columns show the contribution for class 1 patterns, and by duality there is an identical contribution from class -1. To calculate higher order coefficients, the first order contributions are added for the respective rows, ignoring any component with $\sigma_j = 0$. For example

$s_1 = 2 \times (1 - 1 + 1) = +2$ using row 1.

$s_{12} = 2 \times ((1 \times 1) + (-1 \times -1) + (1 \times 1)) = +6$ using row 1,2.

$s_{123} = 0 + 2 \times (-1 \times -1 \times 1) + 0 = +2$ using row 1,2,3.

From spectral summation we can deduce information about the separability of the function [8]. The existence of $\sum_X \sigma_j^+ > 0$ and $\sum_X \sigma_j^- > 0$ for given j provides evidence that the set of patterns is not 1-monotonic in the jth component and therefore non-separable. In the above example we find that $\sum_X \sigma_j^+ / \sum_X \sigma_j^-$ for $j = 1, 2, 3$ evaluates to $[4/2, 4/2, 2/0]$, showing that the function is not 1-monotonic in the first two components.

For noisy, incompletely specified and perhaps contradictory patterns, the following modification to equation (2) is proposed

$$
\sigma_{mj} = \sum_{X_n} \left(\frac{1 - x_{mj} x_{nj}}{2 D_H(X_m, X_n)} \right), \qquad f(X_m) \neq f(X_n) \tag{3}
$$

and $\sigma_{mj}^+, \sigma_{mj}^-$ are defined as in equation (2). In equation (3), $\sum_{X_n}$ sums contributions from each pattern pair assuming the contribution to be inversely proportional to D_H and, with no evidence to the contrary, equally shared between components that differ.

For a given pattern pair, component x_j has associated σ_j^- after applying equation (3) only if the jth base classifier mis-classifies both patterns. Therefore we expect that a pattern with relatively large $\sum_{j=1}^b \sigma_j^-$ is likely to come from regions where the two classes overlap. In Section 3.2 we consider the relative contribution of σ_j^+ and σ_j^- with respect to $\sum_X \sigma_j^+$ and $\sum_X \sigma_j^-$.

3   Vote Counting Measures

3.1   Margin

Margin was originally used in Support Vector Machines and Boosting. It was used to analyse Adaboost and thereby understand its effectiveness in generalising well even though the training error drops exponentially fast. In [10] margin was defined to be a number between -1 and $+1$, positive for correct classification with its absolute value representing confidence of classification. The margin for mth training pattern X_m is given by

$$Margin(X_m, f(X_m)) = \frac{f(X_m) \sum_{j=1}^b \alpha_j x_{mj}}{\sum_{j=1}^b |\alpha_j|} \tag{4}$$

where α_j is the weight associated with jth base classifier. Note that Margin for majority vote ($\alpha_j = 1/b$) in equation (4) is identical to s_0 in section 2 so that Margin may be regarded as a special case of spectral summation.

It is customary to plot Margins as cumulative distribution graphs, that is $f(z)$ versus z where z is the Margin and $f(z)$ is the fraction of patterns with Margin at least z. It is proved in [10] that larger Margins are associated with superior upper bounds on the generalisation error and that the derived bound is independent of the number of classifiers. However, as pointed out by the authors, the bounds are not necessarily tight and therefore of limited practical usefulness.

3.2   Spectral Contribution and Weighted Vote

A measure of pattern separability σ_T is proposed which reflects the difference between relative excitatory and inhibitory contributions, normalised so that $-1 \leq \sigma_T \leq 1$.

$$\sigma_T = \frac{1}{N} \times \sum_{j=1}^b \left[\frac{\sigma_j^+}{\sum_X \sigma_j^+} - \frac{\sigma_j^-}{\sum_X \sigma_j^-} \right] \tag{5}$$

where

$$N = \sum_{j=1}^b \left[\frac{\sigma_j^+}{\sum_X \sigma_j^+} + \frac{\sigma_j^+}{\sum_X \sigma_j^+} \right]$$

Cumulative distribution graphs for σ_T can be defined similar to cumulative distribution graphs for Margin as explained in Section 3.1. The σ_T distribution measures the relative contribution of a pattern, and hence is able to reflect a re-distribution of correlation between patterns.

The principle behind weighted voting is to reward classifiers that perform well. One way to categorise weighting methods is constant versus non-constant depending on whether weights change as a function of the particular pattern being classified [7]. Adaboost is then regarded as a constant weighting function with weights chosen to be a logarithmic function of errors on the training set. In this paper, we propose a constant weighting function based on first order spectral coefficients computed over the training set as follows

$$\alpha_j = \sum_X \sigma_j^+ - \sum_X \sigma_j^-, j = 1, 2, ...b \qquad (6)$$

3.3   Bias/Variance

Bias/Variance for analysing multiple classifiers is motivated by what appears to be analogous concepts in regression theory. However there are reported difficulties with the various Bias/Variance definitions for 0/1 loss functions. It is shown in [4] that no definition can satisfy both zero Bias/Variance for Bayes classifier and additive Bias/Variance decomposition of error (as in regression theory). Also, as the authors of the various Bias/Variance definitions acknowledge, the effect of bias/variance on error rate cannot be guaranteed. It is easy to think of example probability distributions for which bias and variance are constant but error rate changes with distribution, or for which reduction in variance leads to increase in error rate [2]. There is the additional difficulty that for real problems the Bayes classification needs to be known or estimated, although some definitions, for example [5], do not account for Bayes error.

In our experiments, we use Breiman's definition [2] which is based on defining Variance as the component of classification error that is eliminated by aggregation. Patterns are divided into two sets (criticised in [4]), the Bias set B containing patterns for which the Bayes classification disagrees with the aggregate classifier and the Unbias set U containing the remainder. Bias is computed using B patterns and Variance is computed using U patterns, but both Bias and Variance are defined as the difference between the probability that the Bayes and base classifier predict the correct class label. This definition has the property that the error of the base classifiers can be decomposed into additive components of Bayes error, Bias and Variance.

4   Experimental Evidence

We have selected natural two-class benchmark problems from [1] and [9], and use random 50/50 or 20/80 training/testing splits. The artificial data is described in [2], and uses 300 training and 3000 test patterns. Experiments are performed with one hundred single hidden-layer MLPs connected in parallel and using Levenberg-Marquardt training algorithm with default parameters. While all the parameters of the MLPs are fixed at the same values, we systematically vary the numbers of hidden nodes and training epochs. The number of nodes varies from $2 - 16$ and number of epochs from $1 - 32$. Each node-epoch combination is repeated twenty times for Diabetes and ten times for all other datasets. In the

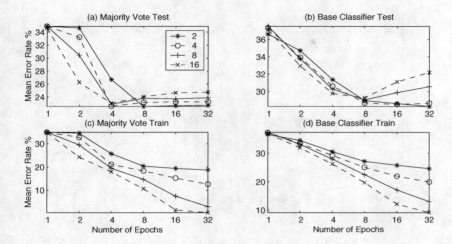

Fig. 1. Base classifier and Majority Vote training and testing error rates, Diabetes 50/50 for 1-32 epochs, 2-16 nodes

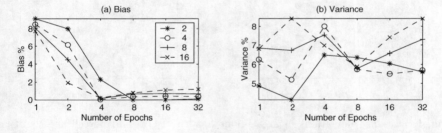

Fig. 2. Bias and Variance, Diabetes 50/50 for 1-32 epochs, 2-16 nodes

experiments described here, random perturbation is caused by different starting weights on each run.

For Diabetes 50/50, we have produced a set of curves shown in Figure 1 to Figure 4. The Diabetes dataset is well-known to over-fit and perform poorly with Boosting. Figure 1 shows the majority vote and base classifier error rates for training and testing. Comparison of Figure 1 (a) with Figure 1 (c) demonstrates that over-training of the majority vote classifier begins at 4 epochs for 8 and 16 nodes. Similarly Figure 1 (b) and (d) show that over-fitting of the base classifier begins at 8 epochs for 8 and 16 nodes.

Figure 2 shows Bias and Variance (Breiman definition Section 3.3) calculated on the test set. Since we need to know the Bayes classification to compute Bias and Variance, we make the optimistic assumption that the lowest majority vote test error rate (for this problem 2 nodes at 8 epochs) corresponds to Bayes classification. Hence, Bias in Figure 2 is 0 percent at 2 nodes, 8 epochs. The decomposition of Bias and Variance means that Figure 1 (b), the base classifier

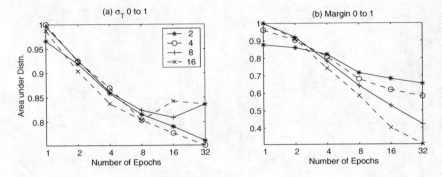

Fig. 3. Normalised area under distributions for $(0 \leq margin \leq 1)$ and $(0 \leq \sigma_T \leq 1)$ Diabetes 50/50 for 1-32 epochs, 2-16 nodes

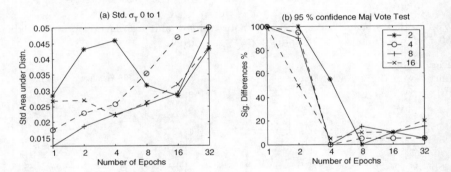

Fig. 4. Standard deviations of area under $(0 \leq \sigma_T \leq 1)$ and percentage significant (McNemar) differences of Majority vote compared to best error rate, Diabetes 50/50 for 1-32 epochs, 2-16 nodes

error rate, can be found by adding together the estimated Bayes rate (23 %), Figure 2 (a) and Figure 2 (b).

The margin distribution graphs (not shown) indicate that, as base classifier complexity is increased, margins of all patterns are increased representing an increase in confidence. To quantify this increase, we show normalised area under distributions for Margin and σ_T in Figure 3. The area under $(0 \leq \sigma_T \leq 1)$ shown in Figure 3 (a) indicates that σ_T for some patterns decreases, in contrast to area under $(0 \leq Margin \leq 1)$ shown in Figure 3 (b). Comparison of Figure 1 (a) (b) and Figure 3 suggests that the area under $(0 \leq \sigma_T \leq 1)$ may correlate with test error. To appreciate the significance of the results, Figure 4 shows the standard deviation of area under σ_T distribution and the number (percentage) of significant differences of majority vote (McNemar 5 percent) with respect to best majority vote error rate (2 nodes at 8 epochs).

Other natural datasets tested were cancer, vote, credita, heart and card for 50/50 and diabetes,cancer, heart, card, ion for 20/20 . The artificial datasets

Table 1. Correlation coefficient between area under distribution $(0 \leq \sigma_T \leq 1)$ and test errors as number of epochs is varied (Mean natural 50/50, Mean natural 20/80, Ringnorm, Threenorm, Twonorm)

Test error	nat50	nat20	Rnorm	3norm	2norm
Base classifier	0.94	0.90	0.92	0.86	0.89
Majority vote	0.81	0.77	0.81	0.85	0.21

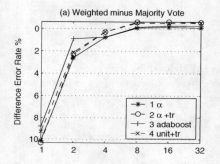 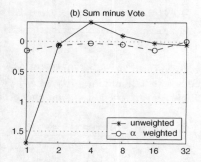

Fig. 5. Natural Datasets 50/50% Train/Test (a) Mean difference between weighted (defined Setion 3.2) and majority vote (b) Mean difference between (α)-weighted (equation (6) vote and (α)-weighted sum and between vote and sum

tested were Ringnorm, Threenorm, Twonorm. Table 1 shows the correlation coefficient between area under $(0 \leq \sigma_T \leq 1)$ and test errors (base classifier and majority vote) over 50/50 (mean), 20/80 (mean) and three artificial datasets. To compare across different datasets, for each dataset the correlation is with respect to training epochs with number of nodes fixed at the value that gave minimum majority vote test error. From Table 1 it can be seen that area under distribution $(0 \leq \sigma_T \leq 1)$ is well correlated with base classifier test error. It is conjectured that, as base classifier complexity is increased beyond optimal, the σ_T distribution is dominated by patterns in and and around the overlap region. An overall decrease in $\sum_X \sigma_{mj}^-$ leads to an increase in $\dfrac{\sigma_{mj}^-}{\sum_X \sigma_{mj}^-}$ and subsequent decrease in σ_T for many patterns. From another perspective, an increase in variance results in a decrease in correlation.

Four weighted voting schemes were compared, two of them trained with a constrained single layer perceptron (SLP) using the full training set

1. Weights fixed using α equation (6)
2. Orientation weights of SLP fixed using α equation (6) and trained bias
3. Weights fixed using Adaboost logarithmic scheme
4. Orientation weights of SLP fixed at unity and trained bias

Figures 5 6 and 7 (a) show the mean difference between the weighted schemes with respect to majority vote over 50/50, 20/80 and artificial datasets respectively. To compare across different datasets, the number of nodes is set to the

284   T. Windeatt, R. Ghaderi, G. Ardeshir

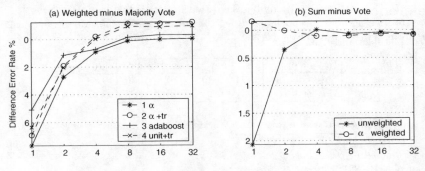

Fig. 6. Natural Datasets 20/80% Train/Test (a) Mean difference between weighted (defined Setion 3.2) and majority vote (b) Mean difference between (α)-weighted (equation (6) vote and (α)-weighted sum and between vote and sum

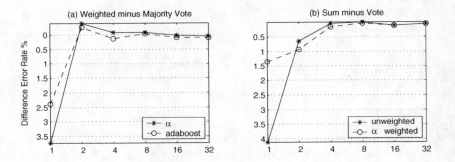

Fig. 7. Artificial Datasets 300/3000 train/test (a) Mean difference between weighted (defined Setion 3.2) and majority vote (b) Mean difference between (α)-weighted (equation (6) vote and (α)-weighted sum and between vote and sum

value that gave minimum majority vote test error. Weighted vote performance is seen to be less sensitive to number of training epochs than majority vote, with α-weighted vote performing best of the four schemes. For 50/50 datasets, training the bias of a SLP performs nearly as well as the weighted schemes, but it is less effective for 20/80 datasets as would be expected. Similarly Figures 5, 6 and 7 (b), show the mean difference between α-weighted vote and α-weighted sum and between vote and sum over 50/50, 20/80 and artificial datasets. As number of epochs is reduced sum outperforms vote but there is little difference for the weighted schemes.

5   Conclusion

In the MCS framework, estimating first order spectral coefficients from the training set provides a measure that correlates with base classifier test error as number of training epochs is varied. When the estimated coefficients are used to set weights for a weighted vote, generalisation is less sensitive to number of epochs.

References

1. C.L. Blake and C.J. Merz. UCI repository of machine learning databases, 1998. http://www.ics.uci.edu/~mlearn/MLRepository.html.
2. L. Breiman. Arcing classifiers. *The Annals of Statistics*, 26(3):801–849, 1998.
3. S. L. Hurst and D. M. Miller. *Spectral Techniques in Digital Logic*. Academic Press, 1985.
4. G. M. James. Variance and bias for general loss functions. *Machine Learning*, 2003. to appear.
5. E.B. Kong and T.G. Dietterich. Error-correcting output coding corrects bias and variance. In *Proceedings of the 12th International Conference on Machine Learning*, pages 313–321. Morgan Kaufmann, 1995.
6. L.I. Kuncheva, M. Skurichina, and R.P.W. Duin. An experimental study on diversity for bagging and boosting with linear classifiers. *Information Fusion*, 3(4):245–258, 2002.
7. C. J. Merz. Using correspondence analysis to combine classifiers. *Machine Learning*, 36(1-2):33–58, 1999.
8. S. Muroga. *Threshold Logic and its Applications*. Wiley, 1971.
9. L. Perchelt. Proben1: Set of neural network benchmark problems and benchmarking rules. Technical Report 21/94, Univ. of Karlsruhe, Germany, 1994.
10. R. E. Schapire, Y. Freund, and P. Bartlett. Boosting the margin: A new explanation for the effectiveness of voting methods. *Annals of Statistics*, 26(5):1651–1686, 1998.
11. T. Windeatt. Recursive partitioning technique for combining multiple classifiers. *Neural Processing Letters*, 13(3):221–236, 2001.
12. T. Windeatt and G. Ardeshir. Boosted tree ensembles for solving multiclass problems. In F. Roli and J. Kittler, editors, *3rd Int. Workshop Multiple Classifier Systems*, pages 42–51. Springer-Verlag, Lecture Notes in Computer Science, 2002.
13. T. Windeatt and R. Ghaderi. Binary labelling and decision level fusion. *Information Fusion*, 2(2):103–112, 2001.
14. T. Windeatt and R. Tebbs. Spectral technique for hidden layer neural network training. *Pattern Recognition Letters*, 18(8):723–731, 1997.

Ensemble Construction *via* Designed Output Distortion

Stefan W. Christensen

Department of Chemistry, University of Southampton, Southampton, SO17 1BJ, UK

Abstract. A new technique for generating regression ensembles is introduced in the present paper. The technique is based on earlier work on promoting model diversity through injection of noise into the outputs; it differs from the earlier methods in its rigorous requirement that the mean displacements applied to any data points output value be *exactly* zero.

It is illustrated how even the introduction of extremely large displacements may lead to prediction accuracy superior to that achieved by bagging.

It is demonstrated how ensembles of models with *very* high bias may have much better prediction accuracy than single models of the same bias-defying the conventional belief that ensembling high bias models is not purposeful.

Finally is outlined how the technique may be applied to classification.

1 Introduction

The inescapable dilemma in ensemble construction, stated in its most succinct form by Krogh and Vedelsby [1] and Sollich and Krogh [2], is this:

$$E_{ensemble} = <E_{individual\ models}> - <A> \tag{1}$$

where E is the prediction error with $<...>$ denoting averaging over all included models, and $<A>$ is the ensemble ambiguity, which provides a measure for the degree to which the individual models in the ensemble differ from one another:

$$A = (f_k(x) - f_{ens}(x))^2 \tag{2}$$

where $f_k(x)$ is the prediction of model k, and $f_{ens}(x)$ is the ensemble prediction.

There are therefore two fundamentally different approaches to building ensembles with low prediction error: (i) making sure that the individual models are very accurate on average, in which case $<E_{individual\ models}>$ is low, and (ii) making sure that the individual models are very unlike one another, in which case the ambiguity, $<A>$, is large.

These two approaches counteract each other; if all the models have very low prediction error, then they must be very similar to the actual system underlying the data, but in that case they must necessarily also all be very similar to one another. If, on the other hand, the models are all very unlike one another, then at most one may be close to the underlying system, the others subsequently having high prediction error.

Unfortunately, there is as yet no known mathematical tool for deciding in any given case, how the trade-off is to be settled. In the absence of such a tool much work has gone into developing methods that try to provide satisfying answers to the dilemma. A common theme is the "weak learner ensemble" in which the models are all

T. Windeatt and F. Roli (Eds.): MCS 2003, LNCS 2709, pp. 286–295, 2003.

supposed to be at least moderately accurate. A problem in this respect has been to ensure that the models differ adequately from one another, and a mesmerising array of methods have appeared, all trying to address this issue. Possibly the most famous of these is bagging [3], which "fools" the modelling algorithm into building different models *via* supplying different training data sets for all of them; these data sets are randomly resampled from the original data set with replacement, such that none of the models is fooled into building models on completely wrong data points. The expectation is therefore that the individual models will all be fairly good, although not as good as a model built on the full set of original data points, and they will all differ from one another, since their data sets are not exactly the same. Bagging has proven itself a valuable modelling approach, but other methods have been developed and are being developed. One of the newer pursuits in ensemble theory is the introduction of "noise" into the outputs, whereby the individual models again differ with respect to their training data sets, but not *via* individual resampling of the original data set; instead the original output values are altered by fairly small amounts in a random manner according to a distribution, typically normal, always with zero mean. E.g. in a regression context a particular data point with original output value y^* might be changed to y^*+2 when constructing one model, but changed to $y^*-1.7$ when constructing another. In this manner the modelling algorithm would use different training data sets when building the different models, but the mean data set, i.e. that obtained through averaging over all the individual data sets, would be the original one, provided the noise has zero mean. Output noise has been the focal point in studies by e.g. Breiman [4] and Raviv and Intrator [5], [6].

The method introduced in this paper differs from the earlier efforts in this field in two important ways:

1) The displacements in output values are not random in the conventional sense, since they are meticulously designed to ensure that their *actual* mean for each data point is always exactly zero. In the earlier works the only concern was to make sure that the mean would be zero in the limit of infinitely many models via simply drawing the noise from a probability distribution with zero mean. Since the changes to the output values are no longer random in this same sense, the word "noise" is also no longer appropriate, and instead the term "output distortion" is used.

2) In earlier works the noise was generally fairly small compared to the output values; the frequent use of a normal distribution, from which the noise contributions were drawn, made this the obvious choice. In the present paper is demonstrated how *very* large amounts of output distortion may have a clearly beneficial effect on ensemble performance. The individual displacements may exceed the range of original output values drastically and still promote very low ensemble prediction error.

2   Designed Output Distortion

The proposed Output Distortion Design algorithm, or ODD for short, is as follows.

0) Decide the number of models to include in the ensemble, M
1) Choose a maximum displacement value, D_{max}

2) For each data point in turn, choose the displacements for each of the M models from the set of possible values given by:

$$d = -D_{max} + 2D_{max} \, i/(M-1) \quad \text{where i is an integer number } \chi \, [0,M-1] \text{ and } M>1$$

such that each possible value of d, given by the corresponding index i, is used for exactly one of the models, and such that the particular value of i for any given model is chosen randomly. This randomness has the effect of ensuring that the displacements for a particular model are not all the same for all the data points.

3) Construct the M models based on their new, unique data sets where the output values are augmented by the chosen displacements: $y_{new} = y_{original} + d$.

4) Combine the models into an ensemble, with ensemble predictions being the average of the individual model predictions.

The ensemble may be weighted such that the individual models are given unequal weights. This would require that the weighting be incorporated into the design of the d values, ensuring that the mean would remain zero, thus adding complication. It is not purposeful to do so, however, since there is no *a priori* reason to assume larger or lesser significance of any of the models in the ensemble. Once the models have been built they perform as an ensemble, and the absence of any weighting in the design of the d values necessitates that there be no individual weighting of the models predictions either. In the experimental work reported on in the next section, all models were given equal weight.

In summary, the special features of ODD are (i) the mean of the output distortion applied to each data point, across all the models, is always *exactly* zero, (ii) a linear distribution of displacements is employed across the range $(-D_{max}, D_{max})$, from which the displacements are sampled, this differs from most previous work, where the favoured distribution has generally been the normal distribution. Finally, (iii) the width of the distribution is given by D_{max} and there is no set upper limit to this parameter; indeed as will be illustrated in the next section, this value can be set larger than the entire range of output values in the original data set. In the present study D_{max} is given as a percentage of this output range.

3   Test Results

The four problems investigated here are the three well known regression problems: Boston Housing, Ozone, and Miles per Gallon (all obtained from the UCI repository, [7]) and the lesser known Schwefel 3.2 problem (adapted from [8]). The features of the data sets and the corresponding modelling parameters are given in table 1.

The models were all of the same general type: feed-forward neural network, with one single hidden layer and tanh as activation function.

Two different principles were used for optimisation, depending on the problem: (i) Stochastic hill climber, and (ii) Downhill simplex [9], [10]. The stochastic hill climber is a global optimisation technique, which has proven useful in many situations; the downhill simplex is a lesser known local optimisation technique, which likewise has shown itself useful, provided it is used in a multiple restart context. In the present experiments, in which it was used, the number of restarts was always 15.

Table 1. Outline of modelling problems

Problem name	Boston Housing	Miles per Gallon	Ozone	Schwefel 3.2
Problem type	Real-life	Real-life	Real-life	Artificial noise free
Inputs	13	7	8	3
Data points	506	392	330	40
Hidden layer neurons	1	1	1	1
MLP weights*	4	5	5	5
Optimisation	Hill climber	Hill climber	Hill climber	Downhill simplex
Cross-validation	3-fold	4-fold	3-fold	4-fold
Ensemble sizes	2, 5, 10, 20, 40, 80	5, 20, 40, 80	5, 20, 40, 80	2, 5, 10, 20, 40, 80
No. of runs at these sizes**	120, 48, 24, 12, 6, 3	64, 16, 8, 4	48, 12, 6, 3	160, 64, 32, 16, 8, 4
ODD D_{max} levels	200%	100%, 500%	100%, 500%	5%, 25%, 50%, 100%, 200%

* All problems except Schwefel 3.2 were modelled via sparsely connected MLP's to further limit model complexity.
** In order to obtain stable statistical averages for the mse's, many runs were needed. The number of runs was chosen such that each ensemble size involved equally many models; i.e. smaller ensembles imply larger number of runs and vice versa.

Evaluation of model and ensemble quality was due to the mean squared error, mse, on training and test data respectively. Cross validation was used in all cases. The results reported here are not the mse values themselves; instead relative mse's are reported, which are mse value relative to the mse obtained by a single model trained on the full original (i.e. unaltered) data set. I.e. a relative ensemble mse of 0.9 corresponds to a 10% reduction in mse over that found for a single model.

As the maximum output value displacements were to attain very large values in this study, the data sets used for the different models in an ensemble might bear exceedingly little resemblance to one another. As a consequence, the differences between the models would tend to be very large even if the models were constrained to having quite low complexity; i.e. the model ambiguity would be large, leaving little reason to try to attain very accurate agreement between the underlying system and the individual models. For this reason the model complexity was chosen very low in all the studies: in none of the tests did the models contain more than one single neuron in the hidden layer.

This also would pose an interesting challenge to the oft-cited idea that ensembling works through lowering the variance of the individual models, whereas it cannot lower the models inherent bias significantly; the models used in this study all would have very large bias. Thus the test conditions were chosen to be presumably particularly unfavourable for ensembling.

For benchmarking, all problems were also modelled via bagging.

3.1   Boston Housing

For Boston Housing one single level of output distortion is included (fig. 1): 200%, meaning D_{max} was set to twice the original output range. This is a severe level of dis-

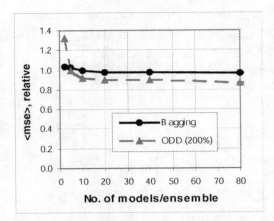

Fig. 1. Boston Housing test results; ODD curve is dashed, bagging solid

tortion, entirely unlike the noise levels used in earlier studies. As fig. 1 reveals, ODD is clearly superior to bagging for ensemble sizes of ≥10 models; similar to bagging at 5 models per ensemble, and outdone completely at 2 models per ensemble. It is notable that baggings performance improves only very slightly as ensemble size increases and bagging never yields a substantial improvement over a single model, whereas the effect of ensemble size on ODD is much more pronounced, and ODD manages to lower mse by more than 10% with respect to that of a single model.

3.2   Miles per Gallon

For the Miles per Gallon problem, fig. 2, two series of ODD results are shown, corresponding to 100% and 500% maximum distortion respectively. Both are very large distortions; in the 500% case, the larger displacements dwarf the original output values. For this latter case, the effect of ensemble size is very pronounced: larger ensembles lead to better predictions, but even at 80 models per ensemble does ODD fail to perform as well as a single model. At the lower level, 100%, ODD does however perform better than that and manages to yield a 20% reduction in mse at 20 models per ensemble; for this D_{max} there does not seem to be a clear effect of ensemble size however. Bagging is seen to be superior to the 500% ODD, but inferior to the 100% ODD, at all ensemble sizes. It also is seen to be performing roughly equally well at all ensemble sizes.

3.3   Ozone

Again, for the ozone problem, fig. 3, two ODD levels, 100% and 500% are illustrated, and here the 500% level is dramatically superior to both bagging and the 100% ODD at ensemble sizes of ≥20 models, but worse than both at 5 models. Bagging, again not showing much effect of ensemble size, is clearly inferior to the 100% ODD at all ensemble sizes. The latter ODD displays only a small reduction in relative mse as ensemble size is increased.

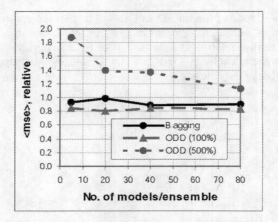

Fig. 2. Miles per Gallon test results; two series of ODD are shown: 100% distortion (dashed) and 500% (dotted), against bagging (solid)

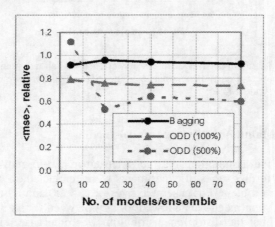

Fig. 3. Ozone test results; two ODD series shown: 100% distortion (dashed) and 500% (dotted), against bagging (solid)

3.4   Schwefel 3.2

The Schwefel problem is based on sampling the equation:

$$f(x) = \sum_{i=2}^{3} [(x_1 - x_i^{2})^2 + (1 - x_i)^2] \tag{3}$$

with input values randomly distributed over the interval [-5,5] for all inputs. In fig. 4, 5 different levels of maximum output distortion are shown against bagging: 5%, 25%, 50%, 100% and 200%. ODD displays a clear size effect at all distortion levels, though less drastic for the lower distortion levels than for the larger; bagging also shows some effect, albeit not as pronounced as ODD. The two largest distortion levels lead to poor mse's at all considered ensemble sizes, but the other three achieve considerable reductions in mse relative to a single model for ensembles with at least 10 models. At the two lowest levels, 5% and 25%, ODD is seen to be superior to bagging; at the two largest, bagging is clearly superior.

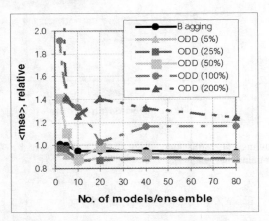

Fig. 4. Schwefel 3.2 test results; 5 different distortion levels shown against bagging. 2 ODD distortion levels appear clearly better than bagging: 5% and 25%. Two appear clearly worse than bagging: 100% and 200%

3.5   Effect of Maintaining Zero-Mean Distortion

In order to test the assumption that the strict adherence to zero-mean distortion is advantageous, a further series of experiments were conducted on the ODD (25%) for the Schwefel 3.2 problem. For ensemble sizes of 2, 5, 20 and 80 models, the magnitude of the distortion mean was allowed to vary between 0 and 30% of the original output range, whilst the distortion distribution was otherwise unaltered (i.e. still a linear distribution, symmetric around the mean). Each point in the plot, fig. 5, represents an average over 2560 models. Clearly, the effect of allowing the mean distortion to stray from 0 is a damaging one.

3.6   Ambiguity of Models

In order to assess the degree to which the models differ from one another, for each of the four problems (and all distortion levels), the ambiguity was calculated via querying the models at a large number of random locations across the input space. These ambiguities were averaged over the different ensemble sizes to yield a single <A> for each problem, modelling method and distortion level. The result appears in table 2, where the values are given relative to the corresponding bagging value. Evidently, higher levels of output distortion lead to higher ambiguities.

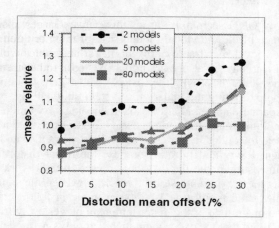

Fig. 5. Effect of allowing non-zero mean distortion for the Schwefel 3.2 ODD (25%). For each training data point a mean distortion was chosen (between 0 and 30% of the output range); the sign chosen randomly

Table 2. Ambiguity of models, relative to bagging

Problem	Boston		MpG			Ozone			Schwefel 3.2					
Method*	B	O	B	O		B	O		B	O				
Dist. /%	-	200	-	100	500	-	100	500	-	5	25	50	100	200
Rel. <A>	1.0	5.9	1.0	4.5	13.7	1.0	6.7	26.7	1.0	0.4	0.8	1.5	5.0	14.6

* B is bagging; O is Output distortion.

4 Discussion

The first result of the present study is a confirmation of an earlier observation [4] that introducing output noise, or as here distortion, as the means to create model diversity, may perform better than bagging. It is evident that for all 4 problems better ensemble prediction accuracy could be achieved *via* ODD than *via* bagging.

Equally evident is the fact that poorer ensemble prediction accuracy may also be achieved via ODD than via bagging; it would seem that there can indeed be introduced too massive distortion for the given ensemble size. Herein lies clearly an added complication of the ODD algorithm over bagging; the latter works "out of the box" but ODD requires the user to choose the distortion level, and this choice may crucially affect ensemble performance.

An important result is that whilst ensemble size as expected was found to be of little importance for the performance of bagging, when operating on models of such little complexity (and therefore necessarily with high bias) as was the case for the present problems, the number of models incorporated into an ODD ensemble may be of major significance, with larger ensembles generally found to have lower prediction errors, especially for high distortion levels. This stands square against the common belief that ensembling is not a fruitful use of models with large bias.

The reason why ODD seemingly defies this conventional wisdom is that it provides large variance of the individual models *even* if these are quite simple, cf. table 2; if the distortion level is extraordinarily high, as has been the case in the present work, the model variance is also extraordinarily high, and the ensembling will be successful. It is best thought of with the Krogh/Vedelsby eq. 1 in mind: the individual models are all approximating the underlying system quite poorly, but they have been trained on so disparate data sets that they have become very unlike one another, and this increased ambiguity more than compensates for the poor individual performance.

It is not possible to conduct a fair comparison between ODD and the methods proposed by Breiman, Raviv and Intrator, because the linear distortion distribution in ODD is not commensurate with the distribution used in their works (e.g. it would be unclear how to set the maximum distortion level), however, the significance of ensuring zero mean distortion is illustrated by the example in fig. 5; clearly performance deteriorates as the magnitude of the distortion mean moves away from zero, though it should be kept in mind that the experiment included only one modelling problem, and further testing will be needed to elucidate the issue thoroughly.

4.1   Application to Classification

ODD is designed to be utilised in a regression context. It cannot immediately be used in classification as the concept of larger or lesser noise/distortion on a particular output value is not directly meaningful; an output value in classification is either the right one, in which case the noise/distortion is zero, or it is a wrong one, in which case the noise/distortion level is not zero but may be difficult, or impossible, to ascertain.

It is, however, possible to use ODD in classification in those situations where the classification ensemble is actually a secondary model, which interprets the output of a primary regression ensemble. E.g. if in a two-class problem the output value for the first class is set to -1 and the output value for the second class is set to +1, it is possible to construct a regression ensemble to predict the correct output value, given the input values, and a secondary model would then classify according to the output value of the regression ensemble (most naturally with the class border lying where the regression ensemble attains an output value of 0).

ODD can be directly applied to the initial part of this two-step model, the regression ensemble. There has as yet been no experimental testing of this approach, and whether or not encouraging results, like those for the regression problems reported on here, can also be found in classification is not presently known, albeit there is no clear reason to suspect that similar results would not be found.

5   Conclusions

In the present paper a novel ensembling technique for regression has been introduced; it operates via encouraging model diversity through distorting the output values differently when training the different constituent models, whilst ensuring that the average distortion applied to each data points output value is *exactly* zero.

Experimental testing of the technique reveals that: (i) it may perform dramatically better than bagging if the level of distortion is not set too high, (ii) extremely high distortion levels may promote very low prediction errors though at these levels large ensembles may be required to bring the prediction errors down, and (iii) even ensembles of models with very high bias may be useful, as the model ambiguity can be driven to such large levels as to overcome the poor individual performance of the constituent models.

Though the technique is firmly rooted in regression, it may be used in classification, where the classifying model bases its predictions on the output of a regression model.

References

1. Krogh, A. and Vedelsby, J. Neural network ensembles, Cross Validation, and Active Learning. In: G. Tesauro, D. S. Touretzky and T. K. Leen, eds. Advances in Neural Information Processing Systems 7, p. 231-238, MIT Press, Cambridge, MA, 1995.
2. Sollich, P. and Krogh, A. Learning with ensembles: How over-fitting can be useful. In: D. S. Touretzky, M. C. Mozer and M. E. Hasselmo, eds. Advances in Neural Information Processing Systems 8, p. 190-196, MIT Press, 1996.
3. Breiman, L. Bagging predictors. Machine Learning 24 (2):123-140,1996.
4. Breiman, L. Randomizing outputs to increase prediction accuracy. Machine Learning, 40 (3): 229-242, September 2000.
5. Raviv, Y. and Intrator, N. Bootstrapping with noise: An effective regularization technique. Connection Science, Special issue on Combining Estimators, 8:356-372, 1996.
6. Raviv, Y. and Intrator, N. Variance reduction via noise and bias constraints. In: Sharkey, A. J. C. (Ed.) Combining Artificial Neural Nets. Springer Verlag. 1999.
7. Murphy, P. M. & Aha, D. W. UCI Repository of machine learning databases. University of California, Department of Information and Computer Science. Irvine, CA 1994.
8. Schwefel, H. Numerical Optimization of Computer Models. Wiley, New York, 1981.
9. Nelder, J. A and Mead, R. Computer Journal, 7, p. 308. 1965.
10. Press, W. H., Flannery, B. P., Teukolsky, S. A., Vetterling, W. T. Numerical Recipes in Pascal. Cambridge University Press, Cambridge, 1989.

Simulating Classifier Outputs
for Evaluating Parallel Combination Methods

H. Zouari[1], L. Heutte[1], Y. Lecourtier[1], and A. Alimi[2]

[1] Laboratoire Perception, Systèmes, Information (PSI), Université de Rouen, France
Laurent.Heutte@univ-rouen.fr
[2] Groupe de Recherche sur les Machines Intelligentes (REGIM), Université de Sfax, Tunisie

Abstract. The use of artificial outputs generated by a classifier simulator has recently emerged as a new trend to provide an underlying evaluation of classifier combination methods. In this paper, we propose a new method for the artificial generation of classifier outputs based on additional parameters which provide sufficient diversity to simulate, for a problem of any number of classes and any type of output, any classifier performance. This is achieved through a two-step algorithm which first builds a confusion matrix according to desired behaviour and secondly generates, from this confusion matrix, outputs of any specified type. We provide the detailed algorithms and constraints to respect for the construction of the matrix and the generation of outputs. We illustrate on a small example the usefulness of the classifier simulator.

1   Introduction

One of the problems that are to be faced in designing a multiple classifier system is the choice of a suitable combination method among the set of existing ones for a given problem of classification [1, 2, 4, 8, 10, 12]. Usual experiments consist in testing exhaustively the possible combination methods that can be used and retain the best one according to some criteria. However the obtained results depend closely on the specific application which has served the experimental proof. On the other hand, there do exist some interesting works in which the combination methods are evaluated on real data sets [3, 4, 7, 9, 10]. But, it is a fact that the use of real data can not yield sufficient variability in classifier performance to evaluate in a deeper manner the combination methods.

Very recently, the use of artificial data (outputs of classifier) generated by a classifier simulator has emerged to address the problem of the evaluation of classifier combination methods [5, 6, 7]. In [5] for example, the author proposes a comprehensive study of the random generation of dependent classifiers to evaluate class type combination methods especially the majority voting. She derives formulas according to how two classifiers can be generated with specified accuracies and dependencies between them. Based on these formulas, the author proposes an algorithm for generating multiple dependent classifiers. Lecce [6] has also studied the influence of correlation among classifiers to evaluate combination methods of class type. The performance of a combination method is measured on several sets of classifiers, each set differing from the others in terms of recognition rate and level of correlation. Each classifier is

T. Windeatt and F. Roli (Eds.): MCS 2003, LNCS 2709, pp. 296–305, 2003.

simulated at output level and a similarity index is used to estimate the stochastic cor-relation among the classifiers of each set. Parker [7] proposed a system based on two steps of simulation for evaluating ranking combination methods. The first step of simulation consists of a process for generating confusion matrices from fixed global recognition rates. The second simulation step consists of a function that uses the probabilities derived in this confusion matrix to generate outputs which can be cor-rect, incorrect or rejected. The proposed method has also been used to evaluate com-bination methods of class type. Although interesting, two drawbacks can be re-proached to the previous works: the first one is that the studies are rather limited since the classifier simulators used aimed at simply generating abstract-level type outputs and are thus not applicable to measurement type combination methods; the second one is that the behaviour of the developed classifier simulators is only controlled by one global parameter (recognition rate).

Building a classifier simulator that exhibits sufficient variability to move nearer a real behaviour needs to be able to control other parameters. To this end, we propose a classifier simulator which is able to generate automatically as many lists of outputs as desired according to a user-specified behaviour. Now, the classical way to evaluate the performance of a classifier is to measure on a test set of outputs provided by the classifier some global performance such as the overall recognition rate and/or rejec-tion rate. More precise analysis of the classifier performance can be measured through a confusion matrix which highlights the behaviour of the classifier on each class. Simulating a classifier is the inverse operation: starting from input parameters such as overall recognition or rejection rates which represent the desired behaviour we want to simulate, we build a confusion matrix to fix the behaviour of the classifier for each class then we generate, according to this confusion matrix, as many lists of outputs as desired. To fit the reality (i.e. simulate any classifier behaviour), we must thus man-age as input parameters the number of classes, the recognition and rejection rates and their standard deviations (to fix each class behaviour) but also and at the same time the maximum number of solutions in output lists and the corresponding recognition rates within the lists of solutions.

The paper is organized as follows. Section 2 describes the methodologies in devel-oping the classifier simulator and the different parameters (desired behaviour) used for this issue. Section 3 presents the construction of the confusion matrix according to these parameters and the main constraints to respect for this construction; Section 4 presents the algorithm for the generation of outputs. Simple experimental results are reported in section 5 to prove the efficiency of the simulator. Conclusion is drawn in section 6.

2   Proposed Method

The aim of the proposed classifier simulator is to generate randomly measurement type outputs i.e. a confidence value is associated to each solution proposed by the classifier (an example is shown in figure 1). Note that we have chosen to generate this type of outputs because it can also be easily transformed into ranked outputs (by "for-getting" confidence values) or into class-label outputs (by retaining only the first solution in the list).

The inputs of the classifier simulator are parameters which allow to define the classification problem and the global performance of the classifier. These parameters are:

The number N of classes: This parameter enables to simulate any pattern recognition problem. We could for example simulate a 2-class problem or a handwritten digit recognition problem (N=10) as well as a handwritten Corean character recognition problem (N=3755) [11].

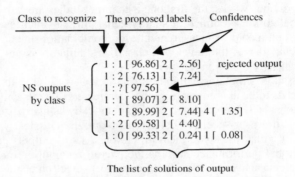

Class to recognize   The proposed labels   Confidences

```
        1 : 1 [ 96.86] 2 [  2.56]    rejected output
        1 : 2 [ 76.13] 1 [  7.24]
NS outputs   1 : ? [ 97.56]
by class     1 : 1 [ 89.07] 2 [  8.10]
        1 : 1 [ 89.99] 2 [  7.44] 4 [  1.35]
        1 : 2 [ 69.58] 1 [  4.40]
        1 : 0 [ 99.33] 2 [  0.24] 1 [  0.08]
```

The list of solutions of output

Fig. 1. Description of the simulator outputs

(a)
```
0 : 0 [72.50]
0 : 0 [35.92]
0 : 0 [44.08]
0 : 2 [51.85]
0 : ? [ 1.24]
```

(b)
```
0 : 1 [50.56] 0 [45.91]
0 : ? [43.03]
0 : 0 [87.71]
0 : 0 [98.51] 2 [ 0.12]
0 : 2 [99.63] 1 [ 0.13]
```

(c)
```
0 : 2 [52.85] 1 [34.43] 0 [ 1.23]
0 : 1 [92.75] 0 [ 7.12] 2 [ 0.10]
0 : 1 [89.51] 2 [ 7.90] 0 [ 1.12]
0 : ? [49.76]
0 : 1 [36.62] 0 [29.22] 2 [ 8.20]
```

Fig. 2. Different types of outputs generated by the classifier simulator for a 3 class problem (a) with K=1; (b) with K=2; (c) with K=3

The number NS of outputs: This parameter will be used to fix the number of outputs to be generated for each class by the simulator (same number for all the classes).

The number K of maximal labels: It corresponds to the length of the solution list that will be generated for each output. K may vary from 1 to N : for K=1, the simulator generates only one solution for each output (fig. 2a); for K between 2 and N-1, at most K solutions are generated except in the case of a rejected output for which there is only one label '?' (fig. 2b); for K=N, each output contains N labels excepted for the rejected outputs (fig. 2c).

Mean recognition rate TL^K: It stands for the overall recognition rate in the K first solutions that is the ratio of the number of outputs for which the true class appears among the K first solutions on the total number of outputs.

Mean rejection rate TR^K: It stands for the overall rejection rate that is the ratio of the number of rejected outputs on the total number of outputs. Of course, $TR^1 = ... = TR^K = ... TR^N$ since a rejected output contains only one label.

Note that we do not include as input parameter the confusion rate TC^K that would represent the ratio of the number of outputs for which the true class does not appear at all in the K first solutions on the total number of outputs. Indeed, TL^K, TR^K and TC^K are linked with the relation : $TL^K + TC^K + TR^K = 100\%$.

TL^K and TR^K enable to control the global performance of the simulated classifier. The classifier behaviour will be completely determined through the confusion matrix CM^K. Note that formally speaking, CM^K can be called "confusion matrix" only for K=1. For K varying from 2 to N, we would rather have to call it "matrix of presence". The matrix CM^K consists of N rows and N+1 columns, where N denotes the number of classes and the column (N+1) the rejection column. The diagonal elements TL_i^k are the top K recognition rate per class (i.e. the ratio of the number of outputs labelled i for which the label i appears in the K first solutions on the number of outputs labelled i). Their mean gives the mean recognition rate TL^K. The off-diagonal elements $TC_{i,j}^k$ (confusion rates) represent the ratio of the number of outputs labelled i for which a solution labelled j (j≠i) appears in the K first solutions. Note that for K=1, $TC_{i,j}^k$ is a true confusion rate between class i and class j. Otherwise, it is rather a co-occurrence rate. The other elements TR_i^k (in the column N+1) represent the ratio of rejected outputs for each class i. The mean of these rates is TR^K.

Standard deviations α^k and β^k: These two parameters will just allow to fill the matrix CM^K. They enable to introduce sufficient variability in the classifier behaviour while controlling this variability. α^K (respectively β^K) will be used to fix the range of variation of TL_i^k (resp. TR_i^k), i.e. each TL_i^k (resp. TR_i^k) will be randomly drawn in the range $[TL^K - \alpha^K; TL^K + \alpha^K]$ (resp. $[TR^K - \beta^K; TR^K + \beta^K]$).

Now, the role of the simulator is to generate, for each class, NS outputs with a list of K solutions. The generation of outputs respects a specified performance in the K first solutions and is realized in two steps:

- Building of the matrix CM^K according to TL^K, α^K, TR^K, β^K.
- Generation of the list of K solutions at most for each output using the matrix CM^K and association of a confidence value to each solution.

Now that the involved parameters are defined, we describe in the following section the two-step algorithm which first builds the matrix CM^K according to TL^K, α^K, TR^K, β^K and secondly generates, for each class, NS outputs with a list of K solutions using the matrix CM^K and association of a confidence value to each solution. The generation of outputs respects a top K behaviour (i.e. specified performance in the K first solutions).

3   Building of the Matrix CM^K

In order to illustrate the different constraints that must be respected, consider first the outputs of class 0 generated previously in figure 2. The list of outputs generated in figure 2a contains three outputs recognized as 0, one confused as 2 and one rejected. This corresponds to a recognition rate of 60%, a confusion rate of 20% and a rejection rate of 20%. Consequently, to generate type I outputs (K=1), we may use the confusion matrix CM^1 in which the sum of rates for each class i (row) must be equal to 100%. Then, the construction of CM^1 consists in respecting the following constraint :

$$TL_i^1 + \sum_{j=1, i \neq j}^{N} TC_{i,j}^1 + TR_i^1 = 100\% . \tag{1}$$

In figure 2c where K=N, the total number of solutions generated for each class is equal to N*NS. This corresponds in the matrix CM^N to the sum of rates that is equal to N*100%. As the rejected outputs are composed of only one solution, we must multiply the rejection rate by N. Then, to generate this type of outputs, we must construct the matrix CM^N respecting the following constraint for each class i :

$$TL_i^N + \sum_{j=1, i \neq j}^{N} TC_{i,j}^N + N*TR_i^N = N * 100\% . \tag{2}$$

In figure 2b, the list of solutions can vary from 1 to K for each output. From the example, we can establish that 60% of outputs include the true class "0" in the top two solutions. Likewise 40% of outputs include the label "1", 40% of outputs include the class label "2" in the top two solutions and 20% of outputs are rejected. In this case, the sum of rates for each class can be lower or at most equal to K*100%. For this reason, we must respect the constraint (3) to construct the matrix CM^K:

$$TL_i^K + \sum_{j=1, i \neq j}^{N} TC_{i,j}^K + K*TR_i^K \leq K* 100\% . \tag{3}$$

The filling of the matrix CM^K begins with the generation of the rejection rates TR_i^K for each row i of the matrix. Each rate TR_i^K is drawn from normal distribution with mean TR^K and standard deviation β^K. Let F be the interval in which all rejection rates must be drawn. Initially, the lower bound of F is equal to $TR^K - \beta^K$ and the upper bound to $TR^K + \beta^K$. As draws are done, the bounds of F get closer and draws become more restrictive. If the matrix were filled row by row starting from 1 up to N, the last rows would always be drawn in the closest bounds. To cope with this bias, the row number is also drawn randomly. Next, the recognition rates TL_i^K for each class i (the diagonal elements of CM^K) are computed in the same manner but according to the rejection rates already fixed. Each recognition rate TL_i^K must thus respect two constraints: $TL_i^K \in \left[TL^K - \alpha^K ; TL^K + \alpha^K \right]$ and $TL_i^K \leq 100 - TR_i^K$. Finally, the confusion rates $TC_{i,j}^K$ for each row i and each column j are generated. As for the recognition rates TL_i^K , the confusion rate $TC_{i,j}^K$ must be also lower or equal to $100 - TR_i^K$.

4   Algorithm of Output Generation

Given the matrix CM^K as constructed above and the number NS of outputs, the next issue is to generate the list of outputs for each class (Table 1). For that, the matrix of probabilities CM^K is first transformed into a matrix of numbers MN^K. This is simply done by multiplying the probabilities in CM^K for each class i by the number of solutions NS*K and then divide them by the sum of rates of this class. Given the matrix MN^K, we must next assign a list of K class labels to each output. This could be done completely randomly. But, if the class labels are chosen arbitrarily, the same class label can be drawn several times in the same list of solutions (this would happen for the last outputs to generate). This case is of course impossible to produce by a real classifier. For this reason, we draw the class labels for each output in the most numerous classes.

Now, an output can be composed of one reject label or a list of K labels. To affect one of these two types of solutions (reject or not) for each output, an integer value X is randomly drawn in the range $[1..C_i+R_i]$ where C_i is the number of remaining class labels and R_i the number of remaining reject labels for class i (at the beginning of the output generation, C_i is initialized to $\sum_{j=1}^{N} MN^K[i][j]$ and R_i to $MN^K[i][N+1]$. $X \in$ $[1..C_i]$ indicates that a list of K labels must be generated for this output; otherwise (when $X \in [C_i..C_i+R_i]$) the output must be rejected.

Actually, when the input value of K is between 2 and N-1, a list of at most K solutions is generated for each output. In other words, the length of the list of solutions is determined for each output. Let $nlab_i^l$ be the number of class labels to be drawn randomly in the range $[1..K]$ for the lth output of class i. As outputs are treated, it becomes more and more difficult to respect both the constraints imposed by the matrix MN^K (the choice of labels) and the random draw of $nlab_i^l$, particularly for the latest outputs. This can however be avoided by taking into account the number of solutions it remains to generate. This is done using the following principles: let S_i^l be the lth output labelled i among the NS outputs of the class i (i=1..N) and O_i^l be the number of outputs already treated; the minimum number of possible labels that can be generated for S_i^l is given by:

$min\_lab = \max(1, C_i-(NS-R_i-O_i^l)*K)$ and $max\_lab = \min(K, C_i-(NS-R_i-O_i^l))$.

Therefore, $nlab_i^l$ will be drawn randomly in the range $[min\_lab..max\_lab]$

The algorithm of the procedure for generating outputs from CM^K is thus the following (where $S_{i,j}^l$ is the jth solution within the list of solutions associated to output S_i^l ($j = 1..nlab_i^l$)):

Table 1. Generation of output lists from CMK

```
Inputs:     MN^K: matrix of numbers of labels to generate;
            NS: number of outputs by class
```

Outputs: S_i^l for i=1 to N and l=1 to NS

```
Begin
For each class i from 1 to N Do
```

Initialize C_i to $\displaystyle\sum_{j=1}^{N} MN^K[i][j]$

Initialize R_i to $MN^K[i][N+1]$

```
    While all outputs are not treated Do
        Choose a random number l between 1 and NS
        Draw X randomly in [1, C_i+R_i]
```
        If X ∈ $\left]C_i, C_i + R_i\right]$ Then
```
            Assign the reject solution
            Decrement R_i
        Else
```
            Draw $nlab_i^l$ in [min_lab, max_lab]
            Choose $nlab_i^l$ labels from the most numerous classes
            Place these labels randomly in $S_{i,j}^l$
            $C_i \leftarrow C_i - nlab_i^l$
```
End
```

Finally, we associate a random confidence to each generated label within the list of solutions. All the confidences are ordered in a decreasing way. The confidence of the first solution of the outputs must be higher than $100/nlab_i^l$. This constraint is available only for outputs which are composed of two solutions at least.

5   Experimental Results

In this section, we report experiments aimed at demonstrating the effectiveness of the proposed simulator in determining the relationship between the performance of a mean rule combination method and diversity in classifier behaviour. We focus on the evaluation of this particular method for different ensembles of 3 classifiers in a 10-class classification problem without rejection. For this experiment, we simulate two classifiers with the same recognition rate p varying from 50% to 90% to which is added a third one whose recognition rate performance vary from 50% to 95% by 5% steps. Each classifier provides 10000 outputs according to the fixed recognition rate (the confidences generated are not normalized). The results are averaged over 100 runs for each of the different sets of classifiers. The recognition rate performance of mean rule versus the best individual classifier are depicted in figure 3. The results show that the mean rule can achieve a significant improvement over the best classifier for the most balanced sets. The improvement decreases as the difference between the recognition rates of the worst and the best individual classifier increases. This means that the integration of the additional classifier by mean rule is interesting only if its performance is near to those of the other classifiers in the same ensemble. Our experiments point out that the performance of the mean rule depends on the degree of classifier imbalance. This idea is also confirmed in [Roli02]. Figure 4 shows the performance of mean rule for the different values of *p*. These results suggest that the difference in the performance of the combined classifiers strongly influences the mean behaviour whatever the values of p (strong or weak sets).

From the experiments, we highlight the interest of our simulator in helping to clarify the behaviour of combination methods and the conditions under which they can be used.

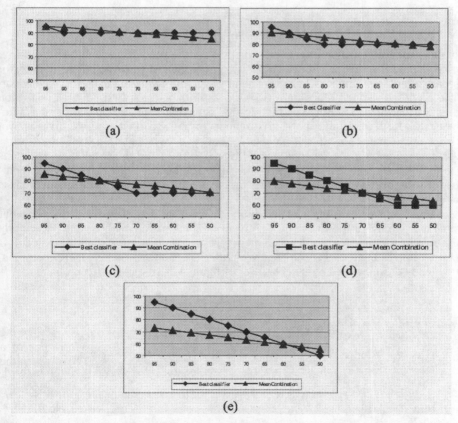

Fig. 3. The performance of mean rule vs the best individual classifier for different values of p (where the X-axis stands for the recognition rate of the 3rd classifier)
(a) *p*= 90% (b) *p* = 80% (c) *p* = 70% (d) *p* = 60% (e) *p* = 50%

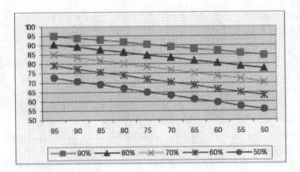

Fig. 4. Combination results of different sets of three classifiers for different values of p (where the X-axis stands for the recognition rate of the 3rd classifier)

6   Conclusion

In this paper, we have proposed a new method for the artificial generation of classifier outputs based on several parameters which provide sufficient diversity to simulate, for a problem of any number of classes and any type of output, any classifier behaviour. The proposed method relies on a two-step algorithm which first builds a confusion matrix according to a user-specified desired behaviour and secondly generates automatically, from this confusion matrix, outputs of any specified type. We have shown that simulating any classifier behaviour (i.e. any pattern recognition problem) requires the management of the recognition and rejection rates and their standard deviations (to fix the behaviour for each class) but also and at the same time the maximum number of solutions in output lists and the corresponding recognition rates within the lists of solutions.

Thanks to its flexibility and its ability to simulate any classifier behaviour, our simulator will be useful to evaluate all types of combination methods and particularly the combination methods of measurement type which are not sufficiently studied. It is thus an interesting tool that can help to clarify the conditions under which a combination method can be used or is the best for different pattern recognition problems.

References

1. Duin, R.P.W., Tax, D.M.J.: Experiments With Classifier Combining Rules. In Proc. First Int. Workshop On Multiple Classifier System, MCS 2000, Vol. 1857, Springer, Berlin, (2000) 16-29
2. Ho, T.K., Hull, J.J., Srihari, S.N.: Decision Combination In Multiple Classifier Systems. IEEE Transactions On Pattern Analysis And Machine Intelligence, Vol.16, No. 1, (1994) 66-75
3. Impedovo, S., Salzo, A.: Evaluation Of Combination Methods. Proc. ICDAR, Bangalore, India, (1999) 394-397
4. Kittler, J., Hatef, M., Duin, R.P.W., Matas, J.: On Combining Classifiers. IEEE Transactions On Pattern Analysis And Machine Intelligence, Vol. 20, No. 3 (1998)

5. Kuncheva, L.I., Kountchev, R.K.: Generating Classifier Outputs Of Fixed Accuracy And Diversity. Pattern Recognition Letters, Vol. 23. (2002) 593-600
6. Lecce, V.D., Dimauro, G., Guerrierro, A., Impedovo, S., Pirlo, G., Salzo, A.: Classifier Combination: The Role Of A-Priori Knowledge. In Proc. Of The 7th International Workshop On Frontiers In Handwriting Recognition, Amsterdam, The Netherlands (2000) 143-152
7. Parker, J.R.: Rank And Response Combination From Confusion Matrix Data. Information Fusion, Vol. 2. (2001) 113-120
8. Roli, F., Fumera, G., Kittler, J.: Fixed And Trained Combiners For Fusion Of Imbalanced Pattern Classifiers. The Fifth International Conference On Information Fusion, Annapolis (Washington) USA (2002)
9. Tax, D.M.J., Breukelen, M.V., Duin, R.P.W., Kittler, J.: Combining Multiple Classifiers By Averaging Or By Multiplying ?. Pattern Recognition, Vol. 33. (2000) 1475-1485
10. Van Erp, M., Vuurpijl, L., Schomaker, L.: An Overview And Comparison Of Voting Methods For Pattern Recognition. 8th International Workshop On Frontiers In Handwriting Recognition, Niagara-on-the-Lake, Ontario, (2002) 195-200
11. Xiao, B.H., Wang, C.H., Dai, R.W.: Adaptive Combination Of Classifiers And Its Application To Handwritten Chinese Character Recognition. In Proc. ICPR, Barcelona, Spain, Vol. 2. (2000) 2327-2330
12. Xu, L., Krzyzak, A., Suen, C.Y.: Methods Of Combining Multiple Classifiers And Their Applications To Handwriting Recognition. IEEE Transaction On Systems, Man, and Cybernetics, Vol. 22. No 3 (1992) 418-435

A New Ensemble Diversity Measure Applied to Thinning Ensembles

Robert E. Banfield[1], Lawrence O. Hall[1], Kevin W. Bowyer[2], and W. Philip Kegelmeyer[3]

[1] Department of Computer Science and Engineering, University of South Florida
4202 E. Fowler Ave, Tampa, Florida 33620, USA
{rbanfiel,hall}@csee.usf.edu
[2] Department of Computer Science and Engineering, University of Notre Dame
384 Fitzpatrich Hall, Notre Dame, IN 46556, USA
kwb@cse.nd.edu
[3] Sandia National Labs, Biosystems Research Department, PO Box 969, MS 9951
Livermore, CA 94551-0969, USA
wpk@ca.sandia.gov

Abstract. We introduce a new way of describing the diversity of an ensemble of classifiers, the Percentage Correct Diversity Measure, and compare it against existing methods. We then introduce two new methods for removing classifiers from an ensemble based on diversity calculations. Empirical results for twelve datasets from the UC Irvine repository show that diversity is generally modeled by our measure and ensembles can be made smaller without loss in accuracy.

1   Introduction

Multiple classifier systems have become the subject of attention because they can provide significant boosts in accuracy for many datasets [1-6]. They can be created in a variety of ways. Classifiers of the same type that perform differently may be created by modifying the training set through randomly re-sampling with replacement, as in bagging [2], or successively choosing training sets based on errors made by the previous set of classifiers, as in Ivoting [3]. They can also be created by approaches that exploit randomization within the learner; for example, different initial random weights in neural networks or a random choice of the test at a node in a decision tree from among the top **n** choices [5]. The boost in performance from using an ensemble is at least partially due to diversity [4,7] – examples that are incorrectly classified by some classifiers are correctly classified by others, in such a way that the voted accuracy is greater than that of any single classifier. This paper considers the concept of diversity, develops a new approach to describing it, and then uses this to create a better ensemble by removing the less useful classifiers.

2   Diversity

Diversity is a property of an ensemble of classifiers with respect to a set of data. Diversity is greater when, all other factors being equal, the classifiers that make incor-

T. Windeatt and F. Roli (Eds.): MCS 2003, LNCS 2709, pp. 306–316, 2003.

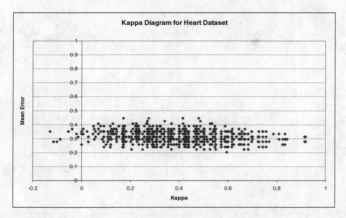

Fig. 1. A Kappa Diagram showing a large spread of Kappa and mean error scores

rect decisions for a given example spread their decisions more evenly over the possible incorrect decisions. The more uniformly distributed the errors are, the greater the diversity, and vice versa.

The Kappa statistic from Dietterich [4], which measures the degree of similarity between two classifiers, serves as an illustrative starting point for examining diversity. Referring to Figure 1, the Kappa value can be plotted on the x-axis for each pair of classifiers, against the mean error for the pair on the y-axis. A broad scatter of points along the x-axis indicates that the pairs of classifiers have significantly different levels of agreement. Ideally, the best classifiers would be both individually accurate and comparatively diverse. The average of all paired Kappa values can be used as a measure of ensemble diversity. One of the drawbacks of using Kappa diagrams is the computational complexity associated with calculating all of the pair-wise combinations which would be required to generate a single number for the overall diversity.

Kuncheva and Whitaker [7] compare ten statistics that can measure diversity among binary classifier outputs. They looked at four statistics that are averaged pair-wise results, and six that are non-pair-wise results. Since they found the importance of diversity to be unclear, they recommend the pair-wise Q statistic [11] based on the criteria that it is understandable and relatively simple to implement. As every set of paired classifiers produces a Q value, the average, Q_{av}, is used for the diversity value of the ensemble as shown in Figure 2. In this algorithm, classifications are compared as a function of correctness or incorrectness with regard to a validation or test set. This differs from Dietterich's Kappa algorithm where classifications are compared based solely on the class they represent.

Dietterich's Kappa statistic is a variant of the Inter-rater Agreement function (also referred to as Kappa). In this algorithm, the rate of coinciding classifications is generated while taking into account the probability that the agreement is based solely upon chance. Like the Q statistic, it does not take into account the actual classification but rather whether the classification was correct or incorrect. However the Inter-rater Agreement function is not pair-wise and hence is polynomially faster than either aforementioned method. The Inter-rater Agreement function is defined in Figure 3.

The approach closest to our new diversity metric is the "measure of difficulty" [8]. This measure looks at the proportion of classifiers that correctly classify an example.

308   Robert E. Banfield et al.

$$Q_{av} = \frac{2}{L(L-1)} \sum_{i=1}^{L-1} \sum_{k=i+1}^{L} \frac{N^{11}N^{00} - N^{01}N^{10}}{N^{11}N^{00} + N^{01}N^{10}}$$

L = Number of classifiers
N^{00} = Classifier$_i$ is incorrect, Classifier$_k$ is incorrect
N^{01} = Classifier$_i$ is incorrect, Classifier$_k$ is correct
N^{10} = Classifier$_i$ is correct, Classifier$_k$ is incorrect
N^{11} = Classifier$_i$ is correct, Classifier$_k$ is correct

Fig. 2. The averaged Q statistic

$$\kappa = 1 - \frac{\frac{1}{L}\sum_{j=1}^{N} l(z_j)(L - l(z_j))}{N(L-1)p(1-p)}$$

N = Number of examples
L = Number of classifiers
p = Average classifier accuracy
$l(z_j)$ = Correct classifications for classifier j

Fig. 3. The Inter-rater Agreement function

One can consider plotting a histogram of the proportions. The variance of this histogram is considered to be a measure of diversity. Our approach measures the proportion of classifiers getting each example right. However, rather than building a histogram of proportions, we examine the percent correct per example.

We propose the percentage correct diversity measure (PCDM) algorithm shown in Figure 4. It works by finding the test set examples for which between 10% and 90% of the individual classifiers in the ensemble are correct. In this way, examples for which there is general consensus are not considered to be useful in the determination of ensemble diversity. Rather, if an example's classification is ambiguous, as indicated by having only the aforementioned percentages of classifiers vote correctly, then the classifiers, for at least that example, are said to be diverse. The bounds of ten and ninety percent were chosen empirically because they cause the algorithm to yield a somewhat uniform distribution of PCDM values over a wide array of ensemble creation techniques. Tighter bounds would place greater strictness on the examples deemed difficult. The use of tighter bounds might be appropriate if comparing two extremely diverse ensembles.

```
Tally = 0
For each example
    For each classifier
        Classify example
    If 10 ≤ % Classifiers Correct ≤ 90
        Tally = Tally + 1
                      Tally
    Diversity = ─────────────────
                Number of Examples
```

Fig. 4. The Percentage Correct Diversity Measure algorithm

For visualization purposes, let $f(x_i)$ be the percent of classifiers voting correctly on example $x_i \in \{x_1, ..., x_N\}$ where N is the number of examples. Sorting the list of N, $f(x)$ values and plotting them on a graph generates a monotonically increasing function showing the "spread" of diversity for different examples. A single classifier, or a multiple classifier system where every classifier returns identical classifications, generates the graph shown in 5A which appears similar to a digital signal (0 or 1) with zero classifiers in between the 10% and 90% bounds. Multiple classifiers outputting diverse classifications on the other hand cause different percentages of correct classifications to appear relative to the number of classifiers. Diversity, in a sense, transforms the line from a discrete to a continuous function as in Figure 5B. Greater numbers of examples appearing between .1 and .9 equate to greater PCDM values.

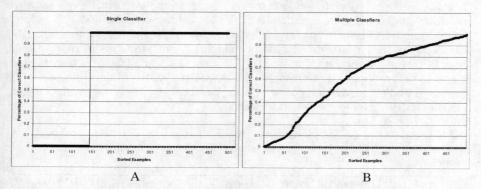

A   B

Fig. 5. After sorting the x-axis based on $f(x)$ to create a non-decreasing graph, it is easy to visualize the number of examples that are diverse. (A) shows a single classifier and (B) shows multiple classifiers having diversity

3   Diversity Experiments

Breiman introduced the concept of creating ensembles of trees that he called random forests [5]. He discussed several methods of creating trees for the forests, one of which was to use bagging and randomly choose an attribute for a test at each node in the decision tree. The best split possible for that attribute would then be chosen. The resultant tree is called a random tree. An ensemble of them, 100 in his experiments, is a random forest. He found that this approach was comparable in accuracy to AdaBoost [6].

We modified C4.5 release 8 to produce random trees by randomly choosing a single attribute to test on at every node. We chose to build 1000 trees in our random forest so that the resultant ensemble is almost certainly larger than necessary and we can better evaluate using diversity to remove trees. Our experiments use a ten-fold cross validation. We build 10,000 trees (1000 per fold) for each of twelve experimental datasets from the UC Irvine Repository [12]. The accuracy of unpruned and pruned ensembles (using the default certainty factor of 25 for pruning) is calculated for each dataset. Table 1 shows the experimental results of the diversity algorithms in measuring the diversity of ensembles as well as the boost in accuracy when comparing average single classifier accuracy and voted accuracy. Decreasing values of Q and Kappa correspond to higher diversity whereas PCDM increases as diversity increases.

There are several instances where the accuracy of the ensemble of pruned trees is greater than that of the unpruned trees. Dietterich, though he generated the trees in a

different fashion, found this as well [4]. However, in no case are the diversity scores
for the pruned trees greater than the unpruned trees. Likewise, in no case is the increase in accuracy of the forest of pruned trees greater than that of the unpruned trees.
Figure 6, which compares the PCDM against other diversity measures, shows that it
picks up the trend of increasing accuracy corresponding to increasing diversity values.
In fact, it outperforms the Q metric, which barely exhibits such a trend. The Q metric
is also capable of generating divide by zero errors in the event that any one of the
classifiers in the ensemble is either 100% or 0% accurate on the test set. In order to
compensate for Q generating a divide by zero error, we invalidate the fold since this
can occur no matter how diverse the two classifiers are. In terms of running time,
both PCDM and Kappa are significantly faster than Q, while PCDM is only marginally faster than Kappa. For example on a 2.53 GHz Intel Pentium 4 it takes 0.008
seconds with PCDM, 0.018 seconds with Kappa, and 111.133 seconds with Q to generate diversity values from the Letter dataset.

Table 1. Diversity vs. accuracy results from datasets appearing in the UCI Data Repository. Q
was unable to be calculated for any fold in the Glass dataset due to divide by zero errors in
every fold

Dataset	Pruning?	Single Accuracy	Forest Accuracy	Accuracy Increase	κ	PCDM	Q
Letter	Unpruned	78.36%	95.61%	17.25%	0.37	0.49	0.74
Letter	Pruned	79.37%	94.97%	15.60%	0.39	0.46	0.76
Led-24	Unpruned	61.85%	74.96%	13.11%	0.41	0.68	0.71
Waveform	Unpruned	73.83%	84.88%	11.05%	0.23	0.72	0.49
Glass	Unpruned	85.95%	95.71%	9.76%	0.34	0.35	--
Waveform	Pruned	75.36%	84.56%	9.20%	0.28	0.64	0.58
Australian	Unpruned	77.47%	86.67%	9.19%	0.32	0.58	0.65
Cleveland	Unpruned	74.90%	84.00%	9.10%	0.29	0.63	0.55
Glass	Pruned	87.20%	96.19%	8.99%	0.37	0.32	--
German	Unpruned	66.82%	75.60%	8.78%	0.25	0.82	0.49
Satimage	Unpruned	83.65%	91.79%	8.14%	0.37	0.39	0.78
Heart	Unpruned	74.70%	81.85%	7.15%	0.31	0.60	0.56
Cleveland	Pruned	77.86%	85.00%	7.14%	0.39	0.46	0.70
Pendigits	Unpruned	92.87%	99.08%	6.21%	0.23	0.22	0.74
Pendigits	Pruned	93.20%	98.92%	5.72%	0.25	0.21	0.76
Satimage	Pruned	85.41%	91.12%	5.71%	0.46	0.30	0.86
Segmentation	Unpruned	93.38%	97.97%	4.58%	0.33	0.17	0.83
Heart	Pruned	77.10%	81.11%	4.01%	0.40	0.47	0.67
Segmentation	Pruned	93.88%	97.84%	3.96%	0.36	0.15	0.86
Iris	Unpruned	92.52%	95.33%	2.82%	0.42	0.20	0.38
Australian	Pruned	83.26%	85.22%	1.96%	0.63	0.20	0.89
Led-24	Pruned	73.09%	74.96%	1.87%	0.74	0.24	0.96
German	Pruned	71.02%	72.30%	1.28%	0.58	0.39	0.85
Iris	Pruned	92.26%	92.67%	0.41%	0.47	0.19	0.46

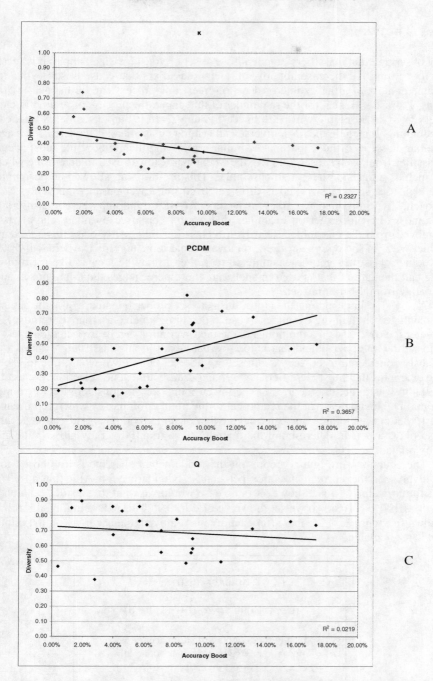

Fig. 6. Graphs showing the boost in accuracy vs. the diversity score for each of the three methods (A-C)

4   Thinning

By observing that classifiers obtain a diverse set of votes for an example, it is feasible to try to improve the ensemble by removing classifiers that cause misclassifications. In the context of an ensemble of decision trees, this process can be likened to "thinning a forest." Hence, for the remainder of this paper, the process of removing classifiers from an ensemble will be dubbed "thinning." In [9] an ensemble is thinned by attempting to include the most diverse and accurate classifiers. They create subsets of similar classifiers (those that make similar errors) and then choose the most accurate classifier from each subset. In [10], the McNemar test was used to determine whether to include a decision tree in an ensemble. This pre-thinning allowed an ensemble to be kept to a smaller size and is different from our "over-produce and choose" approach. We introduce Accuracy in Diversity (AID) thinning, where classifiers that are most often incorrect on examples that are misclassified by many classifiers are removed from the ensemble. That is, if a classifier incorrectly classifies an example which 99% of the others get right, removal would have no effect, whereas if 50% of the other classifiers get the example correct, then it may be a candidate for removal. We call the dataset that is used in analyzing these percentages the thinning set, and is separate from the training set.

A key step in designing the algorithm is to set proper boundaries for the accuracy percentages on thinning examples to use in deciding which classifiers to remove. The greater the diversity on a thinning set, the more variation can be expected on a test set, and setting an upper bound that is too low can result in misclassifying examples previously considered to be "easy." In setting a lower bound, we would like to exclude the examples that most classifiers get wrong because almost no selection of classifiers will allow us to get these correct. The lower bound for the consideration of examples should be no smaller than the reciprocal of the number of classes which represents, at best, random guessing. One can imagine that mean individual classification accuracy also plays a part in determining the bounds, since it and diversity are so fundamentally related.

The equations in Figure 7 represent the fundamental characteristics chosen to effectively set the correct classifier percentage boundaries for AID thinning. The maximum value of d is 1, however in no case would we want to consider examples as high as 100% correct, so we set the value of α to 0.9. The AID thinning algorithm is shown in Figure 8. Note that after each tree is removed, the accuracy on the thinning set is recalculated.

$$LowerBound = \mu \cdot d + \frac{1-d}{N}$$

$$UpperBound = \alpha \cdot d + \mu \cdot (1-d)$$

μ = Mean individual classification accuracy
α = Approximate maximum upper bound allowed
d = Percentage correct diversity measure
N = Number of classes

Fig. 7. Boundary equations for AID thinning

```
While number removed ≤ Maximum number to remove
   Recompute boundary points.
   Remove the classifier that has the lowest individual accuracy rate for the set of
   examples between the boundary points.
```

Fig. 8. The AID thinning algorithm

Since greater diversity typically leads to larger boosts in the accuracy of the forest, we also have created a thinning algorithm that works off of the aforementioned Inter-rater Agreement function called Kappa thinning. In Figure 9, we compare all possible ensembles of n-1 classifiers, and eliminate the classifier whose removal causes the diversity to increase the most.

```
While number removed ≤ Maximum number to remove
   For each classifier $C_i$ of ensemble $C_1 \ldots C_N$
      Calculate $\kappa$ of ensemble $C_1 \ldots C_{i-1}, C_{i+1} \ldots C_N$
   Remove classifier $C_i$ causing the lowest $\kappa$ value.
```

Fig. 9. The Kappa thinning algorithm

Finally, we implement a sequential backwards selection (SBS) approach to removing classifiers. We calculate the voted accuracy after generating all possible ensembles of n-1 classifiers and remove the classifier which causes the accuracy to increase the most. The SBS algorithm shown in Figure 10 is similar to Kappa thinning except it looks at accuracy rather than diversity.

```
While number removed ≤ Maximum number to remove
   For each classifier $C_i$ of ensemble $C_1 \ldots C_N$
      Calculate voted accuracy of ensemble $C_1 \ldots C_{i-1}, C_{i+1} \ldots C_N$
   Remove classifier $C_i$ causing the highest voted accuracy
```

Fig. 10. Thinning by sequential backwards selection

To investigate the properties of these thinning algorithms, we performed a ten-fold cross validation, where 10% of the overall data was removed from the training data to create a thinning set. One thousand trees were built on the training data in each fold. Classifiers were chosen for removal based on the thinning set until only 100 classifiers remained. We compared various thinning methods against a randomly constructed ensemble of 100 classifiers, the number Brieman used in his forests [5]. Table 2 shows both AID and Kappa thinning were better than random construction in 21 of the 24 experiments while SBS was better in 20. A thinned ensemble of trees built and pruned on the Australian and Cleveland datasets shows a decrease in accuracy no matter the type of thinning used. This tends to suggest either that the diversity was too great for only 100 classifiers to overcome, or that thinning set selection was poor. Indeed all of these thinning algorithms will learn to overfit the thinning set, negatively affecting the generalization potential of the ensemble.

SBS ties twice with the other methods in accuracy but is better only once. While Kappa thinning produces a larger accuracy boost over AID thinning 14 times, the majority of these cases occur at the bottom half of the table where the maximum increase is smaller. Kappa thinning also has a greater running time than AID thinning. The method to use thusly depends on the needed gain in accuracy and the CPU time available.

Statistical significance tests will not show the small increases in accuracy to be significant; however, we note there is not a significant difference in accuracy even if 90% of the classifiers are removed because of the large variances between folds. With up to 90% of the classifiers removed from an ensemble, ensemble accuracy is generally clearly lower than the best accuracy. However, there is still significant variation between folds and a significance test will not show the change in accuracy to be significant.

Table 2. Thinning methodologies are compared against randomly constructing ensembles. Double asterisks indicate the highest performing AID, Kappa, or SBS thinning algorithm. The table is sorted by the highest maximum gain

Dataset	Pruning?	AID Acc	κ Acc	SBS Acc	Rand Acc	AID Over Rand	κ Over Rand	SBS Over Rand
Iris	Pruned	92.00%	94.67%	92.67%	88.46%	3.54%	6.20%**	4.20%
Iris	Unpruned	94.67%	94.67%	94.67%	89.21%	5.45%**	5.45%**	5.45%**
Heart	Pruned	81.11%	83.70%	81.11%	78.38%	2.73%	5.32%**	2.73%
German	Pruned	72.80%	74.30%	72.70%	69.92%	2.88%	4.38%**	2.78%
German	Unpruned	76.10%	76.00%	74.60%	74.09%	2.01%**	1.91%	0.51%
Heart	Unpruned	82.22%	82.78%	81.48%	81.32%	0.90%	1.46%**	0.16%
Cleveland	Unpruned	83.67%	83.33%	82.67%	82.47%	1.19%**	0.86%	0.19%
Australian	Unpruned	86.52%	85.07%	86.09%	85.62%	0.90%**	-0.55%	0.47%
Segmentation	Pruned	97.71%	98.01%	97.71%	97.37%	0.34%	0.64%**	0.34%
Led-24	Unpruned	75.40%	75.10%	75.10%	74.78%	0.62%**	0.32%	0.32%
Waveform	Unpruned	84.94%	84.72%	84.44%	84.38%	0.56%**	0.34%	0.06%
Led-24	Pruned	75.08%	75.14%	74.86%	74.63%	0.45%	0.51%**	0.23%
Glass	Pruned	95.24%	96.67%	95.71%	96.17%	-0.93%	0.50%**	-0.45%
Letter	Pruned	94.75%	95.04%	94.85%	94.55%	0.20%	0.49%**	0.30%
Satimage	Pruned	91.34%	91.42%	91.35%	90.95%	0.39%	0.47%**	0.41%
Letter	Unpruned	95.44%	95.41%	95.36%	95.22%	0.22%**	0.19%	0.13%
Segmentation	Unpruned	97.88%	97.92%	97.97%	97.77%	0.11%	0.15%	0.20%**
Pendigits	Pruned	98.86%	98.98%	98.90%	98.79%	0.08%	0.19%**	0.11%
Satimage	Unpruned	91.73%	91.79%	91.76%	91.62%	0.11%	0.17%**	0.14%
Pendigits	Unpruned	99.03%	99.00%	98.98%	98.90%	0.13%**	0.10%	0.08%
Waveform	Pruned	84.46%	84.50%	84.30%	84.41%	0.05%	0.09%**	-0.11%
Glass	Unpruned	96.19%	96.19%	96.19%	96.17%	0.02%**	0.02%**	0.02%**
Australian	Pruned	85.07%	84.49%	84.93%	85.11%	-0.04%**	-0.62%	-0.18%
Cleveland	Pruned	83.00%	83.67%	83.00%	85.88%	-2.88%	-2.21%**	-2.88%

5   Discussion

The concept of diversity is of interest because its effects can easily be seen. However, its quantification and manipulation are not quite well defined. The percentage correct diversity measure allows for some degree of predictability in foreseeing how much of an increase in accuracy can be expected by increasing the diversity of the ensemble. Furthermore, the PCDM is more understandable and efficiently calculated than the Q statistic, and those are the grounds on which Kuncheva and Whitaker originally recommended Q. Finally, the basis for the AID thinning algorithm, removing classifiers that incorrectly classify examples that generate a diverse vote, shows how the diversity concept can be used to shrink ensembles while maintaining or improving accuracy. Kappa thinning shows this as well.

Comparing the original 1000 randomly assembled classifiers to the 100 thinned classifiers, there are generally small losses in accuracy across the board, though these are obviously less than comparing them with the 100 randomly assembled classifiers. A means of dynamically setting the stopping point of thinning and working backwards towards the smallest ensemble with the greatest accuracy has been created, and will be described and compared as part of future work.

Finally, the algorithms presented here could be used to combine multiple different types of classifiers. That is, decision trees, neural networks, and so on could all contribute classification boundary suggestions, the least diverse of which would be thinned away.

Acknowledgments

This work was supported in part by the United States Department of Energy through the Sandia National Laboratories ASCI VIEWS Data Discovery Program, contract number DE-AC04-76DO00789, and the National Science Foundation NSF EIA-013-768.

References

1. Dietterich T., Ensemble methods in machine learning, *Proceedings of the First International Workshop on Multiple Classifier Systems*, pp. 1-15, 2000.
2. Breiman L., Bagging predictors, Machine Learning, Volume 24, No. 2, pp. 123-140, 1996.
3. Breiman L., Pasting small votes for classification in large databases and on-line, Machine Learning, Volume 36, No. 1-2, pp. 85-103, 1999.
4. Dietterich T., An experimental comparison of three methods for constructing ensembles of decision trees: Bagging, boosting, and randomization, *Machine Learning,* Volume 40, No. 2, pp. 139-158, 2000.
5. Breiman L., Random Forests, Machine Learning, Volume 45, No. 1, pp. 5-32, 2001.
6. Freund Y. and Schapire R.E., Experiments with a new boosting algorithm, Proc. 13th International Conference on Machine Learning, pp 148-156, 1996.
7. Kuncheva L.I., Whitaker C.J., Measures of diversity in classifier ensembles, Machine Learning , Volume 51, pp. 181-207, 2003.

8. Hansen L. and Salamon P., Neural network ensembles, IEEE Transactions on PAMI, 1990, V. 12, No. 10, pp. 993-1001.
9. Giacinto G. and Roli F., An approach to automatic design of multiple classifier systems, Pattern Recognition Letters, v. 22, pp. 25-33, 2001.
10. Latinne P., Debeir O., and Decaestecker C., Limiting the number of trees in random forests, Second International Workshop on Multiple Classifier Systems, pp. 178-187, 2001.
11. Kuncheva L., Whitaker C., Shipp C., and Duin R., Is independence good for combining classifiers?, 15th International Conference on Pattern Recognition, pp. 168-171, 2000.
12. Merz C.J. and Murphy P.M., UCI Repository of Machine Learning Databases, Univ. of CA., Dept. of CIS, Irvine, CA., http://www.ics.uci.edu/~mlearn/MLRepository.html

Ensemble Methods for Noise Elimination in Classification Problems

Sofie Verbaeten and Anneleen Van Assche

Department of Computer Science
Katholieke Universiteit Leuven
Celestijnenlaan 200 A, B-3001 Heverlee, Belgium
{sofie.verbaeten,anneleen.vanassche}@cs.kuleuven.ac.be

Abstract. Ensemble methods combine a set of classifiers to construct a new classifier that is (often) more accurate than any of its component classifiers. In this paper, we use ensemble methods to identify noisy training examples. More precisely, we consider the problem of mislabeled training examples in classification tasks, and address this problem by pre-processing the training set, i.e. by identifying and removing outliers from the training set. We study a number of filter techniques that are based on well-known ensemble methods like cross-validated committees, bagging and boosting. We evaluate these techniques in an Inductive Logic Programming setting and use a first order decision tree algorithm to construct the ensembles.

1 Introduction

In many applications of machine learning the data to learn from is imperfect. Different kinds of imperfect information exist, and several classifications are given in the literature (see e.g. [9]). In this paper, we consider the problem of noise or random errors in training examples.

One of the problems created by learning from noisy data is overfitting, that is, the induction of an overly specific hypothesis which fits the (noisy) training data well but performs poor on the entire distribution of examples. Classical noise-handling mechanisms modify the learning algorithm itself to make it more noise-tolerant. Another approach, which we explore in this paper, is to pre-process the input data before learning. This approach consists of filtering the training examples (hopefully removing the noisy examples), and applying a learning algorithm on the reduced training set. As pointed out in [7], this separation of noise detection and hypothesis formation has the advantage that noisy examples do not influence the hypothesis construction, making the induced hypothesis less complex and more accurate.

Many of the methods for filtering training data are in fact removing outliers from the training data. An outlier is a case that does not follow the same model as the rest of the data[1]. For instance in [3], the basic idea is to use a set of

---

[1] Note that, as such, an outlier does not only include erroneous data but also surprising correct data.

T. Windeatt and F. Roli (Eds.): MCS 2003, LNCS 2709, pp. 317–325, 2003.

classifiers (induced by a number of possibly different learning methods) formed from part of the training data to test whether instances in the remaining part of the training data are mislabeled. By taking a consensus or majority vote of these classifiers, it is decided whether or not to remove a particular instance. The noise detection algorithm of [7] is based on the observation that the elimination of noisy examples, in contrast to the elimination of examples for which the target theory is correct, reduces the CLCH value of the training set (CLCH stands for the Complexity of the Least Complex correct Hypothesis). In [8] robust decision trees are presented. Robust decision trees take the idea of pruning one step further: training examples which are misclassified by the pruned tree are removed from the training set and the tree is rebuilt using this reduced set. This process is repeated until no more training examples are removed. In [12], we presented filter techniques for Inductive Logic Programming (ILP) that are based on the idea of [3]. We also applied the robust decision tree technique of [8] to the ILP setting. We already obtained some good results with the filters proposed in [12].

In this paper, we further explore a number of other, new techniques. We propose filter techniques that are based on well-known ensemble methods [4], namely cross-validated committees, bagging and boosting. We present two approaches: (1) filtering based on (unweighted) voting of classifiers that are built on different subsets of the training set (obtained by either cross-validation or bagging), (2) filtering based on removing training examples that obtain high weights in the boosting process. We introduce these filter techniques in the next section, and evaluate them in an ILP setting in section 3. We conclude and discuss topics for future research in section 4.

2   Filter Algorithms

2.1   Base Classification Algorithm

The filters that are presented below make use of a learning algorithm for classification. With L we denote this base classification algorithm.

In our experiments, we evaluate the different filters in an ILP setting, and use Tilde [1] as the base learning algorithm L. Tilde (Top-down Induction of Logical Decision Trees) is an ILP extension of the C4.5 decision tree algorithm [11]. Instead of using attribute-value tests in the nodes of the tree, logical queries (which may contain logical variables) are used. The test to select the best query in each node is information gain ratio. After a tree is constructed, a post-pruning algorithm, based on an estimate of the error on unseen cases, is used.

2.2   Voting Filters

Voting filters are (as many other filter methods) based on the idea of removing outliers from a training set: an instance is removed if it can not be classified correctly by all, or the majority of, the classifiers built on parts of the training set. A motivation for using ensembles for filtering is pointed out in [3]: when we assume that some instances in the data have been mislabeled and that the label errors are independent of the particular model being fit to the data, collecting information from different models will provide a better method for detecting mislabeled instances than collecting information from a single model. As noted in many articles (see e.g. [4]), constructing ensembles of classifiers by manipulating the training examples works especially well for unstable learning algorithms. Decision tree algorithms, like Tilde, are unstable. We expect that ensembles of decision trees will act well as a filter for noisy data sets.

The general scheme of our voting filters is as follows:

1. L induces n classifiers on different subsets of the training set,
2. these n classifiers give labels to every example in the training set,
3. the filter compares the original class of each example with the n labels it has, and decides whether or not to remove the example.

A variation of instances of this general scheme exists depending on the way these n classifiers are induced, the value of n and the decision procedure in step 3.

Concerning step 3, we consider two possibilities: (1) a consensus filter (C filter), where a training example is removed only if all the n labels it has differ from its class; (2) a majority vote filter (M filter), where a training example is removed if the majority of the labels it has differ from its class.

Concerning step 1, we present two approaches for building these n classifiers. In the first approach, the training set is partitioned in n subsets of (approximately) equal size. L is trained n times, each time leaving out one of the subsets from the training set. This results in n classifiers. Such a filter is called a cross-validated committees filter (X filter). In the second approach, n bootstrap replicates are taken from the training set, and L learns on these n sets. Such a filter is called a bagging filter (Ba filter). In [5], a motivation is found for using bagging as a filter. In that paper, it is experimentally shown that bagged C4.5 gains advantage over C4.5 when noise is added to the training sets. More precisely, it is observed that for most data sets, noise improves the diversity of bagging, which permits it to perform better.

We performed experiments with cross-validated committees - consensus (XC) filters, cross-validated committees - majority vote (XM) filters, bagging consensus (BaC) and bagging majority vote (BaM) filters. The parameter n was set to 5, 9, 15, and 25.

2.3   Boosting Filters

Boosting is known to perform poorly with respect to noise. According to [5] a plausible explanation for the poor response of boosting to noise is that mislabeled training examples will tend to receive very high weights in the boosting process. Hence, after a few iterations, most of the training examples with high weights will be mislabeled examples. This gives a good motivation to use boosting as a noise filter.

The idea is to use Adaboost [6] and to remove, after a number of rounds (n), the examples with the highest weights. Since the filter has no idea what the exact percentage of noise is, we chose to give this as input to the filter[2]. Note that there might be several examples with the same weight (especially in the first rounds of the boosting process), so the filter might remove more examples than is given as input[3].

We tested the boosting (Bo) filter with 3, 5, 10 and 17 rounds.

3   Experiments

We evaluate the different filters in an ILP setting. As opposed to propositional or attribute-value learning systems that use a single table to represent the data set, ILP systems use a first order representation. This makes ILP very suitable for dealing with complex data structures.

We first describe the data sets that we used in the experiments. Then we explain how the experiments were carried out, and finally we discuss the results. For more details, we refer to [13].

3.1   Data Sets and Noise Introduction

We want to evaluate how well the different filter techniques perform on data sets with different amounts of classification noise. We therefore considered noise-free ILP data sets, and artificially introduced different levels of classification noise.

We considered the following noise-free data sets: an (artificial) Bongard data set [2] (392 examples), three (artificial) eastbound/westbound trains data sets [10] (200, 400, and 800 examples), and a (non-artificial) KRK data set for learning illegal positions in a chess endgame [9] (200 examples). These are all 2-class problems.

We introduced different levels of classification noise in the data sets. A noise level of $x\%$ means that for a randomly chosen subset of $x\%$ of the training examples, the class-value of these examples was flipped[4]. We introduced noise levels of 0%, 5%, 10%, 15%, 20%, 25%, 30%, 35%, and 40%.

3.2   Experimental Method

In order to obtain a more reliable estimate of the performance of the filters, all experiments were carried out in 10-fold cross-validation and the results were averaged over the 10 folds. For each of the 10 runs, the data set was divided in a training set (9 parts) and a test set (remaining 1 part). The training set was then corrupted by introducing classification errors. Each of the above described

---

[2] In a later stage, we will try to estimate this.

[3] Another possibility is to remove less examples than is given as input; we chose the greedy approach here.

[4] Positive examples are made negative and vice versa.

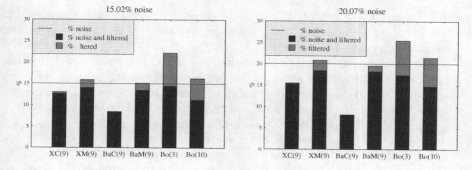

Fig. 1. Filter precision on the Bongard data set.

filter techniques was then run on the (noisy[5]) training set. After filtering the
training set, Tilde was used to learn a decision tree on the reduced training set.
This decision tree was then validated on the (noise-free) test set. Results were
obtained by taking the mean of the results of the 10 runs. For each of the 9 noise
levels and each of the 10 runs, we also run Tilde directly on the (unfiltered)
training set.

In the next subsections, we report results concerning filter precision, tree size
and accuracy.

3.3   Filter Precision

We evaluate the different filters by looking at the percentage of examples that
are removed, as well as the percentage of examples that are removed and are
actually noisy[6].

In Fig. 1, we show the precision of some of our filters on the Bongard data
set with 15% and 20% of noise.

In general, we observe the following. The BaC filters are the most conservative
filters: they remove the fewest examples. But, especially for the artificial data
sets, these filters are also very precise: almost no correct examples are removed.
One might choose to use a BaC filter when data is sparse. Also the XC filters are
rather conservative. The XM and BaM filters perform well. On the KRK data
set the Ba and X filters are not as precise as on the artificial data sets: relatively
more correct examples are also removed. The best results concerning precision
are obtained on the Bongard data sets. This can be explained by the fact that
Tilde reaches an accuracy of 100% on the noise-free Bongard data set, whereas
the other (noise-free) data sets, especially the KRK data set, are harder to learn
from.

---

[5] For each noise level and each of the 10 training sets, the classification errors were
introduced only once (in a random way), and the different filter techniques were run
on the same noisy training sets.

[6] For the detailed results, including an estimated probability of making type 1 and
type 2 errors for all filters, we refer to [13].

In general, the precision of the Bo filters is not very good: a great deal of filtered examples is not noisy. This shows that in the boosting process, also correct examples get high weights.

The influence of the number of classifiers n is as follows. For the $XC(n)$ filters, when there is not too much noise, the higher n, the higher the number of filtered examples, and also the higher the number of filtered and noisy examples. Indeed, when n increases, the training sets on which the n classifiers are built become more similar, and hence the classifiers will obtain a consensus in more cases. This is especially the case when there is not too much noise (up to 20%). For the $XM(n)$ filters, the parameter n does not have much influence.

For the $BaC(n)$ filters, the higher n, the lower the number of filtered examples, and also the lower the number of filtered and noisy examples. This is exactly the opposite behaviour as for the $XC(n)$ filters. This is because with bagging very diverse classifiers are built (especially when there is a lot of noise, see [5]). When the number (n) of such diverse classifiers increases, it becomes more difficult to obtain a consensus, hence less examples will be removed. The $BaM(n)$ filters seem to improve their precision when n is increased, meaning that more noisy examples, and at the same time less correct examples, are removed.

Despite the fact that the exact percentage of noisy examples is given as input to the $Bo(n)$ filters, these filters will remove more examples. This is because there might be examples that have the same weight. Since this is especially the case in the first rounds of the boosting process, we observe that, the higher n, the lower the number of filtered examples. At the same time we observe that, the higher n, the less noisy examples are filtered. When we look at the ratio of noisy examples in the set of examples that are filtered, we notice that, for noise levels up to 15%, this ratio is smaller in the first rounds of the boosting process. For higher noise levels however, the situation is completely reversed: when n is small, there are relatively more noisy examples in the set of filtered examples. This can be explained as follows. If there is a lot of noise in the training set, boosting will first force the learning algorithm to concentrate on these noisy examples. But, by doing this, the correct examples become harder to classify, and will receive higher weights further on in the boosting process. So when n increases, more correct examples will receive high weights and will be filtered.

Finally, by looking at the results on the three trains data sets, we observe that the more training examples we have at our disposal, the more precise the filters are.

3.4   Tree Size

A decision tree that is built from a noisy training set might be overly complex due to overfitting of this set. Therefore, it can be expected that the sizes of the trees induced from a filtered (and hopefully non-noisy) training set are smaller than the sizes of the trees induced from the non-filtered, noisy training set.

In Fig. 2, we show the number of nodes in the decision trees induced from (un)filtered Bongard training sets. More precisely, we report the results for the $XM(9)$, $BaM(9)$ and $Bo(10)$ filters.

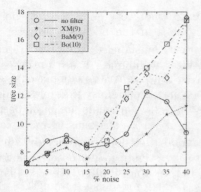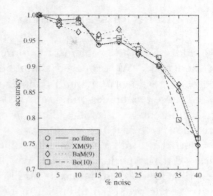

Fig. 2. Results concerning tree size (left) and accuracy (right) on the Bongard data set.

For noise levels up to 15% it is indeed the case that the sizes of the trees induced from a filtered training set are smaller than the sizes of the trees induced from the unfiltered set. For higher noise levels however there is, for many of the cases, no decrease in tree size if a filtered training set is used. One plausible explanation is that, for high noise levels, the filters still leave some amount of noise in the training sets. Also, we should note that Tilde with pruning is used (both in the filter algorithms and for inducing decision trees from the (un)filtered training sets), so the effect of overfitting is already largely reduced.

3.5 Accuracy

Decision trees built on a non-noisy training set will (in general) be more accurate (on a separate test set) than trees induced from a noisy training set. We compare the accuracies of the trees induced from the filtered sets (on the non-noisy test sets) with the accuracies (also on the non-noisy test sets) of the trees induced from the unfiltered, noisy sets.

In Fig. 2, we show our results for the XM(9), BaM(9) and Bo(10) filters on the Bongard data set. For this data set and also for the trains data sets, we observe that for noise levels up to 10%, Tilde still performs well on an unfiltered training set. For higher noise levels, it seems better to first filter the training set. No one filter outperforms the other filters in this respect. For the KRK data set, it is better to also filter the training set for low noise levels.

A hypothesis of interest is whether a majority vote ensemble classifier can be used instead of filtering, or whether the best method is to first filter the training set and then use a majority vote ensemble classifier. This hypothesis was tested in [3]. It was concluded that (for the filters proposed in [3]) a majority vote ensemble classifier can not replace filtering. We did some initial experiments to test this hypothesis in our setting. More experiments are needed to see if this conclusion also holds in our setting.

4   Conclusions and Future Work

We addressed the problem of training sets with mislabeled examples in classification tasks. We proposed a number of filter techniques, based on ensemble methods, for identifying and removing noisy examples. We experimentally evaluated these techniques on noise-free ILP data sets which we artificially corrupted with different levels of classification noise. We reported results concerning filter precision, tree size and accuracy.

Both the BaM and XM filters have a good precision. Surprisingly, the Bo filters did not perform so well. We plan to investigate in more detail how the boosting process can be used/modified to obtain a noise filter. We also plan to evaluate the proposed filters on more data sets.

When the data set is small and the cost of finding new training examples is high, one can choose to use a conservative filter, e.g. a BaC or XC filter. A better solution would be to detect and also correct labelling errors (and thus not removing any example). One way to do this is to present the suspicious data to a human expert and ask what to do with it. Another way is to automatically switch the class labels of the examples which are identified as noise. We will evaluate the performance of such an extension.

Acknowledgements

Sofie Verbaeten is a Postdoctoral Fellow of the Fund for Scientific Research - Flanders (Belgium) (F.W.O.- Vlaanderen). Anneleen Van Assche is supported by the GOA/2003/08(B0516) on Inductive Knowledge Bases.

References

1. H. Blockeel and L. De Raedt. Top-down induction of first order logical decision trees. *Artificial Intelligence*, 101(1-2):285–297, 1998.
2. M. Bongard. *Pattern Recognition*. Spartan Books, 1970.
3. C.E. Brodley and M.A. Friedl. Identifying mislabeled training data. *Journal of Artificial Intelligence Research*, 11:131–167, 1999.
4. T.G. Dietterich. Ensemble methods in machine learning. In J. Kittler and F. Roli, editors, *Multiple Classifier Systems, First International Workshop*, volume 1857 of *Lecture Notes in Computer Science*, pages 1–15. Springer, 2000.
5. T.G. Dietterich. An experimental comparison of three methods for constructing ensembles of decision trees: Bagging, boosting, and randomization. *Machine Learning*, 40(2):139–157, 2000.
6. Y. Freund and R.E. Schapire. Experiments with a new boosting algorithm. In L. Saitta, editor, *Proceedings of the Thirteenth International Conference on Machine Learning*, pages 148–156. Morgan Kaufmann, 1996.
7. D. Gamberger, N. Lavrač, and S. Džeroski. Noise detection and elimination in data preprocessing: experiments in medical domains. *Applied Artificial Intelligence*, 14:205–223, 2000.

8. G.H. John. Robust decision trees: Removing outliers from databases. In U.M. Fayyad and R. Uthurusamy, editors, *Proceedings of the First International Conference on Knowledge Discovery and Data Mining*, pages 174–179. AAAI Press, 1995.

9. N. Lavrač and S. Džeroski. *Inductive Logic Programming: Techniques and Applications*. Ellis Horwood, 1994.

10. R.S. Michalski and J.B. Larson. Inductive inference of VL decision rules. Paper presented at Workshop in Pattern-Directed Inference Systems, Hawaii, 1977. SIGART Newsletter, ACM, 63, 38-44.

11. J.R. Quinlan. *C4.5: Programs for Machine Learning*. Morgan Kaufmann series in machine learning. Morgan Kaufmann, 1993.

12. S. Verbaeten. Identifying mislabeled training examples in ILP classification problems. In M. Wiering and W. de Back, editors, *Twelfth Dutch-Belgian Conference on Machine Learning*, pages 1–8, 2002.

13. S. Verbaeten and A. Van Assche. Ensemble methods for noise elimination in classification problems. Technical report, Department of Computer Science, K.U.Leuven, Belgium,
http://www.cs.kuleuven.ac.be/publicaties/rapporten/cw/CW358.abs.html, 2003.

New Boosting Algorithms
for Classification Problems
with Large Number of Classes Applied
to a Handwritten Word Recognition Task

Simon Günter and Horst Bunke

Department of Computer Science, University of Bern
Neubrückstrasse 10, CH-3012 Bern, Switzerland
{sguenter,bunke}@iam.unibe.ch

Abstract. Methods that create several classifiers out of one base classifier, so-called ensemble creation methods, have been proposed and successfully applied to many classification problems recently. One category of such methods is Boosting with AdaBoost being the best known procedure belonging to this category. Boosting algorithms were first developed for two-class problems, but then extended to deal with multiple classes. Yet these extensions are not always suitable for problems with a large number of classes. In this paper we introduce some novel boosting algorithms which are designed for such problems, and we test their performance in a handwritten word recognition task.

Keywords: Multiple Classifier System; Ensemble Creation Method; Boosting; Large Number of Classes; Hidden Markov Model (HMM); Handwriting Recognition.

1   Introduction

The field of off-line handwriting recognition has been a topic of intensive research for many years. First only the recognition of isolated handwritten characters was investigated [24], but later whole words [22] were addressed. Most of the systems reported in the literature until today consider constrained recognition problems based on vocabularies from specific domains, e.g. the recognition of handwritten check amounts [10] or postal addresses [23]. Free handwriting recognition, without domain specific constraints and large vocabularies, was addressed only recently in a few papers [11,15]. The recognition rate of such systems is still low, and there is a need to improve it.

The combination of multiple classifiers was shown to be suitable for improving the recognition performance in difficult classification problems [13]. Also in handwriting recognition, classifier combination has been applied. Examples are given in [2,25]. Recently new ensemble creation methods have been proposed in the field of machine learning, which generate an ensemble of classifiers from a single classifier [4]. Given a single classifier, the base classifier, a set of classifiers

T. Windeatt and F. Roli (Eds.): MCS 2003, LNCS 2709, pp. 326–335, 2003.
© Springer-Verlag Berlin Heidelberg 2003

can be generated by changing the training set [3], the input features [9], the input data by injecting randomness [6], or the parameters and architecture of the classifier [16]. Another possibility is to change the classification task from a multi-class to many two-class problems [5]. Examples of widely used methods that change the training set are Bagging [3] and Boosting [8]. Random subspace method [9] is a well-known approach based on changing the input features. A summary of ensemble creation methods is provided in [4].

Boosting is one of the most popular ensemble methods. In [20] a good overview of this approach is given. The first boosting algorithms were introduced by Schapire in 1989 [18] and by Freund in 1990 [7]. The most prominent algorithm, AdaBoost, was developed in 1995 [8]. The original AdaBoost algorithm only works for two-class problems, but several extensions were proposed and tested in applications. AdaBoost.M1 [8] is a straightforward extension that basically regards the multi-class problem as a two-class problem with the two classes "correct" and "not correct". It is quite obvious that this simplification has its drawbacks. AdaBoost.MH [21] and AdaBoost.M2 [8] work by reducing the multi-class problem to a larger binary problem. Those methods need well adapted base learners to work properly. Another approach is to combine the method of error-correcting output codes [5] with boosting [1,19]. Here any two-class base classifier may be used. However, a disadvantage of all these approaches is that for problems with a large number of classes the complexity or the number of the induced two-class problems may be too large. In this paper some new boosting algorithms are presented which are especially designed for classification tasks involving a large number of classes. They are all derived from on the original AdaBoost algorithm.

The rest of this paper is organized as follows. In Section 2, the new boosting methods are introduced. The classifier for handwriting recognition used in the experiments is presented in Section 3. Then, in Section 4, results of an experimental evaluation of the proposed methods are given. Finally, conclusions from this work are drawn in Section 5.

2 New Boosting Algorithms for Classification Tasks with Large Number of Classes

In this section four new boosting algorithms are introduced which are designed for classification tasks with a large number of classes. All methods work with a distribution d of weights over the training set, similarly to AdaBoost [8]. Here we interpret the weight $d(x)$ of an element x of the original training set T as the probability of being selected when sampling elements for the training set of the next classifier of the ensemble. This means that $\sum_{x \in T} d(x) = 1$. The basic algorithm of all new boosting methods is given in Table 1.

This algorithm is very similar to AdaBoost where also the weights are adapted according to the results of the previously created classifiers on the training set. Note, however, that in contrast with the AdaBoost algorithm, the first classifier is trained with the full training set. The difference of the four new

Table 1. Basic algorithm of the new boosting algorithms

Input: base classifier (weak learner) C, training set T of size n, and number of runs m.
Output: m classifiers.

$d(x)$ is set to $\frac{1}{n}$ for all $x \in T$;
train C with $T \rightarrow$ classifier C_1;
for(i=2;i $\leq$ m;i++)

    test classifier C_{i-1} on T;
    modify $d(x)$ using information derived from the results of $C_1, \ldots, C_{i-1}$ on T; (*)
    sample m elements of T (without replacement) using the weights $d(x) \rightarrow T_i$;
    train C with $T_i \rightarrow$ classifier C_i;

return $C_1, \ldots, C_m$;

boosting methods is the modification of the weights $d(x)$ (line with star sign in Table 1).

In the following the details of the novel weight modification schemes and their underlying ideas are presented.

2.1 Simple Probabilistic Boosting (SPB)

The main idea of this boosting algorithm is to set the weight $d(x)$ of a training element x proportional to the probability $e(x)$ that the ensemble of classifiers will misclassify elements similar to element x. Similarly to AdaBoost, the weights of "hard" elements, i.e. elements which are likely to be misclassified, are set to a high value. It was decided to make the weights linearly dependent on the misclassification probability, because this approach is simple and the optimal function $o : e(x) \rightarrow d(x)$ is unknown anyway. The question remains how to calculate $e(x)$ from the results of the classifiers $C_1, \ldots, C_m$ that were already created. Four different functions will be considered:

1. If the ensemble of the classifiers $C_1, \ldots, C_m$ classifies x correctly then $e_1(x)$ is set equal to 0, otherwise it is set equal to 1.
2. Let $k(x)$ be the number of classifiers of $C_1, \ldots, C_m$ which output the correct labels for x. Then $e_2(x)$ is 0 if the ensemble of the classifiers $C_1, \ldots, C_m$ classifies x correctly. Otherwise it is $\frac{1-k(x)}{m}$. In contrast with $e_1(x)$, we take here also the information of the number of classifiers which had a correct output although the ensemble output was incorrect.
3. Let $k(x, y)$ be the number of occurrences of label y in the output of the classifiers $C_1, \ldots, C_m$ for training element x. The probability that one classifier of the ensemble outputs y is therefore $\frac{k(x,y)}{m}$. The probability of the ensemble to be wrong is then defined as the probability that the correct label c is not output more often than all other labels y, given the output probabilities $\frac{k(x,y)}{m}$ for label y. This is the most exact estimation of the probability of the misclassification of elements similar to element x, but may be very difficult to calculate. Consequently, two approximations will be considered in the following:

(a) Only the label i of the incorrect class that occurs most frequently and the correct label c are considered.

(b) The output probabilities $\frac{k(x,y)}{m}$ are used and a number of simulations of the output of an ensemble of size m are run. The fraction of simulations were the correct label c was not the most frequent label is the error probability $e_4(x)$. In the experiments of Section 4 the number of simulation was set to 1000.

Note that under $e_3(x)$ and $e_4(x)$ the results of $C_1, \ldots, C_m$ are only used for the calculation of the probability $k(x,y)$ that one classifier outputs label y for training element x. This means that $e(x)$ may be less than 1 even when the actual ensemble misclassifies the element. The reason why the actual results are not directly used is that we are not interested in the optimization of the ensemble for the training set, but in the optimization for elements similar to the ones in the training set. So by using the results only indirectly we may avoid overfitting effects.

For a better understanding of the functions $e_1(x), e_2(x), e_3(x)$ and $e_4(x)$ consider the following example: Assume four classifiers were produced for a classification problem with three classes X, Y and Z. The correct class of the test pattern t is X and the output of the classifiers for t are X, Y, Y and Z. Function $e_1(t)$ is equal to 1, because the wrong label Y appears more often than the correct label X. Function $e_2(t)$ is equal to 0.75, because one of the four labels in the output is correct. For $e_3(t)$ and $e_4(t)$ the value of k must be calculated first. Here, $k(t,X) = k(t,Z) = \frac{1}{4}$ and $k(t,Y) = \frac{1}{2}$. The value of $e_3(t)$ is the probability that Y appears more often than X using the output probabilities of the labels given by k. Here $e_3(t) = 0.81640$.

2.2 Effort Based Boosting (EBB)

The main idea of this method is the following. The weights $d(x)$ of the training elements are regarded as resources. Those resources should be distributed to, or shared among, the elements, for which a high value of $d(x)$ has the largest positive effect on the ensemble performance. Unlike in SPB when using $e_2(x)$, $e_3(x)$ or $e_4(x)$, the results of the ensemble of already produced classifiers are directly used to optimize the ensemble performance on the training set.

The effort $ef(x)$ of a training element x is defined as the average number of instances of x required to be present in the training set so that the trained classifier makes a correct decision for x. We can estimate $ef(x)$ as follows

$$ef(x) = \frac{\text{total number of instances of } x \text{ in all training sets of all classifiers}}{\text{number of correct decisions for } x \text{ made by all classifiers}} \quad (1)$$

Note that, because of the above given interpretation of the weights $d(x)$, the average number of elements in a training set of size n is $d(x) \cdot n$.

As mentioned before, the performance of the ensemble should be optimized. So the resources should be distributed to the elements, for which a correct voting result of the ensemble is achieved with minimum effort, i.e. with as few resources as possible. Quantity $r(x)$ is defined as the average total number of required resources, i.e. the number of training instances, so that the ensemble consisting of the already produced classifiers and some new classifiers outputs the correct result. Moreover, $n(x)$ is the number of classifiers with correct result for x needed to be added to the actual ensemble to get a correct voting result for x. From the definitions introduced above we get $r(x) = n(x) \cdot ef(x)$. If $n(x)$ is larger than the number of classifiers which will be added, then it is impossible to achieve a correct voting result for x and $r(x)$ is set to ∞.

Consider the following example: The training set consists of the elements A and B. The first classifier is trained with both A and B and tested on the training set. A is classified correctly, but B isn't. The second classifier is then trained with two instances of B and when tested on the training set it classifies both A and B correctly. The effort of A is the number of instances in the training sets of the classifiers (which is equal to 1) divided by the number of classifiers with correct result (which is equal to 2), so $ef(A) = \frac{1}{2}$. Similarly, we get $ef(B) = \frac{3}{1} = 3$. Because the voting result for A is correct, $n(A) = 0$ and $r(A) = 0$. For B, we need one more classifier which outputs the correct result to achieve a correct voting result, so $n(B) = 1$ and $r(B) = 3$.

For setting the weights $d(x)$ of the training elements all elements with $r(x) > 0$ are considered in ascending order of $r(x)$ and then the weights are set to $ef(x) \cdot \alpha \cdot \frac{1}{n}$ until the sum of the weights reaches 1. Note that with this formula the average number of instances in the training set of the new classifier for elements selected by the algorithm is $ef(x) \cdot \alpha$. If the sum of weights gets larger than 1 for a set of elements $\{x_1, \ldots, x_n\}$ with the same value of r then the weight of all those elements is set equal to $cc\dot{e}f(x) \cdot \alpha \cdot \frac{1}{n}$ where c it the constant which leads to a sum of weights equal to 1. If the sum of the weights of the elements with $r(x) \neq \infty$ doesn't reach the value 1, then the "rest" of the total weight is equally distributed among the elements with $r(x) = \infty$. Note that the elements with $r(x) = 0$, i.e. the elements which are classified correctly by the actual ensemble, have weight 0. As mentioned before, unlike SPB, the focus of this method is on the optimization of the actual ensemble.

The main idea of the algorithm is to train only on the elements of the original training set for which a correct voting result may be achieved by the inclusion of a few instances in the training sets of the classifiers. Because $ef(x)$ is the number of training instances of x needed on the average for a correct classification of x by the new classifier, the training set should contain more elements than $ef(x)$ to ensure that the classifier correctly classifies x. This is the reason why the parameter α is introduced. The larger the value of α, the more likely the elements with $d(x) > 0$ are classified correctly by the created classifier. On the other hand the smaller α is, the more elements have positive weights. The optimal value of α is application dependent and must be determined in experiments.

2.3   Effort Based Boosting with Doubling of Training Set (EBBD)

In some preliminary experiments it was observed that EBB produces training sets containing instances of only a small fraction of the original training set.

This can possibly lead to a poor performance of the individual classifiers in the application of handwritten word recognition. The reason for this is that the HMM classifiers used for this test have a large number of of free parameters which are poorly estimated if the training set consists of only a few different patterns. To avoid this problem the following modification of EBB is proposed. The individual classifiers are trained with the union of the training set produced by EBB and the original training set. With this approach some of the training samples still have several instances in the training set, and are emphasized therefore, but it is ensured that all original training elements are used for the training.

2.4 Simple Probabilistic Boosting with Effort (SPBE)

The idea of this algorithm is to train on elements for which a correct voting result may be easily achieved and for which, at the same time, the probability of a misclassification of similar elements by the ensemble is high.

The only modification to SPB is a different procedure for the calculation of the weight $d(x)$:

$$d(x) \propto e(x) \cdot (1 + \frac{\alpha}{ef(x)}) \tag{2}$$

The effect of α is the following. The higher the value of α, the higher is the weight for elements with low effort values, but the less weight is "distributed" to elements with higher effort values. Similarly to EBB, there is a tradeoff between the number of elements to be emphasized and the likelihood of the correct classification of an element when emphasizing it. Also here, the optimal value of α is application dependent and must be experimentally determined. In this paper we are only using a special case of SPBE where α is set to a very high value. The formula for $d(x)$ can then be simplified to $d(x) \propto \frac{e(x)}{ef(x)}$.

3 Handwritten Text Recognizer

In the experiments described in Section 4, an HMM-based handwritten word recognizer is used as base classifiers. The recognizers is similar to the one described in [15]. We assume that each handwritten word input to the recognizers has been normalized with respect to slant, skew, baseline location and height (for details of the normalization procedures see [15]). A sliding window of width one pixel is moved from left to right over the word and nine geometric features are extracted at each position of the window. Thus an input word is converted into a sequence of feature vectors in a 9-dimensional feature space. The geometric features used in the system include the fraction of black pixels in the window, the center of gravity, and the second order moment. These features characterize the window from the global point of view. The other features give additional information. They represent the position of the upper- and lowermost pixel, the contour direction at the position of the upper- and lowermost pixel, the number of black-to-white transitions in the window, and the fraction of black pixels between the upper- and lowermost black pixel. In [15] a more detailed description of the feature extraction procedures can be found.

For each uppercase and lowercase character, an HMM is build. For all HMMs the linear topology is used, i.e. there are only two transitions per state, one to itself and one to the next state. The character models are concatenated to word models. There is exactly one model for each word from the underlying dictionary. This approach makes it possible to share training data across different words. That is, each word in the training set containing character x contributes to the training of the model of x. Thus the words in the training set are more intensively utilized than in the case where an individual model is build for each word as a whole, and characters are not shared across different models.

The Baum-Welch algorithm is used for training of the system and the Viterbi algorithm for recognition [17]. The output of the HMM classifiers is the word with the highest rank among all word models together with its score value.

4 Experiments

For isolated character and digit recognition, a number of commonly used databases exist. However, for the task considered in this paper, i.e. recognition of handwritten words, there exists only one suitable database to the knowledge of the authors, holding a sufficiently large number of words produced by different writers [14]. Consequently, a subset of this database was used for the experiments. The training set contains 9861 and the test set 1066 words over a vocabulary of size 2296. That is, a classification problem with 2296 different classes is considered in the experiments. The test set was chosen in such a way that none of its writers was represented in the training set. Hence all experiments described in this paper are writer independent. The total number of writers who contributed to the training and test set is 81. The prototype classifier described in Section 3, trained on the full training set, has a recognition rate of 66.23 %. 74To compare the new methods to classical ensemble methods, also Bagging [3] and AdaBoost.M1 [8] were tested.

The following classifier combination schemes were used:

1. Voting scheme (voting): Initially, only the top choice of each classifier is considered. The word class that is most often on the first rank is the output of the combined classifier. Ties are broken by means of the maximum rule, which is only applied to the competing word classes.
2. Weighted voting (perf-v): Here we consider again the top class of each classifier. In contrast with regular voting, a weight is assigned to each classifier. The weight is equal to the classifier's performance (i.e. recognition rate) on the training set. The output of the combined classifier is the word class that received the largest sum of weights.
3. ga weighted voting (ga-v): Like weighted voting, but the optimal weights are calculated by a genetic algorithm based on the results of the classifiers on the training set.

All methods were tested three times and the averaged results of the experiments are shown in Table 2. In each experiment 10 classifiers were produced. The entries in column error/α denote the function used for error calculation or

Table 2. Results of the experiments with the new boosting algorithms. The recognition rate of the classifier trained on the whole training set is 66.23 %

algorithm	error/α	voting	perf-v	ga-v
Bagging	-	67.51 (0.19) %	67.73 (0.09) %	67.89 (0.24) %
AdaBoost	-	68.17 (0.31) %	68.67 (0.25) %	68.35 (0.38)%
SPB	e_1	68.45 (0.53) %	68.7 (0.46) %	68.67 (0.36) %
SPB	e_2	68.29 (0.41) %	68.23 (0.33) %	68.64 (0.77) %
SPB	e_3	68.04 (0.43) %	68.45 (0.38) %	68.2 (0.71) %
SPB	e_4	68.17 (0.52) %	68.17 (0.52) %	68.26 (0.61) %
EBB	1	69.11 (0.39) %	69.11 (0.54) %	69.29 (0.62) %
EBB	1.5	69.42 (1.07) %	69.45 (1.05) %	69.82 (1.52) %
EBBD	1.5	68.67 (0.26) %	68.73 (0.54) %	68.61 (0.73) %
EBBD	2	68.42 (1.12) %	68.54 (0.94) %	68.42 (0.91) %
SPBE	e_1	69.2 (1.27) %	69.01 (1.03) %	69.04 (1.07) %
SPBE	e_2	67.85 (0.71) %	67.7 (0.98) %	68.32 (1.17) %
SPBE	e_3	68.95 (0.73) %	68.76 (0.92) %	68.42 (0.67) %
SPBE	e_4	69.04 (0.41) %	69.36 (0.6) %	69.04 (0.8) %

the value of parameter α. The number in brackets is the standard deviation of the recognition rate.

For almost all boosting algorithms and all combination schemes better results than by Bagging were achieved (there is only one exception). This shows that the Boosting algorithms really produce superior results. In the following the new boosting algorithms are compared with AdaBoost. The SPB algorithms produced comparable or inferior results for error functions e_2, e_3 and e_4. Only with error function e_1 SPB is slightly better. EBB produced very good results, especially for $\alpha = 1.5$. When using EBB with double training set, i.e. the EBBD algorithm, the results are only slightly better than AdaBoost. It seems that the use of double training set doesn't increase the stability of the recognition rate of the ensemble much and leads to an inferior performance when compared to EBB. The two error functions e_1 and e_4 seem to be suited for use with the SPBE algorithm and lead to very good results. Also with error function e_3 better results than AdaBoost were achieved, yet when using e_2 SPBE can't compete with AdaBoost.

To compare the new algorithms to AdaBoost more systematically the sign test is used. In the sign test we compare corresponding results and count how often the result of the new algorithm is better. The null hypothesis of the test is that both algorithms have the same performance. So a binomial distribution of the counter variable mentioned above is expected (with $p = 0.5$). The results of SPB and Boosting seem to be similar. In 4 of 11 experimental settings the new method obtained better results. This doesn't allow us to reject the null hypothesis. On the other hand the results of EBB, EBBD and SPBE seem to be superior to the results of AdaBoost, because in 20 out of 24 experimental cases a better result was achieved by the methods. Here the null hypothesis of similar performance is rejected using a low significance level of 1 %.

The different combination schemes produced comparable results. It has to be finally noted that all algorithms proposed in this paper have a very high time consumption. This limits the number of repetitions that can be performed.

5   Conclusions

For classification problems with significantly more than two classes only one multi-class AdaBoost version, AdaBoost.M1, is easily applicable, AdaBoost.M1 incorporates an element weighting mechanism which is similar to the one of the two-class AdaBoost. However, this mechanism is not suited for classification problems with a large number of classes. In this paper three new boosting methods, which are all based on AdaBoost, were introduced. Those methods use heuristics for the weighting mechanism which are totally independent of the number of classes. Consequently they are suitable for classification problems with a large number of classes. The first method proposed in this paper sets the weight of an element of the training set proportional to the probability of the misclassification of similar elements. Different functions for the calculation of this probability were introduced. The second method regards weight as resource and distributes it in such a way that the performance of the final ensemble is maximized. A third method combines these two approaches.

The new boosting algorithms were tested in a handwritten word recognition task that involves almost 2,300 classes. The results of the first method produced results comparable to AdaBoost, but the other two methods achieved superior results in most cases. In our experiments, we observed a rather high variance of the recognition rate. In future research we will address this problem by using larger training sets and a higher number of classifiers. In addition we may also execute more runs of the algorithms to get more stable results.

Acknowledgment

This research was supported by the Swiss National Science Foundation (Nr. 20-52087.97). The authors thank Dr. Urs-Victor Marti for providing the handwritten word recognizer and Matthias Zimmermann for the segmentation of a part of the IAM database. Additional funding was provided by the Swiss National Science Foundation NCCR program "Interactive Multimodal Information Management (IM)2" in the Individual Project "Scene Analysis".

References

1. A. Allwein, R. Schapire, and Y. Singer. Reducing multiclass to binary: A uniying approach for margin classifiers. *Journal of Machine Learning Research*, 1:113–141, 2000.
2. A. Brakensiek, J. Rottland, A. Kosmala, and G. Rigoll. Off-line handwriting recognition using various hybrid modeling techniques and character n-grams. In *7th International Workshop on Frontiers in Handwritten Recognition*, pages 343–352, 2000.

3. L. Breiman. Bagging predictors. *Machine Learning*, (2):123–140, 1996.
4. T. G. Dietterich. Ensemble methods in machine learning. In *[12]*, pages 1–15.
5. T. G. Dietterich and G. Bakiri. Solving multiclass learning problems via error-correcting output codes. *Journal of Artifical Intelligence Research*, 2:263–286, 1995.
6. T.G. Dietterich and E.B. Kong. Machine learning bias, statistical bias, and statistical variance of decision tree algorithms. Technical report, Departement of Computer Science, Oregon State University, 1995.
7. Y. Freund. Boosting a weak learning algorithm by majority. *Information and Computation*, 121(2):256–285, 1995.
8. Y. Freund and R. Schapire. A decision-theoretic generalization of on-line learning and an application to boosting. *Journal of Computer and System Science*, 55(1):119–139, 1997.
9. T. K. Ho. The random subspace method for constructing decision forests. *IEEE Transactions on Pattern Analysis and Machine Intelligence*, 20(8):832–844, 1998.
10. S. Impedovo, P. Wang, and H. Bunke, editors. *Automatic Bankcheck Processing*. World Scientific Publ. Co, Singapore, 1997.
11. G. Kim, V. Govindaraju, and S.N. Srihari. Architecture for handwritten text recognition systems. In S.-W. Lee, editor, *Advances in Handwriting Recognition*, pages 163–172. World Scientific Publ. Co., 1999.
12. J. Kittler and F. Roli, editors. *First International Workshop on Multiple Classifier Systems*, Cagliari, Italy, 2000. Springer.
13. J. Kittler and F. Roli, editors. *Third International Workshop on Multiple Classifier Systems*, Cagliari, Italy, 2002. Springer.
14. U. Marti and H. Bunke. The IAM-database: an English sentence database for off-line handwriting recognition. *Int. Journal of Document Analysis and Recognition*, 5:39–46, 2002.
15. U.-V. Marti and H. Bunke. Using a statistical language model to improve the performance of an HMM-based cursive handwriting recognition system. *Int. Journal of Pattern Recognition and Art. Intelligence*, 15:65–90, 2001.
16. D. Partridge and W. B. Yates. Engineering multiversion neural-net systems. *Neural Computation*, 8(4):869–893, 1996.
17. L. Rabiner. A tutorial on hidden Markov models and selected applications in speech recognition. *Proceedings of the IEEE*, 77(2):257–285, 1989.
18. R. Schapire. The strength of weak learner. *Machine Learning*, 5(2):197–227, 1990.
19. R. Schapire. Using output codes to boost multiclass learning problems. In *Proc. of the 14th International Conference on Machine Learning*, pages 313–321, 1997.
20. R. Schapire. The boosting approach to machine learning. an overview. In *MSRI Workshop on Nonlinear Estimation and Classification*, pages 149–172, 2002.
21. R. Schapire and Y. Singer. Improved boosting algorithms using confidence-rated predictions. *Machine Learning*, 37(3):297–336, 1999.
22. J.-C. Simon. Off-line cursive word recognition. *Special Issue of Proc. of the IEEE*, 80(7):1150–1161, July 1992.
23. S. Srihari. Handwritten address interpretation; a task of many pattern recognition problems. *Int. Journal of Pattern Recognition and Art. Intell.*, 14:663–674, 2000.
24. C.Y. Suen, C. Nadal, R. Legault, T.A. Mai, and L. Lam. Computer recognition of unconstrained handwritten numerals. *Special Issue of Proc. of the IEEE*, 80(7):1162–1180, 1992.
25. L. Xu, A. Krzyzak, and C. Suen. Methods of combining multiple classifiers and their applications to handwriting recognition. *IEEE Transactions on Systems, Man and Cybernetics*, 22(3):418–435, 1992.

Automatic Target Recognition Using Multiple Description Coding Models for Multiple Classifier Systems

Widhyakorn Asdornwised[1] and Somchai Jitapunkul[1]

Digital Signal Processing Research Laboratory (DSPRL)
Department of Electrical Engineering
Chulalongkorn University, Bangkok, 10330, Thailand
{Widhyakorn.A,Somchai.J}@chula.ac.th

Abstract. In this paper, we proposed a new multiple classifier system (MCS) based on multiple description coding (MDC) models. Our proposed method was inspired from the framework of transmitting data over heterogeneous network, especially wireless network. In order to support the idea of MDC in pattern classification, parallels between transmission of concepts (hypothesis) and transmission of information through a noisy channel are addressed. Furthermore, preliminary surveys on the biological plausible of the MDC concepts are also included. One of the benefits of our approach is that it allows us to formulate a generalized class of signal processing based weak classification algorithms. This will be very applicable for MCS in high dimensional classification problems, such as image recognition. Performance results for automatic target recognition are presented for synthetic aperture radar (SAR) images from the MSTAR public release data set.

1 Introduction

In this paper, we propose a new multiple classifier systems (MCS) [1] by generalizing a model of weak classifiers based on the concepts of transmitting data over heterogeneous network, called MDC. Parallels between transmission of concepts and transmission of information through noisy channel are discussed in order to describe MDC applications in pattern classification.

As discussed in [2], decision of boosting based MCS, called Adaboost, could be interpreted as an instance of threshold decoding for a T-repetition code under the assumption of a binary discrete memoryless channel constructed by the ensemble of binary weak classifiers. Based on the work in [2], we can further verify that pattern classifying using overcomplete wavelet representations (OWR) for MDC and the threshold decoding for a T-repetition code are also equivalent. As a result, a diverse pool of classifiers can be generated from our MDC approach.

The remainder of this paper is organized as follows. Section 2 introduces a model of transmission of concepts. In Section 3, we describe multiple description coding and its biological plausible motivation. Section 4 gives a brief explanation

T. Windeatt and F. Roli (Eds.): MCS 2003, LNCS 2709, pp. 336–345, 2003.

of overcomplete wavelet representations and theirs extensions. We discuss our proposed method in Section 5. The experimental results are presented on an automatic target recognition task using MSTAR data set, and the discussion concludes the paper.

2 Transmission of Concepts (Hypothesis)

Based on the fact that Kolmogorov entropy estimation and optimal encoding are equivalent [3], let the function classes of concepts c belong to a target class $C : X \to \{0,1\}$ in a metric space with distance function ρ, E is the mapping that map C into a subset $\mathcal{B}$ of bitstreams and the mapping D decodes B, $B \in \mathcal{B}$, and c_B is the decoded concept based on the bitstreams. Then we can find an encoding pair of concepts E, D with distortion ¡ ε, the ball $B(c_B, \varepsilon)$, $B \in \mathcal{B}$, give an ε cover of C such that

$$H_\varepsilon(C) = \log_2 N_\varepsilon(C), \tag{1}$$

and

$$H_\varepsilon(C) < R(C, E, D), \tag{2}$$

where $H_\varepsilon(C)$ is the Kolmogorov ε-entropy of concepts, $N_\varepsilon(C)$ is the smallest integer n for which there is such an ε-covering of concepts (C), $R(C, E, D)$ denotes the largest length of bitstreams that appear when E encodes the concepts, and for each c the encoder E selects an integer $l \in \{1, ..., N_\varepsilon(C)\}$ such that $B(c_l, \varepsilon)$ contains c and map c into the binary digits of l.

From Equation 2, the optimal encoding of concepts can be interpreted further in the framework of communication transmission models, where the mapping E can be models as a Discrete Memoryless Source (DMS) with output alphabet X, $|X| = N_\varepsilon(C)$.

Basically, we can further conclude that pattern classifying using overcomplete wavelet representations (OWR) for MDC models and the threshold decoding for a T-repetition code are equivalent. However, we will skip the explanation of such equivalency in this paper since it can be derived straightforwardly from the equations in [2].

As a result, based on the parallels between transmission of concepts and transmission of information through a noisy channel using MDC models, any signal processing based algorithms that can be explained in the framework of MDC can be applicable for MCS.

3 Multiple Description Coding Models

The problem of breaking an image into pieces and then being able to reconstruct it from an arbitrary subset of these pieces have been long discussed, i.e., the problem of source coding [4] and optical holography [5]. In source coding, the proposition of jointly coding of many source descriptions is based on the original questions posed by Gersho, Ozarow, Witsenhausen, Wolf, Wyner, and Ziv at the

Shannon Theory Workshop in the September 1979 (see [6] and the references therein). The question was that if an information source is described by two separate descriptions, what are the concurrent limitations on qualities of these descriptions taken separately and jointly? This problem would come to be known as the multiple description problem.

Multiple Description Coding (MDC) is a source coding technique, in which the source is encoded into multiple descriptions, which are transmitted over different channels to the receiver. When all the descriptions are available at the receiver (i.e. when all channels are received), a high quality reconstruction of the source is possible. However, in the absence of some of the descriptions at the receiver (when one or more channels are not received), the quality of reconstruction should still be acceptable.

3.1   Biological Plausible Motivation

Our motivation on multiple description wavelet based pattern classification is to ensure that the model used in our classification system should be resembling the models that are evidently found in some biological organizations, i.e. biological vision organizations and auditory models.

As argued in biological vision [7] that both retina and cortical data indicate extensive oversampling (manifested by overlap of adjacent receptive fields), especially in the position dependence Gabor representation scheme. Furthermore, results from vision research indicate that an image is represented in logarithmic scale along the frequency axis, so called "Gaborian Pyramid", which is also a basic type of wavelet representations. Similarly, in auditory model [8], [9], it is argued that several models of the early processing in the mammalian auditory system are developed under wavelet transforms. Note that irregular sampling has been used for the latter case, which its representation is with respect to frames (with high redundancy or oversampling). Similarly to the reconstruction quality improvement in source encoding using MDC, biological organizations also use oversampling or high redundancy representations to improve classification accuracy.

At the best of our knowledge, we have not seen other works using MDC in pattern classification, except the approach using multiple descriptions of data in the context of rule based classification system [10], and the plausible models of vision and auditory systems mentioned above. Hence, with the inspiration from the biological plausible motivation, we believe that MDC could be applied with MCS in the applications of pattern classification.

4   Overcomplete Wavelet Representations (OWR) and Their Extensions

In this section, we first describe OWR for MDC. Then, an extension to OWR suitable for pattern classification tasks is presented.

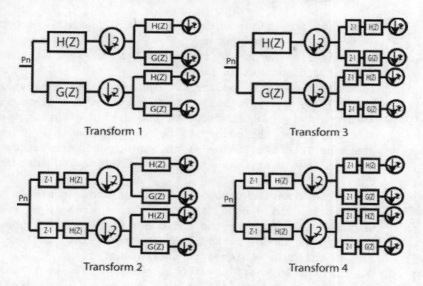

Fig. 1. One level of a 2-D overcomplete wavelet representation with four transforms

4.1 Overcomplete Wavelet Representations for Multiple Description Coding [11]

The overcomplete wavelet representation (OWR) combines coefficients from several critically subsampled discrete wavelet transforms (DWTs) computed for different circular shifts of the input image. The most straightforward approach is to compute in parallel several critically subsampled transforms, each for a different shift of the input image. We will treat it as a special case of the OWR and call it the Parallel Wavelet Representation (PWR). An example of the PWR is shown in Figure 1 for a redundancy ratio of four, which we will refer to each such set of coefficients as one transform even if they were computed using several different DWTs. We separately compute four one-level 2D DWTs for the input image shifted by (0,0), (3,0), (0,3), and (3,3). The four transforms share only the input signal. Generally, more descriptions can be generated by using different circular shifts of the input image before computing DWTs.

4.2 Local Discriminant Basis [12]

Algorithm 1 The Local discriminant basis algorithm (LDB) [12]

```
Step A0: Decompose a given set of training patterns belonging to
         each class into a full wavelet packet decomposition tree
         upto proper resolution.
Step A1: In each node corresponding to a subspace of the input
         pattern, calculate the accumulation of the square of the
         of all expansion coefficients of a given class and then
```

Step A2:
normalize its with total energy of the training patterns belonging to a given class.

Step A2: Continue Step A0 and A1 for all of the classes of the classification task in hand.

Step A3: In each node corresponding to a subspace of the pattern input, calculate discriminant measure for all classes using pairwise combinations of the distance norm between two classes of the values calculated in Step A2.

Step A4: Starting from the bottom of the tree, mark all bottom nodes as the best basis for the classification task in hand.

Step A5: If the information cost of the parent node is higher than that of the child node, then the parent node is marked. On the other hand, if the child has higher cost, then the parent node is not marked, but the total information cost of the child is assigned to the parent.

Step A6: Repeat Step A5 until the top is reached. The best basis is then obtained by collecting the topmost marked nodes.

Step A7: Retain K most discriminant subbands from the information costs selected from Step A6.

5   Our Proposed Method

The following multiple description wavelet based pattern classification algorithm performs classification voting on a set of multiple descriptions of data generated from spatially partitioned images with different numbers of features. These features are transformed by different overcomplete wavelet transforms (OWR).

Algorithm 2 The Multiple Description Wavelet Based Method

Step B0: Spatially partition the original input images into N subimages.

Step B1: In each subimage, use a specific overcomplete wavelet
(LDB)   representations to create a set of features by performing a linear transformation and retain a set of K new, informative features based on the LDB algorithm.

Step B2: Continue Step B1 using a different overcomplete wavelet representations for M times to create M image descriptions.

Step B3: Assemble a set of multiple descriptions (MD). Each MD is composed of N subimages. Each subimage contains LDB features generated using different OWR from Step B2.

Step B4: Classify each description using Fisher's linear discrimi-
(LDA)   nant analysis (LDA) based classification method.

Step B5: Vote all M descriptions to obtain the final classifica-
(MDC)   tion.

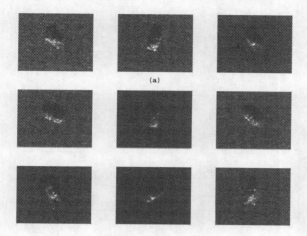

Fig. 2. Sample SAR images of military vehicles (a) BMP2 APCs, (b) BTR70 APCs, and (c) T72 tanks

Through out the rest of this paper, MD-LDB-LDA will be used to represent our proposed algorithm. This term is coined regarding to the operations in Steps B5, B1, and B4, respectively. Specifically, LDB in Step B1 performs both functions of feature extraction/selection with a purpose to reduce dimensionality of the original input. In Step B3, a diverse set of MD are generated by varying the amount of redundancy with the important of discriminant power. In this paper, we use the almost same number of features for each subimages in our experiments. In Step B4, each LDA based classifier with its corresponding MD becomes a weak classifier for a committee of classifiers implemented in Step B5.

6   Experimental Results

We have compared our approach with seven baseline classifier systems on the MSTAR public release data set. In the first system, feature extraction method based on the modified differential box-counting (MDBC) [13] was used to estimate the fractal dimension of the original images. These MDBC features were then used to train and test feed-forward neural networks (NN). In the second system, algorithms based upon a conditionally Gaussian signal models (CGSM) [14] were used to jointly estimate both target type and target pose. We implemented error correcting output coding (ECOC) [15] using original and LDB training data sets as the third and forth baseline classifiers, respectively. Furthermore, we implemented Adaboost with stochastic weighting [16] using original and LDB training data sets as the fifth and sixth baseline classifiers, respectively. We used 7 bits linear block code to generate ECOC classifiers, where each experiment is run for six times. Similarly, we evaluated each Adaboost experiment using 30 weak networks. Here, we trained both ECOC and Adaboost networks for 500 it-

Table 1. MSTAR images comprising training set

	Vehicle No.	Serial No.	Depression	Images
BMP-2	1	9563	17^0	233
	2	9566		231
	3	c21		233
BTR70	1	c71	17^0	233
T-72	1	132	17^0	232
	2	812		231
	3	s7		228

Table 2. MSTAR images comprising testing set

	Vehicle No.	Serial No.	Depression	Images
BMP-2	1	9563	15^0	195
	2	9566		196
	3	c21		196
BTR70	1	c71	15^0	196
T-72	1	132	15^0	196
	2	812		195
	3	s7		191

Table 3. The CGSM Method: Recognition test of a three class problem for 80 x 80 images

	BMP-2	BTR-70	T-72	Percent
BMP-2	580	0	7	98.81%
BTR-70	12	183	1	94.90%
T-72	0	0	582	100%

erations using one hidden-layer backpropagation network with various numbers of hidden nodes. The reason for comparing with ECOC and Adaboost is that our proposed method, ECOC and Adaboost are considered as Majority Voted Learners (MaVL). Finally, our seventh classifier is implemented using Fisher's linear discriminant analysis (LDA) based classification on the selected LDB features of the original images.

The MSTAR public release data set contains high resolution synthetic aperture radar data collected by the DARPA/Wright laboratory Moving and Stationary Target Acquisition and Recognition (MSTAR) program. The data set contains SAR images of three different types of military vehicles – BMP2 armored personal carriers (APCs), BTR70 APCs, and T72 tanks. The sample of SAR images at different orientations are shown in Figure 2. The size of each image is 128x128.

In our experiments, we used the first order Coiflet filters for the LDB algorithm. Four different image sizes from 32x32 to 80x80 have been used in our experiments. Image chips of different image sizes were reconstructed by extracting a small rectangular region at the center of the MSTAR images. The reason

Table 4. Our Proposed Method: Recognition test of a three class problem for 80 x 80 images using 7 descriptions

	BMP-2	BTR-70	T-72	Percent
BMP-2	584	2	1	99.49%
BTR-70	1	194	1	98.98%
T-72	1	1	580	99.66%

Table 5. Comparison of difference methods in overall percentage of images correctly recognized as a function of image size

Methods / Image Size	32x32	48x48	64x64	80x80
MDBC+NN	75.88	N/A	N/A	N/A
CGSM	N/A	N/A	N/A	98.53
SVM-ECOC(orignal)	84.46	90.16	91.76	92.70
SVM-ECOC(LDB)	85.42	90.81	92.51	92.14
Adaboost(orignal)	88.24	93.35	93.48	93.68
Adaboost(LDB)	**89.66**	93.16	94.26	93.97
LDB-LDA	73.78	95.24	97.14	97.29
MDC-LDB-LDA	84.69	**98.53**	**99.34**	**99.47**

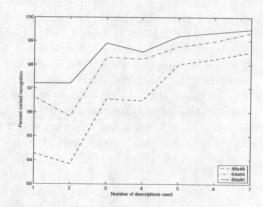

Fig. 3. Percent of correct recognition as a function of number of descriptions used and image size

for windowing target images is that the classification should be sensitive to a region corresponding to the vehicle, not to background clutter or target shadow. The larger image chip used, the more target, shadow, and background clutter pixels are included. Inversely, portions of shadow and background are eliminated and the target occupies a larger portion of image chip, when a smaller image chip are used.

Tables 1 and 2 detail the training and testing set, where the depression angle means the look angle by antenna beam at the side of the flying aircraft pointed to target. Based on the different depression angles SAR images acquired at different

Widhyakorn Asdornwised and Somchai Jitapunkul

time, test sets can be used as a representative sample sets of the SAR images of the targets for testing the recognition performance. Tables 3 and 4 detail the recognition performance through confusion matrices for 80 x 80 images of the CGSM and our approaches (MD-LDB-LDA), respectively. As presented in Table 5, our proposed method gives the best overall performance among all approaches. It should be noted that we evaluated our algorithm at various image sizes compared to the available recognition accuracy given in [13] and [14]. By implementing Steps B1 to B5 for M descriptions, the performance results in term of percent of correct recognition as functions of number of descriptions used and image size can be shown as in Figure 3. Evidently, the computation complexity of our proposed method is much less than ECOC and Adaboost methods when they are evaluated at the original image sizes. This is also being true when all methods are evaluated using LDB. The computational complexity of computing basis for N training targets is $O(N.n.log(n))$, and the cost of searching best basis is $O(n)$, where n is the number of pixels of target chip.

7 Discussion and Conclusion

In this paper, we try to bridge the gap between signal processing and pattern classification by proposing a new algorithm, called multiple description wavelet based pattern classi cation method. Our proposed technique is inspired by the current successful techniques in both pattern classification and signal processing concepts, e.g. divide and conquer approaches, combining classifiers, local discriminant bases, and multiple description coding models etc. Based on our experiment results, our proposed method gave the best performance among all multiple classifier methods. Our future work will be on unifying our method to the random subspace method [17], implementing an approach for jointly feature extracting and classifying based on local discriminant basis.

Acknowledgment

We would like to thank the Rachadapisek Research Fund and the support of the Ministry of the University Affair, Thailand. The MSTAR data sets provided through the center for imaging science, ARO DAAH049510494.

References

1. Dietterich, T.G.: Machine Learning Research: Four Current Directions. AI Magazine **18(4)**(1997) 97-136
2. Tapia, E., Gonzalez, J.C., Villena, J.: A Generalized Class of Boosting Algorithms Based on Recursive Decoding Models. In: Kittler, J., Roli, F. (Eds.): Multiple Classifier Systems. Lecture Notes in Computer Science, Vol. 2096. Springer-Verlag, Berlin Heidelberg New York (2001) 22-31

3. Cohen, A., Dahmen, W., Daubechies, I., DeVore, R.: Tree Approximation and Optimal Encoding. Institut Für Geometrie und Praktische Mathematik, Bericht Nr. 174 (1999)
4. Goyal, V.K.: Beyond Traditional Transform Coding. Ph.D. Thesis, University of California, Berkeley, 1998
5. Bruckstein, A.M., Holt, R.J., Netravali, A. N.: Holographic Representation of Images. IEEE Trans. Image Proc. **7(11)** (1998) 1583-1597
6. El Gamal, A.A., Cover, T.: Achievable Rates for Multiple Descriptions. IEEE Trans. Inform. Theory **IT-28(6)** (1982) 851-857
7. Porat, M., Zeevi, Y.Y.: The Generalized Gabor Scheme of Image Representation in Biological and Machine Vision. IEEE Trans. Pattern Anal. and Machine Intell. **10(4)** (1988) 452-468
8. Yang, X., Wang, K., Shamma, S.: Auditory Representations of Acoustic Signals. IEEE Trans. Information Theory bf 38(2) (1992) 824-839
9. Benedetto,J.J., Teolis,A.: A Wavelet Auditory Model and Data Compression. Applied and Computational Harmonic Analysis **1(1)** (1993) 3-28
10. Ali, K., Brunk, C., Pazzani, M.: On Learning Multiple Descriptions of a Concept. Sixth Int. Conf. on Tools with Artificial Intell. (1994) 476-483
11. Miguel, A.C: Image Compression Using Overcomplete Wavelet Representations for Multiple Description Coding. Ph.D. Thesis, Dept. of Electircal Engineering, University of Washington (2001)
12. Saito, N.: Local Feature Extraction and Its Applications Using a Library of Bases. Ph.D. Thesis, Dept. of Mathematics, Yale University (1994)
13. Theera-Umpon, Nipon: Fractal Dimension Estimation Using Modified Differential Box-Counting and Its Application to MSTAR Target Classification. IEEE Int.Conf. on SMC (2002).
14. O'Sullivan, J.A., DeVore, M.D., Kedia, V., Miller, M.I.: SAR ATR performance using a conditionally Gaussian model. IEEE Trans. Aerospace and Electronic Systems, **37(1)** (2001) 91-108
15. Dietterich, T.G. and Bakiri, G.: Error-Correcting Output Codes: A General Method for Improving Multiclass Inductive Learning Programs. Proc. of the Ninth AAAI. (1991) 572-577
16. James, G.: Majority Vote Classifiers: Theory and Applications. Ph.D. Thesis, Dept. of Statistics, Stanford University (1998)
17. Ho, T. K.: The Random Subspace Method for Constructing Decision Forests. IEEE Trans. Pattern Anal. and Machine Intell. **20(8)** (1998) 832-844

A Modular Multiple Classifier System for the Detection of Intrusions in Computer Networks

Giorgio Giacinto, Fabio Roli, and Luca Didaci

Department of Electrical and Electronic Engineering – University of Cagliari, Italy
Piazza D'Armi – 09123 Cagliari, Italy
{giacinto,roli,luca.didaci}@diee.unica.it

Abstract. The security of computer networks plays a strategic role in modern computer systems. In order to enforce high protection levels against threats, a number of software tools have been currently developed. Intrusion Detection Systems aim at detecting intruders who elude "first line" protection. In this paper, a pattern recognition approach to network intrusion detection based on the fusion of multiple classifiers is proposed. In particular, a modular Multiple Classifier architecture is designed, where each module detects intrusions against one of the services offered by the protected network. Each Multiple Classifier System fuses the information coming from different feature representations of the patterns of network traffic. The potentialities of classifier fusion for the development of effective intrusion detection systems are evaluated and discussed.

1 Introduction

Despite the effort devoted to protect computer networks, they are exposed to new attacks that are constantly developed. The main reason is the presence of unknown weaknesses or bugs, always contained in system and application software (McHugh et al., 2000; Proctor, 2001). Intrusion Detection Systems (IDS) are the software tools placed inside a computer network, looking for known or potential threats in network traffic and/or audit data recorded by hosts.

Two approaches to intrusion detection are currently used. One is called *misuse* detection, and is based on attack *signatures*, i.e., on a detailed description of the sequence of actions performed by the attacker. This approach allows the detection of intrusions perfectly matching the signatures. Their effectiveness is strictly related to the extent to which IDSs are updated with the signatures of the latest attacks developed. In principle, this problem could be solved by designing *general* signatures that capture the "root-cause" of an attack, thus allowing for the detection of all the attack variants designed to exploit the same weakness. Unfortunately, general signatures designed by security experts usually generate high volumes of "false alarms" (Proctor, 2001), i.e., normal traffic events matching an attack signature. This is currently a challenge for the development of effective IDSs, since very small false alarm rates translate to a number of false alarms greater than the number of true alarms, as the volumes of normal traffic are some orders of magnitude greater than those related to the attacks (Axelsson, 2000).

The second approach to intrusion detection is based on statistical knowledge about the *normal* activity of the computer system, i.e., a statistical profile of what consti-

T. Windeatt and F. Roli (Eds.): MCS 2003, LNCS 2709, pp. 346–355, 2003.
© Springer-Verlag Berlin Heidelberg 2003

tutes legitimate traffic in the network. In this case, intrusions correspond to *anomalous* network activity, i.e., to traffic whose statistical profile deviates significantly from the normal (McHugh et al., 2000; Proctor, 2001). This IDS model has been the first to develop on account of its theoretical ability to detect intrusions, regardless of the system type, the environment, the system vulnerabilities, and the type of intrusions. Unfortunately, the acquisition of profiles of "normal" activity is not an easy task, due to the high variability of network traffic over time.

The above discussion points out that the trade-off between the ability to detect new attacks and the ability to generate a low rate of false alarms is the key point to develop an effective IDS. Therefore, the misuse (signature-based) detection model is currently the most widely used due to its ability to produce very low false alarm rates at the price of a very limited ability to detect new attacks.

The difficulties in detecting novel attacks have led researchers to apply statistical pattern recognition approaches (Bonifacio et al., 1998; Cannady, 2000; Debar et al., 1992; Ghosh and Schwartzbard, 1999; Giacinto et al., 2003; Lee and Heinbuch, 2001; Ryan et al., 1998; Yeung and Ding, 2003). The main motivation in using pattern recognition approaches to develop advanced IDSs is their generalization ability, which may support the recognition of previously unseen intrusions that have no previously described patterns. In particular, pattern recognition approaches should allow the detection of the so-called attack "variants", i.e. attacks that produce the same effect of known attacks but with different signatures that are not recognised by signature-based IDSs.

An extensive evaluation of pattern classification techniques was carried out on a sample data set of network traffic during the KDD'99 conference. The results pointed out the feasibility of the pattern recognition approach to intrusion detection (Elkan, 2000). Nevertheless, a number of issues should be still solved before such systems can be used in operational environments (Allen et al., 2000). For network managers, one of the main drawbacks of such systems appears to be the high false alarm rate often produced.

In this paper an experimental evaluation of the use of Multiple Classifier Systems (MCSs) for the detection of intrusions in computer networks is proposed. In particular, this is an extension of the work presented in (Giacinto et al., 2003), where the feasibility of the MCS approach to intrusion detection was assessed. While the experimental results of the previous paper were related to one network service, in this paper a modular MCS architecture is designed to take into account the number of services offered in a TCP/IP computer network.

The paper is organised as follows. A formulation of the intrusion detection problem in the framework of MCSs is presented in Section 2. The modular architecture designed to take into account a number of network services is illustrated in section 3. Section 4 briefly outlines the function used to fuse the outputs of different classifiers. The experimental evaluation of the MCS architecture a data set available to the public is reported in Section 5. Conclusions are drawn in Section 6.

2   Problem Formulation

Intrusions in computer networks basically exploit weaknesses of the network transmission protocol and weaknesses and bugs exhibited by system and application software. The solution proposed hereafter is a network-based IDS (NIDS), as it allows detecting both types of intrusions by processing the network traffic flow (Proctor, 2001).

From the MCSs point of view, the network intrusion detection problem can be formulated as follows (see Figure 1): given the information about network connections between pairs of hosts, assign each connection to one out of N data classes representing normal traffic or different categories of intrusions (e.g., Denial of Service, access to root privileges, etc.). It is worth noting that various definitions of data classes are possible (McHugh et al., 2002; Proctor, 2001).

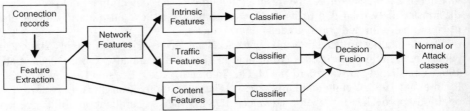

Fig. 1. Intrusion Detection formulated in the framework of MCSs

The term "connection" refers to a sequence of data packets related to a particular service, e.g., the transfer of a web page via the http protocol. As the aim of a network intrusion detector is to detect connections related to malicious activities, each network connection can be defined as a "pattern" to be classified.

Extraction of suitable features representing network connections is based on expert knowledge about the characteristics that distinguish attacks from normal connections. These features can be subdivided into two groups: features related to the data portion of packets (called *payload*) and features related to the network characteristics of the connection, extracted from the TCP/IP headers of packets (Northcutt and Novak, 2001). The latter group of features can be further subdivided into two groups: intrinsic features, i.e., characteristics related to the current connection, and traffic features, related to a number of *similar* connections. Therefore, the following three feature sets can be used to classify each connection (Lee and Stolfo, 2000):

- *content features*, i.e., features containing information about the data content of packets ("payload") that could be relevant to discover an intrusion, e.g., errors reported by the operating system, root access attempts, etc.
- network related features
  - *intrinsic features*, i.e., general information related to the connection. They include the duration, type, protocol, flag, etc. of the connection;
  - *traffic features*, i.e., statistics related to past connections similar to the current one e.g., number of connections with the same destination host or connections related to the same service in a given time window or within a predefined number of past connections.

This feature categorisation is general enough to take into account the high number of features that can be used to describe network traffic, while the features depend on the services, software, etc. used in the protected network.

The MCS approach based on distinct feature representations is motivated by the observation that human experts design signatures that try to "combine" different attack characteristics in order to attain low false alarm rates and high attack detection rates according to their experience and intuition (Allen, 2000; Northcutt et al., 2001). Unfortunately, the manual development of such types of signatures is very difficult and tedious. The fusion of multiple classifiers can automate such an approach. In addition, the generalization capabilities of pattern recognition algorithms can allow for the detection of novel attacks that signatures designed by human experts usually do not detect. Finally, the MCS approach should produce a low rate of false alarms, as the authors showed in another application field (Giacinto et al., 2000).

3   An MCS Modular Architecture for Intrusion Detection

The traffic flow over a TCP/IP computer network is made up of sequences of packets related to different services. Each service is characterised by peculiar patterns of traffic, e.g., the traffic generated by the http service is different from that generated by the smtp service. In addition, as different services involve different software programs, attacks to different services are characterised by different patterns of traffic. Thus it follows that the patterns of traffic related to different services should be described by different feature sets.

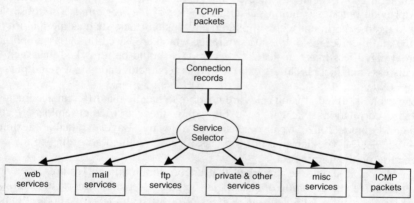

Fig. 2. Network connections related to different services are processed by mutually exclusive modules.

In order to take into account the peculiarities of each service, we propose a *modular* architecture, where a dedicated MCS is designed for each service. In this paper we propose to divide the network services into six groups. Each group is made up of a number of services with similar functions (Figure 2). A "miscellaneous" group is also used to take into account services that are rarely used in the computer network at hand. It is worth noting that the proposed division depends hardly on the computer network to be protected, as different networks may provide different services. As an example, the traffic flow depends highly on the prevalent type of the users of the network services (i.e., home users, corporate users, etc.). As the modular architecture shown in Figure 2 is related to the dataset described in Section 5, it can be regarded as an example of the design of a modular MCS for IDS.

For each service, an MCS made up of three classifiers is designed. Each classifier is related to one of the feature subsets outlined in the previous section. For each service, a feature selection process is performed first to select the more suitable content, traffic and intrinsic features (see Section 2). Then, for each feature subset (i.e., content, intrinsic and traffic), a number of classifiers are designed and the one that attained the best performances is selected. Finally, the fusion rule that better exploits the complementarity of the three selected classifiers is chosen among a number of candidate rules (see Section 4).

4   Decision Fusion Functions

As a first "user's guide" to choose the decision function, the expected degree of *diversity* among classifiers should be taken into account (Roli and Fumera, 2001). It can be seen easily that the three feature sets presented in Section 2 are associated to *unrelated* connection characteristics. For example, for a given set of values of the intrinsic features (e.g., the number of bytes transmitted), there is no relationship with the values assumed by the content features (e.g., an attempt to log in the system as user "root"). According to the current achievements of the multiple classifiers theory (Roli and Fumera, 2002), it can be expected that classifiers trained on such different feature types provide outputs exhibiting a certain degree of *uncorrelation*. This observation allowed us to experiment with simple, "fixed" fusion rules, such as the majority voting rule and the average of classifier outputs, which are based on the assumption that different classifiers make uncorrelated errors. (It should be remarked that such fixed rules also assume that classifiers exhibit similar accuracies and pair-wise output correlations) (Xu et al., 1992).

However, as "fixed" fusion rules are not able to handle the different accuracies and pair-wise correlations that can be exhibited by the classifier ensemble effectively (Roli and Fumera, 2002), we also considered the Naive-Bayes "trainable" fusion rule (Xu et al., 1992). The decision of each classifier is weighted according to the confusion matrix on the training set.

In addition, it should be remarked that uncorrelation among features does not always guarantee uncorrelation of classifiers' outputs (Roli and Fumera, 2002). In some cases classifiers may exhibit strong degrees of positive and negative correlations. For example, some attacks can be detected effectively only by one classifier of the ensemble, or by the combination of a subset of classifiers. To handle these cases, we have considered an additional "trainable" fusion technique: the "decision template" fusion rule (Kuncheva et al., 2001), based on the set of outputs of the classifier ensemble on the training set. This fusion method also allows effectively handling different accuracies and pair-wise correlations exhibited by individual classifiers.

5   Experimental Results

Experiments were carried out on a subset of the database created by DARPA in the framework of the 1998 *Intrusion Detection Evaluation Program* (http://www.ll.mit .edu/ IST/ ideval). We used the subset that was pre-processed by the Columbia University and distributed as part of the UCI KDD Archive (http://kdd.ics.uci.edu/ databases/kddcup99/kddcup99.html). The available database is made up of a large number of network connections related to normal and malicious traffic. Each connection is represented with a 41-dimensional feature vector according to the set of features illustrated in section 2. In particular, 9 features were of the intrinsic type, 13 features were of the content type, and the remaining 19 features were of the traffic type.

Connections are also labelled as belonging to one out of five classes, i.e., normal traffic, Denial of Service (DoS) attacks, Remote to Local (R2L) attacks, User to Root (U2R) attacks, and Probing attacks. Each attack class is made up of different attack variants, i.e., attacks designed to attain the same effect by exploiting different vulnerabilities of the computer network.

The training set was made up of 491837 patterns related to different attacks belonging to one of the four attack categories. As the number of patterns related to the "Smurf" and "Neptune" attacks (DoS type) was very large compared to the number of attacks related to other attacks, we generated a new training set with "balanced" classes by "pruning" the patterns related to these attacks. This procedure was motivated by the experimental evidence that a training set with 1% of randomly chosen patterns of the two above attacks had the same generalisation capability than the entire training set. This propriety allowed to us to use a training set made up of 107670 patterns.

The test set was made up of 311029 patterns, where 19091 patterns were related to attack types not included in the training set. These patterns allow testing the ability of the pattern recognition approach to detect novel attack types.

Classification results are reported in terms of the overall classification error, the sum of the false alarm and the missed alarm rates, and the average classification cost computed according to the cost matrix shown in Table 1. (The cost is computed by multiplying each entry of the confusion matrix with the corresponding entry in the cost matrix and dividing by the total number of test samples (Elkan, 2000)).

Table 1. Cost matrix used to evaluate the confusion matrix related to each classifier

		Assigned class				
		Normal	U2R	R2L	Probing	DoS
Trueclass	Normal	0	2	2	1	2
	U2R	3	0	2	2	2
	R2L	4	2	0	2	2
	Probing	1	2	2	0	2
	DoS	2	2	2	1	0

It is worth noting that the false alarm and missed alarm rates do not take into account class confusion among attack classes. The false alarm rate measures the fraction of alarms produced by the classifier that are related to normal traffic patterns. On the other hand, the missed alarm rate measures the fraction of attack traffic patterns that are assigned to the "normal" class. Typically, an effective IDS should provide very small rates of false and missed alarms. In particular, as the number of normal connections is some degrees of magnitude higher than that of the attacks, small rates of false alarms can translate to a number of alarms unacceptable for operational environments (Axelsson, 2000).

The experiments have been carried out by designing a large number of classifiers for each task. In particular, neural networks (MLP and RBF), k-NN, Gaussian, Mixture of Gaussians, and decision trees have been used. For each classifier, different

values of the design parameters have been used in order to assess the best performances on the test set. As the performances of the classifiers can be evaluated according to the overall error rate, the classification cost, and the sum of false and missed
alarms, different classifiers may be selected according to the considered performance
measure. The experiments carried out clearly showed that no individual classifier was
able to provide the minimum values for all the performance measures, but different
classifiers should be selected according to the performance measure to be minimised.

The first experiment aimed to train a single classifier on the whole data set and to
assess the best performances in terms of overall error rate. Table 2 shows the results
of this experiment. The best results have been attained by an MLP neural network
trained with the standard backprop algorithm. The error rate, the classification cost,
and the sum of the false and missed alarms rates are higher than the best results attained during the KDD99 contest (the best results have been attained by a mixture of
Bagging and Boosting). However, according to the results of the contest reported in
(Elkan, 2000), the single MLP would have been ranked between the fifth and sixth
results.

Table 2. Performances on the test set of the classifier that attained the minimum overall error.
The performances of an MCS made up of three classifiers, each trained on distinct feature sets
are also shown for comparison.

Classifier	Overall error	Cost	false + missed alarm rates
MLP	7.97%	0.2424	6.79%
MCS	7.59%	0.2254	6.34%
Best KDD99 Result	7.29%	0.2331	6.70%

Table 2 also shows the performances attained by an MCS made up of classifiers
trained on distinct feature sets. Each classifier is trained with patterns from all the
services included in the training set. The reported results are related to the combination by majority voting. This result clearly shows that the fusion of information coming from different sources provides lower error than an individual classifier trained on
the entire feature set. In addition, the MCS fusion scheme provides a classification
cost lower than the best KDD99 result. It is worth remarking that this is a more indicative performance measure for this application as it is designed to weight the se-
verity of errors. Finally, the sum of the false and missed alarms produced by an MCS
fusion scheme is lower than that provided by the individual MLP and the best KDD99
result. Thus an MCS based on distinct feature representation is suitable for an effective IDS.

The second experiment was aimed at assessing the performances of the modular
MCS architecture proposed in Section 3. For each service, a feature selection process
has been performed first. A forward selection algorithm has been used with the leave-
one-out option. The number of features selected for each of the three subsets is shown
in Table 3. It is worth noting that for the ICMP and the "Private and Other" services
the content features are not useful for classification. This is motivated by the fact that
the ICMP packets have no data portion, while it is reasonable that the data portion of
the packets related to the "Private and Other" services doesn't help to discriminate
between normal and attack patterns. It is also worth noting that almost all the traffic
features are always useful in the classification process. This result can be explained
by observing that a large number of attacks are made up of a sequence of connections,
each of which does not represent an attack per se. The traffic features take into ac-

count this aspect by coding a number of statistics related to past connections in order to capture malicious sequences of connection.

Table 3. List of selected features for each service

Service	Feature Subsets		
	Intrinsic	Content	Traffic
Http	6	6	19
Ftp	5	9	19
Mail	5	9	19
ICMP	3	-	13
Private&Other	6	-	18
Misc	7	11	19

Table 4 shows the classification results of the modular MCS architecture illustrated in Section 3. For each service, and for each feature subset, a number of classifiers have been trained and the one that attained the minimum overall error has been chosen. Then, the fusion techniques outlined in Section 4 have been applied for each service, and those that attained the minimum overall error has been chosen. In other words, the reported result represent the highest performance achieved on the test set by optimizing the design of the classifiers and the choice of the fusion rule. It is easy to see that the proposed method provided better performances than the best one presented during the KDD99 contest. In particular the proposed MCS architecture outperformed the best KDD99 results in terms of the classification cost, which provides a more effective performance measure than the overall error rate.

Table 4. Performances on the test set of the modular MCS architecture.

Classifier	Overall error	Cost	false + missed alarm rates
Modular MCS (min overall error)	6.82%	0.2074	5.74%
Modular MCS (min false + miss. alarm rate)	7.48%	0.1688	2.54%
Best KDD99 Result	7.29%	0.2331	6.70%

In addition Table 4 also shows the results of the MCS architecture obtained by choosing the classifiers and the fusion rules that minimized the sum of the false and missed alarm rates. It can be easily seen that both the classification cost and the false and missed alarm rates decrease dramatically with respect to the best KDD99 results, at the price of a slightly higher error rate. However, it has already been noticed that the classification cost and the false and missed alarm rates are the more significant performance parameter to assess the effectiveness of an IDS. Thus it follows that the proposed MCS architecture provides a significant step towards the use of pattern recognition tools for the intrusion detection problem.

Table 5 shows the results related to the http service, as an example of the behavior of the MCSs related to different services. For comparison purposes, Table 5 also shows the results of the individual classifier that attained the minimum overall error on the entire feature set, after the feature selection procedure. The overall error and the classification cost attained by the considered fusion rules are always lower than those provided by the individual classifier trained using all the available features. The majority voting rule and the decision templates also provided low rate of false and missed alarms. It is easy to see that the majority-voting rule provides the best performances. It can be concluded that the independence assumption can be deemed

354   Giorgio Giacinto, Fabio Roli, and Luca Didaci

realistic for the classifier trained on the three feature subsets, as far as the http service is concerned. It is worth noting that the majority voting provided the best results for the ftp, the ICMP and the "private & other" services, while the Naive Bayes worked better for the mail services, and the decision templates for the "Misc" group of services. The detailed results have not been reported here for the sake of brevity.

Table 5. Performances related to the http service. The classifier that attained the minimum overall error on the entire feature set is also shown.

	Classifier	Overall error	Cost	false + missed alarm rates
Fusion	Majority	3.41%	0.039	0.54%
	Naive-Bayes	4.22%	0.081	3.87%
	Decision Templates	4.32%	0.083	0.09%
Entire Feature Set	MLP	4.74%	0.093	0.97%

6   Conclusions

In this paper, we have proposed a modular multiple classifier architecture based on distinct feature representation, and experimented a number of different classifiers and fusion rules. The reported results showed that the proposed MCS approach provides a good trade-off between generalization abilities and false alarm generation. In particular, as far as the KDD99 data set is concerned, the proposed MCS architecture provided better performances than those provided by the winner of the KDD99 contest in terms of the classification cost, and the sum of false and missed alarm rates.

Among the fusion rules evaluated, the majority voting rule provided the best results in four out of six MCS modules, as the classifier trained on distinct feature representation can be deemed to be *independent*.

As one of the main criticisms raised from network security experts against previously proposed pattern recognition methods in intrusion detection was related to the high false alarm rates that such methods usually produce (Allen, 2000), we believe that our work can contribute to designing future pattern-recognition-based IDSs that should satisfy the operational requirements, and, consequently, increase the degree of acceptance of network security experts for the pattern recognition approach to intrusion detection. This main conclusion of our work is clearly supported by the reported results, which show that fusion of multiple classifiers allows achieving a good trade-off between generalization abilities and false alarm generation.

References

Allen J., Christie A., Fithen W., McHugh J., Pickel J., Storner E., 2000. State of the Practice of Intrusion Detection Technologies. Tech. Rep. CMU/SEI-99-TR-028, Software Engineering Institute, Carnegie Mellon University.

Axelsson S., 2000. The Base-Rate Fallacy and the Difficulty of Intrusion Detection. ACM Trans. on Information and System Security 3(3), 186-205.

Bonifacio J.M., Cansian A.M., de Carvalho A.C.P.L.F., Moreira E.S., 1998. Neural Networks applied in intrusion detection systems. Proc. of the IEEE World congress on Comp. Intell. (WCCI '98).

Cannady J., 2000. An adaptive neural network approach to intrusion detection and response. PhD Thesis, School of Comp. and Inf. Sci., Nova Southeastern University.

Debar H., Becker M., Siboni D., 1992. A Neural Network Component for an Intrusion Detection System. Proc. of the IEEE Symp. on Research in Security and Privacy, Oakland, CA, USA, 240-250.

Elkan C., 2000. Results of the KDD'99 Classifier Learning. ACM SIGKDD Explorations 1, 63-64.

Ghosh A.K., Schwartzbard A., 1999. A Study in Using Neural Networks for Anomaly and Misuse Detection. Proc. of the USENIX Security Symposium, August 23-26, 1999, Washington, USA.

Giacinto G., Roli F., Bruzzone L., 2001. Combination of Neural and Statistical Algorithms for Supervised Classification of Remote-Sensing Images. Pattern Recognition Letters, 21(5), 385-397.

Giacinto G., Roli F., Didaci L., 2003. Fusion of multiple classifiers for intrusion detection in computer networks. Pattern Recognition Letters (in press).

Kittler J., Hatef M., Duin R.P.W., Matas J., 1998. On Combining Classifiers. IEEE Trans. on Pattern Analysis and Machine Intelligence 20(3), 226-229.

Kuncheva L.I., Bezdek J.C., Duin R.P.W., 2001. Decision Templates for Multiple Classifier Fusion. Pattern Recognition 34(2), 299-314.

Lee S.C., Heinbuch D.V., 2001. Training a Neural-Network Based Intrusion Detector to Recognize Novel Attacks. IEEE Trans. on Systems, Man, and Cybernetics Part A 31, 294-299.

Lee W., Stolfo S.J., 2000. A framework for constructing features and models for intrusion detection systems. ACM Trans. on Inform. and System Security 3(4), 227-261.

McHugh J., Christie A., Allen J., 2000. Defending Yourself: The Role of Intrusion Detection Systems. IEEE Software, Sept./Oct. 2000, 42-51.

Northcutt S., Cooper M., Fearnow M., Frederick K., 2001. Intrusion Signatures and Analysis. New Riders Pub.

Northcutt S., Novak J., 2001. Network Intrusion Detection (2nd ed). New Riders Pub.

Proctor P.E., 2001. The Practical Intrusion Detection Handbook. Prentice Hall.

Roli F., Fumera G., 2002. Analysis of Linear and Order Statistics Combiners for Fusion of Imbalanced Classifiers. Multiple Classifier Systems, Roli and Kittler, Eds. Springer-Verlag, Lecture Notes in Computer Science, vol. 2364, 252-261.

Ryan J., Lin M.J., Miikkulainen R., 1998. Intrusion Detection with Neural Networks. In: Advances in Neural Information Processing Systems 10, M. Jordan et al., Eds., Cambridge, MA: MIT Press, 943-949.

Sharkey A.J.C., 1999. Combining Artificial Neural Nets. Springer.

Xu L., Krzyzak A., Suen C.Y., 1992. Methods for combining multiple classifiers and their applications to handwriting recognition. IEEE Trans. Systems, Man and Cybernetics 22, 418-435.

Yeung D.-J., Ding Y., 2003. Host-based intrusion detection using dynamic and static behavioral models. Patter Recognition 36, 229-243.

Input Space Transformations for Multi-classifier Systems Based on n-tuple Classifiers with Application to Handwriting Recognition

K. Sirlantzis, S. Hoque, and M.C. Fairhurst*

Department of Electronics, University of Kent, Canterbury, Kent, UK
{K.Sirlantzis,S.Hoque,M.C.Fairhurst}@kent.ac.uk

Abstract. In this paper we investigate the properties of novel systems for handwritten character recognition which are based on input space transformations to exploit the advantages of multiple classifier structures. These systems provide an effective solution to the problem of utilising the power of n-tuple based classifiers while, simultaneously, addressing successfully the issues of the trade-off between the memory requirements and the accuracy achieved. Utilizing the flexibility offered by multi-classifier schemes we can subsequently exploit this complementarity of different transformations of the original feature space while at the same time decompose it to simpler input spaces, thus reducing the resources requirements of the sn-tuple classifiers used. Our analysis of the observed behaviour based on Mutual Information estimators between the original and the transformed input spaces showed a direct correspondence of the values of this information measure and the accuracy obtained. This suggests Mutual Information as a useful tool for the analysis and design of multi-classifier systems. The paper concludes with a number of comparisons with results on the same data set achieved by a diverse set of classifiers. Our findings clearly demonstrate the significant gains that can be obtained, simultaneously in performance and memory space reduction, by the proposed systems.

1 Introduction

The study of Multiple Classifier Systems has now grown to an established research area accumulating a significant body of work on the analysis of the procedures contributing to the design of increasingly more successful schemes. Within this body of research, the importance of the input spaces on which the individual classification devices used in a multi-classifier system are trained has been widely recognised. However, these efforts have been mainly focusing either on methods for the selection of subsets of the original feature space (e.g. the random subspace method [6]), or on techniques to partition the set of training examples (e.g. boosting [5] and bagging [1]). Our previous work on the design of high

---

* The authors gratefully acknowledge the support of the EPSRC, UK.

T. Windeatt and F. Roli (Eds.): MCS 2003, LNCS 2709, pp. 356–365, 2003.

performance handwriting recognition systems suggested that input space transformations of the originally available set of measurements can also significantly contribute to the creation of a successful classification system [8,9].

The motivation for the investigation of the potential importance of input space transformations arises from the study of a particular problem in handwritten character recognition, which is still one of the most challenging problems in pattern classification. Among the large number of algorithms that have been developed to tackle this difficult task, some of the simplest yet most successful are the so-called 'n-tuple' based classifiers. Unfortunately, there is usually a trade-off between high performance and either increased computational load or increased memory requirements. The Scanning n-tuple classifier (SNT) [13] is a typical example of a case where superior recognition rates are attained at the expense of significant storage requirements, especially in applications with samples of realistic size. On the other hand, the Frequency Weighted Scheme (FWS) [3] is the opposite example with low memory requirements accompanied by moderate performance. Hence we propose a novel system which can exploit the representational power of sn-tuple based classifiers while addressing successfully the issue of containing storage requirements.

Typically the sn-tuple classifier uses the so-called Freeman chain code which describes the contour of the object of interest, as its input space. The memory requirements of the sn-tuple classifier are mainly defined by the representational complexity (i.e. number of symbols in the code). Fortunately, there exist transformations of this input space able to achieve significant reductions of the representational complexity [8]. Another difficulty is the possible loss of information resulting from applying these transformations. This can be overcome if, after training classifiers on the transformed simpler input spaces, we create a scheme based on the ideas of multiple classifier fusion in which the constituent members are simplified, 'low-requirement' versions of the sn-tuple classifier. Although the individual performances of these classifiers can be poor, it is demonstrated by our findings, that significant gains can be obtained, simultaneously, in performance and storage space reduction, by this method.

Although our previous proposals have been shown to be effective, the fact that every transformation of the initial feature space can cause some loss of information which is reflected in the final performance, is worth special consideration. The information loss due to one transformation can be potentially counteracted by complementary information captured through a different transformation technique. Utilizing the flexibility offered by multi-classifier schemes we can subsequently exploit this complementarity of different transformations of the original feature space while at the same time decompose it to simpler input spaces, thus reducing the resources requirements of the sn-tuple classifiers used. The conditions under which such combinations are effective and advantageous have not yet been investigated systematically, and this is addressed here. We have, already, at our disposal three transformation methods, two of which have a common background while the third is based on totally different principles. In this initial set of experiments we also use an FWS scheme which uses the raw binary character images as input space and, as noted has low memory overheads. In our preliminary analysis of the resulting multi-classifier schemes we considered mutual information between the original and the transformed input spaces as a natural measure of possible information loss and analyze performance based on statistical estimators of this measure.

In the following sections we initially give a brief description of two classification devices and the three input space transformations we propose. Then we present the multiple classifier system in which the group of classifiers trained on the transformed spaces will be constituent components. To demonstrate the statistical properties of our schemes, we discuss results obtained over a series of 10-fold cross-validation experiments and the estimated mutual information statistic. Finally, we present a number of comparisons with results on the same data set achieved by a diverse set of classifiers reported in the literature.

2   Description of the Proposed System

2.1   The Classification Devices Used

Frequency Weighed ntuple Scheme (FWS): In a conventional n-tuple classifier, the n-tuples are formed by selecting multiple sets of n distinct locations from the pattern space. Each n-tuple thus sees an n-bit feature derived from the pattern. For classification, a pattern is assigned to that class for which the number of matching features found in the training set is maximum. The training process, therefore, requires remembering the occurrences of different features as seen by individual n-tuples. This is usually achieved by setting a 'flag' bit in a large memory array [3]. The FWS is the simplest enhancement of the basic n-tuple classification system. In this, instead of setting the flag to record the occurrence of a certain feature in the training set, the relative frequencies are recorded. The sum of these frequencies corresponding to a particular test image determine its class label. The FWS forms different simple discriminators according to different n-tuple configurations the outputs of which are finally fused by a maximum selector combination rule. In that sense FWS can be considered collectively to form another group of multiple classifiers trained on a different transformation of the original input space which is the raw binary image of the characters.

Scanning n-tuple Classifier (sn-tuple): The Scanning n-tuple Classifier is an n-tuple based classifier. It has been introduced by Lucas et al[13] and is shown to have achieved very high recognition rates while retaining many of the benefits of the simple n-tuple algorithm. In an sn-tuple system, each sn-tuple defines a set of relative offsets between its input points which then scans over a 1-D representation of the character image. This uni-dimensional model of the character image is obtained by tracing the contour edges of the image and representing the path by Freeman chain-codes [4]. In the case of multiple contours, all strings are mapped to a single string by concatenation after discarding the positional information. As different characters produce contour strings of widely varying lengths, all these chains are proportionately expanded to a predefined fixed length.

2.2 Transformations of the Contour Chain-Code String

The first two transformation strategies have already been reported by the authors [7,8,9,17], but are summarized as follows:

Ordered Decomposition Technique: Both in this and the next transformation methods, the Freeman direction codes are represented in binary. (It is also possible to use other forms of binary notation, for example, Gray coding, etc., to express the direction codes prior to decomposition and classifier performance is sometimes dependent on this choice. See [7] for details). Since there are 8 possible distinct direction codes, 3-bit binary numbers are sufficient to represent them. For Ordered decomposition (also known as bit plane decomposition, the chain-code string is decomposed into 3 separate strings (called Layers) such that Layer-i is composed only of the ith bits of the corresponding direction code.

Random Decomposition: In contrast to the Ordered decomposition, in the Random Decomposition technique (which was inspired by the Random Subspace Method [6], as well as the chromosome generation process in Genetic Algorithms [9]), bits for decomposed layers are chosen arbitrarily from the Freeman direction-codes. Since the same bits must always be chosen from a given contour position, an array of randomly selected numbers from the set $\{0,1,2\}$ is generated identifying the bit to be sampled from the corresponding chain element. An arbitrary number of templates can be generated, hence the random transformation approach can create many different binary layers, while for the ordered scheme only as many layers as the number of bits representing each symbol in original chain code can be generated.

Directional Filtering Transformation: The Directional Quantization is, in fact, a filter detecting the presence, as well as the location, of a particular direction code in a given contour chain. Since there are 8 possible Freeman directions, only 8 directional layers can be created. If C_f denote a contour chain using Freeman codes d_k such that, $C_f = d_1d_2\ldots d_k\ldots d_N$ where $d_k \in \{0,1,\ldots,7\}$, and N is the length of chain. If i is the direction of interest, then after filtering, $C_d^i = b_1b_2\ldots b_k\ldots b_N$, where $b_k = 1$ if $d_k = i$, otherwise $b_k = 0$.

For example, the Freeman chain-coded fragment '...566566566710...' will be transformed to '...100100100000...' if the direction of interest is direction-5, or to '...011011011000...' for direction-6. These corresponds to input data for the decomposed layers 5 and 6 respectively.

2.3 Measuring Mutual Information

The estimation of Mutual Information between two sets of features is based on entropy metrics and information theoretic considerations, as described in [14].

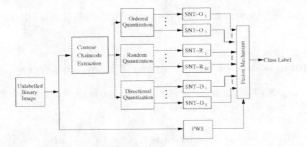

Fig. 1. A Schematic of the Proposed Systems

The Mutual Information values we present are expressed in bits since they are calculated using base-2 logarithms. The choice of Mutual Information as measure appropriate to examine the properties of our transformed feature or input spaces is additionally supported by the recent development of methods which use this as a criterion to select effective nonlinear transforms of raw features in pattern recognition problems [18].

2.4 Proposed Multi-classifier Architecture

The proposed recognition system is illustrated in Figure 1. It is a parallel combination of many groups of sn-tuple classifier implementations. Unlike the conventional sn-tuple [13], the classifiers used in the proposed system are all trained on the transformed input spaces obtained from the Freeman chain-code. In our experiments, we attempted all possible combinations of these groups/components with or without the FWS classifier. The best performing structure proved to be the one actually illustrated in Figure 1 which include FWS along with all three different transformations groups of classifiers. Finally, the decision fusion stage combines the outputs of these groups of individual classifiers and generates a final class label for the test image.

3   Experiments and Discussion of Results

A database of pre-segmented handwritten character images has been used for the experiments [11]. This database consists only of digits and uppercase letters with no distinctions made between '0'/'O' and '1'/'I' character pairs. There are 300 binary images for each character class, each of resolution 24×16 pixels. This dataset is randomly partitioned into two disjoint sets for training and testing. For the experiments reported here, 150 images per character class were used for training. Experiments were conducted in two task domains, the first involving only the digits and the second significantly more difficult involving all 34 alphanumeric characters. For multi-classifier combination, five fusion schemes were investigated. These are sum, median, min, max, and simple majority voting. The choice of simple, fixed rules were made for higher interpretability of the produced results. Details of these rules can be found in [12]. All the tables presented

Table 1. Recognition performance for the individual classifiers (error rates in %)

Task Domain	Transformation Type	Layer No.									
		1	2	3	4	5	6	7	8	9	10
Numeric	Ordered (O)	23.89	21.28	22.45	–	–	–	–	–	–	–
	Random (R)	25.31	27.39	27.09	27.79	26.21	25.97	27.23	27.60	26.21	27.44
	Directional (D)	30.48	39.81	27.68	49.95	27.47	43.49	23.92	45.15	–	–
Alpha-numeric	Ordered (O)	44.92	40.68	42.09	–	–	–	–	–	–	–
	Random (R)	43.05	43.54	42.33	44.29	41.91	41.93	44.32	45.12	43.07	45.04
	Directional (D)	56.71	67.90	46.50	68.70	51.95	66.58	41.80	64.64	–	–

Table 2. Fusion of the sn-tuple classifier trained on the transformed spaces

Fusion rules applied	Classification Error Rates					
	Numerals			Alphanumerics		
	Ordered	Random	Directional	Ordered	Random	Directional
Sum	11.41%	17.28%	10.93%	23.69%	30.45%	22.10%
Median	13.07%	17.44%	12.43%	28.30%	31.04%	26.89%
Majority Vote	15.73%	17.09%	13.95%	34.97%	31.47%	31.21%

include performance statistics averaged over the 10-fold cross validation experiments performed on the unseen test sets from the above database,consisting of 75 images per class[1].

Table 1 shows the mean error rates achieved by the individual classifiers trained on the different input data (layers) produced by the decomposition for each one of the three transformation methods we described. Note that the original sn-tuple (trained on untransformed input space) achieved 4.6% and 12.4% error rates for the two task domains. There are two important observations to be made: (a) Both in the 10 class (digits) and the 34-class (alphanumeric) cases, significant performance differences can be observed among the classifiers trained on different layers only for the directional method. It seems that layers 1,3,5,7 corresponding to the main directions (i.e., directions along the Cartesian axes) are more informative and hence more successful in discriminating the shapes of different characters. (b) we see that directional filtering is the worst performing among the three decomposition schemes as far as individual layer performances are concerned. However, Table 2 shows that, for all the fusion rules tested, the combination of the classifiers trained on the layers resulting from directional filtering exhibit significantly better performance than the other two transformation methods in both tasks.

Table 3 presents error rates corresponding to all possible combinations of the groups of classifiers (based on the sum-rule) trained on the layers obtained by the three input space transformation methods as well as the FWS, as an example of a classifier using a distinctly diverse input space (i.e., raw images). For ease of comparison, we also included the original sn-tuple and the FWS results

---

[1] 75 patterns per class were used for the evaluation phase of the GA algorithm and consequently these samples were not used in testing the proposed algorithms to retain comparability of the results.

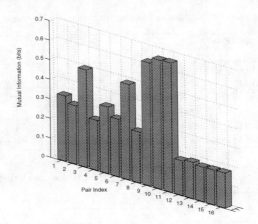

Fig. 2. Mutual Information (in bits) for pairs of the original Freeman chain code data set and each one of the sets corresponding to the decomposed 'layers' produced using the three transformation methods (Pair indexes are explained in the text)

in the first two rows. Before proceeding to discuss further the results in this Table, it is important to observe that since, as shown in Table 1, the individual classifiers of the directional layering are the worst performers, one should reasonably expect that if they do not encapsulate information complementary to that of the classifiers obtained from the other two decomposition schemes, their combination should not result in any performance improvement. However, all combinations presented in Table 3 exhibit significant improvements not only with respect to individual classifiers but also with respect to the combinations in Table 2 and the original FWS and sn-tuple. This observation, we believe, supports the existence of complementarity in the information captured by the three decomposition methods presented.

Figure 2 shows the estimated Mutual Information values (in bits) for pairs of the original Freeman chain code input data set and each one of the data sets corresponding to the decomposed 'layers' produced using the three transformation methods defined previously. Pairs 1-8 correspond to the directional technique, pairs 9-11 to the ordered decomposition and pairs 12-16 to the random transformation method. It is not difficult to observe the following: (a) There is a direct correspondence between the qualitative characteristics of the Mutual Information values and the accuracies of the individual classifiers for each of the transformation schemes presented in Table 1. For instance, the diversity in accuracies among the classifiers/layers in the directional scheme is almost identically reflected in the diversity of the Mutual Information values corresponding to these same layers. (b) As was expected, the classifiers obtained by the Ordered technique which have the best individual performances correspond also to input spaces which have the highest Mutual Information with the original Freeman chain code input space. (c) Finally, from a careful examination of Table 2 in conjunction with Figure 2, we can observe that transformation methods

Table 3. Mean error rates of the proposed combinations using the 'mean' rule

Row No.	Layers Fused	Classification Error Rates	
		Numerals	Alphanumerics
1	*Original* Sn-tuple	4.59%	12.42%
2	FWS	10.00%	22.28%
3	SNT-D + SNT-R	4.08%	10.96%
4	SNT-D + SNT-O	3.28%	9.93%
5	SNT-O + SNT-R	12.69%	24.74%
6	SNT-D + SNT-O + SNT-R	2.96%	8.96%
7	FWS + SNT-O	2.56%	8.73%
8	FWS + SNT-R	2.91%	10.09%
9	FWS + SNT-D	4.96%	13.65%
10	FWS + SNT-O + SNT-R	3.04%	9.27%
11	FWS + SNT-O + SNT-D	1.73%	6.84%
12	FWS + SNT-D + SNT-R	2.08%	7.33%
13	FWS + SNT-O + SNT-R + SNT-D	1.28%	5.65%

which produce layers (input sets) with approximately uniform distribution of the Mutual Information level values among the members of the group (such as the Ordered and Random methods) are not as successful, when the group members are combined, as those resulting in a more diverse distribution of the Mutual Information values among the transformed input spaces obtained. Furthermore, the combination of the two groups based on the former type of transformed inputs can be seen in Table 3 (row 5) to be the less successful of all possible group combinations included in the Table. The same can be observed for the combination of these two groups with the alternative classifier we used, i.e. the FWS (see row 10 of the same Table). These observations hold despite the fact that the three input spaces based on the Ordered transformation have the highest values of Mutual Information and hence the lowest loss of information with respect to the original chain code. It seems, again, that diversity, as expressed by the Mutual Information values' distribution (such as the one observed in Directional layering), has precedence in the determining the combination accuracy.

Finally in Table 4, additionally to the error rates of the proposed architecture, error rates achieved by four other classifiers are shown. The MLP is the standard multi-layer perceptron [10] trained using Back-propagation learning. The reported MLP had 40 hidden nodes and used zonal pixel density as the input feature. The MPC is a Maximum-likelihood-based [15] statistical classifier which explores possible cluster formation with respect to a distance measure. The particular implementation reported here used the Mahalanobis distance metric calculated on geometric moments (up to 7th order) of the binary image as features. The MWC [2] is an n-tuple based system where features are extracted from a sub-image isolated by a scanning window. The reported results are based on an MWC using a 21×13 pixel window and 12-tuples. The GA is a parallel multiple classifier system optimized using genetic algorithm techniques, originally introduced in [16]. It is readily evident from Table 4 that the proposed layout is capable of producing very high performance. Even when compared to

364   K. Sirlantzis, S. Hoque, and M.C. Fairhurst

Table 4. Comparison with Different Classifiers

Classifiers	Classification Error Rates	
	Numerals	Alphanumerics
Proposed system	**1.28%**	**5.65%**
MPC	15.00%	21.29%
MLP	7.20%	18.22%
MWC	5.84%	14.59%
GA	3.40%	8.62%

the GA which uses a trainable fusion scheme, the proposed system performed very favourably although it is using a very simple fixed (i.e., non-trainable) fusion mechanism. The proposed architecture outperformed the GA system in both classification tasks.

4   Conclusion

The main purpose of this paper was to investigate the properties of novel systems for handwritten character recognition which use input space transformations to exploit the advantages made available by the multiple classifier structures. We have chosen as an illustrative application domain the particular problems of high memory requirements in exchange for higher accuracy arising in the use of the sn-tuple classifiers. Our experiments demonstrated that input space transformations in this particular exercise (although we believe our finding are more generally applicable and will investigate this) form a useful tool for the design and creation of recognition systems with highly desirable characteristics and performance. Further analysis of the behaviour of the proposed multi-classifier structures based on Mutual Information estimators between the original and the transformed input spaces showed a direct correspondence of the values of this information measure and the accuracy obtained from the examined combination schemes. This suggests Mutual Information as a useful tool for the design and analysis of multi-classifier systems to address specific problems in realistic applications.

One of the additional merits of the proposed architecture is in the savings of physical memory space. The conventional sn-tuple implementation demands the presence of a large physical memory (in the order of 8^n, where n is the tuple size) whereas, for sn-tuple classifiers using the transformed feature space, this requirement is in the order of 2^n. Thus, in spite of using 21 distinct sn-tuple classifiers, the total memory requirement is slightly more than 2% of the physical memory needed by a single sn-tuple system using the original chain code. The last point of concern may be the classification speed. However, the main part of computational load in an sn-tuple classifier comes from the extraction of the contour chain code from the off-line image while the load for the actual classification task is very small. In all our proposed schemes, the chain code needs to be extracted only once (as in conventional sn-tuple classification). The additional computation imposed by the input space transformations is minimal, and hence classification by the individual sn-tuple classifiers is very fast and the overall computational speed is comparable to that of a conventional sn-tuple classifier.

References

1. L. Breiman. Bagging predictors. *Machine Learning*, 24(2):123–140, 1996.
2. M. C. Fairhurst and M. S. Hoque. Moving window classifier: Approach to off-line image recognition. *Electronics Letters*, 36(7):628–630, March 2000.
3. M. C. Fairhurst and H. M. S. Abdel Whab. An approach to performance optimisation in frequency-weighted memory network pattern classifiers. *Electronics Letters*, 23:1116–1118, 1987.
4. H. Freeman. Computer processing of line-drawing images. *ACM Computing Surveys*, 6(1):57–98, March 1974.
5. Y. Freund and R.E. Schapire. Experiments with a new boosting algorithm. In *Machine Learning: Proceedings of the 13th Int. Conference*, pages 148–156, 1996.
6. T. K. Ho. The random subspace method for constructing decision forests. *IEEE Trans Pattern Analysis and Machine Intelligence*, 20(8):832–844, 1998.
7. M. S. Hoque and M. C. Fairhurst. Face recognition using the moving window classifier. In *Proceedings of the 11th British Machine Vision Conference (BMVC2000)*, volume 1, pages 312–321, Bristol, UK., September 2000.
8. S. Hoque, K. Sirlantzis, and M. C. Fairhurst. Bit plane decomposition and the scanning n-tuple classifier. In *Proc. of 8th Intl. Workshop on Frontiers in Handwriting Recognition*, pages 207–211, NOTL, Ontario, Canada, 6-8 August 2002.
9. S. Hoque, K. Sirlantzis, and M. C. Fairhurst. Intelligent chain-code quantization for multiple classifier-based shape recognition. In John A. Bullinaria, editor, *Proc. of the 2002 U.K. Workshop on Computational Intelligence (UKCI-02)*, pages 61–67, Birmingham, UK, September 2002.
10. A. K. Jain, J. Mao, and K. M. Mohiuddin. Artificial neural networks: A tutorial. *Computer*, pages 31–44, March 1996.
11. Digital Systems Research Group (DSRG), Department of Electronics, University of Kent, Canterbury CT2 7NT, United Kingdom.
12. J. Kittler, M. Hatef, R. P. Duin, and J. Matas. On combining classifiers. *IEEE Transactions on Pattern Analysis and Machine Intelligence*, 20(3):226–239, 1998.
13. S. Lucas and A. Amiri. Statistical syntactic methods for high performance ocr. *IEE Proceedings Vision, Image and Signal Processing*, 143(1):23–30, February 1996.
14. D. Michie, D. J. Spiegelhalter, and C. C. Taylor, editors. *Machine Learning, Neural and Statistical Classification*. Ellis Horwood, New York, 1994.
15. R. Schalkoff. *Pattern Recognition: Statistical, Structural and Neural Approaches*. John Wiley and Sons, New York, 1992.
16. K. Sirlantzis, M. C. Fairhurst, and M. S. Hoque. Genetic algorithms for multiclassifier system configuration: A case study in character recognition. In J. Kittler and F. Roli, editors, *Multiple Clasifier Systems*, pages 99–108. Springer, 2001.
17. K. Sirlantzis, S. Hoque, and M. C. Fairhurst. Classifier diversity estimation in a multiclassifier recognition system based on binary feature quantization. In *Proceedings of 4th International Conference on Recent Advances in Soft Computing (RASC 2002)*, pages 97–101, Nottingham, UK., 12-13 December 2002.
18. K. Torkkola. Nonlinear feature transforms using maximum mutual information. In *Proceedings of the International Joint Conference on Neural Networks (IJCNN'01)*, pages 2756–2761, Washington D.C., USA., 15-19 July 2001.

Building Classifier Ensembles
for Automatic Sports Classification

Edward Jaser, Josef Kittler, and William Christmas

Centre for Vision, Speech and Signal Processing, University of Surrey
Guildford GU2 7XH, UK
{E.Jaser,J.Kittler,W.Christmas}@eim.surrey.ac.uk
tel:+44 (0)1483 689294, fax:+44 (0)1483 686031

Abstract. Technology has been playing a major role in facilitating the capture, storage and communication of multimedia data, resulting in a large amount of video material being archived. To ensure its usability, the problem of automatic annotation of videos has been attracting the attention of much researches. This paper describes one aspect of the development of a novel system which will provide a semantic annotation of sports video. The system relies upon the concept of "cues" which attach semantic meaning to low-level features computed on the video and audio. We will discuss the problem of classifying shots, based on the cues they contain, into the sports they belong to. We adopt the multiple classifier system (MCS) approach to improve classification performance. Experimental results on sports video materials provided by the BBC demonstrate the benefits of the MCS approach in relation to this difficult classification problem.

1 Introduction

There is a vast amount of sports footage being recorded and stored every day. Ideally, all this sports video should be annotated, and the meta-data generated on it should be stored in a database along with the video data. Such a system would allow an operator to retrieve any shot or important event within a shot at a later date. Also, the level of annotation provided by the system should be adequate to facilitate simple text-based queries. Such a system has many uses, such as in the production of television sport programmes and documentaries.

Due to the large amount of material being generated, manual annotation is both impractical and very expensive. However, automatic annotation is a very demanding and extremely challenging computer vision task as it involves high-level scene interpretation. It is unlikely that an efficient, fully automated video annotation system will be realised in the near future.

This paper describes one aspect of the development of a novel system which will provide a semantic annotation of sports video. This annotation process segments the sports video into semantic categories (e.g. type of sport) and permits the user to formulate text-based queries to retrieve events that are significant to that particular sport (e.g. goal, foul). The system will aid an operator in the

T. Windeatt and F. Roli (Eds.): MCS 2003, LNCS 2709, pp. 366–374, 2003.
© Springer-Verlag Berlin Heidelberg 2003

generation of high-level annotation for incoming sports video. The basic building blocks of the system are low-level audio and video analysis tools, which we term cue-detectors. Examples of cue-detectors include: grass, swimming pool lanes, ocean, sprint frequency, referee whistle and crowd cheering.

In this paper we discuss the classification of shots into sports categories they belong to using the cues that the shot contains. Four learning algorithms are used to build the classification models. We discuss improving the classification performance by building classifier ensembles using two state-of-the-art methods: bagging and boosting. We compare the performance of the individual classifiers as well as the performance of the ensembles created.

The paper is organised as follows. In Section 2 we briefly describe the cue detector methods used to create the necessary cues in this study. The problem of classifying shots into the sports category is addressed in Section 3. In Section 4 we overview two approaches for building ensembles of classifiers, Bagging and Boosting. The results of experiments designed to demonstrate the system performance and the improvement in performance achieved by adopting ensemble methods are presented in Section 5. The paper is concluded in Section 6.

2   Cue Detectors

The objective in the automatic annotation of video material is to provide indexing material that describes as usefully as possible the material itself. In much of the previous work in this area (for example [4]), the annotation consisted of the output of various feature detectors. By itself, this information bears no semantic connection to the actual scene content — it is simply the output of some image processing algorithms. In this project we are taking the process one stage further. By means of a set of training processes, we aim to generate an association between the feature detector outputs and the occurrence of actual scene features. Thus for example we might train the system to associate the output of a texture feature detector with crowds of people in the scene. We can then use this mechanism to generate confidence values for the presence of a crowd in a scene, based on the scene texture. We denote the output of this process as a "cue". These cues can then be combined to generate higher-level information, e.g. the type of sport being played.

We have developed many different cue detection methods. In this section we briefly discuss three visual cue generation methods. Each method can be used to form a number of different cue-detectors provided that suitable training data is available. These methods are:

- neural network
- multimodal neighbourhood signature
- texture codes

and they are briefly described in the following subsections.

2.1   Neural Network

Each cue-detector is a neural network trained on colour and texture descriptors computed at a pixel level on image regions containing the cue of interest (see [6]) and on image regions which are known not to contain the cue. The resulting trained network is then able to distinguish between the features of cue and non-cue pixels. A high output represents the case when the feature vector of the pixel belongs to the same distribution as the cue and vice-versa.

To check for the presence of a cue in a test image, the same colour and texture features are computed for each test image pixel and the feature vector is passed to the neural network. If many high outputs are observed then this gives an indication of how likely it is that the given cue is present in the image. Cues suitable for this method include ClayTennisSurface and AthleticsTrack.

2.2   Multimodal Neighbourhood Signature

In the Multimodal Neighbourhood Signature approach (described in detail in [5]), object colour structure is represented by a set of invariant features computed from image neighbourhoods with a multimodal colour density function. The method is image-based – the representation is computed from a set of examples of the object of interest, a cue in this context.

In the implemented method, MNS are sets of invariant colour pairs corresponding to pairs of coordinates of the located density function modes from each neighbourhood. The MNS signatures of all the example images are then merged into a composite one by superimposing the features (colour pairs). Considering each colour pair as an independent object descriptor (a detector), its discriminative ability is measured on a pre-selected training set consisting of positive and negative example images. A simple measure, the absolute difference of true and false positive percentages is computed. Finally, the n most discriminative detectors are selected to represent the object of interest. For the reported experiments n was set to 3.

For testing, we view each detector as a point in the detector space. A hypersphere with radius h is defined around each point. Given test image of the object, measurements are likely to lie inside the detector hyperspheres. A binary n-tuple is computed for each test image, each binary digit assigned 1 if at least one test measurement was within the corresponding detector sphere, 0 otherwise. One of 2^n possible n-tuples are the measurements output from the matching stage. The relative frequency of each possible n-tuple over the positive and negative cue examples of the training set define an estimate of the probability of each measurement given the cue and not given the cue respectively. These 2 numbers are output to the decision making module.

2.3   Texture Codes

The texture-based cue-detector consists of two components: a training phase, in which a model for the cue is created using ground truth, and the cue extractor (see [3]). In the training stage, template regions from the key-frames are selected for each cue. Several templates are needed for each cue to account for appearance variations. Textural descriptors are extracted from the templates using a texture analysis module based on Gabor filters. These descriptors, with the number of occurrences, form the model for the cue.

In the testing mode, the whole image is presented to the texture analysis module. Then, by comparing the result with the model, a coarse detection component selects the three templates which are most likely to be visually similar to an area of the image being annotated. The similarity is evaluated using the histogram intersection. We increase the computational efficiency by hashing the meta-data; this also enables us to compute the similarity measure only for templates which share descriptors with the input image. A localisation component finally identifies the areas of the image which the selected templates match most closely, and the image location which yields the best match confidence is retained. The highest confidence, with its location, are the output for the cue.

3 Sport Shots Classification

In this section we discuss classifying shots into the sport categories using the cue values extracted by the cue-detectors. Let us suppose that we have a set of m trained cue-detectors. This set of detectors is built using the neural net (NN), texture code (TC) and/or multi-modal neighbourhood signatures (MNS) methods described previously in Section 2. The cues have been chosen so that they are representative of objects occurring within the set of n sports being investigated. The cue-detectors operate on a key-frame image and generate two pdf values per cue which are then, assuming equals prior probabilities, used to compute the posterior probability $P(C|x)$ as:

$$P(C|x) = \frac{p(x|C)}{p(x|C) + p(x|\bar{C})} \tag{1}$$

where x denotes the measurement vector used by the cue-detector. Thus, each shot is represented by a vector $\mathcal{S} = (\mathcal{C}_1, \mathcal{C}_2, ..., \mathcal{C}j, ..., \mathcal{C}_m)$ where $\mathcal{C}_j$ is the mean value of the posterior probabilities computed by the jth cue-detector on the key frames that belong to the shot $\mathcal{S}$.

In this paper, we selected four different learning algorithms to build the models for solving the classification problem in hand. An implementation of the C4.5 algorithm [7] for building decision trees, neural networks, naive Bayes and k-nearest neighbour (k-NN) algorithms were trained using a set of training shots. The performance of each classifier is discussed in Section 5.

4 Ensemble Methods

Much research has shown that the classification performance of classifiers constructed using multiple classifiers system approaches is superior to that of individual classifiers. In this section we will summarise two state-of-the-art methods widely used in constructing classifier ensembles: bagging and boosting.

4.1 Bagging

In this method, proposed by Breiman [1], the training algorithm is used to construct T individual classifiers using T training sets (bootstrap) each of which is drawn with replacement from the original training set. The classifiers are then aggregated by voting to form a final classifier. The bagging algorithm can be summarised as follows:

Algorithm 1: Bagging

---

1. construct a set of instances I for training purposes
2. For $t = 1$ to T do:
   - Create bootstraps I_t from I.
   - Use the learning algorithm to build a classifier CL_t from I_t.
3. Classify new instance by majority vote of the T trained classifiers.

4.2 Boosting

In this paper we are investigating a version of boosting (AdaBoost.M1) proposed by Freund and Schapire [2]. Boosting attaches a weight to each instance in the training set. The higher the weight the more attention the instance will receive from the learning algorithm. The weights get updated at each trial in a way that reflects the performance at that trial. After T trials, the classifiers constructed are combined as in bagging except that the vote casted by individual classifier is weighted according to its accuracy. The algorithm can be summarised as follows:

Algorithm 2: AdaBoost.M1

---

1. Construct a set I_1 of m instances for training purposes
2. For each instance i in I_1, assign weight $w_i = 1/m$
3. For $t = 1$ to T do:
   - Use the learning algorithm to build a classifier CL_t from I_t.
   - Calculate error $\epsilon_t = \sum_{i \in \mathcal{E}} w_i$, where $\mathcal{E}$ is the set of misclassified samples.
   - If $\epsilon_t = 0$ or $\epsilon_t \geq 0.5$ then stop and set $T = t - 1$
   - Compute $\beta_t = \epsilon_t/(1 - \epsilon_t)$
   - Create I_{t+1} from I_t by multiplying w_i for each $i \in$ set of correctly classified samples by β_t and normalise
   - Assign weight $log(1/\beta_t)$ to CL_t
4. Classify new instance by the weighted majority vote of the T trained classifiers.

Table 1. Sports investigated

Boxing	S_1
Cycling	S_2
Gymnastics	S_3
Hockey	S_4
Interview	S_5
Judo	S_6
Medal Ceremony	S_7
Shooting	S_8
Swimming	S_9
Taekwondo	S_{10}
Tennis	S_{11}
Track Events	S_{12}
Weight-lifting	S_{13}
Yachting	S_{14}

5   Experimental Results

Experiments were conducted on a database comprising video material from the 1992 Barcelona Olympic games. The material includes twelve Olympic sport disciplines, medal ceremonies and interviews (Table 1). The experiments have been performed using the WEKA data mining suite [10].

There are 2253 shots in the data base. Two configurations were considered. In the first configuration, 30% of the data base was used for training purposes, leaving the remaining 70% to serve as a test set. In the second configuration we increased the data available for training to include 50% of the data base to study the effects of providing more training data on the performance of each classifier as well as of the ensembles. In both configurations the experiments were repeated 10 times and the average performance was reported. The number of iterations for bagging and boosting T was set to 20. Although choosing T greater than 20 might increase the accuracy gain, it was shown [8] that choosing T to be between 10 and 25 can achieve a significant improvement over a single classifier. We did an experiment to see the effect of T on bagging and boosting using decision trees. We noticed that out of 100 iterations the lowest misclassification rate was recorded on the 48th iteration for bagging and the 82nd iteration for boosting. For both methods however, we noticed that to significantly improve the performance of a decision tree the number of iterations need to be greater than 10.

The results of the experiments are summarised in Table 2 and Table 3. The associated standard deviations suggest that even improvements by a percentage point are statistically significant as the standard error of the sampling distribution of means is 3 (i.e. $\sqrt{no.\ of\ experiments\ -1}$) times smaller than the reported standard deviations.

From the first configuration results we can see that, as a single classifier, neural network performance was the best. Naive Bayes classifier, on the other hand, delivered the worst results. When we used bagging, decision trees recorded the

Table 2. Configuration 1: Correct classification rates (Standard deviation)

	Single Classifier	Bagging	Boosting
naive Bayes	40.74 (2.97)	47.11 (3.00)	43.12 (3.58)
k-NN	57.37 (2.19)	60.98 (1.86)	53.92 (2.15)
Decision Trees	54.57 (1.61)	65.00 (0.80)	**67.38** (0.97)
Neural Network	**59.40** (1.80)	**66.08** (1.12)	67.14 (1.39)

Table 3. Configuration 2: Correct classification rates (Standard deviation)

	Single Classifier	Bagging	Boosting
naive Bayes	36.86 (1.98)	42.94 (1.67)	39.91 (2.97)
k-NN	58.23 (2.19)	63.92 (1.14)	54.38 (2.85)
Decision Trees	56.58 (1.96)	67.50 (0.88)	**70.33** (1.22)
Neural Network	**58.50** (1.89)	**68.53** (1.35)	69.39 (1.12)

highest improvement on classification rate (10.43%). The same behaviour was observed when we experimented with boosting, the decision trees classification rate improving by (12.81%). Neural network classification was also improved by bagging and boosting. In both cases boosting performed better than bagging. However, an ensemble of naive Bayes classifiers or k-NN classifiers built by bagging proved to perform better than boosting. This is consistent with the fact that, for the given dimensionality defined by the number of cues (37) and the number of classes, we are dealing with a small sample size problem. Decision trees, which implicitly group classes to super classes at the higher levels of the tree, effectively increase the number of training samples per class and are therefore more likely to benefit from boosting. In the case of neural networks, these classifiers are inherently unstable due to slow learning rates and either method of data set manipulation will result in performance improvements. We did not expect the k-NN classifier to improve by boosting as the boosting process tends to increase the overlap of the estimated posteriori class probabilities which will lead to degraded performance. This has been confirmed by the results in both configurations.

The results of the second configuration experiments, shown in Table 3, demonstrate that both neural network and k-NN achieved the best results of the single classifiers. The performance of the naive Bayes classifier did not improve by increasing the number of instances for training purposes but actually deteriorated. When we experimented with bagging and boosting, we noticed that it exhibited the same behaviour as in the first configuration.

An experiment was conducted to combine the four base-level classifiers instead of bagging or boosting each of them individually. The Meta Decision Trees (MDTs), introduced by Todorovski and Dzeroski [9], for combining multiple experts was used in the experiment. MDTs share the same structure with decision trees. The decision nodes specify tests to be carried out on individual attributes. Leaf nodes predict which base-level classifier to use for classifying an instance. For the first configuration, using MDTs achieved a classification rate

Table 4. Confusion matrix for sports classification of decision trees ensemble using boosting. 50% of the shots in the data base were used for training. Error = 29.64%

	S_1	S_2	S_3	S_4	S_5	S_6	S_7	S_8	S_9	S_{10}	S_{11}	S_{12}	S_{13}	S_{14}
S_1	**23**	0	0	0	3	1	4	2	0	4	0	2	2	1
S_2	1	**6**	0	1	0	0	8	0	3	0	1	8	0	0
S_3	0	0	**18**	0	3	0	8	0	1	0	0	4	0	0
S_4	0	1	1	**79**	1	0	22	1	2	0	0	7	3	0
S_5	1	0	0	0	**47**	1	8	1	0	0	0	3	2	0
S_6	0	2	0	0	2	**35**	9	1	0	4	0	0	0	1
S_7	5	1	1	5	7	3	**169**	4	0	1	2	7	11	2
S_8	1	1	1	3	2	0	10	**14**	0	2	2	2	1	0
S_9	0	1	1	0	0	0	12	0	**135**	1	0	3	2	8
S_{10}	3	0	0	1	0	1	6	0	2	**28**	0	1	0	0
S_{11}	0	0	0	3	0	0	10	3	0	0	**32**	4	5	0
S_{12}	0	1	1	3	0	0	13	0	3	0	1	**132**	1	4
S_{13}	1	1	1	5	4	0	13	0	3	0	0	0	**30**	2
S_{14}	0	0	0	0	0	0	1	0	4	0	0	1	0	**45**

of (59.23%). In the second configuration, the classification rate obtained was (59.25%). In both configurations, bagging and boosting k-NN, decision trees and neural network classifiers for the problem in hand achieved better results than using MDTs for combining the different classifiers.

Table 4 presents the confusion matrix of one of the experiments conducted using a boosted decision tree. We notice that the classification performance on some sports was good (i.e. swimming, yachting and track events). However, the results for some sports (i.e. cycling, shooting, weight lifting and gymnastics) were disappointing. For cycling, weight-lifting and gymnastics, this can be explained by the fact that we do not extract cues that are sufficiently characteristic of them. From the list of cues in Table 5 we can see that weight-lifting and gymnastics are not represented, and cycling is represented with two cues. For shooting, from the shots database we found that, out of 74 shots representing shooting, only 13 contain a view of the cue Shooting Target which was the only shooting cue.

6   Conclusion

In this paper we have described a process for the automatic sports classifications within the ASSAVID system. We demonstrated that the system, which relies upon the concept of "cues" that attach semantic meaning to low-level features, is working well, especially if we discount the errors injected by the usually ambiguous content of medal ceremony which often includes the cues of the respective disciplines. We demonstrated as well that adopting the multiple classifiers system approach of bagging and boosting can significantly improve the classification performance in this application. The results also provides a feedback on the capacity of the existing cues to represent the various sport categories. This feedback will be taken into account in future studies.

374   Edward Jaser, Josef Kittler, and William Christmas

Table 5. Cues

MNS Cues	NeuralNet Cues	TexureCodes Cues
AthleticsTrack	AthleticsTrack	AthleticsTrack
ClayTennisSurface	BoxingRing	BoxingRing
HockeyGround	ClayTennisSurface	ClayTennisSurface
IndoorCrowd	HockeyGround	CloseUp
JudoMat	IndoorCrowd	HockeyGround
Ocean	Net-JudoMat	IndoorCrowd
OutdoorCrowd	Ocean	JudoMat
ShootingTarget	OutdoorCrowd	Ocean
SwimmingPool	ShootingTarget	OutdoorCrowd
TaekwondoMat	SwimmingLanes	ShootingTarget
	SwimmingPool	SwimmingLanes
	TaekwondoMat	SwimmingPool
	WoodCycleTrack	TaekwondoMat
		WoodCycleTrack

Acknowledgements

This work was supported by the IST-1999-13082 ASSAVID project funded by the European IST Programme.

References

1. Leo Breiman. Bagging predictors. *Machine Learning*, 24(2):123–140, 1996.
2. Y Freund and R E Schapire. Experiment with a new boosting algorithm. In *In Proceedings of the Thirteenth International Conference on Machine Learning*. Morgan Kaufmann, 1996.
3. B Levienaise-Obadia, J Kittler, and W Christmas. Defining quantisation strategies and a perceptual similarity measure for texture-based annotation and retrieval. In *In IEEE, editor, ICPR'2000*, volume volume III, 2000.
4. B V Levienaise-Obadia, W Christmas, J Kittler, K Messer, and Y Yusoff. Ovid: towards object-based video retrieval. In *In Proceedings of Storage and Retrieval for Video and Image Databases VIII (part of the SPIE/ITT Symposium: Electronic Imaging'2000)*, 2000.
5. J Matas, D Koubaroulis, , and J Kittler. Colour image retrieval and object recognition using the multimodal neighbourhood signature. In *In D Vernon, editor, Proceedings of the European Conference on Computer Vision LNCS*, volume 1842, page 48 64, 2000.
6. K Messer and J Kittler. A region-based image database system using colour and texture. In *Pattern Recognition Letters*, page 1323 1330, 1999.
7. J R Quinlan. *C4.5 : Programs for machine learning*. Morgan Kaufmann, 1993.
8. John Tobler. Building decision tree ensemles: A comparative analysis of bagging, adaboost and a genetic algorithm, 2001. http://www.cs.wisc.edu/~tobler/_private/DTEnsembles.pdf.
9. Ljupco Todorovski and Saso Dzeroski. Combining classifiers with meta decision trees. *Machine Learning*, 50(3):223–249, 2003.
10. I Witten and E Frank. *Data Mining: Practical Machine Learning Tools and Techniques with Java Implementation*. Morgan Kaufmann, 1999.

Classification of Aircraft Maneuvers
for Fault Detection

Nikunj C. Oza, Kagan Tumer, Irem Y. Tumer, and Edward M. Huff

Computational Sciences Division
NASA Ames Research Center
Mail Stop 269-3
Moffett Field, CA 94035-1000
{oza,itumer,kagan,huff}@email.arc.nasa.gov

Abstract. Ensemble classifiers tend to outperform their component base classifiers when the training data are subject to variability. This intuitively makes ensemble classifiers useful for application to the problem of aircraft fault detection. Automated fault detection is an increasingly important problem in aircraft maintenance and operation. Standard methods of fault detection assume the availability of data produced during all possible faulty operation modes or a clearly-defined means to determine whether the data represent proper operation. In the domain of fault detection in aircraft, the first assumption is unreasonable and the second is difficult to determine. Instead we propose a method where the mismatch between the actual flight maneuver being performed and the maneuver predicted by a classifier is a strong indicator that a fault is present. To develop this method, we use flight data collected under a controlled test environment, subject to many sources of variability. In this paper, we experimentally demonstrate the suitability of ensembles to this problem.

1   Introduction

Ensembles have been shown to improve the generalization performance of many types of classifiers in many real world pattern recognition problems (e.g., [3]). The improvement tends to increase as the variability among the classifiers in the ensemble increases [10]. This property of ensembles intuitively makes them useful in understanding aircraft data, which is subject to considerable variability. In this paper, we discuss the results of applying ensemble methods to aircraft data for fault detection.

A critical aspect of operating and maintaining aircraft is detecting problems in their operation in flight. This allows maintenance and flight crews to fix problems before they become severe and lead to significant aircraft damage or a crash. Fault detection systems are becoming a standard requirement in most aircraft [1,8]. However, most systems produce too many false alarms, mainly due to an inability to compare real behavior with modeled behavior, making their reliability questionable in practice [7]. Other systems assume the availability of

T. Windeatt and F. Roli (Eds.): MCS 2003, LNCS 2709, pp. 375–384, 2003.

Table 1. Conceptual open loop model illustrating assumed causal relationships.

Flight ⟶ Maneuver (M)	Aircraft ⟶ Attitude (A)	Physical ⟶ Input (I)	Internal ⟶ Response (R)	Measured Output (O)
•Fwd. Flight	•Radar Alt.	•Engine Torque	•*[Tooth Bending]*	•Vibration
•Side Flight	•Airspeed	•Engine Speed		- x axis
•Fwd. Climb	•Climb Rate	•*[Mast Lifting]*	•*[Backlash]*	- y axis
•Fwd. Descent	•Heading	•*[Mast Bending]*	•*[Friction]*	- z axis
•Hover	•Bank	•*[other]*	•*[Heat]*	•*[Temp]*
•Hover Turn	•Pitch		•*[other]*	•*[Noise]*
•Coord. Turn	•Side Slip		•*[DAMAGE]*	•*[other]*
•*[other]*	•*[other]*			

data produced during all possible faulty operation modes [1,4,8]. Because of the highly safety-critical nature of the aircraft domain application, most fault detection systems must function well even though fault data are non-existent and the set of possible faults is unknown. Models are often used to predict the effect of damage and failures on otherwise healthy (baseline) data. However, while models are a necessary first start, the modeled system response often does not take operational variability into account, resulting in high false-alarm rates [5,7].

In this paper, we use in-flight aircraft data that were collected as part of a research effort to understand the sources of variability present in the actual flight environment, with the purpose of reducing the high rates of false alarms [5,9]. That work described aircraft operation conceptually according to the open-loop causal model shown in Table 1. We assume that the maneuver being performed (M) influences the observable aircraft attitudes (A), which in turn influence the set of possibly observable physical inputs (I) to the transmission. The physical inputs influence the transmission in a variety of ways that are not typically observable (R); however, they influence outputs that can be observed (O).

Our approach to fault detection in aircraft depends fundamentally on the assumption that the nature of the relationships between the elements M, A, I, R, and O described above change when a fault materializes. As mentioned earlier, the many approaches that try to model only the set of possible outputs (O) and indicate the presence of a fault when the actual outputs do not match the model do not account for operational variability. Also, the output space is often too complicated to allow faithful modeling and measuring differences between the model and actual outputs. This latter difficulty remains even if one attempts to model the output as a function of the flight maneuver or other influence due to noise, wind, and other conditions. Approaches to fault diagnosis (e.g., [12]) attempt to predict either normal operation or one of a designated set of faults. As stated earlier, this is not possible in the aircraft domain because the set of possible faults is unknown and fault data are non-existent. In this work, we create a system diagrammed in Figure 1. We create classifiers that predict the flight maneuver (M) as a function of other available data such as the outputs (O). The data that we use contain the actual maneuver, but in general, this may be calculated using pilot input and/or attitude data. We propose that mismatches

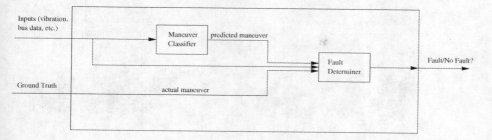

Fig. 1. Online Fault Detection System Block Diagram.

between the predicted maneuver and the actual maneuver being performed is a strong indicator for the presence of a fault.

In order for our method to have a low false-alarm rate, we need a maneuver classifier with the highest performance possible. In addition to using Multilayer Perceptrons (MLPs) and Radial Basis Function (RBF) networks, we use ensembles [2,10] of MLPs and RBF networks. We have also identified sets of maneuvers (e.g., three different hover maneuvers) that are similar enough to one another that misclassifications within these groups are unlikely to imply the presence of faults. Additionally, we smooth over the predictions for small windows of time in order to mitigate the effects of noise.

In the following, section 2 discusses the aircraft under study and the data generated from them. We discuss the ensemble methods that we used and the associated data preparation that we performed in section 3. We discuss the experimental results in section 4. We summarize the results of this paper and discuss ongoing and future work in section 5.

2   Aircraft Data

The data used in this work were collected from two helicopters: an AH1 Cobra and OH58c Kiowa [5]. The data were collected by having two pilots each fly two designated sequences of steady-state maneuvers according to a predetermined test matrix [5]. It uses a modified Latin-square design to counterbalance changes in wind conditions, ambient temperature, and fuel depletion. Each of the four flights consisted of an initial period on the ground with the helicopter blades at flat pitch, followed by a low hover, a sequence of maneuvers drawn from the 12 primary maneuvers (e.g., high-speed forward flight), a low hover, and finally a return to ground. Each maneuver was scheduled to last 34 seconds in order to allow a sufficient number of cycles of the main rotor and planetary gear assembly to apply the signal decomposition techniques used in the previous studies [5].

Summary matrices were created from the raw data by averaging the data produced during each revolution of the planetary gear. The summarized data consists of 31475 revolutions of data for the AH1 and 34144 revolutions of data for the OH58c. Each row, representing one revolution, indicates the maneuver being performed during that revolution and the following 30 quantities: Rev-

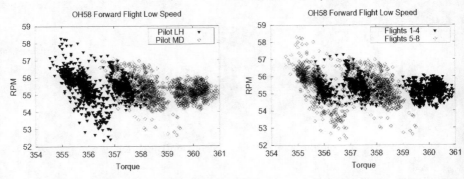

Fig. 2. OH58 Maneuver A (Forward Flight Low Speed) Pilot-Separated.

Fig. 3. OH58 Maneuver A (Forward Flight Low Speed) Flight-Separated.

olutions per minute of the planetary gear, torque (mean, standard deviation, skew, and kurtosis), and vibration data from six accelerometers (root-mean-square, skew, kurtosis, and a binary variable indicating whether signal clipping occurred). For the AH1, also available were the mean and standard deviation values for the following attitude data from a 1553 bus: altitude, speed, rate of climb, heading, bank angle, pitch, and slip.

3   Methodology

Sample torque and RPM data from one maneuver separated by pilot and by flights are shown in Figures 2 and 3, respectively. The highly-variable nature of the data and differences due to different pilots and different times of day when the aircraft were flown, are clearly visible and make this a challenging classification problem. We chose multilayer perceptrons (MLPs) with one hidden layer and radial basis function (RBF) networks as base classifiers. We also constructed ensembles of each type of classifier and ensembles consisting of half MLPs and half RBF networks, because ensembles have been shown to improve upon the performances of their base classifiers, particularly when the correlations among them can be kept low [10,11]. In particular, we use averaging ensembles (the output of the ensemble is the average of the outputs of the base classifiers) because of its combination of simplicity and high performance relative to many more sophisticated methods [2].

We created data sets for each of the two aircraft by combining its 176 summary matrices. This resulted in 31475 patterns (revolutions) for the AH1 and 34144 for the OH58. Both types of classifiers were trained using a randomly-selected two-thirds of the data (21000 examples for the AH1, 23000 for the OH58) and were tested on the remainder for the first set of experiments. Each aircraft's complete set of available inputs (described in section 2) was used.

We calculated the confusion matrix of every classifier we created. Entry (i, j) of the confusion matrix of a classifier states the number of times that an exam-

Table 2. Sample confusion matrix for OH58 (MLP).

True Class	Predicted Class													
	1	2	3	4	5	6	7	8	9	10	11	12	13	14
1	693	0	7	6	79	0	0	0	0	0	0	0	0	0
2	0	679	0	0	0	0	0	0	0	0	0	0	47	0
3	55	1	568	64	31	6	0	11	9	1	11	7	0	3
4	26	0	43	691	15	0	0	3	0	0	0	2	0	1
5	196	0	68	41	412	0	0	0	0	0	2	16	0	0
6	0	0	0	0	0	719	0	0	0	0	0	0	0	0
7	0	0	0	0	0	0	1079	0	0	0	0	0	0	0
8	0	9	22	16	0	0	0	**748**	**177**	**97**	11	6	3	0
9	0	1	1	6	0	0	0	**172**	**381**	**162**	4	7	6	0
10	0	4	1	6	0	0	0	**186**	**170**	**376**	0	8	13	0
11	4	0	15	4	3	0	0	2	1	0	**494**	**217**	0	0
12	3	0	7	6	4	0	0	2	1	0	**200**	**531**	0	0
13	0	63	0	0	0	0	0	4	1	0	0	0	712	0
14	0	0	0	0	0	0	0	0	0	0	0	0	0	685

ple of class i is classified as class j. The confusion matrices (see Table 2 for an example of a confusion matrix—entry $(1,1)$ is in the upper left corner), indicate that particular maneuvers were continually confused with one another. In particular, the three hover maneuvers (8-Hover, 9-Hover Turn Left, and 10-Hover Turn Right) were frequently confused with one another and the two coordinated turns (11-Coordinated Turn Left and 12-Coordinated Turn Right) were also frequently confused (the counts associated with these errors are shown in bold in Table 2.) The maneuvers within these groups are similar enough that misclassifications within these groups are unlikely to imply the presence of faults. Therefore, for the second set of experiments, we recalculated the classification accuracies allowing for these misclassifications. In section 4, we refer to the results of these experiments as "Post-Consolidated" because the class consolidation was performed after the learning.

For our third set of experiments, we consolidated these two sets of maneuvers in the data before running the experiments. That is, we combined the hover maneuvers into one class and the coordinated turns into one class, yielding a total of 11 possible predictions instead of the original 14. In section 4 we refer to these as "Pre-Consolidated" results since the consolidation was done before the learning. We expected the performance to be best for this third set of experiments because, informally, the classifiers do not have to waste resources distinguishing among the two sets of similar maneuvers.

Finally, we used the knowledge that a helicopter needs some time to change maneuvers. That is, two sequentially close patterns are unlikely to come from different maneuvers. To obtain results that use this "prior" knowledge, we tested the classifiers from the previous experiments on sequences of revolutions by averaging the classifiers' outputs on a window of examples surrounding the current one. In one set of experiments, we averaged over windows of size 17 (8 revolutions before the current one, the current one, and 8 revolutions after the current

Table 3. OH58c Single Revolution Test Set Results.

Base Type	N	Single Rev	Corr	Post-Run Consolidated	Corr	Pre-Run Consolidated	Corr
MLP	1	79.789 ± 0.072	–	92.709 ± 0.055	–	93.566 ± 0.060	–
	4	81.997 ± 0.065	0.4193	93.820 ± 0.044	0.4118	94.422 ± 0.038	0.4443
	10	82.441 ± 0.045	0.4193	94.015 ± 0.028	0.4133	94.672 ± 0.032	0.4395
	100	82.771 ± 0.016	0.4199	94.133 ± 0.011	0.4139	94.672 ± 0.032	0.4374
RBF	1	75.451 ± 0.103	–	89.305 ± 0.080	–	90.460 ± 0.169	–
	4	75.817 ± 0.048	0.7164	89.485 ± 0.047	0.7046	90.912 ± 0.056	0.5877
	10	75.871 ± 0.040	0.7185	89.498 ± 0.034	0.7058	90.987 ± 0.032	0.6009
	50	75.908 ± 0.016	0.7162	89.506 ± 0.011	0.7058	91.018 ± 0.014	0.6028
MLP/ RBF	2	80.190 ± 0.079	0.3687	92.834 ± 0.065	0.3176	93.777 ± 0.046	0.2905
	4	80.946 ± 0.059	0.4352	93.189 ± 0.042	0.3997	94.097 ± 0.048	0.3788
	10	81.406 ± 0.043	0.4574	93.403 ± 0.039	0.4273	94.348 ± 0.025	0.3941
	100	81.543 ± 0.020	0.4681	93.463 ± 0.017	0.4392	94.457 ± 0.011	0.4056

one) which corresponds to about three seconds of real time. Because the initial training and test sets were randomly chosen from the original data sequence, this averaging could not be performed on the test set alone. Instead it was performed on the full data set for both helicopters. In order to isolate the benefits of window averaging, we also compute the errors of the single-revolution classifiers on this full dataset[1].

4   Experimental Results

In this section we describe the experimental results that we have obtained so far. We first discuss results on the OH58 helicopter. In Table 3, the column marked "Single Rev" shows the accuracies of individual networks and ensembles of various sizes on the summary matrices randomly split into training and test sets. We only present results for some of the ensembles we constructed due to space limitations and because the ensembles exhibited relatively small gains beyond 10 base models. MLPs and ensembles of MLPs outperform RBFs and ensembles of RBFs consistently. The ensembles of MLPs improve upon single MLPs to a greater extent than ensembles of RBF networks do upon single networks, indicating that the MLPs are more diverse than the RBF networks. This is corroborated by the fourth column (marked "Corr")[2] which shows that the av-

---

[1] We performed this windowed averaging as though the entire data were collected over a single flight. However, it was in fact collected in stages, meaning that there are no transitions between maneuvers. We show these results to demonstrate the applicability of this method to sequential data obtained in actual flight after training the network on "static" single revolution patterns.

[2] Each correlation in this paper is the average of the correlations of every pair of base classifiers in the ensemble. We calculate the correlation of a pair of classifiers as the number of test patterns that the two classifiers agree on but misclassify, divided by the number of patterns that at least one classifier misclassifies. Note that this is not the posterior-based correlation used in [10,11].

Table 4. OH58c Full Data Set Results.

Base Type	N	Window of 17	Corr	Window 17 Post-Consolidated	Corr	Window 17 Pre-Consolidated	Corr
MLP	1	89.905 ± 0.121	–	96.579 ± 0.066	–	97.586 ± 0.078	–
	4	90.922 ± 0.074	0.5014	96.799 ± 0.026	0.6145	97.635 ± 0.041	0.6258
	10	91.128 ± 0.064	0.5013	96.820 ± 0.018	0.6255	97.729 ± 0.031	0.6067
	100	91.307 ± 0.015	0.5052	97.063 ± 0.140	0.6290	97.695 ± 0.006	0.6086
RBF	1	82.564 ± 0.154	–	92.831 ± 0.103	–	94.611 ± 0.124	–
	4	82.634 ± 0.059	0.7509	92.882 ± 0.047	0.7755	94.548 ± 0.063	0.5870
	10	82.618 ± 0.055	0.7543	92.895 ± 0.043	0.7758	94.517 ± 0.029	0.6001
	50	82.644 ± 0.019	0.7505	92.901 ± 0.013	0.7747	94.524 ± 0.012	0.6072
MLP/ RBF	2	88.674 ± 0.108	0.3652	95.910 ± 0.059	0.3596	97.155 ± 0.045	0.3419
	4	88.895 ± 0.078	0.4520	95.902 ± 0.040	0.4791	97.145 ± 0.067	0.4383
	10	89.140 ± 0.057	0.4788	95.980 ± 0.033	0.5143	97.226 ± 0.032	0.4576
	100	89.320 ± 0.025	0.4937	96.003 ± 0.012	0.5335	97.204 ± 0.009	0.4706
Base Type	N	Single Rev	Corr	Single Rev Post Consolidated	Corr	Single Rev Pre-Consolidated	Corr
MLP	1	82.097 ± 0.072	–	93.539 ± 0.058	–	94.495 ± 0.064	–
	4	84.304 ± 0.049	0.4069	94.622 ± 0.039	0.4019	95.321 ± 0.035	0.4443
	10	84.750 ± 0.043	0.4075	94.805 ± 0.028	0.4029	95.540 ± 0.029	0.4372
	100	85.048 ± 0.012	0.4081	94.922 ± 0.011	0.4036	95.595 ± 0.008	0.4355
RBF	1	76.406 ± 0.099	–	89.680 ± 0.077	–	90.788 ± 0.147	–
	4	76.799 ± 0.040	0.7164	89.872 ± 0.039	0.7142	91.187 ± 0.045	0.6027
	10	76.836 ± 0.033	0.7186	89.902 ± 0.027	0.7162	91.244 ± 0.027	0.6157
	50	76.910 ± 0.011	0.7162	89.948 ± 0.007	0.7143	91.271 ± 0.013	0.6182
MLP/ RBF	2	82.146 ± 0.075	0.3613	93.523 ± 0.061	0.3172	94.587 ± 0.049	0.2883
	4	82.877 ± 0.053	0.4293	93.854 ± 0.041	0.4022	94.876 ± 0.051	0.3783
	10	83.332 ± 0.036	0.4516	94.066 ± 0.029	0.4291	95.089 ± 0.024	0.3948
	100	83.505 ± 0.015	0.4618	94.142 ± 0.015	0.4406	95.163 ± 0.014	0.4076

erage correlations among the base models are much higher for ensembles of RBF networks than ensembles of MLPs. Mixed ensembles perform worse than pure-MLP ensembles and better than pure-RBF ensembles for all numbers of base models. The standard errors of the mean performances decrease with increasing numbers of base models as is normally the case with ensembles. The column marked "Post-Run Consolidated" shows the single revolution results after allowing for confusions among the hover maneuvers and among the coordinated turns, consolidating them into single classes. As expected, the performances improved dramatically. The column "Pre-Run Consolidated" shows the single revolution results on the summary matrices in which the hovers and coordinated turns were consolidated before learning as described in section 3. The performances here were consistently the highest as we had hypothesized. In all these experiments, the improvement due to adding base models to the ensemble increases as the average correlation decreases, as expected.

The top half of Table 4 shows the results of performing the windowed averaging described in the previous section in the column marked "Window of 17." The columns "Window 17 Post-Consolidated" and "Window 17 Pre-Consolidated" give the results allowing for the confusions mentioned earlier. The bottom half

Table 5. AH1 Results.

Base Type	N	Single Rev Test	Corr	Single Rev Full	Corr	Window of 17	Corr
MLP	1	96.752 ± 0.059	–	96.933 ± 0.060	–	98.344 ± 0.059	–
	4	97.284 ± 0.031	0.4155	97.555 ± 0.025	0.3966	98.757 ± 0.031	0.4052
	10	97.448 ± 0.027	0.4130	97.683 ± 0.013	0.3973	98.779 ± 0.021	0.4105
	100	97.542 ± 0.006	0.4128	97.762 ± 0.008	0.3981	98.861 ± 0.006	0.4055
RBF	1	95.669 ± 0.059	–	95.743 ± 0.067	–	96.662 ± 0.102	–
	4	95.946 ± 0.029	0.6462	96.063 ± 0.032	0.6369	96.988 ± 0.042	0.6668
	10	95.911 ± 0.023	0.6561	96.042 ± 0.026	0.6456	96.968 ± 0.028	0.6764
	50	95.946 ± 0.009	0.6538	96.067 ± 0.005	0.6321	97.003 ± 0.008	0.6735
MLP/ RBF	2	97.040 ± 0.054	0.3120	97.231 ± 0.055	0.2933	98.256 ± 0.064	0.2313
	4	97.318 ± 0.025	0.3698	97.502 ± 0.028	0.3539	98.482 ± 0.034	0.3148
	10	97.429 ± 0.018	0.4040	97.570 ± 0.018	0.3899	98.475 ± 0.028	0.3577
	100	97.521 ± 0.011	0.4160	97.659 ± 0.008	0.3978	98.553 ± 0.005	0.3739

of the table gives the full set errors of the single-revolution classifiers. We can clearly see the benefits of windowed averaging, which serves to smooth out some of the noise in the data.

Table 5 gives all the AH1 results. The column marked "Single Rev" shows the results with the AH1 summary matrices randomly split into training and test sets. The next column has the results of the same single-revolution classifiers on the full data set (training and test combined). The final column gives the results of the windowed averaging method. We do not present the results of the second and third set of experiments (with maneuver consolidation) because they ranged from 99.404% to 100%. The AH1 results are substantially better than the OH58 results. We expected this because the AH1 is a heavier helicopter, so it is less affected by conditions that introduce noise such as high winds. With the AH1 pure-MLP ensembles always outperform mixed ensembles when using windowed averaging. However, in the single-revolution case, the mixed ensembles outperform the pure ensembles for small numbers of base models but perform worse than the MLP ensembles for larger numbers of base models. This is also true with maneuvers consolidated; however, all these performances are very high. Once again, we can see that ensembles of MLPs outperform single MLPs to a greater extent than ensembles of RBFs outperform single RBFs, so the RBFs are not as different from one another. The average correlations among the base models are consistent with this. Because of this, it does not help to add large numbers of RBF networks to an MLP ensemble. The standard errors of the mean performances tend to decrease with increasing numbers of base models just as with the OH58.

On the AH1, the hover maneuvers were frequently confused just as they were on the OH58, but the coordinated turns were not confused. Taking this confusion into account boosted performance significantly. The windowed averaging approach did not always yield improvement when allowing for the maneuver confusions, but helped when classifying across the full set of maneuvers. However, in all cases when windowed averaging did not help, the classifier performance was at least 99.6%, so there was very little room for improvement.

Table 6. AH1 Bus and Non-Bus Results.

Inputs	Single Rev	Single Rev Consolidated	Window of 17	Window of 17 Consolidated
All	96.752 ± 0.059	99.843 ± 0.032	98.344 ± 0.059	99.737 ± 0.028
Bus	90.380 ± 0.110	95.871 ± 0.091	91.209 ± 0.126	96.027 ± 0.086
Non-Bus	87.884 ± 0.228	93.731 ± 0.171	92.913 ± 0.355	96.110 ± 0.236
$P(agree)$	79.523 ± 0.247	90.063 ± 0.202	85.609 ± 0.320	93.393 ± 0.247

5   Discussion

In this paper, we presented an approach to fault detection that contains a subsystem to classify an operating aircraft into one of several states, with the idea that mismatches between the predicted and actual state is a strong indicator that a fault is present. The classifier predicts the maneuver given vibration data and other available data and compares that prediction with the known maneuver. Through experiments with two helicopters, we demonstrated that the classifier predicts the maneuver with good reliability, especially when using ensemble classifiers. These results show great promise in predicting the true maneuver with high certainty, enabling effective fault detection. Future work will involve applying this approach to "free-flight data", where the maneuvers are not static or steady-state, and transitions between maneuvers are recorded.

We are currently constructing classifiers using different subsets of the available data as inputs. For example, for the AH1, we have constructed some classifiers that use only the bus data as input and others that use only the vibration data. We hypothesize that disagreement among these classifiers that use different sources of information may indicate the presence of a fault. For example, if the vibration data-based classifier predicts that the aircraft is flying forward at high speed but the bus data-based classifier predicts that the aircraft is on the ground, then the probability of a fault is high. Table 6 shows the results of training 20 single MLPs on these data using the same network topology as for the other MLPs trained on all the AH1 data. They performed much worse than the single MLPs trained with all the inputs presented at once. The last line in the table indicates the percentage of maneuvers for which the two types of classifiers agreed. We would like these agreement probabilities to be much higher because none of our data contains faults. However, simpler uses of the bus data may lead to better performance. For example, if a vibration data-based classifier predicts forward flight, but the bus data indicate that the altitude is zero, then the probability of a fault is high. We did not need a classifier that uses all the bus data to draw this conclusion. We merely needed to know that a zero altitude is inconsistent with a forward flight. We plan to study the bus data in detail so that we may construct simple classifiers representing knowledge of the type just mentioned and use them to find inconsistencies such as what we just described.

References

1. Robert Campbell, Amulya Garga, Kathy McClintic, Mitchell Lebold, and Carl Byington. Pattern recognition for fault classification with helicopter vibration signals. In *American Helicopter Society 57th Annual Forum*, 2001.
2. Thomas G. Dietterich. Ensemble methods in machine learning. In J. Kittler and F. Roli, editors, *First International Workshop on Multiple Classifier Systems*, pages 1–15. Springer Verlag, Berlin, 2000.
3. Thomas G. Dietterich. An experimental comparison of three methods for constructing ensembles of decision trees: Bagging, boosting, and randomization. *Machine Learning*, 40:139–158, Aug. 2000.
4. Paul Hayton, Bernhard Schölkopf, Linel Tarassenko, and Paul Anusiz. Support vector novelty detection applied to jet engine vibration spectra. In Todd K. Leen, Thomas G. Dietterich, and Volker Tresp, editors, *Advances in Neural Information Processing Systems-13*, pages 946–952. Morgan Kaufmann, 2001.
5. Edward M. Huff, Irem Y. Tumer, Eric Barszcz, Mark Dzwonczyk, and James McNames. Analysis of maneuvering effects on transmission vibration patterns in an AH-1 cobra helicopter. *Journal of the American Helicopter Society*, 2002.
6. J. Kittler. Combining classifiers: A theoretical framework. *Pattern Analysis and Applications*, 1:18–27, 1998.
7. D.A. McAdams and I.Y. Tumer. Towards failure modeling in complex dynamic systems: impact of design and manufacturing variations. In *ASME Design for Manufacturing Conference*, volume DETC2002/DFM-34161, September 2002.
8. Sunil Menon and Rida Hamza. Machine learning methods for helicopter hums. In *Proceedings of the 56th Meeting of the Society for Machinery Failure Prevention Technology*, pages 49–55, 2002.
9. I.Y. Tumer and E.M. Huff. On the effects of production and maintenance variations on machinery performance. *Journal of Quality in Maintenance Engineering*, 8(3):226–238, 2002.
10. K. Tumer and J. Ghosh. Error correlation and error reduction in ensemble classifiers. *Connection Science, Special Issue on Combining Artificial Neural Networks: Ensemble Approaches*, 8(3 & 4):385–404, 1996.
11. K. Tumer and J. Ghosh. Linear and order statistics combiners for pattern classification. In A. J. C. Sharkey, editor, *Combining Artificial Neural Nets: Ensemble and Modular Multi-Net Systems*, pages 127–162. Springer-Verlag, London, 1999.
12. V. Venkatasubramanian, R. Vaidyanathan, and Y. Yamamoto. Process fault detection and diagnosis using neural networks—i. steady-state processes. *Computers and Chemical Engineering*, 14(7):699–712, 1990.

Solving Problems Two at a Time: Classification of Web Pages Using a Generic Pair-Wise Multiple Classifier System

Hassan Alam, Fuad Rahman[*], and Yuliya Tarnikova

BCL Technologies Inc. 990 Linden Dr., Suite #203
Santa Clara CA 95050, USA
{halam,fuad,yuliyat}@bcltechnologies.com
www.bcltechnologies.com

Abstract. We propose a generic multiple classifier system based solely on pairwise classifiers to classify web pages. Web page classification is getting huge attention now because of its use in enhancing the accuracy of search engines and in summarizing web content for small-screen handheld devices. We have used a Support Vector Machine (SVM) as our core pair-wise classifier. The proposed system has produced very encouraging results on the problem web page classification. The proposed solution is totally generic and should be applicable in solving a wide range of multiple class pattern recognition problems.

1   Introduction

Web page classification is attracting huge interest in recent years. As the number of web pages is increasing exponentially with time, finding information is becoming more and more difficult. Search engines are becoming very important in this scenario. It is also known that 90% of traffic to commercial web sites comes from search engine referrals. Most search engines use a brute force method of indexing "all" web pages, and the match, in most cases, is either directly related to the extracted keywords or the hyperlink mapping. Classification of web pages into a set of predefined categories gives the search engines additional accuracy by making sure that number of false positives is decreased. In addition, it is known that most users (~80%) give up after the first two pages of the results returned by the search engines. So limiting the number of false positives by conducting the search within a sub-class of documents does not only improve the user experience, but also boosts commerce by not losing a prospective buyer.

Another important application area is the automated reformatting of web pages for different types of display devices. With the advent of many types of small screen devices, such as cell phones, pagers, PDAs, wearable computers etc., and most, if not all, of these devices being used for accessing the web wirelessly, it is very important to re-author content of live web pages on-the-fly into a format best suited for the device. Since finding a generic solution for re-authoring all possible types of web pages

---

[*] Corresponding author

T. Windeatt and F. Roli (Eds.): MCS 2003, LNCS 2709, pp. 385–394, 2003.

is a very daunting task, a pre-classification stage categorizing web pages into set of classes and then use specific algorithms for each of those classes is a very attractive solution. Web page classification is, therefore, a very important step in this process.

In addition, the subjectivity of the web classification adds to the complexity of the problem. It is almost impossible to arrive at a classification that is going to solve the requirements of all applications. Hence a web classification strategy that is easily trainable with different types of class definitions is very important. And since categorizing billions of web pages is not possible by humans, finding an automated solution for this problem is also very important.

The rest of the paper is organized as follows. Section 2 sets the background of pair-wise classifiers within the framework of a multiple classifier system (MCS) paradigm for web page classification. Section 3 presents a concise summary of previous research on web page classification and pair-wise classifiers; specifically on their use in multiple-layer hierarchical MCSs. Section 4 introduces the proposed generic pair-wise MCS. Section 5 introduces an illustrative pair-wise classifier, a Support Vector Machine (SVM), used exclusively for the rest of the paper. Section 6 presents some results and finally, in Section 7, some conclusions are drawn and future work is discussed.

2   Pair-Wise Classifiers and MCSs

Pair-wise classifiers are specifically designed and employed to separate two classes. Aside from the theoretical interest and applications in feature level separation, these classifiers have now become important tools in the framework of MCSs. In many cases, MCSs take the form of hierarchical classifiers, where classification is achieved not in a single layer, but in multiple layers. More often than not, many of these hierarchical multiple level classifiers have a mechanism of deferring difficult classification between closely resembling classes ("conflicting classes") to specific classifiers in separate layers. The pair-wise classifiers are then exclusively used for "conflict resolution" purposes. In this paper, we propose a generic self-configurable MCS composed entirely of an ensemble of pair-wise classifiers and apply it in classifying web pages.

3   Previous Research

As previously discussed, web page classification is getting a lot of attention in recent times and the number of research papers appearing in the relevant scientific literature is a proof of that. The precursor to web page classification, text categorization, has been studied for years [1]. Soonthornphisaj and Kijsirikul [2] have extended some of these ideas to iteratively cross-train two naive Bayes classifiers for web page classification. Yu et al.[3,4] have reported a heterogeneous learner for web page classification where no negative data is required. Wong and Fu[5] have reported an incremental clustering approach for web page classification. Mlandenić [6] reported an approach for turning Yahoo! into a web page classifier by using n-grams instead of single words (unigrams). Many of these algorithms assume the web as an unstructured "bag of words". However, other researchers have treated web pages as structured and often hierarchical representation of multi-modal information. Kovacevic et al.[7,8] have used web page structures based on spatial coordinates of objects, such as left bars, right bars etc., to classify web pages. Glover et al.[9] have extended this approach by ranking words and phrases in the citing documents according to expected entropy loss. Others, such as Sirvatham and Kumar[10], have used additional information about embedded images in addition to the textual information to classify web pages. Significant contributions are also made by other researchers [11-15].

Pair-wise classification is also not a new phenomenon. Separating two classes using an optimal decision boundary has always been the core problem of pattern recognition. A technique for finding areas of maximum dissimilarity between the statistical models of two closely resembling classes was introduced by Rahman and Fairhurst[16]. In [17], Rahman and Fairhurst have presented a pair-wise conflict resolution framework within an MCS. Argentiero et al.[18] have analyzed an automated technique for effective decision tree design, which relies only on *a priori* statistics. They utilize canonical transforms and Bayes look-up decision rules and also produce a procedure for computing the global probability of correct classification.

Pair-wise classifiers have been used extensively as "conflict resolvers" in MCSs. In the most generic representation, a single or an ensemble of classifiers take primary classification decision at the first layer. Based on previous experience, or by using an "evaluating training set", classes most likely to be confused with each other are identified and dedicated pair-wise classifiers are used in the second stage to solve these problems. Research on these concepts have been reported by Anisimovich et al.[19], Jonghyun et al.[20], Zhou et al.[21], Rahman and Fairhurst[22], and Tung and Lee[23], to name a few.

Researchers are also actively exploring use of SVMs in MCSs. Specifically Wang et al.[24], Vuurpijl and Schomaker[25], Schwenker and Palm[26] and Frossyniotis and Stafylopatis[27] have extensively used SVMs in various configurations of MCSs over the last three years.

4   A Generic Pair-Wise MCS

We propose a generic pair-wise MCS for pattern classification. The philosophy of this MCS is that each classifier in this configuration is a pair-wise classifier. Assuming we are dealing with an N class classification problem, the first stage of the configuration has N pair-wise classifiers, one for each class (Fig. 1). Each of these classifiers is trained with positive samples for that particular class and negative samples of all the other classes. Classification for a pattern is accepted only when there is a single positive response from a class-specific classifier. Other cases are not accepted and are sent for further evaluation to an ensemble of classifiers (A in Fig. 1) in the second layer. On the other hand, all patterns that are classified as belonging to the negative classes are sent to a different ensemble of classifiers (B in Fig. 1), also in the second layer.

Fig. 2 shows that each of the patterns sent for further evaluation because of multiple conflicting classifications is fed to an ensemble of dedicated pair-wise classifiers. In this case, the number of classifiers used in the configuration is directly related to the number multiple conflicting classification in the first layer. For example, if a pattern is classified as belonging to classes i and j simultaneously, there will a single

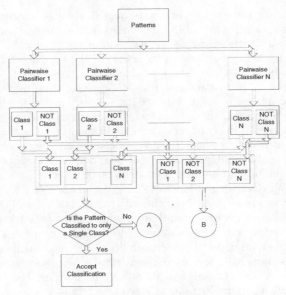

Fig. 1. The generic pair-wise MCS

classifier at this stage performing pair-wise classification between i and j. So assuming M pair-wise conflicts, $M(M-1)/2$ classifiers will be part of the ensemble. Once classified, the classification recommended by most classifiers is accepted as the final decision. If, at this stage, there is conflict on the top choice (e.g. the same number of votes for classes i and j), then the normalized confidence scores of the classification by the individual classifiers are used for conflict resolution.

On the other hand, the patterns classified as negative samples (B in Fig. 1) are sent to another ensemble of classifiers. In this case, $N(N-1)/2$ pair-wise classifiers are used for pair-wise classification, since patterns for all possible classes can be present in this mixture. Fig. 3 shows how this is achieved. In terms of decision mechanism, this is identical to Fig. 2, the only difference being that number of classifiers in the ensemble is different. In practical implementation, the ensemble shown in Fig. 2 is a sub-set of the ensemble shown in Fig. 3, and in our implementation, we simply activated the required classifiers depending on the requirement of the particular decision requirement.

5   A Pair-Wise Classifier: Support Vector Machine (SVM)

The previous section has introduced a generic pair-wise MCS. In this paper, SVM has been chosen as the core pair-wise classifier. SVM is being extensively studied in recent years because of its ability to create very accurate decision boundary in multi-dimensional feature spaces. The following is a generalized description of the principal concepts in an SVM based largely on [28]. A function $f:\mathrm{R}^N \rightarrow \{\pm 1\}$ is estimated from the training data, i.e. for N-dimensional patterns x_i and class labels $y_i, (x_1, y_1),..,(x_l, y_l)$

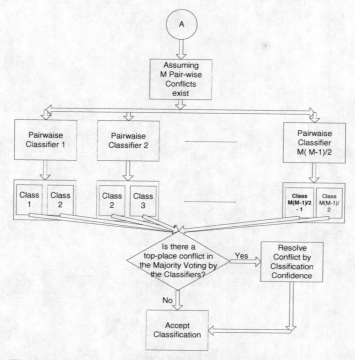

Fig. 2. Re-evaluation of patterns with specific ensemble of classifiers

$\in R_N X \{ (+/-)1 \}$, such that f will correctly classify new examples (x,y) - that is, $f(x) = y$ for examples (x,y), which were generated from the same underlying probability distribution $P(x,y)$ as the training data. If no restriction is put on the class of functions that f is chosen from, a function that does well on the training data may not generalize well to unseen examples. Assuming no prior knowledge about f, the values on the training patterns carry no information whatsoever about values on novel patterns. Therefore learning is not possible, and minimizing the training error does not necessarily imply a small test error. Statistical learning theory, or VC (Vapnik-Chervonenkis) theory, shows that it is crucial to restrict the class of functions that the learning machine can implement to one with a capacity that is suitable for the amount of available training data.

To design solid learning algorithms, a class of functions is required whose capacity can be computed. Support Vector classifiers are based on the class of hyperplanes $(w.x) + b = 0$, $w \in R_N$, $b \in R$ corresponding to decision functions $f(x) = sign((w.x) + b)$. It is possible to show that the optimal hyperplane, defined as the one with the maximal margin of separation between the two classes, has the lowest capacity. It can be uniquely constructed by solving a constrained quadratic optimization problem whose solution w has an expansion $w \sum_i v_i x_i$ in terms of a subset of training patterns that lie on the margin. These training patterns, called support vectors (SV), carry all relevant information about the classification problem. One crucial property of the algorithm is that both the quadratic programming problem and the final decision func-

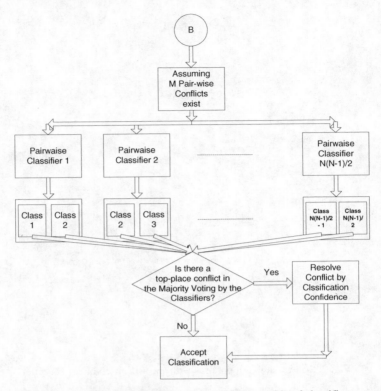

Fig. 3. Re-evaluation of patterns with specific ensemble of classifiers

tion depend only on dot products between patterns. This makes it easier to generalize this solution to the nonlinear case. SV machines map the data into some other dot product space (called the feature space) F via a nonlinear map $\Phi:R^N \rightarrow F$, and perform the above linear algorithm in F, which only requires the evaluation of dot products $k(x, y)=(\Phi(x).\Phi(y))$. If F is high dimensional, the right-hand side of this equation is very expensive to compute. In some cases, however, there is a simple kernel k that can be evaluated efficiently.

For instance, the polynomial kernel $k(x, y)=(x.y)^d$ can be shown to correspond to a map F into the space spanned by all products of exactly d dimensions of R^N. For $d=2$ and x, $y \in R^2$, for example, $(x.y)^2 = \left(\left(\begin{pmatrix} x_1 \\ x_2 \end{pmatrix} \begin{pmatrix} y_1 \\ y_2 \end{pmatrix} \right) \right)^2 = \left(\begin{pmatrix} x_1^2 \\ \sqrt{2}x_1x_2 \\ x_2^2 \end{pmatrix} \begin{pmatrix} y_1^2 \\ \sqrt{2}y_1y_2 \\ y_2^2 \end{pmatrix} \right) = (\Phi(x)\Phi(y))$, defining

$\Phi(x)=(x_1^2, \sqrt{2}x_1x_2, x_2^2)$. More generally, it can be shown that for every kernel that gives rise to a positive matrix $(k(x_i,x_j))_{ij}$, a map F can be constructed such that this equation holds. It is also possible to use radial basis function (RBF) kernels such as $k(x, y)=\exp(-\|x-y\|^2/(2\sigma^2))$ and sigmoid kernels (with gain κ and offset Θ), $k(x,y)=tanh(\kappa(x.y)+\Theta)$. Support Vector Machines use a nonlinear decision function of the form $f(x)=sign\left(\sum_{i=1}^{l} v_i.k(x,x_i)+b\right)$. The parameters v_i are computed as the solution of a quadratic programming problem. In input space, the hyperplane corresponds to a nonlinear decision function whose form is determined by the kernel.

We have adopted an implementation of SVM^{light}, which is an implementation of Vapnik's Support Vector Machine [29]. The optimization algorithm used in SVM^{light} is described in [30]. The algorithm has scalable memory requirements and can handle problems with many thousands of support vectors efficiently. All SVMs discussed in this paper assumes a Dot Product function implementation.

6   Experimental Results

At BCL Technologies, we have created and reported a web database [31]. Recently there have been some changes to that database. Currently we have 400 samples in that database. Three-fourth is used for training and one one-fourth is used for testing. The classes are (a) Reference pages (pages primarily of links and referrals, sites such as Yahoo!), (b) Story pages (pages primarily of textual content, sites such as CNN), and (c) Form pages (pages with large interactive forms, sites that deal with banking and transactions).

The features calculated for the SVM included ratio of text to links, largest chunk of text, maximum size of text per column, ratio of largest continuous chunk of text to links, ratio of text to embedded links, ratio between contiguous text and contiguous links, ratio of contiguous chunk of text to total text, number of images, images with and without links, average contiguous text and link between images, ratio of non-repeating links to repeating links, boldness, underlines, highlighting, headline or other tags, links in navigation columns, number of active form-related tags, ratio of forms to links, ratio of forms to text and ratio of text chunks that are preceded by a link. As can be easily seen, this is a comprehensive feature set describing not only the textual, image and link geometry, but also the structure of the web page in terms of contiguous blocks of text or images or forms.

The proposed pair-wise MCS achieved an overall accuracy of 87.88%. Individually 81.81% forms, 87.88% of the reference pages and 93.94% of the story pages were correctly classified. In order to check the flow of decisions within the MCS framework, it was noted that there were conflicts from the first layer of the ensemble in 8% of the cases. The second layer ensemble corrected 25% of the wrong classifications delivered by the first layer ensemble. In the other 75% cases, the second layer ensemble supported the (either correct or wrong) decision of the first layer ensemble. And what is more important, in no cases a correct decision was discarded.

The pair-wise MCS as reported here makes a somewhat arbitrary decision of placing the ensemble of pair-wise classifiers resolving one-to-many conflicts before resolving one-to-one conflicts. The first layer pair-wise classifiers are trained to recognize one class (positively trained) over all others (negatively trained), and in the second layer, pair-wise classifiers separate one class from its conflict class, both positively trained. We wanted to see what happens if we reversed that placement. The accuracy of this configuration was 86.87%, lower than that achieved with the first configuration. In this case, the second layer was activated in 4% of the cases, in 25% of the cases the incorrect decisions were corrected, in 25% of the cases correct decisions were discarded in favor of incorrect decisions and in 50% of the cases, first layer decisions were supported. This shows that the original configuration is much

392 Hassan Alam, Fuad Rahman, and Yuliya Tarnikova

more stable, especially in terms of the false positive and false negative conflict resolution.

We also tried switching off one of the layers to see the effect of the conflict resolution. When the second layer was turned off, the accuracy was 86.86% and when the first layer was turned off the accuracy dropped to 85.86%. This is obviously supported by the results evaluated earlier in terms of decision flow through the pair-wise MCS.

7 Conclusions

We have presented a new generic solution to the web classification problem. A generic pair-wise multiple classifier system was presented and discussed in this respect. It has been shown that this MCS configuration made up of individual pair-wise classifiers is able to provide very high accuracy in a very difficult problem domain. It is also shown how decision flow through the system can be tracked and how individual layers of this two-layer ensemble can be separately controlled.

Given the complexity of the web page classification problem, and the novelty of using only pair-wise classifiers in creating an easily trainable MCS, some comments need to be made concerning the database on which the experiments were conducted. Although it is possible to draw certain conclusions by testing on a dataset of this magnitude, it is required to have access to a larger statistically representative database to make definite conclusions about the overall effectiveness of the proposed pair-wise MCS. In addition to that, we have reported a three-class problem, and a finer granularity of the classification is also desirable. Creating a database of web pages is very easy; a web-crawler can easily collect thousands of web pages overnight. The problem is the manual annotation, classification and verification of that database. Recently there have been reports on efforts [32] to establish a globally accessible large benchmark web database. In future, we will continue to enlarge our own database and collaborate with others in establishing a larger benchmark database to further test the proposed system.

On the other hand, there are significant advantages of the proposed system. It is easily trainable, it can theoretically handle very high granularity in the patterns, it is able to accommodate feature vectors of significant size, and the solution is generic. Although presented within the context of a web page classification problem, the pair-wise MCS should be applicable to any pattern recognition problem. Currently we are using the same ensemble in face recognition and hand-written character recognition. Preliminary results suggest a very stable system with very high accuracy. We are also planning to use this system as a pre-processing stage to a natural language web page summarization system.

References

1. C. Apte and F. Damerau. Automated learning of decision rules for text categorization. ACM TOES 12(2):233-251, 1994.
2. N. Soonthornphisaj and B. Kijsirikul. Proc. National Computer Science and Engineering Conf., Thailand, 2000.

3. H. Yu, K. Chang and J. Han. Heterogeneous learner for web page classification, IEEE Int. Conf. on Data Mining (ICDM), pages 538-545, 2002.
4. H. Yu, J. Han and K. Chang. Positive example based learning for web page classification using SVM. Proc. ACM SIGKDD, 2002.
5. W. Wong and A. Fu. Incremental document clustering for web page classification. IEEE Int. Conf. on Information Society in the 21st Century: Emerging Technologies and New Challenges (ISO), 2000.
6. D. Mladenic. Turning Yahoo! into an automatic web-page classifier. Proc. of the 13th European Conf. on Artificial Intelligence (ECAI'98), pages 473-474, 1998.
7. M. Mlandenić, M. Diligenti, M. Gori, M. Maggini and V. Milutinovic. Web page classification using special information. Workshop su NLP e Web: la sfida della multimodalita tra approcci simbolici e apprtoacci ststistici, Bulgaria, 2002.
8. M. Mlandenić, M. Diligenti, M. Gori, M. Maggini and V. Milutinovic. Web page classification using visual layout analysis. Proc. IEEE Int. Conf. on Data Mining (ICDM), 2002.
9. E. Glover, K. Tsioutsiouliklis, S. Lawrence, D. Pennock and G. Flake. Using web structure for classifying and describing web pages. Proc. 11th WWW Conf., 2002.
10. A. Sirvatham and K. Kumar. Web page classification based on document structure. IEEE Indian Council National Student Paper Contest, 2001.
11. O. Kwon, J. Lee, Web page classification based on k-nearest neighbor approach. 15th Int. Workshop on Information Retrieval with Asian Languages (IRAL), 2000.
12. G. Attardi; A. Gulli; F. Sebastiani. Automatic Web page categorization by link and context analysis. THAI-ETIS European Symposium on Telematics, Hypermedia and Artificial Intelligence, pages 1-15, 1999.
13. X. Peng, B. Choi. Automatic web page classification in a dynamic and hierarchical way. IEEE Int. Conf. on Data Mining, 2002.
14. V. Loia and P. Luongo. An evolutionary approach to automatic web page categorization and updating. Int. Conf. on Web Intelligence, pages 292-302, 2001.
15. M. Tsukada, T. Washio and H. Motoda: Automatic web-page classification by using machine learning methods. Int. Conf. on Web Intelligence, pages 303-313, 2001.
16. A. F. R. Rahman and M. C. Fairhurst. Selective partition algorithm for finding regions of maximum pair-wise dissimilarity among statistical class models. Pattern Recognition Letters, 18(7):605-611, 1997.
17. A. F. R. Rahman and M. C. Fairhurst, "A novel pair-wise recognition scheme for handwritten characters in the frame-work of a multi-expert configuration". Lecture Notes in Computer Science: 1311, A. Del Bimbo (Ed.), pages 624-631, 1997.
18. P. Argentiero, R. Chin, and P. Beaudet. An automated approach to the design of decision tree classifiers. IEEE Trans. Pattern Analysis and Machine Intelligence, 4(1):51-57, 1982.
19. K. Anisimovich, V. Rybkin, A. Shamis, and V. Tereshchenko. Using combination of structural, feature and raster classifiers for recognition of handprinted characters. In Proc. 4th Int. Conf. on Document Analysis and Recognition, ICDAR97, vol. 2, pages 881-885, 1997.
20. P. Jonghyun, C. Sung-Bae, L. Kwanyong, and L. Yillbyung. Multiple recognizers system using two-stage combination. In Proc. of the 13th Int. Conf. on Pattern Recognition, pages 581-585, 1996.
21. J. Zhou, Q. Gan, and C. Y. Suen. A high performance hand-printed numeral recognition system with verification module. In Proc. 4th Int. Conf. on Document Analysis and Recognition, ICDAR97, vol. 1, pages 293-297, 1997.
22. M. C. Fairhurst and A. F. R. Rahman. A Generalised approach to the recognition of structurally similar handwritten characters. Int. Jour. of IEE Proc. on Vision, Image and Signal Processing, 144(1), pp. 15-22, 1997.
23. C. H. Tung and H. J. Lee. 2-stage character recognition by detection and correction of erroneously-identified characters. In Proc. of the Second Int. Conf. on Document Analysis and Recognition, pages 834-837, 1993.
24. F. Wang, L. Vuurpijl and L. Schomaker. Support vector machines for the classification of western handwriting capitals. Proc. IWFHR 2000, pages 167-176.

25. L. Vuurpijl, and L. Schomaker. Two-stage character classification: A combined approach of clustering and support vector classifiers. Proc. IWFHR 2000, pages 423-432.
26. F Schwenker and G. Palm. Tree structured support vector machines for multi-class pattern recognition. In Proc. MCS 2001, pages 409-417.
27. D. S. Frossyniotis and A. Stafylopatis. A multi-SVM classification system. Proc. MCS 2001, pages 198-207.
28. B. Scholkopf, S. T. Dumais, E. Osuna and J. Platt. Support Vector Machine. In IEEE Intelligent Systems Magazine, Trends and Controversies, Marti Hearst, ed., 13(4), pages 18-28, 1998.
29. V. Vapnik, The Nature of Statistical Learning Theory. Springer, 1995.
30. T. Joachims. In Making large-Scale SVM Learning Practical. Advances in Kernel Methods - Support Vector Learning, B. Schölkopf and C. Burges and A. Smola (ed.), MIT Press, 1999.
31. A. F R. Rahman, Y. Tarnikova and H. Alam. Exploring a Hybrid of Support Vector Machines (SVMs) and a Heuristic Based System in Classifying Web Pages. Document Recognition and Retrieval X, 15th Annual IS&S/SPIE Symposium, pages 120-127, 2003.
32. M. Sinka and D. Corne. A large benchmark dataset for web document clustering. Int. Conf. on Hybrid Intelligent Systems (HIS'02), 2002.

Design and Evaluation of an Adaptive Combination Framework for OCR Result Strings

Elke Wilczok and Wolfgang Lellmann

Océ Document Technologies GmbH, Constance, Germany
{Elke.Wilczok,Wolfgang.Lellmann}@odt-oce.com

Abstract. Frequently changing applications require combination systems with flexible architectures: depending on the recognition problem at hand, different sets of recognizers may be selected or different algorithms for ranking alternatives may be preferred. This paper presents an adaptive combination framework for OCR result strings and describes methods of finding suitable parametrizations automatically. Given an image of a text-line, string results are obtained from geometrical decomposition followed by character recognition. The combination strategy described tries to improve both steps by synchronizing input strings according to geometric criteria before applying classical voting algorithms (like Majority Vote or Borda Count) on the character level. The best string candidate is determined by an incomplete graph search. Quantitative results showing the difference between various voting strategies are presented for a two-recognizer system.

1 Introduction

While theoretical investigations concentrate on questions like

- *How to measure classifier diversity?* [KuWh02,RoGi01,RuGa02],
- *How to construct a set of diverse classifiers starting from a limited training sample?* [Diet00,Ho01]
- *Given several ranked lists of alternatives - how to find a better ranking?* [AlKi99,ErSc00,SiHo02,TaBr00],

practical applications of multi-expert techniques impose completely different problems.

In the OCR context, a typical question is the following:
Given a set of commercial OCR systems (most of them black boxes) - which combination strategy produces satisfying results for very general input data?
Due to the variety of problems, there is little hope that even some carefully chosen recognizers complement one another perfectly. One possibility to balance missing diversity is to analyze the recognizers on many different test sets and to consider their so found strengths and weaknesses during the combination process (e.g. by using situation-specific weights). Often, this leads to intricate combination code. Keeping recognizer-specific information in a separate data base - as it is done in section 2.2 - all recognizers look the same from the perspective

T. Windeatt and F. Roli (Eds.): MCS 2003, LNCS 2709, pp. 395–404, 2003.
© Springer-Verlag Berlin Heidelberg 2003

of combination algorithms. The integration of a new recognizer becomes much easier by that.

Another important aspect is recognition time which grows about linearly with the number of recognizers involved in the combination process. A sensible strategy is to call the 'best' recognizer first and to abandon further calls if its result seems reliable enough (as can be seen e.g. from confidence values).

Apart from questions of system control, this paper describes a strategy for combining OCR results obtained from text-line images. Here text-line denotes an arbitrary sequence of characters, digits, blanks and punctuation marks - handwritten or printed. As a consequence, text-line recognition is not a mere classification problem, but a two-step process: line geometries have to be decomposed into single character geometries, before character recognition algorithms can be applied. OCR systems vary in their segmentation strategies as well as in their classification strategies. Often, no single recognizer produces the correct result. But the correct string may be combined from parts of the results, e.g. taking the first three characters from result A, the next four characters from result C and the rest from result B. Consequently, classical voting algorithms (like Borda Count or Majority Vote) cannot be applied directly to improve result strings. They may be applied on the character level, however, provided some common character geometries can be found in the different strings. Detecting these is the job of the geometrical synchronization procedure described in section 2.3. Its output is a graph, with nodes corresponding to characters, edges to segmentation decisions. Consequently, finding the n best strings is reduced to a classical graph search problem, where different quality measures may be used.

2   Description of the Adaptive Combination Framework

2.1   Overview

Starting from a fully functional, but highly specialized and therefore rather rigid two-reader system, the adaptive combination framework was designed to get a clear separation between recognizer-specific, application-specific and algorithm-specific program code. Considering the mutual interactions between the components lead to the structure sketched in fig. 1.

Mainly, the framework consists of four blocks of algorithms and several data bases, governed by a central control unit.

Given an input image and possibly some additional parameters (like 'font', 'country' or 'image quality'), the present recognition setting is identified with some setting from the (manually composed) "data base of recognition settings". Missing parameters are estimated by suitable algorithms. With help of the assignment table, the most suitable expert team is called, where expert means a recognizer with fixed recognition parameters, including a weighted character set (cf. section 2.2).

Using the expert concept, combining different OCR systems becomes equivalent to combining different parametrizations of the same OCR system (e.g. the

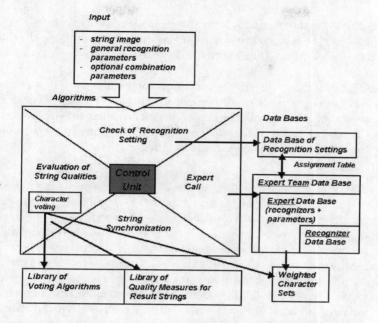

Fig. 1. Structure of the adaptive combination framework

'handwriting' version with the 'machinetype' version). Such strategies may prove helpful in cases of bad quality print.

Time being more important than accuracy in some applications, the control unit may stop calling experts as soon as the quality measure of the temporary combination result exceeds a given threshold. Correspondingly, the most promising expert should be called first. To preserve quality, string results were excluded from combination, if their confidence values were much lower than those of their competitors.

Given some input strings, a so called *result graph* (cf. section 2.2) is built using the *geometrical synchronization* algorithm (cf. section 2.3). Consulting a suitable voting algorithm on character level (cf. section 2.3), the best string candidate can be found by standard graph search algorithms (cf. e.g. [Flam95]). Various string quality measures may be used.

2.2   Data Structures

Result Graph: The most natural data structure for administering string alternatives seems to be a graph. From the two possibilities of modelling characters - by edges or by nodes - the latter one is chosen. More precisely, a result graph is an acyclic, connected, directed graph with two special nodes marking start and end of text-line. Each inner node corresponds to a character geometry and contains the results of all experts which support that geometry. It does not matter, whether the experts produce unique results (*decision level*) or ranked lists of alternatives with/without confidence values (*measurement/rank level*) [XuKr92]. Each node may be associated with a new alternative ranking by calling one of the voting algorithms from section 2.3. Graph edges represent segmentation decisions.

Result graphs may represent synchronization results as well as segmentation alternatives obtained by a single expert. In the latter case, all nodes contain exactly one list of alternatives. A uniquely segmented text-line image corresponds to a linear result graph, in which each node has exactly one successor. Such linear graphs are the input of the synchronization algorithm.

Expert Teams: As mentioned in section 2.1, the adaptive combination system differentiates between recognizers and experts. A *recognizer* may be considered as an arbitrary OCR system. From such, several *experts* can be constructed by prescribing various sets of system parameters (e.g. 'use handprint algorithms' or 'use a special image preprocessing method'). An ordered set of experts is called an *expert team*. To each team there corresponds a weighted character set containing all characters known to the team members, together with weights describing each experts reliability. Referring to this (manually composed) table, the voting algorithms of section 2.3 may give more trust to an 'A' coming from expert 1 than to an 'A' coming from expert 2, while 'Z's may preferably be taken from expert 2. Even experts specialized in different countries and therefore different national characters (e.g. 'à' and 'ë' in France, or 'ö' and 'ß' in Germany) may be combined with help of the weighted character set.

To keep things clear, there are two data bases: one contains all possible experts, the other all possible expert teams. Further, there is a data base of recognition settings (with entries such as 'dot matrix' or 'thick lines'), each setting corresponding to an expert team. The correspondence between teams and settings can be seen from a heuristically generated assignment table.

2.3   Algorithms

Character Voting: There are various strategies to *vote* results on the character level, i.e. to attain a new, better ranked list of alternatives from some rankings given. While any strategy may be used for results on the measurement level, rankings without confidence values are usually treated by variants of the Borda Count [ErSc00] algorithm. Majority Vote suits every setting, even the case of unique decisions. In case of mixed data, the least informative result determines the voting strategy to be used. Statistical methods using recognition results as features for an additional training step are not considered in the following.

The combination system under consideration contains a library of voting algorithms, including Majority Vote *(MV)*, Borda Count *(BC)* and sum, maximum and product rule for confidence values *(CVA, CVMax, CVMult)* [AlKi99]. *MV* is actually a Weighted Majority Vote method, with character-specific weights given by the character set described in 2.2. Besides the classical, average-rank-based Borda Count method, a median-rank-based version was tested *(BCM)*. Assigning first alternatives an additional reward in CVA, while higher alternatives retain their original confidence values, lead to the strategy $CVBA$.

The library of voting algorithms may easily be extended. The common interface of all voting algorithms is the following:

Input:

- an arbitrary number of (possibly 1-element) ranked lists of alternatives

- a weighted character set (cf. section 2.2)

Output:

- a ranked list of alternatives with confidence values (independent of the type of the input data).

Majority vote leads to a (rough) confidence value on the scale $[0, MaxConfVal]$ using the formula

$$ConfVal(x) = \frac{Number\ of\ Votes\ for\ x}{Number\ of\ Experts} * MaxConfVal, \qquad (1)$$

which takes only three values $(MaxConfVal, MaxConfVal/2, 0)$ for a two-expert system. Considering not more than $MaxAlt$ alternatives, a confidence value for Borda Count results may be computed as follows:

$$ConfVal(x) = \frac{Inverse\ Rank\ Sum\ of\ x}{(MaxAlt - 1) * Number\ of\ Experts} * MaxConfVal, \qquad (2)$$

where

$$Inverse\ Rank\ Sum\ of\ x = \sum_{Experts\ i} (MaxAlt - Rank_i(x)),$$

and $Rank_i(x)$ denotes the rank assigned to x by the i-th expert.

The voting strategy may be specified by the combination parameters or may be determined automatically by checking the type of input data (using as much information as possible). The weighted character set allows to confirm or to weaken single character decisions using knowledge about individual talents of the experts (cf. section 2.2). Missing such detailed information, the only entries in the character set are usually ones and zeros (standing for 'character known / unknown by the expert'). If a result contains a character marked as 'unknown' in the weighted character set, the character set may 'learn' this character with hindsight by setting the corresponding entry to one.

Voting algorithms like those described above are only applicable to 'true classification problems', i.e. to problems of the type: Given a finite set of classes (e.g. A-Z,0-9), which is the class of the sample at hand? Text-line recognition does not fit into this scheme: except for applications based on a finite dictionary, the probability for two result strings confirming each other is rather low. Voting algorithms may be applied on character level after synchronization. A possible algorithm is described in the following section.

Geometrical Synchronization integrates a result string into a given reference graph using a kind of restricted breadth-first graph search based on character geometries. The algorithm requires characters sorted by their horizontal positions. Ambiguities (as they may result from overlapping handwritten characters) should be resolved during preprocessing (cf. section 2.4). Result strings without character geometries may be treated by interpolation techniques as described in [Klin97] or synchronized according to character labels.

Finding the n Best Strings corresponds to the well-known problem: Find the n 'cheapest' paths between node 'start' and node 'end' in the (weighted) result graph. (Cf. e.g. [Flam95].) To reduce computing time, an incomplete graph search is performed, i.e. only the n best partial paths are kept in each step. The quality of a path (resp. string) depends on the weights of its nodes (resp. characters) and edges (resp. segmentation decisions). More precisely, the weight of a result graph node corresponds to the confidence value of the best character alternative resulting from voting the lists of alternatives contained in that node. Voting algorithms are activated only during string search (cf. fig.1).

There are various strategies for estimating the (length-independent) quality of a path starting from node weights and edge weights (weighted average, minimum, maximum...). Some of them are implemented in the library of quality measures. For many OCR applications considering 'minimal node weight' leads to the most satisfying results.

2.4   Integration of New Readers

The adaptive combination framework was primarily designed to be used with an arbitrary number of arbitrary OCR systems. Especially, the integration of new recognizers should not cause severe problems. To achieve this, an abstract 'recognizer'-class was implemented which owns a virtual method 'recognize' accepting the following input data: text-line image, recognition parameters (like 'country', 'font' etc.) and - optionally - image preprocessing parameters. The latter were included to combine strings resulting from different images. This may be useful in case of bad quality images such as facsimiles or blueprints, where line-thickening or -thinning may be applied. Each OCR system corresponds to a derived class of the recognizer class. The associated 'recognize'-method provides the necessary transformations between the different data structures of the OCR system and the combination framework, including the scaling of geometries and confidence values. Furthermore, it checks the consistency of character order and activates the recognition ability of the respective OCR system. The implementation of the data transformations for input parameters and result data structures is the main work that has to be done for integrating a new recognizer. The structure of the combination framework offers a systematic approach.

2.5   Control

The adaptive combination framework is designed as an all-purpose string recognizer. Likewise it may be used as a testing environment for various combination strategies. Depending on the application at hand, some of the combination parameters are determined automatically while others may be user-specified. Analyzing, e.g., the mean size of connected components or the pixel density, one gets an estimate of the image quality. Using the assignment table, one may find an expert with a suitable preprocessing method which improves image quality and therefore recognition results.

During combination, the control unit monitors the quality of temporary results to stop further processes as soon as possible. The various data bases (containing experts, teams, settings and their connections, as well as weighted character sets) are generated heuristically at the moment.

3   Comparison with Literature

Probably due to the high costs expected for implementing and running algorithms on the string level, OCR results were almost exclusively combined on character level in literature. Som papers concerning string techniques are [Klin97,MaBu01,WaBr02,YeCh02]. All of those seem to use graph-based methods for synchronization purposes, but none of them describes any control mechanism: independent of the nature of input data or the quality of temporary results, all experts are called unconditionally. Most authors restrict to word input, avoiding the combination of different line partitions. In our work, word separators (like blanks or commas) are treated as special characters, whose existence may be proved or disproved by voting algorithms.

4   Experiments

Various experiments were performed with different parametrizations of two commercial OCR systems. Both systems rely on (independent implementations) of a pairwise hyperplane classification strategy and use different training sets and features. Recognition results were obtained at the measurement level (confidence values reflecting inverse hyperplane distances) and included geometry data for each character. To get a better impression of the true effect of the combination strategies, postprocessing steps (like n-grams or dictionary algorithms) were suppressed during measurements.

Testing material originated from five real-life German handwriting applications (two alphanumeric, three numeral) and two machineprint applications (both alphanumeric). Single test sets consisted of 10.000 to 50.000 characters contained in 800 to 3600 lines. The experts were trained on completely different data bases. Measurements were made at a low reject threshold of 10, where confidence values ranged on a scale of 0 (=bad) to 255 (=optimal).

The first experiment analyzed the influence of the different voting strategies at character level (cf. 2.3) on the string combination result. Results are presented in table 1 and may be interpreted as follows: in each column, the first number denotes the fraction of misclassified characters, while the second number denotes the fraction of rejected characters (in percent). Experiment names correspond to those introduced in section 2.3.

Table 1. Substituted / rejected characters (%) for different voting strategies

Strategy	Handwriting 1	Handwriting 2	Machine 1	Machine 2
Expert 1	20.73 / 0.78	11.85 / 0.68	9.17 / 0.59	5.76 / 1.82
Expert 2	25.99 / 0.51	22.48 / 2.23	11.29 / 0.26	7.15 / 0.89
MV	21.24 / 0.06	12.73 / 0.20	9.58 / 0.05	6.43 / 0.31
BC	20.82 / 0.06	12.41 / 0.20	9.15 / 0.05	6.23 / 0.31
BCM	21.28 / 0.07	12.57 / 0.08	9.57 / 0.05	6.41 / 0.32
CVA	19.12 / 2.74	13.33 / 0.55	9.27 / 0.13	5.65 / 0.42
CVBA	18.45 / 2.06	13.19 / 0.32	9.20 / 0.06	5.82 / 0.23
CVMax	19.26 / 2.50	13.33 / 0.55	9.32 / 0.13	5.65 / 0.42
CVMult	17.36 / 6.99	11.01 / 11.34	8.73 / 1.51	4.10 / 3.62

Strategy	Numerics 1	Numerics 2	Numerics 3
Expert 1	0.37 / 0.11	0.85 / 0.34	1.62 / 0.33
Expert 2	0.95 / 0.03	1.22 / 0.02	2.89 / 0.11
MV	0.40 / 0.00	1.04 / 0.03	1.62 / 0.02
BC	0.39 / 0.00	0.97 / 0.03	1.56 / 0.02
BCM	0.39 / 0.00	1.03 / 0.03	1.62 / 0.02
CVA	0.30 / 0.12	0.65 / 0.25	1.39 / 0.05
CVBA	0.31 / 0.08	0.67 / 0.20	1.38 / 0.02
CVMax	0.31 / 0.12	0.65 / 0.24	1.38 / 0.05
CVMult	0.31 / 0.24	0.60 / 0.53	1.24 / 0.82

CVMult turns out to be too overcautious through all the test sets: only labels suggested by both experts can survive. This leads to an inacceptably high reject rate. All other voting strategies showed recognition rates comparable to or higher than the recognition rate of the better single expert. Improvements were achieved by either reducing reject rate (MV,BC,BCM) or substitution rate (CVA, CVBA, CVMax). The low reject rates of MV and BC(M) may be explained by the discrete confidence scales produced by formulas as (1) or (2). Expert 1 remained superior to all combination strategies on test set Handwriting 2. Here, expert 2 seems to be no adequate partner. Improvements were achieved by confidence-based voting strategies on the less difficult Machine and Numerics test sets. In most cases, CVBA seems to be optimal.

Strategies for saving computation time were tested in experiment 2: Further expert calls were abandoned as soon as the quality of the temporary string result exceeded a given threshold (150 resp. 200 on a scale [0,255]). Measures of string quality under consideration were: average and minimal confidence value of the best character alternatives in the string.

While minimum strategy guaranteed higher recognition rates using the same thresholds over all test sets and voting strategies, average criterion achieved higher time reduction (up to 33%) producing more rejects. The effect of time-saving strategies strongly depends on the test set under consideration. For difficult material (e.g. handwriting, alphanumerics) and a two-expert-system, the additional quality check may balance the time-savings achieved by avoiding a second expert call. Of course, the effect of time-saving strategies grows with the number of experts in the expert team, relativizing the cost of global pre- and postprocessing steps.

The third experiment concerned the dependency of recognition results on expert order (in case of conditional combination). Calling expert 2 before expert 1 using the minimum criterion with threshold 200 lead to a time-saving (up to 6%) on most test sets. Regarding recognition quality, slight improvements were observed as well as substitution rates growing with a factor 2.5, depending on the test set. This shows once more the importance of an adaptive choice of the combination strategy.

5   Conclusions

An adaptive framework for the combination of OCR result strings has been presented. Quantitative results have been shown for a two-reader system using various voting strategies on the character level. Different time-saving strategies have been tested. Further work will be done to enlarge the data base of recognition settings and to automatize the training process. For example, weighted character sets should be generated automatically, based on representative recognition statistics. Since confidence values for segmentation decisions are rarely provided by OCR systems, alternative strategies (based e.g. on character geometries) have to be tested.

Acknowledgements

This work was supported by BMBF (German Federal Ministery of Education and Research), project: Adaptive READ.

References

AlKi99.   Alkoot, F.M., Kittler.J, Experimental evaluation of expert fusion strategies, Pattern Recognition Letters **20** (1999) 1361–1369

Diet00.   Dietterich, Th.G., Ensemble Methods in Machine Learning, in [KiRo00] 1-15

ErSc00.   van Erp, M., Schomaker, L., Variants of the Borda Count Method for combining ranked classifier hypotheses, Proceedings FIHR 2000, 443 - 452

Flam95.   Flamig, B., Practical Algorithms in C++, Wiley, New York, 1995

Ho01.   Ho, T.K., Data Complexity Analysis for Classifier Combination, in [KiRo01] 53-67

KiRo00.   Kittler, J., Roli, F. (Eds.), Multiple Classifier Systems, Proceedings MCS 2000, Cagliari, Springer Lecture Notes in Computer Science 1857, Berlin 2000

KiRo01.   Kittler, J., Roli, F. (Eds.), Multiple Classifier Systems, Proceedings MCS 2001, Cambridge, Springer Lecture Notes in Computer Science 2096, Berlin 2001

Klin97.   Klink, S., Entwurf, Implementierung und Vergleich von Algorithmen
            zum Merge von Segmentierungs- und Klassifikationsergebnissen unter-
            schiedlicher OCR-Ergebnisse. Master Thesis, Kaiserslautern 1997
KuWh02.   Kuncheva, L.I., Whitaker, C.J., Using Diversity with Three Variants of
            Boosting: Aggressive, Conservative and Inverse, in [RoKi02] 81-90
MaBu01.   Marti, U.-V., Bunke, H., Use of Positional Information in Sequence Align-
            ment for Multiple Classifier Information, in [KiRo01] 388-398
RoGi01.   Roli, F., Giacinto, G., Vernazza, G., Methods for Designing Multiple Clas-
            sifier Systems, in [KiRo01] 78-87
RoKi02.   Roli, F., Kittler, J. (Eds.), Multiple Classifier Systems, Proceedings MCS
            2002, Cagliari, Springer Lecture Notes in Computer Science 2364, Berlin
            2002
RuGa02.   Ruta, D., Gabry, B., New Measure of Classifier Dependency in Multiple
            Classifier Systems, in [RoKi02] 127-136
SiHo02.   Sirlantzis, K., Hoque, S., Fairhurst, M.C., Trainable Multiple Classifier
            Schemes for Handwritten Character Recognition, in [RoKi02] 169-178
SuLa00.   Suen, Ch.Y., Lam, L., Multiple Classifier Combination Methodologies for
            Different Output Levels, in [KiRo00] 52-66
TaBr00.   Tax, D.M.J., van Breukelen, M., Duin, R.P.W., Kittler, J., Combining mul-
            tiple classifiers by averaging or by multiplying? Pattern Recognition **33**
            (2000) 1475-1485
WaBr02.   Wang, W., Brakensiek, A., Rigoll, G., Combination of multiple classifiers
            for handwritten word recognition, in: 8th Int. Workshop on Frontiers in
            Handwriting Recognition (2002) 117-122
XuKr92.   Xu, L., Krzyzak, A., Suen, Ch.Y., Methods of Combining Multiple Clas-
            sifiers and Their Applications to Handwriting Recognition, IEEE Transac-
            tions on Systems, Man and Cybernetics **22** (1992) 418-435
YeCh02.   Ye, X., Cheriet, M., Suen, Ch.Y., StrCombo: combination of string recog-
            nizers, Pattern Recognition Letters **23** (2002) 381-394

Author Index

Ahmad, Khurshid   236
Ahmadyfard, Ali   106
Aksela, Matti   84
Alam, Hassan   385
Alimi, A.   296
Ardeshir, G.   276
Arenas-García, J.   45
Artola, F.A.V.   246
Asdornwised, Widhyakorn   336
Assche, Anneleen Van   317
Ayad, Hanan   166

Banfield, Robert E.   306
Baumgartner, Richard   65
Baykut, Alper   94
Bowyer, Kevin W.   306
Brown, Gavin   266
Bunke, Horst   326
Byun, Hyeran   146

Casey, Matthew   236
Christensen, Stefan W.   286
Christmas, William   366
Chu, Wei   125
Cohen, Shimon   227
Cutzu, Florin   115

Didaci, Luca   346
Duan, Kaibo   125

Eckley, Idris A.   35
Erçil, Aytül   94
Estruch, V.   206

Fairhurst, M.C.   356
Ferri, C.   206
Figueiras-Vidal, A.R.   45
Fontoura, S.A.B. da   246
Fumera, Giorgio   74

García-Villalba, Javier   156
Ghaderi, R.   276
Giacinto, Giorgio   346
González, José Carlos   156
Günter, Simon   326

Hall, Lawrence O.   306
Hand, David J.   35
Hernández-Orallo, J.   206
Heutte, L.   296
Hoque, S.   356
Huff, Edward M.   375

Inoue, Hirotaka   256
Intrator, Nathan   227

Jaeger, Stefan   196
Jaser, Edward   366
Jitapunkul, Somchai   336

Kamel, Mohamed S.   1, 166
Keerthi, S. Sathiya   125
Kegelmeyer, W. Philip   306
Kittler, Josef   106, 186, 366
Ko, Jaepil   146
Kuncheva, Ludmila I.   25

Lecourtier, Y.   296
Lellmann, Wolfgang   395
Lewitt, Michael   176
Luttrell, S.P.   217

Magee, Derek   135
McDonald, Ross A.   35

Nakagawa, Masaki   196
Narihisa, Hiroyuki   256

Oza, Nikunj C.   15, 375

Polikar, Robi   176
Poo, Aun Neow   125

Rahman, Fuad   385
Ramírez-Quintana, M.J.   206
Raudys, Šarunas   55, 65
Roli, Fabio   55, 74, 346

Santos, R.O.V.   246
Saragiotis, Panagiotis   236
Sharkey, A.J.C.   45
Shevade, Shirish Krishnaj   125
Sirlantzis, K.   356

Somorjai, Ray   65

Tapia, Elizabeth   156
Tarnikova, Yuliya   385
Tumer, Irem Y.   375
Tumer, Kagan   375

Velek, Ondrej   196
Vellasco, M.M.B.R.   246
Verbaeten, Sofie   317

Vrusias, Bogdan   236

Wanas, Nayer M.   1
Wilczok, Elke   395
Windeatt, Terry   276
Windridge, David   106, 186
Wyatt, Jeremy   266

Zouari, H.   296

Lecture Notes in Computer Science

For information about Vols. 1–2601

please contact your bookseller or Springer-Verlag

Vol. 2602: C. Priami (Ed.), Computational Methods in Systems Biology. Proceedings, 2003. IX, 214 pages. 2003.

Vol. 2603: A. Garcia, C. Lucena, F. Zambonelli, A. Omicini, J. Castro (Eds.), Software Engineering for Large-Scale Multi-Agent Systems. XIV, 285 pages. 2003.

Vol. 2604: N. Guelfi, E. Astesiano, G. Reggio (Eds.), Scientific Engineering for Distributed Java Applications. Proceedings, 2002. X, 205 pages. 2003.

Vol. 2606: A.M. Tyrrell, P.C. Haddow, J. Torresen (Eds.), Evolvable Systems: From Biology to Hardware. Proceedings, 2003. XIV, 468 pages. 2003.

Vol. 2607: H. Alt, M. Habib (Eds.), STACS 2003. Proceedings, 2003. XVII, 700 pages. 2003.

Vol. 2609: M. Okada, B. Pierce, A. Scedrov, H. Tokuda, A. Yonezawa (Eds.), Software Security – Theories and Systems. Proceedings, 2002. XI, 471 pages. 2003.

Vol. 2610: C. Ryan, T. Soule, M. Keijzer, E. Tsang, R. Poli, E. Costa (Eds.), Genetic Programming. Proceedings, 2003. XII, 486 pages. 2003.

Vol. 2611: S. Cagnoni, J.J. Romero Cardalda, D.W. Corne, J. Gottlieb, A. Guillot, E. Hart, C.G. Johnson, E. Marchiori, J.-A. Meyer, M. Middendorf, G.R. Raidl (Eds.), Applications of Evolutionary Computing. Proceedings, 2003. XXI, 708 pages. 2003.

Vol. 2612: M. Joye (Ed.), Topics in Cryptology – CT-RSA 2003. Proceedings, 2003. XI, 417 pages. 2003.

Vol. 2613: F.A.P. Petitcolas, H.J. Kim (Eds.), Digital Watermarking. Proceedings, 2002. XI, 265 pages. 2003.

Vol. 2614: R. Laddaga, P. Robertson, H. Shrobe (Eds.), Self-Adaptive Software: Applications. Proceedings, 2001. VIII, 291 pages. 2003.

Vol. 2615: N. Carbonell, C. Stephanidis (Eds.), Universal Access. Proceedings, 2002. XIV, 534 pages. 2003.

Vol. 2616: T. Asano, R. Klette, C. Ronse (Eds.), Geometry, Morphology, and Computational Imaging. Proceedings, 2002. X, 437 pages. 2003.

Vol. 2617: H.A. Reijers (Eds.), Design and Control of Workflow Processes. Proceedings, 2002. XV, 624 pages. 2003.

Vol. 2618: P. Degano (Ed.), Programming Languages and Systems. Proceedings, 2003. XV, 415 pages. 2003.

Vol. 2619: H. Garavel, J. Hatcliff (Eds.), Tools and Algorithms for the Construction and Analysis of Systems. Proceedings, 2003. XVI, 604 pages. 2003.

Vol. 2620: A.D. Gordon (Ed.), Foundations of Software Science and Computation Structures. Proceedings, 2003. XII, 441 pages. 2003.

Vol. 2621: M. Pezzè (Ed.), Fundamental Approaches to Software Engineering. Proceedings, 2003. XIV, 403 pages. 2003.

Vol. 2622: G. Hedin (Ed.), Compiler Construction. Proceedings, 2003. XII, 335 pages. 2003.

Vol. 2623: O. Maler, A. Pnueli (Eds.), Hybrid Systems: Computation and Control. Proceedings, 2003. XII, 558 pages. 2003.

Vol. 2624: H.G. Dietz (Ed.), Languages and Compilers for Parallel Computing. Proceedings, 2001. XI, 444 pages. 2003.

Vol. 2625: U. Meyer, P. Sanders, J. Sibeyn (Eds.), Algorithms for Memory Hierarchies. Proceedings, 2003. XVIII, 428 pages. 2003.

Vol. 2626: J.L. Crowley, J.H. Piater, M. Vincze, L. Paletta (Eds.), Computer Vision Systems. Proceedings, 2003. XIII, 546 pages. 2003.

Vol. 2627: B. O'Sullivan (Ed.), Recent Advances in Constraints. Proceedings, 2002. X, 201 pages. 2003. (Subseries LNAI).

Vol. 2628: T. Fahringer, B. Scholz, Advanced Symbolic Analysis for Compilers. XII, 129 pages. 2003.

Vol. 2631: R. Falcone, S. Barber, L. Korba, M. Singh (Eds.), Trust, Reputation, and Security: Theories and Practice. Proceedings, 2002. X, 235 pages. 2003. (Subseries LNAI).

Vol. 2632: C.M. Fonseca, P.J. Fleming, E. Zitzler, K. Deb, L. Thiele (Eds.), Evolutionary Multi-Criterion Optimization. Proceedings, 2003. XV, 812 pages. 2003.

Vol. 2633: F. Sebastiani (Ed.), Advances in Information Retrieval. Proceedings, 2003. XIII, 546 pages. 2003.

Vol. 2634: F. Zhao, L. Guibas (Eds.), Information Processing in Sensor Networks. Proceedings, 2003. XII, 692 pages. 2003.

Vol. 2636: E. Alonso, D, Kudenko, D. Kazakov (Eds.), Adaptive Agents and Multi-Agent Systems. XIV, 323 pages. 2003. (Subseries LNAI).

Vol. 2637: K.-Y. Whang, J. Jeon, K. Shim, J. Srivastava (Eds.), Advances in Knowledge Discovery and Data Mining. Proceedings, 2003. XVIII, 610 pages. 2003. (Subseries LNAI).

Vol. 2638: J. Jeuring, S. Peyton Jones (Eds.), Advanced Functional Programming. Proceedings, 2002. VII, 213 pages. 2003.

Vol. 2639: G. Wang, Q. Liu, Y. Yao, A. Skowron (Eds.), Rough Sets, Fuzzy Sets, Data Mining, and Granular Computing. Proceedings, 2003. XVII, 741 pages. 2003. (Subseries LNAI).

Vol. 2641: P.J. Nürnberg (Ed.), Metainformatics. Proceedings, 2002. VIII, 187 pages. 2003.

Vol. 2642: X. Zhou, Y. Zhang, M.E. Orlowska (Eds.), Web Technologies and Applications. Proceedings, 2003. XIII, 608 pages. 2003.

Vol. 2643: M. Fossorier, T. Høholdt, A. Poli (Eds.), Applied Algebra, Algebraic Algorithms and Error-Correcting Codes. Proceedings, 2003. X, 256 pages. 2003.

Vol. 2644: D. Hogrefe, A. Wiles (Eds.), Testing of Communicating Systems. Proceedings, 2003. XII, 311 pages. 2003.

Vol. 2645: M.A. Wimmer (Ed.), Knowledge Management in Electronic Government. Proceedings, 2003. XI, 320 pages. 2003. (Subseries LNAI).

Vol. 2646: H. Geuvers, F, Wiedijk (Eds.), Types for Proofs and Programs. Proceedings, 2002. VIII, 331 pages. 2003.

Vol. 2647: K.Jansen, M. Margraf, M. Mastrolli, J.D.P. Rolim (Eds.), Experimental and Efficient Algorithms. Proceedings, 2003. VIII, 267 pages. 2003.

Vol. 2648: T. Ball, S.K. Rajamani (Eds.), Model Checking Software. Proceedings, 2003. VIII, 241 pages. 2003.

Vol. 2649: B. Westfechtel, A. van der Hoek (Eds.), Software Configuration Management. Proceedings, 2003. VIII, 241 pages. 2003.

Vol. 2651: D. Bert, J.P. Bowen, S. King, M, Waldén (Eds.), ZB 2003: Formal Specification and Development in Z and B. Proceedings, 2003. XIII, 547 pages. 2003.

Vol. 2652: F.J. Perales, A.J.C. Campilho, N. Pérez de la Blanca, A. Sanfeliu (Eds.), Pattern Recognition and Image Analysis. Proceedings, 2003. XIX, 1142 pages. 2003.

Vol. 2653: R. Petreschi, Giuseppe Persiano, R. Silvestri (Eds.), Algorithms and Complexity. Proceedings, 2003. XI, 289 pages. 2003.

Vol. 2655: J.-P. Rosen, A. Strohmeier (Eds.), Reliable Software Technologies – Ada-Europe 2003. Proceedings, 2003. XIII, 489 pages. 2003.

Vol. 2656: E. Biham (Ed.), Advances in Cryptology – EUROCRPYT 2003. Proceedings, 2003. XIV, 429 pages. 2003.

Vol. 2657: P.M.A. Sloot, D. Abramson, A.V. Bogdanov, J.J. Dongarra, A.Y. Zomaya, Y.E. Gorbachev (Eds.), Computational Science – ICCS 2003. Proceedings, Part I. 2003. LV, 1095 pages. 2003.

Vol. 2658: P.M.A. Sloot, D. Abramson, A.V. Bogdanov, J.J. Dongarra, A.Y. Zomaya, Y.E. Gorbachev (Eds.), Computational Science – ICCS 2003. Proceedings, Part II. 2003. LV, 1129 pages. 2003.

Vol. 2659: P.M.A. Sloot, D. Abramson, A.V. Bogdanov, J.J. Dongarra, A.Y. Zomaya, Y.E. Gorbachev (Eds.), Computational Science – ICCS 2003. Proceedings, Part III. 2003. LV, 1165 pages. 2003.

Vol. 2660: P.M.A. Sloot, D. Abramson, A.V. Bogdanov, J.J. Dongarra, A.Y. Zomaya, Y.E. Gorbachev (Eds.), Computational Science – ICCS 2003. Proceedings, Part IV. 2003. LVI, 1161 pages. 2003.

Vol. 2663: E. Menasalvas, J. Segovia, P.S. Szczepaniak (Eds.), Advances in Web Intelligence. Proceedings, 2003. XII, 350 pages. 2003. (Subseries LNAI).

Vol. 2665: H. Chen, R. Miranda, D.D. Zeng, C. Demchak, J. Schroeder, T. Madhusudan (Eds.), Intelligence and Security Informatics. Proceedings, 2003. XIV, 392 pages. 2003.

Vol. 2667: V. Kumar, M.L. Gavrilova, C.J.K. Tan, P. L'Ecuyer (Eds.), Computational Science and Its Applications – ICCSA 2003. Proceedings, Part I. 2003. XXXIV, 1060 pages. 2003.

Vol. 2668: V. Kumar, M.L. Gavrilova, C.J.K. Tan, P. L'Ecuyer (Eds.), Computational Science and Its Applications – ICCSA 2003. Proceedings, Part II. 2003. XXXIV, 942 pages. 2003.

Vol. 2669: V. Kumar, M.L. Gavrilova, C.J.K. Tan, P. L'Ecuyer (Eds.), Computational Science and Its Applications – ICCSA 2003. Proceedings, Part III. 2003. XXXIV, 948 pages. 2003.

Vol. 2670: R. Peña, T. Arts (Eds.), Implementation of Functional Languages. Proceedings, 2002. X, 249 pages. 2003.

Vol. 2671: Y. Xiang, B. Chaib-draa (Eds.), Advances in Artificial Intelligence. Proceedings, 2003. XIV, 642 pages. 2003. (Subseries LNAI).

Vol. 2672: M. Endler, D. Schmidt (Eds.), Middleware 2003. Proceedings, 2003. XIII, 513 pages. 2003.

Vol. 2674: I.E. Magnin, J. Montagnat, P. Clarysse, J. Nenonen, T. Katila (Eds.), Functional Imaging and Modeling of the Heart. Proceedings, 2003. XI, 308 pages. 2003.

Vol. 2675: M. Marchesi, G. Succi (Eds.), Extreme Programming and Agile Processes in Software Engineering. Proceedings, 2003. XV, 464 pages. 2003.

Vol. 2676: R. Baeza-Yates, E. Chávez, M. Crochemore (Eds.), Combinatorial Pattern Matching. Proceedings, 2003. XI, 403 pages. 2003.

Vol. 2678: W. van der Aalst, A. ter Hofstede, M. Weske (Eds.), Business Process Management. Proceedings, 2003. XI, 391 pages. 2003.

Vol. 2679: W. van der Aalst, E. Best (Eds.), Applications and Theory of Petri Nets 2003. Proceedings, 2003. XI, 508 pages. 2003.

Vol. 2686: J. Mira, J.R. Álvarez (Eds.), Computational Methods in Neural Modeling. Proceedings, Part I. 2003. XXVII, 764 pages. 2003.

Vol. 2687: J. Mira, J.R. Álvarez (Eds.), Artificial Neural Nets Problem Solving Methods. Proceedings, Part II. 2003. XXVII, 820 pages. 2003.

Vol. 2688: J. Kittler, M.S. Nixon (Eds.), Audio- and Video-Based Biometric Person Authentication. Proceedings, 2003. XVII, 978 pages. 2003.

Vol. 2692: P. Nixon, S. Terzis (Eds.), Trust Management. Proceedings, 2003. X, 349 pages. 2003.

Vol. 2694: R. Cousot (Ed.), Static Analysis. Proceedings, 2003. XIV, 505 pages. 2003.

Vol. 2695: L.D. Griffin, M. Lillholm (Eds.), Scale Space Methods in Computer Vision. Proceedings, 2003. XII, 816 pages. 2003.

Vol. 2701: M. Hofmann (Ed.), Typed Lambda Calculi and Applications. Proceedings, 2003. VIII, 317 pages. 2003.

Vol. 2702: P. Brusilovsky, A. Corbett, F. de Rosis (Eds.), User Modeling 2003. Proceedings, 2003. XIV, 436 pages. 2003. (Subseries LNAI).

Vol. 2706: R. Nieuwenhuis (Ed.), Rewriting Techniques and Applications. Proceedings, 2003. XI, 515 pages. 2003.

Vol. 2707: K. Jeffay, I. Stoica, K. Wehrle (Eds.), Quality of Service – IWQoS 2003. Proceedings, 2003. XI, 517 pages. 2003.

Vol. 2709: T. Windeatt, F. Roli (Eds.), Multiple Classifier Systems. Proceedings, 2003. X, 406 pages. 2003.

Vol. 2716: M.J. Voss (Ed.), OpenMP Shared Memory Parallel Programming. Proceedings, 2003. VIII, 271 pages. 2003.